DATE DUE

OCT - 7 1995	
MAR 22 1996	
APR 15/96	
APR 29/96	
OCT 31 1996	
FEB -7 1997	
NOV 12 1997	
Nov 19	
Nov 30	
Dec 15	
JAN 2	
MAR - 4 1998	
MAR 19 1998	
APR 02 1998	
APR 17 1998	
OCT 24 2000	

BRODART   Cat. No. 23-221

Nicotine Addiction

Nicotine Addiction:
Principles and Management

EDITED BY

C. Tracy Orleans, Ph.D.
Division of Behavioral Research
Fox Chase Cancer Center

John Slade, M.D.
Department of Medicine
St. Peter's Medical Center
University of Medicine and Dentistry of New Jersey

New York   Oxford
OXFORD UNIVERSITY PRESS
1993

Oxford University Press

Oxford   New York   Toronto
Delhi   Bombay   Calcutta   Madras   Karachi
Kuala Lumpur   Singapore   Hong Kong   Tokyo
Nairobi   Dar es Salaam   Cape Town
Melbourne   Auckland   Madrid

and associated companies in
Berlin   Ibadan

Published by Oxford University Press, Inc.,
200 Madison Avenue, New York, New York 10016

Oxford is a registered trademark of Oxford University Press

Library of Congress Cataloging-in-Publication Data
Nicotine addiction : principles and management / edited by C. Tracy
Orleans, John Slade.
p.   cm.   ISBN 0-19-506441-0
1. Tobacco habit.   I. Orleans, C. Tracy.
II. Slade, John D.), 1949–
RC567.N5235   1993
616.86′5—dc20   92-29443

9 8 7 6 5 4 3 2 1

Printed in the United States of America
on acid-free paper

To Jeffrey, Jesse, Alexander, Phyllis
and the friends, family, and colleagues
who sustain me
C.T.O.

To Frances
J.S.

Foreword

Future historians will look back with amazement that it took society so long to control the use of tobacco. After all, the health effects of tobacco use and the pharmacologic effects of nicotine have been known for many decades. And any doubts about the dangers of smoking were removed with publication of the first reports on smoking and health from the Royal College of Physicians of London (1962) and the U.S. Surgeon General (1964).

The important point is *not* that smoking is merely harmful. Harmful behaviors, pathogens, chemicals, occupations, and consumer products are commonplace today. What *is* important is *how* dangerous smoking is. Public health officials have been sounding the alarm for quite some time. As early as 1979, in the first Surgeon General's report on health promotion and disease prevention *(Healthy People),* the U.S. Public Health Service called cigarette smoking "the largest single preventable cause of illness and premature death in the United States." In his 1982 report on smoking and cancer, former Surgeon General C. Everett Koop went even further, calling smoking "the most important public health issue of our time."

Statistics back up the rhetoric. The Centers for Disease Control and Prevention estimates that smoking is responsible for 434,000 deaths each year in the United States, or more than 1,000 deaths each day, or one-fifth of deaths from all causes. That toll, as tobacco control advocates are fond of pointing out, exceeds the *combined* number of deaths from alcohol, cocaine, heroin, suicide, homicide, motor-vehicle accidents, fires, and AIDS.

At the international level, the numbers are even more staggering. The World Health Organization (WHO) estimates that, worldwide, smoking causes approximately 2.5 million deaths annually. The WHO predicts that if current smoking patterns continue, the yearly toll will increase to 10 million deaths by the year 2025. If that happens, 500 million people now alive—10% of the entire world population—will ultimately die of diseases caused by smoking.

Most of the resources devoted to tobacco and health have been in the area of research. Tens of thousands of studies have explored the relationship between smoking and disease. In her 1990 report on the health benefits of smoking cessation, former Surgeon General Antonia Novello noted that "smoking represents the most extensively documented cause of disease ever investigated in the history of biomedical research." But where we have utterly failed, as a society, is in the prevention of tobacco use and the treatment of nicotine addiction. Despite the statistics, despite the research, despite the streams of government reports and the outrage often expressed about the actions of the tobacco industry and its allies, progress in tobacco *control* is agonizingly slow, and in many parts of the world, totally nonexistent.

Effective tobacco control will require the involvement of clinicians, educators, community organizations, policy-makers, and the media. Prevention and treatment of nicotine addiction must focus on individuals as well as on the environments that affect individual behavior. Success in these efforts will depend on effective combination and information dissemination. And it is in this area where significant progress is being made. A few specific achievements are worth noting. In 1990 the Advocacy Institute and the American Cancer Society developed an electronic communications system linking anti-tobacco advocates around the world. The U.S. and international networks— called Smoking Control Advocacy Resource Network (SCARCNet) and GLOBALink, respectively—had enrolled about 500 participants from more than thirty countries by May 1993. In March 1992 the British Medical Association launched *Tobacco Control,* the first peer-reviewed scientific journal dedicated to the prevention and control of tobacco use.

Nicotine Addiction: Principles and Management is another critical development in the dissemination of information on tobacco control. Previous books and government reports have explored various aspects of tobacco, such as the history of tobacco in our culture, the health effects of its use, the costs of smoking, smoking behavior, tobacco policies and politics, methods to quit, and so on. But this is the first book that attempts to bring all this information together in one place. It will be an indispensable tool for use by teachers, researchers, clinicians, and policy-makers.

Nicotine Addiction: Principles and Management will also be valuable in the training of health professionals. Individuals seminars on tobacco, much less entire courses on the subject, are rare in schools of medicine, nursing, public health, health education, and psychology. In the case of medicine, for example, the "tobacco curriculum" addresses the histology of lung cancer, the interpretation of pulmonary function tests, and the effect of smoking on theophyllin dosing. But most schools teach little if anything about how to prevent and treat nicotine addiction. The availability of this book provides the opportunity to change that situation, to give nicotine addiction its rightful place in the curriculum of students in the health professions.

Ronald M. Davis, M.D.
Chief Medical Officer
Michigan Department of Public Health

Preface

Knowledge about nicotine addiction and its treatment has advanced enormously since the publication of the first U.S. *Surgeon General's Report,* which, nearly 30 years ago, concluded that there is a causal link between smoking and lung cancer. Tremendous progress has been made, especially in the past 10 years, in recognizing and developing the essential elements of effective behavioral, motivational, and pharmacologic treatments for nicotine addiction. However, no book has yet organized this knowledge as a guide for clinicians and public health specialists. This book is offered as an attempt to fill the gap and to foster better training and improved clinical practice.

We believe this volume will be especially useful at the present time—a critical juncture in U.S. tobacco control history. The *Healthy People 2000* goal of reducing the prevalence of smoking among adult Americans to no more than 15% by the year 2000, unimaginable in 1964, is now clearly in sight and in range. Nearly half of all adults now alive who ever have smoked have quit, and smoking prevalence has fallen dramatically, from 40% in 1965 to 26% in 1991. We have also seen a major shift in public attitudes toward tobacco. Unfortunately, we still have a long way to go. Over 50 million Americans continue to smoke or use oral snuff or chewing tobacco, and thousands of teenagers start smoking every day. Despite the enormous prevalence of the problem, professional advice and treatment to help tobacco users overcome their addiction are by no means universally given. If the nation is to achieve the Year 2000 Health Objectives—both reducing adult cigarette smoking to a prevalence of no more than 15% and increasing to at least 75% the proportion of health care providers who routinely advise cessation and provide assistance and follow-up for *all* of their tobacco-using patients—we must help clinicians recognize and treat nicotine addiction as a primary problem or disease in its own right, not just as a "risk factor" for other disease. This means translating the enormous scientific and clinical advances of the 1980s and early 90s into practical action plans for practitioners and public health advocates.

As work on the clinical and public health aspects of tobacco control has grown in recent years, practitioners in the field have made increasing use of a comprehensive disease model of nicotine addiction that considers more than just the *agent* (tobacco products) and the *host* (the consumer). The *vector* of nicotine addiction (tobacco product manufacturers), as well as the *environment* (cultural, economic, political, historical) in which vector, agent, and host interact, plus the interactions themselves, have become the focus of a growing number of investigations and interventions. Since exposure to environmental tobacco smoke harms some who do not themselves consume tobacco products, the complete disease model of nicotine addiction also includes the *incidental host.*

Nicotine Addiction: Principles and Management works within this model. The book integrates an up-to-date summary of the scientific literature on the etiology, complications, and treatment of nicotine addiction with a stepped-care clinical model similar to models used in the treatment of other chronic medical conditions such as hypertension. This model involves patient-treatment matching (i.e., triage) and a progression over time and quit attempts from the least intense, lowest-cost proven approaches to more intensive, more specialized programs. It is our hope that the systematic use of this stepped-care model will significantly increase the efficacy of treatment and increase the rate at which people are able to achieve stable abstinence from nicotine.

A few words about language are in order. Many of the terms commonly used to describe nicotine addiction or its treatment evolved from and reflect an outdated paradigm for understanding nicotine addiction, one that defined tobacco use as merely a *habit* rather than a full-fledged *addiction.* In this book, *dependence* and *addiction* are used synonymously to define the medical condition involving loss of control over use of a psychoactive drug plus continued use of that drug despite problems. Unfortunately, *dependence* has not always been a synonym for *addiction;* sometimes its meaning has been hedged and has actually connoted *habit* instead. After weighing these considerations, we chose the term *addiction* for the title of this book. Also, in preparing this volume, we became more keenly aware of the need for more careful use of the language used to describe the *treatment* of nicotine addiction. Much of the literature on managing nicotine dependence refers to the process of stopping smoking as *smoking cessation.* This phrase is a carry-over from the *habit* paradigm and may connote that achieving abstinence from tobacco involves little more than the willful decision to stop. While ingrained habits are only slowly extinguished, in this book we have attempted to describe the clinical approach to nicotine addiction as *treating* or *managing nicotine dependence* rather than as smoking cessation treatment. In addition, drawing on the traditions of chemical dependency treatment, the process of becoming a former smoker is sometimes discussed as *recovering from nicotine addiction.*

Nicotine Addiction: Principles and Management includes contributions from many of the nation's leading authorities on tobacco use, nicotine addiction and its treatment—representing a variety of clinical, behavioral science, and public health backgrounds. It was written for a wide audience of clinical and public health professionals, including physicians, nurses, respiratory therapists, physician assistants, health educators, psychologists, chemical dependency treatment professionals and other therapists, medical educators, and public health specialists. It was designed primarily to be used as a "how to" manual for the practicing clinician and as a textbook in schools of medicine, nursing, public health, health education, health psychology and related programs. However, the theoretically—and empirically—based reviews in each chapter will be of value to the researcher as well, providing direction for the next decade of research into critical issues surrounding tobacco use and its treatment.

This volume is organized into three major sections, following the general outline used in traditional texts on medical disease:

I. **The Disease of Nicotine Addiction.** Chapters 1–7 cover the epidemiology, etiology, economics, and medical complications of nicotine addiction. This section also presents a public health model of nicotine addiction and tobacco use, with concise summaries of the known biological, psychological, social and societal factors that contribute to tobacco dependence. The pharmacology and economics of nicotine addiction are also reviewed. Recent "stage" models for understanding the acquisition of smoking behavior and recovery from nicotine addiction are introduced.

II. **Management.** Chapters 8–16 offer practical guidelines and conceptual tools for diagnosing, treating and managing nicotine addiction. Practical, empirically-tested interventions for office, clinic, and hospital settings are emphasized. Management guidelines are modeled after those for chronic medical conditions or diseases and follow a stepped-care approach emphasizing brief interventions that can be easily incorporated into routine medical care. The topics covered in this section include: creating a practice environment that promotes quitting tobacco use and reinforces routine anti-tobacco advice and treatment; the essential elements of brief medical interventions in outpatient and inpatient settings; the use and efficacy of pharmacologic and formal treatment programs; the key role of non-M.D. health care providers; treatments for addiction to smokeless tobacco; and guidelines for treating nicotine addiction in the face of medical and psychiatric conditions that are caused or complicated by tobacco use.

III. **Public Health and Prevention.** Chapters 17–21 combine public health and practical clinical perspectives. Emphasis is given to youth-oriented prevention and treatment programs, the special needs of smokers in high-risk populations, and to promising worksite and community intervention strategies.

This book is the result of remarkable work by many people. As editors, we are grateful to the chapter authors for their gracious sharing of knowledge and art, and to Dr. Ronald Davis for his thoughtful review and foreword. We also appreciate the cheerful assistance of the many people who reviewed this work at various stages, the invaluable help of the staff at Oxford University Press, especially Al Ritchie, Edith Barry, Stanley George, and Sharon Lahaye, Joan Magee at the Fox Chase Cancer Center, and Natalie Mendelson at St. Peter's Medical Center. It has been a privilege to work in collaboration with so many wonderful colleagues, friends, and associates. Finally, we express gratitude to our mentors, clients, patients, and students. They have taught and inspired us.

June 1993   C.T.O.
Cheltenham, Pa.   J.S.
New Brunswick, N.J.

Contents

Contributors

David M. Burns, M.D.
Associate Professor of Medicine,
Department of Medicine, Pulmonary
    Division
University of California, San Diego
Medical Center
San Diego, California 92103

Caroline Cohen, Ph.D.
Research Associate,
Addiction Research Center
National Institute on Drug Abuse
Baltimore, Maryland 21224

Kay M. Eberman, M.S.
Nicotine Dependence Counselor,
Nicotine Dependence Center
Mayo Clinic
Rochester, Minnesota 55905

Michael C. Fiore, M.D., M.P.H.
Director,
Tobacco Research and Intervention
    Program
Department of Medicine
University of Wisconsin
Madison, Wisconsin 53792

Edwin B. Fisher, Jr., Ph.D.
Director,
Center for Health Behavior Research
Professor of Psychology,
Departments of Medicine and Psychology
Washington University
St. Louis, Missouri 63108

Brian R. Flay, D.Phil.
Director and Associate Professor,
Prevention Research Center
School of Public Health
University of Illinois at Chicago
Chicago, Illinois 60607

Brian S. Flynn, Sc.D.
Associate Director,
Department of Health Promotion Research
University of Vermont
Burlington, Vermont 05405

Kipling J. Gallion, M.A.
Communication Coordinator for Media
    Research and Production,
Department of Media Research and
    Production
South Texas Health Research Center
The University of Texas Health Science
    Center
San Antonio, Texas 78284-7791

Thomas J. Glynn, Ph.D.
Acting Associate Director, Cancer Control
    Science Program, and Program Director,
    Smoking Research,
Division of Cancer Prevention and Control
National Cancer Institute
Rockville, Maryland 20853

Ellen R. Gritz, Ph.D.
Professor and Chair
Department of Behavioral Science
University of Texas
M.D. Anderson Cancer Center
Houston, TX 77030

Jessie Gruman, Ph.D.
Executive Director,
Center for the Advancement of Health
Washington, D.C. 20036

Debra Haire-Joshu, Ph.D.
Associate Director,
Center for Health Behavior Research
Department of Medicine
Washington University
St. Louis, Missouri 68108

Jack E. Henningfield, Ph.D.
Chief,
Clinical Pharmacology Branch
Addiction Research Center
National Institute on Drug Abuse
Baltimore, Maryland 21224

Richard D. Hurt, M.D.
Chairman,
Division of Community Internal Medicine
and Director,
Nicotine Dependence Center
Mayo Clinic
Rochester, Minnesota 55905

Murray E. Jarvik, M.D., Ph.D.
Veterans Administration Medical Center
Brentwood Division and
Professor of Psychiatry and Pharmacology,
Department of Psychiatry and
   Biobehavioral Sciences
The Neuropsychiatric Institute
University of California, Los Angeles
School of Medicine
Los Angeles, California 90024

Lori Karan, M.D.
Medical Director, Inpatient Unit
Department of Substance Abuse
Medical College of Virginia
Richmond, Virginia 23298-0001

Jean L. Kristeller, Ph.D.
Associate Professor,
Department of Psychology
Indiana State University
Terre Haute, Indiana 47809

Harry A. Lando, Ph.D.
Associate Professor,
Division of Epidemiology
University of Minnesota
School of Public Health
Minneapolis, Minnesota 55455

Edward Lichtenstein, Ph.D.
Professor,
Department of Psychology
University of Oregon
and
Research Scientist
Oregon Research Institute
Eugene, Oregon 97401

William Lynn, B.A.
Project Officer for COMMIT,
Prevention and Control Research
National Cancer Institute
Bethesda, Maryland 20892

Marc W. Manley, M.D., M.P.H.
Medical Officer and Acting Chief of Public
   Health,
Division of Cancer Prevention and Control
National Cancer Institute
Rockville, Maryland 20853

Patrick McBride, M.D., M.P.H.
Assistant Professor,
Tobacco Research and Intervention
   Program
Department of Medicine
University of Wisconsin
Madison, Wisconsin 53792

Polly Newcombe, Ph.D.
Assistant Professor,
Tobacco Research and Intervention
   Program
Department of Medicine
University of Wisconsin
Madison, Wisconsin 53792

C. Tracy Orleans, Ph.D.
Director, Tobacco Control Research,
Division of Behavioral Research
Fox Chase Cancer Center
Cheltenham, Pennsylvania 19012

Wallace B. Pickworth, Ph.D.
Pharmacologist,
Addiction Research Center
National Institute on Drug Abuse
Baltimore, Maryland 21224

Amelie G.Ramirez, Dr. P.H.
Faculty Associate
Department of Community Health
   Promotion
South Texas Health Research Center
The University of Texas Health Science
   Center
San Antonio, Texas

James L. Repace, M.Sc.
Bowie, Maryland

Michael P. Resnick, M.D.
Director, Psychiatric Education,
Providence Medical Center
Portland, Oregon 97213

Barbara K. Rimer, Dr.P.H.
Director,
Division of Cancer Control Research
Duke Comprehensive Cancer Center
Durham, North Carolina 27710

Herbert H. Severson, Ph.D.
Research Scientist,
Oregon Research Institute
Eugene, Oregon 97401

Donald R. Shopland
Public Health Advisor,
Smoking and Tobacco Control
    Program
National Cancer Institute
Bethesda, Maryland 20892

John Slade, M.D.
Associate Professor of Medicine,
Department of Medicine
St. Peter's Medical Center
University of Medicine and Dentistry of
    New Jersey
Robert Wood Johnson Medical School
New Brunswick, New Jersey 08903

Leif I. Solberg, M.D.
Clinical Director of Research
Department of Family Practice and Health
University of Minnesota School of
    Medicine
Minneapolis, Minnesota 55455

Laura J. Solomon, Ph.D.
Clinical Associate Professor,
Department of Psychology
University of Vermont
Burlington, Vermont 05405

Kenneth E. Warner, Ph.D.
Professor and Chairman,
Department of Public Health Policy and
    Administration
School of Public Health
University of Michigan
Ann Arbor, Michigan 48109

PART I

THE DISEASE OF NICOTINE ADDICTION

Nicotine Delivery Devices

JOHN SLADE

... [T]he cigarette is ... among the most awe-inspiring examples of the ingenuity of man. ... The cigarette should be conceived not as a product but as a package. The product is nicotine. The cigarette is but one of many package layers. There is the carton, which contains the pack, which contains the cigarette, which contains the smoke. The smoke is the final package. The smoker must strip off all these package layers to get to that which he seeks. ... Smoke is beyond question the most optimized vehicle of nicotine and the cigarette the most optimized dispenser of smoke.

William L. Dunn, Jr.,
Philip Morris, 1972

At the time of Columbus's voyages to the New World, tobacco use was widespread in the Americas (Garner 1946; Spinden 1950; Brooks 1952). Native Americans smoked, snuffed, and drank tobacco preparations; tobacco featured prominently in religious ceremonies, and it was used as a medication. In fact, the first recorded prohibition against tobacco use grew out of its religious role. A clash of Peruvian native and Christian ritual led to a ban on tobacco use in church by the Archbishop of Lima in 1583. This decree was followed by a Papal directive in 1586 which declared that "under pain of mortal sin no priest, before celebrating and administering Communion, [may] take tobacco in smoke or in powder" (Spinden 1950). Ritual use of tobacco continues today among American native groups (California Rural Indian Health Board 1991).

Most tobacco use, however, bears little resemblance to traditional patterns. As will be discussed in this chapter, contemporary tobacco products are intricately engineered devices that deliver finely graded doses of nicotine. They require varieties of tobacco leaf which were only developed in the last 150 years and which are still being refined. The patterns of use most associated with commercial tobacco products are the compulsive ones typical of drug dependencies (Chapter 2; USDHHS 1988), and tobacco and tobacco smoke from these products causes enormous morbidity (Chapters 6 and 7; USDHHS 1989).

This chapter reviews the pharmacokinetics of nicotine and the major types of tobacco and tobacco derivatives found in commercial products. It then describes the major tobacco products presently available in the United States, how they work, and some of the practical results of differences among them. This is followed by a brief consideration of a rapidly emerging class of nicotine delivery devices that are relatively free of tobacco. Some of these novel designs have been produced by tobacco companies with the intention of sustaining dependence on nicotine while others have been developed by ethical pharmaceutical companies as adjuncts for the management of nicotine dependence (Chapter 12). The chapter concludes with a discussion of some of the considerations which have a bearing on how one might approach policy issues posed by these devices.

A specific nicotine delivery device, whether a cigarette or a nicotine patch, emerges from a crucible of technical feasibility and commercial viability. For more than 40 years, both product development and commercial viability in this industry have been heavily influenced by concerns about the toxicity of the product. Moreover, a specific device is but a single part of the entire product package, which also includes its associated design, wrappings, imagery, and marketing (Slade 1985; Warner 1986; Davis 1987). These themes will be touched on as specific nicotine delivery devices are examined.

ABSORPTION AND DELIVERY OF NICOTINE

Nicotine (Figure 2–1) is the major pharmacologically active alkaloid in tobacco (USDHHS 1988). Its pKa is 8.0, which means that at this pH, half the nicotine is ionized and half is un-ionized. In acidic environments, where the pH is lower, the drug is largely ionized and does not easily cross biologic membranes, while it crosses them readily in the un-ionized, alkaline state. For instance, nicotine gum is buffered with sodium carbonate to raise the pH of the mouth from 7.0 to 8.0 to facilitate nicotine absorption. If the pH of the mouth is lowered by drinking a beverage such as coffee or carbonated beverages, absorption of nicotine from the gum is temporarily blocked (Henningfield et al. 1990).

Accordingly, tobacco products designed to promote oral absorption of nicotine present the drug in an alkaline state. For instance, traditional preparations of oral tobacco in Central America and betel quid containing tobacco in South Asia both include powdered lime in the recipe (see Brooks 1952). Smokes from traditional pipe and cigar tobaccos are puffed rather than inhaled, with nicotine absorption being assured by their alkalinity (pH 8.5). In contrast, smokes derived from flue-cured tobaccos are acidic (pH 5.5), and there is virtually no absorption of nicotine in the mouth from smoking devices such as cigarettes which use these tobaccos (Benowitz 1988).

Nicotine itself is irritating to the back of the throat, especially in the nonionized, alkaline form (USDHHS 1988). In the ionized form, more nicotine is dissolved in the "tar" droplets of the smoke, and the tars are thought to cushion the sensory impact of cigarette smoke on the throat. Tobacco smokes with low pH values are less irritating to the back of the throat, making them easier to inhale (see, e.g., Lawson, Bullings, Perfetti 1989).

The lungs present an enormous surface area for inhaled smoke, and even ionized nicotine is readily absorbed across the respiratory epithelium with an efficiency of over 90% (USDHHS 1988). Absorption into the pulmonary circulation results in the rapid delivery of nicotine to the arterial system and from there to the brain. Inhaled nicotine reaches the brain in less than half the time required for orally absorbed nicotine. Moreover, the peak arterial drug concentration immediately after smoking a cigarette is up to three times higher than the simultaneous venous level (Henningfield, London, Benowitz 1990). Inhalation provides higher, more rapid, and briefer surges of nicotine to the brain compared to oral or nasal administration. Ginzel (1987) has suggested that inhaled nicotine can also produce central effects in less than two seconds by stimulation of the vagus nerve (USDHHS 1988). These characteristics make inhaled nicotine more reinforcing and hence more capable of initiating and sustaining dependence on nicotine. This is similar to the differences seen between the nasal insufflation of cocaine and the inhalation of cocaine taken as crack.

The tobacco in cigarettes contains about 10 mg of nicotine, regardless of brand and regardless of Federal Trade Commission (FTC) rated nicotine yield (Benowitz et al. 1983). The average daily intake of nicotine among a group of heavy smokers was 37 mg, with a range of 10–72 mg (Benowitz 1988). The nicotine intake from a single cigarette averaged 1.0 mg with a range of 0.37–1.56 mg.

TOBACCO AND TOBACCO DERIVATIVES

Four major types of leaf are major ingredients in nearly all tobacco products in the United States. Two types, flue-cured and light air-cured (comprising Burley and Maryland varieties), are known as blond tobaccos because of their lighter coloring. Dark tobaccos comprise the third type, and oriental leaf the fourth. In addition, several derivatives of tobacco leaves contribute to various products in important ways. These include tobacco sheet, expanded tobacco, and tobacco extracts, including nicotine itself.

Types of Tobacco

Flue-cured Tobacco

Flue-cured tobacco was developed in North Carolina in the mid-nineteenth century. The farmers of Caswell County are generally credited with discovering and popularizing this now dominant variety (Tilley 1948; Slade 1990). Flue-cured is also called bright leaf or Virginia tobacco. Flue-cured leaf is the only tobacco variety used in conventional British cigarettes, and it is the major ingredient in American blend brands (Akehurst 1984).

Flue-cured tobacco is notable for having a high sugar:nitrogen ratio; good quality leaf contains 15–24% sugars (Wolf 1967; Tso 1972; Akehurst 1984). This is accomplished by harvesting leaves past their prime and by controlling moisture loss in the dark curing barn with heat transmitted from wood or fossil fuel furnaces via flues. This results in chemical changes that preserve much of the sugar content. Flue-curing requires an enormous amount of energy, and in developing countries, where most flue-cured tobacco is now grown, it is common for trees to be felled to fuel the curing barns on a nonsustainable basis (Chapman and Wong 1990).

The abundant sugars and low nitrogen content produce an acidic smoke when flue-cured tobacco is burned.

Light Air-cured Tobacco

Burley Tobacco. The blond form of Burley tobacco originated in Brown County, Ohio in 1864 (Robert 1949). The large cellular structure of the Burley leaf permits it to absorb relatively large amounts of casings, especially sugars. Burley leaf can absorb up to 25% of its own weight in casing materials, which is about three times the absorptive power of flue-cured leaf (Akehurst 1984). This characteristic has made Burley leaf a staple of the chewing tobacco trade and also explains its popularity in American blend cigarettes. This variety is also a major ingredient in many mixtures for pipe smoking.

Burley tobacco is cured in a shaded, well-ventilated structure without external heat. The resulting cured leaf contains virtually no sugar (Wolf 1967), but because of its absorptive capacity, sugars are easily added back during processing.

Maryland Tobacco. This light variety is also air-cured. As its name implies, production was, until recently, exclusive to Maryland, although there is now limited production in Italy to serve the Swiss market. This variety is distinguished by its "extreme fluffiness, good burning properties, relatively low nicotine content and a neutral aroma" (Akehurst 1984, p. 377). Maryland leaf has a density which is only 75% of flue-cured or Burley leaf. In burning, it tends to sustain a smolder which reduces the likelihood that a burning cigarette will self-extinguish. This characteristic has led to the inclusion of Maryland tobacco in American blend cigarettes since R. J. Reynolds added a small amount of the leaf to the blend used for the cigarette brand Camel in 1916 (Tilley 1985).

Dark Tobaccos

The dark tobaccos most closely resemble the traditional tobacco varieties originally used by native Americans. They are air-cured and often fermented (Akehurst 1984). As a result, they have exceedingly low sugar contents and produce an alkaline smoke. Dark tobaccos are the traditional tobaccos for cigar wrappers and fillers, and they comprise much of the tobacco used for chewing and for many pipe mixtures around the world. Dark tobaccos have also been used in cigarettes, for instance in the traditional cigarettes of France and Spain. Dark tobaccos for cigarettes are rapidly being supplanted by blond tobaccos with the breakdown of traditional national monopolies in these countries and as the European Community begins to impose ceilings on permissible tar deliveries in cigarettes. Dark tobacco is used in the bidi of India and the kretek, or clove cigarette, of Indonesia (see later).

Oriental Tobaccos

Tobacco cultivation in southeastern Europe and Turkey began in the sixteenth century. The small-leafed "oriental" varieties from this region are cured in the sun and allowed to ferment during storage. Their characteristic aroma is derived from resins and waxes produced by trichomes on the leaf surface (Cerwenka 1984). They have a moderate sugar content (Wolf 1967). These varieties are an essential minor ingredient in American blend cigarettes, valued for their aroma.

Cigarette Blends

Until the introduction of Camel by R. J. Reynolds in 1913, cigarette brands in the United States depended on three different formulas: Turkish (oriental) leaf, flue-cured leaf, and a blend of the two. Camel represented an important departure from this formula with the addition of Burley tobacco to a flue-cured/Turkish blend (Tilley 1985). Reynolds was originally a manufacturer of chewing tobacco, and he had extensive experience in the use of Burley tobacco for those products since this variety permitted the greatest addition of flavorings without the product becoming soggy. He had pioneered the addition of Burley tobacco in smoking mixtures with the introduction of Prince Albert smoking mixture in 1907, so adding Burley to a cigarette blend was a short step for him to take.

Camel was the first American blend cigarette. Its success, relying on a novel product with a coherent, national marketing strategy and distribution network (Sobel 1978; Tilley 1985; Slade 1989), forced other companies to follow its lead with a repositioning of Chesterfield, and the launching of Lucky Strike (1916) and Old Gold (1926) (Sobel 1978; Tilley 1985). Formulas for specific brands vary, but American blend cigarettes are reported to be 40–75% flue-cured, 15–45% Burley, 1–5% Maryland, and 5–15% oriental leaf (Wolf 1967). Conventional British cigarettes are based entirely on flue-cured leaf.

Tobacco Derivatives

Tobacco Sheet

Tobacco paper or tobacco sheet, often termed *reconstituted tobacco* by the industry, was developed in the 1950s at the R. J. Reynolds Tobacco Company as a way to utilize scrap and stems which otherwise were wasted (Moshy 1967; Tilley 1985). Made with a variety of processes, tobacco sheet has become an important ingredient in a variety of products. By the mid-1960s, it had come to substitute for an average of 15% of the tobacco in cigarette blends (Moshy 1967). The material is used instead of conventional cigarette paper for products such as the so-called little cigars, smokes that are manufactured and packaged like cigarettes but that are subject to lower taxes and no federal health warning requirements because they are regulated as cigars.

An advantage of tobacco sheet is that its composition can be adjusted precisely as it is synthesized. Adhesives, binders, humectants, and other additives can be easily included. As Moshy has noted, "It is difficult to obtain uniform distribution of an additive in an blend of natural tobacco shreds. On the other hand, it is relatively easy to make a reconstituted sheet with an additive as part of the formulation and thus obtain uniformity in the distribution of the additive" (1967, p. 82; Silberstein 1985). The deliveries of tar and nicotine from various tobacco sheets are somewhat less than that from tobacco leaf itself (because of the stems), so the use of sheet as a substitute for tobacco is also a factor in the design of so-called low tar cigarettes.

Expanded Tobacco

Expanded or "puffed" tobacco is used to decrease the amount of tobacco needed per unit volume of cigarette. Using rapid thermal transfer techniques to volatilize a liquid impregnated into a tobacco leaf, the cellular structure of the leaf can be permanently expanded. Materials which have been used for this process include alcohol, freons, carbon dioxide, ammonia, ammonium carbonate, nitrogen, and water (Voges 1984). The first commercially utilized process for expanding tobacco was a freon-based process developed by the R. J. Reynolds Tobacco Company. Over the last 20 years, the use of expanded tobacco has increased markedly. There are substantial amounts of expanded tobacco in today's cigarettes: Regular, "full flavor" brands have about 15% expanded tobacco; "light" brands, 25%; and "ultralight" brands up to 50% (Boxman 1992).

Tobacco Extracts and Nicotine

Various extracts of tobacco are easily prepared using a variety of solvents. Nicotine can be further purified from such extracts and converted to various salts as well. There are numerous allusions to the use of nicotine as an additive in tobacco products among industry patents (e.g., Lawson, Bullings, Perfetti 1989), and the director of research for American Tobacco testified at a product liability trial that the company used alcohol "denatured with nicotine" as an additive (Leek 1988). Silberstein has discussed the "fortification" of reconstituted tobacco sheet with nicotine as a routine procedure at LTR Industries, a cigarette paper-making division of Kimberly Clark (1985). The use of nicotine as an additive permits precise titration of the amount of this alkaloid in the finished product. The nicotine used in the Favor inhaler, in Premier, and in nicotine gum is extracted from tobacco (see next section).

TOBACCO PRODUCTS

Cigarettes

> A cigarette is the perfect type of a perfect pleasure. It is exquisite, and it leaves one unsatisfied.
>
> Oscar Wilde
> *Picture of Dorian Gray*

Although cigarettes make up 95% of all tobacco products consumed in the United States today (Grise 1992), this device is a relative newcomer to the marketplace. Cigarettes were a novelty for well-to-do ladies and dandies in the mid-nineteenth century. They were initially made by hand of oriental leaf by largely immigrant labor in New York. Production began to move to Virginia and North Carolina after the Civil War, but in the days before matches, most tobacco was consumed as chew (Robert 1949; Brooks 1952), and this, not the cigarette, was the dominant form of tobacco in the United States until the 1920s.

The cigarette's coming of age was made possible by the confluence of several factors: the invention and refinement of the cigarette-making machine (1884), the availability of capital to expand what had been a modest enterprise into a large monopoly, transport and communication systems that permitted widespread product distribution and promotion, and a portable and safe source of ignition—the match (Tennant 1950; Wagner 1971; Slade 1989).

James Bonsack won a contest for a cigarette-making machine held by the Allan and Gintner cigarette company of Richmond. The rights to Bonsack's invention were returned to the inventor when the company realized it did not know how to sell as many cigarettes as this machine could make (Valentine Museum 1990). Bonsack took his invention to James Duke in Durham, North Carolina, and Duke's engineers refined the mechanism while Duke devised ways to sell the vastly increased output of lower-priced smokes made possible by the machine. Duke moved his offices to New York to be closer to sources of capital. Presaging efforts in the 1990s to use foreign markets to absorb excess cigarette-making capacity, Duke's first scouting expedition to develop overseas sales began in 1884 (Chandler 1977). This international interest eventually led to the establishment of the British American Tobacco Company whose entire production in the early years came from Duke factories in the United States. Duke's domestic success became the Tobacco Trust which monopolized cigarette production and controlled much of the chewing tobacco market from 1890 until it was dismantled in 1911. In 1909, the American Tobacco Company was the third largest industrial enterprise in the United States behind U.S. Steel and Standard Oil (Chandler 1962).

Despite its substantial growth from the 1880s through the breakup of the trust, the cigarette industry was still in its infancy. In 1900, adult per capita cigarette consumption in the United States was only 54 sticks per year. In 1911, the figure was 173. A variety of laws were passed in 14 states outlawing selling and using cigarettes (Dillow 1981; Tate 1989), but enforcement became impossible and these laws were gradually repealed in the wake of the growing popularity of cigarettes after the first American blend cigarette, Camel, was introduced and popularized beginning in 1913. Cigarette consumption began to rise more briskly, reaching a peak in per capita consumption in 1963 of 4,345 cigarettes per person over 18 years of age (Figure 5–1).

Over the last 80 years, a number of innovations have been made in the cigarette and its packaging (Slade 1989). The following discussion will emphasize two which have particular importance to health care professionals: the development of filters and the evolution of low tar smokes. Before examining these two strategies in detail, though, I will first review additional details about cigarette ingredients, the FTC testing method for determining yields of tar, nicotine, and carbon monoxide and a general description of available engineering techniques to modify cigarettes.

Ingredients

There are no legal restrictions on what may be added to tobacco products. Besides tobacco and tobacco derivatives, numerous other ingredients are used. They can be added to parts of the tobacco blend itself as casing (a soaking solution) or as top dressing (sprayed onto the blend and mechanically mixed in) or they can be added to tobacco sheet during the sheet-making process (see earlier; Silberstein 1985). Similarly, ingredients can be added to the cigarette paper and to the filter during their respective manufacture. There is even a technique for adding menthol by putting it in the packaging and letting it sublimate into the finished product.

The range of additives is enormous, ranging from humectants, salts, and sugars to pharmacologically active agents such as menthol to complex flavorants.

Sugars are added to casing sauces to balance the overall chemical composition of a tobacco blend, so the smoke is not too alkaline and harsh, and licorice is a common ingredient to reinforce the sweetness of the sugars and to bring out a specific, desired flavor (Leffingwell, Young, Bernasek 1972). The tobacco industry uses most of the world's supply of licorice. Other classic casing ingredients include cocoa, acids, fruit extracts, and humectants. "Reaction flavors" may also be included (see later; Silberstein 1985).

Humectants such as glycerol and diethylene glycol prolong shelf life by helping retain moisture. In the 1930s, this class of additive was the basis for claims of reduced nose and throat irritation from Philip Morris cigarettes (Flinn 1935; Mulinos and Osborne 1935).

The first mentholated cigarette, introduced in 1927, was Spud, developed by race car driver Lloyd "Spud" Hughes. The local anesthetic qualities of menthol were features in initial advertising promoting it as an ideal cigarette for the smoker who had a sore throat (Sobel 1978). Kool, which has long been the dominant player in the menthol market, was introduced in 1932.

Various inorganic salts are used to alter the burning characteristics of cigarette paper, and a wide variety of essential oils and fragrances have been used as ingredients in tobacco products (Leffingwell, Young, Bernasek 1972), but the lists of additives are treated as trade secrets. It is widely believed that the use of flavoring agents has increased as tar deliveries have decreased (USDHHS 1981, 1989), but the government has no authority to force disclosure in this area. The only regulatory concession the industry has made to concerns about these ingredients has been the sharing of a master list of additives with no brand specificity with the secretary of the Department of Health and Human Services (DHHS).

The industry reportedly relies mostly on additives that are recognized food additives or are constituents of tobacco (Tobacco International staff 1992), although a substance's being on such a list of additives does not ensure that its inhalation is without hazard or that its combustion products are safe.

An additive that had long been an ingredient but has been set aside because it is banned from food products is coumarin, from the herb named deer tongue. "Reaction flavors," certain pyrazine compounds that result from the reaction of amino acids with carbohydrates and other compounds when heated, cause what food flavorists call the "browning effect." Reaction flavors are important for low tar brands even though many are not heat stable: some "continue to react after formulation creating additional compounds" (Tobacco International staff 1992). The toxicology of these families of compounds based on reaction flavors would seem to be incompletely understood.

Silberstein (1985) has recounted how casing materials, flavorings, and additional nicotine can be added to the final blend via reconstituted tobacco sheet.

The FTC testing method

There are at least 2,550 known compounds in processed, unadulterated tobacco, and tobacco smoke contains over 4,000 compounds (USDHHS 1989). Table 7–1 lists 43 cigarette smoke constituents recognized by the International Agency for Research on Cancer (IARC) as carcinogenic, and the major components of the vapor and particulate phases are detailed in the 1989 Report of the Surgeon General (USDHHS 1988). Alpha radiation from ^{210}Pb and ^{210}Po found in cigarette smoke also contributes to the carcinogenic risk (Martell 1982; Cohen and Harley 1982). Reported values for the tar content of cigarette smoke only provide a crude index of what is being consumed.

From 1967 to 1985, standardized yields of tar and nicotine from nationally sold cigarette brands were regularly published by the FTC. Since 1988, the Tobacco Institute has continued the practice. Carbon monoxide yield was added to the other two measures in 1981.[1] Test results are printed in small type on cigarette advertising, and comparisons among various brands based on these values have been staples of advertising in the low

tar segment for 25 years (Coalition on Smoking OR Health 1988).

Although the standardized testing method used for these assays has come to be known as the *FTC test method* (Pillsbury et al. 1969), its key parameters originated in the laboratories of the American Tobacco Company in the 1930s (Kozlowski 1983; Bradford, Harlan, Hammer 1936). These parameters are: 35 ml puffs taken over 2 seconds 1 minute apart until the test cigarette has been shortened to a specific butt length. The parameters were "arbitrarily selected" (Bradford, Harlan, Hammer 1936) after consideration of a set of measurements reported by Pfyl in 1933. The standard puff volume seems low, however. Pfyl had reported air intakes during smoking of from 29 to 61 ml, which correspond to puff volumes (considering the additional gas contributed by the cigarette) of 35–73 ml (Kozlowski 1983). This wide range has been confirmed in more recent studies. The range of *mean* puff volumes observed in 18 studies conducted between 1978 and 1986 was 21–66 ml, the range of *mean* puff durations in 27 studies was 1.0–2.4 sec, and the range of *mean* interpuff intervals in 24 studies was 18–64 sec (USDHHS 1988). The ranges of these puffing behaviors are wide, and they are skewed toward values that would result in higher deliveries of smoke than the values used in the "standard" machine-based test.

Finally, the standard test does not record the number of puffs taken from a given cigarette, and this may vary widely. In one series, various brands of king size filter cigarettes had from 6.9 to 11.5 average puffs per cigarette in the assay (USDHHS 1981).

Engineering Techniques to Modify Cigarette Yields

Table 1–1 summarizes the ways a cigarette designer can lower tar yields on standard smoke assays. The available techniques fall into two categories: those that reduce the number of puffs taken by the machine and those that lower the concentration of material in the smoke.

Shorter tobacco rods lead to fewer puffs. Even an average reduction of one puff per cigarette can lead to a commercially impor-

---

[1] A tabulation of the entire data set from 1967 to 1988 is available from the Tobacco Merchants Association (1989).

Table 1–1   Lowering Machine-measured Cigarette
Yield

I. Reduce the number of puffs per cigarette
   A. Shorten the tobacco rod
      1. Longer filters
      2. Longer overwrap of tipping paper
   B. Increase the burn rate of the tobacco rod
      1. Chemical additives
      2. Higher porosity paper
      3. Less tobacco per unit volume

II. Reduce the concentration of smoke constituents
   A. Use tobaccos and tobacco substitutes with lower
      yields
   B. Decrease the amount of tobacco per unit
      volume
      1. Expanded tobacco
      2. Increased use of flavorings and additives
   C. Increase amount of room air diluting
      mainstream smoke
      1. Increased porosity of cigarette paper
      2. Increased porosity of filter plug wrap
      3. Ventilation holes in filter tipping paper
   D. Increase efficiency of the filter
      1. Longer filter
      2. Denser filter

Source: Modified from Kozlowski 1983.

tant reduction in tar yield: Apparent tar
yield from a cigarette with a tar value of 15
at 10 puffs might only rate 13.5 at 9. Shorter
tobacco rods result when longer filters are
used (USDHHS 1981; Grunberg et al.
1985). Smoking less of the tobacco rod also
leads to fewer puffs. Since the FTC test only
smokes a cigarette down to within 3 mm of
the tipping paper overwrap, wider tipping
paper leads to fewer puffs on the machine.
(Tipping paper is the relatively stiff paper at
the proximal end of the cigarette which
holds the filter onto the tobacco rod.) Between 1967 and 1979, 18 brands of filter cigarette underwent increases in overwrap
width that reduced the amount of tobacco
smoked in the cigarettes on the machine,
even though the remaining tobacco is still
smokable. This design change led to decreases in tar yield. Over the same period, 11
other brands achieved decreases in tar yield
by lengthening the filter (Grunberg et al.
1985).

Increasing the rate at which cigarettes
burn can also lower the puff count. Increasing the efficiency of combustion by mixing
more air with the puff through the use of
high porosity paper, using additives which
promote burning, and reducing the amount

of fuel in a given volume by using expanded
tobacco contribute to this phenomenon
(Kozlowski 1985).

Lowering the concentration of smoke
constituents can be accomplished in several
ways. The first is by reducing the amount of
precursors in the material to be burned. Tobacco sheet prepared from stems produces
less tar and lower levels of polycyclic aromatic hydrocarbons (PAH) than an equivalent amount of conventional tobacco leaf.
Changing agronomic practices and the selection of lower yielding leaves can also contribute to this effect. The use of higher quantities of burley tobacco in the blend can
lower the overall tar yield and reduce PAH
and phenol levels, but this substitution increases the yield of nitrogen oxides which
has the potential to increase the levels of
N-nitrosamines (USDHHS 1989). The
amount of tobacco and tobacco derivatives
in the rod can also be decreased by diluting
the blend with cellulose fibers from other
plant sources. The most celebrated attempt
to do this was the failed effort by three British
cigarette companies in the 1970s to include
what they called "new smoking material"
(NSM) and "Cytrel" in their blends (see
later).

The use of expanded tobacco reduces the
amount of raw material needed to fill out a
tobacco rod. This technique has been extensively employed (Boxman 1992). Between
1967 and 1979, the average 33% reduction
in tar yield seen among U.S. cigarettes was
associated with a 20% reduction in the
weight of tobacco used to make them
(USDHHS 1981). Reducing the amount of
tobacco and tobacco derivatives carries with
it the need to include more additives and flavor enhancers in the recipe.

Following the dictum that the solution to
pollution is dilution, concentrations, and
hence machine-measured deliveries, of
smoke constituents can be lowered by mixing more ambient air with the smoke. This is
done by increasing the porosity of the cigarette paper and the filter plug wrap and by
drilling holes in the cigarette paper or, more
commonly, in the tipping paper (Durocher
1985; Maeda 1985). The use of papers of
varying porosity is well illustrated by the
availability of three varieties of E-Z Wider

rolling papers on the U.S. market: regular, light, and ultra-light. The only way a rolling paper by itself can affect yield is by changes in porosity.

The first entry into the low tar sweepstakes, Carlton, featured the ventilation hole approach in its initial advertising campaign.[2] For instance, an advertisement from July 1964 illustrates 13 rings of ventilation holes around the filter end of the cigarette (American Tobacco Company 1964).

Patients who complain that smoking "ultra low tar" cigarettes is like smoking air are in large measure correct. The dramatic effects of both dilution techniques are evident in the widely varying results of tar and nicotine testing of one "roll your own" (RYO) tobacco blend packed into 17 different preassembled, commercially available filter tubes (Kaiserman and Rickert 1992).

Kozlowski, Pope, and Lux (1988) have called attention to the fact that people who smoke vented cigarettes often block the holes, even though smoking machines never do. Because blocked ventilation holes result in different staining patterns on filters than unblocked holes, the researchers were able to estimate the prevalence of hole blocking that defeats this aspect of cigarette design. Among butts from 135 cigarettes with a machine-rated tar yield of 4 mg or less, ventilation holes in 19% had been completely blocked, and a partial block was evident in 39%. Only 42% had been smoked without the ventilation holes being obstructed.

The final method for reducing specific constituents of tobacco smoke is filtration. Cellulose acetate filters have some ability to reduce the levels of phenol and of volatile N-nitrosamines in smoke, and charcoal particles may reduce volatile aldehydes and hydrogen cyanide (USDHHS 1989). These benefits are very modest in comparison with the promise manufacturers have held out for their filters.

In practice, the combination of these techniques has been effective in lowering the machine-measured yields of tar and nicotine. Since 1967, when the FTC began performing machine smoking tests, there has been a

[2]The reader is invited to examine the tipping paper of "low tar" cigarettes. Circumferential holes will usually be found.

steady decline in sales-weighted average tar and nicotine yields. Average tar values declined from about 22 to 14 mg (36% decline), and nicotine yields fell from about 1.4 to 0.9 mg (36% decline). Nearly all of these changes occurred before 1980: the sales-weighted yields have been virtually unchanged over the past dozen years. In a single, unfiltered king-sized cigarette brand, the yield of benzo[a]pyrene fell by 50% between the early 1950s and 1980 (USDHHS 1981).

Whether the changes in cigarette construction described in this section have been important for the health of people who smoke and for the public at large is considered later in this chapter.

Filters

The first successful cigarette filter designed to reduce the inhalation of toxins was marketed by the Wix brothers in Great Britain in 1930 as the key feature of Du Maurier. Previous filters had been novelties designed to keep particles of tobacco from getting into the mouth or had been marketed with no accompanying basis for their claims of benefit. In contrast, Du Maurier was launched with a data-filled booklet titled *Pharyngolaryngeal Inflammation* aimed at the medical profession. The filter was designed "as a valuable means of preventing 'smoker's cough' and other adverse effects on the pharynx, larynx, or general health, traceable either directly or indirectly to the irritants and acrids in tobacco smoke" (Technical Research Department 1930). Not only did this filter remove irritants, the claim went, it also allowed the virtually unimpeded passage of nicotine into the mainstream smoke "so that *the 'normalising' effect of tobacco smoke, which constitutes the main reason for smoking, remains unimpaired"* (emphasis in original) (Technical Research Department 1930, p 17).

The rolled crepe paper design of the Du Maurier filter was copied in the United States by Viceroy, introduced in 1935. A legend on the back of a 1944 pack of Viceroy claims, "Throat irritants checked." By 1952, the health claim had become bolder. An advertisement for the brand bearing the headline, "Leading N.Y. doctor tells his patients what to smoke!" proclaimed, "Filtered cigarette smoke is better for health" (Brown and Williamson 1952).

The publication of authoritative data linking cigarette smoking with lung cancer led to a sharp decline in overall cigarette sales in the early 1950s. Putting filters on the product gave tobacco companies the opportunity to claim that they were doing what they could to make smoking safe (Wagner 1971; Slade 1989). Because there was no regulatory oversight of cigarette design and only incomplete regulation of advertising claims, companies made overt claims of benefit that were far grander than any actual protection afforded.

Among the most extreme claims were those made by P. Lorillard for the Kent brand, which was launched in 1952. It boasted that Kent with the Micronite filter afforded the "greatest health protection" of all cigarettes on the market (P. Lorillard 1953). Kent accomplished this feat by employing a filter based on crocidolite, a form of asbestos (Slade 1988). Although the manufacturer claimed the filtering agent was "a pure, dust-free, completely harmless material" (P. Lorillard 1954), asbestos was known at the time to be hazardous, and the "dust-free" claim was contrary to the findings of two electron microscopists the company had hired to examine smoke from Kent cigarettes. An epidemic of asbestos-caused disease has occurred among workers in the factory that made the filters (Talcott et al. 1989), and several lawsuits have recently been filed against the cigarette company by people with mesothelioma whose only credible exposure to asbestos was the Kent cigarettes they smoked in the early to mid 1950s. The asbestos was finally removed from Kent cigarettes in 1956 or 1957.

By 1955, filter cigarettes commanded 19% of the market, up 30-fold from the 1950 level (Table 1–2), and within another 5 years, more than half of all cigarettes had filters. This amazing shift in the market reversed the cigarette's declining fortunes, and the sag in per capita consumption produced by the cancer scare reversed by mid-decade (Figure 5–1).

The cigarette makers used a variety of measures to reinvigorate sales. Besides the

Table 1–2   Market Share for Filter and Low Tar Cigarettes in the U.S. 1950–89

Year	% Filters	% Tar <15 mg
1950	0.6	—
1955	19	—
1960	51	—
1965	64	2
1970	80	3.6
1975	87	13.5
1980	92	44.8
1985	95	51.9
1989	95	55.9

Sources: Warner 1986; FTC 1991.

addition of filters with unsubstantiated promises of health protection, the industry professed to have "an interest in people's health as a basic responsibility, paramount to every other consideration in our business" in full page advertisements in major newspapers across the country (Tobacco Industry Research Committee 1954). It promised to get to the bottom of the smoking and health controversy. In contrast to usual prudence in such matters, however, the industry saw no reason to advise people to stop smoking while they awaited the final results.

Health claims for filter cigarettes became muted following the issuance of FTC guidelines on such claims in 1955. However, as discussed at a congressional hearing on filtered cigarettes, the idea had already been planted in the public mind that filters were devices to reduce the risks of smoking (Committee on Government Operations 1957). Ironically, a Department of Agriculture spokesman testified at the same hearing that tobacco leaves that had long been regarded as of poorer quality because of their harshness when smoked had become popular with major cigarette manufacturers as the production of filter cigarettes gathered momentum. The testimony suggested that harsher tobaccos were being used in some filter brands to produce the sensations and satisfaction customers had come to expect from their unfiltered smokes.

Low Tar

A week before the first Surgeon General's Report on Smoking and Health was issued in February 1964 (USPHS 1964; Terry

1983), the American Tobacco Company tried to gain an advantage on Dr. Luther Terry. American introduced Carlton nationwide in advance of the bad news from Washington without first trying it out in test market. As Camel had done in 1913, as Kent had done in 1952, so now with Carlton: this brand established an important new market segment, the low tar, low nicotine cigarette (Wagner 1971).

By the mid-1960s, it was apparent that filters were not a panacea. While there remained hope that filters provided some protection, it was becoming clear that people who used filtered cigarettes still got sick from smoking. The 1964 report sparked a major flurry of activity against cigarettes among the FTC, the Federal Communications Commission, and the Congress which only abated with the ban on cigarette advertising in electronic media (Wagner 1971). In this climate, cigarette companies increasingly offered an alternative to smoking conventional cigarettes on the one hand and to quitting altogether on the other. This alternative was the low tar smoke.

Occasionally, the sales talk was explicit, pitching a brand to people who would otherwise be quitting. For instance, an advertisement for True quotes an earnest young woman, "All the fuss about smoking got me to thinking I'd either quit or smoke True. I smoke True" (P. Lorillard 1975). Vantage weighed in with "How many times have you tried to give up smoking?" (R. J. Reynolds 1976).

In 1977, three British tobacco companies offered a dozen brands made with 25% "tobacco substitute," materials like NSM and Cytrel (Taylor 1984). By replacing some of the tobacco in the blends, tar delivery was reduced. Scientific articles praising these efforts appeared (Russell 1976; Freedman and Fletcher 1976), but the public health community objected that these products offered a false hope of safer smoking and confused and diluted the public health message about smoking (Taylor 1984). The products never caught on with the public, and they were abandoned after about a year.

Around the world, "light" smokes are promoted in response to health concerns. These brands are introduced into a market not as a way to offer customers the least hazardous way to enjoy the product but as a response to increased visibility of the serious health hazards of smoking. Two examples from the Far East are illustrative.

Although Marlboro Lights was introduced in the United States in 1971, it was launched in a major way in Hong Kong only in 1982. An executive with the Philip Morris advertising agency in Hong Kong noted a few years later, "We started advertising Marlboro Lights in 1982. That's when we were feeling the pressure of the government's antismoking campaign" (Kwok 1986).

Indonesia's clove cigarettes are notorious for their extraordinarily high tar deliveries. Yields of 40 mg and higher are not uncommon (see later). The clove cigarette industry only began marketing a version with substantially reduced tar when the government began to talk seriously about requiring a health warning on cigarette packs for the first time.

Finally, in the winter of 1991–92, nicotine patches were introduced into the United States with much fanfare (Hwang and Valeriano 1992). In light of the many other examples of propitious timing, it is not surprising that Philip Morris chose this occasion to launch the brand extension, Merit Ultima ("Surprising Flavor at only 1 mg Tar") (Philip Morris 1992). It is as though Philip Morris were inviting people who found themselves still smoking despite the patch to comfort themselves by taking up Ultimas.

As with filters, so, too, with low tar: the companies develop and introduce products to suit their public relations needs, not the needs of public health (Slade 1989).

Table 1–2 summarizes the rise of the low tar segment since the mid-1960s. In 1989, cigarettes with 12.1–15.0 mg FTC rated tar comprised 6.7% of the market, brands with 9.1–12.0 mg had 26.9%, those with 6.1–9.0, 10.1%, those with 3.1–6.0, 9.0%, and brands with a tar yield of 3.0 mg or less had only 2.4% of the market (FTC 1991).

What have been the effects of these products on public health? The obvious issue raised by this question, namely, the toxicologic effects of smoking "light" cigarettes compared to "regular" smokes on people who would be smoking anyway, is discussed in the next section. The less obvious, but equally important question is this: How does the presence of cigarettes that have connotations of being less hazardous affect the dynamics of tobacco use among the entire population at risk for smoking? This second question will be considered in the section on public policy.

Toxicology of Low Tar Cigarettes

Individuals who smoke show remarkable consistency in plasma nicotine and breath carbon monoxide levels from day to day and even from year to year when smoking the same brand (Lynch and Benowitz 1987). Subjects smoking cigarettes through ventilated cigarette holders smoke more intensely as the dilution factor is increased (USDHHS 1988), and in experiments with ventilated cigarettes, the number of puffs taken on each cigarette decreases if ventilation holes are experimentally blocked (USDHHS 1988).

Numerous studies have been done since the late 1970s to correlate machine-rated yields and actual exposures in individuals. Some find no correlation between FTC ratings and nicotine, tar, and carbon monoxide absorption except at the very lowest yields (1 mg tar) (Benowitz et al. 1986), while others find small positive correlations, albeit ones that are still far less than would have been predicted on the basis of the machine-estimated yields (Woodward and Tunstall-Pedoe 1992). The strongest predictor of nicotine intake in these studies is the number of cigarettes smoked per day.

Maron and Fortmann (1987) have provided an especially useful analysis of their population based study of 713 smokers. In this group, the number of cigarettes smoked increased as FTC rated nicotine yield decreased. "In multivariate analysis, the number of cigarettes smoked per day accounted for 28 per cent and 22 per cent of the variance in observed expired-air carbon monoxide and plasma thiocyanate levels, respectively, whereas nicotine yield accounted for only 1 per cent and 2 per cent of the variance, respectively." (p. 546)

Kozlowski (1989) examined the proportion of cigarette advertising spending on brands of various tar yields in relationship to their market share. While sales of moderately low tar brands increased with boosts in spending on advertising, consumption of brands in the lowest tar category, 1–3 mg, fluctuated in the narrow range of 2.6–3.7% of all sales over an 8-year period despite remarkably large relative advertising expenditures on this category early in the period. Kozlowski interprets these data as suggesting that the cigarette brands in the "ultra-low tar" category are unacceptable to most people who smoke. The experimental data of Benowitz et al. (1986) of smokers switched from their usual brand to brands of varying yield corroborate these findings from the marketplace: tar, nicotine, and carbon monoxide exposure were similar for all but the lowest yield brands. The "ultra-low yield" brands (1 mg of tar) were associated with reductions of only 49% for tar, 56% for nicotine, and 36% for carbon monoxide.

There are many ways smokers can adjust smoking behavior to titrate the dose of nicotine. The major ones include the number of cigarettes consumed per day, the number of puffs taken with each cigarette, the puff volume, the depth and duration of inhalation, and whether hole blocking is practiced. These modulations of smoking behavior tend to be in the direction of a consistent level of intake which markedly blunts the supposed benefits of lower yield smokes as measured by the intake of smoke constituents.

Are low tar cigarettes less hazardous? Unfortunately, the answer is not by much, if at all, at least within the range of tar yields among brands popular in the United States in recent decades (Benowitz 1989).[3] While most of the literature addressing this question for lung cancer concludes that there is a modest reduction in lung cancer risk among

[3] There is no doubt, however, that cigarettes with a yield of, say, 15 mg tar are less toxic than those with yields of 30 mg tar or higher. But the latter sort of cigarette has not been sold in the United States for 30 years. Thus, imposing ceilings on tar yields where these levels remain unusually high, for instance China and Indonesia, is sound public health policy while further tar reductions may make little sense for the United States.

low tar smokers (USDHHS 1981, 1989; Kaufman et al. 1989), one recent study found no risk reduction at all in the low tar group after the number of cigarettes smoked was taken into account (Wilcox et al. 1988). The risk of heart disease appears to be unchanged (USDHHS 1981, 1989; Palmer, Rosenberg, Shapiro 1989).

Despite industry-fueled hype that genuinely less hazardous cigarettes might be practical (Gori and Lynch 1978; Barclay 1978), this promise has not been kept, and the National Cancer Institute abandoned its search for a less hazardous cigarette more than a decade ago (Warner and Slade 1992). Smokers of nearly all low yield cigarettes do not take in substantially lower amounts of toxins compared to smokers of other brands on the U.S. market today, and they do not experience substantially lower rates of serious illness. These data have led informed observers to recommend abstinence (Benowitz et al. 1985; USDHHS 1989; Benowitz 1989). As recently as 1983, major textbooks in internal medicine and family medicine advised physicians to recommend low tar smokes for patients who would not or who could not quit smoking (Warner and Slade 1992). This recommendation had uniformly disappeared from all major textbooks of primary care medicine by the mid-1980s.

Other Gimmicks in Cigarette Design

In the 1920s, cigarettes with reduced nicotine content were introduced with extravagant health claims, and a decade earlier, perfumed cigarettes made an appearance as smokes for ladies. Cigarette makers in the late 1980s revived these ideas with trials of brands such as Next De-nic, Merit De-nic, Horizon, and Chelsea (Slade 1989; Broder 1990). The latter two brands, which incorporated an incense in the cigarette paper, were promoted with "scratch 'n sniff" advertisements proclaiming them to be "the first cigarette that smells good." So-called low smoke cigarettes have been tried: Passport, Vantage Excel, and Virginia Slims Superslims. The claim made for these smokes was that they produce less visible sidestream smoke when smoldering. This effect is achieved by adding large quantities of a variety of organic or inorganic salts to the cigarette paper (Hampl, Fields, Bullwinkel 1989). While use of these papers may reduce *visible* sidestream smoke, the levels generated of many smoke constituents is not lessened (Slade 1989).

A company named CA Blockers marketed Spectra that featured an additive called N-Bloctin. On remarkably scanty evidence, the company claimed that N-Bloctin lowered the risk of lung cancer from smoking by interfering with the absorption of N-nitrosamines in cigarette smoke (Slade 1989). The Food and Drug Administration (FDA) examined the situation and determined that N-Bloctin was a drug because it was intended to prevent a disease (lung cancer) and, by extension, that cigarettes containing N-Bloctin were also drugs (Slade et al. 1992b).

In China, several brands of cigarette containing traditional Chinese herbal medicines such as ginseng and bluish henbane are widely available. Ginseng is reputed to have general restorative powers, and bluish henbane is regarded as a specific remedy for bronchitis. The Pecs Cigarette Factory in Hungary, now managed by the British American Tobacco Company, produces a filter impregnated with granules of vitamin C, allegedly to reduce certain toxins in cigarette smoke (Doolittle 1991).

These and other similar gimmicks share a basic characteristic: they appeal to yearnings for safe or socially acceptable smokes without altering the fundamental toxicity inherent in the product for smokers or for bystanders (Chapters 6 and 7).

Clove Cigarettes

Kretek, or the clove cigarette, was developed in Indonesia early in the century. Kreteks are composed of cloves (up to 40%) and dark tobaccos, although blond tobaccos have begun to find their way into some blends. The mixture probably became popular because the local anesthetic in clove, eugenol, permitted the inhalation of the harsh smoke from locally grown, sun-cured, dark tobaccos. Since the mid-1960s, kretek manufacture has gradually grown from a cottage industry with factories of hand rollers to an oligopoly dominated by a few large companies who increasingly rely on machinery. Kretek has come to dominate the Indonesian cigarette market at the expense of blond tobacco cigarettes in a way unparalleled anywhere else in the world. While blond cigarettes are rapidly overtaking dark tobacco cigarettes elsewhere in Asia and Europe, the category is in retreat in Indonesia. Although once dominant, only 11% of cigarettes in Indonesia were conventional blond cigarettes by 1989. The rest were kretek (Tobacco Journal International 1991). The major kretek manufacturers operate marketing and distribution systems strikingly similar to those of the major cigarette companies in the United States and Europe, and several have forged alliances with some of the industry's multinational corporations.

A study of smoke yields from kretek found tar levels between 48 and 113 mg, of which from 10 to 23 mg was eugenol (Wise and Guerin 1986). Nicotine yields varied from 2.2 to 4.5 mg. High nicotine yields such as these are characteristic of markets in developing countries where consumption per consumer is low because of low levels of disposable income. Lower yield brands are just being introduced in Indonesia as the government takes small steps toward increasing the visibility of health concerns about smoking.

Kretek imports into the United States began to rise in the 1970s. The novelty was especially popular among teenagers, and in California, it was said to be a training device for people interested in learning how to smoke marijuana. In the mid-1980s, the market suffered a temporary collapse in the wake of a series of case reports of acute health problems associated with this device (Schechter et al. 1985). Review of several of the cases suggested that eugenol anesthetized the throat sufficiently to contribute to aspiration of food or stomach contents. Suspicions were also raised of direct toxicity to the respiratory passages from eugenol or other substances in the smoke. Several states banned the sale of kretek and others considered such action.

A trade organization representing the importers responded to these reports with a public relations campaign based on animal inhalation studies of kretek smoke (Gooch 1986). Staff at the American Medical Association prepared a report on clove cigarettes at the request of the House of Delegates (Council on Scientific Affairs 1988). The report concluded that kretek was toxic in the same way as other cigarettes, that the presence of eugenol was likely associated with an increased risk of aspiration, and that some individuals were probably susceptible to "severe lung injury" from inhaling smoke from kretek.

Since the late 1980s, kretek consumption has again begun to rise in the United States. It is likely that use remains highest among the young.

Fire Safety

Most cigarettes continue to smolder if left unattended. This characteristic is responsible for fires caused by lit cigarettes which become caught in upholstery and bedding (McGuire 1989). The design defect leads to 1,500 deaths from fire each year, including the deaths of 130 children (McLoughlin and McGuire 1990).

The Technical Study Group established by the Fire Safe Cigarette Act of 1984 established the feasibility of making fire safe cigarettes. Its research established that the ignition propensity of cigarettes could be reduced by "low tobacco density, small circumference, low paper porosity, and in some cases elimination of citrate addition to the paper. Considerably larger reductions were achieved with combinations of these properties" (McGuire 1990). Furthermore, fire safety could be achieved with cigarettes that matched the tar, nicotine, and carbon monoxide yields of the leading commercial brands.

The Fire Safe Cigarette Act of 1990 takes these findings a step further. It is developing a standard assay that can be used to assess the fire safety of a given cigarette. Once a standardized assay is develped and approved by the National Institute of Standards and Technology in the Commerce Department, it is expected that legislative efforts to require that cigarettes comply with this standard will move forward.

Cigars and Pipe Tobaccos

Cigars are dark tobacco leaves that have been rolled together and covered with a wrapper or a binder plus a wrapper. These coverings have traditionally also been tobacco leaves, but in recent years, reconstituted tobacco sheet has often been substituted. Cigars comprised only 1.5% of the tobacco product market in 1991 (Grise 1992), the result of a steady decline from 5.5% in the 1970–74 period.

Pipe tobaccos can be blends of a wide variety of leaf types, including dark tobacco blends as well as blond blends which are very similar to cigarette blends (such as Half and Half, a mixture of equal parts flue-cured and Burley tobaccos). They are often heavily cased and flavored to give distinctive aromas and tastes. This, too, is now a small market.

The pathologies most clearly associated with cigar and pipe smoking are a wide variety of oral and laryngeal problems (USDHHS 1989). Cardiovascular disease and lung cancer risks have also been observed (Ockene et al. 1987). This pattern reflects the fact that smoke from these devices is more often puffed than inhaled. Nicotine absorption across the buccal mucosa is facilitated by the alkaline nature of the smoke from dark tobaccos (Benowitz 1988).

Ockene and her colleagues used serum thiocyanate (SCN) measures to estimate exposure of the lungs to tobacco smoke from various nicotine delivery devices in the Multiple Risk Factor Intervention Trial (MRFIT) population (1987). Nearly all absorption of SCN from smoke occurs in the lungs. They found that people who smoked pipes or cigars had lower SCN levels than those who smoked cigarettes, as would be predicted on the basis of presumed inhalation patterns. However, people who had switched from cigarettes to pipes, cigars, or both had SCN levels higher than those smoking these devices who had never smoked cigarettes. This suggests that switchers were more likely to inhale than those who had never smoked cigarettes. Furthermore, those who only smoked pipes had higher SCN levels than those who only smoked cigars, whether or not they had previously smoked cigarettes. This may reflect the heterogeneity of pipe tobaccos, with some mixtures having characteristics more like cigarette tobacco blends.

Moist Snuff and Chewing Tobacco

Although moist snuff and chewing tobacco are a small segment of the U.S. tobacco industry, moist snuff is the only traditional nicotine delivery device that is experiencing *increases* in sales volume (see Chapter 13). Growth in this category is largely explained by increased use among adolescent boys, fueled by a deliberate, comprehensive marketing strategy combining the design of a family of products with advertising and promotion to "graduate" novices from sweet, low nicotine brands such as Skoal Bandit to more alkaline, high nicotine brands such as Copenhagen (Chapter 13; Jarvik and Henningfield 1988).

Among the constituents of oral tobacco products, the preformed carcinogens have caused the greatest concern because of their abundance and the oral cancers associated with the use of these products (Hoffman, Djordjevic, Brunnemann 1991). Moist snuff is by far the leading source of N-nitrosamines in commercial products. Observed levels of one of these carcinogens, Nitrosodiethanolamine, have varied from 40 to 6,800 ng/g of product. Between 1981 and 1990, however, the level of this compound in one brand of moist snuff fell nearly two orders of magnitude to the (still very high) levels prevalent in chewing tobacco. This suggests that, as with the makers of cigarettes, the manufacturers of oral tobacco products sometimes quietly refine the formulation of their mixtures in response to scientific evidence of harm despite official posturing that there is no connection between the use of a given product and disease.

OTHER NICOTINE DELIVERY DEVICES

In the past decade, a number of nicotine delivery devices have appeared that are strikingly different from traditional tobacco products. Some have been marketed for use alongside traditional devices, while others have been developed by ethical pharmaceutical companies for use as therapeutic agents. This is a rapidly emerging category; patents and trade journals offer the interested reader clues to an intriguing array of possible future nicotine delivery devices, the description of which is beyond the scope of this chapter (Dagnoli 1991).

Nontherapeutic Devices

The Favor Smokeless Cigarette, introduced in 1985, was a nicotine inhaler consisting of a plastic tube resembling a cigarette which had a nicotine-impregnated foam plug at the distal end (USDHHS 1989). It delivered a small amount of nicotine vapor to the user. It was marketed as a temporary substitute for tobacco products when it was inconvenient to smoke. Since the manufacturer's literature clearly described the product as a device intended to sustain a dependence on nicotine, the FDA exerted its regulatory authority over it as a drug (USDHHS 1989; Slade 1989). The FDA has also determined that a device strongly resembling Favor, "22 Twenty-two Smoke-free Cigarettes," is a drug (Food and Drug Administration 1989), but the device has been marketed in Japan outside of that nation's drug regulations.

In 1987, the Pinkerton Tobacco Company, the leading producer of chewing tobacco, introduced Masterpiece Tobacs, a chewing gum impregnated with shreds of tobacco (USDHHS 1989). This product, essentially a sweetened, 1 mg, over the counter nicotine gum, was packaged neatly and did not require the use of a spittoon. It, too, was marketed as a socially acceptable alternative to other forms of tobacco. The FDA determined that Masterpiece was a food product (chewing gum), and pointed out that tobacco had not been approved as a food additive. Pinkerton withdrew Masterpiece from the market.

Also in 1987, the R. J. Reynolds Tobacco Company announced the development of a "revolutionary" product, a device that heated, rather than burned, "tobacco" (R.J. Reynolds Tobacco Company 1988; USDHHS 1989; Slade 1990). The device

consisted of an aluminum cylinder containing alumina beads impregnated with glycerin, propylene glycol, and a nicotine-rich tobacco extract called "spray-dried tobacco" by Reynolds, plugged at the distal end with a piece of charcoal. When the charcoal was lit and a puff taken through the device, the alumina beads became hot, generating an aerosol that contained nicotine (nominal delivery 0.4 mg) as well as substantial amounts of carbon monoxide. An elaborate mouthpiece subassembly consisting of a roll of reconstituted tobacco sheet and a piece of polypropylene acted as a cooling chamber for the effluent before it entered the consumer's mouth.

A year after the device was first announced, the company started to test market Premier in St. Louis and in Phoenix amid strong protests from medical and public health groups. The Coalition on Smoking OR Health and the American Medical Association petitioned the FDA to regulate Premier as a drug (USDHHS 1989). In January 1989, scientists at the National Institute on Drug Abuse reported that Premier could be easily modified to deliver crack (Cone and Henningfield 1989). The resulting adverse publicity, combined with continued opposition from public health authorities and poor performance in test markets, forced Reynolds to withdraw the product a month later, before FDA acted on the petitions (Slade, 1990).

Therapeutic Devices

Nicotine gum and several nicotine patches are marketed as adjuncts for the management of nicotine dependence (Chapter 12; Henningfield and Stitzer 1990). In addition, a nicotine nasal spray and a nicotine vapor inhaler are among the other devices being developed for potential therapeutic use. An inhaler from KABI Pharmacia Therapeutics AB is based on the patents for Favor, and highly preliminary clinical results are beginning to appear (Glover et al. 1992).

As discussed in Chapter 12 and elsewhere (Slade et al. 1992a; Hughes, in press), while the approved formulations already have an important supportive role in the therapy of nicotine dependence, there are numerous as yet unanswered questions about the optimal roles these devices might eventually have.

PUBLIC POLICY ISSUES

Policy discussions about the public health value of nicotine delivery devices such as low tar cigarettes have usually focused exclusively on an idealized user who is unalterably committed to continuing the use of nicotine (Gori and Lynch 1978; Gori and Bock 1980; USDHHS 1981; Benowitz et al. 1985; Benowitz 1989; USDHHS 1989). Essays have appeared more recently that advocate making tobacco-free nicotine delivery devices widely available in open market competition with tobacco products (Russell 1991), which is essentially the same approach taken by Reynolds with Premier (R. J. Reynolds Tobacco Company 1988).

In reality, however, nicotine delivery devices have a much broader potential market than people already addicted to nicotine who are uninterested in quitting. It is important to reflect on who else is affected by such products as policy approaches are formulated (Slade et al. 1992a, 1992b).

For instance, Silverstein, Feld, and Kozlowski (1980) have suggested that the widespread availability of low nicotine cigarettes contributed to the increase in smoking among teenage girls seen in the 1970s. The use of low yield cigarettes as starter products by teenagers is an unintended accompaniment of policies intended to provide a "less hazardous" alternative for people who continue to smoke. These policies were pursued between the mid-1950s and 1981 by some medical and public health authorities (Committee on Government Operations 1957; Warner and Slade 1992), and they are still vigorously advocated by the industry.

Something as seemingly simple as pack size has intriguing policy implications as well. Kozlowski (1987) has pointed out that a smaller pack might encourage lower consumption among smokers, which would presumably lead to reduced morbidity because of the striking relationships between number of cigarettes smoked and illness. In response to this editorial, however, Chapman (1988)

noted that smaller pack sizes encourage cigarette purchases among teenagers.

Clearly, there are important groups other than hopelessly addicted smokers that must be considered in developing policy approaches to the design and availability of nicotine delivery devices.

Briefly, the groups that should be explicitly considered in such analyses include the following (Slade et al. 1992b):

Novices: New smokers are needed to replace those who die or who have quit. This is a strikingly dynamic process: over half of current smokers have begun to smoke since the publication of the first Surgeon General's Report in 1964. About 70% of teenagers experiment with cigarettes at least once.

Potential Quitters: Three-fourths of people who smoke want to stop smoking, and a third try to do so each year.

Former Smokers: Nearly half of all men in the United States who have ever smoked regularly have already quit smoking; however, relapse is not uncommon and may occur years after quitting.

The introduction of new nicotine delivery devices with potential appeal to people in these three groups demands thoughtful consideration. The World Health Organization has called for a ban on oral tobacco products in countries that have no tradition of their use, and at least a half dozen countries have adopted this recommendation as national policy (WHO Study Group on Smokeless Tobacco Control 1988). Norway has gone further. It has barred the introduction of any novel nicotine delivery device except as a drug (Slade 1990).

It may be prudent to declare a moratorium on the introduction of nicotine delivery devices outside the drug regulation system until a coherent system for regulation is established (Warner and Slade 1992; Slade et al. 1992b).

CONCLUSION

Tobacco products cause enormous suffering and death, and the chief agent of the pandemic is the cigarette. Attention to the design of nicotine delivery devices and the context in which they are developed and used is informative for clinical practice and essential for public health practice. Experience with these devices over the last 40 years offers many pertinent lessons and suggests useful directions for the future.

REFERENCES

Akehurst, B. C. Leaf types: Flue-cured, light air-cured and dark air-cured. In Voges, E., ed. *Tobacco Encyclopedia.* Mainz, Germany: *Tobacco Journal International,* 1984.

American Tobacco Company. Test results on the pack. *Time* 24 July 1964, 37.

Barclay, W. R. Smoke screens. *JAMA* 240:1271, 1978.

Benowitz, N. L. Pharmacologic aspects of cigarette smoking and nicotine addiction. *N Engl J Med* 319:1318–1330, 1988.

————. Health and public policy implications of the "low yield" cigarette. *N Engl J Med* 320:1619–1621, 1989.

Benowitz, N. L., Hall, S. M., Herning, R. I., Jacob, P. III, Jones, R. T., Osman, A.-L. Smokers of low-yield cigarettes do not consume less nicotine. *N Engl J Med* 309:139–142, 1983.

Benowitz, N. L., Feinleib, M., Feyerabend, C., Garfinkel, L., et al. Is there a future for lower-tar-yield cigarettes? *Lancet* 1111–1114, 16 November 1985.

Benowitz, N. L., Jacob, P. III, Yu, L., Talcott, R., Hall, S., Jones, R. T. Reduced tar, nicotine, and carbon monoxide exposure while smoking ultralow- but not low-yield cigarettes. *JAMA* 256:241–246, 1986.

Boxman, A. R. Unveiling the secrets of primary processing. *Tobacco International* 194(4):16–19, 1 March 1992.

Bradford, J. A., Harlan, W. R., Hammer, H. R. Nature of cigarette smoke. Technic of experimental smoking. *J Indust Engin Chem* 28:836–839, 1936.

Broder, K. New generation cigarettes: safety or smoke screen? *JNCI* 82:89–91, 1990.

Brooks, J. E. *The Mighty Leaf.* Boston: Little Brown and Co., 1952.

Brown and Williamson. Leading N.Y. doctor tells his patients what to smoke! *Time* 17 November 1952, 62.

California Rural Indian Health Board. *Tobacco: Use it in a Sacred Way.* Sacramento, CA: California Rural Indian Health Board, 1991.

Cerwenka, K. Oriental leaf. In Voges, E., ed. *Tobacco Encyclopedia.* Mainz, Germany: Tobacco Journal International, 1984.

Chandler, A. D., Jr. *Strategy and Structure: Chapters in the History of the Industrial Enterprise.* Cambridge, MA: MIT Press, 1962.

————. *The Visible Hand: The Managerial Revolution in American Business.* Cambridge, MA: Belknap Press of Harvard University Press, 1977.

Chapman, S. Smaller packs of cigarettes. *Am J Public Health* 78:92–93, 1988.

Chapman, S., and Wong, W. L. *Tobacco Control in the Third World.* Penang, Malaysia: International Organization of Consumers Unions, 1990.

Coalition on Smoking OR Health. Petition before the Food and Drug Administration to classify "low tar" cigarettes as drugs. Washington, D.C.: Coalition on Smoking OR Health, April 1988.

Cohen, B. S., and Harley, N. J. Radioactivity in cigarette smoke. *N Engl J Med* 307:310–311, 1982.

Committee on Government Operations. *False and Misleading Advertising (Filter-Tip Cigarettes).* Washington, D.C.: House of Representatives, 85th Cong., 1st sess., July 1957.

Cone, E. J., and Henningfield, J. E. Premier "smokeless cigarettes" can be used to deliver crack. *JAMA* 261:41, 1989.

Council on Scientific Affairs. Evaluation of the health hazard of clove cigarettes. *JAMA* 260:3641–3644, 1988.

Dagnoli, J. "Smokeless" cig not out. *Advertising Age* 18 November 1991; 3.

Davis, R. M. Current trends in cigarette advertising and marketing. *N Engl J Med* 316:725–732, 1987.

Dillow G. L. The hundred-year war against the cigarette. *American Heritage* February/March 1981.

Doolittle, D. E. Beauty and order. *Tobacco Reporter* 118(10): 28–29, 1991.

Dunn, W. L., Jr. *Motives and Incentives in Cigarette Smoking.* Richmond, VA: Philip Morris Research Center, 1972.

Durocher, D. F. The influence of paper components on the delivery of low-tar cigarettes. *Tobacco Journal International* 3:186–189, 1985.

Federal Trade Commission (FTC). Report to Congress for 1989 pursuant to the federal cigarette labeling and advertising act. Washington, D.C.: Federal Trade Commission, 1991.

Flinn, F. B. Some clinical observations on the influence of certain hygroscopic agents in cigarettes. *Laryngoscope* 45:149–154, 1935.

Food and Drug Administration. Letter from Kevin M. Budich, compliance officer, Division of Drug Labeling Compliance, to Dominic J. Biondi, president, Mechtronics Corporation, Stamford, CT, 18 April 1989.

Freedman, S., and Fletcher, C. M. Changes of smoking habits and cough in men smoking cigarettes with 30% NSM tobacco substitute. *Br Med J* 1:1427–1430, 1976.

Garner, W. W., *The Production of Tobacco*. Philadelphia: Blakiston Company, 1946.

Ginzel, K. H. The lungs as sites of origin of nicotine-induced skeletomotor relaxation and behavioral and electrocortical arousal in the cat. *Proceedings of the International Symposium on Nicotine*. Goldcoast, Australia: ICSU Press, 1987.

Glover, E. D., Glover, P. N., Sullivan, C. R., Sullivan, P., Nilsson, F., Sawe, U. Nicotine inhaler versus placebo in smoking cessation. Abstract No. 237 presented at the 8th World Conference on Tobacco OR Health, Buenos Aires, Argentina, 1 April 1992.

Gooch, P. U.S. kretek sales hope to benefit from health study. *Tobacco Reporter* May 1986, 44–45.

Gori, G. B., and Lynch, C. J. Toward less hazardous cigarettes. *JAMA* 240:1255–1259, 1978.

Gori, G. B., and Bock, F. G., eds. *Banbury Report 3: A Safe Cigarette?* Cold Spring Harbor, NY: Cold Spring Harbor Laboratory, 1980.

Grise, V. N. The changing tobacco user's dollar. *Tobacco Situation and Outlook Report*. Washington, D.C.: U.S. Department of Agriculture, June 1992.

Grunberg, N. E., Morse, D. E., Maycock, V. A., Kozlowski, L. T. Changes in overwrap and butt length of American filter cigarettes. *NY State J Med* 85:310–312, 1985.

Hampl, V. Jr., Fields, R. D., Bullwinkel, E. P. Sidestream reducing cigarette paper. U.S. Patent No. 4,805,644, 1989.

Henningfield, J. E., London, E. D., Benowitz, N. L. Arterial-venous differences in plasma concentrations of nicotine after cigarette smoking. *JAMA* 263:2049–2050, 1990.

Henningfield, J. E., Radzius, A., Cooper, T. M., Clayton, R. R. Drinking coffee and carbonated beverages blocks absorption of nicotine from nicotine polacrilex gum. *JAMA* 264:1560–1564, 1990.

Henningfield, J. E., and Stitzer, M. L. *New Developments in Nicotine-Delivery Systems*. Ossining, NY: Cortlandt Communications, The Cortlandt Group, 1990.

Hughes, J. R. Risk-benefit of nicotine preparations in smoking cessation. *Drug Safety,* in press.

Hwang, S. L., and Valeriano, L. L. Marketers and consumers get the jitters over severe shortage of nicotine patches. *Wall Street Journal,* 22 May 1992, B1.

Jarvik, M. E., and Henningfield, J. E. Pharmacological treatment of tobacco dependence. *Pharmacol Biochem Behav* 30:279–294, 1988.

Hoffman, D., Djordjevic, M. V. Brunnemann, K. D. New brands of oral snuff. *Food and Chemical Toxicology* 29:65–68, 1991.

Kaiserman, M. J., and Rickert, W. S. Handmade cigarettes: It's the tube that counts. *Am J Public Health* 82:107–109, 1992.

Kaufman, D. W., Palmer, J. R., Rosenberg, L., Stolley, P., Warshauer, E., Shapiro, S. Tar content of cigarettes in relation to lung cancer. *Am J Epidemiol* 129:703–711, 1989.

Kozlowski, L. T. Physical indicators of actual tar and nicotine yields of cigarettes. In Grabowski, J., and Bell, C. S., eds. *Measurement in the Analysis and Treatment of Smoking Behavior*. NIDA Research Monograph 48. Department of Health and Human Services, Public Health Service, Alcohol, Drug Abuse, and Mental Health Administration, National Institute on Drug Abuse, 1983.

————. Less hazardous smoking and the pursuit of satisfaction. *Am J Public Health* 77:539–541, 1987.

Kozlowski, L. T., Pope, M. A., Lux, J. E. Prevalence of the misuse of ultra-low-tar cigarettes by blocking filter vents. *Am J Public Health* 78:694–695, 1988.

Kwok, K.C.H. Interview with Scott Ellsworth in the offices of Philip Morris Asia, Hong Kong. From an oral history of Marlboro advertising. Washington, D.C.: Archive Center, National Museum of American History, Smithsonian Institution, 27 October 1986.

Lawson, J. W., Bullings, B. R., Perfetti, T. A. Improving smoking characteristics of higher nicotine delivery low "tar" cigarettes with levulinic acid and nicotine levulinate. U.S. Patent No. 4,836,224, 1989.

Leek, P. Testimony at trial. *Horton v. American Tobacco*. Cause #9050, Circuit Court, Holmes County, Mississippi, 1988.

Leffingwell, J. C., Young, H. J., Bernasek, E. *Tobacco Flavoring for Smoking Products*. Winston-Salem, NC: R. J. Reynods Tobacco Company, 1972.

Lynch, C. J., and Benowitz, N. L. Spontaneous cigarette brand switching: Consequences for nicotine and carbon monoxide exposure. *Am J Public Health* 78:1191–1194, 1987.

McGuire, A. Fires, cigarettes and advocacy. *Law, Medicine and Health Care,* 17:73–77, 1989.

McLoughlin, E., and McGuire, A. The causes, cost, and prevention of childhood burn injuries. *Am J Dis Child* 144:677–683, 1990.

Maeda, K. The design of ventilated filter cigarettes. *Tobacco Journal International* 3:228–233, 1985.

Maron, D. J., and Fortmann, S. P. Nicotine yield and measures of cigarette smoke exposure in a large population: Are lower-yield cigarettes safer? *Am J Public Health* 77:546–549, 1987.

Martell, E. A. Radioactivity in cigarette smoke. *N Engl J Med* 307:309–310, 1982.

Moshy, R. J. Reconstituted tobacco sheet. In Wynder, E. L., and Hoffman, D., eds. *Tobacco and Tobacco Smoke.* New York: Academic Press, 1967.

Mulinos, M. G., and Osborne, R. L. Irritating properties of cigarette smoke as influenced by hygroscopic agents. *NY State J Med* 35:590–592, 1935.

Ockene, J. K., Pechacek, T. F., Vogt, T., Svendsen, K. Dose switching from cigarettes to pipes or cigars reduce tobacco smoke exposure? *Am J Public Health* 77:1412–1416, 1987.

P. Lorillard. Which cigarette gives you the greatest health protection? *Life* 19 October 1953, 148–149.

———. Why Kent gives you more for your money than any other filter cigarette. *Life* 31 May 1954.

———. Advertisement for True cigarettes. *Ms* October 1975.

Palmer, J. R., Rosenberg, L., Shapiro, S. "Low yield" cigarettes and the risk of nonfatal myocardial infarction in women. *N Engl J Med* 320:1569–1573, 1989.

Pillsbury, H. C., Bright, C. C., O'Connor, K. J., et al. "Tar" and nicotine in cigarette smoke. *J Assoc Off Anal Chem* 52:458–462, 1969.

R. J. Reynolds. Ad for Vantage cigarettes. *Ms* 1976.

R. J. Reynolds Tobacco Company. *New Cigarette Prototypes that Heat Instead of Burn Tobacco.* Winston-Salem, NC: R. J. Reynolds Tobacco Company, 1988.

Robert, J. C. *The Story of Tobacco in America.* New York: Alfred A. Knopf, 1949.

Russell, M.A.H. Low-tar medium-nicotine cigarettes: A new approach to safer smoking. *Br Med J* 1:1430–1433, 1976.

———. The future of nicotine replacement. *Br J Addict* 86:653–658, 1991.

Schechter, F. G., Hackett, P., Rodriguez, Z., et al. Illnesses possibly associated with smoking clove cigarettes. *MMWR* 34:297–299, 1985.

Silberstein, D. A. Flavouring reconstituted tobacco. *Tobacco Journal International* 1:26–29, 1985.

Silverstein, B., Feld, S., Kozlowski, L. T. The availability of low-nicotine cigarettes as a cause of cigarette smoking among teenage females. *J Health Soc Behav* 21:383–388, 1980.

Slade, J. D. A disease model of cigarette use. *NY State J Med* 85:294–298, 1985.

———. Learning to fight *Nicotiana tabacum. NJ Med* 85:102–106, 1988.

———. The tobacco epidemic: Lessons from history. *J Psychoactive Drugs* 21:281–291, 1989.

———. Premier: The demise of a nicotine delivery system. In Durston, B., and Jamrozik, K., eds. *Tobacco & Health 1990: The Global War.* East Perth, Western Australia: Health Department of Western Australia, 1990.

Slade, J., Connolly, G. N., Davis, R. N., Douglas, C. E., Henningfield, J. E., Hughes, J. R., Kozlowski, L. T., Myers, M. L. Report of the tobacco policy research study group on adjunctive medications for managing nicotine dependence. *Tobacco Control,* 1(Suppl):S10–S13, 1992a.

———. Report of the tobacco policy research study group on tobacco products. *Tobacco Control,* 1(Suppl):S4–S9, 1992b.

Sobel, R. *They Satisfy.* Garden City, NY: Anchor Press/Doubleday, 1978.

Spinden, H. J., *Tobacco is American.* New York: New York Public Library, 1950.

Talcott, J. A., Thurber, W. A., Kantor, A. F., et al. Asbestos-associated diseases in a cohort of cigarette-filter workers. *N Engl J Med* 321:1220–1223, 1989.

Tate, C. In the 1800s, antismoking was a burning issue. *Smithsonian* July 1989, 107–117.

Taylor, P. *The Smoke Ring.* New York: Pantheon, 1984.

Technical Research Department. *Pharyngolaryngeal Inflammation.* London: Peter Jackson (Tobacco Manufacturer), Ltd., 1930.

Tennant, R. B. *The American Cigarette Industry.* New Haven, CT: Yale University Press, 1950.

Terry, L. L. The Surgeon General's first report on smoking and health. *NY State J Med* 83:1254–1255, 1983.

Tilley, N. M. *The Bright-Tobacco Industry,*

1860–1929. Chapel Hill: University of North Carolina Press, 1948.

———, *The R. J. Reynolds Tobacco Company*. Chapel Hill: University of North Carolina Press, 1985.

Tobacco Industry Research Committee. A frank statement to cigarette smokers. *New York Times* 4 January 1954.

Tobacco International staff. Too many cooks spoil the flavor. *Tobacco International* 194, no. 2 (1 February 1992):22–24.

Tobacco Journal International. Indonesian market dominated by kreteks. *Tobacco Journal International* (5):46–47, 1991.

Tobacco Merchants Association. *Directory of Cigarette Brands, 1864–1988*. Princeton, NJ: Tobacco Merchants Association of the United States, 1989.

Tso, T. C. *Physiology and Biochemistry of Tobacco Plants*. Stroudsburg, PA: Dowden, Hutchinson and Ross, 1972.

U. S. Department of Health and Human Services (USDHHS). *The Health Consequences of Smoking. The Changing Cigarette: A Report of the Surgeon General*. U.S. Department of Health and Human Services, Public Health Service, Office of the Assistant Secretary for Health, Office on Smoking and Health. DHHS Publication No. (PHS) 81-50156, 1981.

———. *The Health Consequences of Smoking: Nicotine Addiction. A Report of the Surgeon General*. U.S. Department of Health and Human Services, Public Health Service, Centers for Disease Control, Center for Health Promotion and Education, Office on Smoking and Health. DHHS Publication No. (CDC) 88-8406, 1988.

———. *Reducing the Health Consequences of Smoking: 25 Years of Progress. A Report of the Surgeon General*. U.S. Department of Health and Human Services, Public Health Service, Centers for Disease Control, Center for Chronic Disease Prevention and Health Promotion, Office on Smoking and Health. DHHS Publication No. (CDC) 89-8411, 1989.

U.S. Public Health Service (USPHS). *Smoking and Health. Report of the Advisory Committee to the Surgeon General of the Public Health Service*. U.S. Department of Health, Education and Welfare, Public Health Service, Center for Disease Control. PHS Publication No. 1103, 1964.

Valentine Museum. Cigarette Advertising: An Exhibition. Richmond, VA: Valentine Museum, 1990.

Voges, E. *Tobacco Encyclopedia*. Mainz, Germany: Tobacco Journal International, 1984.

Wagner, S. *Cigarette Country*. New York: Praeger, 1971.

Warner, K. E. *Selling Smoke: Cigarette Advertising and Public Health*. Washington, D.C.: American Public Health Association, 1986.

Warner, K. E., and Slade, J. Low tar, high toll. *Am J Public Health* 82:17–18, 1992.

Wilcox, H. B., Schoenberg, J. B., Mason, T. J., Bill, J. S., Stemhagen, A. Smoking and lung cancer: Risk as a function of cigarette tar content. *Prev Med* 17:263–272, 1988.

Wise, M. B., and Guerin, M. R. Chemical analysis of the major constituents in clove cigarette smoke. In Hoffman, D., and Harris, C. C., eds. *Banbury Report 23: Mechanisms in Tobacco Carcinogenesis*. Cold Spring Harbor, NY: Cold Spring Harbor Laboratory, 1986.

Wolf, F. A. Tobacco production and processing. In Wynder, E. L., and Hoffman, D., eds. *Tobacco and Tobacco Smoke*. New York: Academic Press, 1967.

Woodward, M., and Tunstall-Pedoe, H. Do smokers of lower tar cigarettes consume lower amounts of smoke components? Results from the Scottish Heart Health Study. *Br J Addic* 87:921–928, 1992.

World Health Organization (WHO). Study Group on Smokeless Tobacco Control. *Smokeless Tobacco Control*. Geneva: World Health Organization, Technical Report Series 773, 1988.

2

Psychopharmacology of Nicotine

JACK E. HENNINGFIELD, CAROLINE COHEN, and WALLACE B. PICKWORTH

Nicotine as delivered by use of tobacco products is highly addictive (see also Chapter 1). Regular ingestion of the alkaloid often produces a drug dependence in exactly the same sense that regular ingestion of heroin, cocaine, and alcohol can produce dependence. While the cultural context of drug use may influence the prevalence of dependence on a particular drug and the chances that a casual user will become addicted, pharmacologically, nicotine is as addictive as heroin and cocaine, although not more so (Henningfield, Cohen, Slade 1991). This chapter discusses the psychopharmacology of nicotine in the context of drug dependence in general.

The focus of this chapter is on the pharmacologic actions of nicotine that are important in the establishment and maintenance of nicotine dependence. Other chapters address the equally important social and environmental determinants of tobacco use, such as social pressures to use tobacco (Chapter 4) and the availability and financial cost of tobacco products (Chapter 3). Chapter 10 provides clinical guidelines for assessing the degree of nicotine dependence in an individual patient.

Nicotine produces a broad and diverse range of effects of which only some are clearly relevant to the behavior of smoking. For example, nicotine, like morphine, can elicit vomiting and reduce skeletal muscle tone; nicotine, like cocaine, can increase heart rate and produce vasoconstriction; nicotine, like alcohol and barbiturates, can induce marked intoxication, especially during early use episodes. These effects of nicotine do not, however, appear to be prominent influences on tobacco use. How does nicotine affect mood and behavior? What physiologic actions of nicotine are important in determining why people smoke? Among the effects of nicotine that smokers find desirable, which might be considered specific effects of nicotine administration and which are more appropriately considered suppression of undesirable nicotine withdrawal effects? Answers to these questions are not only important for better understanding of the reasons people smoke and the difficulties many face in their attempts to quit, but they also can help patients and health care providers understand which factors they can manipulate in the management of addiction to nicotine.

GENERAL PHARMACOLOGY OF NICOTINE

An overview of the chemistry, pharmacodynamic, and pharmacokinetic properties of nicotine is included because these properties influence its psychopharmacologic characteristics. The material is supplemented in this book in Chapters 1 and 10, the 1988 Surgeon General's Report (USDHHS 1988), and Gilman and associates (1985). The interested reader may consult these sources for original references.

As shown in Figure 2–1, nicotine is composed of a pyridine and a pyriolidine ring. It is one of the few natural alkaloids that exist in the liquid state. The pure alkaloid is a clear, volatile, alkaline liquid that turns

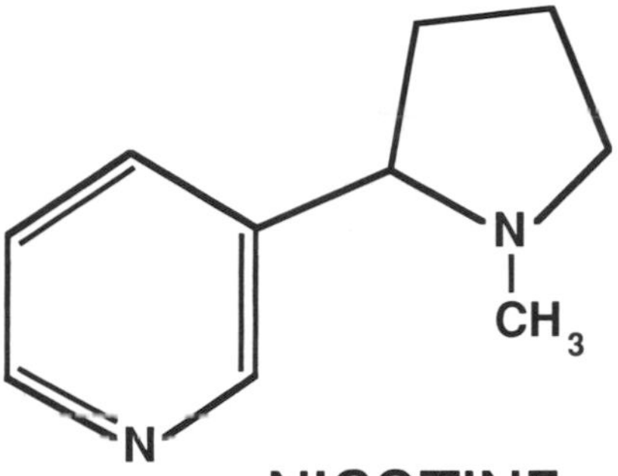

Fig. 2–1   Nicotine.

brown on exposure to air. It has the smell of tobacco. Nicotine may exist in two different stereoisomers. Pharmacologically active 1-nicotine is the only form found naturally, although cigarette smoke contains about 10% d-nicotine apparently derived from racemization during the combustion process.

Various forms of tobacco contain differing amounts of nicotine; the tobacco in cigarettes contains about 8 mg of nicotine. This amount is similar across all brands of cigarettes whether they are "low yield" or not. However, the amount of nicotine delivered to the smoker varies widely across cigarette brands from 0.1 to 1.9 mg per cigarette.

Although nicotine is the major alkaloid in tobacco accounting for about 1.5% of the dry weight of tobacco, other alkaloids are present in smaller quantities. These substances make up about 8–12% of the total alkaloid content and may have pharmacologic importance. Among these alkaloids are: nornicotine, anabasine, myosmine, anabatine, and cotinine. Smoking topography and cigarette design influence the delivery of the component alkaloids including nicotine.

Pharmacokinetics and Metabolism of Nicotine

Absorption of Nicotine

Nicotine is distilled from burning tobacco and is carried on "tar" droplets and in the vapor phase. Absorption across membranes is dependent on the drug being available in the nonionized state. Nicotine is a weak base with a pK of 8.0: in alkaline media, the mol-

ecule is nonionized, while in acidic media, it is ionized. Most cigarette smoke (from flue-cured tobacco and "American blend" mixtures) is acidic and the acidity increases as the cigarette is smoked. Consequently, there is little buccal absorption of nicotine after cigarette smoking. Smoking from air-cured tobacco (used in cigars, pipes, and some European cigarettes) has an alkaline pH, and considerable nicotine absorption occurs in the mouth. After cigarette smoking, nicotine is rapidly absorbed from the lung where the pH rises to 7.4 and the surface area is large. Smokers absorb up to 90% of the nicotine in the mainstream cigarette smoke.

Chewing tobacco, snuff, and nicotine polacrilex gum have an alkaline pH that facilitates the buccal absorption of nicotine. Nicotine base is also readily absorbed through the intact skin. Such absorption accounts for cases of toxicity in tobacco field workers and from nicotine-containing pesticides. Transdermal absorption is applied therapeutically in the nicotine patch, which is available as an adjunct to smoking cessation (Chapter 12).

Bioavailability of nicotine in the gastrointestinal tract is limited. Nicotine is poorly absorbed from the stomach due to the acidity of the gastric fluid. Nicotine is absorbed from the intestine, but it largely undergoes metabolism on first pass through the liver before it enters into the systemic circulation.

Metabolism of Nicotine

Nicotine is extensively metabolized before elimination. Depending on urine flow and pH, from 2 to 35% of nicotine is excreted unchanged, but typically the range is from 5 to 10%. Most metabolism (85–90%) occurs in the liver to the primary metabolites cotinine and nicotine oxide. The cotinine pathway is a cytochrome p 450-dependent, two-step oxidation process. Cotinine itself is extensively metabolized (only about 17% is excreted unchanged) to further oxidized products including (among others): cotinine oxide, norcotinine, and cotinine methonium ion. The liver metabolism is rapid and nearly complete. Total clearance averages 1,300 ml/min and nonrenal clearance averages 1,100 ml/min. Nonrenal clearance represents about 70% of liver blood flow, indicating that about 70% of nicotine is cleared from the blood during each pass through the liver.

After an intravenous dose of nicotine, there is rapid distribution to body tissue—especially the brain. After tissue equilibrium, the half-life of nicotine in the blood is about 120 minutes. The half-life is useful in describing the blood nicotine levels observed in smokers over a 24-hour period. Upon arising, blood nicotine averages 5 ng/ml. These levels rise with the day's smoking to a plateau of 30–40 ng/ml over 3–4 half-lives (6–8 hr). The blood nicotine levels then gradually decline after the subject discontinues smoking at bedtime. Peaks and troughs follow the smoking of each cigarette, but as the day progresses the overall level increases and the influence of each cigarette diminishes. Thus, nicotine is not a drug to which the smoker is intermittently exposed. Rather, considerable accumulation occurs over the day and appreciable levels of nicotine persist in the plasma.

The metabolism and elimination of cotinine is of interest because of blood and urine levels of cotinine are used as qualitative indices of nicotine ingestion. Cotinine blood levels average about 250 ng/ml. After stopping smoking, the levels decline with a half-life of 18–20 hours. The long half-life is consistent with the observation that cotinine levels show little fluctuation with each cigarette over the day.

Pharmacologic Properties

Nicotine is a powerful pharmacologic agent that changes cardiovascular, neural, endocrine, and skeletal muscle functions. Its effects are dependent on dose, rate of administration, tolerance level of the person, and rate of elimination. While the focus of this chapter is on the effects of nicotine responsible for its abuse liability, it is important to recognize that other actions of nicotine are present, and the person may associate these with the reinforcing effects of tobacco.

Nicotine readily crosses biological membranes and acts upon specific receptors in the brain and the periphery. Activities at receptors in the brain are associated with changes in electrical cortical activity as well as with the generation of evoked potentials and motor potentials.

Nicotine affects nearly all components of the endocrine and neuroendocrine systems. For example, it stimulates the release of anterior and posterior pituitary hormones including: prolactin, adrenocorticotropic hormone (ACTH), B-endorphin, B-lipotropin, growth hormone, vasopressin, and neurophysin.

Nicotine has direct and indirect effects on several neurotransmitters. At peripheral autonomic ganglia, nicotine is a cholinergic agonist at low doses and an antagonist at high doses. Besides its direct action at ganglionic cholinergic receptors, nicotine releases acetylcholine (ACh) from the myenteric plexus. Release of ACh from neurons in the cerebral cortex is thought to be responsible for the electroencephalogram (EEG) activation seen after nicotine administration.

Nicotine releases epinephrine and norepinephrine from the adrenal gland and from peripheral nervous tissue. The pressor response to nicotine in the cat is due in part to epinephrine release from the adrenals. The increase in heart rate after nicotine in humans is also due to adrenal mechanisms. Nicotine also releases norepinephrine and dopamine from neurons in the brain. These effects are thought to be involved in its neuroendocrine activation.

Receptor Interactions

Nicotine binds to specific receptors on neurons in the central nervous system (CNS) and to receptors in the periphery located on cells in autonomic ganglia and on skeletal muscle cells. The binding sites on the autonomic ganglia and adrenal medulla (C6 or ganglionic type) are ordinarily activated by ACh. Nicotine binding at these sites is blocked by hexamethonium. Binding sites on skeletal muscle (C10), are located at the muscle end plate. ACh ordinarily activates these sites, which are blocked by decamethonium and alpha-bungarotoxin. Generally, higher doses of nicotine are required to stimulate C10 receptors than C6 receptors. Doses of nicotine in ordinary smoking do not affect the muscle end plate. In the brain, C6-type receptors have been identified, and the action of nicotine at these sites alters electrophysiologic responses, local metabolism, neurotransmitter release, and behavior. Many of these actions are prevented or reversed by mecamylamine, a C6 nicotine antagonist with central and peripheral actions.

Cardiovascular Effects

Among the most prominent and easily measured effects of nicotine are increases in heart rate and blood pressure, and decreased skin temperature due to vasoconstriction in the extremities. These actions are due to stimulation of the sympathetic autonomic ganglia, release of catecholamine from the adrenal medulla, and discharge of catecholamines from sympathetic nerve endings. Nicotine also stimulates chemoreceptors in the carotid artery and the aortic arch causing reflex tachycardia, increases in blood pressure, and vasoconstriction.

Gastrointestinal Effects

Nicotine stimulates parasympathetic autonomic ganglia and the release of ACh from the myenteric plexus and nerve endings. These changes increase tone and motor activity of the bowel and occasionally produce diarrhea. Nausea and vomiting also occur, but these effects are due to nicotine's effect on the brain stem.

PERCEPTIONS OF NICOTINE DEPENDENCE

In the 1950s, World Health Organization (WHO) experts made a distinction between "habituating" and "addicting" drugs based largely on whether a characteristic withdrawal syndrome was evident following abrupt cessation of a drug and on the apparent strength of the resulting drug-seeking behavior (WHO 1952). At the time, the addictions were widely considered to be personality disorders. The requirements that there be a withdrawal illness for a drug to be regarded as addictive was dropped in 1964 (WHO 1964). This same group of experts recognized that the strength of drug-seeking

could vary widely both within and across drugs so that this feature was not useful in attempting to differentiate drugs according to whether they were *addictive* or *habituating.* Another landmark came in 1980, when the American Psychiatric Association classified drug addictions separately from personality disorders (APA 1980). For several centuries references had been made to compulsive or addictive tobacco use, but it was not until the 1970s that biomedical research and epidemiologic observations left little doubt that nicotine was a highly addicting drug (Russell 1976). In the 1980s, the National Institute on Drug Abuse, and then the U.S. Surgeon General, came to similar conclusions (USDHHS 1984, 1987; see Kanigel 1988; USDHHS 1988).

We now understand that drug dependence, or addiction, is a compulsive behavior in which the role of a specific psychoactive drug is prominent. Important to this concept is the notion that dependence-producing drugs can be identified independent of specific examples of drug addiction in humans. That is, the abuse or addiction liability as well as physical dependence potential of chemicals can be predicted from the results of various human and animal test procedures. It is helpful to consider the status of nicotine as a dependence-producing drug and tobacco use as an instance of drug dependence from both epistemological and empirical perspectives. The epistemology of nicotine dependence has evolved with those of other drug dependencies over the past several decades. It is interesting to identify the conceptual threads that have remained common and those that have changed as clinical observations and experimental data have accrued over time. The empirical perspective compares the pharmacology of nicotine and the behavior of tobacco self-administration to the pharmacology of and the behaviors associated with other drug dependence disorders (e.g., opioid, cocaine, and alcohol dependence). We will draw such comparisons later in this chapter.

Epistemology

From the earliest recorded uses of the term *addiction,* its primary connotation has been of the behavior of individuals, for example, "addicted to others for stipendes" (in the year 1560), "addicted to virginitie" (in 1590), "addicted to wine or strong drinke" (in 1612), and "addicted to useful reading" (in 1771) (Murray et al. 1933). The referent for the term *addiction* was the behavior of the individual, and the connotation was that the behavior was very strong, excessive, irrational, or compulsive. The term *drug addiction* came to describe compulsive self-administration of substances such as alcohol, opiates, marijuana, and cocaine which directly alter behavior and which produce effects that promote readministration. In the 1940s and early 1950s, the term *drug addiction* assumed additional meaning. It came to carry the implication that, following a period of continuous use, deprivation of an addictive substance would lead to a withdrawal syndrome (WHO 1952). This refinement emerged largely from studies documenting the withdrawal syndrome occurring when morphine use was suddenly discontinued. The notion that a chronic state of intoxication was produced was also frequently referred to and appears to have arisen from observations of chronic high dose alcohol use because this characteristic did not apply to the tolerant morphine user. More recent clinical and research formulations of drug addiction do not place such central emphasis on withdrawal syndromes and intoxication (WHO 1964; APA 1980, 1987; USDHHS 1988). The common thread through the twentieth century has been the same as that which started centuries earlier, namely, the compulsive-ppearing behavior of drug self-administration.

Laboratory evaluations of abuse liability identify drugs that produce the effects which appeal to addicted users with a high degree of specificity (Jasinski and Henningfield 1989). Thus, the abuse liability can be estimated even before addictive patterns of use are observed. The ability to specify and measure such features of drugs, and to make accurate predictions, has not only been of enormous value in protecting public health, it has also validated many of the theoretical underpinnings of the testing procedures.

Definitions

Drug dependence is synonymous with drug addiction; however, the term *dependence* is preferred by the WHO and other organizations that are concerned with public health (WHO 1982). The term *drug dependence* will be used throughout this chapter since it is also somewhat less encumbered by overly general use (e.g., the so-called addictions to love, sugar, and video games), and it has fewer antisocial connotations than the term drug addiction. Drug dependence may be defined as a substance-seeking behavior involving a psychoactive drug that acts in the CNS; tolerance and physiologic withdrawal may or may not be present (WHO 1982; Jaffe 1985). Drug dependencies are not distinct from habitual or compulsive behaviors but, rather, they form a subset of habitual or compulsive behaviors in which the role of a specific, exogenously administered, centrally active chemical is critical. The term *drug abuse* is often used synonymously with drug dependence; however, at times this term is used to designate a broad range of inappropriate or nontherapeutic drug use in which the actual level of dependence might be negligible.

As is increasingly well understood, tobacco use is often a form of drug dependence in which nicotine is the dependence-producing drug. In fact, tobacco use and nicotine meet criteria set forth not only by the 1964 and subsequent definitions of drug dependence by the WHO, but data available today also show that nicotine would have met the 1950s definition of the WHO for an "addicting" drug (USDHHS 1988).

ABUSE LIABILITY AND PHYSICAL DEPENDENCE POTENTIAL

What distinguishes tobacco use from compulsive gambling, eating potato chips, or compulsive sexual behavior? In part it is that tobacco use involves the self-administration of a specific psychoactive substance that shares critical features in common with prototypic dependence-producing substances such as morphine, cocaine, and alcohol. In fact, the role of nicotine in the use of tobacco is similar to the roles of morphine, cocaine, and ethanol in the use of opium, coca, and alcohol-based products, respectively. This conclusion stands whether these substances are termed *addicting, habituating,* or *dependence-producing.* Furthermore, experimental laboratory studies have shown that nicotine meets objective criteria as a drug with the pharmacologic actions that frequently lead to a state of dependence in those exposed. The distinguishing characteristics of dependence-producing drugs are listed in Table 2–1 (USDHHS 1988). The following is a brief review of these criteria and the data obtained in studies of nicotine.

The abuse liability and physical dependence potential of drugs may be assessed in laboratory studies by tests designed to quantitate these factors (Jasinski, Johnson, Henningfield 1984; Brady and Lukas 1984). Abuse liability studies measure the effects of a drug that will result in its continued self-administration, even in the face of harm. Physical dependence potential studies measure physiologic and behavioral sequelae to repeated drug administration: specifically, physical dependence (evidenced by the occurrence of an abstinence-induced withdrawal syndrome) and tolerance (evidenced by decreased responsivity when doses are repeatedly given).

Drug Delivery to the CNS

Typical methods of use of marijuana, opium, coca leaf, and alcoholic beverages all result in the delivery of a specific exogenous drug to the CNS. Similarly, all common forms of tobacco use result in the delivery of nicotine to the plasma, from which it is rapidly carried to the CNS. This observation is not incompatible with the finding that certain effects of nicotine are mediated by the peripheral nervous system, as well as by modulation of endocrine function. Moreover, certain subjective effects of substances of abuse may mimic those occurring during various activities (e.g., jogging and sex) or consumption of food: The intact nervous system has a large but limited variety of final common pathways that must be followed to effect responses.

Among the earlier quantitative data on

Table 2–1   Criteria for Drug Dependence

Primary criteria
  Highly controlled or compulsive use
  Psychoactive effects
  Drug-reinforced behavior

Additional criteria
  Addictive behavior often involves:
    stereotypic patterns of use
    use despite harmful effects
    relapse following abstinence
    recurrent drug cravings
  Dependence-producing drugs often produce:
    tolerance
    physical dependence
    pleasant (euphoriant) effects

Source: USDHHS 1988.

nicotine distribution were those collected by Schmiterlow and colleagues (1967), who used radiotracer techniques to characterize the distribution of nicotine accumulation throughout the body, including the CNS. Nicotine was found to be quickly distributed to all highly blood-perfused tissues, including the brain. More recently, London and co-workers (London, Waller, Wamsley 1985; London, Connolly, Szikszay et al. 1985) have shown that nicotine binds to specific receptors in the rat brain with a distribution that closely parallels the patterns of metabolic stimulation in response to nicotine. They found that the density of nicotine binding sites was highest in the interpeduncular nucleus, the medial habenula, and the superior colliculus. They have used the autoradiographic 2-deoxy-D-[1-^{14}C] glucose (or 2-DG) method to evaluate the possible changes in local cerebral glucose utilization as a function of the administration of a variety of dependence-producing drugs. Subcutaneous administration of nicotine to rats resulted in specific regional increases in glucose utilization. The greatest increases occurred in the habenulointerpeduncular system and portions of the thalamus. Increases were related to nicotine dose and were blocked by the centrally and peripherally acting nicotinic antagonist mecamylamine, but not by the peripherally acting antagonist hexamethonium.

Abuse Liability of Nicotine

Heroin, cocaine, ethanol, and other dependence-producing drugs produce certain effects that distinguish them from drugs that are not generally abused. When given to persons with histories of drug abuse under double-blind, placebo-controlled conditions, such drugs produce characteristic responses on standard tests (Jasinski, Johnson, Henningfield 1984). (1) Subjects can discriminate drug from placebo and the reliability of the discrimination is related to the dose of the drug. If these effects are centrally mediated, then the drug is defined as *psychoactive*. (2) Scores on the empirically derived morphine-benzedrine-group (MBG) scale of the Addiction Research Center Inventory (ARCI) and scores on drug liking scales are elevated in a dose-related manner. If these effects are also centrally mediated, then they define the drug as a *euphoriant*. (3) Presentation of the drug can condition and control behavior in such a way that the person will seek the drug. Demonstration of such potential of a drug to control subsequent behavior in both human subjects and animals shows that the biologic activity of the drug apart from the various aspects of the vehicle (e.g., cigarettes) is critical: the drug is then said to serve as a *positive reinforcer*.

When nicotine was tested in a series of such studies, the results showed that nicotine, in doses comparable to those delivered by cigarette smoking, is an abusable drug. That is, as will be described later, nicotine meets the criteria of being psychoactive, producing euphoriant effects, and serving as a reinforcer.

Nicotine as a Psychoactive Drug

By the 1920s, Lewin and others had concluded that nicotine produced effects on "mental function" and mood that were similar in some respects to those of other psychoactive drugs (Henningfield and Goldberg 1988). By the 1970s it had been definitively established that such effects were due to nicotine's actions in the CNS (see review in USDHHS 1988).

To permit a quantitative comparison of nicotine to other dependence-producing drugs, researchers at the Addiction Research Center (ARC) conducted a series of studies which used standardized procedures for evaluating dependence potential (Henning-

field, Miyasato, Jasinski 1983, 1985). Volunteer subjects with histories of drug abuse were tested because they could identify drugs with a potential for abuse and could compare the effects to those of other abused drugs. Nicotine in a wide range of doses was given both intravenously and in the form of tobacco smoke. By both routes of administration, nicotine produced a similar profile of effects across a variety of measures, thereby confirming the importance of nicotine itself in these effects of tobacco.

In brief, nicotine was psychoactive as evidenced by its reliable discrimination from placebo. Its self-reported effects peaked within 1 minute after administration (by either route) and dissipated within a few minutes. Peak response and duration of response were directly related to the dose. In other subjects pretreated with mecamylamine, the effects of nicotine were attenuated in a dose-related fashion.

Nicotine as a Euphoriant and Discriminative Stimulus

In the ARC study, nicotine was shown to be a potent euphoriant causing dose-related increases on scores of the drug liking scale (Henningfield, Miyasato, Jasinski 1985). Interestingly, intravenous nicotine was found to be approximately 5 to 10 times more potent than intravenous cocaine in producing elevated liking scale scores (Fischman et al. 1976). Another measure of euphoria is the MBG scale which provides an empirically derived means of estimating addictive opioid and stimulant-like effects of a compound. On this measure, as well, nicotine elevated scores relative to placebo (Henningfield, Miyasato, Jasinski 1985).

Analogous studies have been conducted using animals as research subjects. Animal studies are critical since they permit an objective differentiation of the effects of the drug from any possible influence or bias carried by human research subjects. In the discrimination or psychoactivity tests, the animals were given either the test drug or placebo. They were trained to press one lever when given placebo and to press another lever when given the test drug. When tested in this fashion, animals were found to readily learn to discriminate nicotine from placebo as evidenced by their nicotine-specific lever pressing (Rosecrans and Meltzer 1981). Furthermore, the degree of discrimination was dose-related and was blocked by pretreatment of the animals with centrally (but not peripherally) acting nicotinic antagonists. In the animal analog of euphoriant tests, animals are trained to press one lever when given the standard drug (e.g., amphetamine) and another lever when given another drug (e.g., sedative) or placebo. When tested in this manner, nicotine has been found to be unique but more similar to stimulants than to sedatives (Henningfield and Goldberg 1984). These findings may be considered systematic extensions of research conducted by Johnston (1942) and Jones and his co-workers (Jones, Farrell, Herning 1978).

Nicotine as a Positive Reinforcer

To determine whether or not nicotine can control behavior, animals and human subjects can be given the opportunity to take intravenous injections. Nearly all drugs that are widely abused by humans are voluntarily taken by animals (Griffiths, Bigelow, Henningfield 1980), ruling out the possibility that specific personality factors and other unique human traits are necessary for these drugs to control behavior. The drug-taking behavior must be voluntary in that the animal or person is not required or specifically induced to take the drug following initial training and exposure to it.

In one such study, human subjects were tested during 3-hour sessions in which 10 presses on a lever resulted in either a nicotine or a placebo injection (Henningfield, Miyasato, Jasinski 1983). A variety of safeguards ensured the safety of the subjects. The subjects self-administered the intravenously available nicotine but discontinued lever pressing when saline was substituted for the nicotine. Similarly, when subjects were given access to both nicotine and placebo at the same time (by pressing alternate levers) they chose nicotine, confirming that nicotine was functioning as a positive reinforcer (Henningfield and Goldberg 1983). When dose was increased, fewer injections were ob-

tained; however, the subjects obtained more nicotine per session.

Tolerance to Nicotine

Studies of tolerance to nicotine have been conducted since near the turn of the twentieth century when Langley and Dixon and others demonstrated that repeated administration of nicotine led to diminished responsiveness which could be partially overcome by increasing the dose of nicotine (see review, Swedberg, Henningfield, Goldberg 1990). Human subjects given nicotine at 10 minute intervals reported rapidly decreased positive subjective effects; by the sixth or seventh injection, subjects could not distinguish nicotine from placebo (Henningfield 1984a; see also Jones et al. 1978).

The development of tolerance is likely an important factor early in the natural history of nicotine dependence. A survey of patterns of tobacco use over time showed that the self-reported number of cigarettes or the amount of smokeless tobacco (SLT) used steadily increased from the first day of tobacco use to the fourth (SLT) or eighth (cigarettes) year (Henningfield, cited in USDHHS 1987). For most of the more than 800 smokers and former smokers surveyed, it took at least several years before a stable level of consumption, usually from one to two packs per day, was reached. Use of smokeless tobacco appeared to level off more rapidly, but this, too, followed a period of gradually escalating use.

Physical Dependence on Nicotine: Deprivation and Substitution for Tobacco

Physical dependence is measured by the demonstration of an abstinence syndrome characterized by an orderly pattern of signs and symptoms when regular drug administration is discontinued. These signs and symptoms are often opposite in direction from effects produced by acute drug administration (Jaffe 1985). For instance, in the case of opiate withdrawal, pupillary constriction is replaced with pupillary dilation, constipation is replaced with diarrhea, and so forth. With nicotine (as with opiates and sedatives), a prominent characteristic is an increased tendency to want to use the drug, sometimes reported as "craving."

In a series of studies at the ARC, the tobacco abstinence syndrome was experimentally analyzed (Henningfield and Nemeth-Coslett 1988; Snyder, Davis, Henningfield 1989; Pickworth, Herning, Henningfield 1989). Heavy cigarette smokers volunteered for a study in which a baseline period of regular cigarette smoking was followed by a 10-day period of tobacco abstinence, then voluntary reexposure to regular cigarette smoking. In a separate phase of the study, subjects volunteered for three alternating cycles of 4 days of regular cigarette smoking interspersed with 3 days of abstinence. During each 3-day abstinence period, varying doses of nicotine polacrilex were administered every hour.

During the nicotine deprivation phase of the ARC studies, ratings of desire to smoke increased to near peak levels within the first 24 hours of deprivation. After this, ratings of desire to smoke began to decline for the remainder of the deprivation period. Changes in heart rate showed a similar time course with decreases averaging about 5 bpm. However, reversal in the trend of falling heart rate did not begin until the 6th day. Performance deficits peaked during the first few days of nicotine deprivation and only partially recovered by the 10th day.

In the nicotine replacement phase of the ARC studies, the rate of gum administration and the rate of chewing were carefully controlled. From 8:00 A.M. until 7:00 P.M., subjects used one piece of gum per hour for 15 minutes at a chew rate of one chew every 3 seconds. With regard to overall venous plasma nicotine levels, 12 pieces of 4 mg of gum chewed under controlled conditions provided adequate replacement for the smoked tobacco. Hourly chewing of 2 mg of gum did not maintain plasma nicotine levels at the cigarette-smoking level.

As in the first phase of the study, baseline heart rate for the subjects was about 70 bpm; during the nonsmoking days when placebo gum was administered, heart rate decreased about 5 bpm to levels approximating those seen during days two and three of the 10-day deprivation phase of the study. Administration of 2 mg gum attenuated the decrease

and 4 mg of nicotine completely abolished this withdrawal effect. Cognitive performance deficits occurred during the nicotine gum placebo condition, but were blocked by nicotine gum administration: the blockade of these withdrawal effects was most reliable in the 4 mg gum condition.

A number of important electrophysiologic effects were also observed. Beginning as early as 29 hours after tobacco deprivation, changes in the resting EEG were evident. Pickworth and associates (1989) found that theta power increased and alpha frequency decreased at the onset of tobacco deprivation. These results confirm the observations made in other EEG studies on the effects of nicotine deprivation (Ulett and Itil 1969; Knott and Venables 1977; Herning, Jones, Bachman 1983). The EEG effects persisted for up to 7 days in this study, and, with the resumption of smoking, they rapidly (within 4 hr) reverted to predeprivation levels. Similar EEG findings occurred in the placebo gum phase of the replacement experiment. These effects were prevented by the hourly chewing of the 2 and 4 mg nicotine polacrilex. These results indicate that slowing of alpha frequency, an indication of decreased CNS arousal, paralleled the discontinuation of tobacco and could be prevented with the administration of nicotine gum. In recent studies, changes in the EEG were evident on a puff to puff analysis, suggesting the changes in CNS arousal may be under very fine, discrete control of the smoker (Knott 1988).

Desire to Smoke

As described earlier, abstinence from tobacco regularly produces an orderly syndrome that is largely attenuated by replacement of the usual intake of nicotine in the form of the gum. There is one important exception, however; that is, there was no significant difference in ratings of desire to smoke during placebo, 2 or 4 mg gum administration. This suggests that whereas patients can expect nicotine gum to help them to be more comfortable by suppressing many features of nicotine withdrawal, this preparation will not as readily reduce thoughts, urges, desires, or cravings for cigarettes.

These findings, that nicotine replacement can alleviate various signs and symptoms of withdrawal without appreciably altering desire to smoke, are consistent with the notion that the desire to smoke is more closely related to learning factors and to environmental stimuli (Henningfield and Brown 1987; Henningfield 1986). An analogous finding is that nicotine replacement in the form of intravenous injections or nicotine gum can decrease the behavior of cigarette smoking and intake of carbon monoxide, whereas ratings of desire to smoke remain relatively constant.

Additional clinical features of the nicotine withdrawal syndrome are described in Chapters 10 and 12, and nicotine replacement therapy is discussed in Chapter 12.

COMPARISON OF NICOTINE DEPENDENCE WITH OTHER DRUG DEPENDENCIES

Drug dependence is characterized by features that can be distinguished on the basis of the specific pharmacology of a particular drug and clinical signs and symptoms described by the American Psychiatric Association (APA) (Gilman et al. 1985; APA 1987). At the same time, many features are common across different drug dependencies as discussed in the 1988 Report of the Surgeon General, *Nicotine Addiction* (USDHHS 1988), and clinically described by the APA (1987). Comparisons of nicotine dependence to other drug dependencies (summarized later) have revealed commonalities of both theoretical and clinical relevance (Jaffe and Kanzler 1979; Henningfield, Griffiths, Jasinski 1981; Henningfield and Nemeth-Coslett 1988).

Drug Use in the Face of Harm

The simplest and perhaps most fundamental behavioral commonality engendered by dependence-producing drugs is persistent use despite knowledge of harm that may result from such use. The persistence of drug taking despite such risks and often despite wanting to stop has led to the concept of "loss of control" over drug seeking and drug ingestion. Most tobacco users believe that their use of tobacco is harmful to their health and would like to quit (American College of Physicians Health and Public Policy Committee 1985). In fact, while the presence of an imminent health risk substantially increases the likelihood of quitting smoking, most smokers who experience a myocardial infarction relapse to smoking after hospitalization (Burling, Singleton, Bigelow 1984).

Individual Vulnerability to Dependence

The persistence of certain forms of drug dependence despite known health risks has led to the postulation of specific vulnerability factors and/or an addictive personality type which are necessary to establish the dependence. Whereas the data bearing on these issues are considerable and diverse, the following conclusion can be reasonably made: while there is some degree of overlap in personality type of individuals who have become dependent on drugs (e.g., elevated extroversion, psychopathy, and risk-taking scores on various scales), and there is some overlap in situations that are related to drug relapse (e.g., stress and anxiety) (USDHEW 1979), no specific vulnerability factors have been consistently found across drug classes and/or populations which are either necessary or sufficient to produce drug dependence, including dependence on nicotine (Lang 1983; see also Chapter 4).

The most critical factor is simple: exposure to the drug. Tobacco differs quantitatively from other drugs of abuse since an apparently greater percentage of those who sample tobacco become regular daily users than those who sample other drugs of abuse (Pollin and Ravenholt 1984). A variety of factors probably contributes to this relationship, including greater social acceptability of tobacco than many other drugs, relatively low cost, and ready availability. A factor which has received less attention is that tobacco use tends to begin at an earlier age than use of most other dependence-producing drugs (Johnston, O'Malley, Bachman 1985). Still, it remains plausible that individual factors (possibly genetically mediated) might influence an individual's vulnerability to becoming dependent upon tobacco, but this issue is unresolved for tobacco.

Deprivation Increases Drug Seeking

With the opioid drugs it is well known clinically that the probability of opioid self-administration and the self-reported craving strength is a direct function of the length of the deprivation period. Similarly, deprivation of tobacco increases the desire of the smoker to smoke cigarettes and decreases the latency to smoke when the opportunity arises. Commonly observed during the "cigarette break," "theater intermission," or when cigarettes had been unavailable for a few hours, this effect has also been experimentally studied. One study showed that the deprivation effect is directly related to the time since the last cigarette (Henningfield and Griffiths 1979). That nicotine plays a specific role in the tobacco deprivation effect has been established by several lines of evidence. For instance, the effect is inversely related to the magnitude of nicotine preloading when nicotine is given either in tobacco smoke (Herman 1974) or via other routes of administration, including the transdermal route (Rose et al. 1985). Although the suppression effect is a behavioral component of drug withdrawal in the physiologically dependent person, measurable effects of deprivation on subsequent drug intake or desire to use the drug may occur in the absence of any other measured signs of withdrawal.

Increased Tobacco Cost Decreases Intake

For tobacco, as for many other addictive substances, increasing the cost in terms of effort or money decreases intake; analogously, specific monetary incentives can be used to reduce intake of heroin and other drugs (Bigelow et al. 1981). This phenomenon has been observed in animal experiments as well (Griffiths, Bigelow, Henningfield 1980). In fact, this relation even holds when per capita cigarette consumption is examined as a function of cigarette tax rates across many different countries (Grossman 1983). One experimental treatment approach that has been evaluated with opioids, sedatives, and tobacco is the use of monetary incentives to reduce or eliminate target drug intake (Stitzer et al. 1982; Stitzer et al. 1983; Stitzer and Bigelow 1985; Stitzer et al. 1986). Increasing the price of tobacco products through increased tobacco taxes would appear to be one way to apply this phenomenon at the level of public health policy (Warner and Murt 1973; see Chapter 3).

Paired Stimuli Can Increase Drug Use

The role of environmental stimuli in strengthening the control of dependence-producing drugs over behavior has been well known, although not widely studied, for decades. The fundamental observation is that a drug can produce discrete and readily identifiable effects. Given that a drug can function as a stimulus, it follows that its stimulus properties can be extended through other stimuli that are paired with it. Nicotine in its usual vehicle (i.e., tobacco and/or tobacco smoke) seems to provide innumerable opportunities for confluence of drug exposure paired with a huge variety of stimuli. Some of these stimuli are the tobacco and the smoke themselves.

Wikler (1965) showed that the effects of opiates could be elicited by environmental stimuli previously associated with the administration of opiates. In alcoholic patients, the desire to use alcohol is increased by presentation of alcohol-associated stimuli (Pickens, Bigelow, Griffiths 1973; Ludwig 1986). Recent studies with opioid-dependent persons have found that the effects of both drug administration and withdrawal can be elicited by various environmental stimuli (O'Brien et al. 1981). Only preliminary work has been done with respect to tobacco; however, the role of nicotine-paired stimuli would appear to function analogously to the role of such stimuli in other dependence-producing drugs. For instance, Gritz (1978) found that amount of smoking decreased as nicotine-paired stimuli were removed. The subject smoked most in the full presence of the cigarette and smoke, less when a clear screen attenuated the direct smell of smoke in the room, and the least when an opaque screen blocked the sight and smell of the smoke. Using experimental animals, Katz and co-workers (Katz and Goldberg 1987) studied the role of environmental stimuli in the maintenance of behavior ultimately controlled by morphine, cocaine, nicotine, and other drugs. They found that the total amount of drug-seeking behavior was greatly increased when stimuli which had been systematically paired with the drug were presented intermittently. Taken together, the results of these studies suggest that part of the demonstrably strong behavioral controlling properties of tobacco are due to the seemingly ideal combination of a drug that has well-discriminated interoceptive effects along with the equally well-discriminated extroceptive stimuli which accompany every puff on a cigarette or chew on a tobacco wad; namely, the sight, smell, feel, and taste of the tobacco and/or smoke. Beyond this, the settings, circumstances, and mental states associated with nicotine ingestion likely operate as conditioned stimuli for smoking as well.

Conditioning Factors in Nicotine Dependence

Pharmacologically active agents act as unconditioned stimuli in animals and humans. Collins and Tatum (1925) recognized that stimuli associated with opiate administration in dogs developed the ability to elicit salivation, an effect produced by the drug itself. Pavlov and others (reviewed in Pert, Post, Weiss 1990) described similar findings with other drugs in different animal models. Wikler was among the first drug abuse researchers to describe the importance of context in drug effect and withdrawal states in humans. Wikler (1973) found that opiate withdrawal symptoms could be conditioned to the circumstances in which they occurred. In smokers, greater withdrawal is experienced in natural rather than laboratory environments presumably because the natural environment contains cues associated with prior smoking (Hatsukami, Hughes, Pickens 1985). These findings suggest that stimuli formerly associated with nicotine ingestion will induce cigarette cravings and other withdrawal signs which engender cigarette smoking.

Opponent process theory (Solomon and Corbit 1973) suggests that the reduction of an aversive withdrawal syndrome is the result of the immediate (pleasurable) response to the drug, called the A state, and the delayed (aversive) response, the B state. The A and B states are opposite or opposed, hence the term *opponent process.* The theory applied to nicotine dependence posits that during the onset of smoking, the pleasurable A state prevails and smoking increases. Eventually, with regular smoking, the aversive B state begins to dominate which the smoker attempts to reverse or reduce by the A state consequences of further smoking. That is, smoking perpetuates itself by reducing displeasure rather than by inducing the pleasure that initially engendered the behavior. It is important to acknowledge that neither the Wikler theory nor the opponent process theory has been empirically tested on smoking behavior (USDHHS 1988).

In contrast to these explanations that emphasize the relief of withdrawal, a recent review (Niaura et al. 1988) proposes an appetitive model of cues associated with smoking. Cues that are associated with the positively perceived effects of smoking (stimulation, relaxation), such as those cues associated with nicotine intake (holding a cigarette, the smell of smoke, etc.), elicit conditioned responses similar to the effects of nicotine. These associations strongly encourage the individual to obtain and ingest the drug. In the appetitive model, negative emotions are not necessarily withdrawal symptoms, although negative emotions formerly alleviated by nicotine may serve as a cue for repetitively administering the drug (Stewart, DeWitt, Eikelboom 1984).

Cigarette smoking has been described as a behavior thoroughly interwoven among the fabric of daily life (Pomerleau and Pomerleau 1987). The average pack-a-day smoker of 20 years duration has inhaled cigarette smoke over 1 million times. Each inhalation provides an occasion to associate nicotine with the numerous and varied circumstances of daily life. Over years of smoking, the emotional states and life events conditional to smoking continue to increase. These associated stimuli complicate the task of maintaining abstinence (USDHHS 1988).

Tobacco Taking Is Controlled by Delivered Nicotine Dose

Among the most fundamental of pharmacologic phenomena is the relationship between absorbed dose and a drug effect. Demonstration that certain effects were related to the administered dose of the drug shows that the drug was relevant to the response. The role of nicotine dose as a determinant of a wide variety of centrally and peripherally mediated actions of nicotine has been systematically studied for nearly a century in a wide variety of species and preparations. Physiologic and behavioral responses to nicotine which have been studied as a function of dose include: nicotine receptor binding, effects on skeletal muscle, cardiovascular function, cortical electrical activity (EEG), appetite, mood and emotional state, and even changes in the ability to learn and memorize. Nicotine produces dose-related effects on peripheral or CNS tissue affecting these and other phenomena (Gilman et al. 1985).

The extensive literature on the effects of nicotine dose as a determinant of tobacco self-administration (Benowitz et al. 1983; Finnegan, Larson, Haag 1945) supports an unequivocal general conclusion; namely, that nicotine dose is one determinant of tobacco self-administration behavior (Henningfield 1984b; Gritz 1980). The most consistent findings may be summarized as follows: increasing the amount of nicotine circulating in the plasma of the smoker (e.g., by preloading with other forms of nicotine, decreasing excretion rate, increasing unit delivered dose) results in diminished cigarette smoking (Griffiths and Henningfield 1982). This effect is often termed *downward compensation* and appears to be somewhat a more robust phenomenon than *upward compensation.* However, upward compensation does occur when, for instance, subjects are given preloads of the ganglionic blocker mecamylamine (Stolerman et al. 1973; Nemeth-Coslett et al. 1986). The quantitative aspects of the nicotine dose-effect relations in studies of cigarette smoking have been widely debated (Gori and Bock 1980). Much of the debate has centered around the degree to which smokers regulate their intake of nicotine. Specific data have led to dichotomous interpretations. On the one hand, cigarette smokers are often viewed as titraters who carefully adjust their nicotine intake in order to maintain stable plasma nicotine levels (Schacter et al. 1977).

On the other hand, cigarette smokers have also been viewed as being remarkably insensitive to changes in nicotine dose (Russell 1979). The issues concerning the disparate interpretations of dose-response data in human studies are both empirical and theoretic. Review of the empirically based portion of this literature shows that few studies of the effects of nicotine dose on cigarette smoking provide confirmation that intended manipulations of nicotine dose had actually been affected. Many factors can determine the actual dose of nicotine delivered to the plasma. When major factors are not controlled, and there is no physiologic means of verifying that the dose manipulation obtained was intended, then the finding of a relatively monotonic dose-effect function may accurately reflect the fact that plasma levels were not varied as intended.

Theoretical issues surrounding the role of dose in the control of tobacco use have been as much a cause for debate as the data themselves. It has been widely observed that decreasing plasma nicotine levels are associated with the occurrence of tobacco withdrawal signs and symptoms, including feelings of discomfort. It has also been observed that increasing plasma levels produce desirable effects (although tolerance may attenuate these effects),with continued increases eventually producing acute nicotine toxicity and feelings of discomfort. These upper and lower thresholds of nicotine intake at which discomfort occurs, and the theory that smokers will change their behavior in such a fashion as to avoid either threshold, has been termed the *boundary hypothesis* by Kozlowski and Herman (1984). Dimensions of the boundary vary across individuals and even within a single day of smoking in a single individual as he or she becomes increasingly tolerant. However, at a descriptive level this appears to be a generally accurate and useful concept. It is also a useful model to consider when nicotine replacement therapy is used as an adjunct in the management of tobacco dependence. For example, the Nicotine Reduction Therapy Formula is an empirically derived formula based on estimated nicotine intake (Henningfield et al. 1990).

What happens to plasma nicotine levels during the course of the day of the usual smoker? Smoking produces a brief surge in arterial nicotine concentrations to levels many times higher than those simultaneously observed in venous blood (Henningfield et. al. 1990) (see also Chapter 1). Following each dose of nicotine, plasma levels rapidly decline as nicotine is redistributed throughout the body; the rate of decline subsides after about 15–30 minutes to reach a fairly stable half-life of about 2 hours. The initial redistribution phase has sometimes been confused with nicotine's metabolic half-life (Rosenberg et al. 1980). Imposed on this pattern of elimination, small boli of nicotine obtained by smoking cigarettes or by rapid intravenous injection may produce plasma spikes (Feyerabend, Ings, Russell 1985; Russell and Feyerabend 1978). By comparison, venous plasma level increases from smokeless tobacco use are somewhat attenuated, and they lack the marked surge in arterial level seen with inhaled nicotine from cigarette smoke (Russell et al. 1985). Within a smoker's day, these nicotine boli produce an overall accumulation of nicotine in the plasma until the point is reached (usually after about 4–6 hours of smoking) at which overall rates of nicotine excretion approximate overall rates of intake. Then, there is relatively little change from hour to hour, although between and immediately following each cigarette there remains considerable variation in plasma level. During sleep, plasma nicotine levels may fall to less than 15% of the previous day's average (Benowitz, Kuyt, Jacob 1982; Griffiths, Bigelow, Henningfield 1980). This variable pattern of plasma nicotine probably enhances the effects of nicotine, by permitting the partial loss of tolerance each day. Such effects would otherwise be greatly attenuated by the rapid onset of tolerance or tachyphylaxis which accompanies exposure of neural tissue to nicotine.

Remission from and Relapse to Drug Use

People addicted to a wide variety of drugs may permanently discontinue their drug use without formal treatment programs. At the same time, relapse is common, regardless of the nature of the quitting attempt. However, patterns of remission and relapse are not random; they are related to specific factors that are similar across several drug types. Some of the remission and relapse factors can be manipulated or otherwise taken advantage of when understood. Data that come from studies of the course of drug use and quitting patterns (cf. Vaillant 1970) have contributed substantially to theory and basic research, and research of this type could probably be conducted more easily with tobacco than with substances which are illicit and for which smaller numbers of users are available for study.

When people achieve abstinence outside the setting of a formal treatment program, the phenomenon is sometimes referred to as *spontaneous remission.* The term is a misnomer, however, in that far from being a spontaneous event, identifiable factors are often associated with such quitting, and the factors are often equivalent in their potential power to modify behavior to those offered in drug treatment programs. For example, life-threatening health problems prompt 40–50% of patients to quit smoking (Burling, Singleton, Bigelow 1984; West and Evans 1986). Other factors associated with quitting include: social sanctions, pressure from significant others, financial problems, significant accidents, management of cravings, positive reinforcement for quitting, internal psychic change/motivation, and change in life-style (see review by Henningfield, Clayton, Pollin 1990 and Chapter 10).

Relapse to drug use is also determined, in part, by environmental pressures. Treatment programs have responded to this insight by recognizing that efforts to prevent relapse are as important as the efforts to achieve abstinence from the drug in the first place (Marlatt and Gordon 1985; USDHHS 1988). Developing better techniques to prevent relapse might be facilitated with more extensive data concerning the relative role of various factors leading to relapse and to the most effective means to reduce their impact. In general, prominent relapse factors include the following: degree of dependence, psychiatric impairment, treatment length, modality, use of drugs and alcohol, positive expectations of outcome, peers, isolation, lack of involvement in work, lack of active leisure, negative emotional states, negative physical states, skills deficits, negative life events, lack of needed services (see review by Henningfield, Clayton, Pollin 1990). The risk factors for relapse to nicotine that have been specifically validated include negative affect (anger, frustration, anxiety), interpersonal conflict, and social pressure (including simply being in the presence of other smokers) (USDHHS 1988).

In the case of tobacco, the nicotine withdrawal syndrome is a particularly important relapse factor in the first few weeks of abstinence. The nicotine withdrawal syndrome may be a relatively weak factor for relapse after several months of abstinence, but it appears powerful enough that most would-be quitters do not remain abstinent during the early period of nicotine withdrawal. This phenomenon has led to what may be termed the fallacy of Mark Twain (Henningfield et al. 1990)—"To cease smoking is the easiest thing I ever did; I ought to know because I've done it a thousand times."—that quitting smoking is easy. The fact is that both quitting and remaining abstinent are very difficult for most people. For example, if quitting smoking is defined as abstinence for more than 1 week, even with some professional guidance, most people do not achieve this seemingly modest goal. That is, after deciding to quit, most people resume smoking before the approximately 2 weeks during which the physical withdrawal symptoms are most prominent.

Useful Effects of Drug Administration

Tobacco, like many other abused substances, produces effects often considered useful or beneficial to the user. In fact, many drugs of widespread abuse (or forms of them) were originally developed as therapeutic agents and continue to be used as such. Furthermore, people who are dependent on drugs often report desirable and/or useful effects derived from the drug. Specifically, nicotine ingestion in the tobacco-dependent person can alleviate stress and anxiety, facilitate learning and memory, and can function to control appetite and weight (Pomerleau and Pomerleau 1984; Henning-

field 1984b). Some of these effects have also been observed in animals, indicating that they may be at least partially due to direct actions of nicotine and not due simply to the alleviation of withdrawal.

Effects of nicotine administration to restore concentration and performance in tobacco-deprived people are particularly interesting. For instance, common complaints among people who have quit smoking are that their concentration is impaired, they are easily distracted, and that they cannot work as effectively on certain tasks. Cognitive impairments secondary to tobacco abstinence are measurable in laboratory settings. They are specific to nicotine since administration of alternate forms of nicotine (e.g., nicotine polacrilex) are effective, and there are a variety of electroencephalographic correlates (Pickworth, Herning, Henningfield 1986). Recent laboratory studies at the ARC confirm the organic basis of these complaints. Pickworth (Pickworth, Herning, Henningfield 1986) and Herning (Henningfield et al. 1986) and their co-workers showed altered EEG responses during nicotine withdrawal including impaired evoked "cognitive potentials" and enhancement of distractive effects of background noise; certain effects were nicotine-specific since nicotine gum could reverse them. Correlated in time with the EEG changes were impairments in performance on tests of ability, performance on rapid arithmetic, logical reasoning tasks, and so forth; these impairments, too, were reversed by nicotine gum administration (Henningfield et al. 1986). The degree to which these useful effects of nicotine persist beyond the short-term withdrawal syndrome (protracted abstinence), resulting from many years of tobacco use, is not clear at this point.

It is worth noting that such effects are sometimes termed *therapeutic.* However, such a statement has misleading implications when the drug is delivered in a vehicle as toxic as tobacco or the smoke of burning tobacco. Additionally, it is not clear to what degree the effects of nicotine which are useful to the user are only useful because of a long history of use. In other words, it is possible that the development of dependence to nicotine changed the person in such a way that the individual might never, or perhaps at least not for an extended amount of time, function at peak levels and feel normal or comfortable in the absence of nicotine. For such persons, nicotine administration might be considered useful, indeed; but the term *therapeutics* might best be reserved for the case of nicotine administration in approved medical products and under the guidance of a health professional.

Given the power and potency of nicotine as a behaviorally active drug, it is plausible that chronic exposure beginning in adolescence (the age at which most smokers begin), before CNS maturation, might have lasting behavioral effects. Yet, relatively little developmental behavioral research with nicotine has been undertaken. In this regard, it is of interest and concern to learn whether the even younger population (preteenage) that has begun using smokeless tobacco products will become even more dependent on nicotine. Another issue of interest may also be of relevance in the treatment of tobacco dependence: the possibility that the useful effects of nicotine administration (and conversely, the adverse effects of nicotine abstinence) are related to the life circumstances of the individual patient. For instance, are the effects of chronic nicotine use in sustaining concentration and logical reasoning of special importance for writers? Are the possible anxiolytic effects of nicotine of special importance for people in high stress occupations? These questions will be important to consider clinically as more pharmaceutical grade nicotine delivery systems come into widespread use.

Tobacco Use Is a Preventable Risk Factor for Abuse of Other Drugs

Although not necessarily a causal determinant of illicit drug use, tobacco is a common part of the developmental sequence lending to such use and may be considered a preventable risk factor. For example, one study showed that among persons who had used both cigarettes and marijuana 10 times or more, 67% of males and 79% of females reported using cigarettes first (Yamaguchi and Kandel 1984; USDHHS 1988). Furthermore, levels of tobacco and alcohol use have

generally been found to be higher in persons who had progressed to illicit drugs (Kandel et al. 1978; Huba, Wingard, Bentler 1981; O'Donnell and Clayton 1982; USDHHS 1988). Tobacco also holds a special status as a "gateway" substance in the development of drug dependencies not only because tobacco use reliably precedes use of illicit drugs, but also because use of tobacco is more likely to escalate to dependent patterns of use than use of other dependence-producing drugs (USDHHS 1988).

The incidence and severity of various drug dependencies are related to the level of tobacco use. Patterns of tobacco use predict the extent of use of other psychoactive drugs, especially in youth. Clayton and Ritter (1985) found that alcohol drinking and cigarette smoking were the most powerful predictors of marijuana use for both males and females. The relationship was strongest when cigarette smoking had begun before the individuals were 17 years old. In a longitudinal study, Ary and associates (1987) interviewed more than 300 male adolescents twice, at 9-month intervals, to determine their use of various psychoactive substances. They found that users of smokeless tobacco were more likely to use cigarettes, marijuana, or alcohol than nonusers, and that smokeless tobacco users who were using these other substances at the time of the first interview showed substantially greater increases in levels of use of these other substances by the time of the second interview. Analogously, students in grades 7–12 in New York State showed a positive correlation between frequency of drinking alcoholic beverages and daily cigarette consumption (Welt and Barnes 1987). The 1985 National Household Survey also revealed a crude but consistent dose response relationship between smoking and other drug use (USDHHS 1988; Henningfield, Clayton, Pollin 1990).

CONCLUSION

The pharmacologic properties of nicotine and its patterns of use share many characteristics with other prototypic dependence-producing drugs. Nicotine satisfies the major and minor criteria (Table 2–1) that define a dependence-producing drug. Initial use—usually on a trial basis—often escalates as a process of dose graduation to a full level of dependence (physical as well as behavioral). The enhancement of performance, mood, and feeling are critical factors in the drug's ability to control behavior, and the high availability, low cost, and high acceptability of the product promote (rather than deter) dependence. When cigarette smoking was regarded as a voluntary pleasure or a simple habit, there was little reason to treat it as anything else and, in fact, there were limited resources available to the smoker who wanted to quit other than his own determination and motivation. Now that tobacco use has been more universally accepted as a form of drug dependence in which nicotine is the critical abuse-producing agent, there is a rational basis for the treatment of cigarette smoking based on experience with other forms of drug dependence (APA 1987).

While such a conclusion may discourage some, for most it should come as a relief to discover that their difficulties in quitting and the pleasures they associate with tobacco are not merely psychological; they are physically based. Moreover, they can be treated. In fact, the acknowledgment and acceptance that much of tobacco use is an addictive disease is actually reason for encouragement in treating cigarette smoking, for it provides a rational basis for combining adjunctive pharmacologic intervention with behavioral and other management techniques.

The role of nicotine in the compulsive use of tobacco products is now known to be equivalent to the role of cocaine in coca leaf use, ethanol in alcoholic beverage consumption, and morphine in opium poppy use. That is, these substances produce effects in the CNS that can be reinforcing to animals and humans alike, they all produce a range of effects that users may report to be "useful" or "beneficial," and at least with respect to nicotine, alcohol, and morphine, a distinct state of physical dependence may result from repetitive administration of the drug. Tobacco use, particularly in the form of cigarette smoking, is an orderly behavior that is controlled by the same behavioral and pharmacologic variables as are the more commonly studied forms of drug dependence

(Jasinski, Johnson, Henningfield 1984). These common factors suggest that treatment programs for cigarette smoking could be enhanced by incorporation of clinical strategies proven effective with people dependent on other drugs.

Various issues involving the nature and development of drug dependence continue to be investigated and debated. In this regard, drug dependence is no different from any other disease state that is well understood along several dimensions and less well understood along others. For example, the relative contribution of individual vulnerability to development of addiction, the reasons for the persistent drug craving that can occur at extraordinarily high levels years after abstinence from the drug, and explanation of the powerful gateway effect of nicotine to other forms of drug dependence remain issues of controversy. While much remains to be learned, the fact that the tobacco user is subject to the behavioral and direct pharmacologic influences of an addicting drug, nicotine, and that many of these can be mitigated by medical treatment, is now well understood.

REFERENCES

American College of Physicians Health and Public Policy Committee. Methods for stopping cigarette smoking. *Ann Intern Med* 105:281–291, 1985.

American Psychiatric Association (APA). *Diagnostic and Statistical Manual of Mental Disorders* (DSM-III), 3d ed. Washington, D.C.: American Psychiatric Association, 1980.

———. *Diagnostic and Statistical Manual of Mental Disorders* (DSM-III-R), 3d ed. rev. Washington, D.C.: American Psychiatric Association, 1987.

Ary, D. V., Lichenstein, H. H., Severson, H. H. Smokeless tobacco use among male adolescents: Patterns, correlates, predictors, and the use of other drugs. *Prev Med* 16:385–401, 1987.

Benowitz, N. L., Kuyt, F., Jacob P. III. Circadian blood nicotine concentration during cigarette smoking. *Clin Pharmacol Ther* 32:758–764, 1982.

Benowitz, N. L., Hall, S. M., Herning, R. I., Jacob P. III, Jones, R. T., Osman, A. L. Smokers of low-yield cigarettes do not consume less nicotine. *N Engl J Med* 309:139–142, 1983.

Bigelow, G. E., Stitzer, M. L., Griffiths, R. R., Liebson, I. A. Contingency management approaches to drug self-administration and drug abuse: efficacy and limitations. *Addict Behav* 6:241–252, 1981.

Brady, J. V., Lukas, S. C., eds. *Testing Drugs for Physical Dependence Potential and Abuse Liability.* NIDA Research Monograph 52. U.S. Department of Health, Education and Welfare, Public Health Service, Alcohol, Drug Abuse, and Mental Health Administration, National Institute on Drug Abuse. DHEW Publication No. (ADM) 84-1332, 1984.

Burling, T. A., Singleton, E. G., Bigelow, G. E. Smoking following myocardial infarction: A critical review of the literature. *Health Psychol* 3:83–96, 1984.

Clayton, R. R., and Ritter, C. The epidemiology of alcohol and drug abuse among adolescents. *Adv Alcohol Subst Abuse* 4:69–97, 1985.

Collins, K. H., and Tatum, A.L. A conditioned salivary reflex established by chronic morphine poisoning. *Am J Physiol* 74:14–15, 1925.

Feyerabend, C., Ings, R. M., Russell, M.A.H. Nicotine pharmacokinetics and its application to intake from smoking. *Br J Clin Psychol* 19(2):239–247, 1985.

Finnegan, J. K., Larson, P. S., Haag, H. B. The role of nicotine in the cigarette habit. *Science* 102:94–96, 1945.

Fischman, M. W., Schuster, C. R., Resnekov, L., Shick, J. F. E., Krasnegor, N. A., Fennell, W., Freedman, D. X. Cardiovascular and subjective effects of intravenous cocaine administration in humans. *Arch Gen Psychiatry* 33:983–989, 1976.

Gilman, A. G., Goodman, L. S., Rall, T. W., Murad, F., eds. *Goodman and Gilman's Pharmacological Basis of Therapeutics.* New York: Macmillan, 1985.

Gori, G. B., and Bock, F. G., eds. *Banbury Report 3: A Safe Cigarette?* Cold Spring Harbor, NY: Cold Spring Harbor Laboratory, 1980.

Griffiths, R. R., Bigelow, G. E., Henningfield, J. E. Similarities in animal and human drug-taking behavior, In Mello N. K., ed. *Advances in Substance Abuse: Behavioral and Biological Research.* Greenwich, CT: JAI Press, 1980, 1–90.

Griffiths, R. R., and Henningfield, J. E. Pharmacology of cigarette smoking behavior. *Trends Pharmacol Sci* 3:260–263, 1982.

Gritz, E. R. Patterns of puffing in cigarette smokers. In Krasnegor, N. A., ed. *Self-Administration of Abused Substances: Methods for*

Study. National Institute on Drug Abuse Research Monograph No. 20. Washington, D.C.: U.S. Government Printing Office, 1978, 221–235.

———. Smoking behavior and tobacco abuse. In Mello N. K., ed. *Advances in Substances Abuse: Behavioral and biological research.* Greenwich, CT: JAI Press, 1980, 91–158.

Grossman, M. Taxation and cigarette smoking in the United States. In Forbes, W. F., Frecker, R. C., Nostbakken, D., eds. *Proceedings of the Fifth World Conference on Smoking and Health,* vol. 1. Ottawa, Canada: Canadian Council on Smoking and Health, 1983, 483–487.

Hatsukami, D. K., Hughes, J. R., Pickens, R. W. Blood nicotine, smoke exposure and tobacco withdrawal symptoms. *Addict Behav* 10:413–417, 1985.

Henningfield, J. E. Behavioral pharmacology of cigarette smoking. In Thompson, T., Dews, T. B., Barrett, J. E., eds. *Advances in Behavioral Pharmacology,* vol. 4. New York: Academic Press, 1984a, 131–210.

———. Pharmacologic basis and treatment of cigarette smoking. *J Clin Psychiatry* 45:24–34, 1984b.

———. How tobacco produces drug dependence. In Ockene, J. K., ed. *The Pharmacologic Treatment of Tobacco Dependence: Proceedings of the World Congress.* Cambridge, MA: Institute for the Study of Smoking Behavior and Policy, 1986, 19–31.

Henningfield, J. E., and Brown, B. S. Do replacement therapies treat craving? *NIDA Notes* 2:8–9, 1987.

Henningfield, J. E., Clayton, R., Pollin, W. The involvement of tobacco in alcoholism and illicit drug use. *Br J Addict* 85:279–292, 1990.

Henningfield, J. E., Cohen, C., Slade, J. D. Is nicotine more addictive than cocaine? *Br J Addict* 86:565–569, 1991.

Henningfield, J. E., and Goldberg, S. R. Nicotine as a reinforcer in human subjects and laboratory animals. *Pharmacol Biochem Behav* 19:989–992, 1983.

———. Stimulus properties of nicotine in animals and human volunteers: A review. In Seiden, L. S., and Balster, R. L., eds. *Behavioral Pharmacology: The Current Status.* New York: Alan R. Liss, 1984, 433–449.

Henningfield, J. E., Goldberg, S. R., Herning, R. I., Jasinski, D. R., Lukas, S. E., Miyasato, K., Nemeth-Coslett, R., Pickworth, W. B., Rose, J. E., Sampson, A., Snyder, F. Human studies of the behavioral pharmacological determinants of nicotine dependence. In Harris, L. S., ed. *Problems of Drug Dependence,*

1985. NIDA Research Monograph 67. U. S. Department of Health, Education and Welfare, Public Health Service, Alcohol, Drug Abuse, and Mental Health Administration, National Institute on Drug Abuse. DHEW Publication No. (ADM) 86-1448, 1986, 54–65.

Henningfield, J. E., and Goldberg, S. R. Progress in understanding the relationship between the pharmacological effects of nicotine and human tobacco dependence. *Pharmacol Biochem Behav* 30:217–220, 1988.

Henningfield, J. E., Griffiths, R. R. A preparation for the experimental analysis of human cigarette smoking behavior. *Behav Res Meth Instru* 11:538–544, 1979.

Henningfield, J. E., Griffiths, R. R., Jasinski, D. R. Human dependence on tobacco and opioids: Common factors. In Thompson, T., and Johanson, C. E., eds. *Behavioral Pharmacology of Human Drug Dependence.* NIDA Research Monograph 37. U.S. Department of Health, Education and Welfare, Public Health Service, Alcohol, Drug Abuse, and Mental Health Administration, National Institute on Drug Abuse. DHEW Publication No. (ADM) 81-1137, 1981, 210–234.

Henningfield, J. E., London, E. D., Benowitz, N. L. Arterial-venous differences in plasma concentrations of nicotine after cigarette smoking. *JAMA* 263:2049–2050, 1990.

Henningfield, J. E., Miyasato, K., Jasinski, D. R. Cigarette smokers self-administer intravenous nicotine. *Pharmacol Biochem Behav* 19:887–890, 1983.

————. Abuse liability and pharmacodynamic characteristics of intravenous and inhaled nicotine. *J Pharmacol Exp Ther* 234:1–12, 1985.

Henningfield, J. E., and Nemeth-Coslett, R. Nicotine dependence: Interface between tobacco and tobacco-related disease. *Chest* 93:37S–55S, 1988.

Henningfield, J. E., Radzius, A., Cooper, T. M., Clayton, R. R. Drinking coffee and carbonated beverages blocks absorption of nicotine from nicotine polacrilex gum. *JAMA* 264:1560–1564, 1990.

Herman, C. P. External and internal cues as determinants of the smoking behavior of light and heavy smokers. *J Pers Soc Psychol* 30:664–672, 1974.

Herning R. I., Jones, R. T., Bachman, J. EEG changes during tobacco withdrawal. *Psychophysiology* 20:507–512, 1983.

Huba, G. J., Wingard, J. A., Bentler, P. M. A comparison of two latent variable causal models

for adolescent drug use. *J Pers Soc Psychol* 40:180–193, 1981.

Jaffe, J. H. Drug addiction and drug abuse. In Gilman, A. G., Goodman, L. S., Rall, T. W., Murad, F., eds. *Goodman and Gilman's Pharmacological Basis of Therapeutics.* New York: Macmillan, 1985, 532–581.

Jaffe, J. H., and Kanzler, M. Smoking as an addictive disorder. In Krasnegor N. A., ed. *Cigarette Smoking as a Dependence Process.* NIDA Research Monograph 23. U.S. Department of Health, Education and Welfare, Public Health Service, Alcohol, Drug Abuse, and Mental Health Administration, National Institute on Drug Abuse. DHEW Publication No. (ADM) 79-800, 1979, 4–23.

Jasinski, D. R., Johnson, R. E., Henningfield, J. E. Abuse liability assessment in human subjects. *Trends Pharmacol Sci* 5:196–200, 1984.

Jasinski, D. R., and Henningfield, J. E. Human abuse liability assessment by measurement of subjective and physiological effects. In Fischman, M. W., and Mello, N. K., eds. *Testing for Abuse Liability of Drugs in Humans.* NIDA Research Monograph 92. U. S. Department of Health and Human Services. DHHS Publication No. (ADM) 80-1613, 1989, 73–100.

Johnston, L. D., O'Mally, P. M., Bachman, J. G. *Use of Licit and Illicit Drugs by America's High School Students, 1975–1984.* National Institute on Drug Abuse. U.S. Department of Health and Human Services. DHHS Publication No. (ADM) 85-1394, 1985.

Johnston, L. M. Tobacco smoking and nicotine. *Lancet* 2:742, 1942.

Jones, R. T., Farrell, T. R., Herning, R. I. Tobacco smoking and nicotine tolerance. In Krasnegor, N. A., ed *Self-Administration of Abused Substances: Methods for Study.* NIDA Research Monograph 20. U.S. Department of Health, Education and Welfare, Public Health Service, Alcohol, Drug Abuse, and Mental Health Administration, National Institute on Drug Abuse. DHEW Publication No. (ADM) 78-727, 1978.

Kandel, D. B., Marguilies, R. Z., Davies, M. Analytical strategies for studying transitions into development stages. *Soc Educat* 51:162–176, 1978.

Kanigel, R. Nicotine becomes addictive. *Science Illustrated* 2:10–21, 1988.

Katz, J. L., and Goldberg, S. R. Second-order schedules of drug injection: Implications for understanding reinforcing effects of abused drugs. In Mello, N. K., ed. *Advances in Sub-*

stance Abuse, vol 3. Greenwich, CT: JAI Press, 1987.

Knott, V. J. Dynamic EEG changes during cigarette smoking. *Neuropsychobiology* 19:54–60, 1988.

Knott, V. J., and Venables, P. H. EEG alpha correlates of nonsmokers, smokers and smoking deprivation. *Psychophysiology* 14:150–156, 1977.

Kozlowski, L. T., and Herman, C. P. The interaction of psychosocial and biological determinants of tobacco use: More on the boundary model. *J Appl Soc Psychol* 14:244–256, 1984.

Lang, A. R. Addictive personality: A viable construct. In Levison, P. K., Gerstein, D. R., Maloff, D. R., eds. *Commonalities in Substance Abuse and Habitual Behavior.* Lexington, MA: Lexington Books DC Health and Company, 1983, 157–235.

London, E. D., Connolly, R. J., Szikszay, M., Wamsley, J. K. Distribution of cerebral metabolic effects of nicotine in the rat. *Eur J Pharmacol* 110:391–392, 1985.

London, E. D., Waller, S. B., Wamsley, J. K. Autographic localization of [^{3}H] nicotine binding sites in rat brains. *Neurosci Lett* 53:179–184, 1985.

Ludwig, A. M. Pavlov's "bells" and alcohol craving. *Addict Behav* 11:87–91, 1986.

Marlatt, G. A., and Gordon, J. R. *Relapse Prevention: Maintenance Strategies in the Treatment of Addictive Behaviors.* New York: Guilford Press, 1985.

Murray, J.A.H., Bradley, H., Craigre, W. A., Onions, C. T., eds. *New England Dictionary on Historical Principles.* Oxford: Clarendon Press, 1933.

Nemeth-Coslett, R., Henningfield, J. E., O'Keefe, M. K., Griffiths, R. R. Effects of mecamylamine on human cigarette smoking and subjective ratings. *Psychopharmacology* 88:420–425, 1986.

Niaura, R. S., Rohsenow, D. J., Binkoff, J. A., Monti, P. M., Pedraza, M., Abrams, D. B. Relevance of cue reactivity to understanding alcohol and smoking relapse. *J Abnorm Psychol* 97(2):133–152, 1988.

O'Brien, C. P., Ternes, J. W., Grabowski, J., Ehrman, R., eds. Classically conditioned phenomena in human opiate addiction. In Thompson, T., and Johanson, E. C., eds. *Behavioral Pharmacology of Human Drug Dependence.* NIDA Research Monograph 37. U. S. Department of Health, Education and Welfare, Public Health Service, Alcohol, Drug Abuse, and Mental Health Administration, National Institute on Drug Abuse.

DHEW Publication No. (ADM) 81-1137, 1981, 107–115.

O'Donnell, J. A., and Clayton, R. R. The stepping stone hypothesis marijuana, heroin, and causality. *Chem Depend* 4:229–241, 1982.

Pert, A., Post, R., Weiss, S.R.B. Conditioning as a critical determinant of sensitization induced by psychomotor stimulants. In Erinoff, L., ed. *Neurobiology of Drug Abuse: Learning and Memory.* NIDA Research Monograph 97, U. S. Department of Health and Human Services, Public Health Service, Alcohol, Drug Abuse, and Mental Health Administration, National Institute on Drug Abuse, 1990, 208–241.

Pickens, R., Bigelow, G., Griffiths, R. An experimental approach to treating chronic alcoholism: A case study and one-year follow-up. *Behav Res Ther* 11:321–325, 1973.

Pickworth, W. B., Herning, R. I., Henningfield, J. E. Electroencephalographic effects of nicotine chewing gum in humans, *Pharmacol Biochem Behav* 25:879–882, 1986.

———. Spontaneous EEG changes during tobacco abstinence and nicotine substitution in human volunteers. *J Pharmacol Exp Ther* 251:976–982, 1989.

Pollin, W., and Ravenholt, R. T. Tobacco addiction and tobacco mortality: Implications for death certification. *JAMA* 252:2849–2854, 1984.

Pomerleau, O. F., and Pomerleau, C. S. Neuroregulators and the reinforcement of smoking: Towards a biobehavioral explanation. *Neurosci Biobehav Rev* 8:503–513, 1984.

———. A biobehavioral view of substance abuse and addiction. *J Drug Issues* 17:111–131, 1987.

Rose, J. E., Herskovic J. E., Trilling, Y., Jarvik, M. E. Transdermal nicotine reduces cigarette craving and nicotine preference. *Clin Pharmacol Ther* 38:450–456, 1985.

Rosecrans, J. A., and Meltzer, L. T. Central sites and mechanisms of action of nicotine. *Neurosci Biobehav Rev* 5:497–501, 1981.

Rosenberg, J., Benowitz, N. L., Jacob, P., Wilson, K. M. Disposition kinetics and effects of intravenous nicotine. *Clin Pharmacol Ther* 28:517–522, 1980.

Russell, M.A.H. Tobacco smoking and nicotine dependence. In Gibbins, R. J., Israel, Y., Kalant, H., Popman, R. E., Schmidt, W., Smart, R. G., eds. *Research Advances in Alcohol and Drug Problems.* New York: John Wiley and Sons, 1976, 1–47.

———. Tobacco dependence: Is nicotine rewarding or aversive? In Krasnegor, N. A., ed. *Cigarette Smoking as a Dependence Process.*

NIDA Research Monograph 23. U.S. Department of Health, Education and Welfare, Public Health Service, Alcohol, Drug Abuse, and Mental Health Administration, National Institute on Drug Abuse. DHEW Publication No. (ADM) 79-800, 1979, 100–122.

Russell, M.A.H., and Feyerabend, C. Cigarette smoking: A dependence on high-nicotine boli. *Drug Metab Rev* 8:29–57, 1978.

Russell, M.A.H., Jarvis, M. J., West, R. J., Feyerabend, C. Buccal absorption of nicotine from smokeless tobacco sachets. *Lancet* 2:84-86:1370, 1985.

Schacter, S., Silverstein, B., Kozlowski, L. T., Perlick, D., Herman, C. P., Liebling, B. Studies of the interaction of psychological and pharmacological determinants of smoking. *J Exp Psychol* [Gen] 106:1–40, 1977.

Schmiterlow, C. G., Hansson, G., Andersson, L., Applegren, E., Hoffman, P. C. Distribution of nicotine in the central nervous system. *Ann NY Acad Sci* 142:2–14, 1967.

Snyder, F. R., Davis, F. C., Henningfield, J. E. The tobacco withdrawal syndrome: Performance decrements assessed on a computerized test battery. *Drug Alcohol Depend* 23:259–266, 1989.

Solomon, R. L., and Corbit, J. D. An opponent-process theory of motivation. II. Cigarette addiction. *J Abnorm Psychol* 81:158–171, 1973.

Stewart, J., DeWit, H., Eikelboom, R. The role of unconditioned and conditioned drug effects in the self-administration of opiates and stimulants. *Psychol Rev* 91(2):251–268, 1984.

Stitzer, M. L., Bigelow, G. E., Liebson, I. A., Hawthorne, J. W. Contingent reinforcement for benzodiazepine-free urines: Evaluation of a drug abuse treatment intervention. *J Appl Behav Anal* 15:493–503, 1982.

Stitzer, M. L., McCaul, M. E., Bigelow, G. E., Liebson, I. A. Oral methadone self-administration: Effects of dose and alternative reinforcers. *Clin Pharmacol Ther* 34:29–35, 1983.

Stitzer, M. L., and Bigelow, G. E. Contingent reinforcement for reduced breath carbon monoxide levels: Target-specific effects on cigarette smoking. *Addict Behav* 10:345–349, 1985.

Stitzer, M. L., Rand, C. S., Bigelow, G. E., Mead, A. M. Contingent payment procedures for smoking reduction and cessation. *J Appl Behav Anal* 19:197–202, 1986.

Stolerman, I. P., Goldfarb, T., Fink, R., Jarvik, M. E. Influencing cigarette smoking with nicotine antagonists. *Psychopharmacologia* 28:247–259, 1973.

Swedberg, M.B.D., Henningfield, J. E., Goldberg, S. R. Evidence of nicotine dependence from animal studies: Self-administration, tolerance and withdrawal. In Russell, M.A.H., Stolerman, I. P., Wannacott, S., ed. *Nicotine: Action and Medical Implications.* Oxford University Press, Oxford, 1989.

U.S. Department of Health, Education and Welfare (USDHEW). *Smoking and Health. A Report of the Surgeon General.* DHEW Publication No. (PHS) 79-50066, 1979.

U. S. Department of Health and Human Services (USDHHS). *Drug Abuse and Drug Abuse Research. The First in a Series of Triennial Reports to Congress from the Secretary. U. S. Department of Health and Human Services.* Public Health Service, Alcohol, Drug Abuse, and Mental Health Administration, National Institute on Drug Abuse. DHHS Publication No. (ADM) 85-1372, 1984.

———. *Drug Abuse and Drug Abuse Research. The Second Triennial Report to Congress from the Secretary.* Department of Health and Human Services, Public Health Service, Alcohol, Drug Abuse, and Mental Health Administration, National Institute on Drug Abuse, DHHS Publication No. (ADM) 87-1468, 1987.

———. *The Health Consequences of Smoking: Nicotine Addiction. A Report of the Surgeon General.* DHHS Publication No. (CDC) 88-8406, Public Health Service, Centers for Disease Control, Center for Health Promotion and Education, Office on Smoking and Health, 1988.

———. *Reducing the Health Consequences of Smoking: 25 Years of Progress. A Report of the Surgeon General.* DHHS Publication No. (CDC) 89-8411. Public Health Service, Centers for Disease Control, Center for Health Promotion and Education, Office on Smoking and Health, 1989.

Ulett, J. A., and Itil, T. M. Quantitative electroencephalograph in smoking and smoking deprivation. *Science* 164:969–970, 1969.

Valliant, G. E. The natural history of narcotic drug addiction. *Sem Psychiatry* 2:486–490, 1970.

Warner, K. E., and Murt, H. A. Premature deaths avoided by the antismoking campaign. *Am J Public Health* 73:672-677, 1973.

Welt, J. W., and Barnes, G. M. Youthful smoking: Patterns and relationships to alcohol and other drug use. *J Adolesc* 10:327–340, 1987.

West, R. R., and Evans, D. A. Lifestyle changes in long term survivors of acute myocardial infarction. *J Epidemiol Community Health* 40:103–109, 1986.

Wikler, A. Conditioning factors in opiate addiction and relapse. In Wilner, D. M., and Kassebaum, G. G., eds. *Narcotics*. New York: McGraw-Hill, 1965, 85–100.

———. Requirements for extinction of relapse-facilitating variables and for rehabilitation in a narcotic-antagonist program. *Adv Biochem Psychopharmacol* 8:399–414, 1973.

World Health Organization (WHO). Expert Committee on Drugs Liable to Produce Addiction. *Third Report, World Health Organization Technical Report Series No. 67.* Geneva: World Health Organization, March 1952.

———. Expert Committee on Addiction-Producing Drugs. *Thirteenth Report, World Health Organization Technical Report Series No. 273.* Geneva: World Health Organization, 1964.

———. *Sixth Review of Psychoactive Substances for International Control.* Geneva: World Health Organization, 1982.

Yamaguchi, K., and Kandel, D. B. Patterns of drug use from adolescence to young adulthood: Sequence of progression. *Am J Public Health* 74:668–672, 1984.

3

The Economics of Tobacco

KENNETH E. WARNER

The leading cause of premature mortality and avoidable morbidity, tobacco, is also the fuel of a powerful economic engine. The financial yield from sales of tobacco products, primarily cigarettes, marks the cultivation of tobacco and the manufacture, distribution, marketing, and retailing of tobacco products as one of this nation's leading economic activities.

The relationship between tobacco's health toll and its economic yield is not coincidental. The profitability of the enterprise—both its absolute magnitude and its rate of return—have provided the tobacco industry with economic incentive and political clout that have contributed to high rates of addiction to nicotine, and hence to tobacco's unique burden of disease (Taylor 1984; White 1988). Given the role of economics in the etiology of nicotine addiction and disease, this chapter examines essential ingredients in the economics of tobacco and tobacco products.

The chapter covers the following topics: (1) the economic structure, magnitude, and importance of the tobacco products industry, including consideration of the nature and effects of the federal government's tobacco "subsidy"; (2) the major economic consequences of tobacco outside of the formal market for tobacco products; and (3) the nature, magnitude, and implications of tobacco excise taxation. Other major issues in tobacco economics are discussed elsewhere. For example, the marketing of tobacco products—the largest enterprise of its kind for any product in America—is examined in Chapter 1.

While this chapter focuses on domestic economic matters, international economic issues have assumed growing importance in recent years. The efforts of the multinational tobacco companies to move into markets in Asia and the Third World, aided and abetted by the U.S. Government, are the major economic, political, and health story of the 1990s. Interested readers should consult Connolly (1989) and Barry (1991) for an introduction to this topic.

STRUCTURE, MAGNITUDE, AND IMPORTANCE OF THE TOBACCO INDUSTRY

Economic Importance of Tobacco and Tobacco Products

In 1988, over 50 million Americans spent almost $38 billion on tobacco products, with 95% of this sum paying for 562 billion cigarettes (Tobacco Institute 1989). The typical smoker consumed close to 11,000 cigarettes during the year (30 cigarettes/day), spending over $700 (at just under $1.30/pack of 20).

This aggregate expenditure ranks the tobacco industry as a major national economic activity. Among nondurable consumer goods, tobacco products ranked ninth in 1987 in terms of manufacturing output (U.S. Dept. of Commerce, Bureau of the Census 1989). Among agricultural commodities, the principal raw ingredient in tobacco products, tobacco leaf, ranked as the sixth largest cash crop in 1988, behind corn, soybeans, hay, wheat, and cotton. At a value of $2.2 billion, the tobacco crop constituted more than 3% of the total expended on all cash crops and farm commodities. The six "tobacco bloc" states of North Carolina, Kentucky, South Carolina, Tennessee, Virginia, and Georgia accounted for 93% of tobacco sales, with North Caroline ($890 million) and Kentucky ($554 million) alone producing almost two-thirds of the national total (Tobacco Institute 1989).

These figures indicate two dimensions of the economic importance of tobacco: the sheer magnitude of the enterprise and its concentration, as illustrated by the dominance of six (or even two) states in tobacco growing. Concentration also occurs at the manufacturing level. The cigarette market is a classic oligopoly consisting of six major firms, two of which, Philip Morris and R. J. Reynolds, control almost three-quarters of the market. While domestic cigarette sales continue to drop, price increases by the manufacturers more than compensate for lost customers. Profits rise annually within the industry, and the profit margin—the percent of sales revenues that are profit—is one of the largest ever enjoyed by any industry group. This concentration of profit has been successfully converted into disproportionate political influence from the White House down to state and local legislatures (Taylor 1984).

The profitability of the cigarette business, and hence its importance to its parent companies, has been vividly illustrated by White (1988), who compared the 1986 tobacco and nontobacco product sales and earnings for the two largest companies. For Philip Morris, tobacco and nontobacco products brought in equal revenues, $12.7 billion each. Three-quarters of operating income, however, was attributable to cigarette sales, a total of $2.9 billion (or 23% of operating revenues from tobacco products). Nontobacco products yielded only $1 billion in income, representing a still healthy rate of return of close to 8%. For R. J. Reynolds, tobacco products generated just over a third (36%) of $16 billion in total revenue, but accounted for almost two-thirds (64%) of earnings. The earnings-to-sales ratio for tobacco products was 28%; for nontobacco products, 9.5%.

The tobacco industry regularly turns its economic power into political influence. The industry's aggressive lobbying, supported by its largesse in contributions to legislators' campaigns and personal incomes, has blocked or moderated legislation at all levels of government, ranging from the content of cigarette pack warning labels, determined by Congress, to limits on smoking in public places, largely to date the purview of state governments and municipalities (Taylor 1984; White 1988; Samuels and Glantz 1991).

While the economic and associated political clout of tobacco have derived from the products' profitability, influence may also flow in part from federal, state, and some local governments' receipt of excise tax revenues from the sale of tobacco products, primarily cigarettes. In fiscal year 1990, these taxes yielded over $9.6 billion, split roughly equally between the federal government ($4.07 billion) and the states ($5.56 billion), with local government units receiving a minor share (Tobacco Insitute 1989, 1991). The role and impact of excise taxes are discussed later in this chapter.

The economic importance of tobacco also extends to its macroeconomic consequences. The United States is both the world's leading exporter and importer of tobacco and tobacco products. Exports significantly exceed imports, with the former accounting for $4.15 billion in 1988 while the latter totaled $546 million. The difference defines tobacco's role as a positive contributor to the nation's balance of payments. Exports have increased dramatically in recent years, with the total dollar value rising by 22% in 1988 alone. The lion's share of the export total ($2.6 billion) consists of sales of cigarettes, numbering 118.5 billion in 1988, an increase of 18% over the preceding year. In comparison, America imported only 2 billion cigarettes in 1988, valued at $36.7 million (Tobacco Institute 1989). American cigarette manufacturers import a large volume of tobacco leaf for use in domestic cigarette production.

Given America's chronic balance of payments problem, tobacco's role as a positive contributor has both practical and symbolic value at the level of national policy. Industry representatives emphasize the importance of tobacco in this context whenever critics complain that government encouragement of tobacco sales abroad constitutes a national policy of exporting death and disease (Connolly 1989; Barry 1991).

In sum, the economic and hence political clout of the tobacco industry derives from the sheer magnitude of the enterprise and from its concentration, geographic in the case of tobacco farming and corporate in the extraordinarily profitable manufacture and sale of tobacco products. To combat its critics in the legislative arena and elsewhere, the industry regularly points to its role in employment, generation of tax revenue, and the trade balance. The strategy is to convince legislators, journalists, and the public that, whatever they may think of the health consequences of tobacco, they are highly dependent on the contribution tobacco makes to the economic health of their communities and the nation as a whole. The *objective* economic importance of the tobacco industry differs significantly from its subjectively and politically perceived importance, however. This distinction, and an assessment of the objective economic contribution of the industry, are discussed at the end of this section.

Structure of the Industry

The tobacco industry can be characterized as consisting of four major core sectors: tobacco growing, product manufacturing, wholesaling, and retailing. There are additional discrete core activities, including auctions and warehousing; given their proportionately small contribution to the whole, they will be subsumed under wholesaling in this discussion. (Thus defined, wholesaling includes activities at both the pre- and post-manufacturing stages of production.) In addition to the core sectors, a number of industries constitute the tobacco industry's supply network. This includes the equipment, energy, and chemicals needed for tobacco farming, the chemicals and other supplies used in manufacturing cigarettes, and so on.

According to an industry funded study (Chase Econometrics 1985), in 1983 the largest single group of workers involved in the tobacco industry consisted of the esti-mated 504,000 people who helped with the cultivation and harvesting of tobacco—the farm workers. Given the sporadic nature of their employment, however, average annual employment in tobacco growing (on a full-time basis) was estimated at 100,000 people. Farm workers toiled on approximately 200,000 farms.

The next largest core sector, in terms of number of individuals employed during the year, fell at the opposite end of the production spectrum: in retailing, 192,720 people owed their employment to tobacco (in terms of average annual employment). Manufacturing employed 76,900 people, while wholesaling employed 35,357 (both average annual figures). All told, the core sectors were responsible for the employment of 414,000 Americans, on an average annual basis. An additional 296,000 people were employed by the tobacco industry's supplier industries as a consequence of tobacco-related economic activities. Combined, the core sectors and supplier industries employed 710,000 people, or three-quarters of 1% of U.S. employment during 1983.

Of nontax revenues produced by the sale of tobacco products that year, the lion's share went to manufacturers. The direct manufacturers of tobacco products received $4.3 billion, or nearly 30% of the nontax total of $14.8 billion; tobacco manufacturing suppliers received $2.1 billion, an additional 14%. Wholesalers' and their suppliers' share equaled $3.5 billion (24%), while that of retailers and their suppliers was $2.4 billion (16%). Tobacco growers and their suppliers received a like amount, $2.5 billion (17%) (Chase Econometrics 1985).

These figures indicate that the manufacturers and their employees reap the greatest rewards from the nontax component of tobacco product sales. As observed earlier, the profitability of tobacco products, and specifically cigarettes, has few parallels in the world of commerce. At the opposite end of the economic spectrum, farmers—the "heart and soul" of tobacco's political appeal—receive much more modest benefits from the tobacco business. As just noted, the farming enterprise as a whole received only 17% of the nontax portion of tobacco product sales. Taxes constituted almost half of the tobacco sales dollar in 1983 (including employees' income and Federal Insurance Contributions Act, or FICA, taxes, in addition to consumers' excise and sales taxes); accordingly, farming accounted for less than 9% of the money spent on cigarettes and other tobacco products in 1983. The raw ingredient in cigarettes—tobacco—is only a minor share of the price of a pack of cigarettes.

One feature of tobacco economics is often misinterpreted by the lay public. The financial yield per acre is dramatically higher for tobacco than for virtually all other legal crops. This does not mean, however, that tobacco farming is more profitable than farming other crops. The U.S. Department of Agriculture (USDA) estimates the gross income per acre of tobacco at $3,500 in 1989. In contrast, tree nuts are estimated to yield $2,200, peanuts $670, sweet corn $540, cotton $350, corn for grain $220, soybeans $210, hay $170, and wheat $120 (Tobacco Institute 1989). While these figures specify gross yield, they do not indicate profitability because they ignore the cost side of the ledger. On that side, tobacco farming is labor-intensive, particularly given its typical small-scale nature, a function in part of the allotment system (discussed in the next section). Labor-intensive activities, other things being equal, are more expensive. Consequently, while tobacco's gross yield per acre is high, so are its costs; and the small scale of most tobacco farmers' tobacco acreage limits its profit potential for the farmer.

The Tobacco "Subsidy"

One of the more interesting, and confusing, aspects of tobacco economics relates to the system of federally mandated tobacco allotments and price supports, commonly known as the *tobacco subsidy*. A product of the Depression era farming crisis, the system was intended to bring stability and security to the nation's tobacco farmers. Since the mid-1960s, the tobacco subsidy has become, for many observers, a symbol of entrenched economic and political interests and of government hypocrisy: on the one hand, the health arm of the government warns Americans not to smoke; on the other hand, the USDA subsidizes the growing of tobacco. The latter, it is commonly assumed, increases smoking.

The structure of the allotment/price support system is too complex to describe in detail here; interested readers should consult Miller and Tarczy (1987). In broad form, the system assures farmers a buyer for their tobacco at a guaranteed minimum price in exchange for their agreement to limit production to quantities decided by the USDA according to complicated formulas and following consultation with the tobacco products manufacturers. Both minimum prices and quantity limitations vary by tobacco type.

The allotment feature requires growers to possess an allotment—a legal authorization—in order to grow tobacco. Farmers can own allotments or rent them. This component of the system limits the acreage devoted to tobacco growing and tends to encourage small-scale farming. The latter, in turn, encourages labor-intensive farming (since economical use of heavy machinery requires large farms). Most tobacco farms in the United States are small: tobacco was harvested from an estimated 632,000 acres on 180,000 farms in 1988 (Tobacco Institute 1989).

When farmers fail to sell their tobacco to private buyers at auction, regional tobacco cooperatives buy this "surplus" tobacco under the price support system at the guaranteed minimum price and store it for later sale. The costs of acquiring and storing this tobacco are covered by low-interest government loans (hence the subsidy).

The price support system was altered several times during the 1980s, including one major attempt to make it "no net cost" to taxpayers through legislation in 1982, and, in 1986, an enormous bailing out of farmers whom the no net cost system was bankrupting. The 1986 legislation was not unlike the more recent bailout of the savings and loan industry. Government analysts estimated the ultimate cost of the bailout at about $1 billion, or $5,000 of taxpayer monies for each of the nation's tobacco farms (Warner 1988).

The preeminent issue in the debate about the system is whether it is appropriate for the federal government to help subsidize a crop that, by the government's own well-publicized estimates, is responsible for more avoidable premature mortality than any other product. This issue has two dimensions. One is the moral question; the other pertains to the direct impact of the subsidy system on the price of cigarettes.

The moral question cannot be addressed empirically. The direct impact of the system on cigarette price can be. Contrary to the conventional wisdom, the direct effect of the subsidy is to *raise* the price of cigarettes, since the system increases the cost of a raw material, tobacco, to manufacturers of tobacco products. To the extent that consumers are price responsive (Warner 1986), the subsidy thus might have the effect of *decreasing* the demand for cigarettes and other tobacco products. Because tobacco constitutes such a small fraction of the cost of manufacturing and marketing cigarettes, however, elimination of the allotment/price support system would probably decrease the price of cigarettes by no more than 2–3 cents per pack (Sumner and Alston 1984).

The indirect effect of the subsidy system might work in the opposite way, however, The political interests the system has created and perpetuated may have helped protect farmers and manufacturers from more stringent public health legislation that would have the effect of increasing the price of cigarettes, such as substantially higher federal excise taxes. Thus, the net effect of the system on the price of tobacco products, and hence on their consumption, is indeterminant (Warner 1988).

The Economic Importance of Tobacco Revisited

As described earlier, representatives of the tobacco industry frequently employ the statistics on tobacco's economic contributions in an attempt to convince the public and legislators that tobacco is indispensable to the economy. The Tobacco Institute has commissioned at least three studies of the economic impacts of tobacco on the economies of the individual states and the country as a

whole (Wharton ARC 1980; Chase Econometrics 1985; Price Waterhouse 1990). Data from these studies have been compiled in reports and booklets that detail estimated national and state-specific contributions of tobacco to employment, income, and tax revenues; in some instances, data have even been developed for major cities and counties. Simply because tobacco products are bought and sold in all states, in all instances the documents describe positive economic "benefits" of tobacco to the citizenry of the relevant jurisdiction. The cynical political argument these supposed "benefits" support is that policies that reduce tobacco consumption will wreak havoc with the economic vitality and even stability of any community.

This argument contains a fatal flaw, however, one that has been acknowledged in the complete reports of the consulting firms that have produced the analyses of tobacco's economic contributions. The flaw is not described in any of the documents distributed by the industry for public relations purposes, and it is not appreciated by the targets of the industry's propaganda. The flaw is that the economic benefits associated with tobacco would exist in the complete absence of the industry. Money now spent on tobacco products would, instead, be spent on other goods and services. This spending, in turn, would generate jobs, incomes, and taxes just as spending on tobacco products does today. For the country as a whole, there is no reason to believe that there would be any net loss of economic output (or "benefits") were the nation to attain the Surgeon General's goal of a smoke-free society.

The following quotation from the industry-commissioned report by Chase Econometrics (Vol. I, Chapt. V, p. 3, 1985) demonstrates that the industry's consultants concur with this assessment but were instructed to ignore it:

It can be argued, of course, that without the tobacco industry, the expenditures on, and resources devoted to, the production of tobacco products would simply be shifted elsewhere in the economy. That is, if consumers were faced with no available tobacco products, they would reallocate their spending to other goods and services. This reallocated spending would generate additional business opportunities in other sectors of the economy along with the associated employment and incomes. Therefore, except for transitional problems and differential industry levels of productivity, *the aggregate economic results would be substantially the same.... [T]he compensatory responses that would occur automatically within the economy and within the Chase Econometrics U.S. Macroeconomic Model in a total impact-type of study were constrained from taking place within this analysis.* (Emphasis added)

While the net economic effect of the elimination of tobacco products would be negligible for the nation as a whole, individual states would experience true economic gains or losses. The six major tobacco bloc states likely would suffer net losses in employment and incomes, although as Schelling (1986) has observed, these losses would occur gradually during the period of transition to a tobacco-free society. Regarding employment effects, he concluded that few tobacco farmers would be driven out of business. Rather, the children of tobacco farmers would be more likely to farm other crops or enter nonfarm occupations.

In contrast, the nontobacco states would experience economic gains as spending was redirected from tobacco products to indigenous goods and services. Much of the spending on tobacco products in these states is exported out of state. In the state of Michigan, for example, 50 cents of every dollar spent on tobacco products is immediately "shipped" to North Carolina and the other tobacco states. A large percentage of the jobs and incomes created by tobacco spending in a nontobacco state thus goes to residents of the tobacco states and to tobacco company stockholders. Spending redirected at least partially to indigenously produced goods and services would create jobs and incomes within the states. Therefore, tobacco produces a net drain on the economies of the nontobacco states (Warner 1987; Warner and Fulton 1993).

ECONOMIC CONSEQUENCES OUTSIDE OF THE MARKET FOR TOBACCO PRODUCTS

Social Costs of the Health Consequences of Smoking

As substantial as the tobacco industry's gross economic contribution to the nation's output (gross national product, or GNP) may be, the economic value of the adverse consequences of tobacco use equal or exceed the GNP figure. The adverse consequences include everything from the costs of smoking-caused fire damage, to extra ventilation costs in buildings in which smoking is permitted, to the expense of the additional cleaning of clothes necessitated by exposure to smoke. While these might constitute important economic costs, however, they pale in comparison with the two principal economic burdens of smoking and other tobacco use: the costs of tobacco-related medical care and the productivity lost to society due to tobacco-related morbidity and premature mortality.

Several analysts have developed estimates of these two major costs to society in the case of cigarette smoking. Recent prominent estimates are those of Rice and associates (1986) and the Office of Technology Assessment (1985) in Congress. The work of Rice and colleagues is particularly noteworthy for its methodological rigor and its analytical detail. Employing conservative assumptions concerning the risks of smoking, these scholars estimated smoking-related medical care costs in 1984 at $23.3 billion. Productivity losses associated with premature mortality were $21.1 billion and those associated with smoking-related morbidity equaled $9.3 billion, for a total of $30.4 billion in productivity, or indirect, losses. Combined, the medical care costs and productivity losses represented a cost to society of $53.7 billion. The authors explicitly excluded the non-health-related costs of smoking. The only prominent previous study to consider any such costs found that the most likely candidate to represent a large loss, fire damage, constituted only 1.5% of the total estimated costs of smoking (Luce and Schweitzer 1978).

The study by the Office of Technology Assessment produced an estimate of $62.2 billion in costs of smoking in 1984 dollars (as adjusted by Rice et al. for purposes of comparison). Increasing the estimates of Luce and Schweitzer to 1984 dollars yielded a figure of $52.8 billion. While these estimates all appear to be quite close, Rice and co-workers note that they mask differences in the estimated costs associated with the three major disease categories: neoplasms, circulatory diseases, and respiratory diseases. Still, the overall consistency has been interpreted as suggesting that these estimates are a reasonable "ballpark" figure for the economic burden of the morbidity and mortality caused by smoking.

Each of these studies likely underestimates that burden considerably, however. The reason is that the analysts were forced to rely upon data on the risks of smoking derived from now-dated epidemiologic studies. Analysis of data from the American Cancer Society's new Cancer Prevention Study II, covering deaths between 1982 and 1988, shows that the relative risks of smoking are much higher for several disease categories than previously believed, particularly among women (see Chapter 6). These findings likely reflect the earlier age of initiation of smoking and greater smoking "intensity" (cigarettes/day) by study enrollees, as compared with the earlier generations of smokers who comprised the previous study populations. As a consequence, the Centers for Disease Control estimated that smoking was responsible for 390,000 deaths in 1985 (USDHHS 1989) and 434,000 deaths in 1988 (Schultz 1991). In contrast, Rice and co-workers estimated the annual mortality toll at only 270,000 deaths and the Office of Technology Assessment placed it at 314,000. In each case, the lower estimate reflects specific exclusions, as well as outdated estimates of relative risks.

No one has yet used the new estimates of relative risk to assess the costs of smoking-related disease in the late 1980s. Use of the epidemiologic evidence available from the new Cancer Society study, combined with inflation in the years between the earlier studies and the present, would push the contemporary figure close to $100 billion (in 1990 dollars).

Net Social Costs

While the tobacco industry insists that society is economically dependent on tobacco, the antismoking community argues the opposite: smoking imposes an unaffordable economic burden on society, reflecting the social costs of tobacco's health consequences. Just as the industry's claim is no more than a half truth, the antismoking argument presents an incomplete picture as well, for it ignores economic "benefits" of smokers' premature demise. Specifically, the premature deaths of many smokers mean that substantial costs of health care experienced by the elderly are avoided, since the victims of tobacco do not realize the full life expectancy of nonsmokers. Of greater consequence, smokers' premature deaths mean that they do not live to collect pension and Social Security benefits comparable to those received by nonsmokers.

Each of these economic phenomena has been studied by economists in recent years. While more interest has focused on the health care cost issue, the pension phenomenon is likely of greater consequence. In one study of the implications of a workplace smoking cessation program, for example, Gori, Richter, and Yu (1984) concluded that the increased burden on firms of later pension obligations to successful quitters dwarfed all of the other economic outcomes—all benefits—associated with the smokers' quitting. More recently, Shoven, Sundberg, and Bunker (1989) estimated that the median-wage male smoker lost $20,000 in Social Security benefits due to smoking-related loss of life expectancy, while the median-wage female smoker lost $10,000. In essence, they concluded, smokers subsidize nonsmokers' Social Security incomes. A similar finding by Manning and colleagues (1989) influenced the assessment of the net social costs of smoking.

Several economists have tackled the question of whether smoking increases or decreases net health care costs. In 1983, Leu and Schaub published an analysis of the aggregate health care costs in 1976 of two populations of Swiss males: the actual population, born since 1876, and a hypothetical population including only nonsmokers. The authors found that the health care costs of the two groups would have been about the same, because the nonsmoking population's greater longevity would have balanced the smokers' higher annual health care costs. While the absence of smoking would not have produced significant health care cost savings, it would have resulted in a larger population of longer-lived men.

Several analyses undertaken since Leu and Schaub's article was published have challenged the specifics of their findings while supporting the basic point; namely, that the complete elimination of smoking would not substantially reduce aggregate health care costs. For example, Lewit (1983) estimated that aggregate costs would eventually fall, although they might rise in the near term following the elimination of smoking.

Some of the cost analysis has focused on the impact of stopping smoking on Medicare costs. Wright (1986) estimated that a 45-year-old male light smoker's quitting would increase Medicare's liabilities by $204 to $2,745 (in 1980 dollars). However, Pickett and Bridgers (1987) noted that an analysis like Wright's tends to ignore salutary changes in health status and hence in the health care utilization patterns of the elderly. It also misses the fact that some Medicare expenditures on chronic disease now reflect the morbidity and disability toll of smoking. Indeed, to date no one has determined whether Medicare would, on balance, gain or lose, much less how much, by the advent of a smoke-free society. On the one hand, the elimination of smoking clearly would increase the number of Medicare beneficiaries in any given year; in and of itself, this would increase Medicare liabilities. On the other hand, the reduction of smoking-related chronic disease morbidity among Medicare claimants could have the effect of decreasing costs.

The best and most recent analysis of the relationship between smoking and health care costs concludes that, on balance, smoking does increase costs, even during the Medicare years (Hodgson 1992). The importance of resolving the "net" medical cost of smoking lies almost exclusively in the intellectual realm of puzzle-solving, since a finding that smoking raises medical costs a little or decreases them some is unlikely to have any impact on tobacco-and-health policy. The qualitative point the analyses have already made, however, *is* important: the impact of smoking on the nation's total health care costs is neither a wholly meaningful nor an important measure of smoking's social burden.

A corollary to this finding deserves emphasis: lack of definitive knowledge of whether smoking increases or decreases costs in the aggregate reflects the essential fact of smoking—it kills people. None of the cost analyses disagrees that smokers incur greater health care costs than nonsmokers at any given age. The possibility that nonsmokers incur greater (or comparable) lifetime costs results exclusively from the fact that, on average, they live longer. In essence, additional health care costs associated with the avoidance of smoking—if any occur—represent an exceedingly small price to pay for a major health benefit. Surely, this is a social outcome to be sought with enthusiasm (Warner 1987).

Independent of the net health care costs associated with tobacco, the productivity losses associated with tobacco-related morbidity and premature mortality represent a definite drain on the economy. These indirect costs of smoking's health consequences have constituted the majority of social costs estimated in each of the cost-of-smoking analyses. As such, smoking imposes a real economic burden in the tens of billions of dollars annually in the United States. As the net production contribution of tobacco to the economy is minimal (relative to what would exist in the absence of tobacco) and the health care cost issue is ambiguous (and also likely minor), the productivity loss is the most important true economic cost of tobacco. The pension/Social Security issue represents a major redistribution of resources. Whether one considers this a true social cost or dismisses it as a transfer payment will determine how one ranks this factor in the ultimate social calculus of tobacco's "bottom-line" effect on the economy (Rice et al. 1986; Manning et al. 1989).

TOBACCO EXCISE TAXATION

Excise Tax Revenues

As was indicated in the first section of this chapter, almost half of the tobacco dollar goes to taxes, including those imposed on the consumers of tobacco products (excise and sales taxes) and those associated with employment within the industry (income taxes and FICA). With the exception of the excise tax, all of these taxes apply to the production and sale of virtually all other goods. Consequently, from the perspective of the "uniqueness" of tobacco, only the excise tax is of interest.

The excise tax is also the largest component of all tax revenues associated with tobacco. In fiscal year 1990, the federal excise tax on cigarettes—then 16 cents per pack of 20 cigarettes—grossed $4.07 billion. (The tax increased to 20 cents in 1991 and to 24 cents in 1993.) All states imposed excise taxes on cigarettes, ranging from 2 cents per pack in North Carolina to 42 cents in Hawaii in 1990. Collectively, state cigarette excise taxes grossed $5.56 billion. In addition, almost 400 cities, towns, and counties imposed local cigarette taxes, in most instances amounting to a penny or two per pack; collectively, these local-level taxes generated $191 million in revenue (Tobacco Institute 1991).

While all states tax cigarettes, only 35 states impose taxes on other tobacco products, a number that has been increasing since the mid-1980s. Collectively, however, these taxes yield only a small fraction of total tobacco product excise tax revenue: in 1990, excise taxes on cigarettes constituted 98% of all tobacco excise tax revenues. Since 1863, cigarettes have produced 96% of all tobacco excise taxes collected at all levels of government (Tobacco Institute 1991).

The importance of tobacco taxes as a revenue source has varied over the past 130 years. During wartime in the nineteenth century, tobacco taxes provided significant revenue to the federal government. Since imposition of the personal income tax in 1913, however, tobacco excise taxes have never been a major source of federal revenue. In 1950, cigarette excise taxes generated 3% of federal revenues, a figure that fell steadily to only one-half of 1% in 1987. In part this reflects the development of other revenue sources. In part it reflects the failure of the federal excise tax rate to have kept pace with inflation. While the nominal rate was doubled from 8 to 16 cents per pack in 1983, the real value of the tax (i.e., accounting for inflation) eroded by almost 50% between 1951 and 1988 (USDHHS 1989). During the same period, the federal tax as a fraction of total cigarette retail price plummeted from more than a third to only 12%. Four cent increases in 1991 and 1993 will do little to compensate. Including state taxes, which have yielded less ground to inflation, excise taxes have fallen from half of retail price during the two decades from the mid-1950s to the mid-1970s to just over a quarter (25.6%) in 1990 (Tobacco Institute 1991).

Consumption and Health Effects of Cigarette Excise Taxes

The small and declining share of federal government revenues produced by cigarette taxes, and the generally small contribution to state and local governments (USDHHS 1989), means that the importance of excise taxes lies not primarily in their ability to generate needed government revenues, although historically this has been their principal purpose (Warner 1981; USDHHS 1989). Rather, their import lies in their effects on the consumption of tobacco products. Over the past quarter century, a major line of economic inquiry has examined how consumers' demand for cigarettes has responded to changes in their price. With excise tax a major component of price, and a policy tool that can be wielded to affect price, excise taxation has become an issue of great interest.

The literature on the price elasticity of demand for cigarettes (price elasticity being the standard measure of consumers' responsiveness to price changes) has been reviewed thoroughly by the Surgeon General (USDHHS 1989). Price elasticity of demand is defined as the percentage decrease (increase) in consumer demand that is produced by a 1% increase (decrease) in retail price. Thus, an elasticity of −0.4 would mean that a 1% price increase should reduce demand by 0.4%, or a 10% price increase should decrease it by 4%.

Among a dozen prominent studies of adult price elasticity of demand published during the decade of the 1980s and reviewed by the Surgeon General, estimates ranged from a low (in absolute value) of −0.14 to a high of −1.23 for adults. While this range looks considerable, the studies exhibited substantial clustering in the vicinity of −0.4, with more recent studies tending toward a lower estimate (in absolute value). Consequently, despite methodologic differences, economists in general concur on the magnitude of the price elasticity of demand for cigarettes (USDHHS 1989), and experience supports their agreement. The doubling of the federal cigarette excise tax in 1983 was associated with a pattern of price and consumption changes consistent with an elasticity of roughly −0.4 (Harris 1987; Lewit 1985), as was experience with tax increases in Canada during the 1980s (Ferrence et al. 1991). A 25 cent increase in the California state cigarette excise tax in 1989 has been associated with a somewhat lower estimate of price elasticity, but one consistent with the expectation that a price increase of a given percentage should decrease the demand for cigarettes by one-fifth to two-fifths as much (Flewelling et al., 1992).

Price changes can have different effects in different socioeconomic groups. Townsend (1987) analyzed how the five major social classes in England have responded to cigarette price increases in that country. She found that the lower social classes were much more price responsive than were the higher social classes. This finding is as expected, since responses to price include an "income effect," that is, consumers will react to a price in part based on its implications for their disposable income.

The importance of the finding is that tax increases are most likely to encourage less affluent members of society to avoid smoking—to quit or not to start. This segment of society has proven more resistant to the smoking-and-health message conveyed by public health organizations since the mid-1960s (see Chapter 5). Also, the relationship between price responsiveness and socioeco-nomic status mitigates a prominent industry argument against increasing excise taxes: namely, that excise taxes are highly regressive (see also Harris 1982).

In a similar vein, little research has addressed the price responsiveness of children and teenagers, as compared with adults. Lewit, Coate, and Grossman (1981) produced the most widely cited study focusing on teens. These authors found that children tend to be more price responsive with regard to smoking than adults. Specifically, the authors estimated teenagers' price elasticity of demand at −1.44, with the majority of the response reflecting teens' decisions of whether or not to smoke, rather than how much; the prevalence elasticity was −1.2, meaning that a 10% increase in cigarette price would decrease the number of teenage smokers by 12%. Utilizing a different data set, Grossman, Coate, and Lewit (see Grossman 1983) found a smaller prevalence elasticity among teens, −0.76. The authors cautioned, however, that the latter result came from analysis of a much smaller data set. Even so, this elasticity estimate is considerably higher (in absolute value) than that of the vast majority of studies of adult price elasticities. A study in Canada concluded that teenagers' price elasticity of demand was even greater than that estimated by Lewit, Coate, and Grossman (Ferrence et al. 1991). In contrast, recent research failed to find a significant difference between teens' and adults' price responsiveness (Wasserman et al. 1991).

Lewit and Coate's (1982) analysis of adult price elasticities found a consistent inverse relationship between age and price responsiveness. Assuming that this pattern holds in still younger age classes, as the work of Lewit, Coate, and Grossman indicates, the pattern has direct health and policy relevance, in that it suggests that cigarette price increases will be particularly effective smoking deterrents for children. The recent Canadian evidence provides strong supportive evidence.

Harris (1982) and Warner (1986) have used two of the price elasticity of demand studies (Lewit and Coate 1982; Lewit, Coate, Grossman 1981) to estimate the effects that specific increases in the federal cigarette excise tax would have on the numbers of smokers and on their daily consumption. Harris estimated that doubling the federal excise tax from 8 to 16 cents would lead to a decline in the number of adult smokers of 1.5 million and in the number of teenage smokers of 700,000. When Congress was considering whether to make the 1983 doubling of the tax permanent, Warner estimated that failure to do so would increase the number of adult smokers by 1.5 million and the number of teen smokers by almost half a million. In 1985, Lewit examined the actual decline in total cigarette consumption following the 1983 doubling of the excise tax and found it to be consistent with expectations predicted by the earlier demand elasticity studies.

Both Warner (1986) and Harris (1987) have attempted to convert predicted consumption changes into their implications for smoking-produced mortality. Warner estimated that permitting the 1983 doubling of the federal tax to "sunset" (i.e., return to the pre-1983 level, as scheduled) ultimately would be responsible for an additional 480,000 premature deaths. Although most of these would occur decades into the future, the estimated health toll is extraordinary, when one contemplates that the change envisioned amounted to only 8 cents per pack of cigarettes. Warner's analysis assumed maintenance of any tax changes at their real value. As federal excise taxes are set in nominal terms, however, that real value would erode over time and the health impact similarly would decline.

Harris (1987) analyzed the health implications of the 1983 doubling of the federal tax and of associated price increases by the cigarette manufacturers. He concluded that these price changes would result in 100,000 additional Americans living to age 65 years, half of whom would now be teenagers. The smaller estimate reflected, in part, relaxing the assumption that the real value of the tax change would be maintained over time. Together, these analyses demonstrate that cigarette excise taxation is a potentially powerful tool of public health policy.

Excise Tax Policy Initiatives

Interest in the health implications of excise taxation has prompted new legislative activity to raise taxes and to utilize revenues in creating new ways, especially at the state level. In recent years, several states have earmarked cigarette excise activities for public health activities, and specifically for tobacco use control. These include Minnesota, which employed such revenues to mount a televised antismoking campaign and to assist local school boards in implementing tobacco use prevention programs; Nebraska, which has earmarked a penny-per-pack to fund the state's Cancer and Smoking Disease Research Program; and Utah, which dedicates a portion of excise tax revenues for tobacco control programs. Other states, including New Jersey, Indiana, and Michigan, earmark portions of their cigarette excise tax revenues for other (nontobacco) social programs (USDHHS 1989).

The most dramatic tax-and-earmark package to date was inaugurated in California in 1989, after that state's voters approved a 25 cent per pack increase in the state's excise tax—the largest single cigarette excise tax increase in U.S. history—with the majority of hundreds of millions of new annual tax dollars earmarked for health education, research, treatment, and environmental conservation programs (USDHHS 1989). In 1992, Massachusetts voters also passed a referendum raising the state's tax by 25 cents per pack.

At the federal level, several pieces of legislation have been proposed to increase the federal tax by a doubling or more; health organizations have called for an increase of $2 in the federal tax (Coalition on Smoking OR Health 1993). An additional policy measure currently under consideration, at both the state and federal level, calls for switching the excise tax from a nominal tax to an ad valorem tax. The latter would tie the tax to the nontax price of cigarettes, thereby assuring that the nominal tax rate would rise automatically as manufacturers' price increases raised the nontax portion of cigarette price (USDHHS 1989; Tobacco Reduction Task Force 1990).

CONCLUSION

Tobacco is deeply rooted in the cultural and economic history of this nation; from these roots have sprung hardy economic and political interests. While tobacco's health consequences remain the principal battleground on which the war against tobacco is waged, skirmishes are fought daily on the terrain of economic argumentation. Thus, to fight the health battle effectively, one must be armed with an understanding of the economic terrain as well. One must appreciate the magnitude of tobacco's economic and political power, and also comprehend the complicated nature of its significance. One must understand, too, the nature of tobacco's social burden as it has been defined in economic terms. Finally, the tobacco excise tax has important implications beyond its role as a revenue source. It is a particularly potent tool of public health policy.

REFERENCES

Barry, M. The influence of the U.S. tobacco industry on the health, economy, and environment of developing countries. *N Engl J Med* 324:917–920, 1991.

Burns, D., and Pierce, J. P. *Tobacco Use in California, 1990–91.* Sacramento, CA: California Department of Health Services, 1992.

Chase Econometrics. *The Economic Impact of the Tobacco Industry on the United States Economy.* Bala Cynwyd, PA: Chase Econometrics, 1985.

Coalition on Smoking OR Health. Saving lives and raising revenue: the case for major increases in state and federal tobacco taxes, Washington, D.C.: Coalition, January 1993.

Connolly, G. N. The international marketing of tobacco. In Blakeman, E. M., ed. *Tobacco Use in America.* Washington, D.C.: American Medical Association, 1989, 49–54.

Ferrence, R. G., Garcia, J. M., Sykora, K., Collishaw, N. E., Farinon, L. Effects of pricing on cigarette use among teenagers and adults in Canada, 1980–89. Toronto: Addiction Research Foundation, February 1991.

Flewelling, R. L., Kenney, E., Elder, J. P., Pierce, J., Johnson, M., Bal, D. G. First-year impact of the 1989 California cigarette tax increase on cigarette consumption. *Am J Public Health,* 82(6):867–869, 1992.

Gori, G. B., Richter, B. J., Yu, W. K. Economics

and extended longevity: A case study. *Prev Med* 13:396–410, 1984.

Grossman, M. Taxation and cigarette smoking in the United States. In Forbes, W. F., Frecker, R. C., Nostbakken, D., eds. *Proceedings of the Fifth World Conference on Smoking and Health,* vol. 1. Ottawa, Canada: Canadian Council on Smoking and Health, 1983, 483–487.

Harris, J. E. Increasing the federal excise tax on cigarettes. *J Health Econ* 1(2):117–120, 1982.

———. The 1983 increase in the federal cigarette excise tax. In Summers, L. H., ed. *Tax Policy and the Economy,* vol. 1. Cambridge, MA: MIT Press, 1987, 87–111.

Hodgson, T. A. Cigarette smoking and lifetime medical expenditures. *Milbank Q* 70(1):81–125, 1992.

Leu, R. E., and Schaub, T. Does smoking increase medical care expenditure? *Soc Sci Med* 17:1907–1914, 1983.

Lewit, E. M. Some economic issues raised by reduced smoking. Paper presented at the Allied Social Sciences Annual Meeting, San Francisco, CA, December 1983.

———. Regulatory and legislative initiatives. In *Proceedings of the Pennsylvania Conference on Tobacco and Health Priorities.* Pennsylvania Department of Health, October 1985, 113–121.

Lewit, E. M., Coate, D., Grossman, M. The effects of government regulation on teenage smoking. *J Law Econ* 24:545–569, December 1981.

Lewit, E. M., and Coate, D. The potential for using excise taxes to reduce smoking. *J Health Econ* 1(2):121–145, 1982.

Luce, B. R., and Schweitzer, S. O. Smoking and alcohol abuse: A comparison of their economic consequences. *N Engl J Med* 298(10):569–571, 1978.

Manning, W. G., Keeler, E. B., Newhouse, J. P., Sloss, E. M., Wasserman, J. The taxes of sin: Do smokers and drinkers pay their way? *JAMA* 261(11):1604–1609, 1989.

Miller, R. H., and Tarczy, R. L. Implications of the Tobacco Improvement Program Act on the various sectors of the tobacco economy and the federal budget. In Delman, F., ed. *Current Issues in Tobacco Economics,* vol. 2. Princeton, NJ: Tobacco Merchants Association, 1987.

Office of Technology Assessment. *Smoking-related Deaths and Financial Costs.* OTA Staff Memorandum. Washington, D.C.: Office of Technology Assessment, Health Program, U.S. Congress, 1985.

Pickett, G., and Bridgers, W. F. Prevention, declining mortality rates, and the cost of Medicare. *Am J Prev Med* 3:76–80, 1987.

Price Waterhouse. *The Economic Impact of the Tobacco Industry on the United States Economy.* 1990.

Rice, D. P., Hodgson, T. A., Sinsheimer, P., Browner, W., Kopstein, A. N. The economic costs of the health effects of smoking, 1984. *Milbank Mem Fund Q* 64(4):489–547, 1986.

Samuels, B., and Glantz, S. A. The politics of local tobacco control. *JAMA* 266:2110–2117, 1991.

Schelling, T. C. Economics and cigarettes. *Prev Med* 15:549–560, 1986.

Shoven, J. B., Sundberg, J. O., Bunker, J. P. The Social Security cost of smoking. In Wise, D. A., ed. *The Economics of Aging.* Chicago, IL: Univ. of Chicago Press, 1989.

Shultz, J. M. Smoking-attributable mortality and years of potential life lost—United States, 1988. *MMWR* 40:62–71, 1 February 1991.

Sumner, D. A., and Alston, J. M. Consequences of elimination of the tobacco program. N.C. Agriculture Research Service, Bull. No. 469. Raleigh: North Carolina State University, March 1984.

Taylor, P. *The Smoke Ring: Tobacco, Money, and Multinational Politics.* New York: Pantheon Books, 1984.

Tobacco Institute. *Tobacco Industry Profile 1989.* Washington, D.C.: Tobacco Institute, 1989.

———. *The Tax Burden on Tobacco. Historical Compilation,* vol. 25. Washington, D.C.: Tobacco Institute, 1991.

Tobacco Reduction Task Force. *Report.* Lansing: Michigan Department of Public Health, 1990.

Townsend, J. Cigarette tax, economic welfare and social class patterns of smoking. *Appl Econ* 19:335–365, 1987.

U.S. Department of Commerce, Bureau of the Census. *Statistical Abstract of the United States 1989,* 109th ed. Washington, D.C.:

U.S. Bureau of the Census, U.S. Department of Commerce, 1989.

U.S. Department of Health and Human Services, (USDHHS). *Reducing the Health Consequences of Smoking: 25 Years of Progress. A Report of the Surgeon General.* U.S. Department of Health and Human Services, Public Health Service, Centers for Disease Control, Center for Chronic Disease Prevention and Health Promotion, Office on Smoking and Health. DHHS Publication No. (CDC) 89-8411, 1989.

Warner, K. E. State legislation on smoking and health: A comparison of two policies. *Policy Sciences* 13:139–152, 1981.

———. Smoking and Health implications of a change in the federal cigarette excise tax. *JAMA* 255(8):1028–1032, 1986.

———. Health and economic implications of a tobacco-free society. *JAMA* 258(15):2080–2086, 1987.

———. The tobacco subsidy: Does it matter? *JNCI* 80(2):81–83, 1988.

Warner, K. E., and Fulton, G. A. The economic implications of tobacco product sales in a nontobacco state. Working paper. Ann Arbor, MI: Univ. of Michigan, March 1993.

Wasserman, J., Manning, W. G., Newhouse, J. P., Winkler, J. D. The effects of excise taxes and regulations on cigarette smoking. *J Health Econ* 10(1):43–64, 1991.

Wharton ARC. *A Study of the U.S. Tobacco Industry's Economic Contribution to the Nation, Its Fifty States, and the District of Columbia, 1979.* Philadelphia: Wharton Applied Research Center and Wharton Econometric Forecasting Associates, Inc., 1980.

White, L. C. *Merchants of Death: The American Tobacco Industry.* New York: Beech Tree Books, 1988.

Wright, V. B. Will quitting smoking help Medicare solve its financial problems? *Inquiry* 23:76–82, Spring 1986.

4

Multiple Determinants of Tobacco Use and Cessation

EDWIN B. FISHER, JR., EDWARD LICHTENSTEIN, and
DEBRA HAIRE-JOSHU

Considering the easy availability of cigarettes, the billions of dollars spent marketing them, the ease with which they are consumed in almost every setting of daily life, and their strongly addictive properties, it is no wonder that over a quarter of the adult population smokes. Considering all of these forces, however, it is remarkable that a campaign of public information and related community efforts to encourage nonsmoking has helped a substantial number of smokers to quit. The 1989 Surgeon General's Report estimated that 50% of all adults who had ever smoked regularly had quit. Dr. C. Everett Koop suggested in his preface to the 1989 report that "This achievement has few parallels in the history of public health. It was accomplished despite the addictive nature of tobacco and the powerful economic forces promoting its use" (USDHHS 1989, p. iv).

In the United States, smoking is the most prevalent form of nicotine addiction. In recent years, clear understanding of nicotine addiction has increased our understanding of how smoking develops and why it is so resistant to change. For these reasons and because it is the most studied and best understood example of nicotine addiction, this chapter focuses on smoking. Chapter 13 covers the determinants of smokeless tobacco use and cessation.

SYNTHESIS OF BIOLOGICAL, PSYCHOLOGICAL, AND SOCIAL DETERMINANTS OF SMOKING

Medicine and psychology have often reflected an assumed dichotomy between soma and psyche, nature and nurture. Frequently, the two realms are thought to be mutually exclusive. From this perspective, if a problem includes chemical addiction, then only biological interventions will be useful and behavioral, psychological, or educational efforts would be doomed to failure. Several years ago, a positron emission tomography (PET) finding of neurophysiological correlates of hyperkinesis (Zametkin et al. 1990) was described in the *New York Times* as showing that hyperkinesis is "not psychological" (15 November 1990, p. 1). Similarly, Jensen (1969) found evidence that genetic factors account for a *portion* of the variability in IQ as grounds for limiting governmental investment in educational efforts to improve intellectual performance of disadvantaged children.

More recent thinking has synthesized the antitheses of psyche and soma. We understand that course, morbidity, and even mortality of medical diseases like diabetes are strongly associated with behavioral and social forces (e.g., Davis, Hess, Hiss 1988; Fisher, Delamater, Bertelson et al. 1982).

Eclipsing past arguments that schizophrenia was either a disease or a behavior pattern, either genetically or environmentally determined, current thinking integrates genetic and other biological factors along with psychosocial influences in etiology (e.g., Zubin and Spring 1977), familial and social factors in expression, course, morbidity (e.g., Leff and Vaughn 1985), utility of family therapy in preventing relapse and rehospitalization (e.g., Falloon et al. 1982), and neuropsychological models of pathognomonic behavior patterns (Spaulding and Cole 1984).

Multiple Determinants of Smoking and Nicotine Addiction

Understanding smoking and nicotine addiction, too, has benefited from perspectives integrating biological, psychological, social, and other determinants. At the level of basic physiological processes, we now have a sharper understanding of the role of nicotine addiction. At the other end of the spectrum of causes, we can also articulate economic forces such as the influence of the profitability of cigarettes on the ubiquity of cigarette advertising.

Current explanations assume that smoking is determined by an interplay of multiple causes, no one sufficient, no one necessary. Work reviewed in this chapter and elsewhere in this book shows how conditioning interacts with nicotine addiction, how social and economic factors may heighten the appeal of smoking, or how educational and psychological interventions enhance pharmacological treatment of nicotine addiction. Various pharmacologic, biochemical, and psychological processes interact in nicotine addiction. In fact, conditioned drug-taking behavior, not physical dependence, is now thought to be central to the concept of addiction (USDHHS 1988). The biological power of nicotine may make the learned behaviors that form smoking patterns stronger and more resistant to change. At the same time, the plenitude of daily circumstances, activities, and emotions to which smoking is conditioned ties this behavior to numerous rituals of daily life and contributes to the difficulty of breaking the addiction (Fisher et al. 1990; Pomerleau and Pomerleau 1987).

That interplay among multiple influences is important in all addictions was well stated by the editor of a special issue of the *Journal of Abnormal Psychology* devoted to addiction.

> [A]ddiction occurs in the *milieu externe,* not in the *milieu interne.* Addiction occurs in the environment, not in the liver, genes, or synapse. Certainly drugs exert effects on the liver and synapse, and certainly physiological systems must be understood in order to appreciate the nature of addiction. However, an individual chooses to take drugs in the world. The likelihood of a person trying a drug or eventually becoming addicted is influenced by his or her friends, marital happiness, the variety and richness of alternatives to drug use, and so on. Any complete addiction treatment or prevention program must appraise drug use in the context of an individual's general life situation, not just in the context of those behaviors or attitudes temporally or situationally associated with drug use.
>
> (Baker 1988, p. 117)

In addition to the multiple determinants of smoking onset and cessation, this chapter will also emphasize a series of stages in smoking, from initial exploration to quitting and maintaining abstinence. Stages and determinants interact. The importance of the various determinants change from stage to stage. For instance, peer pressure may encourage initial experimentation and, later, quit efforts. In some instances, physical responses may discourage initial smoking but make cessation almost unattainable. However, the multiple determinants also influence the nature and form of the stages. For example, changes in social acceptability may have substantial impacts on the nature, duration, and culmination of the stages of initiation of smoking or contemplation of quitting. Recognition of both the multiple forces that influence smoking and the multiple roles they can take at different stages is critical to the clinician's judgment in discouraging it.

The next section of this chapter reviews three basic concepts in understanding smoking: nicotine addiction, conditioning, and the stages of onset and cessation. The chapter then goes on to review influences on the initiation and maintenance of smoking.

These range from personality variables to social class and economic factors. In a subsequent section, several of these influences are considered as they are especially pertinent to smoking cessation. Other chapters in this book will review in greater detail specific approaches to encouraging smoking cessation. The perspective of the present chapter is generally confined to major influences that cut across varying approaches to encouraging smoking cessation. The chapter closes with brief consideration of implications for clinicians' efforts to encourage nonsmoking.

BASIC CONCEPTS: NICOTINE ADDICTION, CONDITIONING, AND THE STAGES OF SMOKING

Nicotine Addiction

To call a habit an addiction, it must meet the following criteria: (1) highly controlled or compulsive pattern of drug use, (2) psychoactive or mood-altering effects involved in pattern of drug taking, and (3) drug functioning as reinforcer to strengthen behavior and lead to further drug ingestion. As documented by extensive research reviewed in the 1988 Surgeon General's Report, smoking meets all these criteria.

Expanding on this, the 1988 report noted the following major conclusions: (1) cigarettes and other forms of tobacco are addicting, (2) nicotine is the drug in tobacco that causes addiction, and (3) the pharmacologic and behavioral processes that determine tobacco addiction are similar to those that determine addiction to drugs such as heroin and cocaine (USDHHS 1988, p. 9).

Mechanisms of Nicotine Addiction

The pharmacology of nicotine is reviewed in detail in Chapter 2. As noted there, much research in the 1970s on the behavioral effects of nicotine has been guided by the nicotine regulation or titration model put forth over the years by Jarvik (1977). According to this model, smokers regulate their smoking to maintain a certain level of blood nicotine within a range of upper and lower limits (Kozlowski and Herman 1984). This includes the avoidance of withdrawal symptoms or anticipated withdrawal by maintaining a nicotine level above a and avoidance of toxicity by m below an upper limit.

This formulation has been failing to explain the self-perceived positive effects or benefits of smoking that may promote use (Leventhal and Cleary 1980). In the last few years, several investigators (e.g., Pomerleau and Pomerleau 1987) have proposed that smoking, by virtue of the varied actions of nicotine, provides several positively perceived effects and is employed by many smokers as a responsive and effective coping strategy. This implies that smokers can be reinforced for continued smoking without maintaining a minimum blood nicotine level. In essence, critics of the nicotine regulation model argue that smoking is governed not only by actual physical presence or absence of nicotine, but also by the conditioning effects into which nicotine has entered. The next section reviews evidence on the conditioning of smoking and concludes with a discussion of models which integrate conditioning effects and the direct effects of nicotine and the current physiological state of the organism.

Conditioning of Smoking

The range of possible conditioning effects surrounding nicotine addiction is great. First, of course, the effects of nicotine may reinforce those behaviors that lead to them. Second, the circumstances in which smoking occurs may become discriminative stimuli for smoking, signaling the likelihood of reinforcement of smoking. Third, the circumstances surrounding smoking may also become conditioned to nicotine so that they evoke conditioned responses that resemble the organismic response to nicotine, itself. The complexity of these conditioning effects is increased by the fact that smoking is a sequence of behaviors. Thus, behaviors in the middle of the smoking chain may (1) elicit conditioned responses resembling the pharmacological effects of nicotine, which may (2) reinforce the same, previous behaviors which elicited them, (3) be reinforced themselves by the conditioned responses they elicit, and (4) serve as discriminative stimuli for subsequent links, signaling the likelihood of their reinforcement by nicotine. (For clar-

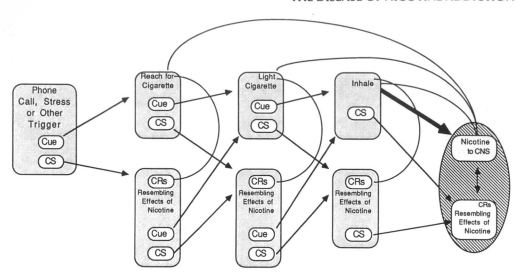

Fig. 4–1 Relationships among behaviors, conditioned responses, cues, and reinforcers in a chain leading to nicotine delivery. CS = conditioned stimulus; CR = conditioned response; CSs elicit CRs; Cues set the occasion for subsequent behaviors (e.g., lighting the cigarette). *Curved lines* indicate reinforcement of reach for cigarette, light cigarette, and inhale by the CRs resembling effects of nicotine (e.g., Niaura et al. 1988) and by the arrival in the central nervous system (CNS) of nicotine. Even at the central level, CRs and the actual effect of nicotine on the CNS likely interact, as depicted by the *double pointed arrow.*

ification of these aspects of operant and classical conditioning, consult a text on the psychology of learning such as Rachlin 1991.) For instance, a phone call and the stressful content of the call may each serve as discriminative stimuli, signaling a situation in which the pharmacologic effects of nicotine would be especially reinforcing (see Figure 4–1). This may result in reaching for a cigarette which may then serve as a conditioned stimulus, eliciting conditioned responses that resemble the effects of nicotine. These conditioned effects of nicotine may reinforce reaching for the cigarette. All of these—the conditioned effects, reaching, the phone call, the stress—may serve as discriminative stimuli for further steps in the chain and may elicit further conditioned responses reinforcing earlier steps. All of these steps and relationships are organized and strongly maintained by the reinforcement of nicotine which follows them. The importance of these conditioning and reinforcing effects is that they create a tightly and intricately woven fabric of smoking in daily life—not one likely to unravel with the loosening of a few threads.

The biological potency and speed of action of nicotine also contribute to the strength of conditioning surrounding smoking. Research in classical conditioning has established that stronger unconditioned stimuli, as measured by intensity, amount, and so on, lead to more rapid conditioning, stronger conditioned responses, and greater resistance to extinction (Rachlin 1991). The many and easily discriminated effects of nicotine (USDHHS 1988) would be expected, then, to lead to powerful conditioning of cues which accompany them. This is especially true after a period of deprivation. For instance, the cues surrounding the first cigarette in the morning would be especially strongly conditioned to smoking since the nicotine unconditioned stimulus which they accompany will be especially strong after overnight deprivation.

In addition to the strength of nicotine as an unconditioned stimulus, its delivery to the central nervous system is rapid, about 7 seconds from inhalation (Pomerleau and Pomerleau 1987, p. 117). This supports stronger classical conditioning of cues which accompany smoking. Brief intervals between such cues and the unconditioned stimuli and responses to which they are conditioned enhance that conditioning. Rapidity of delivery also makes nicotine an effective reinforcer of behaviors that lead to inhalation since short durations between behavior and reinforcer enhance the effects of reinforcers, especially in early phases of learning (Rachlin 1991). In contrast, most disincentives for smoking are subtle, insidious, or much delayed, reducing their ability to discourage it.

Withdrawal symptoms, themselves, may be conditioned to the circumstances in which smoking has occurred (Wikler 1973). This sets the stage for withdrawal being psychologically prolonged. Stimuli associated with prior drug taking elicit withdrawal symptoms and cravings even after the organism has returned to physiological homeostasis following cessation of drug ingestion. Following cessation, reports of withdrawal symptoms have been greater in natural rather than artificial environments, presumably because those natural environments contain numerous cues associated with prior smoking (Hatsukami, Hughes, Pickens 1985). Work by Abrams and colleagues (1988) demonstrates that former smokers manifest psychophysiological reactivity to smoking cues long after they have quit.

The importance of the conditioning of withdrawal is illustrated by findings that, although nicotine replacement may reduce withdrawal symptoms, it seems to have little effect on desire to smoke. Subjects giving up cigarettes for 3-day periods received varying doses of nicotine or placebo. Nicotine reduced several withdrawal symptoms, supporting the view of smoking as a specific addiction to nicotine. However, nicotine did not reduce subjects' reported desire to smoke more than did placebo (Henningfield and Nemeth-Coslett 1988). Desire to smoke was apparently more dependent on cues and circumstances associated with previous smoking than on blood nicotine levels.

The conditioning of smoking is complicated by the varied effects of nicotine (Pomerleau and Pomerleau 1987). Nicotine may reduce arousal, reduce anxiety, or function as a stimulant. So, arousal, anxiety, or lethargy may come to serve as discriminative stimuli for smoking and conditioned stimuli for withdrawal symptoms or cravings following cessation. The effect of such association would be for such moods to elicit urges to smoke (Leventhal and Cleary 1980), an effect mirrored in reports of antecedents of relapse (Shiffman 1986). Additionally, the circumstances which give rise to such emotions or moods—e.g., time of day, work demands, family conflict, or loneliness—may come to signal the occasion for smoking or elicit conditioned withdrawal symptoms. Finally, moods or arousal states that merely resemble those which have been associated with smoking may come, by stimulus generalization, to signal occasions to smoke. If the effects of smoking improve those moods or states, the individual will have extended his or her smoking repertoire.

Once established in an individual, is smoking maintained by *reduction* of aversive urges or withdrawal symptoms or is it reinforced by *positive* consequences of nicotine ingestion? Niaura and colleagues (1988) reviewed the evidence on this issue and concluded that the positive consequences of nicotine drive relapse, often cued by stimuli associated with smoking and these consequences. Thus, the ex-smoker is prone to relapse not to reduce withdrawal symptoms per se but because of the likelihood of reinforcement by nicotine. This analysis does not mean that negative affect cannot be a cue for smoking. Low mood, for instance, may cue smoking and reinforcement by nicotine's euphoriant effects. The reinforcer, though, is not the reduction of a withdrawal symptom but the euphoriant effects of nicotine which may have been cued and enhanced by the prior low mood. This analysis suggests treatments should not focus solely on supposed withdrawal symptoms, but should minimize cues associated with smoking and should teach other ways of copying with affects that trigger it.

As can be seen, the many ways in which smoking is conditioned to circumstances around it explain ". . . the thorough interweaving of the smoking habit in the fabric of daily life" (Pomerleau and Pomerleau 1987, p. 119). The sheer repetition of smoking also strengthens such interweaving. It is estimated that the average, pack-a-day smoker of 20 years has inhaled cigarettes over 1 million times (Fisher and Rost 1986), each inhalation providing opportunity for conditioning smoking to many settings or situations of daily life. The million conditioning trials link the many actions of a smoking career. As the person recently retired from a job or business career may "not know what to do with myself," so the quitter may feel overwhelmed by the ubiquity of cues and cravings, complaining that smoking is almost constantly "on my mind."

Stages of Development and Cessation of Smoking

A number of stages have been identified in the path from first to last cigarette. These include (1) preparation, initiation, experimentation, and transition to regular smoking (Biglan and Lichtenstein 1984; Leventhal and Cleary 1980); (2) habitual use; and, often, (3) several phases leading to cessation (Prochaska and DiClemente 1983). The identification of these stages helps clarify that beginning or quitting smoking are not just simple steps that may be taken or not taken with ease. Rather, smoking and quitting evolve gradually, determined by a wide range of influences. Furthermore, different influences are prominent at different stages, as noted earlier and discussed in greater detail later.

Initiation of Smoking

Research has tended to pay little attention to the role of pharmacologic effects of nicotine and conditioning in the initiation of smoking. Of course, ethical concerns would discourage experiments with children to identify early stages of nicotine addiction. However, available evidence does indicate that, as a smoker starts to inhale, the pharmacologic properties of nicotine contribute to continued smoking (Kozlowski 1989). A few studies have investigated the potential role of individual-specific psychophysiological responses to nicotine and the development of smoking (Silverstein et al. 1982). Reactions to initial cigarettes and the interpretation of these reactions may predispose

individuals to continue or not to continue smoking. Hirschman, Leventhal, and Glynn (1984), for example, found that the initial early physical reaction was predictive of continued smoking. Dizziness was related to a rapid progression to a second cigarette, while coughing and a sore throat were related to discontinuation.

It is not clear how long it takes for the transition from experimental to regular smoking and if there is likely to be much variation in this (e.g., Hirschman, Leventhal, Glynn 1984). Results from several recent studies suggest that teenagers become more addicted to smoking than was previously believed (see also Chapter 19). Survey data (Johnson 1986) indicate that teenagers make frequent and often unsuccessful quit attempts. Other studies confirm that teenagers have difficulty stopping and report reasons for the difficulty—social pressure, urges, withdrawal symptoms—similar to those seen with adults (Biglan and Lichtenstein 1984). Because smoking among children and adolescents is generally confined to relatively few situations, the level of nicotine dependence may be limited to such situations. Nevertheless, the reports of withdrawal symptoms and relapses among teenage smokers attest to the strength of nicotine dependence, even among those still in the early stages of smoking.

A major assumption in much thinking about the development and prevention of smoking is that initiation of smoking during adolescence enhances the likelihood of adult smoking. This has recently been tested in a prospective study of 6th–12th graders, assessed 4–8 years later as young adults. Those who reported smoking at least monthly as adolescents were 16–20 times more likely to report smoking at least weekly as young adults. The importance of even minimal exposure was indicated by a relative risk of approximately 2 for those who, as adolescents, had reported having smoked one or two cigarettes but none in the month prior to the survey. The impact of early exposure was supported by evaluation of the grade at initiation. Sixty-nine percent who had reported smoking at least monthly before grade 6 went on to report smoking at least weekly as adults, in comparison to 46% of those who first reported monthly smoking in grade 11 (Chassin et al. 1990). These results provide appreciable support for the importance of early prevention programs. That smoking in adolescence predicts smoking in young adulthood also suggests some continuity in the psychological and biological forces which support smoking.

The arrival at regular or maintained smoking corresponds roughly to the period of transition from adolescence to adulthood. At least until very recently, the social changes that accompany this passage—entering a university, the military, or the work force—have been associated with a marked change in the acceptability of smoking. For high school students, smoking is often prohibited on school property. In the work force, community college, and university setting, smoking has been widely accepted. Until recently, the military had supported smoking among its men and women, as reflected in low prices for cigarettes at military exchanges and commissaries and by the announcement of breaks with "The smoking lamp is lit." The extent to which smoking is a part of the role of the serviceman was shown in a survey of Navy enlisted men with a mean age of 22.6 years and a mean of 3.9 years' service. Seventy-two percent were self-reported smokers (Burr 1984). That the military has had an effect in creating rather than merely selecting smokers is suggested by a comparison of prevalence among naval recruits, 27.6%, and shipboard men, 49.8% (Cronan and Conway 1988).

Smoking Cessation

Prochaska and DiClemente (1983; DiClemente 1991) have suggested five stages of cessation: Precontemplation, Contemplation, Preparation, Action, and Maintenance. These five stages may recur in the smoker's career since repeated relapses and efforts to quit are common, many successful quitters reporting several prior attempts and relapses. Thus the process of quitting may extend over a number of years.

As an example of the ways in which different influences are important at different stages, daily hassles and support from others seem most important at action and relapse stages while a history of smoking in response to negative affect and the number of smoking friends and relatives have been linked to long-term abstinence. As different influences may be critical at different points after quitting, different messages or types of information may be most helpful at different stages of cessation—matter-of-fact information at precontemplation versus specific advice on quitting during the action stage (Prochaska and DiClemente 1983). These and other considerations in promoting smoking cessation are treated in greater detail in Chapters 8 and 10.

Cautions in Using Stages

Talking of stages sometimes suggests an intrinsic sequence which plays itself out independent of events surrounding it. Much talk about early child development, for instance, tends to attribute patterns of behavior to the stage a child "is in" rather than to influences surrounding the child. In contrast, it is the *interplay* of intrinsic and social or environmental factors which direct the development and phases of smoking. How society reacts to smoking influences its nature. A school system's restrictions on smoking; parental actions to punish or model or encourage it; advertisements' presentations of smokers as daring, sophisticated, successful, or attractive; workplace smoking policies; insurance regulations, and other social and governmental responses to smoking will interact with its intrinsic characteristics to determine progress through smoking's stages.

Connected to dangers in ignoring extrinsic influences, there exists in stage theories the risk of circular explanations. We sometimes explain characteristics of a particular stage as caused by that stage. For instance, to say that adolescence is a stage of rebellion and then to explain rebelliousness among adolescents as due to this stage is circular. Calling rebellion "adolescent" may describe it in some interesting way, but does not explain it (Skinner 1953). In the same way, the stages of smoking are not explanations but descriptions of smokers' and quitters' behavior. Smokers do not quit because they are in the action stage. Rather, we say they are in the action stage because they are quitting.

What thinking of stages does promote is greater attention to particular extrinsic or intrinsic factors that may be especially important at a particular phase. However, if attention to these increases our precision in encouraging cessation, it is because of improved interventions, not because the smokers were at the right stage. At the clinical level, observing that someone is at the action stage should help us identify what intervention might be most helpful. Identifying the stage should not cause us to relax and trust that the stage will unfold on its own.

In addition to making the mistake of ignoring extrinsic factors, we may interpret stages too concretely, as rigid orderings of events that take place without regard to their contexts. In fact, their order is not rigid. For instance, some may proceed to cessation directly from transition to regular smoking, without ever going through the phases of habitual use, precontemplation, or contemplation of quitting. Of course, stages can be repeated, as with relapse and action. Indeed, the average successful quitter reports several and often many failed attempts before achieving maintained abstinence (USDHHS 1989).

To emphasize the importance of the interaction of extrinsic and intrinsic forces, smoking has been described as a "career" (Fisher et al. 1990). Borrowed from the sociology of other addictive drugs (Becker 1963), "career" includes periods of development of the habit, habitual use, and, possibly, cessation. Just as a vocational career reflects core skills and training as well as the economic and social circumstances which alter the availability, prestige, and other characteristics of a particular job, so the career of a smoker reflects the influence of intrinsic factors, such as addiction and core habits, social reactions to those intrinsic factors, and the interaction of these intrinsic and social factors (Becker 1963). Social, economic, and environmental factors will influence the natural history or course of a smoking career just as they will influence the path of a vocational career. Indeed, the natural history of a career is not "natural" in the sense of following some preordained plan, but is only "natural" in the sense that the social factors which influence it are viewed themselves as understandable in terms of natural laws of social influence (Krasner and Ullmann 1973).

PERSONAL AND ENVIRONMENTAL INFLUENCES ON SMOKING

Personality Influences in Smoking

An attractive strategy for understanding problems in human behavior is to search for some key incentive, motive, or personality factor that explains why *they* do *that.* In smoking, a popular example of this strategy has been research on extraversion (e.g., Cherry and Kiernan 1976) or, as the 1964 Surgeon General's Report defined it, a tendency "to live faster and more intensely" (USPHS 1964, p. 366). One of the chief proponents of this work, Eysenck, describes the extraversion–introversion dimension as "based on the observed intercorrelations between traits such as sociability, impulsiveness, carefreeness, activity, etc." (1980, p. 91). Reflecting this, research has found relationships with smoking and characteristics such as: coffee and alcohol consumption, circadian phase differences, being an "evening type" as opposed to a "morning type," driving accidents, divorce, frequent job changes, low levels of vocational success, and impulsivity (USDHHS 1989).

The "tendency to live faster and more intensely" has also been linked to the initiation of smoking. Smoking among children and adolescents has been associated with rule breaking in school, general delinquency, age at first intercourse, inadequate contraceptive use, low levels of child compliance within the family, low levels of responsibility, nonconventionality, impulsivity, rebelliousness, and previous use of alcohol and other substances (USDHHS 1989). On the other hand, academic success, as measured by grade point average, is linked to a low rate of smoking (Johnson 1986). High school dropouts (Pirie, Murray, Luepker 1988) and high school seniors not planning to go to college (Johnston, O'Malley, Bachman 1987) are much more likely to smoke than are those planning higher education. Similar factors are observed with other drug addictions (USDHHS 1988). Jessor (1987) views these kinds of covariation as a problem behavior syndrome reflecting an interaction of social forces which equate risk taking with independence and individual needs such as for identity.

Negative Affect and Smoking

A number of investigators have reported high prevalence of smoking among depressed adults (e.g., Anda et al. 1990). Among adolescents, measures of depression are associated with concurrent smoking, even after controlling for peer and family factors often linked to smoking (Covey and Tam 1990). Depression measured during adolescence also predicts later smoking (Kandel and Davies 1986). A history of regular smoking was observed more frequently among individuals who had experienced a major depressive disorder as opposed to those without a history of major depression (Glassman et al. 1990). Similarly, analyses of the National Health and Nutrition Examination Survey (NHANES) found that depressed smokers were 40% less likely to quit than nondepressed smokers, even after adjusting for amount smoked, sex, age, and educational attainment (Anda et al. 1990). In another study (Rausch et al. 1990), participants in an outpatient cessation program who failed to quit had higher pretreatment depression scores than those who were initially successful.

Nicotine's anxiolytic, arousing, and, especially, its euphoriant effects (USDHHS 1988) may make it useful for managing depression as well as reducing other unpleasant emotions. Along these lines, Hughes (1988) suggested that smokers with a history of depression have come to rely on nicotine to prevent depressive episodes.

In addition to managing dysphoria, the anxiolytic effects of nicotine would suggest stress reduction should be a factor in encouraging regular smoking (e.g., Leventhal and Cleary 1980; Pomerleau and Pomerleau 1987). Much evidence for such effects comes from the retrospective reports of relapsers and smokers attempting to stop, reviewed later in this chapter. Other data demonstrate that *heightened* stress leads to *greater* smoking. Among them are Ikard and Tomkin's

observations (1973) of greater incidence among race track spectators *during* horse races, presumed to be times of stress, than in the periods before and after races, and Silverman's (1971) observations of nicotine-induced reductions in aggression among rats. A number of other studies reviewed in the 1988 Surgeon General's Report link smoking and negative affect but, as noted in that review, are not conclusive as to whether reduction of negative affect makes a substantial contribution to regular smoking. Design problems include comparisons of smokers who are smoking with smokers who are deprived, leaving unclear, for instance, whether smoking reduces negative affect or whether, for regular smokers, not smoking merely causes an aversive, deprivation state. As concluded in the 1988 report, ". . . caution must be exercised in generalizing about smoking and nicotine's effects on stress and mood . . ." (USDHHS 1988, p. 405).

The same potential for circular explanations in discussion of stages of smoking also threatens discussion of personality factors in smoking. To say that one smokes because he or she is self-destructive and to argue that smoking's risks are clear evidence of such a self-destructive trend is clearly circular. Beyond this trouble with circularity, the general strategy of looking for the personality pattern responsible for smoking has been severely criticized (e.g., Lichtenstein 1982). Smoking is not alone in this. A popular approach to much psychological research in disease has been to search for the personality type that is associated with a particular disease or problem. For example, the search for the diabetic personality has been discredited (Dunn and Turtle 1981) as oversimplified. There appear to be no personality types which distinguish smokers or diabetics from the rest of us. This is not to say that such psychological variables are of no use. For instance, they are often related to different degrees of success in reducing risks as well as managing chronic diseases (Fisher, Delamater, Bertelson et al. 1982). For example, negative affect appears to complicate both success in quitting smoking and success in diabetes management. But depression is the *cause* of neither smoking nor diabetes and reducing depression may aid but will guarantee neither diabetes management nor smoking cessation.

Peer, Family, and Social Influences

Studies have noted that children of smoking parents are more likely to smoke than children of nonsmoking parents (Wohlford 1970). Smoking teenagers are more likely to have friends who smoke than are nonsmoking teenagers (Gordon and McAlister 1985). The impact of peer smoking on adolescent smoking has been identified in a number of studies (e.g., Chassin et al. 1984; Mittelmark et al. 1987), including their impact on initial smoking episodes (Friedman, Lichtenstein, Biglan 1985) and continuation of smoking among those who already have experimented with cigarettes (Biglan and Lichtenstein 1984). These influences seem to rest on the importance of modeling of smoking (e.g., Antonuccio and Lichtenstein 1980), as well as on the setting of norms among subgroups of adolescents. The importance of bidirectional influences in smoking and smoking cessation among young people has been noted by Chassin, Presson, and Sherman (1984). In some cases, a young person's membership in a particular peer group may expose him or her to the example to smoke or to quit; however, in other cases, a young person may actively seek membership in a peer group that represents or is consistent with his or her established intentions about smoking.

Parent and peer influences may have their greatest impacts at different times during the process from the initial smoking episode to regular use (e.g., Friedman, Lichtenstein, Biglan 1985). The literature has tended to underscore the role of parental example and influence for initiation of smoking by young children and adolescents, and the primacy of peer influences among older youth. Krosnick and Judd (1982) found no evidence for decreases in parental influences on smoking during adolescence, although they did find that peer influence increases during this period. These studies also include important methodological advances wherein interviews and self-monitoring are used to augment questionnaire data.

A growing body of literature implicates family climate or family interaction patterns in smoking. Family characteristics, such as indifference, low levels of trust, parental restrictiveness, and low levels of parental involvement, are associated with smoking as well as with marijuana and alcohol use (Hundleby and Mercer 1987). Other research has demonstrated that low levels of adolescent involvement in family decision making predict subsequent experimentation with cigarettes among adolescents (Mittelmark et al. 1987). Fathers' characteristics, such as harsh criticism, impulsivity, and poor ego integration, were associated with a greater likelihood of sons' smoking (Brook et al. 1983). In contrast, paternal affection, emotional support, participation in meaningful conversations, and higher expectations for their sons were associated with lower likelihood of sons' smoking. It appears that adolescent smoking is more likely in restrictive, punitive, and unempathetic families in which children are uninvolved in decision making. Put in terms of desirable outcomes, families who provide multiple avenues for identity formation and expression of feelings may obviate the utility of smoking or other problem behaviors as a mode of identity expression (Jessor 1987).

This chapter emphasizes the interplay among intrinsic characteristics of drug use, characteristics of the user, and social or external forces. Consistent with this emphasis, an adolescent's personal characteristics and attitudes may mediate peer influence on smoking (USDHHS 1988). Research indicates greater impact of peer smoking among adolescents scoring low on a measure of obedience to parental authority and high on a measure of rebelliousness (McAllister, Krosnick, Milburn 1984). Tenth graders inclined to smoke indicated greater congruity between the value they place on interest in the opposite sex and the extent to which they ascribe such interest to smokers (Barton et al. 1982). The interactions among social influences, personality, and smoking were highlighted in a study in which seventh and eighth graders described the informal reference or affiliation groups they observed among their schoolmates and identified the group with which they felt the closest affiliation (Mosbach and Leventhal 1988). Two of the four groups that emerged, "hot-shots" (78% female, popular leaders in academic and extracurricular activities) and "dirts" (63% male, characterized by problem behaviors such as drinking, poor academic performance, and cutting classes), were identified as primary reference groups by only 14.7% of respondents but accounted for 55.6% of the smokers. In discriminant function analyses, a "macho" dimension was highly associated with one high smoking prevalence group, the "dirts," but not with the "hotshots." In contrast, academic and social leadership was asociated with the "hotshots" but not with the "dirts." As were the "dirts," the "jocks" were also 63% male and high on the macho dimension but low on use of both hard liquor and cigarettes. Adolescent smoking, then, is closely related to individual identification with groups, but these groups differ markedly in their association with other problem behaviors and psychosocial characteristics. Depending on group affiliation, different personality and attitudinal characteristics may be related to smoking.

Cigarette Marketing

Cigarettes are the most heavily marketed consumer product in the United States. (Marketing includes advertising as well as other promotions such as distribution of samples, point-of-sale displays, or distribution of product-related goods such as cigarette lighters, t-shirts, etc.) The Federal Trade Commission estimated that $3.25 billion were spent marketing cigarettes in 1988.

The direct effects of tobacco marketing are hard to characterize. That recruitment of new or reenlistment of former smokers are among these effects is suggested by economic analyses of advertising and cigarette consumption patterns (Tyre, Warner, Glantz 1987). It is also suggested by the extent of the marketing effort and the apparent need to replace smokers who quit—50% of all adults who have ever smoked (USDHHS 1989)—or die. In contrast, the tobacco industry maintains that advertising is directed to brand preference among current smokers, not recruiting new smokers. But only 10% of smokers switch brands each year. This seems

a modest impact for the most extensive marketing effort in our culture (Davis 1987).

Marketing campaigns seem designed to appeal to specific personality characteristics of groups of potential buyers. In this respect, they exemplify interactions between personal characteristics and the environment. The Marlboro brand was the leading choice of a group of white adolescent male (48%) and female (38%) smokers surveyed in Louisiana in 1981 (Hunter et al. 1986). In a sample of 306 high school students in Georgia, Marlboro was the preferred brand of 76% of smokers who identified a single preferred brand (Goldstein et al. 1987). These figures contrast with the overall domestic market share of Marlboro, which was 24% in 1987 (Ticer 1988). The associations of rebelliousness and behavioral problems with adolescent smoking, as reviewed earlier, suggest a relationship between its disproportionate brand preference among adolescents and the emphasis on the tough independence of the "Marlboro Man." In fact, this pattern may be a reflection of extensive market segmentation, in which specific brands are marketed for specific gender or ethnic groups, often with campaign messages and symbols aimed at those groups (Davis 1987).

Marketing to youth shows most clearly the tobacco companies' need to recruit new smokers. The Camel Old Joe campaign has resulted in that brand being more preferred among smokers under 18 than among those over that age (Pierce, Gilpin, Burns, Whalen, Rosbrook, Shopland, et al. 1991). For instance, Camel was the choice of 33% of a sample of Massachusetts smokers under age 18, in contrast to 9% of those over 21 (DiFranza, Richards, Paulman, Wolf-Gillespie, Fletcher, Jaffe, et al. 1991). This striking market segmentation makes clear that the brand is successful for those who are not yet legally smoking. That this is a systematic result of marketing efforts is strongly suggested by responses to the ads; 98% of the Massachusetts sample under 18 recognized the Old Joe character as opposed to 72% of those over 21. In a California survey, respondents under 18 were more likely than adults to name Camel and Marlboro as the most advertised bands, indicative of the greater salience of their ads to youth (Pierce et al.

1991). Among a sample of Georgia 6 year olds, there was no significant difference between the percentage able to pair a cigarette with the Old Joe logo and the percentage able to pair Mickey Mouse with the logo of the Disney Channel—about 90% in each case. Among the entire sample of 3–6 year olds, Old Joe was much better recognized (51%) than Marlboro (33%), the Marlboro man (28%) or than Old Joe's predecessors: camels and pyramids (27%) (Fischer, Schwartz, Richards, Goldstein, Rojas 1991). Thus, in spite of their own industry code that claims they do not advertise to youth, and in spite of their promotion of campaigns to "help youth decide"—which never mention the health effects of smoking—the tobacco companies direct millions of dollars of advertising toward youth who cannot legally buy the product, but who, if they are to become smokers, will most likely do so before the age of 18.

Market segmentation as a strategy of tobacco companies (1) identifies specific groups within a population (older, younger, male, female, black, white, Latino, urban, suburban, rural, etc.) and attempts to develop brands that will either (2) capture groups that already have a high prevalence of smokers or (3) promote smoking in specific groups in which the prevalence is relatively low. For cigarettes, marketing and advertising are especially segmented according to race, ethnicity, and gender (Davis 1987). As a result, three menthol brands have an aggregate share of 60% of the African-American cigarette market (Cummings, Giovino, Mendicino 1987). Even more concentrated market shares may result in some groups. For instance, among adolescent, African American males and females surveyed in Louisiana in 1981, 56% and 77%, respectively, reported Salem as their preferred brand (Hunter et al. 1986).

Other examples of market segmentation are with teenage girls who, relative to boys, are more likely to believe that smoking controls weight (Charlton 1984). This makes them good targets for advertisements that emphasize the desirability of being slender (Gritz 1986). Market segmentation efforts to exploit the women's movement are apparent. Among white adolescent females surveyed in Louisiana in 1981, 31% named Virginia Slims their preferred brand. Ironically, segmentation strategies and the psychosocial characteristics they presume may compete for brand preference. While 31% of the adolescent women said they preferred Virginia Slims, it is still less popular within this group than the macho brand, Marlboro (Hunter et al. 1986).

Some market segmentation appears more subtle, guided by smoker characteristics not as apparent as race and gender. McCarthy and Gritz (1987) surveyed students in 6th, 9th and 12th grade regarding their attitudes about cigarette advertisements. For those youth more likely to be smokers, personality self-ratings were more closely related to personality ratings assigned to models in cigarette advertisements. Thus, the way adolescents see themselves appears to be related to their attraction to certain advertisements. This congruity among psychological correlates of teenage smoking, marketing themes, and teenage preferences is especially striking, again, in light of the tobacco industry's denial that campaigns are aimed at teenagers (Davis, 1987). That this congruity is the result of tobacco companies' marketing strategies was strikingly confirmed in a leaked report of market research for a cigarette brand developed for young women, Dakota (Shore 1989).

As described in a later section, smoking in the United States is increasingly concentrated among groups of lower socioeconomic status. This creates problems for market segmentation, as ironically reflected in two articles about cigarette marketing appearing in the same issue of the *New York Times* (13 April 1991). One noted the problems created for R. J. Reynolds by the decline in sales of its "full price brands . . . like Winston and Salem," the compensating increased demand for lower priced, less profitable brands, and the cost of promotional campaigns featuring product give-aways. According to·one distributor ". . . smokers around here are really bargain hunters and they like to get freebies."Just below this quotation, a separate article described Philip Morris' decision to switch advertising agencies for its Benson and Hedges brand. This followed a decline in market share from 4.3

to 3.5% in spite of advertising strategies centered on showing ". . . young, obviously affluent people puffing Benson & Hedges in social situations." *Sic transit gloria mundi.*

Knowledge of Health Effects of Smoking

To explain how individuals make decisions such as to smoke or not to smoke, psychologists have often used models in which the considerations encouraging and discouraging a particular action are weighed and compared. For instance, in expectancy value models, the decision to smoke is based on the value of its consequences and the expectancy that they will occur. For smoking, influential consequences include enjoyment and disease. Values also reflect the personal importance or weight given to various possible outcomes and can be extended to perceptions about what significant others wish to do (Fishbein 1982). Expectancy value models tend to assume that human behavior is rationally guided by logical or at least internally consistent thought processes (Henderson, Hall, Linton 1979).

If decisions such as whether or not to smoke are guided by rational or logical processes and if 87% of current smokers now understand that smoking is harmful to their health (American Lung Association 1987), one might wonder why so many persist in smoking. After all, the 25-year-old, pack-a-day smoker who does not quit will die, on average, 6–8 years earlier than someone who has never smoked (USDHEW 1979).

One explanation for the persistence of smoking even with widespread awareness of its riskiness is, of course, its addictive properties. Another is the many years smoking's most feared consequences are delayed relative to the virtual immediacy of its biologically addicting and psychosocial consequences. Relative delay of consequences undermines their effects considerably. The relative delay and probability of short- and long term consequences can account in large measure for the kinds of choices and decisions we label "self-control" (Rachlin 1991).

In contrast to 87% of smokers, 97 and 98% of former smokers and nonsmokers, respectively, acknowledge it as harmful. More striking, only 75% of smokers indicated

agreement with the proposition that smoking is "one of the causes of lung cancer." In contrast, 94% of nonsmokers and 90% of former smokers indicated agreement. In a similar pattern, 75% of smokers agreed that smoking is a cause of emphysema, in comparison to 91 and 90% of former smokers and nonsmokers, respectively (American Lung Association 1987). It has been suggested that personalized acceptance ("Cigarette smoking is dangerous to my health") always lags behind general acceptance ("Cigarette smoking is dangerous to health") (Lichtenstein and Bernstein 1980). These considerations suggest that many smokers still find it possible to discount the riskiness of their behavior (Ockene et al. 1987). In this, smoking is similiar to other behavioral problems and addictions in which apparent discounting of risks and negative consequences runs in parallel to persistence in the face of what others see as compelling motives for change. Chapter 20 indicates that older smokers (those born between 1910 and 1940) may be especially likely to discount smoking's health risks.

In addition to smokers' possibly discounting the risks of their habit, surveys indicate the general population is insensitive to the uniquely high level of risk associated with smoking. In 1991, the Office on Smoking and Health estimated the annual mortality attributable to smoking in the United States at 434,175 (CDC 1991) or one out of every six or seven deaths each year in this country (UADHEW 1989). These enormous impacts of smoking dwarf the effects of most other risk. In a Harris survey in 1983, health professionals rated not smoking as the first priority among things Americans can do to protect their health. The public rated not smoking as 10th, behind such important but, for most Americans, less critical needs as consuming adequate vitamins and minerals and drinking water of acceptable quality (UADHHS 1989, pp. 209–210). Thus, while most Americans agree that smoking is risky, they seem unaware of how much its dangers dwarf those of other life-style related risk factors. This *relative* discounting of smoking's risks is mirrored in some responses to proposed smoking restrictions—"What will they want to prohibit next week?"—and in some patients' responses to advice to quit—"Well, I don't have too many other vices." Both responses fail to grasp that smoking *does* deserve to be singled out.

Although our attention is drawn to persistence of smoking among adults in spite of their knowledge of its health effects, children's and adolescents' knowledge also deserves consideration. Knowledge of the health effects of smoking is likely to influence initiation for some teenagers. Teenagers reported that one-third of their earliest refusals of cigarettes were based on fear of the effects of smoking on health, attractiveness, or athletic performance (Friedman, Lichtenstein, Biglan 1985). Cognitive appraisals of the attractiveness or desirability of smoking or of smokers are associated with current smoking or intentions to smoke (Barton, Chassin, Presson 1982), as are beliefs or attributions of the functional role of smoking (Murray and Perry 1984). Murray and Perry's analyses (1984) of the functional meaning of substance use by youth elucidated a variety of attributions correlated with their practices. The belief that smoking is useful for relieving boredom was most highly correlated with smoking. Data from England (Charlton 1984) demonstrated that children who smoke were more likely to agree that "smoking keeps your weight down." This attribution was especially prominent among older girls.

Despite school health education programs, children, especially those who smoke, continue to harbor several misconceptions about smoking. These misconceptions include overestimating the prevalence of both peer and adult smoking, underestimating the negative attitudes of their peers, and minimizing the addictive nature of smoking (Leventhal, Glynn, Fleming 1987). The overestimating of prevalence may represent the combined influence of social context and cognitive factors in determining smoking.

Economic Barriers to Full Public Knowledge

Why have many smokers not gotten the message? One answer is that the lack of forceful government restriction of cigarette marketing may lead citizens to infer that smoking must not be as dangerous as antismoking voices claim (Davis 1987, p. 725). Another answer is that many smokers have not been given the message. Warner and his colleagues have documented persistent efforts of tobacco companies to suppress media coverage of the uniquely risky nature of smoking (Warner et al., 1992; see Chapter 3). Their ability to do this is enhanced by being part of conglomerates with substantial advertising budgets for nontobacco products. The possibility of loss of advertising revenues from these nontobacco products, beyond profits from cigarette advertising, is an effective threat to print and electronic media (Warner et al., 1992). It is also a threat to others in the communication business. In the spring of 1988, RJR-Nabisco canceled nontobacco product accounts with an advertising agency, Saatchi and Saatchi, which had prepared advertisements for Northwest Airline's nonsmoking policy.

Why would a highly diversified conglomerate manipulate its nontobacco marketing and economic power to advance the interests of its cigarette division? The answer may be in the great profitability of cigarettes in comparison to other product lines. Based on profit and sales data from one conglomerate in 1981, the profit per dollar gross sales of cigarettes was four times that of nontobacco products such as alcoholic beverages and food (Fisher and Rost 1986, pp. 551–552). Chapter 3 discusses these and other economic dimensions of smoking and nicotine addiction, including the international expansion of U.S. tobacco companies.

Social Differentiation of Smoking

As noted earlier, racial, ethnic, and gender groups in our society have been targeted for market segmentation in cigarette advertising, resulting in prevalence and brand choices varying according to such social and demographic characteristics (see also Chapter 18). In addition to prevalence and brand choice, other characteristics of smoking careers have been related to group differences. African American smokers report fewer cigarettes per day than whites, but choose brands with higher tar/nicotine yields (Orleans et al. 1989). Until recently, heavy smoking was rare among Hispanics (Chapter 18).

Observed group differences may mislead us to conclude that intrinsic characteristics of those groups are responsible for high or low prevalences. However, there is no evidence that central characteristics of African American culture are responsible for higher prevalences than observed among white groups. Indeed, observed differences by race and sex may be largely attributable to effects of income and education (USDHHS 1989). Income and education effects are, themselves, quite substantial. For instance, results of the 1985 National Health Interview Survey indicated a 35.7% prevalence among adults with less than a high school education, about twice the 18.4% prevalence among those with postgraduate training. For both women and men, prevalence declines with increases in income range. Among unemployed men, the prevalence is 44.3% (USDHHS 1989). Even among health professionals, socioeconomic status appears related to smoking. Physicians smoke less than registered nurses who, in turn, smoke less than licensed practical nurses (USDHHS 1984).

Beyond the general associations of smoking with education and income, several specific characteristics of its distribution suggest it is especially common among those not doing well in our society. Of the 38 subgroups defined by gender and economic, educational, vocational, or marital status in the 1988 Surgeon General's Report (USDHHS 1988, p. 571), divorced or separated men had the highest prevalence of smoking (48.2%). It is interesting to note that these same characteristics, divorce and separation among men, have been closely linked to suicide and alcoholism (Kaplan and Sadock 1985). Among a sample of psychiatric outpatients, 52% reported smoking. Prevalence varied with diagnosis, for example, 88% with schizophrenia, 49% with major depression (Hughes et al. 1986). Among male frequenters of a church-sponsored soup kitchen in Charleston, South Carolina, 76% reported smoking cigarettes (McDade and Keil 1988).

Abstracting some of these and previous findings, racial prejudice, low income, less education, poverty, adolescent problem behavior, lack of optimistic plans for the future, identity as working class, breakdown of affectional bonds, psychopathology—these correlates of smoking and the research on stress, mood, and nicotine suggest a role as response to psychosocial adversity. Indeed, the pharmacological characteristics of nicotine and the delivery characteristics of inhaled tobacco smoke make the cigarette well suited as a drug for mitigating diverse psychological reactions to adversity in our culture.

Multiple Determinants and the Persistence of Smoking

As noted at the beginning of this chapter, the multiplicity of determinants of smoking and the many relationships or interdependencies among them may account for much of the persistence of smoking—a persistence otherwise inexplicable in light of smoking's risks.

As an example of these interdependencies, consider the response of a recent quitter, coming across a cigarette advertisement in a magazine, as outlined in Figure 4–2. To the extent the quitter is part of the "market segment" targeted by the advertisement, he or she may find within the advertisement a number of symbols closely associated with his or her own smoking habits. Prior conditioning of these symbols causes them to elicit some of the individual's responses to cigarettes, experienced as urges to smoke. The symbols and the conditioned responses to them may serve as strong cues for smoking. The conditioned responses to the advertisement are also enhanced by the strength of nicotine as an unconditioned stimulus. Of course, the placement of such advertisements, billboards, point-of-sale marketing displays, free samples, and other instances of cigarette marketing at numerous points in the daily life of the quitter is supported by the great profits associated with the sale of cigarettes.

Summarizing the interplay of these influences, the frequencies of cigarette adveritsements, the responses conditioned to them,

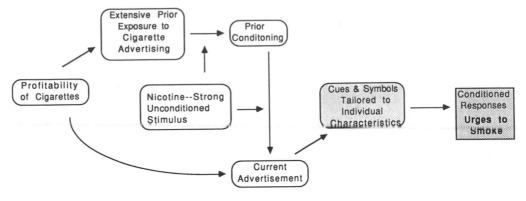

Fig. 4-2 The relationships among cigarette profits, advertising, conditioning, and urges to smoke.

and the responses which they cue are all increased by the profitability of cigarette sales. Cigarette profits make worthwhile the placement of advertisements and other marketing efforts throughout the daily circumstances of the quitter's life. These profits can even drive the largest corporate takeover in the history of our economy—that of RJR-Nabisco in 1988. The smoking career is maintained by forces ranging from physiology to global finance.

FACTORS INFLUENCING SMOKING CESSATION

Personality, Personal and Social Problems in Quitting Smoking

As noted earlier, smoking has been linked to rebelliousness, impulsiveness, and identity assertion in adolescence and adulthood. On the other hand, it is less common among those who are conforming, less impulsive, and apparently secure in their identity. The same factors, rephrased somewhat in accord with how we usually describe adulthood, figure in quitting. Those who are succeeding and who have greater personal and socioeconomic resources are more likely to have quit smoking (see also Chapter 8). Prospective studies indicate that education level, income, and skills in self-management or personal coping are significantly related to success in self-initiated efforts to quit (Blair et al. 1980; Perri, Richards, Schultheis 1977). Other studies indicate that, among a wide

sample of health management organization (HMO) subscribers, for example, those who quit were likely to have been those with fewer health problems (e.g., Friedman et al. 1979). Thus, smoking cessation may be part of a pattern including other individual efforts to enhance health as well as general personal resources.

Negative Affect and Cessation

Of increasing interest are links between smoking cessation and various negative affective states. One source of this research was Tomkin's typology of smoking and affect regulation, very influential in the 1960s and early 1970s (Ikard and Tomkins 1973). Tomkins proposed a fourfold typology including positive affect, negative affect, habitual, and addictive smoking. Validity studies have yielded the most consistent support for the negative affect smoking construct (e.g., Joffe, Lowe, Fisher 1981). Some studies of the role of negative affect in cessation have yielded striking findings. For instance, only 26% of those who had mentioned negative moods as most likely to trigger their own smoking were abstinent at 1-year follow-up in comparison to 50% of those mentioning other events as primary triggers (Pomerleau, Adkins, Pertschuk 1978).

In addition to individual's reports of negative affect, recent years have seen striking associations between smoking and clinical depression. Among participants in a cessation program who had a history of previous depression, 33% were abstinent 4 weeks after quitting. Among those without such a history, 57% were abstinent (Glassman et al. 1988). In another program, depression was related to lapses 2 and 3 weeks after quitting (West, Hajek, Belcher 1989). Glassman and his colleagues (1988) report a much higher than expected 61% of entrants into their program had a prior history of major affective disorder, even though those with major depression at the time of enrollment were referred elsewhere. While previous or current depression may presage greater difficulty in quitting and greater likelihood of seeking help to quit, quitting itself may instigate depression and low mood along with stress and other negative affect. Smokers who have recently quit report more withdrawal symptoms and severe mood disturbances than those continuing to smoke (Hall et al. 1985). Whether such emotional sequelae of quitting are limited to those predisposed to depression or other psychological problems is not yet known.

Stress and Relapse

Relapse crises are often precipitated by stress and negative affect. Bliss and co-workers (1989) found 56% of relapsers attributed their first slip to negative affect. In a prospective study of quitters, Ashenberg, Morgan, and Fisher (1984) found level of stress to predict subsequent relapses. Life stress coupled with an established pattern of using cigarettes to alleviate anxiety or other negative affect (Pomerleau, Adkins, Pertschuk 1978) may increase relapses. In addition to demonstrating an association between increases in stress and relapse following cessation, Cohen and Lichtenstein (1990) found that those who failed to quit reported higher levels of stress over a 6-month follow-up period. But in addition to the apparent role of stress as a barrier to quitting and a prompt to relapse, these authors also found evidence that cessation may influence stress. From pre-quit stress levels somewhat higher than those in a national sample, individuals who remained abstinent reported decreasing stress over a 6-month follow-up period. In cross-lag analyses, decreases in stress followed

quitting. As the authors conclude, ". . . the field's focus on the effects of stress on smoking status may be overly one-sided, distracting us from a practically and theoretically important effect of smoking status on stress" (p. 477).

The evidence that stress often precedes relapses might lead us to assume that relapsers lack skills for coping with stress. Indeed, the virtual lack of coping responses appears predictive of relapse (Shiffman 1982). But Ashenberg and his colleagues (1984) found that relapsers did not differ from smokers in their stress coping skills. Rather, relapsers reported failing to use those skills they did have in the specific situations in which they relapsed. Consistent with this, Shiffman (1982) found that subjects using strategies for coping with temptations were less likely to relapse than subjects who did not use any strategies but, importantly, regardless of the specific strategies they chose. Others have found similar results (Bliss et al. 1989). Thus, the occurrence of stress and failure to use whatever coping skills an individual may possess appear to be important antecedents of relapses. Clinically, the emphasis may best be placed on encouraging people to use the skills they have, not on teaching them new stress management skills.

Marlatt and Gordon (1985) present a model which has been very popular in understanding the observation that "lapses" or "slips" are highly predictive of subsequent relapse (Baer et al. 1988). In addition to being under stress, the quitter may also receive social prompts, encouragement, or direct facilitation by peers to resume smoking. After a slip, Marlatt and Gordon suggest that an "Abstinence Violation Effect" may compound the problem. This may occur in the following sequence: (1) negative affect leads to lowered self-confidence which in turn leads to a smoking slip; (2) the slip, one or two cigarettes, leads to a further reduction in self-confidence; (3) further lowered self-confidence leads to the conclusion that the case is "hopeless"; and (4) abandonment of the quit attempt. Critical to the Abstinence Violation Effect is overemphasizing the implications of a single slip, justifying the conclusion that one's case is hopeless.

Weight and Smoking Cessation

On average, smokers weigh less than non-smokers (e.g., Gordon et al. 1975). Nicotine may aid smokers in maintaining lower body weight (USDHHS 1988). Paradoxically, however, initiation and continuance of smoking may cause harmful patterns of weight distribution in spite of the lower overall weight (Shimokata et al. 1989).

The 1990 Surgeon General's Report on Smoking (USDHHS 1990) reviewed a number of studies of weight gain following cessation. Contrary to previous views that, after quitting, one third gain, one third lose, and one third do not change their weight ". . . approximately four-fifths of smokers who quit will gain weight after cessation . . ." (p. 483). Contrary to some projections of great weight gain, however, ". . . the average weight gain after smoking cessation is approximately 5 pounds" (p. 483). A relatively small percentage, estimated at 3–4%, gain over 20 pounds (USDHHS 1990, pp. 476, 483). A more recent paper based on NHANES data included 11-year follow-up of adults from 25 to 74 years old. After statistical adjustment for confounding factors, differences between quitters and continuing smokers at 1-year follow-up were 6.16 pounds for males and 8.36 pounds for females. In this study, incidence of "major weight gain" (over 13 kg or 28.6 lb) was 9.8% in men and 13.4% in women (Williamson et al. 1991). Weight gain following cessation appears to be a complex but still poorly understood result of changes in total intake (Hall et al. 1989), changes in specific food intake (Rodin 1988) such as increased preference for sugar (Grunberg et al. 1985), and changes in nutrient metabolism or fat storage (Carney and Goldberg, 1984).

Although the direct health effects of weight gain following smoking are, in almost all cases, trivial, the health significance may be great in its discouragement of smoking cessation. In one survey, 27% of smokers who had tried to quit cited weight gain as an incentive for relapse (USDHH 1990, p. ix). The fear of weight gain following cessation may be particularly a problem for women (Abrams et al. 1987; USDHHS 1988) who report using cigarettes as a method of appetite and weight control (Sorenson and Pechacek 1987). Among adolescent women, the links between smoking and concern about being thin may fairly be described as pathological. Amphetamine use for weight loss is positively related to smoking for adolescent women but not men (Gritz and Crane 1991). Also among adolescent women, smoking has been associated with bulimia and purging (Killen, Taylor, Telch, Robinson, Maron, Saylor 1987), and smoking along with binge-eating and purging have been associated with secondary amenorrhea (Johnson and Whitaker 1992).

Nicotine replacement may suppress weight gain following cessation. One study reported a dose-response relation between nicotine gum use and suppression of weight gain and smaller increases in hunger and eating among those receiving nicotine substitution than in those receiving placebo. Unfortunately, differences in weight gain between placebo and nicotine groups were not maintained at follow-up, prompting the authors to conclude that "nicotine replacement delayed but did not prevent typical postcessation weight gain . . ." (Gross, Stitzer, Maldonado 1989, p. 91); (see also Chapter 17).

Gender and Smoking Cessation

Historical differences in prevalence among adult men and women have narrowed to 1 or 2 percentage points in recent years. However, while the percentage of high school seniors reporting daily smoking declined from 27 to 19% from 1975 to 1981, a concurrent shift in prevalence by gender is cause for special concern. Every year since 1977, the prevalence of daily smokers among female high school seniors has exceeded that among males; in 1987, prevalences were 20 and 16%, respectively (USDHHS 1989, pp. 303–304). No compelling factors have yet emerged to account for these historical shifts, although a change in social acceptability seems a likely candidate. No cause for complacency, some data suggest the adolescent male prevalence of nicotine use in all forms, including smokeless tobacco, is greater than that among adolescent females

(Severson et al 1991). This observation reinforces this book's emphasis on nicotine addiction and suggests the focus needs to be on gender differences not in the extent but in the form of the problem.

On the basis of survey data, it has been suggested that women have lower rates of quitting smoking than do men (Remington et al. 1985), although this has been questioned for failing to adjust male quit rates to reflect the proportion of men who switch to other tobacco products (Jarvis 1984). As noted earlier, weight gain following smoking cessation may also be a special concern for women (USDHHS 1988). Stress appears to be a factor especially influencing women's cessation (Abrams et al. 1987; Sorensen and Pechacek 1987), as well as their initiation of smoking (Mitic, McGuire, Neumann 1985). Chapter 17 provides a detailed discussion of smoking among women, including smoking as a palliative for stress and unique quit smoking barriers and motives among women.

Peer, Family Factors, and Social Support in Cessation

As early as 1971, research indicated the importance of peer smoking in adult smoking and its cessation. For instance, those who fail to quit or relapse are more likely to be married to a smoking spouse and/or to report high prevalence of smoking among their friends (Eisinger 1971; Graham and Gibson 1971). Quitters who work with nonsmokers are more likely to be successful in maintaining their abstinence than quitters who work with smokers (Bishop et al. 1985). However, smoking by peers and family members of adult quitters did not receive as much attention as in discussions of determinants of adolescent smoking, probably reflecting popular notions that adolescents are especially influenced by their peers but that adults are more autonomous. Counter to this presumption, a study of the importance of friends' smoking across the life span found no significant influence of subject age (Gottlieb and Baker 1986).

While influences of others on adult smoking were relatively ignored, the popularity of self-control procedures and rhetoric (c.f., Fisher 1986) was manifest in smoking cessation programs of the 1970s. These stressed the individual's control over smoking by manipulating its triggers or antecedents. However, research directed at such procedures failed to yield appreciable improvements in program impacts (Lichtenstein 1982). This led researchers to seek important variables they might have overlooked. The 1980 and 1982 Surgeon General's Reports each identified social support as possibly important in mediating cessation among adults. Since then, a number of papers have explored its effects (USDHHS 1980, 1982). Several studies from smoking cessation clinics have found abstinence related to participants' ratings of support from spouses, living partners, other family members, or friends (e.g., Coppotelli and Orleans 1985; Morgan, Ashenberg, Fisher 1988). But, in addition to supporting cessation, the influence of others may sometimes be negative. Quitters' reports of smokers offering cigarettes or smoking in front of them predicted subsequent relapse (Morgan, Ashenberg, Fisher 1988).

Lichtenstein, Glasgow, and Abrams (1986) noted that, as much as social support measures have been repeatedly correlated with abstinence, social support interventions have not been found to improve markedly on other procedures. For instance, an emphasis on group cohesion to enhance social support led to initial but not long-term advantages over a control group receiving standard intervention (Etringer, Gregory, Lando 1984). Understanding the lack of a long-term effect of intervention strategies that promote interpersonal support may be advanced by considering the nature of support and its functions at different stages of cessation (Cohen et al. 1988). Interpersonal emotional support seems especially related to maintained abstinence in the first several months after cessation (Coppotelli and Orleans 1985; Morgan, Ashenberg, Fisher 1988). On the other hand, long-term abstinence of a year or more may be more closely tied to the number of smoking friends and relatives in the social network (Eisinger 1971; Graham and Gibson 1971; Mermelstein et al. 1986; Cohen et al. 1988).

The importance of the smoking status of members of one's social network for consolidation of long-term abstinence strikes an interesting parallel with consolidation of a smoking career in adolescence. Just as the initiate who goes on to a career of drug use will tend to have friends who are also users, so the quitter who goes on to a career as abstainer is more likely to have friends who are also pursuing the career of nonuser. The implications for programs to promote nonsmoking may be great. Changing norms for smoking behavior may be more effective in deterring uptake and encouraging maintained cessation than promoting interpersonal support for quitting.

One place where smoking norms of important social networks may encourage nonsmoking is at work. Accordingly, worksite programs are attracting considerable attention. Worksites differ in smoking prevalence and cessation rates as well as in norms for supporting cessation attempts (Sorensen, Pechacek, Pallonen 1986). Programs aimed at worksite norms and general support for nonsmoking have reported substantial quit rates, even among smokers who did not join cessation clinics (Fisher et al. 1988). Employees' ratings of management support for such programs and indices of management support such as instituting smoking policies were associated with participation, cessation attempts and with ratings of social support for nonsmoking (Emont and Cummings 1990; Fisher et al. 1988). A still more ambitious approach to changing smoking norms is through programs to promote nonsmoking across entire communities. The National Cancer Institute has supported COMMIT, a large clinical trial evaluating community organization for smoking cessation. This trial compares 11 treated communities against changes in smoking prevalence in 11 untreated communities (Lichtenstein, Wallack, Pechacek 1991, in press). Moving from the community to the state level, the institute recently launched ASSIST statewide nonsmoking programs to be implemented in each of 17 participating states. Chapter 21 includes further details about the rationale and procedures for worksite and community programs, including ASSIST.

Countermarketing

Cigarette consumption declined between 1967 and 1970, a period when television and radio stations were required to run public service advertisements encouraging nonsmoking under a court ruling that "equal time" had to be given antitobacco messages. When Congress passed legislation prohibiting television and radio advertising of tobacco products, the basis for the "equal time" disappeared, the frequency of antismoking public service announcements declined sharply, and the per capita cigarette consumption increased in each year from 1971 to 1973 (USDHHS 1989). Open to conjecture are the motives of the tobacco companies in agreeing to the legislative compromise which removed from the airwaves their own—and most of their opposition's—advertisements.

Countermarketing continues through the efforts of such groups as Doctors Ought to Care (DOC), in the United States, or BUGGA UP in Australia. In New York, inner city African-American groups have recently launched a campaign to deface billboards advertising cigarettes in their neighborhoods, far more numerous than in white and middle-class neighborhoods. Recently, increased state taxes on cigarette sales in California have been partially dedicated by the legislature to public information campaigns countering tobacco. This has resulted in the return to "prime time" of a well-financed campaign. Early 1991 results of California's "Proposition 99 Tobacco Tax Initiative" (see Chapter 21) indicated that "the media component of the campaign was a motivating factor for 33,000 California residents to quit smoking within the last year," and "an additional 140,000 Californians cited the campaign's advertising and marketing efforts as 'significantly related' to their decision to quit smoking." (California Department of Health Services 1991). The latest results, based on a 1992 survey, indicated that smoking prevalence among Californians over age 18 had decreased by 24% between 1988 and 1992, and concluded that: "Some of this decline was associated with the introduction of the Initiative and the tax. However, a good proportion of the decline in [smoking] prevalence in California may be attributed to the interventions funded by the tax initiative" (i.e., the anti-tobacco community-based cessation and prevention programs) (Pierce et al. 1993, page 37).

Cognitive Process and Decision Making

In addition to their use in understanding the initiation and persistence of smoking, expectancy value models have also been applied to smoking cessation (Velicer et al. 1985) and have come to take into account stages of change (Prochaska and DiClemente 1983). Changes in the relative level of pro and con views of smoking, for example, appear related to stages of quitting. Smokers not contemplating quitting report substantially higher levels of pro than con views, while those contemplating quitting report equal pro and con views. For quitters, con views were higher than pro views. These relative pro and con views also predicted subsequent change in smoking (Velicer et al. 1985).

Since the 1960s, the health belief model (Rosenstock 1974) has been a popular instance of expectancy value concepts applied to smoking cessation. According to this model, attempting to stop smoking is a function of three factors: (1) beliefs about the health consequences of smoking and perceived susceptibility to the disease consequences, (2) perceptions of available actions that can reduce one's risk, and (3) perceptions of the costs and benefits of accomplishing these actions (Kirscht and Rosenstock 1979). Johnston and his colleagues (Bachman et al. 1988), for example, have shown that changes in perceived risk have accounted for a considerable reduction in adolescent marijuana use, particularly regular use. They suggest that effects of such beliefs may be more limited in the case of cigarettes because of the addictive properties of nicotine.

That information regarding its health effects might discourage smoking has not always been strongly emphasized. Some views have held that information about health risks or "scare tactics" are ineffective in promoting change. This perspective encouraged many smoking cessation programs to focus

on how to quit rather than why. However, it is important to differentiate the level of *information* versus the level of *arousal* provided by a message. Calm presentation of risk information may increase decisions to quit. Highly frightening scare tactics, on the other hand, may raise arousal to the point that the individual is simply motivated to reduce that arousal, even at the cost of ignoring the information provided (Janis and Mann 1977). The effects of information may also be mediated by the stage in the smoking career. The contemplator of quitting may take in and benefit from information which the precontemplator would resist (Prochaska and DiClemente 1983). The person maintaining abstinence may consolidate change through risk information which confirms its value (Best 1975). Again, it is important to recognize that the several stages of a smoking career differ in their responses to external influences, such as information about health risks.

In addition to the health belief model, other approaches to health behavior change have emphasized individuals' cognitions or beliefs about their own skills. An influential example of this is Bandura's (1982) writing on self-efficacy. Self-efficacy is defined as an individual's belief in his or her ability to perform a specific behavior coupled with outcome expectations concerning the likely impact or utility of that behavior. In this model, efficacy beliefs and outcome expectations represent a final common pathway mediating behavior change. Information from past behavior, modeling of behavior by others, affective states, and instruction combine to produce a performance expectation, which then predicts future behavior. Behavior then influences subsequent efficacy so that behavior and efficacy are reciprocally related (Bandura 1982).

In smoking, research on self-efficacy has focused on predictions of abstinence by ratings of efficacy of participants in cessation clinics. When all clients in treatment are considered, self-efficacy ratings at the end of treatment correlate strongly with short-term maintenance (Condiotte and Lichtenstein 1981). For the most part, efficacy scores seem to correlate with outcome most highly when the follow-up interval is shorter (e.g., 3 months) and diminish over time (McIntyre-Kingsolver, Lichtenstein, Mermelstein 1983). Similar to self-efficacy is self-attribution—the extent to which individuals attribute their behavior to their own skills or efforts rather than to external causes. Statements of self-attribution of quitting also predict subsequent abstinence (Harackiewicz, Sansone, Blair 1987).

Of course, subjects may estimate their own efficacy on the basis of their own smoking patterns. That is, correlations with efficacy might simply derive from a correlation between smoking patterns and subsequent cessation. One approach to disentangling efficacy ratings and current smoking is to confine analyses to subjects who had quit at the time they provided the efficacy ratings. Using this approach, efficacy ratings of clinic participants still predict subsequent follow-up status (e.g., Baer, Holt, Lichtenstein 1986).

The importance of self-efficacy or self-attribution is suggested by national survey data in which smokers indicate that lack of confidence in their ability to quit deters them from trying (Shiffman 1987). However, from a deterministic perspective, it is hard to see how self-efficacy, self-attribution, or feelings of confidence can be independent causes of cessation. Those things which help people to quit are likely to raise feelings of confidence, but it is hard to see how we can raise confidence directly, without influencing other factors. Thus, the feeling of confidence or self-efficacy may be a useful marker of the effects of a cause or influence (Fisher, Levenkron, Lowe et al. 1982; Fisher 1986) rather than itself a cause. That is, those who have been substantially influenced by a public health campaign or a program they have entered are more likely to express confidence in their future ability to quit and remain a nonsmoker. The difference in interpretation has clinical import. The *causes* of smoking cessation are not individuals' feelings about themselves or about the programs they have received, but are the treatments, educational campaigns, interpersonal persuasion, and other interventions which influence both these feelings and smoking cessation.

Circular Explanations and Clinical Blind Alleys

This discussion of self-efficacy recalls that of risks of circular explanations in understanding smoking in general. Such risks also lie in discussions of cessation and relapse. We may hear that the reason for failure to quit is weak motivation. This names the problem "weak motivation," but leaves unexplained the reason "motivation" may be weak.

If explanations are to improve our clinical efforts, they need to identify factors that we can manipulate or influence. We cannot directly influence a relapse stage, adolescence, or motivation. We can coach would be quitters on recruiting family support for cessation resulting in apparent increases in motivation. As one other example, we can help a diabetic smoker understand why smoking cessation may be the most important part of diabetes management, resulting in clearer understanding of the risks of smoking and an attempt at quitting. As indicated for self-efficacy, asking individuals how confident they feel may help us know when, say, a program teaching strategies for avoiding relapse has been well executed. Ultimately, however, it is specification of ways of influencing smoking, not the feelings of smokers, which will constitute the most efficient efforts to combat it.

Coexisting Disease

Coexisting disease related to smoking may facilitate cessation (Sachs 1984; Burt et al. 1974) with the greatest abstinence rates—as high as 50%—obtained with cardiovascular disease (e.g., Ockene 1987; Havik and Maeland 1988). In contrast, research with pulmonary patients indicates poorer results in this group (Tonnesen et al. 1989). Diabetes doubles risks of stroke, myocardial infarction, and peripheral vascular disease; the addition of smoking further increases these risks 4- to 11-fold (Rytter, Troelsen, Beck-Nielsen 1985). Nevertheless, the prevalence of smoking among diabetic adults appears equivalent to the nondiabetic population (Haire-Joshu 1991) with some evidence that cessation rates are lower (Ardron and MacFarlane 1987).

Expectancy value theories' emphases on variations in risks of smoking and incentives for cessation may help make sense of the different cessation rates among patients with cardiovascular disease as opposed to lung disease and diabetes. For example, patients' motivation to quit smoking may be affected by their appraisal of the degree of personal threat presented by the disease and by the likelihood of advantage from quitting. The prospects of full recovery from myocardial infarction may be advanced substantially by smoking cessation and other life-style changes. In contrast, the impacts of quitting for the patient with chronic lung disease are likely to be on course and symptoms of disease, but not mortality.

Diabetes is an interesting example of the numerous interactions that may exist between smoking and a coexisting disease. Unlike cardiovascular or pulmonary diseases, diabetes is not caused by smoking. This may lead diabetic patients as well as clinicians to overlook the impacts on morbidity and mortality of the combination of smoking and diabetes. Even though they smoke, diabetic adults may still be taught to focus on metabolic control as a way to minimize physical conditions. Yet quitting smoking can have as great an impact on reducing the physical threats associated with diabetes. Further complicating the picture, diabetic smokers may believe smoking's effects on body weight or on stress assist diabetes management (Haire-Joshu et al. 1990). Given the widespread emphasis on weight management in diabetes care, diabetic smokers may mistakenly assume that weight management is more important than quitting smoking. Furthermore, the pharmacological effects of nicotine may aid management of stress apparently associated with diabetes and its care, thereby providing another incentive for smoking among those with diabetes.

The multidimensionality of smoking may have effects that vary according to a number of disease characteristics. The perception by the patient of the nature of smoking as a causal versus peripheral factor, the perception of immediate versus long-term health risks in association with other diseases and risks, or the sense that smoking provides immediate benefits to replace those that have been forgone because of coexisting disease, may all influence the persistence of smoking. Further discussion of smoking cessation among high risk groups or those with other diseases is in Chapter 14.

IMPLICATIONS FOR HEALTH PROFESSIONALS

This chapter has emphasized two themes: (1) the multiple determinants of smoking and their interaction with (2) the numerous phases through which smoking and quitting evolve. Both these themes have important implications for clinicians desiring to promote nonsmoking.

Smoking's multiple determinants account for much of the frustration of clinicians faced with the persistence of smoking in spite of its overwhelming health effects. Because the causes of smoking are so strong and varied, the isolated efforts of the professional cannot be decisive in every case. Rather, professionals contribute to smoking cessation in concert with a wide range of other factors, from mass media campaigns, to smoking cessation clinics, to legislation and regulation regarding tobacco use. In many cases, the professional's own actions may catalyze patients' efforts which also benefit from nonsmoking promotions outside the clinical setting. Parts II and III of this book outline many ways in which physicians and other professionals can use such promotions to benefit both their patients and the wider communities in which they practice.

Regarding phases in the development of smoking and quitting, the professional needs to recognize that, just as with any patient, smokers' needs will vary according to the stage to which the problem for which they seek help has developed. Thus, the clinician's tactics may range widely—from discouraging the adolescent who is contemplating initiating smoking, to brief explanations of risks for the adult precontemplator, to counseling about cessation strategies, prescription of a nicotine patch, or even referral to intensive inpatient nicotine addiction treatment programs for the would-be quitter in the or, action stage, to reassuring the relapser not to be overlooked, continuing to support and encourage the long-term quitter. These and other clinical activities are described in Chapters 8, 10, and 11.

ACKNOWLEDGMENTS

Portions of this chapter were based on previous writing of Drs. Fisher and Lichtenstein in "Changes in knowledge about the determinants of smoking behavior" in Chapter 5, Part II (pp. 329–378) of *Reducing the Health Consequences of Smoking: 25 Years of Progress. A Report of the Surgeon General.* U. S. Department of Health and Human Services, Public Health Service, Centers for Disease Control, Office on Smoking and Health. DHHS Publication No. (CDC) 89-8411, 1989. We thank especially Judith Ockene, PhD, who worked with us in developing the chapter in that report. We also thank Ronald Davis, MD, and Kenneth Warner, PhD, who, along with Dr. Ockene, contributed substantially to this chapter through their roles as editors of the Surgeon General's reports.

REFERENCES

Abrams, D. B., Monti, P. M., Pinto, R. P., Elder, J. P., Brown, R. A., Jacobus, S. I. Psychosocial stress and coping in smokers who relapse or quit. *Health Psychol* 6(4):289–303, 1987.

Abrams, D. B., Monti, P. M., Carey, K. B., Pinto, R. P., Jacobus, S. I. Reactivity to smoking cues and relapse: Two studies of discriminant validity. *Behav Res Ther* 26(3):225–233, 1988.

American Lung Association. Survey of attitudes toward smoking. Conducted by the Gallup Organization, Inc., July 1985.

Anda R. F., Williamson D. F., Escobedo L. G., Mast E. E., Giovino G. A., Remington P. L. Depression and the dynamics of smoking. A national perspective. *JAMA* 264(12):1541–1545, 1990.

Antonuccio, D. O., and Lichtenstein, E. Peer modeling influences on smoking behavior of heavy and light smokers. *Addict Behav* 5(4):229–306, 1980.

Ardon, M., Macfarlane, I. A., Robinson, C., Van Heyningen, C., Calverley, P.M.A. Anti-smoking advice for young diabetic smokers: Is it a waste of breath? *Diabetic Med* 5:667–670, 1988.

Ashenberg, Z. S., Morgan, G. D., Fisher, E. B., Jr. Psychological stress and smoking recidivism. Paper presented at Society of Behavioral Medicine, Philadelphia, May 1984.

Baer, J. S., Holt, C. S., Lichtenstein, E. Self-efficacy and smoking reexamined: Construct validity and clinical utility. *J Consult Clin Psychol* 54(6):846–852, 1986.

Baer, J. S., Kamarck, T. W., Lichtenstein, E., Ransom, C. R. The prdiction of smoking relapse from characteristics of prior temptations and slips. Paper presented at the Wilford Hall Health Promotion Conference, San Antonia, TX, May 1988.

Baker, T. F. Models of addiction: Introduction to the special issue. *J Abnorm Psychol* 97:115–117, 1988.

Bandura, A. Self-efficacy mechanism in human agency. *Am Psychol* 37(2):122–147, 1982.

Barton, J., Chassin, L., Presson, C. C., Sherman, S. J. Social image factors as motivators of smoking initiation in early and middle adolescence. *Child Dev* 53:1499–1511, 1982.

Becker H. S. Becoming a marijuana user. In *Outsiders: Studies in the Sociology of Deviance.* New York: Free Press, 1963.

Best, J. A. Tailoring smoking withdrawal procedures to personality and motivational differences. *J Consult Clin Psychol* 43(1):1–8, 1975.

Biglan, A., and Lichtenstein, E. A behavior-analytic approach to smoking acquisition: Some recent findings. *J Appl Soc Psychol* 14(3):207–223, 1984.

Blair, A., Blair, S. N., Howe, H. G., Pate, R. R., Rosenberg, H., Parker, G. H., Pickle, L. W. Physical, psychological and sociodemographic differences among smokers, ex-smokers, and nonsmokers in a working population. *Prev Med* 9:747–759, 1980.

Bliss, R. E., Garvey, A. G., Heinhold, J. W., Hitchcock, J. L. The influence of situation and coping on relapse crisis outcomes after smoking cessation. *J Consult Clin Psychol* 57:443–449, 1989.

Brook, J. S., Whiteman, M., Gordon, A. S., Brook, D. W. Fathers and sons: Their relationship and personality characteristics associated with the son's smoking behavior. *J Gen Psychol* 142(2):271–281, 1983.

Burr, R. G. Smoking among U.S. Navy enlisted men: Some contributing factors. *Psychol Rep* 54:287–294, 1984.

Burt, A., Illingworth, D., Shaw, T.R.D., Thornley, P., White, P., Turner, R. Stopping smoking after myocardial infarction. *Lancet* 1:304–306, 1974.

California Department of Health Services, *California Department of Health Services Releases New Print Advertisement for Historic Tobacco Education Campaign,* Sacramento: California Department of Health Services, July 29, 1991.

Carney, R. M., and Goldberg, A. P. Weight gain after cessation of cigarette smoking. *N Engl J Med* 310(10):614–616, 1984.

Centers for Disease Control (CDC). Smoking-attributable mortality and years of potential life lost. United States, 1988. *MMWR* 40(4):62–71, 1 February 1991.

Charlton, A. Smoking and weight control in teenagers. *Public Health* 98:277–281, 1984.

Chassin, L., Presson, C. C., Sherman, S. J., Corty, E., Olshavsky, R. W. Predicting the onset of cigarette smoking in adolescents: A longitudinal study. *J Appl Soc Psychol* 14(3):224–243, 1984.

Chassin, L., Presson, C. C., Sherman, S. J., Edwards, D. A. The natural history of cigarette smoking. Predicting young-adult smoking outcomes from adolescent smoking patterns. *Health Psychol* 9(6):701–716, 1990.

Cherry, N., and Kiernan, K. E. Personality scores and smoking behaviour. A longitudinal study. *BJPSM* 30:123–131, 1976.

Cohen, S., Lichtenstein, E., Mermelstein, R., Kingsolver, K., Baer, J., Kamarck, T. Social support interventions for smoking cessation. In Gottlieb, B. H., ed. *Marshalling Social Support: Formats, Processes and Effects.* New York: Sage, 1988, 211–240.

Cohen, S., and Lichtenstein, E. Perceived stress, quitting smoking, and smoking relapse. *Health Psychol* 9:466–478, 1990.

Condiotte, M. M., and Lichtenstein, E. Self-efficacy and relapse in smoking cessation programs. *J Consult Clin Psychol* 49(5):648–658, 1981.

Coppotelli, H. C., and Orleans, C. T. Partner support and other determinants of smoking cessation maintenance among women. *J Consult Clin Psychol* 53(4)455–460, 1985.

Covey, L. S., and Tam, D. Depressive mood, the single-parent home, and adolescent cigarette smoking. *Am J Public Health* 80(11)1330–1333, 1990.

Cronan, T. A., and Conway, T. L. Is the navy attracting or creating smokers? *Milit Med* 153(4):175–178, 1988.

Cummings, K. M., Giovino, G., Mendicino, A. J. Cigarette advertising and black–white differences in cigarette brand preferences. *Public Health Rep* 102(6):698–701, 1987.

Davis, R. M. Current trends in cigarette advertising and marketing. *N Engl J Med* 316(12):725–732, 1987.

Davis, W. K., Hess, G. E., Hiss, R. G. Psychosocial correlates of survival in diabetes. *Diabetes Care* 11(7):538–545, 1988.

DiClemente, C. C., Prochaska, J. O., Fairhurst, S. K., Velicer W. F. Velasquez, M. M., Rossi, J.

S. The process of smoking cessation: An analysis of precontemplation, contemplation, and preparation stages of change. *J Consult Clin Psychol* 59(2):295–304, 1991.

Di Franza, J., Richards, J., Paulman, P., Wolf-Gillespie, N., Fletcher, C., Jaffe, R., Murray, D. RJR Nabisco's cartoon camel promotes camel cigarettes to children. *JAMA* 266(22), 3149–3153, 1991.

Dunn, S. M., and Turtle, J. R. The myth of the diabetic personality. *Diabetes Care* 4:640–646, 1981.

Eisinger, R. A. Psychosocial predictors of smoking recidivism. *J Health Soc Behav* 12:355–362, 1971.

Emont, S. L., and Cummings, K. M. Organizational factors affecting participation in a smoking cessation program and abstinence among 68 auto dealerships. Am J Health Promotion 5(2):107–114, 1990.

Etringer, B. D., Gregory V. R., Lando, H. A. Influence of group cohesion on the behavioral treatment of smoking. *J Consult Clin Psychol* 52(6):1080–1086, 1984.

Eysenck, H. J. *The Causes and Effects of Smoking.* Beverly Hills, CA: Sage 1980.

Falloon, I.R.H., Boyd, J. L., McGill, C. W., Razani, J. Moss, H. B., Gilderman, A. Family management in the prevention of exacerbations of schizophrenia: A controlled study. *N Engl J Med* 306:1437–1440, 1982.

Fishbein, M. Social psychological analysis of smoking behavior: In Eiser, J. R., ed. *Social Psychology and Behavioral Medicine.* New York: John Wiley and Sons, 1982, 179–197.

Fischer, P., Schwartz, M., Richards, J., Goldstein, A., Rojas, T. Brand logo recognition by children aged 3 to 6 years: Mickey Mouse and Old Joe the Camel. *JAMA* 266(22):3145–3148, 1991.

Fisher, E. B., Jr. A skeptical perspective: The importance of behavior and environment. In Holroyd, K. A., and Creer, T. L. eds. *Self-management of Chronic Disease: Recent Developments in Health Psychology and Behavioral Medicine.* New York: Academic Press, 1986.

Fisher, E. B., Jr., Delamater, A. M., Bertelson, A. D., Kirkley, B. G. Psychological factors in diabetes and its treatment. *J Consult Clin Psychol* 50:993–1003, 1982.

Fisher, E. B., Jr., Levenkron, J. C., Lowe, M. R., Loro, A. N., Jr., Green, L. Self-initiated self-control in risk reduction. In Stuart, R. B., ed. *Adherence, Compliance, and Generalization in Behavioral Medicine.* New York: Brunner/Mazel, 1982.

Fisher, E. B., Jr., Lowe, M. R., Levenkron, J. C.,

Newman, A. Structured support and reinforcement of maintained risk reduction. In Stuart, R.B., ed. *Adherence, Compliance and Generalization in Behavioral Medicine.* New York: Brunner/Mazel, 1982.

Fisher, E. B., Jr., and Rost, K. Smoking cessation: A practical guide for the physician. *Clin Chest Med* 7(4):551–565, December 1986.

Fisher, E. B., Jr., Bishop, D. B., Mayer, J., Brown, T., White-Cook, T. The physician's contribution to smoking cessation in the workplace. *Chest* 93(2):56S–65S, 1988.

Fisher, E. B., Jr., Haire-Joshu, D., Morgan, G. D., Rehberg, H., Rost, K. State of the art: Smoking and smoking cessation. *Am Rev Respir Dis* 142:702–720, 1990.

Friedman, G. D., Siegelaub, A. B., Dales, L. G., Seltzer, C. C. Characteristics predictive of coronary heart disease in ex-smokers before they stopped smoking: Comparison with persistent smokers and nonsmokers. *J Chronic Dis* 32:175–190, 1979.

Friedman, L. S., Lichtenstein, E., Biglan, A. Smoking onset among teens: An empirical analysis of initial situations. *Addict Behav* 10:1–13, 1985.

Garvey, A. J., Bosse, R., Glynn, R. J., Rosner, B. Smoking cessation in a prospective study of healthy adult males: Effects of age, time period, and amount smoked. *Am J Public Health* 73:446–450, 1983.

Glassman, A. H., Stetner, F., Walsh, T., Raizman, P. S., Fleiss, J. L., Cooper, T. B., Covey, L. S. Heavy smokers, smoking cessation, and clonidine: Results of a double-blind, randomized trial. *JAMA* 259(19):2863–2866, 1988.

Glassman, A. H., Cotler, J. E., Covey, L. S., Cotler, L. B., Stetner, F., Tipp, J. E., Johnson, J. Smoking, smoking cessation, and major depression. *JAMA* 264(12):1546–1549, 1990.

Goldstein, A. O., Fischer, P. M., Richards, J. W., Jr., Creten, D. Relationship between high school student smoking and recognition of cigarette advertisements. *J Pediatr* 110(3):488–491, 1987.

Gordon, T., Kannel, W. B., Dawber, T. R., McGee, D. Changes associated with cigarette smoking: The Framingham study. *Am Heart J* 90:322–328, 1975.

Gottlieb, N. H., and Baker, J. A. The relative influence of health beliefs, parental and peer behaviors and exercise program participation on smoking, alcohol use and physical activity. *Soc Sci Med* 22(9):915–927, 1986.

Graham, S., and Gibson, R. W. Cessation of patterned behavior: Withdrawal from smoking. *Soc Sci Med* 5(4):319–337, 1971.

Gritz, E. R. Gender and the teenage smoker. In Ray, B. A., and Braude, M. C., eds. *Women and Drugs: A New Era for Research.* NIDA Research Monograph 65. U.S. Department of Health and Human Services, Public Health Service, Alcohol, Drug Abuse, and Mental Health Administration, National Institute on Drug Abuse. DHHS Publication No. 83-1268, 1986, 70–79.

Gritz, E., and Crane, L. Use of diet pills and amphetamines to lose weight among smoking and nonsmoking high school seniors. *Health Psychol* 10(5):330–335, 1991.

Gross, J., Stitzer, M. L., Maldonado, J. Nicotine replacement: Effects on post-cessation weight gain. *J Consult Clin Psychol* 57(1):87–92, 1989.

Grunberg, N. E., Bowen, D. J., Maycock, V. A., Nespor, S. M. The importance of sweet taste and caloric content in the effects of nicotine on specific food consumption. *Psychopharmacology* 87:198–203, 1985.

Haire-Joshu, D. Smoking, cessation, and the diabetes health care team: A review. *Diabetes Educator* 17(1):54–67, 1991.

Haire-Joshu, D., Heady, S., Thomas, L., Fisher, E., Jr. The impact of smoking on diabetes care: Beliefs of diabetic smokers. *Diabetes* 39(1):164a, 1990.

Hall, R. G., Sachs, D.P.L., Hall, S. M., Benowitz, N. L. Two-year efficacy and safety of rapid smoking therapy in patients with cardiac and pulmonary disease. *J Consult Clin Psychol* 52:574–581, 1984.

Hall, S. M., Tunstall, C., Rugg, D., Jones, R. T., Benowitz, N. L. Nicotine gum and behavioral treatment in smoking cessation. *J Consult Clin Psychol* 53(2):256–258, 1985.

Hall, S. M., McGee, R., Tunstall, J. D., Benowitz, N. L. Changes in food intake and activity after quitting smoking. *J Consult Clin Psychol* 57:81–86, 1989.

Harackiewicz, J. M., Sansone, C., Blair, L. L., Epstein, J. A., Manderlink, G. Attributional processes in behavior change and maintenance: Smoking cessation and continued abstinence. *J Consult Clin Psychol* 55:372–378, 1987.

Hatsukami, D. K., Hughes, J. R., Pickens, R. W. Blood nicotine, smoke exposure and tobacco withdrawal symptoms. *Addict Behav* 10:413–417, 1985.

Havik, O. E., and Maeland, J. G. Changes in smoking behavior after a myocardial infarction. *Health Psychol* 7(5):403–420, 1988.

Henderson, J. B., Hall, S. M., Linton, H. L. Changing self-destructive behaviors. In Stone, G. C., Cohen, F., Adler, N. E., et al., eds. *Health Psychology: A Handbook.* San Francisco: Jossey-Bass, 1979, 141–160.

Henningfield, J. E., and Nemeth-Coslett, R. Nicotine dependence: Interface between tobacco and tobacco-related disease. *Chest* 93(2):37S–55S, 1988.

Hirschman, R. S., Leventhal, H., Glynn, K. The development of smoking behavior: Conceptualization and supportive cross-sectional survey data. *J Appl Soc Psychol* 14(3):184–206, 1984.

Hughes, J. R. Clonidine, depression, and smoking cessation. *JAMA* 259(19):2901–2903, 1988.

Hughes, J. R., Hatsukami, D. K., Mitchell, J. E., Dahlgren, L. A. Prevalence of smoking among psychiatric outpatients. *Am J Psychiatry* 143(8):993–997, 1986.

Hundleby, J. D., and Mercer, G. W. Family and friends as social environments and their relationship to young adolescents' use of alcohol, tobacco, and marijuana. *J Marriage Family* 49:151–164, 1987.

Hunter, S. M., Croft, J. B., Burke, G. L., Parker, F. C., Webber, L. S., Berenson, G. S. Longitudinal patterns of cigarette smoking and smokeless tobacco use in youth: The Bogalusa heart study. *Am J Public Health* 76(2):193–195, 1986.

Ikard, F. F., and Tomkins, S. The experience of affect as a determinant of smoking behavior: A series of validity studies. *J Abnorm Psychol* 81(2):172–181, 1973.

Janis, I. L., and Mann, L. *Decision Making: A Psychological Analysis of Conflict, Choice, and Commitment.* New York: Free Press, 1977.

Jarvis, M. Gender and smoking. Do women really find it harder to give up? *Br J Addict* 79(4):383–387, 1984.

Jensen, A. R. How much can we boost IQ and scholastic achievement? *Harvard Educational Review* 39:1–23, 1969.

Jessor, R. Problem-behavior theory, psychosocial development, and adolescent problem drinking. *Br J Addict* 82:331–342, 1987.

Joffe, R., Lowe, M. R., Fisher, E. B., Jr. A validity test of the reasons for smoking scale. *Addict Behav* 6(1):41–45, 1981.

Johnson, J., Whitaker, A. Adolescent smoking, weight changes, and binge-purge behavior: associations with secondary amenorrhea. *Am J Pub Health* 82(1):47–54, 1992.

Johnston, L. D., O'Malley, P. M., Bachman, J. G. *National Trends in Drug Use and Related Factors Among High School Students and Young Adults, 1975–1986.* U.S. Department of Health and Human Services, Public Health Service, Alcohol, Drug Abuse, and Mental Health Administration, National Institute on Drug Abuse. DHHS Publication No. (ADM) 87-1535, 1987.

Kandel, D. B., and Davies, M. Adult sequelae of adolescent depressive symptoms. *Arch Gen Psychiatry* 43:255–262, 1986.

Kaplan, H. I., and Sadock, B. J., eds. *Comprehensive Textbook of Psychiatry,* 4th ed. Baltimore: Williams & Wilkins, 1985.

Killen, J., Taylor, C., Telch, M., Robinson, T., Maron, D., Saylor, K. Depressive symptoms and substance use among adolescent binge eaters and purgers: a defined population study. *Am J Pub Health* 77:1539–1541, 1987.

Kirscht, J. P., and Rosenstock, I. M. Patients' problems in following recommendations of health experts. In Stone, G. C., Cohen, F., Adler, N. E., et al., eds. *Health Psychology: A Handbook.* San Francisco: Jossey-Bass, 1979, 189–215.

Klesges, R. C., and Cigrang, J. A. Worksite smoking cessation programs: Clinical and methodological issues: In Hersen, M., Eisler, R. M., Miller, P. M., eds. *Progress in Behavior Modification.* Newbury Park, CA: Sage, 1988.

Kozlowski, L. T. Evidence for limits on the acceptability of lowest-tar cigarettes. *Am J Public Health* 79(2):198–199, 1989.

Krasner, L., and Ullmann, L. P. *Behavior Influence and Personality: The Social Matrix of Human Action.* New York: Holt, Rinehart and Winston, 1973.

Krosnick, J. A., and Judd, C. M. Transitions in social influences at adolescence: Who induces cigarette smoking? *Developmental Psychology* 18(3):359–368, 1982.

Leff, J., and Vaughn, C. *Expressed Emotion in Families.* New York: Guilford Press, 1985.

Leventhal, H., and Cleary, P. D. The smoking problem: A review of the research and theory in behavioral risk modification. *Psychol Bull* 88:370–405, 1980.

Leventhal, H., Glynn, K., Fleming, R. Is the smoking decision an "informed choice"? Effect of smoking risk factors on smoking beliefs. *JAMA* 257(24):3373–3376, 1987.

Lichtenstein, E. The smoking problem: A behavioral perspective. *J Consult Clin Psychol* 50(6):804–819, 1982.

Lichtenstein, E., and Bernstein, D. A. Cigarette smoking as indirect self-destructive behavior. In Farberow, N. L., ed. *The Many Faces of Suicide: Indirect Self-Destructive Behavior.* New York: McGraw Hill, 1980, 243–253.

Lichtenstein, E., Glasgow, R. E., Abrams, D. B. Social support in smoking cessation: In search of effective interventions. *Behavior Therapy* 17:607–619, 1986.

Lichtenstein, E., Wallack, L., Pechacek, T. F. Introduction to the community intervention trial for smoking cessation (COMMIT). *Inter Q Community Health Education* 1991 (in press).

Lowe, M. R., Green, L., Kurtz, S., Ashenberg, Z., Fisher, E. B., Jr. Alternatives to rapid smoking: Self-initiated, cue extinction, and covert sensitization procedures in smoking cessation. *J Behav Med* (3) 357–372, 1980.

McAlister, A. L., Krosnick, J. A., Milburn, M. A. Causes of adolescent cigarette smoking: Tests of a structural equation model. *Soc Psychol Q* 47(1):24–36, 1984.

McArthur, E., Waldron, E., Dickinson, J. The psychology of smoking. *J Abnorm Soc Psychol* 56:267–275, 1958.

McCarthy, W. J., and Gritz, E. R. Teenagers' responses to cigarette advertising. Paper presented at the meeting of the American Psychological Association, New York, August 1987.

McDade, E. A., and Keil, J. E. Characterization of a soup kitchen population. Paper presented at the American Heart Association Conference on Epidemiology, Santa Fe, NM, March 1988.

McIntyre-Kingsolver, K., Lichtenstein, E., Mermelstein, R. J. Spouse training in a multicomponent smoking-cessation program. *Behav Ther* 17:67–74, 1986.

Marlatt, G. A., and Gordon, J. R., eds. *Relapse Prevention: Maintenance Strategies in the Treatment of Addictive Behaviors.* New York: Guilford Press, 1985.

Mermelstein, R., Cohen, S., Lichtenstein, E., Baer, J. S., Kamarck, T. Social support and smoking cessation and maintenance. *J Consult Clin Psychol* 54:447–453, 1986.

Mitic, W. R., McGuire, D. P., Neumann, B. Perceived stress and adolescent cigarette use. *Psychol Rep* 57:1043–1048, 1985.

Mittelmark, M. B., Murray, D. M., Luepker, R. V., Pechacek, T. F., Pirie, P. L., Pallonen, U. E. Predicting experimentation with cigarettes: The childhood antecedents of smoking study (CASS). *Am J Public Health* 77(2):206–208, 1987.

Morgan, G. D., Ashenberg, Z. S., Fisher, E. B., Jr. Abstinence from smoking and the social environment. *J Consult Clin Psychol* 56(2): 298–301, 1988.

Mosbach, P., and Leventhal, H. Peer group iden-

tification and smoking: Implications for intervention. *J Abnorm Psychol* 97(2):238–245, 1988.

Niaura, R. S., Rohsenow, D. J., Binkoff, J. A., Monti, P. M., Pedraza, M., Abrams, D. B. Relevance of cue reactivity to understanding alcohol and smoking relapse. *J Abnorm Psychol* 97(2):133–152, 1988.

Ockene, J. K. Clinical perspectives: Physician-delivered interventions for smoking cessation: Strategies for increasing effectiveness. *Prev Med* 16:723–737, 1987.

Ockene, J. K., Hosmer, D. W., Williams, J. W., Goldberg, R. J., Ockene, I. S., Raia, T. J., III. Factors related to patient smoking status. *Am J Public Health* 77(3):356–357, 1987.

Orleans, C. T., Schoenbach, V. J., Salmon, M. A., Strecher, V. J., Kalsbeek, W., Quade, D., Brooks, E. F., Konrad, T. R., Blackmon, C., Watts, C. D. A survey of smoking and quitting patterns among black Americans. *Am J Public Health* 79:176–181, 1989.

Perri, M. G., Richards, C. S., Schultesis, K. R. Behavioral self-control and smoking reduction: A study of self-initiated attempts to reduce smoking. *Behav Ther* 8:360–365, 1977.

Pierce, J., Farkas, A., Evans, N., Berry, C., Chio, W., Rosbrook, B., Johnson, M., Bal, D. G. *Tobacco Use in California: A Focus on Preventing Uptake in Adolescents.* Sacramento: California Department of Health Services, 1993.

Pierce, J., Gilpin, E., Burns, D., Whalen, E., Rosbrook, R., Shopland, D., Johnson, M. Does tobacco advertising target young people to start smoking? Evidence from California. *JAMA* 266(22):3154–3158, 1991.

Pirie, P. L., Murrary, D. M., Luepker, R. V. Smoking prevalence in a cohort of adolescents, including absentees, dropouts, and transfers. *Am J Public Health* 78(2):176–178, 1988.

Pomerleau, O. F., Adkins, D., Pertschuk, M. Predicters of outcome and recidivism in smoking cessation treatment. *Addict Behav* 3:65–70, 1978.

Pomerleau, O. F., and Pomerleau, C. S. A biobehavioral view of substance abuse and addiction. *J Drug Issues* 17:111–131, 1987.

Prochaska, J. O., and DiClemente, C. C. Stages and processes of self-change of smoking: Toward an integrative model of change. *J Consult Clin Psychol* 51(3):390–395, 1983.

Rachlin, H. *Introduction to Modern Behaviorism.* 3d ed., New York: Freeman, 1991.

Rausch, J. L., Nichinson, B., Lamke, C., Matloff, J. Influence of negative affect of smoking cessation treatment outcome: A pilot study. *Br J Addict* 85(7):929–933, 1990.

Remington, P. L., Forman, M. R., Gentry, E. M., Marks, J. S., Hogelin, G. S., Trowbridge, F. L. Current smoking trends in the United States. The 1981–1983 Behavioral Risk Factor Surveys. *JAMA* 253(20):2975–2978, 1985.

Rodin, J. Weight change following smoking cessation: The role of food intake and exercise. *Addict Behav* 12:303–317, 1987.

Rosenstock, I. M. The health belief model and preventive health behavior. *Health Ed Monogr* 2:354–386, 1974.

Rytter, L., Troelsen, S., Beck-Nielsen, H. Prevalence and mortality of acute myocardial infarction on patients with diabetes. *Diabetes Care* 8(3):230–234, 1985.

Sachs, D.P.L. Cigarette smoking: Health effects and cessation strategies. *Respiratory Dis* 2(2):337–362, 1984.

Severson, H. H., Glasgow, R., Wirt, R., Brozovsky, P., Zoref, L., Black, C., Biglan, A., Ary, D., Weissman, W. Preventing the use of smokeless tobacco and cigarettes by teens: Results of classroom intervention. *Health Educ Res* 6(1):109–120, 1991.

Shiffman, S., Relapse following smoking cessation: A situational analysis. *J Consult Clin Psychol* 50:71–86, 1982.

———. A cluster-analytic classification of smoking relapse episodes. *Addict Behav* 11:295–307, 1986.

———. Psychosocial factors in smoking and quitting: Health beliefs, self-efficacy, and stress. In Ockene, J. K., ed. *The Pharmacological Treatment of Nicotine Dependence.* Cambridge, MA: Harvard University Press, 1987, 48–62.

Shimokata, H., Muller, D. C., Andres, R. Studies in the distribution of body fat. *JAMA* 261(8):1169–1173, 1989.

Shore, G., president of Gene Shore Associates of Narbeth, PA. Letter to Ms. Penny Cohen, Marketing Research, R. J. Reynolds Company, Winston-Salem, N.C., 5 September 1989.

Silverman, A. P. Behaviour of rats given a "smoking dose" of nicotine. *Anim Behav* 19:67–74, 1971.

Silverstein, B., Kelly, E., Swan, J., Kozlowski, L. T. Physiological predisposition toward becoming a cigarette smoker. Experimental evidence for a sex difference. *Addict Behav* 7(1):83–86, 1982.

Skinner, B. F. *Science and Human Behavior.* New York: Macmillan, 1953.

Sorenson, G., Pechacek, T., Pallonen, U. Occupational and worksite norms and attitudes about smoking cessation. *Am J Public Health* 76(5):544–549, May 1986.

Sorenson, G., and Pechacek, T. F. Attitudes toward smoking cessation among men and women. *J Behav Med* 10(2):129–137, April 1987.

Spaulding, W. D., and Cole, J. K., eds. *Theories of Schizophrenia and Psychosis. Nebraska Symposium on Motivation, 1983.* Lincoln: University of Nebraska Press, 1984.

Ticer, S. Where there's smoke, there's trouble. *Business Week* 18 January 1988.

Tonnesen, P., Fryd, V., Hansen, M., Helsted, J., Gunnersen, A. B., Forchammer, H., Stockner, M. Two and four mg nicotine chewing gum and group counseling in smoking cessation: An open, randomized, controlled trial with a 22 month follow up. *Addict Behav* 13(1):17–27, 1988.

Tye, J. B., Warner, K. E., Glantz, S. A. Tobacco advertising and consumption: Evidence of a causal relationship. *J Public Health Policy* 8(4):492–508, 1987.

U.S. Department of Health and Human Services (USDHHS). *The Health Consequences of Smoking for Women. A Report of the Surgeon General.* U.S. Department of Health and Human Services, Public Health Service, Office of the Assistant Secretary for Health, Office on Smoking and Health, 1980.

———. *The Health Consequences of Smoking: Cancer. A Report of the Surgeon General.* U.S. Department of Health and Human Services, Public Health Service, Office on Smoking and Health. DHHS Publication No. (PHS)82-50179, 1982.

———. *The Health Consequences of Smoking: Chronic Obstructive Lung Disease. A Report of the Surgeon General.* U.S. Department of Health and Human Services, Public Health Service, Office on Smoking and Health. DHHS Publication No. (PHS)84-50205, 1984.

———. *The Health Consequences of Smoking: Nicotine Addiction. A Report of the Surgeon General.* U.S. Department of Health and Human Services, Public Health Service, Centers for Disease Control, Center for Health Promotion and Education, Office on Smoking and Health. DHHS Publication No. (CDC)88-8406, 1988.

———. *Reducing the Health Consequences of Smoking: 25 Years of Progress. A Report of the Surgeon General.* U.S. Department of Health and Human Services, Public Health Service, Centers for Disease Control, Center for Chronic Disease Prevention and Health Promotion, Office on Smoking and Health. DHHS Publication No. (CDC) 89-8411, 1989.

U.S. Public Health Service (USPHS). *Smoking and Health: Report of Advisory Committee to the Surgeon General.* U.S. Department of Health, Education and Welfare, Public Health Service, Centers for Disease Control. PHS Publication No. 1103, 1964.

Velicer, W. F., Diclemente, C. C., Prochaska, J. O., Brandenburg, N. Decisional balance measure for assessing and predicting smoking status. *J Pers Soc Psychol* 48(5):1279–1289, 1985.

Warner, K., Goldenhar, L., McLaughlin, C. Cigarette advertising and magazine coverage of the hazards of smoking. A statistical analysis. *N Engl J Med* 326:305–309, 1992.

————. Effects of the antismoking campaign: An update. *Am J Public Health* 79:144–151, 1989.

West, D. W., Graham, S., Swanson, M., Wilkin-son, G. Five year follow-up of a smoking withdrawal clinic population. *Am J Public Health* 67(6):536–544, 1977.

West, R. J., Hajek, P., Belcher, M. Severity of withdrawal symptoms as a predictor of outcome of an attempt to quit smoking. *Psychol Med* 19:981–985, 1989.

Wikler, A. Requirements for extinction of relapse-facilitating variables and for rehabilitation in a narcotic-antagonist program. *Adv Biochem Psychopharmacol* 8:399–414, 1973.

Williamson, D. F., Madans, J., Anda, R. F., Kleinman, J. C., Giovino, G. A., Byers, T. Smoking cessation and severity of weight gain in a national coliont. *N Engl J Med* 324:739–745, 1991.

Zametkin, A. J., Nordahl, T. E., Gross, M., King, A. C., Semple, W. E., Rumsey J., Hamburger, S., Cohen, R. M. Cerebral glucose metabolism in adults with hyperactivity of childhood onset. *N Engl J Med* 323(20):1362–1366, 1990.

5

Natural History and Epidemiology of Tobacco Use and Addiction

MICHAEL C. FIORE, POLLY NEWCOMB, and PATRICK MCBRIDE

While tobacco products have been consumed in the United States for many centuries, cigarette smoking was an uncommon behavior at the beginning of this century. In 1900, approximately 7 pounds of tobacco were consumed on a per capita basis for every adult in the United States (Shopland 1986). Of this, about 4 pounds were in the form of chewing tobacco, 1.6 pounds of pipe tobacco, and 0.3 pounds of snuff. In 1900, less than 1 pound of tobacco was consumed as cigars or cigarettes. By 1918, however, cigarette consumption had surpassed all other forms of tobacco use and the epidemic of cigarette smoking had begun.

Using per capita consumption data from the U.S. Department of Agriculture (USDA 1987), approximately 50 cigarettes were smoked in 1900 for each adult aged 18 years and older (Figure 5–1). The widespread adoption of smoking began during the 1910s with the introduction of Camel cigarettes and its imitators (see Chapter 1). These new products were easily inhaled compared with earlier products, thus directly exposing the pulmonary system to a host of toxins and providing a highly effective means of delivering nicotine.

Per capita cigarette consumption (Figure 5–1) increased rapidly during the first half of this century, at a rate of 5–15% per year. This rate of increase slowed during the 1950s, a phenomenon that coincided with the dissemination of the first scientific reports linking cigarette smoking to lung cancer (Wyn-

der and Graham 1950; Levine 1950; Mills and Porter 1950; Schrenk 1950). Consumption peaked in 1963 when approximately 4,300 cigarettes per year were consumed for every adult in the United States. Per capita cigarette consumption began to decline in 1964, the year the first Surgeon's General's report was released (USDHEW 1964). Consumption has declined in nearly every year since. Since 1964, adult consumption has declined by about a third, to 2,800 cigarettes for every U.S. adult in 1990.

Per capita consumption provided an overall estimate of cigarette use for the U.S. population, but no information regarding the differential smoking rates among various segments of our society. An accurate description of trends in tobacco use is essential in order to estimate the magnitude of the smoking problem and to target public health intervention to those individuals most at risk for the health consequences resulting from cigarette smoking.

In 1955, the National Cancer Institute (NCI) conducted the Current Population Survey (CPS) (NCHS 1958), the first large-scale national survey to assess population characteristics including smoking prevalence. More recently, in 1965 and periodically since that time (1966, 1970, 1974, 1977, 1978, 1979, 1980, 1983, 1985, 1987, and 1990), the National Health Interview Survey (NHIS) conducted by the National Centers for Health Statistics (NCHS 1985) has included an assessment of tobacco use.

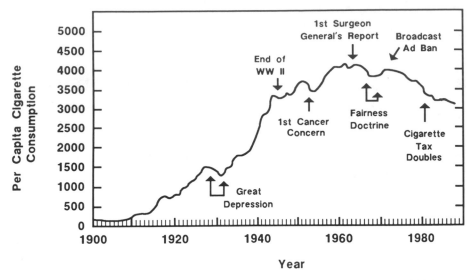

Fig. 5–1   Per capita cigarette consumption in the United States by year from 1900 to 1989. *Source:* USDHHS 1989.

These surveys provide the most detailed estimates of cigarette smoking in the United States over the last 25 years. Other national, representative sources of data to assess tobacco use in the United States have included the National Household Surveys on Drug Abuse conducted by the National Institute on Drug Abuse (Bachman, Johnston, O'Mally 1987), the Adult Use of Tobacco Surveys (AUTS) conducted by the United States Office on Smoking and Health (CDC) (USDHHS 1989), and, the National Health and Nutrition Examination Survey (NHANES-I), and its follow-up, the Epidemiologic Follow-up Study (NHEFS), both conducted by the National Center for Health Statistics (NCHS 1987). In addition, nongovernmental sources such as the Gallup Poll have provided additional sources of information on smoking, including some of the earliest information on tobacco-use prevalence.

TRENDS IN CIGARETTE SMOKING— OVERALL AND BY SEX

The NCI's 1955 CPS showed that approximately 39% of all adults (aged 20 years and older) smoked, with men smoking at more than twice the rate of women (53 vs. 24%, respectively) (NCHS 1958). One decade later, the 1965 and 1966 NHIS demonstrated that overall smoking prevalence had risen to its highest recorded rate of 41% of the adult population (USDHHS 1990). This increase in prevalence was almost exclusively the result of an increase in smoking among women which rose from 24% in 1955 to 34% by 1965. In contrast, smoking among men remained essentially the same over this time period and was measured at 52% in 1965.

Data from the NHIS have shown that the overall prevalence of smoking has declined since 1965 at a slow, but steady, rate of about 0.45 percentage points per year, falling from 40.4% in 1965 to 25.5% in 1990 (Table 5–1) (Fiore et al. 1989; CDC 1992). This decline has not been equal between the sexes. Among women, the prevalence of smoking has declined at a rate of only 0.36 percentage points per year, falling from 31.9% in 1965 to 22.8% in 1990 (Table 5–1). For men, the rate of decline has been four times that observed for females. Smoking prevalence among men has declined at a rate of 0.87 percentage points per year from 50.2% in 1965 to 28.4% in 1990 (Table 5–1). If current trends continue, differences in smoking prevalence between the sexes will disappear and even reverse during the 1990s.

Table 5-1   Trends in Smoking Prevalence (%) in the U.S., Adults Aged 20 Years and Older, 1965-90

Year	Overall Population	Sex		Race		Educational Level			
		Males	Females	Whites	Blacks	Less Than High School Graduate	High School Graduate	Some College	College Graduate
1965[a]	40.4	50.2	31.9	40.0	43.0				
1966	40.7	50.8	32.0	40.4	42.9	36.5	41.1	42.5	33.7
1970	37.0	44.3	30.8	36.5	41.4	34.8	38.3	36.7	28.1
1974	36.9	43.4	31.4	36.1	44.0	36.5	37.6	36.9	28.3
1976	36.1	42.1	31.3	35.6	41.2	35.8	37.8	36.4	27.4
1977	35.6	40.9	31.4	34.9	41.8	35.8	38.4	35.2	25.6
1978	34.0	39.0	29.6	33.6	38.2	35.3	36.5	32.7	23.8
1979	33.5	38.4	29.2	33.2	36.8	34.9	35.4	33.3	23.4
1980	33.3	38.5	29.0	32.9	37.2	35.5	35.7	31.2	24.6
1983	31.8	35.5	28.7	31.4	36.6	34.7	35.6	30.0	19.9
1985	30.4	33.2	28.0	29.9	36.0	35.7	34.2	28.1	18.4
1987	29.1	31.7	26.8	28.8	34.0	35.7	33.1	26.1	16.3
1990	25.5	28.4	22.8	25.6	26.2	31.8	29.6	23.0	13.5
Trend Information (1965-85)									
Change[b]/year	-0.50	-0.84	-0.21	-0.50	-0.39	-0.06	-0.32	-0.70	-0.76
Standard error (±)	0.03	0.04	0.03	0.03	0.08	0.03	0.05	0.07	0.08
R^2	0.97	0.98	0.81	0.97	0.74	NA[d]	0.87	0.94	0.93

Source: National Health Interview Surveys (NHIS) (USDHHS 1989 and CDC 1992).
[a]For 1965, data stratified by education were not available.
[b]In percentage points.
[c]The slope of the regression line was not significantly different from zero, making the R^2 computation inappropriate.

TRENDS IN CIGARETTE SMOKING BASED ON RACE AND ETHNIC ORIGIN

Black, White, and Hispanic Americans

There are significant differences in smoking prevalence between different racial and ethnic groups in the United States. The most detailed information regarding these differences is available for black and white Americans.

Since the early 1960s, smoking prevalence rates have consistently been higher among blacks when compared to whites (USDHHS 1989) although this gap has narrowed considerably. Among blacks overall, the prevalence rate has declined from 43.0% in 1965 to 26.2% in 1990. Among whites overall, the prevalence rate has declined from 40.0% in 1965 to 25.6% in 1990 (Table 5-1). The *rate* of decline per year, however, has not been significantly different between these two races over the last 25 years (Fiore et al. 1989). Since 1965, smoking prevalence among blacks has declined at a rate of 0.67 percentage points per year while smoking prevalence for whites has declined at a rate of 0.58 percentage points per year. For

smoking prevalence rates to equalize between the races, the decline among blacks must accelerate in relation to whites.

While smoking prevalence has been consistently higher among blacks than whites, the proportion of heavier smokers (more than 20 cigarettes per day) among black smokers has been consistently lower when compared to whites. The 1985 NHIS reported that approximately 21.0% of white smokers reported smoking more than 20 cigarettes per day while only 10.4% of black smokers reported smoking more than 20 cigarettes per day (USDHHS 1989).

Smoking prevalence among Hispanics in the United States has consistently been lower than that observed among whites and blacks in this country. These differences, however, are narrowing and are noted primarily among Hispanic females. Using data from the NHIS, the prevalence rate among Hispanic men had fallen to 30.9% by 1990 among males, a rate not markedly different from the overall male rate of 28.4%. Among Hispanic females, the smoking prevalence rate was reported at 16.3%, a rate markedly

Table 5–2 Age-adjusted Smoking Rates (%) for Hispanics Living in the U.S., Adults Aged 20–74 Years, 1982–84

	Males	Females
Mexican-Americans	43	24
Cuban-Americans	42	24
Puerto Ricans	40	30

Source: Hispanic Health and Nutrition Examination Survey (HHANES) (Hayes 1987).

lower than the rate of 22.8% reported for women overall.

The Hispanic Health and Nutrition Examination Survey (HHANES) collected information on smoking among Hispanics between 1982 and 1984 (Hayes 1987). Unlike the NHIS, this survey targeted Hispanics specifically in order to provide a representative sample of the three largest Hispanic groups in the United States (Puerto Ricans in the New York City area; Cuban-Americans in Dade County, Florida; and Mexican-Americans in the Southwest). Utilizing the HHANES, the age-adjusted smoking rates for Hispanic males aged 20–74 years were 43% for Mexican-Americans, 42% for Cuban-Americans, and 40% for Puerto Ricans (Table 5–2). Among Hispanic females, the smoking prevalence rate was 24% for Mexican-Americans, 24% for Cuban-Americans, and 30% for Puerto Rican Americans (Table 5–2).

American Indians and Alaskan Natives

While no national representative data are available for native American populations, surveys have assessed smoking rates among specific Indian tribes and on specific Indian reservations (CDC June 1987). These surveys have reported extremely high rates of smoking prevalence among Northern Plain Indians (42–70%) and Alaskan natives (56%). Lower rates have been reported for Indians from the Southwest (13–28%). Extremely high rates of smokeless tobacco use also have been reported among native American populations.

TRENDS IN CIGARETTE SMOKING BASED ON EDUCATIONAL STATUS

At the time of the release of the first Surgeon General's Report in 1964 (USDHEW 1964),

small differences were noted in smoking rates across educational groups. Using data from the 1966 NHIS, the smoking prevalence rate was reported at 36.5% among high school dropouts (less than 12 years of education), 41.1% among high school graduates (exactly 12 years of education), 42.5% among persons with some college education (13–15 years of education), and 33.7% among college graduates (16 or more years of education) (Pierce et al. 1989a). By 1990, these differences had widened dramatically (Table 5–1). In 1990, the prevalence rate had fallen only slightly among high school dropouts (to 31.8%, −0.20 percentage points per year) and among high school graduates (to 29.5%, −0.48 percentage points per year). In contrast, among persons with some college education (13–15 years of education), smoking prevalence declined 0.81 percentage points per year from 1965 to a level of 23.0% by 1990. Among college graduates, smoking prevalence declined an impressive 0.84 percentage points per year since 1965 to a level of 13.5% by 1990. Educational status has replaced gender as the sociodemographic variable most highly predictive of differences in smoking prevalence rates.

TRENDS IN CIGARETTE SMOKING AMONG TEENAGERS

Unfortunately, systematic surveys to assess smoking among the total population of United States teens have not been conducted on a regular basis over the last 25 years. The United States Office on Smoking and Health recently completed (1990) the first representative survey of all teens since 1979. This telephone survey will provide extensive information of a wide variety of information regarding tobacco usage and attitudes.

The National Institute on Drug Abuse (NIDA) High School Senior Survey (Bachman, Johnston, O'Mally 1987) has provided some tobacco use information on a representative sample of that subpopulation of teenagers who attend their senior year (grade 12) of high school. While a consistent longitudinal source of information on teenage tobacco use, these data must be considered within the constraints inherent in a survey limited to individuals who attend the senior

Table 5–3 Self-Reported Prevalence (%) of Daily Smoking among High School Seniors by Sex, Race, and Educational Plans, U.S., 1975–90

Education	Sex		Race		Plans for Higher Education	
	Males	Females	Whites	Blacks	Yes	No
1975	27	26				
1976	28	28	29	26	21	37
1977	28	30	28	25	20	38
1978	26	29	27	22	18	36
1979	22	28	26	19	17	35
1980	18	24	22	16	14	31
1981	18	22	20	13	13	30
1982	18	24	23	12	13	30
1983	19	23	22	12	14	30
1984	16	21	20	8	11	29
1985	17	21	20	11	13	31
1986	17	20	21	8	12	29
1987	16	20	20	8	14	30
1990	13	13	16	2		

Source: National Institute on Drug Abuse (NIDA) High School Senior Survey (Bachman, Johnston, O'Mally 1987).

year in high school. As described in the previous section, the highest prevalence rate of smoking is found among persons who have dropped out of high school.

With these considerations in mind, the NIDA survey has been an excellent source of information on teenage tobacco for nearly two decades. Table 5–3 highlights some important findings regarding teenage tobacco use during the recent past.

First, during the mid-1970s, the prevalence rate of daily smoking among teenage girls exceeded that observed among boys for the first time. Since 1977, high school senior girls have reported a higher rate of daily cigarette smoking than their male classmates. In that the vast majority of smokers start to smoke during their teenage years (McGinnis, Shopland, Brown 1987), this preponderance of young women starting to smoke is the primary factor leading to the convergence of smoking rates between men and women overall. If young women continue to exceed young men in rates of smoking initiation during the 1990s, the smoking prevalence rate among women will soon equal and then overtake the rate for men (Figure 5–2).

Second, the decline in teenage daily smoking observed during the 1960s and 1970s did not continue in the 1980s. Since 1980, 20–24% of senior high school girls reported daily

smoking, and only 16–19% of boys reported daily smoking. This stagnation in the decline of smoking prevalence among high school seniors means that teenage smoking initiation has not changed in the past decade. This is a leading factor explaining the slow rate of decline in smoking prevalence among adults overall in recent years.

Finally, differences in rates of daily cigarette smoking have been observed among high school seniors based on race and educational aspirations. Black high school seniors have consistently reported a lower prevalence of daily smoking than whites with black prevalence in 1990 less than half that of whites. Also, seniors who plan to pursue higher education consistently report lower daily smoking prevalence than their counterparts who do not plan to continue their formal education.

TRENDS IN CIGARETTE SMOKING AMONG DIFFERENT OCCUPATIONAL GROUPS

The NHIS have provided information on smoking prevalence based on occupational status for the years 1970, 1978–80, and 1985. For each of these years, smoking prevalence was significantly higher among unemployed persons in the United States when compared with employed persons (Table 5–

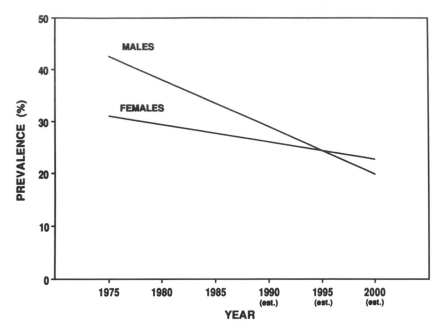

Fig. 5-2 Trends in the prevalence of cigarette smoking for men and women with projections to the year 2000, adults, aged 20 and older, United States. *Source:* USDHHS 1989.

4). In 1985, smoking prevalence among un-employed persons was 36.1% while that for employed persons was 32.1%. This finding was substantiated by Novotny and col-leagues (1988) who performed multivariate logistic regression analysis on data from the 1985 NHIS. Using a model that included sex, occupation, education, race, marital sta-tus, poverty status, and employment status, they reported that unemployed persons were significantly more likely than employed per-sons to be current or former smokers.

Among employed persons, there has been a consistent pattern of higher smoking prev-alence among blue-collar workers when

compared with white-collar workers (Table 5-4). Using data from the 1985 NHIS, smoking prevalence among blue-collar workers overall was 39.7% while prevalence among white-collar workers was 27.5%. The smoking prevalence rate among service workers was reported at an intermediate rate of 37.2%.

TRENDS IN CIGARETTE SMOKING AMONG MILITARY PERSONNEL

Since 1980, the U.S. Department of Defense (USDOD) has periodically surveyed U.S. military personnel regarding their smoking

Table 5-4 Prevalence of Smoking (%) by Occupation, 1970, 1978-80, and 1985

Occupation	1970[a]		1978-80[a]		1985[b]		
	Males	Females	Males	Females	Males	Females	Total
Currently employed	47.9	36.5	39.9	33.3	33.8	30.0	32.1
White collar	40.8	36.1	33.0	31.9	26.4	28.0	27.5
Blue collar	55.0	37.7	47.1	38.1	40.1	33.9	39.7
Service	53.3	39.4	47.5	37.4	40.3	35.4	37.2
Unemployed	55.9	42.3	53.1	39.6	44.3	28.0	36.1

Source: National Health Interview Surveys (NHIS) (USDHHS 1989)
[a] Aged 20-64 years.
[b] Aged 20 years and older.

Table 5-5 Prevalence of Cigarette Smoking (%) among U.S. Military Personnel, 1980, 1982, 1985, and 1988

Rank[b]	Percentage of Current Smokers[a]			
	1980 (n = 15,016)	1982 (n = 21,412)	1985 (n = 17,328)	1988[c] (n = 18,673)
E1–3	55	56	47	47
E4–6	55	55	52	45
E7–9	56	61	56	48
W1–4			40	34
O1–O3				19
O1 O2	24	25	17	
O3	23	24	18	
O4–O10			21	20
O4–O6	27	28		
Total	52	53	46	42

Source: USDHHS 1989.

[a]Persons who had smoked cigarettes during the past 30 days.

[b]In ascending rank, from enlisted personnel (E1–9) to warrant officers (W1–W4) to commissioned officers (O1–O10).

[c]Preliminary data (not adjusted for nonrespondents).

behavior (Herbold 1987; USDOD 1986, 1987, 1988). The results show that smoking prevalence has declined among military personnel over the last decade, falling from 52% overall in 1980 to 42% in 1988 (Table 5–5). For all years reported, the rate of smoking among military personnel was markedly higher than rates observed among their civilian counterparts.

These data also demonstrate an inverse relationship between military rank and smoking prevalence rate; the highest rate was observed among enlisted personnel (E1–E9), followed by warrant officers (W1–W4), followed by commissioned officers (01–06). In 1988, the rate among enlisted military personnel was about 47%, among warrant officers about 34%, and among commissioned officers about 20%. Estimates for the individual military branches showed a 1988 prevalence rate of 37% for the Air Force, 42% for the Marine Corps, 44% for the Army, and 45% for the Navy.

STATE-SPECIFIC TRENDS IN CIGARETTE SMOKING

Since 1982, the United States Centers for Disease Control has periodically conducted the Behavioral Risk Factor Surveillance System (BRFS) (CDC May 1987, June 1987). This telephone survey uses a random digit dialing methodology to provide state-specific estimates regarding a wide variety of

health behaviors including smoking prevalence among adults aged 18 years and older. Not all states have participated in the BRFS. Forty-five states were included in the system in 1990. For this reason, these data are not representative of the entire U.S. population.

Smoking rates have varied widely across states. For example, in 1990, Utah, the state with the lowest prevalence estimate among those surveyed, reported an overall smoking prevalence of 17%. In contrast, Kentucky had the highest prevalence estimate from the BRFS, reporting a smoking rate of 29% in 1990 (Table 5–6). Overall, the BRFS has consistently provided lower smoking prevalence estimates when compared with other large, representative, state-specific surveys such as the CPS. The lower prevalence estimates of the BRFS compared to the CPS (median difference of 1.8 percentage points) has been ascribed to the data collection methodology. The CPS conducts in-person surveys similar to the NHIS while the BRFS conducts telephone surveys which may underreport smoking prevalence (USDHHS 1991).

TRENDS IN THE NUMBER OF CIGARETTES SMOKED PER DAY

Since 1974, the NHIS has asked smokers the number of cigarettes smoked per day. The percentage of smokers who report they are "heavy smokers" (25 or more cigarettes/

Table 5–6 State-specific Smoking Prevalence (%), Behavioral Risk Factor Surveillance System, Adults Aged 18 Years and Older, 1982–90

State	1982	1984	1985	1986	1987	1990
Alabama	31			25	27	22
Alaska	36	34				
Arizona	32	28	26	24	26	21
Arkansas	27					
California	28	26	26	25	21	20
Colorado	34					21
Connecticut			27			22
Delaware	31					23
District of Columbia	33	38	26	27	24	19
Florida	32		27	28	28	24
Georgia	29	37	29	27	25	24
Hawaii				25	23	21
Idaho		25	24	23	21	21
Illinois		34	26	28	26	24
Indiana	33	28	32	27	29	27
Iowa	30					22
Kansas	22					
Kentucky	37		29	35	32	29
Louisiana						25
Maine					28	27
Maryland					25	22
Massachusetts				27	25	24
Michigan	31					29
Minnesota		27	28	25	24	21
Mississippi						29
Missouri				26	29	26
Montana	26	29	25	23	22	19
Nebraska	23					23
New Hampshire	29					22
New Jersey	32					
New Mexico	29			26	21	22
New York			31	27	23	22
North Carolina	38	31	27	27	26	28
North Dakota		28	26	26	24	20
Ohio	30	29	29	28	27	26
Oklahoma						26
Oregon						22
Pennsylvania	34					24
Rhode Island		31	29	39		26
South Carolina		26	29	27	25	25
South Dakota					25	21
Tennessee	32	32	28	28	28	27
Texas	30					23
Utah		16	16	18	15	17
Virginia	34					23
Washington					24	22
West Virginia	32	33	27	29	29	27
Wisconsin		27	25	26	26	25
Minimum	22	16	16	18	15	17
Maximum	38	38	32	35	32	29
Median	37	29	27	26	24	23
No. of States[a]	27	19	22	26	29	44

Source: USDHHS 1989, CDC 1992.

[a]Includes the District of Columbia.

Note: No data were available for the following states: Nevada, and Wyoming.

day) has changed little from a reported 26.0% of current smokers in 1974 to 27.1% of current smokers in 1985 (Table 5–7).

INTERNATIONAL TRENDS IN CIGARETTE SMOKING

While data for the developed world have been regularly collected in a number of countries, less information is available for the developing world. In 1989, Pierce reviewed trends in cigarette smoking prevalence among six developed countries (Australia, Canada, Great Britain, Norway, Sweden, United States). He noted that, since 1974, sex-specific prevalence had decreased in all countries studied with the exception of Norway, where women showed a small increase in smoking prevalence. As in the United States, the rate of decline in adult smoking prevalence followed a linear pattern in most of these countries. By 1987, the lowest smoking prevalence rate among men in the countries studied was in Sweden (24%) while the highest male rate was in Norway (41.3%). Among women, the lowest prevalence rates by 1987 were noted in Canada, the United States, and Sweden (at 26.6, 26.8, and 27%, respectively) while the highest rate was noted in Norway (33.3%). Most of the countries reported an increasing gap in prevalence between higher and lower educational groups.

Chapmen and Wong (1990) reviewed tobacco use in the developing world in a report presented to the Seventh World Conference on Tobacco and Health in Perth, Australia. They emphasized that there has been a sig-

Table 5–7 Self-reported Cigarettes Smoked per Day (Percentage of Current Smokers), NHIS, U.S., Adults Aged 20 Years and Older, 1974–85

| Year | No. of Cigarettes Smoked Per Day | | |
	1–14	15–24	≥25
1974	30.8	43.2	26.0
1976	30.1	44.4	25.5
1977	30.3	43.2	26.5
1978	28.1	42.8	29.1
1979	28.2	43.0	28.8
1980	27.6	42.6	29.8
1983	28.5	44.9	26.6
1985	31.0	41.9	27.1

Source: USDHHS 1989.

nificant growth in tobacco use in the developing world with few efforts to control that use. Specifically, they pointed out that there are already more tobacco users in developing countries than in industrialized nations, with China alone responsible for 29% of the total world cigarette consumption in 1988— 1.5 trillion cigarettes. Moreover, the greater rate of population growth along with rising incomes and fewer marketing restrictions and public health programs leaves the developing world at grave risk for a large epidemic of tobacco use in the twenty-first century with an expected enormous burden of morbid complications.

Unfortunately, there is a dearth of information on prevalence trends in tobacco use among developing countries. Per capita consumption data, however, are available for a number of countries. For those countries, the overall pattern shows per capita consumption to be generally correlated with income, with wealthier developing countries having a much higher per capita consumption than that observed in poorer developing countries. Additionally, within the developing world, cigarette smoking continues to be a behavior practiced almost exclusively by males.

Data from 1985 showed per capita cigarette consumption rates averaged 679/yr in African countries, 1,150/yr in Asian/Pacific countries, and 1,279/yr in Latin American countries (Maisironi and Rothwell 1988). The individual country rates for per capita cigarette consumption in 1985 ranged from a low of 30 in Guinea-Bissau, 50 in Afghanistan, and 60 in Ethiopia, to a high of 1,590 in China, 2,880 in Lebanon, and 3,920 in Cuba. In contrast, per capita cigarette consumption in the United States for 1985 was 3,370.

TRENDS IN SMOKING INITIATION

Reliable, representative data regarding the rate of smoking initiation among the total population of young Americans has not been collected on a regular basis. It is known, however, that for most individuals, experimentation with cigarettes begins at an early age. About 62% of 10th grade students report that they have already smoked at least one cigarette and 50% report that they smoked their first cigarette by the 7th or 8th grade (USDHHS 1989). About 50% of both men and women who become smokers report that they started to smoke regularly by 18 years of age; about 90% report that they started by age 21 years (USDHHS 1989). The age of smoking initiation has remained constant across all age cohorts for men born during this century, while the age of smoking initiation among women has declined for those cohorts born during the latter half of this century.

Because 90% of Americans start to smoke by 20 years of age (McGinnis, Shopland, Brown 1987), the prevalence of smoking among persons aged 20 to 24 years has been used as a surrogate for smoking initiation (Fiore et al. 1989; USDHHS 1989). The NHIS over the last 25 years has collected information on smoking prevalence among persons aged 20–24 years, and this has been used to estimate rates of smoking initiation.

The rate of smoking initiation (as measured using smoking prevalence for persons aged 20–24 years) has declined at a rate of 0.80 percentage points per year from 47.8% in 1965 to 29.5% by 1987 (Table 5–8). The rate of decline for women overall was a modest 0.40 percentage points per year falling from 40.5% in 1965 to 28.1% in 1987 (Table 5–8). In contrast, the rate of decline among men (-1.27 percentage points per year) was more than three times that observed for women, falling from 56.3% in 1965 to 31.1% by 1987 (Table 5–8). This slower decline in the rate of smoking initiation among females is a main contributor to the gradual convergence in smoking prevalence rates between the sexes observed over the last 25 years.

Among blacks, smoking initiation has declined at a rate of 1.13 percentage points per year falling from 50.8% in 1965 to 25.6% by 1987 (Table 5–8). In contrast, the rate of smoking initiation among whites fell at a rate of only 0.75 percentage points per year from 47.5% in 1965 to 30.5% in 1987 (Table 5–8). If this lower rate of smoking initiation among blacks continues into the 1990s, the decline in smoking prevalence for blacks overall will accelerate in relation to whites.

Among educational groups, the rates of

Table 5–8   Trends in Smoking Initiation (%) in the U.S., Adults Aged 20–24 Years, 1965–87

| | | Sex | | Race | | Education Level | | | |
| | | | | | | High School Graduate or Less | | Some College or More | |
Year	Overall Population	Males	Females	Whites	Blacks	Males	Females	Males	Females
1965	47.8	56.3	40.5	47.5	50.8	63.6	42.6	42.7	34.5
1966	47.7	57.7	39.5	48.2	45.5	65.1	41.3	43.5	34.7
1970	41.5	48.5	35.8	41.2	45.2	60.0	40.2	33.2	26.8
1974	39.5	44.3	35.4	38.6	47.1	52.7	40.1	34.7	26.4
1976	39.6	45.9	34.2	39.5	42.3	54.1	41.0	34.4	23.0
1977	38.8	40.4	37.4	38.5	41.5	52.2	43.0	24.0	27.5
1978	35.4	38.5	32.5	35.7	34.8	46.8	39.3	25.9	21.1
1979	35.8	37.7	34.0	35.6	36.7	47.1	41.9	23.8	22.1
1980	36.1	40.0	32.5	35.9	37.9	50.1	40.3	20.1	19.4
1983	36.9	36.9	37.0	36.8	38.7	49.1	45.5	16.2	22.9
1985	31.8	31.0	32.5	32.5	28.2	43.0	43.6	15.5	17.2
1987[a]	29.5	31.1	28.1	30.5	25.6	43.8	37.6	16.3	15.1
Trend Information (1965–85)									
Change[b]/year	−0.69	−1.19	−0.28	−0.68	−0.79	−1.00	0.10	−1.51	−0.72
Standard error	0.09	0.10	0.12	0.09	0.17	0.13	0.10	0.13	0.15
R^2	0.86	0.94	0.40	0.85	0.71	0.87	NA[c]	0.95	0.75

Source: National Health Interview Surveys (NHIS) (USDHHS 1989).

[a]Provisional data only.

[b]In percentage points.

[c]The slope of the regression line was not significantly different from zero, making the R^2 computation inappropriate.

smoking initiation mirror the rates of smoking prevalence overall. By 1987, smoking initiation among persons with a 12th grade education (high school graduate) or less fell only slightly to 43.8% among males and 37.6% among females (Table 5–8). In contrast, for persons with at least some college education, the rate of smoking initiation fell markedly by 1987 to 16.3% for males and 15.1% for females (Table 5–8). The differences in smoking initiation rates based on educational status explain a large part of the increasing gap in overall smoking prevalence rates observed over the last 25 years.

TRENDS IN SMOKING CESSATION

Various measures have been used to measure quit smoking behavior (USDHHS 1989). The "quit ratio," defined as the proportion of ever smokers who are now former smokers, has been used in the recent Surgeon General's Reports on Smoking and Health to measure quit behavior. Other measures such as the percentage of former smokers in the entire population and the smoking continuum have also been used to

describe quitting behavior (USDHHS 1989).

The NHIS (1965–87) provide data which permit the calculation of the quit ratio over time (Table 5–9). The quit ratio among adult Americans overall has increased markedly over the last quarter century, from 29.6% in 1965 to 44.8% by 1987 (Table 5–9). By 1987, almost half of all Americans who had ever smoked had successfully quit.

This pattern of stopping smoking was noted for both men and women (Table 5–9). Among males, the quit ratio increased at a rate of 0.77 percentage points per year from 31.4% in 1965 to 49.8% in 1989. Among females, the quit ratio increased at a similar rate of 0.78 percentage points per year from 24.6% in 1965 to 43.3% by 1989. Large numbers of both men and women in the United States are quitting smoking each year, with a similar rate of increase in the quit ratio for the two genders (Fiore et al. 1989).

The quit ratio among whites increased at a rate of 0.69 percentage points per year from 30.5% in 1965 to 47.0% by 1989. In contrast, the quit ratio for blacks increased

Table 5–9 Trends in Smoking Quit Ratio (%) in the U.S., Adults Aged 20 Years and Older, 1965–89

		Sex		Race		Educational Level			
Year	Overall Population	Males	Females	Whites	Blacks	Less Than High School Graduate	High School Graduate	Some College	College Graduate
1965[a]	29.6	31.4	24.6	30.5	22.8				
1966	29.5	31.4	24.2	30.4	22.6	33.3	28.0	28.7	39.7
1970	35.3	37.9	29.2	36.7	23.2	38.1	33.6	34.9	48.2
1974	36.3	39.3	30.8	38.0	21.8	38.0	35.2	36.6	47.9
1976	37.1	39.9	32.1	38.4	26.3	39.5	35.0	37.2	46.1
1977	36.8	40.3	31.3	38.2	24.8	38.3	34.0	36.8	48.6
1978	38.5	41.3	33.8	39.9	27.5	38.7	36.3	41.0	49.7
1979	39.0	41.5	34.0	40.3	28.0	40.8	36.7	37.5	50.6
1980	39.0	41.5	34.0	40.4	27.7	39.4	36.5	40.6	48.7
1983	41.8	44.1	37.6	43.3	29.3	42.1	38.7	41.2	54.9
1985	45.0	49.0	40.0	46.7	31.8	41.3	40.5	46.0	61.1
1987	44.8	48.7	40.1	46.4	31.5	39.7	40.9	46.9	61.4
1989		49.8	43.3	47.0	39.1				
Trend Information (1965–85)									
Change[b]/year	+0.68	+0.73	+0.73	+0.72	+0.43	+0.41	+0.57	+0.73	+0.85
Standard error (±)	0.05	0.06	0.05	0.06	0.07	0.06	0.07	0.10	0.16
R^2	0.95	0.94	0.96	0.94	0.82	0.85	0.89	0.88	0.78

Source: National Health Interview Surveys (NHIS) (USDHHS 1989).
[a]For 1965, data stratified by education were not available.
[b]In percentage points.
Note: Quit ratio = (former smokers/current + former smokers).

at a slower rate of 0.68 percentage points per year from 22.8% in 1965 to 39.1% by 1989 (Table 5–9). This lower rate of change in the quit ratio among blacks has contributed to the continuing gap in smoking prevalence rates between blacks and whites overall in the United States.

Across educational groups, the quit ratio mirrors the overall prevalence rates for these subpopulations (Pierce et al. 1989a). For high school dropouts, the quit ratio increased at a rate of 0.42 percentage points per year over the last quarter century from 33.3 to 39.7% in 1987 (Table 5–9). Among high school graduates, the quit ratio increased at a rate of 0.65 percentage points per year from 28.0 to 40.9%. Among persons with some college education, the quit ratio increased at a rate of 0.91 percentage points per year from 28.7 to 46.9%. Finally, among college graduates, the quit ratio increased at a rate of 1.13 percentage points per year from 39.7 to 61.4% by 1987. That is, more than 60% of living college-educated persons who had ever smoked had quit by 1987. This high quit ratio combined with the low rate of smoking initiation among college graduates

is responsible for the extremely low overall prevalence rate (16.3% in 1987) observed in this sociodemographic subpopulation. In contrast, the low quit ratio combined with the high rate of smoking initiation among high school dropouts is responsible for the extremely high overall smoking prevalence rate (35.7% in 1987) observed in this group.

CHANGES IN THE TYPES OF CIGARETTES SMOKED

In 1950, less than 1% of the cigarettes sold in the United States had filters (Federal Trade Commission 1990). Since that time, the proportion of filter cigarettes in the United States has steadily increased to: 19% by 1955, 51% by 1960, 64% by 1965, 80% by 1970, 87% by 1975, 92% by 1980, and 95% by 1988 (See Table 1–2).

Additionally, the sales-weighted average yield of tar and nicotine for machine-smoked cigarettes sold in the United States has steadily decreased since the 1960s. For tar, the sales-weighted average yield has fallen from 35 mg in 1957 to 13 mg in 1987 with the proportion of "low tar" (15 mg or less) cigarettes sold in this country increasing from 2% in 1967 to 54% by 1988 (Federal Trade Commission 1990; USDHHS 1989). For nicotine, the sales weighted average yield declined from 1.3 mg in 1968 to 1.0 mg in 1987. For both tar and nicotine, most of the observed decline occurred during the 1960s and 1970s as a result of modifications in the design of cigarettes. For both tar and nicotine, the sales-weighted average yield leveled off during the 1980s. Finally, smokers tend to compensate for changes in average cigarette yield by changing the number of cigarettes smoked per day, by puffing more frequently or more deeply, and by making other, probably inadvertent, changes in smoking behavior (USDHHS 1988).

TRENDS IN CIGAR AND PIPE SMOKING

Unlike cigarette smoking, cigar and pipe smoking has remained primarily a male behavior. The 1986 AUTS reported that 8.7% of males and 0.3% of females were current cigar and/or pipe users and that 41.8% of males and 4.5% of females were former cigar and/or pipe users (USDHHS 1989). The AUTS data since the early 1960s indicate that there was a 80% decline in the prevalence of cigar and pipe smoking among men from 1964 to 1986. From 1964 to 1986, the prevalence of cigar smoking among men declined from 29.7 to 6.2%. The prevalence of pipe smoking among men decreased from 18.7 to 3.8% (Lazarus 1979).

TRENDS IN SMOKELESS TOBACCO USE IN THE UNITED STATES

During most of this century, the use of smokeless tobacco products (chewing tobacco and oral snuff) was concentrated among rural residents and particular occupational groups such as miners and agricultural workers (Maxwell 1980; Shelton 1982). Additionally, observed prevalence was highest among persons over the age of 50 years (USDHHS 1986). During the 1970s and 1980s, however, the use of smokeless tobacco products increased markedly among children and adolescents (USDHHS 1986).

Table 5–10 Prevalence (%) of Male Smokeless Tobacco Use by Age, U.S., 1970 and 1985

Age (yr)	Snuff		Chewing Tobacco	
	1970	1985	1970	1985
16–19	0.3	2.9	1.2	3.0
20–29	0.6	2.7	1.9	4.2
30–39	0.7	1.8	2.8	3.7
40–49	1.2	1.5	3.0	3.3
50+	2.7	1.4	6.5	4.2

Source: 1970 National Health Interview Survey (HHIS) and 1985 Current Population Survey (CPS) (Maxwell 1980).
[a]For 1970, this age group was composed of 17- to 19-year olds.

This coincided with an increase in smokeless tobacco advertising geared toward adolescents (Ernster 1989). Ironically, it also coincided with the publication of new biomedical and epidemiologic evidence which indicated that smokeless tobacco use causes oral cancers (USDHHS 1986; Mattson and Winn 1989) (Chapter 13).

Marcus and colleagues (1989) summarized data from the 1985 CPS regarding chewing tobacco, snuff, and total smokeless tobacco use. They found that smokeless tobacco use varied considerably between regions of the United States with the highest rates noted in the South and the lowest in the Northeast. Additionally, smokeless tobacco users were predominately male, about 5.5% of all males reported use of these products as compared to less than 1% of females. Moreover, more than 90% of all male smokeless tobacco users in 1985 were white. Smokeless tobacco use was also two to three times more prevalent among blue-collar workers when compared with white-collar workers.

These data from the 1985 CPS can be compared with the 1970 NHIS data (Table 5–10). This comparison highlights the enormous increases in smokeless tobacco use among adolescents over this time period. From 1970 to 1985, the use of snuff among 16 to 19 year olds increased nearly 10-fold from 0.3 to 2.4% while the use of chewing tobacco increased from 1.2 to 3.0%.

These findings were substantiated by Novotny and colleagues (1989) who reviewed data from the 1986 AUTS. These authors reported overall current smokeless tobacco use among males aged 17 and older at 5.2%

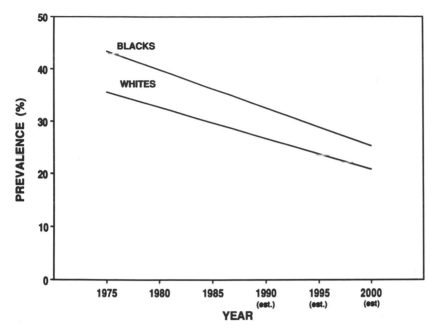

Fig. 5–3   Trends in the prevalence of cigarette smoking for blacks and whites with projections to the year 2000, adults, aged 20 and older, United States. *Source:* USDHHS 1989.

with the highest reported prevalence among males aged 17–19 years who reported a current use rate of 8.2%.

PROJECTIONS OF CIGARETTE SMOKING RATES TO THE YEAR 2000

As described earlier, cigarette smoking rates among adults overall in the United States have declined at a slow but steady rate since the early 1960s, falling by about 0.5 percentage points per year from about 41% in 1965 to 29% in 1987. While this represents significant progress over the last quarter century, 29% of all adults in 1987 still represented approximately 49 million adult Americans who smoke (Pierce et al. 1989b). Investigators at the United States Office on Smoking and Health (Pierce et al. 1989b) used data from the NHIS to project smoking rates through the year 2000. Using a linear regression analysis, they projected that, if present trends continue, smoking among adults in the U.S. overall will fall to 21.7% by the year 2000. This projected smoking rate will represent approximately 43 million adult

smokers in the year 2000. This is in contrast to the estimated 49 million adult smokers in the United States in 1987 (Pierce et al. 1989b).

When examining projections based on sex, cigarette smoking for men and women is projected to equalize by the mid-1990s and, thereafter, women are projected to smoke at a higher rate than men. If current trends continue, the rate of cigarette smoking among women is projected to decline to about 22.7% by the year 2000, while the rate for men is projected to fall to only 19.9% (Figure 5–2). Projections based on race suggest that smoking among blacks will fall to 24.5% by the year 2000, while smoking among whites will fall to about 21.5% (Figure 5–3).

The most dramatic differences in smoking rates are projected for persons across educational groups. If current trends continue (Pierce et al. 1989b), the rate of cigarette smoking for the year 2000 is projected to decline to approximately 5% among college graduates, to 16% among persons with some college education, to 30% among high

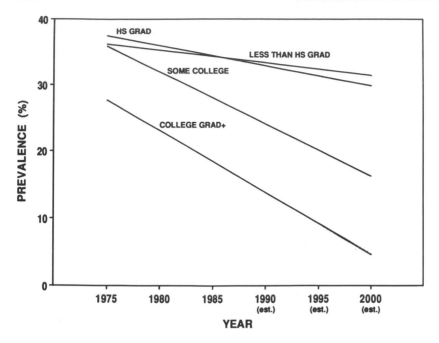

Fig. 5–4 Trends in the prevalence of cigarette smoking by educational status with projections to the year 2000, adults, aged 20 and older, United States. *Source:* USDHHS 1989.

school graduates, and, to 31% among persons who have completed less than 12 years of education (high school dropouts) (Figure 5–4). If these trends continue, cigarette smoking will increasingly be a behavior practiced predominately by poorly educated and socioeconomically disadvantaged segments of our society. Effective prevention and cessation interventions must increasingly focus on less educated Americans to produce the greatest impact on smoking rates into the next century.

REFERENCES

Bachman, J. G., Johnston, L. D., O'Mally, P. M. *Monitoring the Future. Questionnaire Responses from the Nation's High School Seniors, 1986.* Ann Arbor: University of Michigan, 1987.

Centers for Disease Control (CDC). Behavioral risk factor surveillance-selected states, 1986. *MMWR* 36(16):252–254, 1 May 1987.

———. Indian Health Service facilities become smoke-free. *MMWR* 36(22):348–350, 11 June 1987.

———. Cigarette smoking among adults— United States, 1990. *MMWR* 41:354–355, 1992.

Chapman, S., and Wong, W. L. *Tobacco Control in the Third World—A Resource Atlas.* Penang, Malaysia: International Organization of Consumers Unions, 1990.

Ernster, V. L. Advertising and promotion of smokeless tobacco products. In *Smokeless Tobacco Use in the United States.* National Cancer Institute Monographs. National Institutes for Health, National Cancer Institute, Division of Cancer Prevention and Control, Smoking, Tobacco, and Cancer Program. NIH Publication No. 89-3055, 1989, no. 8, pp. 87–94.

Federal Trade Commission. *Report to Congress Pursuant to the Federal Cigarette Labeling and Advertising Act, 1988.* Federal Trade Commission, May 1990.

Fiore, M. C., Novotny, T. E., Pierce, F. P., Hatziandreu, E. J., Patel, K. M., Davis, R. M. Trends in cigarette smoking in the United States. The changing influence of gender and race. *JAMA* 261(1):49–55, 6 January 1989.

Hayes, S. Statement. In *The Impact of Cigarette Smoking on Minority Populations. Proceedings of the Federal Interagency Committee of Smoking and Health.* U.S. Department of

Health and Human Services, Public Health Service, Centers for Disease Control, Center for Health Promotion and Education, Office on Smoking and Health. DHHS Publication No. HH/PHS/CDC-87-8403, 31 March 1987, 129–131.

Herbold, J. R. Smoking habits of U.S. military personnel. *Milit Med* 152(4):194–195, April 1987.

Lazarus, G. Cigar makers can's snuff out sales drop. *Chicago Tribune* 3 June 1979, sec. 5, p. 6.

Levine, M. L., Goldstein, H., Gerhardt, P. R. Cancer and tobacco smoking. A preliminary report. *JAMA* 143:336–338, 1950.

McGinnis, J. M., Shopland, D., Brown, C. Tobacco and health trends in smoking and smokeless tobacco consumption in the United States. *Ann Rev Public Health* 8:441–467, 1987.

Marcus, A. C., Crane, L. A., Shopland, D. R., Lynn, W. R. Use of smokeless tobacco in the United States: Recent estimates from the Current Population Survey. In *Smokeless Tobacco Use in the United States.* National Cancer Institute Monographs. National Institutes for Health, National Cancer Institute, Division of Cancer Prevention and Control, Smoking, Tobacco and Cancer Program. NIH Publication No. 89–3055, 1989, no. 8, 17–23.

Masironi, R., and Rothwell K. Tenderces et effects du tabagisme dans le monde. *Rapp Trimest Statist Sanit Mond* 41:228–241, 1988.

Mattson, M. E., and Winn, D. M. Smokeless tobacco: Association with increased cancer risk. In: *Smokeless Tobacco Use in the United States.* National Cancer Institute Monographs. National Institutes for Health, National Cancer Institute, Division of Cancer Prevention and Control, Smoking, Tobacco and Cancer Program. NIH Publication No. 89-3055, 1989, no. 8, 13–16.

Maxwell, J. R. Chewing snuff is growth segment. *Tobacco Reporter* p. 31, 1980.

National Center for Health Statistics (NCHS). *The Statistical Design of the Household-Interview Survey by the Staff of the U.S. National Health Survey and the Bureau of the Census.* DHEW Publication No. (PHS)583-4-A2, Hyattsville, Maryland, 1958.

———. *The National Health Interview Survey Design, 1973–1984 and Procedures, 1975–1983.* Vital and Health Statistics, ser. 1, no. 18. Public Health Service. DHHS Publication No. (HHS) 85-1320, 1985.

———. In Cohen, B. B., Barbano, H. E., Cox, C. S., Feldman, J. J., Finucane, F. F., Klein-man, J. C., Madans, J. H. *Plan and Operation of the NHANES I Epidemiological Followup Study 1982–1984.* Vital and Health and Statistics, ser. 1, no. 22. Public Health Service. DHHS Publication No. (PHS)87-1324, June 1987.

Novotny, T. E., Warner, K. E., Kendrick, J. S., Remington, P. L. Smoking by blacks and whites: Socioeconomic and demographic differences. *Am J Public Health* 78(9):1187–1189, September 1988.

Novotny, T. E., Pierce, J. P., Fiore, M. C., Davis R. M. Smokeless tobacco use in the United States: The Adult Use of Tobacco Surveys. In *Smokeless Tobacco Use in the United States.* National Cancer Institute Monographs. National Institutes for Health, National Cancer Institute, Division of Cancer Prevention and Control, Smoking, Tobacco and Cancer Program. NIH Publication No. 89-3055, 1989, no. 8, pp. 25–28.

Pierce, J. P. International comparison of trends in cigarette smoking prevalence. *Am J Public Health* 79(2):152–157, February 1989.

Pierce, J. P., Fiore, M. C., Novotny, T. E., Hatziandreu, E. J., Davis, R. M. Trends in cigarette smoking in the United States: Education differences are increasing. *JAMA* 261(1):56–60, 6 January 1989a.

———. Trends in cigarette smoking in the United States: Projections to the year 2000. *JAMA* 261(1):61–65, 6 January 1989b.

Scherk, R., Baker, L. A., Ballard, G. P., Dolgoff, S. Tobacco smoking as an etiologic factor in disease. *Cancer Res* 10:49–58, 1950.

Shelton, A. Smokeless sales continue to climb. *Tobacco Reporter* p. 42, 1982.

Shopland, D. R. Smoking. In *1987 Medical and Health Annual.* Chicago: Encyclopedia Britannica, 1986, 420–424.

U.S. Department of Agriculture (USDA). *Tobacco Situation and Outlook Report.* U.S. Department of Agriculture, Economic Research Service, National Economics Division, TS-199, June 1987.

U.S. Department of Defense (USDOD) *The 1985 Worldwide Survey of Alcohol and Nonmedical Drug Use Among Military Personnel.* Report of the Research Triangle Institute to the Office of the Assistant Secretary of Defense (Health Affairs), U.S. Department of Defense, June 1986.

———. *Updated Report of Smoking and Health in the Military.* U.S. Department of Defense, Office of the Assistant Secretary of Defense (Health Affairs), Office of the Assistant Secretary of Defense (Force Management of Personnel), June 1987.

————. *The 1988 Worldwide Survey of Substance Abuse and Health Behavior Among Military Personnel.* Report of Research Triangle Institue to the Office of the Assistant Secretary of Defense (Public Affairs), U.S. Department of Defense, 1988.

U.S. Department of Health, Education and Welfare (USDHEW). *Smoking and Health. Report of the Advisory Committee to the Surgeon General of the Public Health Service.* U.S. Department of Health, Education and Welfare, Public Health Service, Centers for Disease Control. PHS Publication No. 1103, 1964.

U.S. Department of Health and Human Services (USDHHS). *The Health Consequences of Using Smokeless Tobacco. A Report of the Advisory Committee to the Surgeon General.* U.S. Department of Health and Human Services, Public Health Service. NIH Publication No. 86–2874, April 1986.

————. *The Health Consequences of Smoking: Nicotine Addiction. A Report of the Surgeon General.* U.S. Department of Health and Human Services, Public Health Service, Centers for Disease Control, Center for Health Promotion and Education, Office on Smoking and Health. DHHS Publication No. (CDC)88-8406, 1988.

————. *Reducing the Health Consequences of Smoking: 25 Years of Progress. A Report of the Surgeon General.* U.S. Department of Health and Human Services, Public Health Service, Centers for Disease Control, Center for Chronic Disease Prevention and Health Promotion, Office on Smoking and Health. DHHS Publication No. (CDC)89-8411, 1989.

————. *Smoking, Tobacco and Cancer Program 1985–1989 Status Report.* U.S. Department of Health and Human Services, Public Health Service, National Institutes of Health, National Cancer Institute. NIH Publication No. 90-3107, 1990.

Wynder, E. L., and Graham, E. A. Tobacco smoking as a possible etiologic factor in bronchogenic carcinoma. A study of six hundred and eighty-four cases. *JAMA* 143:329–336, 1950.

6

Medical and Public Health Implications of Tobacco Addiction

DONALD R. SHOPLAND and DAVID M. BURNS

In those Western cultures where cigarette smoking has been an established behavior for many decades, smoking is estimated to be responsible for nearly one-sixth of all deaths annually, including 35% of all cancer deaths, 22% of deaths due to coronary heart disease, 15% of stroke deaths, and 90% of all deaths from chronic obstructive lung disease. The U.S. Public Health Service estimates that in the United States over 400,000 excess deaths each year are directly caused by smoking (*MMWR* 1991), while the World Health Organization has estimated more than 2.5 million such deaths annually are due to smoking worldwide (Mahler 1988). As unbelievable as these totals may seem, these estimates may actually be conservative, as will be discussed in more detail later.

The list of diseases caused by or associated with smoking is truly staggering (Table 6–1). However, considering the thousands of chemical constituents found in tobacco and tobacco smoke—dozens of which are either carcinogenic, toxic, or otherwise harmful to biologic systems—this should not be too surprising (USDHEW 1979). The mortality effects of smoking are so severe that when releasing his first report as U.S. Surgeon General, Dr. C. Everett Koop called smoking ". . . the chief, single, avoidable cause of death in our society and the most important public health issue of our time" (USDHHS 1982).

This view was even shared by the White House and its Office of Management and Budget. In the 1987 Economic Report of the President, Ronald Reagan's Counsel of Economic Advisors categorized smoking as "the greatest avoidable risk" to health and safety in American society far outpacing other known causes of death and disability (U.S. President 1987). The mortality caused by cigarette use is probably at least 6 times greater than that from alcohol (U.S. President 1987; USDHHS 1989) and nearly 75 times greater than that from all legally prohibited substances combined (Godshall 1992).

The title of this chapter reflects the perspective that addiction to tobacco is the primary process leading to a host of morbid consequences (Henningfield 1988; Slade 1985). Those consequences which loom largest among the problems tobacco causes are discussed in some detail, while a number of the less prominent but important conditions are also briefly covered. Complications in nonsmokers from tobacco smoke pollution are addressed in Chapter 7, while problems consequent to smokeless tobacco use are covered in Chapter 13. Chapter 14 explores the effects of smoking on cardiac and pulmonary function, on reproductive health and the fetus, infant and growing child, and on the benefits of quitting smoking for people with cancer.

The second part of this chapter presents smoking and health information in a form especially designed to facilitate routine quit smoking advice in clinical practice.

The varied pathogenetic mechanisms that

Table 6–1 Causes of Death and Their Established Epidemiological Association with Cigarette Smoking

Category	Cause of Death
A	Cancer of lung
	Chronic obstructive lung disease (includes emphysema)
	Peripheral vascular disease
	Cancer of larynx
	Cancer of oral cavity (pharynx)
	Cancer of esophagus
B	Stroke
	Coronary heart disease
	Cancer of bladder
	Cancer of kidney
	Cancer of pancreas
	Aortic aneurysm
	Perinatal mortality
C	Cancer of cervix uteri
	Cancer of stomach
	Gastric ulcer
	Duodenal ulcer
	Pneumonia
	Cancer of the liver
	Sudden infant death syndrome
D	Alcoholism
	Cirrhosis of liver
	Poisoning
	Suicide
E	Endometrial cancer
	Parkinson's disease
	Ulcerative colitis

A = diseases for which a direct causal association has been firmly established and smoking is considered the major, single contributor to excess mortality from the disease; *B* = diseases for which a direct causal association has been firmly established, but smoking is but one of several causes; *C* = diseases for which an increased risk (association) has been epidemiologically demonstrated, but the exact nature of that association has not been firmly established; *D* = diseases for which excess mortality in smokers has been observed, but association is attributed to confounding; *E* = diseases for which smokers have lower death rates than nonsmokers.

underlie tobacco's ability to cause such a huge panoply of suffering are summarized in the various reports of the U.S. Surgeon General. The reports on cancer (USDHHS 1982), cardiovascular disease (USDHHS 1983), and pulmonary disease (USDHHS 1984) are especially detailed and helpful in this regard, as are the summative reports of 1979 and 1989 (USDHEW 1979; USDHHS 1989). Reviews of the data that lead to the inference that the connection between smoking and lung cancer is causal are also available (USDHEW 1964, 1979; USDHHS 1982), and an interesting exchange on this

topic appeared in 1983 (Burch 1983; Lilienfeld 1983).

Much of the basic epidemiologic data on smoking as a cause of chronic diseases comes from a number of large, prospective mortality studies. These investigations are the largest epidemiologic initiatives ever undertaken in public health. Collectively, they involve hundreds of thousands of deaths and represent more than 22 million person-years of observation.

The largest of these investigations were conducted among U.S. populations (Hammond and Horn 1958; Hammond 1966; Hammond et al. 1977; Garfinkel 1985; Garfinkel and Stellman 1988; Kahn 1966; Rogot and Murray 1980); however, studies also have been undertaken in Japan (Hirayama 1977, 1990), Sweden (Cederlof et al. 1975), the United Kingdom (Doll and Hill 1956, 1964a, 1964b; Doll and Peto 1976; Doll et al. 1980), and Canada (Best 1966). These studies have been instrumental both in establishing a causal relationship between smoking and various chronic diseases, and in elucidating the total public health disease burden of smoking (Rice and Hodgson 1986; Office of Technology Assessment 1985). A brief description of each of these studies can be found at the end of this chapter in Appendix 6–A.

In many of the older prospective studies, especially those initiated during the 1950s, women were often not included, and when they were, few reports on their mortality experience were published because so few deaths were available for analysis (USDHHS 1980). Fortunately, information from the two American Cancer Society (ACS) studies (and to a somewhat lesser extent the Japanese and British prospective studies) provide considerable insight into the effects of smoking on the health of women (Hammond 1966; USDHHS 1982; Garfinkel and Stellman 1988). These findings have documented that as women smoke more like men, they die more like men. In addition, research over the past 20 years has established a number of unique health risks of smoking for women of reproductive age, including compounding the cardiovascular disease risks associated with oral contraceptive use,

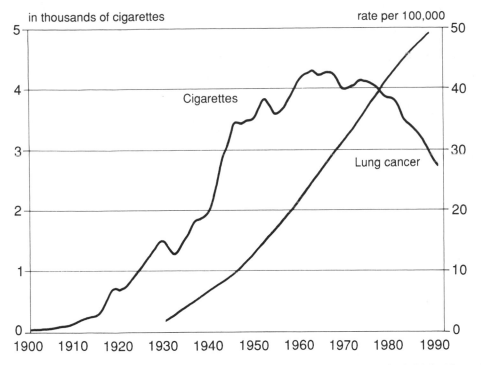

Fig. 6–1 Change in per capita cigarette consumption and lung cancer death rate in the United States between 1900 and 1990. Lung cancer rate is for both men and women combined and age-standardized to 1970 U.S. population. *Source:* U.S. Department of Agriculture and National Center for Health Statistics.

impairing fertility, adverse outcomes of pregnancy, and harm to the fetus (see Chapter 14).

The ACS studies, Cancer Prevention Study I and Cancer Prevention Study II, are referred to as the 25 State and 50 State studies, respectively, in this chapter. The ACS 25 State Study, initiated in 1959, followed 1 million individuals, including 562,000 women for 12 years. The ACS 50 State Study, initiated in 1982, contains 1.2 million individuals including nearly 700,000 women. Individuals in the ACS 50 State Study now have been successfully traced for 6 years. However, only follow-up data corresponding to the first 4 years have been published.

The era of these prospective studies began as tobacco consumption reached its zenith in the United States, some 40-odd years after the American blended cigarette first entered the market (see Chapter 1). The death rate from lung cancer has changed in parallel with changes in per capita cigarette consumption, albeit with a 25–30 year latency (Figure 6–1).

SMOKING AS A CAUSE OF DISEASE

Smoking and Overall Mortality

Overall mortality can be used to measure the cumulative or total effect of a disease-causing agent on the health of a population. It is a particularly useful approach for measuring the health effects of agents, such as cigarette smoking, which influence multiple causes of death, multiple organ systems, and the public health of large populations. As such, it is the best measure of the sum of the risks due to cigarette smoking (USDHEW 1979).

While the effect smoking has on mortality can be measured in various ways, the most common approach is examination of differences in death rates between smokers and nonsmokers. Differences are expressed in the form of mortality ratios. Ratios are calculated by dividing the death rate of one group (smokers) by the death rate of another group (nonsmokers). When the rate in a group is compared to itself, the ratio is, of course, 1.0. If a group experiences twice the mortality rate of the reference group, its mortality ratio is 2.0.

Differences in risks can also be expressed as a percent difference. Throughout this chapter both terms are used to describe mortality differences between smokers and nonsmokers.

Excess mortality among smokers was first documented in the retrospective study by Raymond Pearl in 1938. (This work has been confirmed and extended by numerous prospective studies.) Among the earlier prospective studies (those started in the 1950s), the all-cause mortality rate among male smokers was approximately 70% greater than that seen in men who did not smoke. Among women who smoked, the overall mortality risks were approximately 25–30% higher (Table 6–2). As total smoking exposure increased, mortality risks also increased. Smokers at any given age and level of smoke exposure experienced substantially higher mortality risks than their nonsmoking counterparts. These ratios were especially pronounced at younger age groups and increased with increasing numbers of cigarettes smoked daily. Younger aged males smoking two or more packs per day experienced risks for all causes of death that were between 200 and 300% greater than similarly aged, never-smoking males. As the nonsmoker death rates rose with increasing age, the mortality ratio decreased; however, the absolute difference in the death rate between smokers and nonsmokers increased steadily with age.

Twelve-year follow-up data from the ACS 25 State Study (initiated in 1959) show a similar pattern in both men and women, although overall mortality rates in women were generally not as high as those observed in men at the same age and level of daily consumption. Four-year follow-up data from the more recent ACS 50 State Study (initiated in 1982) show that overall mortality ratios in women smokers now closely parallel

Table 6–2   Smoking and All-cause Mortality Risks

Study	Males	Females
British Physicians	1.63	1.23
ACS 25 State Study	1.83	1.26
U.S. Veterans	1.55	—
Japanese Study	1.29	1.31
Canadian Study	1.54	1.31
Swedish Study	1.58	1.20
ACS 50 State Study	2.34	1.90

Sources: see Appendix 6–A
Nonsmoker ratio = 1.0.

those seen in men, although men still experience higher all-cause smoking related death rates than do women. The mortality experience of women smokers in the 50 State Study mirrors that of men from the earlier 25 State Study begun a generation earlier (see Table 6–2). These findings are entirely consistent with observed differences in smoking behavior between the sexes for the various birth cohorts represented in the two studies.

Data from insurance industry studies parallel findings from the scientific literature. In an analysis of mortality differences in 250,000 insured smoking and nonsmoking policy holders, one report concluded that at age 45 years, male smokers die at an average 80% higher rate than nonsmokers, and at age 55 years, their rate is 110% higher. Though somewhat less affected, women at age 45 years who smoke have a 49% higher death rate than nonsmokers; by age 55 years their death rate differential is 71% higher (Cowell and Hirst 1980).

Quitting Smoking and Overall Mortality

Former smokers have lower mortality risks than do continuing smokers and their excess mortality risk declines as the length of time since stopping increases (Figure 6–2). Generally, those smokers who are abstinent from cigarettes for 15 years or more are observed to have mortality risks that are almost identical to life-long nonsmokers. However, many health benefits, including reduced risk of cardiovascular disease accrue much faster, often within the first 12 months following cessation (see discussion later).

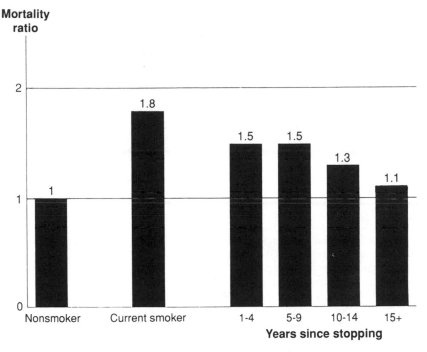

Fig. 6-2   Overall mortality risks in current and former cigarette smokers compared to nonsmokers among male U.S. veterans. *Source:* Kahn 1966; Rogot and Murray 1980.

Overall Mortality in Pipe and Cigar Smokers

In several of the early prospective studies (Hammond 1966; Kahn 1966; Doll and Peto 1976), overall mortality risks among life-long male pipe and cigar smokers were elevated compared to nonsmokers. As with cigarette smoking, individuals who reported higher rates of daily use also experienced higher mortality risks. In the U.S. Veterans Study (Kahn 1966) cigar smokers who smoked five to eight and nine or more cigars daily had mortality risks that were 22 and 40% greater, respectively, than nonsmokers. Generally, pipe smokers have only slightly elevated overall mortality risks compared to nonsmokers. These observations cannot be safely extended, however, to individuals who switch from cigarettes to pipes or cigars, because many continue to inhale the smoke and, thus, do not appreciably change their exposure to tobacco smoke (Ockene et al. 1987).

Smoking and Life Expectancy

Another approach used to measure differences in mortality between smokers and nonsmokers is to examine life expectancy. While this concept is easy to understand, its importance is less apparent since relatively small average differences in life expectancy result from often markedly different risk levels. Thus, seemingly small life expectancy differences often have major public health implications.

Two prospective studies have published detailed information on smoking and life expectancy among men (Hammond 1966; Rogot and Murray 1980; Lew and Garfinkel 1987). The ACS 25 State Study includes information on women as well as men based on 12 years of follow-up (Table 6-3). In both the ACS and U.S. Veterans Study, the total number years of life lost among smoking men increased with increasing levels of daily cigarette consumption. Younger men smoking two or more packs per day experienced a

Table 6-3   Estimated Years of Life Expectancy and Years Lost (YL) for Men and Women at Various Ages, ACS 25 State Study—12 Year Follow-up

Age	Males			Females		
	Non-smoker	Smoker[a]	YL	Non-smoker	Smoker[a]	YL
35	42.4	35.8	6.6	46.2	42.3	3.9
40	37.7	31.2	6.5	41.4	37.6	3.8
45	33.0	26.9	6.1	36.7	33.0	3.7
50	28.5	22.8	5.7	32.1	28.6	3.5
55	24.0	19.0	5.0	27.6	24.4	3.2
60	19.9	15.5	4.4	23.2	20.4	2.8
65	16.1	12.4	3.7	19.0	15.8	3.2
70	12.6	9.8	2.8	15.1	13.3	1.8
75	9.6	7.6	2.0	11.6	10.3	1.3

Source: Lew and Garfinkel, 1987.
[a]One or more packs daily.

8–9 year deficit compared to never-smokers (Hammond 1966; Rogot and Murray 1980). While the average difference in life expectancy between smokers and nonsmokers may appear small (about 4–5 years), this difference is highly important because it represents an average based on the mortality experience of all smokers compared to all nonsmokers. Because only 30–40% of smokers die prematurely from smoking, this 4–5 year difference in life expectancy for all smokers implies that those individuals who die prematurely from smoking experience an approximately 12–15 years shorter life span. Thus quitting smoking could have added significantly to their life expectancy. Such differences are so significant that life insurance companies, even those owned by tobacco companies, set premiums based on accepted actuary risk classification differences between smokers and nonsmokers.

In summary, cigarette smoking exerts a substantial effect on overall mortality risks; these differences can result in a substantial reduction in life expectancy and is greatest at younger ages. Quitting smoking, especially in early adulthood before the medical complications of smoking become evident, can reverse this deficit and after 10–15 years off cigarettes the mortality rate of former smokers is not appreciably different than that of individuals who have never smoked. Moreover, smoking not only reduces the quantity of life; it also profoundly diminishes the quality of life, particularly in later years. Fries and co-workers (1989) point out that stopping smoking, even after 40–50 years of

smoking, will lead to a longer active life span.

SMOKING AND CAUSE-SPECIFIC MORTALITY

Cancer

Tobacco use was first suspected as increasing the risk for developing cancer over 200 years ago (Redmond 1970). However, it was not until publication of four independent retrospective studies on smoking habits of lung cancer patients and controls in 1950 (Wynder and Graham 1950; Doll and Hill 1950; Schrek et al. 1950; Levin et al. 1950) that widespread scientific and public interest in smoking began to develop. Now, 42 years later, the causal link between smoking and cancer is overwhelmingly established, and its toll is simply enormous. Smoking is the leading cause of excess cancer mortality in the United States (USDHHS 1982). For 1991, smoking was estimated responsible for approximately 35% of all U.S. cancer deaths annually. Cigarette smoking alone was responsible for 21.5% of all female cancer deaths, but the combined use of cigarettes, pipes, and cigars were directly linked to an estimated 43% of all male cancer deaths (Shopland, Eyre, Pechacek 1991).

Cigarette smoking is a direct cause of cancer of the lung, larynx, oral cavity, esophagus, and bladder; a contributing factor in the development of cancers of the kidney, pancreas, and stomach for both men and women; cervical cancer in women; and to possibly some additional cases and deaths from cancer of other organ sites (Royal College of Physicians 1962, 1971, 1977, 1986; USDHEW 1964, 1979; USDHHS 1982, 1989, 1990; IARC 1986; WHO 1975, 19770.

Lung Cancer

Lung cancer, once considered a rare medical occurrence in the United States, was not listed as a cause of death in the vital statistics of the United States until 1930; today it is the leading cause of cancer mortality among both men and women, having recently surpassed breast cancer as the leading cause of cancer death in women (NCI 1989). This one disease is now responsible for more than one in every four cancer deaths annually, and the lung cancer death rate among women is increasing faster than the rate among men. In the period 1973–89, the age-adjusted lung cancer mortality rate increased 18% among men but 118% among women (NCI 1991); an estimated 90% of all lung cancer deaths are directly related to active cigarette smoking (Shopland, Eyre, Pechacek 1991).

Table 6–4 provides results from several of the major prospective studies on smoking and lung cancer. Of special interest are data from the ACS 25 State and 50 State Studies. Among the earlier prospective studies—those started during the 1950s—male smokers experienced lung cancer death rates which were approximately 10- to 11-fold higher than male nonsmokers. Lung cancer rates among smoking women in these early studies were in the range of 3- to 4-fold higher, or approximately one-third those seen among men.

Data from the ACS 50 State Study, however, indicate that the risk of death from lung cancer among smokers has increased substantially in both sexes over the intervening two decades. While the relative risk doubled in men from 11.0 to 22.0, the risk for women increased approximately fourfold from less than 3.0 to 12.0. These findings are entirely consistent with the observed changes in smoking behavior and intensity seen in both sexes as represented in the two studies. The men in the 25 State Study had high smoking rates, but many had changed from using

other forms of tobacco to cigarettes prior to and during World War I. Women in the ACS 25 State Study had lower overall smoking rates compared to men, and those who did smoke began smoking much later in life than their male counterparts. In addition, these women had lower levels of smoking prevalence and intensity compared to men as measured by differences in: the number of cigarettes smoked per day, depth of smoke inhalation, use of filtered cigarettes and cigarettes with lower tar/nicotine levels, and total duration of smoking behavior.

In contrast, the men enrolled in the ACS 50 State Study represent a cohort who have primarily smoked cigarettes only, initiated their behavior during adolescence, and have had a high level of daily consumption. Women in the 50 State Study have smoking histories that more closely resemble men in the 25 State Study. Thus, lung cancer mortality ratios now being observed in women are nearly identical to those seen in men one generation earlier. Interestingly, the non-smoker lung cancer mortality rate of both men and women has not increased between the two study periods (Garfinkel 1988; Shopland, Eyre, Pechacek 1991).

A marked dose-response effect between overall exposure to cigarette smoking and lung cancer risk has been a consistent finding in both prospective and retrospective investigations in both sexes. Whether measured in terms of number of cigarettes smoked per day, duration of smoking, age of initiation, inhalation patterns, or tar content of cigarette brand smoked (machine measured), lung cancer mortality increases with each reported increase in exposure (USDHHS 1982; IARC 1986). Figure 6–3 illustrates data for three such measures.

Cancer Sites Other Than Lung

While the correlation between cigarette smoking and lung cancer is best recognized and accepted, smoking also increases mortality risks for a number of other organ sites (Table 6–5).

Among both men and women who smoke, mortality risks for cancers of the larynx, oral cavity, and esophagus are significantly elevated. In the ACS 50 State Study,

Table 6–4 Lung Cancer Mortality by Sex and Number of Cigarettes Smoked Per Day—
Prospective Studies

Study & Population	Males		Females	
	Amount of Cigs./day	Ratio	Amount of Cigs./day	Ratio
ACS 25 State Study	NS	1.0	NS	1.0
1 million males & females	SM	11.4	SM	2.7
	1–9	4.6	1–9	1.3
	10–19	8.6	10–19	2.4
	20–39	14.7	20–39	4.9
	40+	18.7	40+	7.5
British Physicians	NS	1.0	NS	1.0
40,000 doctors	SM	14.0	SM	5.0
	1–14	7.8	1–14	1.3
	15–24	12.7	15–24	6.4
	25+	25.2	25+	29.7
Swedish Study	NS	1.0	NS	1.0
55,000 males & females	SM	7.0	SM	4.5
	1–7	2.3	1–7	1.8
	8–15	8.8	8.15	11.3
	16+	13.7	16+	—
Japanese Study	NS	1.0	NS	1.0
265,000 males & females	SM	4.5	SM	2.3
	1–9	2.1	1–4	2.1
	10–14	3.6	5–9	2.3
	15–19	4.8	10–19	2.6
	20–29	6.1	20–29	4.4
	30–39	5.9	30+	4.7
	40–49	7.4		
	50+	15.1		
ACS 50 State Study	NS	1.0	NS	1.0
1.2 million males & females	SM	22.4	SM	11.0
	<20	18.8	1–10	5.5
	>20	26.9	11–19	11.2
			20	14.2
			21–30	20.4
			31+	22.0
U.S. Veterans	NS	1.0		
290,000 males	SM	11.3		
	1–9	3.9		
	10–20	9.6		
	21–39	16.7		
	40+	23.7		

Source: see Appendix 6–A.
NS = nonsmoker; SM = all levels smoking combined, regardless of amount.

male and female relative risks for cancer of the larynx are 10.5 and 17.8 fold higher, respectively. In a large, retrospective study involving both male and female subjects, a clear dose response effect was observed as measured by number of cigarettes smoked daily and whether individuals smoked filtered, or nonfiltered cigarettes. This finding was similar to the pattern seen in all the major prospective studies with heavy smokers; those consuming two or more packs daily experienced mortality ratios from laryngeal cancer in excess of 20.0.

Mortality risks from oral cavity cancers among smokers are also significantly elevated. Among male smokers in the ACS 50 State Study, ratios approached 30 (27.5), while the risks among women who smoked, while elevated, were not generally as high as those observed in men. Relative risks for cancer of the esophagus were 10.3 and 7.6 for women and men, respectively, and these

Risk by number cigarettes smoked daily

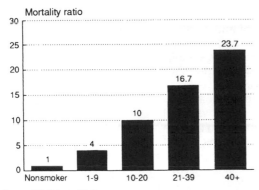

Source: U.S. Veterans Study

Risk by age starting to smoke

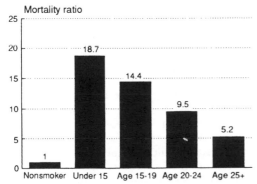

Source: U.S. Veterans Study

Risk by degree of inhalation

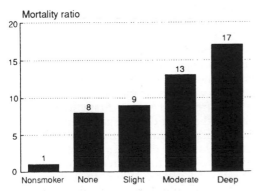

Source: ACS 25 State Study

risks had increased for both sexes compared to those observed in the 25 State Study.

Dose Response and Interaction with Other Factors

For all the major smoking-associated cancer sites, higher mortality risks are observed with increased dose of smoke received as measured by number of cigarettes smoked daily, length of time smoked, and an early age of initiation.

Use of alcohol and tobacco products other than cigarettes each independently elevates the risks for these three sites. Known gender differences in tobacco product use (Marcus et al. 1989; Shopland, Niemcryk, Marconi 1992) as well as differences in inhalation characteristics which exist between men and women probably account for much of the observed gender differences in risks for these cancers.

A number of investigators both in the United States and abroad (USDHHS 1982; IARC 1986) have consistently observed a synergistic effect between reported daily levels of alcohol consumption and daily consumption of cigarettes for cancers of the oral cavity, larynx, and esophagus. One study (McCoy et al. 1980) found that nonsmoking males who consumed 7 ounces or more of alcohol per day had an oral cancer risk of 2.5; however, those individuals consuming 7 ounces of alcohol or more daily had a risk of 5.1 and 24.0 if they smoked less than a pack and more than a pack of cigarettes per day, respectively. Similar findings with respect to cancers of the larynx and esophagus were observed by the same investigators (USDHHS 1982).

Cessation and Cancers Other Than Lung

For all smoking associated cancers, mortality ratios among former smokers are lower than those among continuing smokers, but

Fig. 6–3 Lung cancer mortality risk in cigarette smokers according to three dose measures—risk by number of cigarettes consumed daily, age of smoking initiation, and degree of inhalation from two prospective studies. *Source:* Rogot and Murray 1980; Hammond 1966.

Table 6–5 Mortality Ratios for Cancers Other Than Lung, among Male and Female Current and Former Smokers, ACS 50 State Study—First 4 Years of Follow-up

Cancer Site	Males[a]		Females[a]	
	Current	Former	Current	Former
Lip, oral cavity, pharynx	27.5	8.8	5.6	2.9
Esophagus	7.6	5.8	10.3	3.2
Pancreas	2.5	1.1	2.3	1.8
Larynx	10.5	5.2	17.8	11.9
Cervix uteri	NA		2.1	1.9
Kidney	3.0	2.0	1.4	1.2
Bladder and other urinary	2.9	1.9	2.6	2.9

Source: Shopland et al., 1991.

Nonsmoker ratio = 1.0.

[a]Current and former smoker, regardless of amount smoked.

generally higher than those among subjects who have never smoked (see Table 6–5). This finding has been almost universally observed for more than 30 years and is a consistent finding in both prospective and retrospective studies both in the United States and other countries.

For cancers of the oral cavity and esophagus, cessation of smoking results in an approximately 50% reduction in risk in as little as 5 years with further reductions occurring with additional years off cigarettes. A similar pattern is seen in former smokers for cancers of the bladder and cervix following cessation. Cessation of smoking also reduces the risk for cancer of the pancreas; unfortunately, a measureable reduction is not usually evident until after 10 years of abstinence.

Because diagnosis and 5-year survival rates are so poor for many of the cancers associated with smoking, and has changed little in the past 30 years (lung, 12% 5-year survival; esophagus, 8%; and pancreas, 3%), cessation of smoking—or not starting—presently represent the only method of substantially reducing an individual's chances of developing these serious diseases.

Cardiovascular Disease

While the association between smoking and early cancer mortality was clearly estab-

lished by the time the Advisory Committee to the Surgeon General issued its report in 1964, the causal association between smoking and cardiovascular disease, particularly coronary heart disease (CHD) and stroke, was not established and widely accepted until somewhat later. However, even in the original report (USDHEW 1964), sufficient epidemiological evidence relating smoking to CHD was available for the Advisory Committee to caution "It is [also] more prudent to assume that the established association between cigarette smoking and coronary disease has causative meaning than to suspend judgment until no uncertainty remains." (p 327) By the early 1970s, however, an abundance of epidemiological, clinical, and experimental evidence existed which clearly established cigarette smoking as one of three major causes of CHD (USDHEW 1971; USDHHS 1990).

Coronary Heart Disease (CHD)

In 1983 the Surgeon General issued the first report of the U.S. Public Health Service devoted entirely to an examination of the association between cigarette smoking and cardiovascular disease (USDHHS 1983). In this review, data from both the large prospective studies and several large incidence studies clearly showed the higher risks of CHD morbidity and mortality among current smokers compared to former smokers and nonsmokers. In all of the earlier major prospective studies, a consistent elevation in CHD risk for smokers was observed. These studies showed that male smokers experienced a risk of CHD mortality that was approximately 70% higher, on average, than male nonsmokers. Few of the earlier studies included sufficient numbers of women for evaluation. However, in the ACS 25 State Study women smokers experienced an approximately 25–30% elevation in risk compared to women who did not smoke.

Data from the ACS 25 State Study demonstrated a clear dose-response effect especially when examined by the number of cigarettes smoked daily, an earlier age of initiation, and the degree of inhalation (Hammond 1966). While the effect was more pronounced in male than female

Table 6-6 Mortality Ratios for the Major Cardiovascular Diseases, Male and Female Current and Former Smokers Relative to Nonsmokers, ACS 50 State Study, First 4 Years of Follow-up (1982–86)

CVD Category	Males[a]		Females[a]	
	Current	Former	Current	Former
Coronary heart disease (CHD)	1.94	1.41	1.78	1.31
<Age 65	2.81	1.75	3.00	1.43
>Age 65	1.62	1.29	1.60	1.29
Stroke	2.24	1.29	1.84	1.06
<Age 65	3.67	1.38	4.80	1.41
>Age 65	1.94	1.27	1.47	1.01
Other heart disease	1.85	1.32	1.69	1.16

Source: USDHHS, 1989.

Nonsmoker ratio = 1.0.

[a]Current and former smoker, regardless of amount smoked.

smokers, the data clearly indicated a dose-response association for women as well. In the more recent ACS 50 State Study, mortality risks for both male and female smokers increased with the risk for women smokers almost on a par with that of men (Table 6–6).

Interaction of Smoking with Other Causes of CHD

Numerous investigations have clearly demonstrated that the increase in CHD risk associated with smoking is greater when other risk factors also are present (Dawber 1980; Doyle et al. 1964; Epstein et al. 1965; Kannel 1981; Keys et al. 1963; Liu et al. 1982; Pooling Project Research Group 1978). In the Framingham Heart Disease Study, CHD risk increased with increasing levels of hypertension or elevated serum cholesterol, and at each level of these two risk factors the risk in smokers was greater than the risk in nonsmokers (Kannel 1981). However, the increment of risk with smoking was not constant, but rather increased with increasing levels of hypertension or hypercholesterolemia.

Data from the Pooling Project Research Group (1978), summarized in Figure 6–4, are consistent with a synergistic effect of cigarette smoking with hypertension and hypercholesterolemia. These data provide strong evidence that cigarette smoking interacts with the other two major causes of CHD to produce a combined risk that is greater than the sum of the independent risks. As seen in Figure 6–4, each risk factor, whether smoking, hypertension, or high cholesterol, about equally increases the risk for a major coronary event when compared to individuals who have none of these three factors present. When any two factors are present, the risk doubles and when all three factors are present, the risk is more than eight times greater than when none of the three risk factors are present.

Impact of Smoking on CHD with Increasing Age

Coronary heart disease mortality increases with increasing age in both smokers and nonsmokers. The question of the magnitude of the CHD risk due to smoking at different ages is important because CHD is the most common single cause of death in the United States, accounting for approximately 25% of all deaths annually.

The 1983 Report of the Surgeon General presented information from several of the major prospective studies with respect to smoking and CHD mortality by various age groups in both men and women (USDHHS 1983). Results from the more recent ACS 50 State Study show that risk ratios below age 65 years are higher than those for ages 65 years and older in both men and women (Table 6–6). As can be seen from this table, the CHD mortality ratios for smokers compared to nonsmokers decrease with increasing age. However, this decline in the ratio with increasing age is the result of the rapid rise in CHD rates with age in nonsmokers. The absolute difference between the death rates of cigarette smokers and nonsmokers actually *increases* with age. Thus, the excess risk in smokers is numerically greater in older than in younger populations.

Cessation of Smoking and CHD Risk

The rate of change in CHD mortality risk that occurs after stopping smoking is of great importance both to the individual and to public health. Data summarized in the 1990

Rate per 1,000

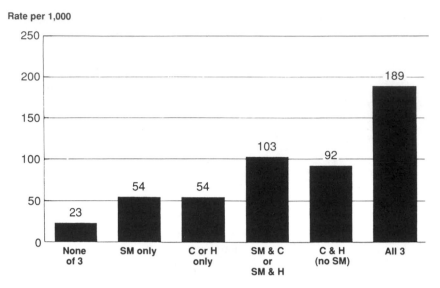

Fig. 6–4 Risk of first major coronary event by major risk factor combinations. C = hypercholesterolemia (>249 mg/dh); H = hypertension (diastolic pressure >90 mm HG); SM = cigarette smoking (any current use of cigarettes at entry). *Source:* Pooling Project Research Group 1978.

Report of the Surgeon General on the benefits of cessation clearly demonstrate that the change in CHD risk following cessation is rapid: About half the risk being eliminated within the first year of abstinence (USDHHS 1990) and within 3–4 years, the CHD risk for former smokers is nearly identical to that of never-smokers. This is in sharp contrast to lung cancer risk where between 30 and 50% of the risk is still evident after 10 years of abstinence (Shopland, Eyre, Pechacek 1990).

The increased risk of CHD mortality from smoking with increasing age combined with the rapid improvement in that risk with quitting smoking combine to explain why there appears to be no age limit for CHD-related quitting benefits (LaCroix et al. 1991). Even individuals over 60 years of age show significantly reduced CHD risks following quitting, regardless of their age or duration of exposure (USDHHS 1990).

Stroke

The contribution of cigarette smoking to increased morbidity and mortality from stroke has been the subject of numerous investigations over the past three decades. In the 1983

Report of the Surgeon General, the causal association between smoking and stroke was believed largely confined to the younger age groups, with little evidence of an effect after 65 years of age. This report also noted that women smokers experienced an increased risk for subarachnoid hemorrhage, and that the concurrent use of both cigarettes and oral contraceptives greatly increased this risk (USDHHS 1983). In the years since publication of the 1983 review, the causal relationship between cigarette smoking and stroke has been clarified in several large studies involving both men and women. This new body of evidence now conclusively establishes a causal link between cigarette use and cerebrovascular disease.

In 1988, Colditz and colleagues examined information on 118,539 nurses followed prospectively for 8 years. They observed a strong dose-response effect with number of cigarettes smoked daily and increased risk for stroke. Compared to women who never smoked, those smoking 1–14 cigarettes daily had a relative risk of both fatal and nonfatal stroke of 2.2; while heavier smokers, those consuming 25 or more cigarettes daily, the relative risk was 3.7. In the ACS 50 State

Study, cigarette smokers under age 65 years experienced increased risks of death from stroke of 3.67 and 4.8 for men and women, respectively. The relative risk for those over age 65 years were 1.9 for men and 1.5 for women (Table 6–6).

Overall, it is estimated that cigarette smoking directly contributes to approximately 15% of the nearly 150,000 stroke deaths that occur in the United States annually (USDIHIS 1989).

Smoking and Other Cardiovascular Diseases

Smoking also is causally related to other cardiovascular diseases and conditions including atherosclerotic peripheral vascular disease and atherosclerotic aortic aneurysm. In the 1983 Surgeon General's Report (USDHHS 1983), it was concluded that "cigarette smoking is the most powerful risk factor predisposing to atherosclerotic peripheral arterial disease," (p 194) and that "death from rupture of an atherosclerotic abdominal aneurysm is more common in cigarette smokers than in nonsmokers." (p 195)

Data for all the major cardiovascular conditions among male and female smokers from the ACS 25 State and 50 State Studies are presented in Table 6–6. These data clearly show that smokers' risk for these diseases are considerably elevated above that of nonsmokers. Further, the risks for both CHD and stroke below age 65 years are higher than that for individuals 65 years and older. When data from the 25 State Study are compared to that of the 50 State Study it becomes quite clear that risks for these diseases have increased between the two study periods. Of particular interest is the fact that risks observed recently in women mirror those seen in men two decades earlier. These studies were initiated nearly a generation apart and thus represent cohorts with different levels of exposure to cigarette smoke.

Although mortality ratios among smokers are much higher for many of the smoking-associated cancer sites than those for many of the cardiovascular diseases, these deaths contribute substantially to the overall public health burden from tobacco because, as a group, they account for slightly more than one-half of all deaths nationally, whereas all cancer deaths account for only approximately one in every four deaths.

Chronic Obstructive Lung Disease

The term chronic obstructive lung disease (also called chronic obstructive pulmonary disease or COPD) traditionally includes the diseases of chronic bronchitis and emphysema. It is now recognized that COPD includes three separate but interconnected disease processes: (1) chronic mucus hypersecretion, resulting in chronic cough and phlegm production; (2) airway thickening and narrowing with expiratory airflow obstruction; and (3) emphysema, which is an abnormal dilation of the distal airspaces along with destruction of alveolar walls.

The association between COPD and cigarette smoking was clearly recognized at the time of the original report in 1964 when the Advisory Committee to the Surgeon General concluded: "Cigarette smoking is the most important of the causes of chronic bronchitis in the United States and increases the risk of dying from chronic bronchitis" and "The smoking of cigarettes is associated with an increased risk of dying from pulmonary emphysema" (USDHEW 1964, p 38).

Twenty years later, in 1984, the Surgeon General devoted an entire volume to the examination of the evidence on smoking and COPD (USDHHS 1984). That report concluded: "Cigarette smoking is the major cause of chronic obstructive lung disease in the United States for both men and women. The contribution of cigarette smoking to chronic obstructive lung disease morbidity and mortality far outweighs all other factors." In 1989, 84,344 COPD deaths were recorded in the United States (NCHS 1992). An estimated 90% of these deaths are directly related to cigarette smoking (USDHHS 1984, 1989).

Smoking and Persistent Cough

Chronic and persistent cough is never a normal condition of the respiratory system and its occurrence is strongly associated with the

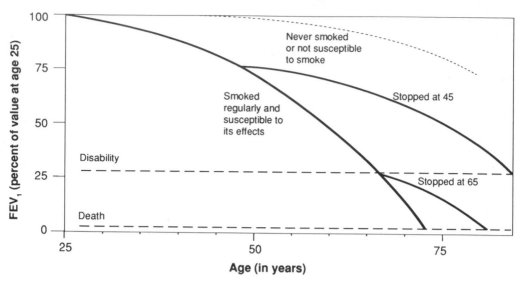

Fig. 6–5   Risk of chronic obstructive lung disease with varying susceptibility to cigarette smoke and benefits of smoking cessation. FEV_1 = forced expiratory volume in 1 second. *Source:* Fletcher and Peto 1977.

long-term use of cigarettes. Standard questions about chronic cough were asked in the National Health and Nutrition Examination Survey I (NHANES) of a representative sample of the U.S. population by the National Center for Health Statistics (USDHHS 1984). For the entire NHANES population, the prevalence of persistent cough was increased threefold in male smokers and twofold in female smokers compared to nonsmokers, and the prevalence increased with increased levels of smoking exposure. Among "heavy smokers," that is, those consuming more than 25 cigarettes daily, 31% of men and 17% of women, reported recurring persistent cough compared to 5.7 and 3.9% of male and female nonsmokers, respectively (USDHHS 1984).

Smoking and Decline in Lung Function

Airflow obstruction is the physiological consequence of disease processes that narrow the airway. In individuals with asthma, the obstruction is reversible with pharmacological intervention such as use of bronchodilation, whereas the obstruction associated with airways damage and emphysema is usually considered permanent.

For epidemiological studies, airflow obstruction is usually defined as a forced expiratory volume in 1 second (FEV_1) less than a given level after standardization for sex, age, and height. Numerous studies both in the United States and in other countries have consistently documented a correlation between cigarette smoking and declines in lung function. In nearly every population studied worldwide, cigarette smoking is the dominant determinant for the prevalence of airflow obstruction. In the 1984 Report of the Surgeon General, nearly 50 studies were reviewed which examined smoking and airflow obstruction; nearly a dozen of these studies were conducted in non-U.S. populations, and 20 involved populations with known occupational status. Striking dose-response relationships have been found in many investigations between the amount smoked and a decline in lung function.

British researchers Fletcher and Peto (1977) have developed a model that depicts the decline in FEV_1 among smokers with varying degrees of susceptibility to cigarette smoke and the benefits of quitting (Figure 6–5). The decline in lung function with age is steeper in smokers than in nonsmokers. This excess decline in lung function in smokers reflects the progressive lung damage that can eventually lead to symptoms of COPD and ultimately death. Beginning in their late twenties, some smokers start to exhibit abnormal measures of expiratory airflow, and an excess rate of decline in function that continues as long as they continue to smoke. Some develop sufficient functional loss to become symptomatic, and some of these develop enough functional loss to become disabled or to die of COPD.

When a smoker quits, the rate of functional decline slows, and with sustained abstinence, the rate of decline in former smokers returns to that of a never-smoker.

Smoking cessation also substantially reduces the rate of respiratory symptoms such as cough, sputum production, and wheezing, and respiratory infections such as bronchitis and pneumonia. And even persons with overt COPD, smoking cessation improves pulmonary function by about 5% within a few months after cessation; there is little evidence to suggest, however, that the smoker can totally regain the lung function that has been lost due to smoking. These findings only serve to emphasize the importance of smoking cessation before long-term damage to the respiratory system occurs.

THE PUBLIC HEALTH BURDEN OF CIGARETTE SMOKING

Smoking clearly causes increased mortality from a number of chronic diseases, especially cardiovascular disease, cancer, and COPD. Collectively, on a national basis, these three disease categories account for well over 75% of all mortality in the United States each year. By using a standard methodology, one can calculate the proportion of these deaths which might reasonably be attributed to cigarette smoking, and thus prevented or delayed, if smoking within the population could be significantly reduced.

The relative risks from each smoking-associated disease among current and former smokers compared to nonsmokers and the proportion of the population classified as current, former, and never-smokers are used. In the example given here, relative risks for each of the major smoking-associated diseases are taken from the ACS 50 State Study as published in the 1989 Report

of the Surgeon General; for data on smoking prevalence, estimates from the 1987 National Health Interview Survey are used (Shopland and Massey 1990). From both sets of data, information was examined separately by gender and smoking status. Based on the model by Walter (1976), the attributable risk (AR) formula for two levels of exposure can be expressed as:

$$AR = \frac{p_0 + p_1(MR_1) + p_2(MR_2) - 1}{p_0 + p_1(MR_1) + p_2(MR_2)}$$

p_0 = proportion of those who never smoked in the U.S. population;

p_1 = proportion of current smokers in the U.S. population;

MR_1 = mortality ratio for current smokers compared with those who never smoked;

p_2 = proportion of former smokers in the U.S. population;

MR_2 = mortality ratio for former smokers compared with those who never smoked.

The resulting smoking attributable risk (percent) is applied to the number of deaths known to have occurred in the United States in 1989, the last year for which complete mortality information is available (NCHS 1992). If only those diseases which the U.S. Public Health Service regard as causally linked to cigarette smoking are used as the basis for calculating smoking attributed mortality, the total number of smoking attributable excess deaths for 1989 is approximately 450,000. However, if all-cause mortality ratios are used (see Table 6–2 for ratios), the number of smoking attributable deaths would be considerably higher, with 37.7% of all male and 23.1% of all female deaths attributed to cigarette smoking. Thus, 420,050 of 1,114,190 male and 239,380 of 1,036,276 female deaths in 1989 could be considered "excess" or preventable in the sense they would not have occurred if cigarette smokers experienced the same death rates as a nonsmoker. This constitutes approximately 30% of all deaths in the United States in 1989.

These calculations, however, are based on

the midpoint of the range for each risk estimate. When conducting formal risk assessments, especially in cases where only a small
number of cases or deaths are available for
analysis, federal regulatory agencies such as
the Environmental Protection Agency and
the Occupational Safety and Health Administration often use the upper bounds of the
confidence interval (CI) to establish a "worst
case scenario" and for establishing a total
cost/benefit ratio as a prelude to implementation of a federal regulation or rule-making
process. This approach is not necessary
when using the ACS 50 State Study because
of the size of the study population (1.2 million participants) and the significant number
of total deaths available for analysis. For example, the all-cause mortality ratio among
male current smokers in the 50 State Study
is 2.34 with a very narrow CI of 2.26–2.43;
for women, the ratio was 1.90 with a CI of
1.82–1.98. Using this approach, however,
would add an additional 40,000 deaths for a
total of nearly 700,000 excess deaths attributed to smoking in 1989.

OTHER DISEASES AND CONDITIONS ASSOCIATED WITH SMOKING AND TOBACCO USE

While tobacco use, especially in the form of
cigarettes, is causally associated with early
mortality from a number of chronic diseases, its use also is associated with a variety
of other diseases and conditions, many of
which can have a profound impact on an individual's health status and quality of life.
This section selectively summarizes several
of these diseases.[1]

Ulcers

An association between cigarette smoking
and peptic ulcer formation has been widely
recognized for nearly 30 years (USDHEW

[1]For a more complete listing of studies in this area, the
reader is referred to the "Other Diseases and Conditions" section of the *Bibliography on Smoking and
Health* published annually since 1967 by the U.S. Public
Health Service's Office on Smoking and Health (OSH).
This publication is available from the Technical Information Center of OSH by calling (404) 488-5708.

1964); this association is significant enough
to strongly suggest a causal correlation (US-
DHEW 1979). Smoking not only causes
peptic ulcer disease but, once formed, ulcers
are less likely to heal if the behavior is not
discontinued (Sontag et al. 1984; Lane and
Lee 1988; Korman et al. 1983). Smoking
cessation reduces the incidence of peptic
ulcer and is, therefore, an important component of peptic ulcer treatment even
with available effective drug treatments
(USDHHS 1989).

Osteoporosis

A number of studies have identified cigarette
smoking as a possible risk factor for osteoporosis (USDHHS 1989). Osteoporosis
leading to fractures of the hip, wrist, and
spine is an important cause of disability and
sometimes even death, especially among
older age, postmenopausal women. The results of these studies suggest that the elevated
risks for osteoporosis and bone fracture
among postmenopausal women who smoke
may be mediated by the inverse relationship
between smoking and obesity. Obesity substantially reduces the risk of hip fracture
(Kiel et al. 1987), and overweight women
have higher endogenous estrogen levels and
greater bone mass (Cauley et al. 1986). It is
also possible that the earlier age of menopause among women smokers also may
raise the risk of osteoporosis (Willett et al.
1983).

Infectious Respiratory Diseases

Independent studies published over the past
25 years have noted that smokers are at increased risk of developing infectious respiratory disease, especially upper respiratory
infections (USDHEW 1971, 1979). In earlier studies Finklea and co-workers (1969
and 1971) found that smokers among a male
college population experienced more clinical illness than did nonsmokers during the
1968–69 influenza epidemic and that this relationship was dose-dependent. Similarly,
Waldman and associates (1969) reported
that cigarette smokers of more than one-half
pack per day had an increased risk of influ-

enza-like illness. Data from several studies cited in the 1984 Report of the Surgeon General suggests that cigarette smoking may actually depress antibody production (USDHHS 1984).

More recently, a number of investigations both in the United States and abroad have noted a strong dose-response relationship between respiratory infections in infants and young children and exposure to very low levels of tobacco smoke that result from living in households where one or more parent smokes (USDHHS 1986; National Academy of Science 1986; USEPA 1990). A connection between pediatric respiratory illness and adult respiratory disease has long been suspected on clinical grounds (Burrows, Knudson, Lebowitz 1977). This area is reviewed in more detail in Chapter 7.

Drug Metabolism

The 1979 Report of the Surgeon General contained an extensive review on the effects of smoking on drug and vitamin metabolism (see Chapter 12 in USDHEW 1979). The most common effect is an alteration in the biotransformation rate, which may affect the efficacy of some therapeutics when given to smokers (Jusko 1978). Phenacetin, antipyrine, theophylline, imipramine, glutethimide, and vitamin C levels are affected by the smoking status of the individual. In the Boston Collaborative Drug Surveillance Program (Jick 1974), for example, propoxyphene was rated ineffective by 10% of nonsmokers, 15% of light smokers, and 20% of heavy smokers. While disposition of phenacetin, theophylline, and antipyrine is known to be increased in smokers, the mechanisms of other drug/smoking interactions is not well established (Jick 1977; Jusko 1978).

Equally important, however, from a clinical viewpoint, a number of drugs have not been found to be influenced by smoking. These include diazepam, phenytoin, warfarin, meperidine, nortriptyline, and ethanol (USDHEW 1979).

Appendix 6–B provides a thumbnail summary of the major complications of smoking and the benefits of quitting.

APPENDIX 6–A

Description of Major Prospective Cohort Mortality Studies

BRITISH PHYSICIANS' STUDY

More than 34,000 men and 6,200 women physicians responded to a questionnaire distributed by the British Medical Association in 1951. With few exceptions, all physicians who replied in 1951 were followed to their deaths or for a minimum of 20 years (for males) and 22 years (for females). Data on changes in tobacco use behavior were collected at various intervals through 1973. More than 11,000 deaths from all causes occurred in this cohort (Doll and Hill 1954, 1964a, 1964b; Doll and Peto 1976; Doll et al. 1980).

AMERICAN CANCER SOCIETY (ACS) 25 STATE STUDY

During 1959 to 1960, ACS volunteers enrolled slightly more than 1 million men and women in Cancer Prevention Study I (ACS 25 State Study). This cohort was followed for a total of 12 years; nearly 93% of all survivors were successfully traced. Although not a representative sample of the U.S. population, all segments of the population were included except groups that were difficult to trace. Enrollees included 440,558 men and 562,671 women; 97% were white and 2% black. More than 150,000 deaths were recorded, including more than 2,500 lung cancer deaths (Hammond 1966; Hammond et al. 1977).

U.S. VETERANS' STUDY

This study followed the mortality experience of nearly 300,000 veterans who held U.S. government life insurance policies in the 1950s. Almost all policyholders were white males. Twenty-six-year mortality experience has been selectively published on this cohort; however, for this chapter data will be limited primarily to information based on the first 16-year mortality experience. More than 107,000 deaths occurred in this population during the first 16 years of follow-up (Kahn 1966; Rogot and Murray 1980).

JAPANESE STUDY OF 29 HEALTH DISTRICTS

In 1965, 265,000 Japanese men and women were enrolled in a prospective study in 29 health districts, representing between 90 and 99% of the total population 40 years and older. Detailed analyses of mortality based on 17 years follow-up of this cohort have recently been published. More than 55,000 total deaths have occurred among the cohort, including nearly 15,000 deaths from cancer (Hirayama 1977, 1990).

AMERICAN CANCER SOCIETY (ACS) 50 STATE STUDY

In September 1982, the ACS initited Cancer Prevention Study II in which 1.2 million men and women in all 50 states, the District of Columbia, and Puerto Rico participated (521,555 men and 685,748 women). In an effort to broader the demographics, the percent of blacks was increased to 4%. Like subjects in the earlier ACS study, participants were predominately white and better educated than the general U.S. population. As of July 1988, death certificates had not been received for about 9% of male and 13% of female deaths (Garfinkel 1985; Garfinkel and Stellman 1988).

APPENDIX 6-B

The Health Consequences of Smoking and the Benefits of Quitting At a Glance

HEALTH CONSEQUENCES

BENEFITS OF QUITTING

Overall mortality risk is two times higher in cigarette smokers compared to non-smokers.

Stopping smoking reduces the risk of premature death with 50% of the risk eliminated within 5 years of quitting. After 15 years off cigarettes, former smokers' risk is nearly identical to that of life-long nonsmoker.

Lung cancer risk in smokers is more than 20 times higher in men and 12 times higher in women.

After 10 years of abstinence, risk of lung cancer is reduced by 30 to 50%. With longer period of cessation, the greater the reduction in risk.

Cancer of the oral cavity risk in men is more than 20 times higher in smokers. The risk in women smokers is between 5 and 10 times greater.

Quitting halves the risks compared to continued smoking, as soon as 5 years after cessation. Further risk reduction occurs over a longer period of abstinence.

Cancer of esophagus among smokers risk is between 5 and 10 times higher.

Quitting significantly reduces risk, 5 years following cessation risk is reduced by 50%.

Pancreatic cancer risks in smokers are 2–3 times higher.

Cessation reduces risk, although may only be measurable after 10 years of abstinence.

Bladder cancer risks in smokers between two- to fourfold greater among both men and women.

Cessation reduces risk by about 50% after only a few years.

Cervical cancer risk among women who smoke is approximately two to three times higher.

Risk in former smoking women substantially lower even in the first few years after cessation.

Coronary heart disease (*CHD*) risks due to smoking are higher at younger than older age groups. For both men and women under age 65 years, CHD risks in smokers are three times higher than nonsmokers.

Risk reduced among men and women of all ages. Excess risk of CHD caused by smoking reduced by about half after 1 year of abstinence. After 15 years of abstinence, risk of CHD is similar to that of persons who never smoked.

Individuals with *diagnosed CHD*

Risk of recurrent infarction or premature death reduced by 50% or more.

Peripheral artery occlusive disease

Cessation substantially reduces risk.

Ischemic stroke and subarachnoid hemorrhage are between two and five times more common in smokers.

After cessation, risk reduced to the level of never-smokers after approximately 10 years of abstinence.

Respiratory symptoms such as cough, sputum production, and wheezing

Rates reduced as compared to continued smoking; often symptoms disappear within 6 months following cessation.

Persons without overt *chronic obstructive pulmonary disease* (*COPD*)

Pulmonary function can improve slightly (about 5%) within a few months after cessation.

Accelerates the *age-related decline in lung function*

With sustained abstinence from smoking, rate of decline in pulmonary function of former smokers returns to that of never-smokers.

COPD mortality rates among smokers is 10 times higher than nonsmokers.

Sustained abstinence reduces COPD mortality rates in comparison with continuing smokers.

Low birth weight babies

Women who stop before pregnancy have infants of same birth weight as those born to never-smokers.

Smoking cessation any time up to the 30th week of gestation results in infants with higher birth weight than continued smoking throughout pregnancy.

Quitting before start of second trimester results in infants with birth weight similar to those born to never-smoking women.

Onset of menopause

Smoking causes women to have natural menopause 1–2 years early. Former smokers have an age at natural menopause similar to that of never-smokers.

Duodenal and gastric ulcers

The increased risk is reduced by smoking cessation. Smoking cessation often medically necessary to promote healing.

REFERENCES

Best, E.W.R. *A Canadian Study of Smoking and Health.* Ottawa: Department of National Health and Welfare, Epidemiology Division, Health Services Branch, Biostatistics Division, Research and Statistics Directorate, 1966.

Burch, P.R.J. The Surgeon General's "epidemiologic criteria for causality": A critique. *J Chronic Dis* 36(12):821–836, 1983.

Burrows, B., Knudson, R., Lebowitz, M. D. The relationship of childhood respiratory illness to adult obstructive airway disease. *Am Rev Respir Dis* 115(2):751–760, 1977.

Cauley, J. A., Gutai, J. P., Sandler, R. B., Laporte, R. E., Kuller, L., Sashin, D. The relationship of endogenous estrogen to bone density and bone area in normal postmenopausal women. *Am J Epidemiol* 124(5):752–761, 1986.

Cederlof, R., Friberg, L., Hrubec, Z., Lorich, U. *The Relationship of Smoking and Some Covariables to Mortality and Cancer Morbidity: A Ten-Year Followup in a Probability Sample of 55,000 Subjects, Age 18–69. Parts 1 and 2.* Stockholm, Sweden: Department of Environmental Hygiene, The Karolinska Institute, 1975.

Colditz, G. A., Bonita, R., Stampfer, M. J., Willett, W. C., Rosner, B., Speizer, F. E., Hennekens, C. H. Cigarette smoking and risk of stroke in middle-aged women. *N Engl J Med* 318(15):937–941, 1988.

Cowell, M. J., and Hirst, B. L. Mortality differences between smokers and nonsmokers. *Trans Soc Actuaries* 32:185–261, 1980.

Dawber, T. R. *The Framingham Study: The Epidemiology of Atherosclerotic Disease.* Cambridge, MA: Harvard University Press, 1980.

Doll, R., and Hill, A. B. Smoking and carcinoma of the lung: Preliminary report. *Br Med J* 2:739–748, 1950.

———. The mortality of doctors in relation to their smoking habits: A preliminary report. *Br Med J* 1(4877):1451–1455, 1954.

———. Mortality in relation to smoking: Ten years' observations of British doctors (part 1). *Br Med J* 1(5395):1399–1410, 1964a.

———. Mortality in relation to smoking: Ten years' observations of British doctors (part 2). *Br Med J* 1(5396):1460–1467, 1964b.

Doll, R., and Peto, R. Mortality in relation to smoking: 20 years' observations on male British doctors. *Br Med J* 2(6051):1525–1536, 1976.

Doll, R., Gray, R., Hafner, B., Peto, R. Mortality in relation to smoking: 22 years' observations on female British doctors. *Br Med J* 280(6219):967–971, 1980.

Doyle, J. T., Dawber, T. R., Kannel, W. B.,

Kinch, S. H., Kahn, H. A. The relationship of cigarette smoking to coronary heart disease: The second report of the combined experience of the Albany, NY, and Framingham, MA, studies. *JAMA* 190(10):108–112, 1964.

Epstein, F. H., Ostrander, L. D., Johnson, B. C., Payne, M. W., Hayner, N. S., Keller, J. B., Francis, T., Jr. Epidemiological studies of cardiovascular disease in a total community—Tecumseh, Michigan. *Ann Intern Med* 62(6):1170–1187, 1965.

Finklea, J. F., Sandifer, S. H., Smith, D. D. Cigarette smoking and epidemic influenza. *Am J Epidemiol* 90(5):390–399, 1969.

Finklea, J. F., Hasselblad, V., Riggan, W. B., Nelson, W. C., Hammer, D. I., Newill, V. A. Cigarette smoking and hemagglutination inhibition response to influenza after natural disease and immunization. *Am Rev Respir Dis* 104(3):368–376, 1971.

Fletcher, C. M., and Peto, R. The natural history of chronic airflow obstruction. *Br Med J* 1(6077):1645–1648, 1977.

Fries, J. F., Green, L. W., Levine, S. Health promotion and the compression of morbidity. *Lancet* 1(8636):481–483, 1989.

Garfinkel, L. Selection, followup, and analysis in the American Cancer Society Prospective Studies. In Garfinkel, L., Ochs, O., Mushinski, M., eds. *Selection, Followup, and Analysis in Prospective Studies: A Workshop. Natl Cancer Inst Monogr* 67:49–52, 1985.

Garfinkel, L., and Stellman, S. D. Smoking and lung cancer in women: Findings in a prospective study. *Cancer Res* 48(23):6951–6955, 1988.

Godshall, W. T. "Smokers' rights": The tobacco companies' latest gasp for survival. *Priorities* (Winter):28–30, 1992.

Hammond, E. C. Smoking in relation to the death rates of 1 million men and women. In Haenszel, W., ed. *Epidemiological Approaches to the Study of Cancer and Other Diseases. Natl Cancer Inst Monogr* 19:127–204, 1966.

Hammond, E. C., and Horn, D. Smoking and death rates: Report on forty-four months of followup on 187,783 men. I. Total mortality. *JAMA* 166(10):1159–1172, 1958.

Hammond, E. C., Garfinkel, L., Seidman, H., Lew, E. A. Some recent findings concerning cigarette smoking. In Hiatt, H. H., Watson, J. D., Winsten, J. A., eds. *Origins of Human Cancer. Book A: Incidence of Cancer in Humans.* Cold Spring Harbor Conference on Cell Proliferation, vol. 4. New York: Cold Spring Harbor Laboratory, 1977, 101–112.

Henningfield, J. E., and Nemeth-Coslett, R. Nicotine dependence: Interface between tobacco and tobacco-related disease. *Chest* 93(suppl):37S–55S, 1988.

Hirayama, T. Changing patterns of cancer in Japan with special reference to the decrease in stomach cancer mortality. In Hiatt, H. H., Watson, J. D., Winsten, J. A., eds. *Origins of Human Cancer. Book A. Incidence of Cancer in Humans.* Cold Spring Harbor Conference on Cell Proliferation, vol. 4. New York: Cold Spring Harbor Laboratory, 1977, 55–75.

———. *Life-Style and Mortality: A Large-Scale Census-Based Cohort Study in Japan.* Basel: Karger Publishing, 1990.

International Agency for Research on Cancer (IARC). Tobacco smoking. *IARC Monogr Eval Carcinog Risks Chem Hum* 38: 1986.

Jick, H. Smoking and clinical drug effects. *Med Clin North Am* 58(5):1143–1149, 1974.

Jusko, W. J. Role of tobacco smoking in pharmacokinetics. *J Pharmacokinet Biopharm* 6(1):7 39, 1978.

Kahn, H. A. The Dorn study of smoking and mortality among U.S. veterans: Report on 8½ years of observation. In Haenszel, W., ed. *Epidemiological Approaches to the Study of Cancer and Other Diseases. Natl Cancer Inst Monogr* 19:1–125, 1966.

Kannel, W. B. Update on the role of cigarette smoking in coronary artery disease. *Am Heart J* 101(3):319–328, 1981.

Keys, A., Taylor, H. L., Blackburn, H., et al. Coronary heart disease among Minnesota business and professional men followed fifteen years. *Circulation* 28(3):381–395, 1963.

Kiel, D. P., Felson, D. T., Anderson, J. J., Wilson, P.W.F., Moskowitz, M. A. Hip fracture and the use of estrogens in postmenopausal women: The Framingham Study. *N Engl J Med* 317(19):1169–1174, 1987.

Korman, M. G., Hansky, J., Eaves, E. R., Schmidt, G. T. Influence of cigarette smoking on healing and relapse in duodenal ulcer disease. *Gastroenterology* 85:871–874, 1983.

LaCroix, A. Z., Lang, J., Scherr, P., Wallace, R. B., Cornoni-Huntley, J., Berkman, L., Curb, J. D., Evans, D., Hennekens, C. H. Smoking and mortality among older men and women in three communities. *N Engl J Med* 324(23):1619–1625, 1991.

Lane, M. R., and Lee, S. P. Recurrence of duodenal ulcer after medical treatment. *Lancet* 1:1147–1149, 1988.

Larson, P. S., Haag, H. B., Silvette, H. *Tobacco: Experimental and Clinical Studies.* Baltimore: William and Wilkins, 1961.

Levin, M. L., Goldstein, H., Gerhardt, P. R. Cancer and tobacco smoking: A preliminary report. *JAMA* 143(4):336–338, 1950.

Lew, E. A., and Garfinkel, L. Differences in mortality and longevity by sex, smoking habits and health status. *Trans Soc Actuaries* 39:107–130, 1987.

Lilienfeld, A. M. The Surgeon General's "epidemiologic criteria for causality": A criticism of Burch's critique. *J Chronic Dis* 36(12):837–845, 1983.

Liu, K., Cedres, L. B., Stamler, J., Dyer, A., Stamler, R., Nanas, S., Berkson, D. M., Paul, O., Lepper, M., Lindberg, H. A., Marquardt, J., Stevens, E., Schoenberger, J. A., Shekelle, R. B., Collette, P., Shekelle, S., Garside, D. Relationship of education to major risk factors and death from coronary heart disease, cardiovascular diseases and all causes: Findings of three Chicago epidemiologic studies. *Circulation* 66(6):1308–1314, 1982.

Lynn, W. R., ed. *1986 Bibliography on Smoking and Health.* Public Health Service Bibliography Series No. 45. Washington, DC: U.S. Department of Health and Human Services, Public Health Service, Office on Smoking and Health, 1987.

Mahler, H. Tobacco or health: Choose health. *World Health Forum* 9:78–83, 1988.

Marcus, A., Crane, L. A., Shopland, D. R., Lynn, W. R. *Use of Smokeless Tobacco in the United States: Recent Estimates from the Current Population Survey. Natl Cancer Inst Monogr* 8:17–32, 1989.

McCoy, D. G., Hecht, S. S., Wynder, E. L. The roles of tobacco, alcohol and diet in the etiology of upper alimentary and respiratory tract cancers. *Prev Med* 9(5):622–629, 1980.

Morbidity and Mortality Weekly Report (MMWR) Smoking-attributable mortality and years of potential life lost: United States, 1988. *MMWR* 40(4):62–63, 69–71, 1991.

National Academy of Sciences. *Environmental Tobacco Smoke: Measuring Exposures and Assessing Health Effects.* Washington, D.C.: National Research Council, National Academy Press, 1986.

National Cancer Institute (NCI). *Cancer Statistics Review 1973–1988.* U.S. Department of Health and Human Services, Public Health Service, National Institutes of Health. NIH Publication No. 91-2789.

————, Division of Cancer Prevention and Control. *1988 Annual Cancer Statistics Review. Including a Report on the Status of Cancer Control.* U.S. Department of Health and Human Services, Public Health Service, National Institutes of Health. NIH Publication No. 89-2789.

National Center for Health Statistics (NCHS). Advance report of final mortality statistics, 1989. *Monthly Vital Statistics Report* 40(8) suppl. 2: 1992.

Ockene, J. K., Pechacek, T. F., Vogt, T., Svendsen, K. Does switching from cigarettes to pipes or cigars reduce tobacco smoke exposure? *Am J Public Health* 77(11):1412–1416, 1987.

Office of Technology Assessment. Smoking-related deaths and financial costs. OTA staff memorandum. Washington, D.C.: U.S. Congress, 1985.

Pearl, R. Tobacco smoking and longevity. *Science* 87(2253):216–217, 1938.

Peto, R., and Lopez, A. D. Worldwide mortality from current smoking patterns. In Durston, B., and Jamrozik, K., eds. *Tobacco and Health: Proceedings of the Seventh World Conference on Smoking and Health.* Perth: Health Department of Western Australia, 1990, 66–68.

Pooling Project Research Group. Relationship of blood pressure, serum cholesterol, smoking habit, relative weight and ECG abnormalities to incidence of major coronary events: Final report of the Pooling Project. *J Chronic Dis* 31(4):201–306, 1978.

Redmond, D. E. Tobacco and cancer: The first clinical report, 1761. *N Engl J Med* 282(1):18–23, 1970.

Rice, D. P., Hodgson, T. A., Sinsheimer, P., et al. The economic costs of the health effects of smoking, 1984. *Milbank Mem Fund Q* 64(4):489–547, 1986.

Rogot, E., and Murray, J. L. Smoking and causes of death among U.S. veterans: 16 years of observation. *Public Health Rep* 95(3):213–222, 1980.

Royal College of Physicians. *Smoking and Health: Summary and Report of the Royal College of Physicians of London on Smoking in Relation to Cancer of the Lung and Other Diseases.* London: Pitman Publishing, 1962.

————. *Smoking and Health Now: A Report of the Royal College of Physicians.* London: Pitman Publishing, 1971.

————. *Smoking or Health: A Report of the Royal College of Physicians.* London: Pitman Publishing, 1977.

————. *Health or Smoking? Followup Report of the Royal College of Physicians.* Edinburgh: Churchill Livingstone, 1986.

Schrek, R., Baker, L. A., Ballard, G. P., Dolgoff, S. Tobacco smoking an etiologic factor in disease. I. Cancer. *Cancer Res* 10:49–58, 1950.

Shopland, D. R. Changes in tobacco consumption and lung cancer risk: Evidence from studies of individuals. In Hakama, M., Beral, V., Cullen, J. W., Parkin, D. M., eds. *Evaluating Effectiveness of Primary Prevention of Cancer.* IARC Scientific Publications No. 103:77–91, 1990.

Shopland, D. R., and Massey, M., eds. *Smoking, Tobacco, and Cancer Program 1985–1989 Status Report.* National Cancer Institute. NIH Publication No. 90-3107, 1990.

Shopland, D. R., Eyre, H. J., Pechacek, T. F. Smoking-attributable cancer mortality in 1991: Is lung cancer now the leading cause of death among smokers in the United States? *JNCI* 83(16):1142–1148, 1991.

Shopland, D. R., Niemcryk, S. J., Marconi, K. M. Geographic and gender variations in total tobacco use. *Am J Public Health* 82(1):103–106, 1992.

Slade, J. D. A disease model of cigarette use. *NY State J Med* 85(7):294–297, 1985.

Sontag, S., Graham, D. Y., Belsito, A., et al. Cimetidine, cigarette smoking, and recurrence of duodenal ulcer. *N Engl J Med* 311(11):689–693, 1984.

U.S. Department of Health, Education and Welfare (USDHEW). *Smoking and Health. Report of the Advisory Committee to the Surgeon General of the Public Health Service.* U.S. Department of Health, Education and Welfare, Public Health Service, Center for Disease Control. PHS Publication No. 1103, 1964.

———. *The Health Consequences of Smoking. A Report to the Surgeon General.* U.S. Department of Health, Education and Welfare, Public Health Service, Health Services and Mental Health Administration. DHEW Publication No. (HSM) 71-7513, 1971.

———. *Smoking and Health. A Report of the Surgeon General.* U.S. Department of Health, Education and Welfare, Public Health Service, Office of the Assistant Secretary for Health, Office on Smoking and Health. DHEW Publication No. (PHS) 79-50066, 1979.

U.S. Department of Health and Human Services (USDHHS). *The Health Consequences of Smoking for Women. A Report of the Surgeon General.* U.S. Department of Health and Human Services, Public Health Service, Office of the Assistant Secretary for Health, Office on Smoking and Health, 1980.

———. *The Health Consequences of Smoking: Cancer. A Report of the Surgeon General.* U.S. Department of Health and Human Services, Public Health Service, Office on Smok-ing and Health. DHHS Publication No. (PHS) 82-50179, 1982.

———. *The Health Consequences of Smoking: Cardiovascular Disease. A Report of the Surgeon General.* U.S. Department of Health and Human Services, Public Health Service, Office on Smoking and Health. DHHS Publication No. (PHS) 84-50204, 1983.

———. *The Health Consequences of Smoking: Chronic Obstructive Lung Disease. A Report of the Surgeon General.* U.S. Department of Health and Human Services, Public Health Service, Office on Smoking and Health. DHHS Publication No. (PHS) 84-50205, 1984.

———. *The Health Consequences of Smoking: Nicotine Addiction. A Report of the Surgeon General.* U.S. Department of Health and Human Services, Public Health Service, Centers for Disease Control, Center for Health Promotion and Education, Office on Smoking and Health. DHHS Publication No. (CDC) 88-8406, 1988.

———. *Reducing the Health Consequences of Smoking: 25 Years of Progress. A Report of the Surgeon General.* U.S. Department of Health and Human Services, Public Health Service, Centers for Disease Control, Center for Health Promotion and Education, Office on Smoking and Health. DHHS Publication No. (CDC) 89-8411, 1989.

———. *The Health Benefits of Smoking Cessation: A Report of the Surgeon General.* U.S. Department of Health and Human Services, Public Health Service, Centers for Disease Control. DHHS Publication No. (CDC) 90-8416, 1990.

U.S. Environmental Protection Agency (USEPA). *Respiratory Health Effects of Passive Smoking: Lung Cancer and Other Disorders.* Washington, DC: U.S. Environmental Protection Agency, EPA/600/6-90/006 F, 1992.

U.S. President. *Economic Report of the President. January 1987.* Washington, D.C.: Council of Economic Advisors, 1987.

Waldman, R. H., Bond, J. E., Levitt, L. P., Hartwig, E. C., Prather, R. L., Baratta-Neill, J. S., Small, P. A. An evaluation of influenza immunization: Influence on route of administration and vaccine strain. *Bull WHO* 41:543–548, 1969.

Walter, S. D. The estimation and interpretation of attributable risk in health research. *Biometrics* 32:829–849, 1976.

Willett, W., Stampfer, M. J., Bain, C., Lipnick, R., Speizer, F. E., Rosner, B., Cramer, D., Hennekens, C. H. Cigarette smoking, relative weight, and menopause. *Am J Epidemiol* 117(6):651–658, 1983.

World Health Organization (WHO). *Smoking and Its Effects on Health: Report of a WHO Expert Committee. WHO Technical Report Series No. 568.* Geneva: World Health Organization, 1975.

———. *Controlling the Smoking Epidemic. Report of the WHO Expert Committee on Smoking and Health. WHO Technical Report Series No. 636.* Geneva: World Health Organization, 1979.

Wynder, E. L., and Graham, E. A. Tobacco smoking as a possible etiologic factor in bronchiogenic carcinoma: A study of six hundred and eighty-four proved cases. *JAMA* 143(4):329–336, 1950.

7

Tobacco Smoke Pollution

James L. Repace

Inhaling the smoke from cigarettes, pipes, and cigars delivers nicotine to the brain more quickly and efficently than chewing tobacco leaf (Chapter 1). However, the practice of burning tobacco leaves indoors exposes other people to indoor air pollution from tobacco combustion products containing many chemicals known to be harmful to human health. Although society, in the interest of public health, has long imposed quality standards for food, water, and indeed, for outdoor air, it has been slow to require that the indoor air be of a quality that will prevent morbidity and mortality. In general, the same amount of contaminant deposited on the lung surface from inhaled air that we breathe has greater potential for harm than an equal amount ingested in food or water, due to differences in absorption efficiency between the pulmonary and gastrointestinal membranes. For example, in a healthy adult, 5% of a gram of lead from a chip of accidentally ingested paint will be absorbed, while 95% of the same amount of lead inhaled as a fume from automobile exhaust will be absorbed.

It is common for there to be strict controls on low-dose general population exposures to toxic agents which have only been proved to be harmful with long-term exposure at high doses. Pollutants such as asbestos, benzene, and radioactivity fall into this category. The 2.5 million deaths per year worldwide caused by the cigarette qualifies tobacco smoke as extraordinarily harmful at high doses (Peto and Lopez 1990). It is astonishing that this fact alone has not led to stringent controls on tobacco smoke pollution. Other environmental agents with the poten-

tial to cause far smaller amounts of harm have been banned from food, water, and air. For example, in 1988, Chilean grapes were banned from U.S. markets because cyanide contamination found on two grapes was of the order of a few percent of that delivered by smoking one cigarette.

In estimating the magnitude of a public health risk from an environmental agent, a technique called *risk assessment* is typically employed by public health agencies. Risk assessment often relies on available data coupled with the use of models to estimate the expected magnitude of a public health risk. If the estimated risk is significant, *risk management,* generally in the form of regulation, is employed to control or eliminate the hazard. Risk assessment is also used to ascertain uncertainties in the estimated risk, as well as to point out directions for future research. Risk assessment has four main components: hazard assessment, exposure assessment, dose-response determination, and risk characterization. This chapter on the pollution of indoor air by tobacco smoke will follow this outline.

HAZARD ASSESSMENT OF TOBACCO SMOKE POLLUTION

Large-dose inhalation exposure to tobacco smoke (ordinary smoking) is a major cause of coronary heart disease, atherosclerotic peripheral vascular disease, lung and laryngeal cancer, oral cancer, esophageal cancer, emphysema, chronic bronchitis, intrauterine growth retardation, and low birth weight. In

Table 7-1 43 Chemical Compounds Identified in Tobacco Smoke for which There is "Sufficient Evidence" of Carcinogenicity in Humans or Animals

acetaldehyde	dibenzo(a,i)pyrene	N-nitrosdi-n-propylamine
acrylonitrile	dibenzo(a,e)pyrene	N-nitrosopyrrolidine
arsenic	dibenzo(a,l)pyrene	N-nitrosodi-n-butylamine
benz(a)anthracene	dibenzo(a,h)pyrene	*ortho*-toluidine
benzene	formaldehyde	styrene
benzo(a)pyrene	hydrazine	urethane
benzo(b)fluoranthene	indeno(1,2,3,-cd)pyrene	vinyl chloride
benzo(k)fluoranthene	lead	1,1-dimethylhydrazine
cadmium	nickel	2-nitropropane
chromium VI	N-nitrosodiethanolamine	2-napthylamine
DDT	N-nitrosodiethylamine	4-(methylnitrosamino)-1-(3-
dibenz(a,h)acridine	N'-nitrosodimethylamine	-pyradyl)-1-butanone
dibenz(a,j)acridine	N'nitrosonornicotine	4-aminobiphenyl
dibenz(a,h)anthracene	N-nitrosopiperidine	5-methychrysene
		7H-dibenzo(c,g)carbazole

Source: IARC 1987.

addition, smoking has also been implicated as a probable cause of unsuccessful pregnancies, increased infant mortality, and peptic ulcer disease, as well as cancers of the bladder, pancreas, and kidney. Associations have been observed between smoking and cancer of the stomach (USDHHS 1989), cervical cancer (Slattery et al. 1989), and breast cancer (Horton 1988; Rohan and Baron 1989). Increased risks among smokers for hepatic cancer (Trichopoulos et al. 1987), leukemia (Kinlen and Rogot 1988), penile cancer (Hellberg et al. 1987), and anal cancer (Daling et al. 1987; USDHHS 1989) have also been reported.

In short, scarcely an organ system of the human body remains undiseased from prolonged inhalation of large doses of tobacco smoke. As a result, there is a significant reduction in life expectancy for smokers compared to nonsmokers (see Chapter 6). Moreover, the lung cancer rate for males smoking as few as one to nine cigarettes per day, as observed in the American Cancer Society's (ACS) 9 State and 25 State studies averaged sixfold times that of nonsmokers (whose annual lung cancer mortality rate was about 12 per 100,000), indicating large risks even at relatively low active smoking exposures, with no evidence of a threshold for the effect (IARC 1986). In fact, cigarette smokers who do not inhale, as well as pipe and cigar smokers, have lung cancer risks which are severalfold that of nonsmokers. This suggests that the dose-response curve between exposure to tobacco smoke and cancer risk rises steeply, and that even relatively small exposures, such as those encountered in passive smoking, might result in significant population risk.

Because thresholds for effect have not been found for the many diseases of smoking, and because air pollution in general can cause human morbidity and mortality, the suspicion that tobacco smoke pollution (also called environmental tobacco smoke, or ETS) in buildings might increase nonsmokers' risk of these diseases has been raised (Repace and Lowrey 1980). Experiments have shown that cigarettes, pipes, and cigars emit copious amounts of air pollution which grossly pollutes indoor atmospheres during smoking (Repace 1987b; Leaderer et al. 1987; USDHHS 1986; NRC 1986). In 1986, an estimated 424,000 metric tons of tobacco were burned indoors annually in the United States, contaminating indoor air with nearly 5,000 chemical substances, many of them toxic. In fact, 43 of these 5,000 meet the stringent criteria for listing as known carcinogens in humans or animals set forth by the International Agency for Research on Cancer (IARC), as shown in Table 7-1 (IARC 1987; Repace and Lowrey 1990). Of the compounds that have been identified in tobacco smoke (Adams, O'Mara-Adams, Hoffman 1987; Guerin 1987; Sakuma et al. 1983, 1984a,b), only about 10% are found in the vapor phase, with the remainder in the particulate phase (Dube and Green 1982).

The particulate phase of tobacco smoke contains more than 40 known or suspected carcinogens, including substances described as tumor-initiators, tumor-promotors, and four classes of organ-specific carcinogens (lung, esophagus, pancreas, and kidney and bladder (USDHHS 1981). Because much of the particulate matter slowly evaporates into the vapor phase (Pritchard 1988), and because material from smoke particles deposited in the mucous/aqueous layer of the alveolar surface may become dissolved, inhalation of tobacco smoke aerosol by nonsmokers may result in the dissemination of carcinogenic particulate phase components to sites distal to the lung.

EXPOSURE ASSESSMENT OF TOBACCO SMOKE POLLUTION

Exposure to an air pollutant is dependent on the product of three quantities: the pollutant concentration in a given microenvironment, the individual's respiration rate during contact with the pollutant cloud, and the length of time the person spends in the contaminated atmosphere. Tobacco smoke concentrations in individual microenvironments may be assessed by measurement, but population exposures, which determine aggregate public health risk, are more generally assessed by a mathematical exposure model. In the case of tobacco smoke, which is a mixture consisting of thousands of different substances, two constituents, nicotine and respirable suspended particulate matter (RSP), have been most commonly selected as surrogates for the entire mixture (USDHHS 1986). Although RSP may be liberated by other combustion processes, during smoking in nonindustrial indoor spaces, RSP from tobacco smoke generally dwarfs the other sources, including kerosene stoves, fireplaces, dust reentrained in room air by pedestrian traffic, and dust infiltrated from the outdoor air (Repace and Lowrey 1980, 1982; Meisner et al. 1988; NRC 1986; Leaderer 1990; Lewtas 1989). For example, Hammond et al. (1988) measured personal exposures to RSP in several hundred railroad workers. Mean calculated ETS-derived RSP exposures for railroad office workers averaged over 90 $\mu g/m^3$; by comparison, all

other sources of RSP for these diesel-exhaust exposed workers averaged less than 40 $\mu g/m^3$.

RSP released indoors from tobacco combustion contributed an estimated 13,000 metric tons into the interiors of the nation's building stock in 1986 (Repace and Lowrey 1990). Surveys of respirable particulate air pollution have shown that, under typical conditions of ventilation and smoking occupancy in indoor microenvironments (i.e., homes, office buildings, sports arenas, bingo games, bowling alleys, waiting rooms, restaurants, and bars), air pollution levels due to tobacco smoke are far higher than those typically encountered indoors in the absence of smoking (Repace 1987b). The levels of RSP from ETS are even higher than levels of RSP observed in vehicles on busy commuter highways (Repace and Lowrey 1980). In fact, whenever smoking occurs indoors, the short-term levels of air pollution generally far exceed the levels of RSP permitted by national outdoor air quality standards for inhalable particles (Figure 7-1) (Repace and Lowrey 1980; Repace 1987b). Personal and area monitoring studies of exposure have confirmed that human exposures to respirable particulate air pollution are dominated by indoor levels of ETS (Repace and Lowrey 1980; NRC 1986; USDHHS 1986; Spengler et al. 1985; Leaderer 1990). This is possible because the population spends 90% of its time indoors—the bulk spent in just two microenvironments, home and work—and because there are few other strong sources of RSP (Leaderer 1990). In addition, tobacco smoke is easily transmitted through mechanical ventilation systems in office buildings and aircraft, and by diffusion in naturally ventilated dwellings (Repace and Lowrey 1987b; Williams 1985; Vaughn and Hammond 1990; USDOT 1990).

Mathematical models have been developed to predict the concentration of RSP from tobacco smoke pollution as a function of the density of smokers in the building space and the rate of exchange of cleansing air between the building and the outdoors. The parameters of importance that determine the impact of tobacco smoke on indoor atmospheres are given in the following equation, which is used to estimate the

Fig. 7-1. RESPIRABLE PARTICLE DENSITY vs ACTIVE SMOKER DENSITY

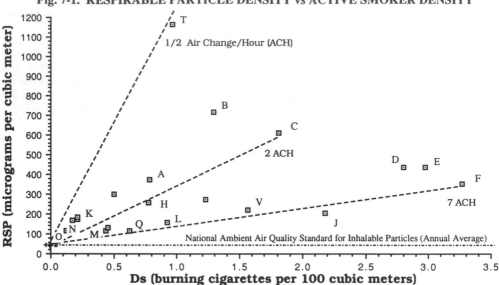

Fig. 7–1 Respirable particle density (RSP) vs. active smoker density (Ds). *Source:* Repace and Lowry 1980, 1982.

quantity of tobacco smoke pollution in indoor spaces. The total concentration of RSP from cigarette smoke plus background sources, in units of micrograms per cubic meter ($\mu g/m^3$), as a function of time, t, in units of hours, in a space is given by the following expression (Repace 1987a):

$$RSP = 21,700 \left(\frac{N}{CV}\right) [1 - e^{-Ct}] + B,$$

where N is the number of smokers (who are assumed to smoke cigarettes at the rate of 2 per hour), V is the space volume in cubic meters, N/V is called the *habitual smoker density,* C is the air exchange rate, in air changes per hour, e is the base of natural logarithms, and B is the background concentration of RSP in the space (Repace 1987a). To understand the enormous impact of smoking on the indoor air, consider, as an illustrative example, the realistic numbers for a typical restaurant, under full occupancy and code-specified ventilation (which is often observed in the breach) for this equation. A typical indoor background RSP level in the absence of smoking is B = 20 $\mu g/m^3$ (Repace and Lowrey 1980, 1982, 1987a,b). A typical restaurant's maximum occupancy is of the

order of 70 persons per 1,000 square feet (about 100 m^2) of floor area (ASHRAE 1989), and assuming that the restaurant is filled to capacity, at a smoking prevalence of 29%, 20 patrons per 1,000 square feet will be smokers. Assuming a 12-foot ceiling, this yields a volume V = 12,000 cubic feet, or 340 cubic meters (a volume approximately the same as a typical single family house). The smoker density is 5.9 × 10^{-2} habitual smokers per cubic meter, equivalent to a burning cigarette density of about 1.8 burning cigarettes per 100 cubic meters (compare with Figure 7–1) (Repace and Lowrey 1980, 1982, 1987a). The American Society of Heating, Refrigerating, and Air Conditioning Engineers (ASHRAE), the design ventilation code-recommending organization, recommends 20 cubic feet of outdoor makeup air per minute per occupant (10 Lps/occ) for a well-ventilated restaurant dining room (ASHRAE 1989), equivalent to an air exchange rate of C = 7 air changes per hour (20 cfm/occ × 70 occ/12,000 cf × 60 min/hr). Applying these numbers to our equation, it is seen that at the end of a half hour, the RSP level increases *10-fold,* from 20 $\mu g/m^3$ to a near steady-state level of 197 $\mu g/m^3$, and, while smoking persists, tobacco smoke pollution constitutes 83% of the RSP levels. (Compare the value just calculated to those shown in Figure 7–1. Data points, E, H, K, L, M, and N are typical restaurants; B and V are reception halls; J is a hospital waiting room; I is a bowling alley; D, G, and T are bingo games; while O is a sports arena [smoking discouraged, but not enforced]; B is a lodge hall dinner-dance; C and Q are bars; F is a nightclub; and A is a private home during a party.) The dashed lines show the calculated air exchange rates.

Given the nature of tobacco smoke particulate matter shown in Table 7–1, should such exposure be considered healthy for the servers or patrons? If the restaurant owner decides to save money by decreasing the air exchange rate to 5 cubic feet of outdoor makeup air per minute per occupant (1.75 air changes/h, a level still common under many "energy-efficient" building ventilation codes), the RSP level after one-half hour is 319 $\mu g/m^3$, and after 3 hours increases to a near steady-state value of 742 $\mu g/m^3$! (Compare this calculation to data point B in Figure 7–1, taken at a dinner-dance.) By way of comparison, the national outdoor air quality standard for inhalable particles ($\leq$ 10 μm in diameter) is 50 $\mu g/m^3$ (shown in Figure 7–1).

Pollution of air in buildings by tobacco smoke is so pervasive that many people are unaware that they are even exposed. This is probably due to the fact that many people believe that because no one is smoking in their immediate environment, they are not being exposed to tobacco smoke. For example, Jarvis and Russell (1984, 1987) showed that among 100 U.K. nonsmokers, only 12 had undetectable cotinine levels, although nearly half reported "no exposure" (IARC 1987). Tobacco smoke recirculated in the central air systems of commercial buildings may expose workers unknowingly, accounting for this result (Repace and Lowrey 1987b). Similar results were reported in the United States by Cummings and associates (1989, 1990): of 663 nonsmokers whose urinary cotinine levels were studied, only 76% reported exposure to ETS; however, 91% had detectable levels. The mean cotinine level in the nonsmokers was 8.84 ng/ml (0.7% of the mean value reported for 130

smokers in the same study), and the range was 0–85 ng/ml; 92% of cotinine values were less than 20 ng/ml. Cotinine levels tended to increase with the number of reported exposures to ETS.

Based on time-budget studies, most people spend the bulk of their time in just two microenvironments: home and work. Since many persons exposed at home are also exposed at work, those exposed both at home and at work represent a most-exposed group of passive smokers (Repace and Lowrey 1985b). Moreover, exposure probabilities are high at work: for example, in the Cummings study (1990), 77% were exposed in the workplace, and 22% were exposed while at home. Similar conclusions about the importance of these two microenvironments were reported by Riboli and colleagues (1990). Cummings et al. (1990) reported that 84% of subjects who did not live with a smoker had detectable cotinine levels. This finding has important implications for epidemiological studies of passive smoking and disease. Most such studies use domestic exposure as a surrogate for total exposure to passive smoking, and unaccounted for exposures outside the home may confound an actual association, since this exposure misclassification tends to bias the mortality ratio toward unity. Insofar as public health measures are concerned, the two most important sites for interventions to control tobacco smoke pollution are the home and the workplace: the former by public information, the latter by public information and regulation.

DOSE-RESPONSE DETERMINATION

Heart Disease

Wells (1988), Glantz and Parmley (1991), and Steenland (1992) have reviewed the evidence that passive smoking increases the risk of death from heart disease. In 10 epidemiological studies on the risk of death from ischemic heart disease or myocardial infarction among nonsmokers living with smokers, the exposed groups experienced an overall 20–30% higher risk than the unexposed groups. Glantz and Parmley (1991) note that these epidemiological studies are complemented by a variety of physiological and biochemical data from human studies that show that exposure to tobacco smoke pollution adversely affects platelet function and damages arterial endothelium in a way that increases the risk of heart disease. These observations have recently been experimentally confirmed in rabbits exposed to passive smoking by Zhu and colleagues (1992). Glantz and Parmley (1991) also reviewed evidence that exposure exerts significant effects on exercise capability of both normal persons and those with heart disease by affecting the body's ability to deliver and utilize oxygen. Further, they report that in animal experiments, exposure to ETS also depresses cellular respiration at the mitochondrial level, and that polycyclic aromatic hydrocarbons in ETS also accelerate, and may initiate, the development of atherosclerotic plaque.

Lung Cancer

Several official bodies have addressed the question of whether passive smoking causes lung cancer. In 1986, the U.S. Surgeon General concluded that "involuntary smoking is a cause of disease, including lung cancer, in healthy nonsmokers" (USDHHS 1986 p 7). Also in 1986, the National Research Council (NRC) concluded that "exposure to ETS increases the incidence of lung cancer in nonsmokers" (NRC 1986 p 10). The NRC estimated that the risk of lung cancer was increased by roughly 30% for nonsmoking spouses of smokers relative to nonsmoking spouses. The following year, the International Agency for Research on Cancer (IARC) stated that "exposure to tobacco smoke gives rise to some risk of cancer" (IARC 1987). In 1992, the U.S. Environmental Protection Agency (EPA) reviewed the original 13 epidemiological studies which had been the basis for these initial findings plus 17 more, for a total of 30 studies of passive smoking and lung cancer, and concluded that ETS is a "class A," or "known human carcinogen" (USEPA 1992). Finally, in 1991, the National Institute for Occupational Safety and Health issued a report which concluded that ETS meets the criteria for classification as an "occupational carcinogen," and called atten-

tion to the "possible association between exposure to ETS and increased risk of heart disease in nonsmokers" (NIOSH 1991). With respect to quantitation of lung cancer risk, EPA used actual epidemiological data and vital statistics to estimate the number of nonsmokers affected. The EPA report concluded that passive smoking is causally associated with lung cancer in adults. This report concluded that, following the EPA guidelines for carcinogen risk assessment, ETS causes approximately 3,000 ($\pm$ 2,000) lung cancer deaths annually in the United States in never-smokers and ex-smokers.

Pediatric Diseases

Tobacco smoke pollution causes the children of parents who smoke to have up to 300,000 cases annually of bronchitis and pneumonia, increased prevalence of asthma, cough, sputum production, wheeze, and middle ear effusions, as well as up to 1,000,000 exacerbated cases of existing asthma annually. (NRC 1986; USDHHS 1986; USEPA 1992). Further, a recent study (Janerich et al. 1990) concluded that exposure to tobacco smoke pollution during childhood was associated with increased susceptibility to lung cancer in adulthood.

Dose-Response Relationship

Suppose it were possible to measure exactly the dose of all lung carcinogens breathed in during passive smoking. Suppose further that the number of lung cancer deaths induced could be precisely measured. A population-based dose-response function could then be defined, yielding the number of lung cancer deaths per year in the population at risk, per average number of milligrams of tobacco smoke carcinogens inhaled per day. Although it is not possible to actually measure the total dose of lung carcinogens from tobacco smoke polluted atmospheres to the nonsmoking population, from measured RSP levels and mathematical models, it is possible to estimate the exposure the nonsmoking population has to the particulate phase of tobacco smoke. Also, although it is also not possible to precisely measure the population response, that is, the number of lung cancer deaths (or other disease end points) per year from passive smoking, its magnitude can be estimated from epidemiological cohort studies. In this manner, a dose-response model can be constructed, based on observed physical and epidemiological phenomena. This model yields an estimate of the true dose-response function. By comparing the predictions of such a mathematical model with the results of independent cohort studies of lung cancer mortality, the accuracy of the approximation can thereby be estimated. This approach permits the prediction of the risk of passive-smoking disease associated with a given level of exposure. This in turn permits the designation of control and abatement procedures which will yield a predetermined level of public health protection.

Repace and Lowrey [1985a, 1986, 1987a, 1993 (in press)] have developed such a dose-response model. This has been utilized in the estimation of the risks of passive smoking in the workplace [Repace and Lowrey 1985b, 1993 (in press)], and in airliner cabins (Repace 1988; USDOT 1990). Repace and Lowrey (1985a) estimated the aggregate average population risk from passive smoking as five lung cancer deaths per 100,000 person-years at risk, per milligram of tobacco tar inhaled per day, for the non-smoking population aged 35 years or older. The implications for public health policy are described in the next section.

RISK CHARACTERIZATION OF TOBACCO SMOKE POLLUTION

How significant is the risk from tobacco smoke? An answer is provided by considering U.S. federal approaches to regulating environmental carcinogens. What level of cancer risk triggers regulation, and is there consistency among various federal agencies? Travis and co-workers (1987) have reviewed the use of cancer risk estimates in prevailing federal standards and in withdrawn regulatory initiatives to determine the relationship between risk level and federal regulatory action. They find definite patterns and consistency in the federal regulatory process. Travis et al. (1987) considered two measures of risk, lifetime cancer risk to the most ex-

posed individual and aggregate or average population risk, which incorporates population size. One-third of the time, federal agencies calculated aggregate risks by multiplying the risk to the most exposed by the population at risk, and two-thirds of the time, risks were calculated by taking into account variations in exposure level. The latter approach is the preferred method. The regulatory actions considered in the analysis were performed by the Consumer Product Safety Commission, the Environmental Protection Agency, the Food and Drug Administration, and the Occupational Safety and Health Administration.

Travis et al. (1987) describe two technical terms current in risk assessment circles: *de manifestis* risk and *de minimis* risk. A *de manifestis* risk is literally a risk of obvious or evident concern, and has its roots in the legal definition of an "obvious risk," one recognized instantly by a person of ordinary intelligence. *De minimis* risk has been used for a number of years by regulators to define an acceptable level of risk that is below regulatory concern. This term stems from the legal principle, *de minimis non curat lex,* "the law does not concern itself with trifles." *De manifestis* risks are so high that agencies almost always acted to reduce them, and *de minimis* risks are so low that agencies almost never act to reduce them. The risks falling in between these extremes were regulated in some cases, but not in others. Two categories were described: small populations and large populations. For low aggregate risk, the *de manifestis* level for individual risk was found to be about 4×10^{-3} (a lifetime probability of four deaths per 1,000 persons at risk), and the *de minimis* level was 1×10^{-4}. For example, the EPA, in declining to regulate natural radionuclide emissions from elemental phosphorus plants with an individual lifetime risk of 1×10^{-3}, weighed the maximum risk to the most exposed individuals against the low aggregate risk (0.06 cancer deaths per year), and against other factors such as cost. However, when the aggregate population risk level was large, that is, above 250 cancer deaths per year, the *de manifestis* risk dropped to about 3×10^{-4}, and the *de minimis* risk dropped to 1×10^{-6}. For example, if the lifetime risks of harm from ex-

Table 7-2 Summary of Risk Assessments of Lung Cancer Deaths (LCDs) in U.S. Nonsmokers from Environmental Tobacco Smoke (ETS) Exposure (Adjusted to 1988)

Study	Range of Estimates (LCDs per year)	Mean or Best Estimate (LCDs per year)
Fong (1982)[a]	960[b]–4,800[c]	2,900
Repace and Lowrey (1985–87)	685[d]–6,850[a]	6,700 ± 340
Russell et al. (1986)[a]		1,107[f]
Rubins (1986)	4314[g]–8,625[h]	6,470
Wells (1988)		3,320[i]
Wald et al. (1986)		8,124[j]
Kuller et al. (1986)[a]	(female LCDs only)	>6,035[k]
Wigle et al. (1987)	(83% workplace)[a]	5,691[l]
Arundel et al. (1987)	19–97	.58[m]
Mean, all 9 studies:		4,500 ± 2,800
Mean, 8 studies, excluding Arundel et al.		5,000 ± 2,400

Source: Repace and Lowrey 1990.

[a]Estimate ours, interpolated from author's overall risk estimate.

[b]Based on sublinearity assumption at low doses.

[c]Based on linearity assumption at low doses.

[d]Lower bound based on smokers' respirable suspended particulate matter (RSP) exposure extrapolation (adjusted to include ex-smokers).

[e]Best estimate based on epidemiology (adjusted to include ex-smokers).

[f]Based on linear extrapolation from nicotine in smokers.

[g]Based on urinary cotinine and ETS epidemiology.

[h]Based on linear multistage from smokers and urinary cotinine.

[i]Based on ETS epidemiology and nonsmokers' LCD rates (adjusted to include ex-smokers).

[j]Based on urine cotinine in U.K. nonsmokers, ETS epidemiology (adjusted to include ex-smokers).

[k]Based on numerical interpretation of qualitative judgment.

[l]Based on extrapolation of Canadian results to U.S. nonsmokers.

[m]Based on linear extrapolation from retained RSP in smokers.

posure to a pollutant were of the order of 1 $\times 10^{-6}$, and 75 million persons were at risk, then this would produce about 75 deaths per lifetime. If 75 years is used as an exposure lifetime, this is 1 estimated death per year. How does the estimated annual mortality of various regulated carcinogenic air pollutants and tobacco smoke pollution compare with the *de minimis* risk level? Nine workers have estimated the lung cancer mortality risk of tobacco smoke pollution. Table 7–2 reproduces the nine estimates. In some cases, the lung cancer deaths are interpolated from an overall estimate that includes estimated tobacco smoke pollution-caused deaths from diseases other than lung cancer, and additionally includes ex-smokers in those cases where the authors did not include them in the original estimate. This facilitates intercomparison of studies. The mean of all estimates is 4,500 ± 2,800, and with the estimates of Arundel et al. (which differ by more than two standard deviations from the remainder) removed, about 5,000 ± 2,400.

Table 7–3 characterizes this estimated risk by comparison with the estimated risks for other indoor and outdoor airborne carcinogens (Repace and Lowrey 1990). It is seen that tobacco smoke pollution poses a far more serious public health risk than all other

Table 7–3 Comparison of Estimated Annual Cancer Deaths from Various Airborne Carcinogens in the U.S.

Indoor Pollutants	No.
Environmental tobacco smoke[a] (homes & workplaces)	5,000[c]
Radon gas in homes	4,000[c]
Outdoor Pollutants[b]	No.
Asbestos	15
Vinyl chloride	<27
Airborne radionuclides	17
Coke-oven emissions	<15
Benzene	<8
Arsenic	<5

Source: Repace and Lowrey 1990.

[a]Lung cancer only.

[b]Before control.

[c]Nonsmokers only.

Table 7–4 Total Annual Estimated Mortality
from Passive Smoking (all causes, rounded figures)

Cause	Estimated Deaths	Reference
Heart disease	35,000	Wells, 1988; Glantz & Parmley 1991; Steenland 1992
Lung cancer	5,000	Repace & Lowrey 1990
Other cancer	10,000	Wells 1988
Total	50,000	Fong 1982; Taylor, et al. 1992, Wells 1988, Glantz & Parmley 1991.

involuntary airborne carcinogenic risks to public health combined.

TOTAL MORTALITY FROM TOBACCO SMOKE POLLUTION

Finally, four groups of workers, Fong (1982), Glantz and Parmley (1991), Wells (1988) and Taylor, et al. (1992) have estimated the total number of passive smoking deaths from all causes (including heart and cancer) at around 50,000 per year in the United States. This ranks the risks of passive smoking as the third leading preventable cause of death, behind only the deaths caused by smoking itself, and those caused by alcohol. Table 7–4 shows the estimated breakdown of the deaths by cause.

RISK MANAGEMENT OF TOBACCO SMOKE POLLUTION

Given the seriousness of the risk from tobacco smoke pollution, how may the public health be protected? The National Institute for Occupational Safety and Health (NIOSH) has recommended that exposures to ETS in the workplace be eliminated by prohibiting smoking there. Until tobacco use can be completely eliminated, NIOSH recommends that exposures be reduced "to the lowest feasible concentration" (NIOSH 1991). What are the residual risks from efforts to control tobacco smoke pollution short of completely eliminating smoking in the building? Repace and Lowrey [1985b, 1993 (in press)] have addressed this question for lung cancer risk.

In the typical workplace, a nonsmoker is estimated to be exposed to about 1.8 mg of tobacco tar per average workday (Repace and Lowrey 1985b). Assuming 40 years of exposure at this average risk level yields an estimate aggregate risk of 3×10^{-3}, and an estimated risk of 3×10^{-2} to the most exposed nonsmokers, who are estimated to inhale 14 mg of tobacco tar per day (Repace and Lowrey 1980). By the criteria elicited by Travis and co-workers (1987), the risk of lung cancer from tobacco smoke pollution is, by itself, a *de manifestis* risk. Repace and Lowrey (1985b) have estimated that the achievement of *de minimis* risk in a typical office workplace would require increases in air exchange rates by 226-fold, a practical impossibility. This analysis also demonstrated that air cleaning and spacial separation of smokers from nonsmokers were equally futile. Repace and Lowrey (1985b) concluded that physical separation of smokers from nonsmokers on separate ventilation systems or complete bans on smoking were the only effective means of protecting nonsmokers from the risk of lung cancer caused by tobacco smoke pollution in buildings.

Although effective separate ventilation will protect nonsmokers adequately, complete protection is difficult to ensure, permitting smoking in the building makes the smoking policy harder to enforce, and, more importantly, smokers appear to be at significantly increased risk of cancer from other smokers' smoke (Sandler et al. 1985; Geng et al. 1988). Moreover, as Stillman et al. (1991) have demonstrated, total bans on smoking in the workplace may have the beneficial result of producing 10–20% 1-year quit rates among smokers, which has the net effect of reducing tobacco smoke pollution in indoor environments other than the workplace.

REGULATORY ISSUES

Given the enormous damage to public health caused by nicotine addiction, why haven't federal regulatory agencies done more to control the risk? The answer lies partly in the fact that in the United States, there are 20 states which grow tobacco, giving these tobacco states 40 senators, and many more congressmen. This strong congressional influence has enabled the tobacco industry to preempt potential federal regulation under every conceivable vehicle: the Federal Hazardous Substances Act, the Consumer Product Safety Act, the Fair Packaging and Labeling Act, the Controlled Substance Act, and the Toxic Substance Control Act. Moreover, a federal court has ruled that Congress did not intend tobacco products to be regulated under the Food Drug and Cosmetics Act (Repace 1981). And the federal cigarette-labeling law prohibits states from regulating tobacco for health reasons.

Although tobacco smoke pollution can be regulated by states, the tobacco industry has fought back with a disinformation campaign to stave off legislation. In a typical example of this multinational effort, the New Zealand Tobacco Institute produced a report entitled "Thru The Smokescreen: A Critique of ETS," a review of the literature on tobacco smoke pollution. This report was found to be fraudulent by Dr. Judith Reinken, in a study sponsored by the New Zealand Department of Health (Reinken 1990). Reinken could find only 256 of 331 references cited, and 196 other pertinent references were not included. References after 1986 consisted mainly of unpublished research, and of 20 unrefereed 1988 citations, 18 were from tobacco industry-funded authors. When other scientists' reports were criticized in the report, the criticisms were presented as if they had gone undefended. Whole areas, such as child health and ETS, were largely ignored, and several studies indicating that ETS affects children's health were quoted out of context so as to imply that factors other than ETS were causal. The effects of tobacco smoke pollution on the unborn were completely ignored. Small studies were accorded as much merit as large ones. The validity of statistical pooling of the results of several studies (meta-analysis) to obtain sufficient numbers for analysis was denied by the Tobacco Institute (TI). Only three of six review articles on ETS published since 1986 were cited. The book most frequently cited by TI in support of its arguments, *Indoor and Ambient Air Quality* (Perry 1988) turned out to be the proceedings of a conference organized by the tobacco industry and held in London in 1988.

As with similar industry-sponsored conferences held in Bermuda, Geneva, Vienna, Essen, Tokyo, and Montreal during the 1970s and 1980s, it presented the invited papers of both tobacco industry representatives and consultants as well as those of a few independent researchers. Despite the range of views offered at these meetings, summary statements added by the editors offer industry positions as the meeting consensus. These biased summaries, in turn, have provided convenient literature citations for industry spokespeople on numerous occasions over the past 15 years around the world. As a result of Reinken's analysis, the New Zealand Health Ministry was directed to henceforth ignore the tobacco industry's arguments by the Minister of Health.

As might be expected, the tobacco industry presents an organized face to respond to difficult questions concerning advertising bans, tobacco addiction, product liability, and ETS. The industry has standard responses to many of these questions for use by its spokesmen worldwide (Mealy's Litigation Reports 1988). For example, in response to the question often posed by journalists: "How do you explain the fact that most medical experts agree that smoking does cause lung cancer?", the stock reply is, "As a matter of fact, there are also scientists who hold the view that smoking has not been scientifically established as a cause of lung cancer. No one knows the cause or causes of lung cancer, or how it develops. Until we have that knowledge, the issue will remain an open question." Similarly, with respect to tobacco smoke pollution, in response to the question, "Isn't it possible for nonsmokers to get lung cancer and other diseases just by being in the same room with a smoker?", the stock reply is, "There is no scientific proof that environmental tobacco smoke is harmful to nonsmokers. Studies on which the Surgeon General's and National Academy of Sciences' reports are based are seriously flawed in a number of key areas of methodology—particularly the fact that they fail to assess the dose of environmental tobacco smoke to which individuals in the study are exposed. They rely instead on questionnaires regarding the smoking habits of spouses and draw conclusions about the amount of exposure. . . ." The reply goes on to cite the 1981 American Cancer Society study by Garfinkel (1981) as being "inconsistent" with two other 1981 studies of passive smoking and lung cancer, ignoring the fact that as of 1988 there were 21 other studies of passive smoking and lung cancer. Taken together these studies convinced several panels of independent experts in the United States and abroad that passive smoking does in fact increase lung cancer among nonsmokers (USDHHS 1986; NRC 1986; IARC 1987; NIOSH 1991; USEPA 1992). In addition, a paradoxical argument frequently cited by tobacco industry consultants to explain the results of the epidemiological studies of passive smoking and lung cancer is to assert that smokers were misclassified as nonsmokers (Lee 1991). While this explanation tacitly concedes that tobacco smoke exposure causes cancer in smokers, it also conveys the assumption that there is a threshold below which tobacco smoke does not induce lung cancer, and that all nonsmokers are beneath it (Repace and Lowrey 1991). Such organized responses are designed by the tobacco industry to slow public health measures aimed at controlling the tobacco pandemic.

The public health measures necessary to control tobacco smoke pollution rest on a solid scientific foundation. Additional data are not needed for policy decisions on basic strategies for protecting the nonsmoking population. However, there are a number of important research needs that should be followed up to advance the general understanding of the health effects from tobacco smoke pollution and to improve our understanding of the risks.

RESEARCH NEEDS

It would be useful to assess the relative magnitude of exposure and risk from passive smoking in the workplace relative to passive smoking at home by means of further atmospheric, biological, and epidemiological measures. Controlled experiments relating atmospheric concentration of nicotine to urinary cotinine in nonsmokers are needed. Further study of the lower risks of smoking-related diseases in life-long nonsmoking populations such as Seventh-Day Adventists and Mormons, who are exposed to less tobacco smoke pollution than most other groups, due to religious proscriptions against smoking (Phillips et al. 1980; Repace and Lowrey 1985a), should be conducted. Also, the relative importance of childhood exposures to passive smoking for adult lung cancer risk and other problems need to be further explored (Janerich et al. 1990; Sandler et al. 1985; Fontham et al. 1991). Further studies of the influence of tobacco smoke pollution on heart disease and other cancers are needed.

CONCLUSION

Tobacco smoke pollution is capable of causing health effects ranging from acute irritation, to chronic respiratory morbidity, to mortality. The most important sites to protect nonsmokers from tobacco smoke pollution are the workplace and the home. Control measures for ETS short of complete bans on smoking are ineffective. Tobacco smoke pollution needs to be taken as seriously as the other major public health threats of our time.

REFERENCES

Adams, J., O'Mara-Adams, K., Hoffmann, D. Toxic and carcinogenic agents in undiluted mainstream smoke and sidestream smoke of different types of cigarettes. *Carcinogenesis* 8:729–731, 1987.

Arundel, A., Sterling, T., Weinkam, J. Never smoker lung cancer risks from exposure to particulate tobacco smoke. *Environment International* 13:409–426, 1987.

ASHRAE. The American Society of Heating, Refrigerating, and Air Conditioning Engineers. *Ventilation for Acceptable Indoor Air Quality.* ASHRAE Standard 62-89, Atlanta, GA, 1989.

Butler, T. The relationship of passive smoking to various health outcomes among Seventh-Day Adventists in California. *Seventh World Conference on Tobacco and Health* 316 (abstr):1990.

Cummings, K. M., Markello, S. J., Mahoney, M. C., Marshall, J. R. Measurement of lifetime exposure to passive smoke. *Am J Epidemiol* 130:122–132, 1989.

Cummings, K. M., Mahoney, M., Bhargava, A.

K., McElroy, P. D., Marshall, J. R. Measurement of current exposure to environmental tobacco smoke. *Arch Env Health* 45:74–79, 1990.

Daling, J. R., Weiss, N. S., Hislop, T. G., Maden, C., Coates, R. J., Ashley, R. L., Beagrie, M., Ryan, J. A., Corey, L. Sexual practices, sexually transmitted disease, and the incidence of anal cancer. *N Engl J Med* 317:973–977, 1987.

Dube, M. F., and Green, C. R. Methods of collection of smoke for analytical purposes. *Recent Adv Tob Sci* 8:42–102, 1982.

Fong, P. The hazard of cigarette smoke to nonsmokers. *J Biol Phys* 10:65–73, 1982.

Fontham, E.T.H., Correa, P., Wu-Williams, A., Reynolds, P., Greenburg, R. S., Buffler, P. A., Cheln, V. W., Boyd, P., Alterman, T., Austin, D. F., Liff, J., Greenburg, S. D. Lung cancer in nonsmoking women. *Cancer Epidemiol Biomarkers Prevention* 1:35–44, 1991.

Glantz, S. A., and Parmley, W. W. Passive smoking and heart disease: Epidemiology, physiology, and biochemistry. *Circulation* 83:1–12, 1991.

Guerin, M. Formation and physicochemical nature of sidestream smoke. In International Agency for Research on Cancer (IARC). *Environmental Carcinogens: Methods of Analysis and Exposure Measurement,* vol. 9, *Passive Smoking.* O'Neill, I., Brunnemann, K. D., Dodet, B., Hoffman, D., eds. Lyon, France: International Agency for Research on Cancer, 1987.

Hammond, S. K., Smith, T. J., Woskie, S. R., Leaderer, B. P., Bettinger, N. Markers of exposure to diesel exhaust and cigarette smoke in railroad workers. *Am Ind Hyg Assoc J* 49:516–522, 1988.

Hellberg, D., Valentin, J., Eklund, T., Staffan, N. Penile cancer: Is there an epidemiological role for smoking and sexual behaviour? *Br Med J* 295:1306–1308, 1987.

Horton, A. W. Indoor tobacco smoke pollution: A major risk factor for both breast and lung cancer? *Cancer* 62:6–14, 1988.

International Agency for Research on Cancer (IARC). *Monographs on the Evaluation of the Carcinogenic Risk of Chemicals in Humans—Tobacco Smoking,* vol. 38. O'Neill, I., Brunnemann, K. D., Dodet, B., Hoffman, D., eds. Lyon, France: International Agency for Research on Cancer, 1986.

———. *Environmental Carcinogens: Methods of Analysis and Exposure Measurement,* vol. 9, *Passive Smoking.* O'Neill, I., Brunnemann, K. D., Dodet, B., Hoffman, D. eds.

Lyon, France: International Agency for Research on Cancer, 1987.

Janerich, D. T., Thompson, W. D., Varela, L. R., Greenwald, P., et al. Lung cancer and exposure to tobacco smoke in the household. *N Engl J Med* 323:632–636, 1990.

Jarvis, M. J. Uptake of environmental tobacco smoke. In International Agency for Research on Cancer (IARC) *Environmental Carcinogens: Methods of Analysis and Exposure Measurement,* vol. 9, *Passive Smoking.* O'Neill, I., Brunnemann, K. D., Dodet, B., Hoffman, D., eds. Lyon, France: International Agency for Research on Cancer, 1987, 43–58.

———. Application of biochemical intake markers to passive smoking measurement and risk estimation. *Mutat Res* 222:101–110, 1989.

Kawachi, I., Pearce, N. E., Jackson, R. T. Deaths from lung cancer and ischaemic heart disease due to passive smoking in New Zealand. *New Zealand Med J* 102:337–340, 1989.

Kinlen, L. J., and Rogot, E. Leukaemia and smoking habits among United States veterans. *Br Med J* 297:657–659, 1988.

Kuller, L. H., Garfinkel, L., Correa, P., Preston-Martin, S., Haley, N., Sandler, D., Hoffmann, D. Contribution of passive smoking to respiratory cancer. *Environ Health Perspect* 70:57–69, 1986.

Leaderer, B. P. Assessing exposures to environmental tobacco smoke. *Risk Analysis* 10:19–26, 1990.

Leaderer, B. P., Cain, W. S., Isseroff, G., Berglund, L. G. Ventilation requirements in buildings. II. Particulate matter and carbon monoxide from cigarette smoking. *Atmos Environ* 18:99–106, 1984.

Leaderer, B. P., and Hammond, S. K. An evaluation of vapor-phase nicotine and respirable suspended particle mass as markers for environmental tobacco smoke. *Environmental Science and Technology,* in press.

Marks, B. E. Respiratory illness and home environment. *Br Med J* 296:1740, 1988.

Mealy's Litigation Reports. *Tobacco.* Wayne, PA: Mealey Publications, 1988.

Miesner, E. A., Rudnick, S. N., Preller, L., Nelson, W. Particulate and nicotine sampling in public facilities and offices. *JAPCA* 39:1577–1582, 1989.

Nagda, N. L., Fortmann, R. C., Koontz, M. D., Baker, S. R., Ginevan, M. E. *Airliner cabin environment: Contaminant measurements, health risks and mitigation options.* Report # DOT P-15-89-5. U. S. Department of Transportation, Washington, DC, December 1989.

National Institute for Occupational Safety and Health (NIOSH). *Current Intelligence Bulletin #54. Environmental Tobacco Smoke in the Workplace, Lung Cancer and Other Health Effects.* U.S. Department of Health and Human Services, National Institute for Occupational Safety and Health, Cincinnati, OH, June 1991.

National Research Council (NRC). *Environmental Tobacco Smoke—Measuring Exposures and Assessing Health Effects.* Washington, D.C.: National Academy Press, 1986.

Perry, R. and Kirk, P. W., eds. *Indoor and Ambient Air Quality.* London: Selper, Press, 1988.

Peto, R., and Lopez, A. D., The future worldwide health effects of current smoking patterns: WHO Consultative Group estimates for the 1990s and beyond, Seventh World Conference on Tobacco and Health, Perth, Australia, 1990.

Phillips, R. L., Kuzma, J. W., Beeson, W. L., Lotz, T. Influence of selection vs. lifestyle on risk of fatal cancer and cardiovascular disease among Seventh-Day Adventists. *Am J Epidemiol* 112:296–314, 1980.

Reinken, J. *Thru The Smoke Screen.* Wellington, New Zealand: New Zealand Department of Health, 1990.

Repace, J. L. Risks of passive smoking. In Wilson, M., and The Center for Philosophy and Public Policy, University of Maryland, eds. *To Breathe Freely.* Paramus, NJ: Rowan and Allenheld, 1985.

———. Indoor concentrations of environmental tobacco smoke: Models dealing with effects of ventilation and room size, vol. 9, *Passive Smoking, scientific publication #81.* O'Neill, I., Brunnemann, K. D., Dodet, B., Hoffman, D., eds. Lyon, France: International Agency for Research on Cancer, 1987a.

———. Indoor concentrations of environmental tobacco smoke: Field Surveys, ch. 10, vol. 9, *Passive Smoking, scientific publication #81.* O'Neill, I., Brunnemann, K. D., Dodet, B., Hoffman, D., eds. Lyon France: International Agency for Research on Cancer, 1987b.

———. Are indoor air quality standards needed? In Berglund, B., and Lindvall, T., eds. *Healthy Buildings '88,* vol. 4, *Conclusions and Recommendations for Healthier Buildings.* Stockholm, Sweden: Swedish Council for Building Research, 1991.

Repace, J. L., and Lowrey, A. H. Indoor air pollution, tobacco smoke, and public health. *Science* 208:464–472, 1980.

———. Tobacco smoke, ventilation, and indoor air quality. *ASHRAE Trans* 88:894–914, 1982.

———. An indoor air quality standard for ambient tobacco smoke based on carcinogenic risk. *NY State J Med* 85:381–383, 1985a.

———. A quantitative estimate of nonsmokers' lung cancer risk from passive smoking. *Environ Int* 11:3–22, 1985b.

———. Rebuttal to criticism of the phenomenological model of nonsmokers' lung cancer risk. . . . *Environmental Carcinogenisis Reviews (J Environ Sci Health)* C4(2):225–235, 1986.

———. Predicting the Lung Cancer Risk of Domestic Passive Smoking (letter). *Am Rev Respir Dis* 136:1308, 1987a.

———. Environmental tobacco smoke and indoor air quality in modern office work environments (editorial). *J Occup Med* 29:628–629, 1987b.

———. Risk assessment methodologies for passive smoking induced lung cancer. *Risk Analysis* 10:27–37, 1990.

———. An enforceable indoor air quality standard for environmental tobacco smoke in the workplace. *Risk Analysis* in press, 1993.

Riboli, E., Preston-Martin, S., Saracci, R., Haley, N. J., Trichopoulos, D., Becher, H., Burch, J. D., Fontham, E.T.H., Gao, Y. T., Jindal, S. K., Koo, L. C., Lemarchand, L., Segnan, N., Shimizu, H., Stanta, G., Wu-Williams, A. H., Zatonski, W. Exposure of nonsmoking women to environmental tobacco smoke, a ten-country collaborative study. *Cancer Causes and Control* 1:243–252, 1990.

Robins, J. Risk assessment—exposure to environmental tobacco smoke and lung cancer. Appendix D, *National Research Council Report on Environmental Tobacco Smoke,* 1986.

Rohan, T. E., and Baron, J. A. Cigarette smoking and breast cancer. *Am J Epidemiol* 129:36–42, 1989.

Russell, M.A.H., Jarvis, M. J., West, R. J. Use of urinary nicotine concentrations to estimate exposure and mortality from passive smoking in non-smokers. *Br J Addict* 81:275–281, 1986.

Sakuma, H., and Kusama, M., et al. The distribution of cigarette smoke components between mainstream and sidestream smoke. I. Acidic components. *Beitr Tabackforsch* 12:63–71, 1983.

———. The distribution of cigarette smoke components between mainstream and sidestream smoke. II. Bases. *Beitr Tabackforsch* 12:199–209, 1984a.

―――――. The distribution of cigarette smoke components between mainstream and sidestream smoke. III. Middle and higher boiling components. *Beitr Tabackforsch* 12:251–258, 1984b.

Sandler, D. P., Everson, R. B., Wilcox, A. J. Passive smoking in adulthood and cancer risk. *Am J Epidemiol* 121:37–48, 1985.

Slattery, J. L., Robinson, L. M., Schuman, K. L., French, T. K., Abbott, T. M., Overall, J. C., Gardner, J. W. Cigarette smoking and exposure to passive smoke are risk factors for cervical cancer. *JAMA* 261:1593–1633, 1989.

Spengler, J. D., Treitman, R. D., Tosteson, T. D., Mage, D. T., Soczek, M. L. Personal exposures to respirable particulates and implications for air pollution epidemiology. *Environ Sci Technol* 19:700–707, 1985.

Steenland, K. Passive smoking and the risk of heart disease. *JAMA* 267:94–99, 1992.

Stillman, F. A., Becker, D. M., Swank, R. T., Hantula, D., Moses, H., Glantz, S., Waranch, R. Ending smoking at the Johns Hopkins medical institutions: An evaluation of smoking prevalence and indoor air pollution. *JAMA* 264:1565–1569, 1991.

Svennsson, C., Pershagen, G., Kominek, J. *Smoking and Passive Smoking in Relation to Lung Cancer in Women.* Stockholm, Sweden: Department of Epidemiology, National Institute of Environmental Medicine, 1988.

Taylor, A. E., Johnson, D. C., Kezemi, H. American Heart Association Position Paper on Environmental Tobacco Smoke and Cardiovascular Disease. *Circulation* 86:1–4, 1992.

Travis, C. C., Richter, S. A., Crouch, E.A.C., Wilson, R., Klema, E. D. Cancer Risk Management: A review of 132 federal regulatory decisions. *Environ Sci Technol* 21:415–420, 1987.

Trichopoulos, D., Day, N. E., Kaklamani, E., Tzonou, A., Munoz, N., Zavitsanos, X., Koumantaki, Y., Trichopoulou, A. Hepatitis B virus, tobacco smoking and ethanol consumption in the etiology of hepatocellular carcinoma. *International Journal of Cancer* 39(1):45–49, January 1987.

U.S. Department of Health and Human Services (USDHHS). The Health Consequences of Smoking. The Changing Cigarette: A Report of the Surgeon General. U.S. Department of Health and Human Services, Public Health Service, Office of the Assistant Secretary for Health, Office on Smoking and Health. DHHS Publication No. (PHS) 81-50156, 1981.

―――――. The Health Consequences of Involuntary Smoking. A Report of the Surgeon General. U.S. Department of Health and Human Services, Public Health Service, Office on Smoking and Health. DHHS Publication No. (CDC) 87-8398, 1986.

―――――. Reducing the Health Consequences of Smoking: 25 Years of Progress. A Report of the Surgeon General. U.S. Department of Health and Human Services, Public Health Service, Centers for Disease Control, Center for Health Promotion and Education, Office on Smoking and Health. DHHS Publication No. (CDC) 89-8411, 1989.

U.S. Department of Transportation (USDOT). *U.S. Department of Transportation Study of Airliner Cabin Air Quality,* Washington, D.C., 1990.

U.S. Environmental Protection Agency (USEPA). *Respiratory Health Effects of Passive Smoking: Lung Cancer and Other Disorders.* EPA/600/6-90/006F, 1992.

Vaughn, W. M., and Hammond, S. K. Impact of "designated smoking area" policy on nicotine vapor and particle concentrations in a modern office building. *J Air Waste Management Assoc* 40:1012–1017, 1990.

Wald, N. J., Nanchanal, K., Thompson, S. G., Cuckle, H. S. Does breathing other people's smoke cause lung cancer? *Br J Med* 293:1217–1222, 1986.

Wells, A. J. An estimate of adult mortality from passive smoking. *Environ Intern* 14:249–265, 1988.

―――――. Breast cancer, cigarette smoking, and passive smoking. *Am J Epidemiol* 133:208–210, 1991.

Wigle, D., Collishaw, N., Kirkbride, J., Mao, Y. Deaths in Canada from lung cancer due to involuntary smoking. *Can Med Assoc J* 136:945–951, 1987.

Williams, D. C., Whitaker, J. R., Jennings, W. G. Measurement of nicotine in building air as an indicator of tobacco smoke levels. *Environ Health Perspect* 60:405–410, 1985.

Wu, A. H., Henderson, B. E., Pike, M. C., Yu, M. C. Smoking and other risk factors for lung cancer in women. *J Natl Cancer Inst* 4:747–751, 1985.

Zhu, B., Sun, Y., Sievers, R. E., Isenberg, W. M., Glantz, S. A. Parmley, W. W. Second hand smoke increases experimental atherosclerosis in rabbits. Paper presented at American College of Cardiology Forty-first Annual Scientific Session, Dallas, TX, 12–16 April 1992.

PART II

MANAGEMENT

8

Treating Nicotine Dependence in Medical Settings: A Stepped-Care Model

C. Tracy Orleans

This chapter presents the rationale for treating nicotine dependence in health care settings and introduces a stepped-care model as a blueprint for intervention. It includes an overview of the patient characteristics associated with success in quitting smoking and of the stages of change smokers progress through as they quit. Treatments for cigarette smokers are emphasized because most clinical work and research has focused on cigarette smoking. Likewise, the chapter focuses on physician interventions, because they have been the most carefully studied. However, applications for allied health care providers (e.g., nurses, physician assistants, health educators, respiratory care practitioners), for dentists and their staffs, for pharmacists, and for chemical dependency counselors also are described. Subsequent chapters give detailed practical guidelines for implementing the interventions outlined here. They also will help the clinician modify this generic treatment model for different settings and for patients in selected high-risk groups (e.g., pregnant smokers, smokers with cardiac or pulmonary disease or cancer, psychiatric and chemical dependency patients) and for smokeless tobacco users.

RATIONALE FOR MEDICAL INTERVENTION

Key Role of Physician

The doctor–patient relationship provides a "unique and powerful" context for nicotine dependence treatments (Glynn and Manley 1989b). Most smokers quit for health reasons and say that advice from their physicians would be compelling (Orleans et al. 1985; Harris 1978). Although the majority of American smokers want to quit smoking (USDHHS 1989b), only a small proportion will ever enroll in organized quit smoking treatments or clinics (Fiore et al. 1990). However, 70% of smokers in the United States see a physician on an annual basis (Davis 1988). Accordingly, physicians in the United States could intervene with about 32 million of the nation's 46 million adult smokers annually.

Moreover, smokers in the United States make an average of 4.3 yearly physician visits per year (Davis 1988). This provides opportunities for intervention over repeated visits, at a variety of "teachable moments" in the medical care of any individual patient (e.g., not limited to, but especially the diagnosis and treatment of smoking-related symptoms/diseases or hospitalization for a smoking-related illness or condition). Increasingly widespread smoke-free hospital policies lead many smokers to quit for at least a few days (Burtaine and Slade 1988; Hurt et al. 1989; Joseph et al. 1990; Orleans and Slade 1992; Orleans et al. in press). If they receive help, these patients might turn short-term abstinence into permanent cessation (Orleans et al. 1990; Taylor et al. 1990). Notwithstanding these multiple opportunities, more than half of American smokers unfortunately still say they never have been advised by their physician to quit smoking (Frank et al. 1991; Gritz 1988).

Other Health Professionals

Of course, the physician is not the only health professional with an important role to play. Motivating and helping smokers to quit increasingly involves the entire health care team in the full range of health care settings (USDHHS 1990a). Nurses make up the single largest group of health care professionals available to intervene with smokers in health care settings. Because of their unique and ongoing contact with patients, nurses can function as key quit smoking counselors on their own, or in concert with the physician in hospital, primary care, and public health settings (Blair, 1989; Fleisher et al. 1990; Goldstein et al. 1987; Taylor et al. 1990; USDHHS 1990b), as well as in occupational health settings (Hourigan, Knapp, Kottke 1989). Quit smoking interventions also have been designed for respiratory care practitioners (Nett 1987; USDHHS 1989a), physician assistants (Cox 1990; Orleans 1984), pharmacists (Pilgrim 1990; USDHHS 1984), and chemical dependency counselors (Joseph et al. 1990).

According to Cohen and co-workers (1989), over half of Americans visit a dentist each year, affording another occasion for quit smoking advice and assistance. Christen (1990) estimates that about 39 million smokers receive routine dental care annually and projects that if 5% of the smokers seen by the nation's 140,000 dentists were to quit in response to an intervention by the dentist and/or a hygienist, the dental profession could help about 1.6 million Americans to become smoke-free each year. Moreover, dentists and dental hygienists are in a unique position to intervene with users of smokeless tobacco (Severson, Stevens, Little et al. 1990) (Chapter 13). A 1990 survey of Oregon dentists found that they were more active and more comfortable intervening with smokeless tobacco users than with smokers (Severson, Eakin, Stevens et al. 1990).

Efficacy of Medical/Dental Intervention and Intervention Characteristics Associated with Positive Outcomes

Many clinical trials have demonstrated the power of physician advice and counseling. Ockene (1987) summarized seven controlled trials, concluding that physicians who intervene with their patients who smoke have a statistically and clinically significant impact, and that better results occur with more intensive interventions. Glynn (1988) reviewed 28 physician-based smoking cessation trials and found that advice or counseling alone produced 6–12 month quit rates of approximately 5–10%, while more intensive physician-based intervention resulted in quit rates of 20–25%. Kottke and colleagues (1988) used meta-analysis to summarize results of 39 controlled smoking trials involving physician intervention. Comparisons between intervention and control groups indicated that physician intervention boosted 1-year quit rates by an average of 5.8 percentage points. Kottke and colleagues found that the most effective interventions were those that involved more than one modality (e.g., face-to-face physician advice, self-help materials, nicotine gum), both physician *and* nonphysician counselors, and a greater number and duration of contacts and smoking follow-up visits. Successful programs were not "one-shot" interventions, but involved repeated efforts over a number of health care visits.

As a blueprint for the 90's, Glynn and Manley (1989a) summarized results of five randomized, controlled clinical trials funded by the National Cancer Institute (NCI) involving more than 30,000 patients and 1,000 providers (mostly physicians, some dentists). Overall, patients in the intervention groups were two to six times more likely to quit than those in usual care conditions. These impressive results were achieved through the application of *a few simple techniques* by physicians/dentists and office staff, *without disrupting routine care:* (1) Ask about smoking at every opportunity; (2) Advise all smokers to stop; (3) Assist the patient in stopping using self-help materials and nicotine replacement when appropriate; and (4) Arrange for follow-up contacts or visits. These techniques, summarized in the NCI's manual for physicians, *How to Help Your Patients Stop Smoking* (Glynn and Manley 1989b), are the ones presented in this chapter and in Chapters 9 and 10.

Similar findings have been reported for interventions involving dentists in private practice. Cohen and associates (1989) randomly assigned 50 dentists briefly trained in smoking management to one of four groups: (1) nicotine gum freely available to patients, (2) the use of chart stickers to identify smokers and remind staff to intervene, (3) gum and reminders, or (4) usual care. Long-term quit rates were almost two times higher when free nicotine gum was supplied (16–17% vs. 9%). Likewise, preliminary analysis of a randomized trial with 450 smokeless tobacco users found short-term quit rates to be twice as high for patients receiving advice to quit from a dentist, combined with brief self-help materials and a 10-minute videotape viewed in the dental clinic (25%) as for patients receiving "usual care" (12%) (Severson, Stevens, Little et al. 1990). The NCI has published a *Manual for the Oral Health Team* (Mecklenburg et al. 1991) that parallels its intervention manual for physicians.

Public Health Impact and Cost-Effectiveness of Medical Intervention

Glynn and Manley (1989a) emphasize that a sustained abstinence rate of even 10% is a very *positive* outcome. If only *half* of U.S. physicians delivered even a brief quitting message to their patients who smoked and were successful with only 1 in 10, this would yield 1.75 million new ex-smokers every year—which would more than double the national annual quit rate (Fiore et al. 1990).

Moreover, Cummings, Rubin, and Oster (1989) estimated that quit smoking advice is at least as cost-effective as other standard preventive medical treatments. Assuming that only 2.7–3.7% of smokers would quit as a result of 4 minutes of physician advice and counseling during routine office visits, they estimated costs of $748–$2,020 per year of life saved, in contrast to estimates of $11,300–$24,408 per year of life saved

through the treatment of moderate–mild hypertension, and $65,511–$108,189 per year of life saved treating hypercholesteremia.

Barriers to Medical Intervention

Most physicians view smoking as a serious health risk and feel responsible for helping their patients quit (Wechsler et al. 1983). However, national physician surveys show that only two-thirds routinely advise most of their smoking patients to quit, and fewer than one-quarter regularly offer systematic treatment either in their practices or via outside referral (e.g., Gottleib, Mullen, McAlister 1987; Orleans et al. 1985). Pessimism about patients' abilities to quit smoking, a lack of time, training, or confidence in their own counseling skills, and a lack of confidence in outside treatments are cited as the major obstacles to more aggressive anti-smoking efforts. Similar barriers have been reported by nurses (Goldstein et al. 1987). The lack of third-party reimbursement for managing this disease also is a major barrier.

Any intervention model must include plans for overcoming systemic barriers as well as step-by-step guidelines for how to intervene with patients who smoke. Any clinician is more likely to intervene when barriers are removed and when he or she is supplied with useful quitting guidelines and aids. For instance, just supplying primary care physicians with free patient self-quitting brochures led them to intervene more frequently and confidently with their patients who smoked (CA 1981). Likewise, in a study of 50 private dental practices, the availability of nicotine gum significantly increased the amount of time spent on quit smoking counseling by private practice dentists and their staff (Cohen et al. 1987).

The lack of training is perhaps the most basic, remediable barrier (Wells, Ware, Lewis 1984). Opportunities for training in state-of-the-art medical behavioral treatments for nicotine dependence in undergraduate medical school, postgraduate training programs, and continuing medical education (CME) programs are increasing. But, they still are surprisingly limited. A survey of U.S. and Canadian medical schools found that only 56% of undergraduate medical school curricula and only 25% of residency training programs included course offerings on smoking cessation (Horton 1986). Unfortunately, only in a handful of select medical schools (e.g., Ockene et al. 1988) do trainees get substantial supervised experience in treating nicotine dependence. Training for other medical professionals, dentists, and dental hygienists is likely to be even less systematic. A recent survey of hospital-based nurses found that only 14% ever had received formal training in smoking cessation counseling (Goldstein et al. 1987). Optimally, training should introduce practical step-by-step guidelines for how to intervene with smokers in the course of routine medical/dental care, and how to steer patients to appropriate resources outside the medical sector for additional help (see Chapter 12).

UNDERSTANDING THE QUITTING PROCESS

Patient Characteristics Associated with Successful Quitting

Whether they quit on their own or through a formal treatment program, smokers are more likely to succeed if they possess certain motivations and expectations, employ certain quitting and self-management skills, and draw on social support and psychosocial resources in their efforts. Table 8–1 summarizes these factors, plus the chemical dependency and smoking habit variables associated with successful recovery from nicotine addiction. The characteristics listed in Table 8–1 are based on over a decade of research to identify factors associated with cessation among *adult* smokers (e.g., Glassman et al. 1990; Gritz 1988; Lichtenstein, Glasgow, Abrams 1986; Orleans 1988; Pechacek and Danaher 1979; Pederson et al. 1982; Schoenbach et al. 1992; USDHHS 1989b; Wilcox et al. 1985). Less is known about predictors of quitting success among adolescents: these factors are noted in Chapter 4 and discussed in more detail in Chapter 19.

Adult smokers motivated to quit for health reasons, particularly those concerned about minor smoking-related symptoms (wheezing, coughing, shortness of breath),

are more likely to succeed. The presence of smoking-related disease also may facilitate quitting; however, as noted in Chapter 4, the effects vary with the nature of the illness. Having cardiovascular disease makes one more likely to quit smoking—in fact, having a heart attack is still the most effective smoking cessation "treatment" known, producing 50–60% 1-year quit rates (Gritz 1988). On the other hand, having other chronic diseases that are exacerbated by smoking (chronic obstructive pulmonary disease or COPD and diabetes) is associated with poorer cessation outcomes. While this may be due to differences in the perceived risks of smoking and incentives for quitting (see Chapters 4 and 14), it also may reflect the fact that the patients with these chronic conditions who continue to smoke represent people more heavily addicted to nicotine, and unable to quit easily in response to clear evidence of disease (Orleans et al. in press).

Smokers who want to quit to achieve greater self-control or mastery are more likely to succeed, as are those who come to the quitting process with confidence that they can succeed (self-efficacy) and the expectation of many benefits from quitting. The presence of nonsmoking norms and supports for not smoking in one's environment, the potential for helpful support for quitting from friends, family, co-workers and/or medical professionals, and the absence of strong smoking norms, all facilitate quitting. Smokers also are more likely to succeed if they possess certain socioeconomic advantages (e.g., education, income, occupation, employment) and psychosocial assets (e.g., manageable life stress, good stress coping skills, self-esteem, freedom from other addictions and health life-style problems and from significant psychopathology). Smokers whose smoking rate and nicotine addiction levels are lower, and those who have quit in the past for 6 months or more, are more likely to succeed. Finally, Table 8–1 lists a variety of prequitting, quitting, and maintenance skills and strategies that are associated with achieving and maintaining cigarette abstinence.

The most effective interventions are those that (1) equip smokers with these requisite quitting motivations, supports, and skills;

Table 8–1 Factors Associated with Better Prognosis for Achieving and Sustaining Cigarette Abstinence

Motivational Factors	Social Support/ Psychosocial Assets	Smoking Habit Factors	Effective Quitting and Maintenance Skills/Strategies
Desire to protect future health and overcome minor smoking-related symptoms (e.g., shortness of breath, coughing, loss of stamina)	Personal medical quit smoking advice and follow-up	Lower smoking rate and nicotine intake (e.g., fewer than 25 cigarettes/day, low nicotine brand)	Using prequitting strategies, such as monitoring smoking rate, reviewing reasons for quitting, systematic brand switching to gradually reduce nicotine intake before quitting
	Support and encouragement from family, friends, and co-workers	Lower nicotine dependence (e.g., first cigarette at least 30 minutes after waking, few past difficulties with withdrawal after quitting)	
Sense of personal vulnerability to smoking health risks	Strong nonsmoking norms in one's immediate social environment		Quitting abruptly on a target date ("cold turkey")
Desire for greater self-mastery, self-control, or self-esteem	Socioeconomic advantage (e.g., education, income, occupation, employment)		Using a variety of methods to cope with withdrawal symptoms (e.g., deep breathing, positive thinking, concrete cigarette substitutes)
Confidence in ability to quit		Shorter smoking history	
	Psychosocial assets (e.g., self-esteem, self-management skills, healthy coping skills, positive health habits, manageable life stress, freedom from other chemical dependencies, no past history of major depression)	Past success quitting for 6 months or longer	Using a variety of methods to remain off cigarettes (e.g., avoiding temptations to smoke, finding alternative ways to relax and cope with stress such as hobbies or exercise, using substitute self-rewards to counteract sense of loss and prevent relapse)
One or more past quit attempts, especially in past year		Less dependence on smoking to regulate negative affect	
Expectation of many quitting benefits (e.g., health, social, psychological, cosmetic)			Taking a long-range, problem-solving approach and making repeated attempts in a cumulative learning process

(2) help them to overcome their physical dependence on nicotine; and (3) help them to overcome any other quitting obstacles they face (e.g., strong smoking norms at home or work, strong fear of weight gain) and to deal constructively with co-morbid factors that might present special difficulties (e.g., insufficient coping skills, problem drinking, over-eating, depression).

The clinician can use Table 8–1 as a "checklist" to assess a patient's quitting prognosis and to help select an appropriate initial quitting program and any adjunctive treatments (e.g., pharmacologic aids for withdrawal, weight control assistance, stress management training). In general, smokers who possess many of the characteristics shown in Table 8–1 will be ideal candidates for minimal-contact, low-intensity approaches offered in the course of routine medical care (e.g., 2–3 minutes physician advice, brief counseling in use of self-help materials, nicotine replacement therapy) (Schoenbach et al. 1992). Smokers who possess few of these characteristics may be better candidates for more intensive formal treatment programs—programs designed to supply or strengthen the motivations, skills, and supports the smoker is missing. In fact, it is useful to think in terms of a continuum severity of addiction based on the severity of psychological and physiological tobacco dependency, the strength and nature of the patient's quitting motivation, and the adequacy of his or her self-change skills and supports.

Quitting as a Multistage Process

Prochaska and DiClemente and their colleagues (Prochaska and DiClemente 1983; Prochaska et al. 1992; USDHHS 1989b, 1990a) have demonstrated that recovery from nicotine dependence is a multistage process (see also Chapter 4). The smoker achieves long-term quitting success by advancing through a sequence of natural stages, often recycling through these stages over repeated quit attempts. As Figure 8–1 shows, there are five major stages through which a quitter may cycle on any given attempt, or over several attempts:

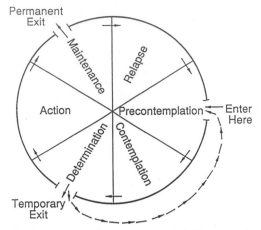

1. *Precontemplation*—not thinking seriously about quitting smoking;
2. *Contemplation and Determination (or preparation)*—planning or deciding to quit;
3. *Action*—preparing to quit and quitting; and finally
4. *Maintenance* of nonsmoking, and
5. *Relapse and "Recycling"* with those who slip or relapse after achieving abstinence returning to any earlier stage.

Fig. 8–1 A stage model of the process of change. *Source:* Prochaska and DiClemente 1983.

Unfortunately, relapse is the norm following the achievement of initial abstinence. In this regard, the management of nicotine dependence is similar to the management of any chronic condition, like hypertension, and to the clinical management of alcoholism or obesity (Brownell et al. 1986). Hunt, Barnett, and Branch (1971) found nearly identical relapse patterns in treated alcoholics, smokers, and heroin addicts. Approximately 70% of all abstinent individuals followed over a year relapsed by 1 year with the vast majority doing so in the first 3 months postabstinence. Kottke et al. (1990) followed smoking patients over 1 year and found that among those who had quit for 24 hours or more, one-quarter had relapsed within 2 days; one-half had relapsed within 1 week—during the early part of the acute withdrawal stage. Subsequent relapse events are less likely to involve withdrawal reactions, but instead, tend to occur in circumstances in-

volving negative affect (anger, frustration, sadness), interpersonal conflicts, and social pressure to smoke (Marlatt and Gordon 1985). Relapse is less likely after 6–12 months of abstinence: but there is no proven "safe" point beyond which relapse is unlikely (Brownell et al. 1986). And data from the National Health and Nutrition Examination Survey indicate that relapse remains a threat even after 1 year—38% of smokers who had been off cigarettes for at least a year reported relapsing at some point; 43% of whom went on to quit again, eventually achieving long-term abstinence most of the time (USDHHS 1990a).

The fact that quitting smoking is a multistage process means that medically based treatments must involve persistent efforts over repeated contacts, not just "one-shot" interventions. Each patient contact presents an opportunity to help the smoker take the *next step* toward permanent cessation. The goal with precontemplators, for instance, is to move them, over time, to contemplation and action stages by bolstering their quitting motivation and self-efficacy. The goal for contemplators is to motivate and assist them to move to a determination to quit, and then to take action and maintain abstinence. The goal for those in action is to assist them to quit smoking and to stay smoke-free. The goal for those in maintenance stages is to help them consolidate a new nonsmoking life-style and to resist relapse cues, triggers, and temptations (Marlatt and Gordon 1985). Finally, the goal for relapsers is to remotivate them, so they return to contemplation, action, or maintenance stages rather than to a precontemplative state.

Research shows that "recycling" is common, and helpful, among relapsed quitters. National survey data show that most current smokers have tried to quit once or more (USDHHS 1989b). There is no clear evidence that relapsers are less likely than "new" quitters to succeed on a given attempt. In fact, one evaluation (Cohen et al. 1989) of more than 5,000 smokers enrolled in several different self-help smoking cessation programs found that the likelihood of quitting did not decrease as a function of number of prior quit attempts. Those with 5–10 quit attempts were no less likely to succeed than those who had tried only a few times.

Moreover, if one takes the view that overcoming nicotine dependence involves incremental learning over time, it follows that smokers might *benefit* from prior quit attempts, learning something with each effort about what it will take for them to succeed. In fact, data from a long-term study of smokers trying to quit on their own found relapsers (people who had made at least one quit attempt and who had stayed off cigarettes for at least 24 hours) were twice as likely to achieve long-term abstinence in the following year as people who had not made a serious quit attempt (Rossi 1988). Similarly, longer duration of abstinence on past quit attempts predicts subsequent quitting success (Gritz 1988; Orleans 1988). Therefore, the model set forth in this chapter is a *cyclical* model—one that assumes most smokers will recycle through multiple interventions, and that many will benefit from referral to more intensive or more specialized treatments over subsequent quit attempt(s).

STEPPED-CARE, CYCLICAL TREATMENT MODEL FOR HEALTH CARE SETTINGS

The model presented here is heuristic—adaptable to a variety of settings, providers, and patient populations (see Figure 8–2; Orleans 1985, 1988). The model starts with a practice environment that encourages nonsmoking and minimizes barriers to quit smoking interventions. It outlines how patients can be offered a variety of opportunities *over time* (and over repeated attempts) to acquire the motivations, skills, and supports needed to achieve sustained abstinence. The model includes treatment and follow-up offered in the practice and/or by referral. The stepped-care approach is a public health model, starting by offering the least intensive, least costly approaches to the largest number of smokers, and reserving more costly and intensive treatments for those who do not succeed with minimal treatments. Similar stepped-care models have been advanced for other preventive medicine interventions, including the treatment of obesity (Brownell 1986) and hypercholesteremia (Blair, Bryant, Bocuzzi 1988).

The essential features of this model are that:

1. it applies to *all* smokers, not just to those already motivated to quit or those seeking treatment;
2. it incorporates notions of staging, encompassing treatment for smokers in all stages of change from precontemplation to maintenance and "recycling";
3. it incorporates an initial assessment and "triage" to steer or match patients to the type or intensity of treatment appropriate to their stage of change, their existing nonsmoking skills, motivations and supports, and the severity of their addiction to nicotine;
4. it is cyclical, offering smokers more specialized or intensive help as they progress through the different stages of recovery from nicotine addiction (precontemplation–contemplation–determination–action–maintenance or "recycling") and through repeated quit attempts; and
5. it can be used in a wide variety of medical settings, inpatient and outpatient, in dental practices and pharmacies, as well as in worksites and community settings.

Each part of the model is described briefly here, and explored in detail in subsequent chapters.

Creating and Maintaining a Facilitative Practice Environment

A facilitative environment is defined as one that provides a high level of nonsmoking cues and supports, and that supplies information to make smokers aware of the negative aspects of smoking and the positive aspects of nonsmoking. In fact, the NCI recommends environmental changes that make nonsmoking cues "persistent and inescapable" (Glynn, Boyd, Gruman 1990). Innovative and inexpensive ways to create an environment that promotes tobacco-free living are discussed in detail in Chapter 9; an overview is provided here.

To start with, there should be visible evidence of a nonsmoking orientation in the health care setting. The setting should be smoke-free, with no smoking signs prominently posted. This includes inpatient and

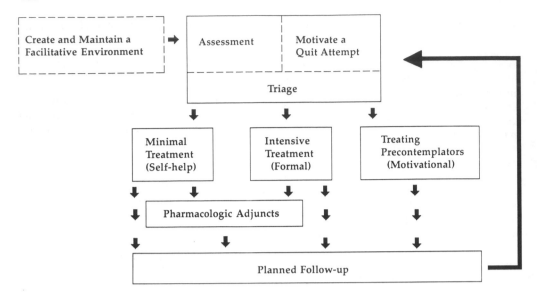

Fig. 8–2 Treating nicotine addiction: A stepped-care, clinical treatment model. *Source:* Orleans, 1988.

outpatient settings (e.g., Hurt et al. 1989). Former smokers on the staff might wear "I Quit" buttons to identify themselves as resources for smokers planning to quit. Patient education materials should be displayed in waiting and treatment areas. Moreover, the NCI's manual for physicians, *How to Help Your Patients Stop Smoking* (Glynn and Manley 1989a) advises that only publications that do not carry tobacco advertising be provided in patient waiting areas. Goldsmith (1991) has compiled a list of approximately 200 suitable "tobacco-free" publications. One recent study found that cigarette advertising in magazines is associated with reduced coverage of the hazards of smoking (Warner, Goldenhar, McLaughlin 1992). In pharmacies offering quit smoking assistance, tobacco products should not be sold (Pilgrim 1990). In some hospital or clinic settings or health maintenance organizations, efforts to publicize available quit smoking treatments and to recruit smokers directly are combined with efforts to identify smokers and inform them of smoking restrictions (e.g., Nett 1987; USDHHS 1989a).

Each practice setting also must have a way to identify smokers (Glynn and Manley 1989a). In most medical settings, asking about smoking status can easily be incorpo-

rated into vital signs checks. Patient histories taken in primary care, hospital, psychiatric, and dental care settings should routinely include questions about tobacco use. Fiore (1991) recommends that smoking status become the "new vital sign" throughout the U.S. medical community. The patient's exposure to environmental tobacco smoke also should be assessed routinely: becoming aware of parental smoking opens an avenue for intervention by pediatricians (Chilmonczyk et al. 1990). Notation should be made in the charts or records of all smokers. Many quit kits designed for medical practice include stickers or stamps designed for this purpose (see Chapters 9 and 10). Cohen and associates (1987) found that physicians and dentists were far more likely to advise their patients to quit and to set quit dates when stickers were placed in the charts of identified smokers. The NCI's kit for pharmacists includes posters and a counter card to prompt patients to ask about smoking (USDHHS 1984).

Another important aspect of creating a facilitative environment, as noted earlier, is to train and motivate (or remotivate) health care providers to intervene effectively with their patients who smoke. Some training in motivational and behavior change strategies will be a prerequisite for quit smoking programs in most health care settings. As Chapter 9 details, effective training can be accomplished in brief CME-type sessions (Ockene et al. 1988). Manley et al. (1991) describe a similar NCI-sponsored 5-hour course for physicians and nurses now being offered nationwide. The goal of the program is to train 100,000 U.S. physicians.

Finally, it must be easy for the physician, dentist, or other health care practitioner to incorporate the treatment of nicotine addiction into routine practice or treatment procedures. It is essential that organizational, financial, and staffing barriers to this intervention be removed or minimized. As a practical matter, Chapter 9 suggests that a "smoking cessation coordinator" be selected within each primary care practice or practice setting. This person assumes responsibility for integrating the treatment of nicotine dependence into the practice's day-to-day activities (i.e., implementing a smoke-free policy, developing procedures to identify all smokers, establishing referral contacts, etc.) (Glynn and Manley 1989a). For inpatient programs, a smoking interventionist or health educator might be identified to assume much of the responsibility for implementing and administering the program, perhaps in concert with the director of the Respiratory Care Department (Emmons and Goldstein 1992; Orleans et al. in press; USDHHS 1989a).

As noted, the barriers most commonly cited by primary care physicians and dentists include: lack of time, lack of coordination between the medical setting and community-based quit smoking programs and resources, and lack of third party reimbursement for the treatment of nicotine dependence (Gottleib et al. 1987; Orleans et al. 1985; Severson, Eakin, Stevens et al. 1990). Many of the same obstacles exist on clinic and hospital settings (Goldstein et al. 1987; Orleans et al. 1990). Additional obstacles in inpatient chemical dependency treatment programs are concerns (unsupported by empirical evidence) that smoking cessation or even restrictive smoking policies might create stress that would jeopardize the outcome of drug or alcohol treatment (Joseph et al. 1990). Emphasizing minimal-

contact, low-intensity treatments, and relying on allied health care staff for more time-consuming counseling and follow-up, can reduce demands on physician time to as little as 2–3 minutes per patient (Glynn and Manley 1989b). Maintaining an up-to-date roster of state-of-the-art community referral programs and resources is essential. Chapter 11 identifies these treatments and gives practical criteria for evaluating community treatment programs; Chapter 10 gives practical referral guidelines. Continuing efforts to secure third party reimbursement for the treatment of tobacco dependence eventually may remove this financial impediment to medically based treatments (USDHHS 1990a).

Essential Elements of Interventions in Health Care Settings

Assessment

It is essential that clinicians take at least a brief smoking and quitting history before offering any treatment—whether minimal contact or a formal treatment program. This can be done by questionnaire or interview. Chapters 9 and 10 offer sample questions and questionnaires, and describe the use of pulmonary function tests and alveolar carbon monoxide testing to assess, and provide "biofeedback" of, smoking health harms and smoke exposure.

At a minimum, the provider should ask about smoking rate, years smoked, whether the first cigarette of the day is smoked within 30 minutes of wakening (a simple but reliable index of nicotine dependency) (Fagerstrom 1978; Pomerleau et al. 1990), desire to quit, stage of quitting (Prochaska and DiClemente 1983), and past quit attempts. Questions about quitting motivations, supports, and obstacles, and about coexisting medical and psychiatric/psychological problems, will help to define the patient's quitting needs and select appropriate treatments, including pharmacologic adjuncts (e.g., nicotine polacrilex or transdermal patch).

A more thorough assessment would cover most or all of the factors listed in Table 8–1 (see, e.g., Orleans and Shipley 1982). Reviewing past attempts allows the provider to assess and bolster quitting motivation, and will help to indicate the most appropriate treatment plan. For instance, even brief probing will reveal whether past difficulties chiefly involved initial withdrawal difficulties, longer-term negative side-effects (e.g., weight gain, stress), a lack of social support, or reliance on ineffective quitting strategies or programs.

Assessment is placed first in the sequence of steps that make up the model in Figure 8–2. This is because intervention starts with identifying patients who smoke. However, the assessment of smoking patterns, quitting problems, and treatment needs must continue into the treatment itself. Any assessment should be conducted in a "therapeutic" manner—reinterpreting past "failure" as "practice"—providing information to correct common misconceptions about smoking, quitting, and formal treatments. Moreover, as the patient makes repeated attempts to quit, both patient and clinician develop more insight into the problems faced by the patient. Information from ongoing assessments should be summarized in the progress notes.

Motivating an Attempt: Risk Education and Quitting Advice

The purpose of this initial step is to enhance quitting motivation among smokers (both contemplators and precontemplators), setting the stage for a serious quit attempt. The percentage of U.S. smokers wishing to quit at any given time is estimated to be 75–80%; yet, each year only about 30% of smokers will make a serious quit attempt (Fiore et al. 1990; Glynn, Boyd, Gruman 1990).

Health motivation is key to successful quitting, so medical quitting advice must include advice about personal health risks of smoking and benefits of quitting (Figure 8–1). The physician, nurse, dentist, or other health professional should capitalize on whatever "teachable moments" arise in the course of their care for any particular smoking patient by pointing out how that patient's presenting symptoms and illnesses are caused or exacerbated by tobacco use. In pediatric settings, links between a parent's smoking and the child's symptoms or illnesses should be made clear. Since medical advice is likely to carry the greatest weight coming from the physician or dentist directly, the physician or dentist should play the key role in this brief "motivating" intervention. Effective medical advice, including a strong "stop smoking" message, can be given in as little as 2–3 minutes.

After reviewing personal health risks and benefits, the provider should go on to briefly explore the patient's interest in and motives for quitting, reviewing any past quit attempts or obstacles. Facts are that 90% of U.S. smokers would like to quit and 60% have tried (many more than once) (Fiore et al. 1990). Hence, most smokers will be at least "contemplating" quitting. Fears that commonly deter smokers from trying to quit also should be addressed (e.g., withdrawal effects, weight gain, lasting sense of loss): Chapter 10 provides suggestions for such "barriers counseling."

Regardless of patient characteristics, medical risk/benefit education should culminate in firm, unambiguous advice to *quit* smoking, with a clear offer of assistance: "As your physician (dentist), I strongly advise that you stop smoking. If we can give you some help, are you willing to give it a try?" Most smokers will agree to try to quit, leading directly to selecting an appropriate treatment, setting a quit date, and arranging planned follow-up. However, smokers who still are in the "precontemplation" stage may not, and they probably should not set a quit date prematurely. As noted later in this chapter, precontemplators should be counseled and followed up in other ways (Miller and Rollnick 1991).

Selecting a Treatment: Triage Guidelines

After eliciting a quit smoking commitment, the next step is to provide or steer the patient to the most appropriate treatment. Many factors will influence this process, beginning with an assessment of the characteristics shown in Table 8–1. Patient preference also plays an important role: the smoker should be actively engaged in making an informed treatment choice. Of course, the cyclical model in Figure 8–2 assures that no matter what the *initial* triage decision, the smoker always has other options for future attempts if unsuccessful with the initial treatment.

Minimal self-help interventions provide the best starting point for most patients unless there is good evidence at the start for believing that a more intensive treatment program is needed or preferred. As Chapter 10 details, about 90% of *ex*-smokers have quit "on their own" and most smokers prefer self-help over formal quitting methods (Fiore et al. 1990; USDHHS 1989b). In fact, as Kristeller and Ockene (1989) point out, the relative impact of minimal-contact interventions is likely to be greater for nicotine dependency than for other addictive disorders.

More intensive formal treatment programs may be a better starting point when the patient expresses a preference for the structure and support that a clinic, group, or counselor can provide; has many prior self-quitting and/or formal treatment failures; and lacks many of the prerequisite quitting motivations, supports, and skills (Table 8–1), indicating that special supports or adjuncts may be helpful. Since over half of all U.S. adults who ever smoked already have quit (USDHHS 1989b), the proportion of heavy, more severely addicted smokers unable to stop on their own has risen. It may be that for this group, more intensive interventions may be especially needed.

Inpatient nicotine addiction treatment programs are emerging as options for the most severely dependent patients who (1) have tried to quit both on their own *and* in clinic or one-to-one counseling programs and/or (2) are unable to remain abstinent even in the face of serious, often life-threatening, smoking-related diseases or conditions. Evaluations of these most intensive programs, now underway, should help to better identify those dependent smokers who are the best candidates for inpatient treatment (Hurt et al. 1992).

Treatment matching also includes choosing from a widening array of *tailored* self-help materials and treatments (Glynn, Boyd, Gruman 1991; USDHHS 1989b). For instance, special self-help guides now are available for women, adolescents, older smokers, African-American and Hispanic smokers, as well as for smokers with certain smoking-related medical risks or problems (including pregnancy, diabetes, cancer, chemical dependency). These guides are reviewed in detail elsewhere (Glynn, Boyd, Gruman 1991) and in subsequent chapters (see especially Chapter 10). Formal treatments also are increasingly tailored and, for instance, might be chosen to address specific quitting barriers, such as concerns about weight control or about problems associated with recovery from another chemical dependency.

Pharmacologic adjuncts to either minimal or formal treatment should be considered whenever they are indicated. In the absence of contraindications, nicotine replacement therapy (gum, patches) should be considered for highly addicted smokers (who smoke within 30 minutes after waking), heavy smokers (25 or more cigarettes/day), and those who suffered severe withdrawal problems in previous quit attempts. As Chapter 12 discusses, other medications also may be helpful (e.g., antidepressants for smokers with a history of major depressive episodes or extreme dysphoria following prior quit attempts, clonidine for patients especially troubled by cravings). To be helpful, pharmacotherapy always should be used as an *adjunct,* never as the sole treatment. When used alone in medical interventions, nicotine gum or patches have been found to have *no* benefit over a placebo (Fiore et al. 1992; Hughes in press; Hughes et al. 1989; Lam et al. 1987).

Minimal Treatment Programs

Helping patients to quit "on their own" potentially is the most cost-effective primary care strategy, and the one most easily incorporated into routine health care. This is why the stepped-care model recommends starting with minimal contact, self-help approaches. Of smokers who make a serious "solo" quit attempt, only 10–15% will be off cigarettes 1 year later, but about 60% will succeed over a lifetime of repeated attempts (Fiore et al. 1990; Schachter 1982).

The health care professional is in a unique position to motivate self-quit attempts and introduce minimal treatments and supports that will enhance their success—usually a self-help quitting guide combined with brief counseling in self-help quitting/maintenance strategies and follow-up (e.g., Cummings et al. 1986; Hourigan et al. 1989; Janz et al. 1987; Kottke et al. 1988). Minimal strategies have been the treatments most extensively refined and tested in primary care (Glynn and Manley 1990a, b) and hospital (Orleans et al. 1990; Taylor et al. 1990) settings, and in dental practices (Cohen et al. 1989; Severson, Eakin, Stevens et al. 1990). They have been distilled down to essential elements that require no more than a few minutes of physician or dentist time and limited additional time from allied health care staff (Glynn and Manley 1989a; Mecklenburg et al. 1991). These same techniques are recommended to nurses (USDHHS 1990b), respiratory care practitioners (USDHHS 1989a), and pharmacists (USDHHS 1984).

Many minimal-contact treatments, involving physicians and allied health professionals (both inpatient and outpatient) achieve 15–25% long-term quit rates with *unselected* patients, including smokers who do and who do not want to quit (Glynn 1988; Janz et al. 1987; Orleans et al. 1990). Quit rates are higher for patients with cardiovascular disease, especially post-acute myocardial infarction (MI) where most quit rates range from 40–60% (Gritz 1988; Ockene 1987; Taylor et al. 1990). Results with self-help treatments can be significantly improved by introducing a number of minimal-contact treatment adjuncts—e.g., brief follow-up counseling in person or by phone, personalized feedback concerning quitting strategies, nicotine replacement (Glynn, Boyd, Gruman 1990). In fact, quit rates may be boosted 50% when self-help adjuncts are used (Orleans et al. 1991). Several effective "add on" activities are described in Chapter 10.

Formal Treatment Programs

Formal treatment programs are a necessary and important backup for the minimal interventions offered in medical care settings. These more intensive treatments, offered ei-

ther within or outside of the health care setting, provide help beyond that of "do-it-yourself" programs, and tend to attract smokers seeking such extra help (Fiore et al. 1990). In fact, formal treatments might be thought of as providing quitters with the motivations, supports, and skills they otherwise lack for a successful *self*-quit attempt (Table 8–1). Most formal treatments produce 1-year quit rates of 15–25% with these selected, motivated smokers. The best, however, achieve 25–40% long-term quit rates (USDHHS 1989b). These are the multicomponent behavioral treatments that include relapse prevention components (see Chapter 11).

Chapter 11 provides a comprehensive overview of existing formal treatment programs, with special emphasis on the most widely available nonprofit and proprietary clinics. Treatment rationales and methods are described, and studies comparing the efficacy of different programs are summarized. Popular smoking aids (filters, lozenges) and unproven treatments (e.g., hypnosis, acupuncture, chemical and dietary treatments) also are reviewed. Chapter 11 includes advice on how to evaluate a formal treatment program before making a referral. Chapter 14 describes formal treatments appropriate for pregnant smokers, and those with cardiac or pulmonary disease or cancer. Chapters 15 and 16 discuss formal treatments for psychiatric and chemical dependency patients, including inpatient nicotine dependency programs.

Pharmacologic Adjuncts

The best studied pharmacological treatment for nicotine dependence is nicotine replacement therapy using nicotine polacrilex (gum). Nicotine gum has been found to be an effective adjunct to minimal quit smoking treatments administered in medical and dental settings (e.g. Cohen et al. 1989), as well as to formal treatment programs (Lam et al. 1987). But, it has been proven *in*effective when provided *only* with medical advice to quit (Hughes et al. 1989; Lam et al. 1987). Therefore, it never should be used alone, but always as an adjunct to a self-help or formal quitting program. Nicotine replacement via transdermal patches promises to be an even more effective adjunct, with more adequate nicotine replacement, fewer unpleasant side effects, and better defined dose and weaning schedules (Fiore et al. 1992; Hurt et al. 1990; Transdermal Nicotine Study Group 1991). Transdermal nicotine patches and other promising pharmacological adjuncts (e.g., clonidine, antidepressants) are described in Chapter 12.

Treating Precontemplators

Patients who are unwilling to make a definite quitting commitment following medical quit smoking advice should be treated and followed up no less diligently than those who are ready to move into action stages. Individuals in precontemplation phases may be resistent in the face of excessive social pressures to quit, pessimistic, or even demoralized in reaction to multiple failed quit attempts, skeptical about smoking health harms and quitting benefits, or just doubtful about their ability ever to succeed in quitting. It is therefore very important to explore with them, in a nonjudgmental, concerned manner, the factors that underlie their lack of quitting motivation. Bolstering quitting motivation and self-efficacy is likely to increase openness to help quitting (Miller and Rollnick 1991).

At the time of initial advice, precontemplators may be supplied with take-home motivational materials, referral information, and/or a self-help guide. Pharmacotherapy, however, should be reserved until they are ready to initiate a minimal or formal *quitting* program. At follow-up visits, further motivational and intervention strategies should be used. Chapter 10 presents several strategies for helping the precontemplator overcome quitting barriers (including resistance) and move ahead into contemplation and action stages.

Planned Follow-up and Recycling

Along with setting a quit date, making arrangements for follow-up contact significantly increases the likelihood that the patient will follow through with agreed upon quitting or prequitting plans (Cummings et al. 1986; Kottke et al. 1988; Janis 1983). In their now famous early study, Russell, Wilson, Taylor, and Baker (1979) found, that even the *warning* of follow-up increased patients' quit attempts and success. As noted earlier, past trials of physician quit smoking interventions show that outcomes are related to the intensity, frequency, and duration of contact, with best results when multiple modalities were used (print, face-to-face, phone, physician- and nurse-delivered, etc.) (Kottke et al. 1988; Ockene 1987).

Follow-up contacts can provide a therapeutic mix of support, surveillance, and assistance, and help to create a relationship of reciprocal commitment (Janis 1982). Follow-up usually consists of return office visits and/or phone calls, often offered in conjunction with personalized mailings (Glynn and Manley 1989a). As noted earlier, several adjuncts to self-help programs constitute effective *follow-up* strategies (Glynn, Boyd, Gruman 1990).

Recycling efforts include assessing what happened, motivating precontemplators and contemplators to move into action stages, and to remotivating relapsers to return to contemplation and action stages. The NCI has recommended that such strategies for recycling should be an *essential* element of all self-help/minimal intervention programs (Glynn, Boyd, Gruman 1990, 1991).

CONCLUSION

The model outlined in this chapter provides a schematic for organizing a comprehensive tobacco addiction treatment in any health care setting. In order to adequately address the needs of *all* smokers, any program should include each of the essential elements in this model, and offer them repeatedly over time, helping smokers recycle through the stages of change as many times as necessary on their way to permanent abstinence. The physician has a unique role to play and physician-initiated interventions can be effectively guided by this model. But, the model provides equally well for important interventions delivered by nurses, respiratory care practitioners, pharmacists, physician assistants, health educators, dentists, and dental hygienists. Subsequent chapters flesh out the model presented here with concrete examples of strategies for a variety of health care professionals and settings, and for smokeless tobacco users.

REFERENCES

Blair, J. E. Smoking intervention: Opportunities for office nurses. *Office Nurse* 2(4):2–7, 1989.

Blair, T. P., Bryant, J., Bocuzzi, S. Treatment of hypercholesterremia by a clinical nurse using a stepped-care protocol in a nonvolunteer population. *Arch Intern Med* 148:1046–1048, 1988.

Brownell, K. D. Public health approaches to obesity and its management. *Annu Rev Public Health* 7:521–533, 1986.

Brownell, K. D., Maratt, G. A., Lichtenstein, E., Wilson, G. T. Understanding and preventing relapse. *Am Psychol* 41:765–782, 1986.

Burtaine, J., and Slade, J. The smoke-free hospital. *J Med Soc* 85:143–147, 1988.

CA—A Cancer Journal for Physicians. The impact of providing physicians with quit-smoking materials for smoking patients. *CA* 31:75–78, 1981.

Chilmonczyk, B. R., Knight, G. J., Palomaki, G. E., Pulkkinen, A. J., Williams, J., Haddow, J. E. Environmental tobacco smoke exposure during infancy. *Am J Public Health* 80:1205–1209, 1990.

Christen, A. G. The dental team: If teeth could talk. Paper presented at the Marion Merrell Dow Meetings, Palm Desert, CA, December 1990.

Cohen, S. J., Christen, A. G., Katz, B. P., Drook, C. A., et al. Counseling medical and dental patients about cigarette smoking: The impact of nicotine gum and chart reminders. *Am J Public Health* 77:313–316, 1987.

Cohen, S. J., Stookey, G. K., Katz, B. P., Drook, C. A., Christen, A. G. Helping smokers quit: A randomized controlled trial with private practice dentists. *J Am Dent Assoc* 118:41–45, 1989.

Cox, J. L. How to help your patients stop smoking. *J Am Acad of Physician Assistants* 3:600–606, 1990.

Cummings, K. M., Giovino, G., Emont, S. L., Sciandra, R., Koenigsberg, M. Factors influencing success in counseling patients to stop smoking. *Patient Education and Counseling* 8:189–200, 1986.

Cummings, S. R., Rubin, S. M., Oster, G. The cost-effectiveness of counseling smokers to quit. *JAMA* 261:75–79, 1989.

Davis, R. M. Uniting physicians against smoking: The need for a coordinated national strategy. *JAMA* 259:2900–2901, 1988.

Emmons, K. M., Goldstein, M. G. Smokers who are hospitalized: A window of opportunity for cessation interventions. *Prev Med* 21:262–269, 1992.

Fagerström, K. O. Measuring degree of physical dependence on tobacco smoking with reference to individualization of treatment. *Addict Behav* 3:235–241, 1978.

Fiore, M. C. The new vital sign. *JAMA* 266:3183–3184, 1991.

Fiore, M. C., Jorenby, D. E., Baker, T. B., Kenford, S. Tobacco dependence and the nicotine patch. Clinical guidelines for effective use. *JAMA* 268:2687–2694, 1992.

Fiore, M.C., Novotny, T. E., Pierce, J. P., Giovino, G. A., Hatziandreu, E. J., Newcomb, P. A., Surawicz, T. S., Davis, R. M. Methods used to quit smoking in the United States: Do cessation programs help? *JAMA* 263:2760–2765, 1990.

Fleisher, L. F., Keintz, M., Rimer, B., Utt, M., Workman, S., Engstrom, P. Process evaluation of a minimal-contact smoking cessation program in an urban nutritional assistance (WIC) program. In Engstrom, P., Rimer, B., Mortenson, L. E., eds. *Advances in Cancer Control: Screening and Prevention Research.* New York: Wiley-Liss, 1990, 95–107.

Frank, E., Winkleby, M. A., Altman, D. G., Rockhill, B., Fortmann, S. P. Predictors of physicians' smoking cessation advice. *JAMA* 266:3139–3144, 1991.

Glassman, A. H., Helzer, J. E., Covey, L. S., Cottler, L. B., Stettner, F., Tipp, J. E., Johnson, J. Smoking, smoking cessation and major depression. *JAMA* 264:1546–1549, 1990.

Glynn, T. J. Relative effectiveness of physician-initiated smoking cessation programs. *Cancer Bull* 40:359–364, 1988.

Glynn, T. J., and Manley, M. W. *How to Help Your Patients Stop Smoking: A National Cancer Institute Manual for Physicians.* U.S. Department of Health and Human Services, Public Health Service, National Institutes of Health. NIH Publication No. 89-3064, 1989a.

————. Physicians, cancer control and the treatment of nicotine dependence: Defining success. *Health Educ Res* 4:479–487, 1989b.

Glynn, T. J., Boyd, G. M., Gruman, J. C. Essential elements of self-help/minimal intervention strategies for smoking cessation. *Health Educ Q* 17:329–345, 1990.

————. *Self-Guided Strategies for Smoking Cessation: A Program Planner's Guide.* U.S.

Department of Health and Human Services, Public Health Service, National Cancer Institute. NIH Publication No. 91-3104, 1991.

Goldstein, A. O., Hellier, A., Fitzgerald, S., Stegall, T. S., Fischer, P. M. Hospital nurse counseling of patients who smoke. *Am J Public Health* 77:1333–1334, 1987.

Gottlieb, N. H., Mullen, P. D., McAlister, A. L. Patients' substance abuse and the primary care physician: Patterns of practice. *Addict Behav* 12:23–31, 1987.

Gritz, E. R. Cigarette smoking: The need for action by health professionals. *CA* 38:194–212, 1988.

Harris, L. *Health Maintenance.* Los Angeles: Pacific Mutual Life Insurance Company, 1978.

Horton, J. Education programs on smoking prevention and smoking cessation for students and housestaff in U.S. medical schools. *Cancer Detect Prev* 9:417–420, 1986.

Hourigan, M., Knapp, J., Kottke, T. E. *Making a Difference: The Occupational Health Nurse's Smoking Cessation Assistance Guide.* Minneapolis: Minnesota Coalition for a Smoke-Free Society 2000, 1989.

Hughes, J. R. Pharmacotherapy for smoking cessation: Unvalidated assumptions, anomalies, and suggestions for future research. *J Consult Clin Psychol*, in press.

Hughes, J. R., Gust, S. W., Keenan, R. M., Fenwick, J. W., Healey, M. L. Nicotine vs. placebo gum in general medical practice. *JAMA* 261:1300–1305, 1989.

Hunt, W. A., Barnett, L. W., Branch, L. G. Relapse in addiction programs. *J Clin Psychol* 27:455–456, 1971.

Hurt, R. D., Berge, K. G., Offord, K. P., Leonard, D. A., Gerlach, D. K., Renquist, C. L., O'Hara, M. R., et al. The making of a smoke-free medical center. *JAMA* 261:95–97, 1989.

Hurt, R. D., Dale, L. C., Offord, K. P., Bruce, B. K., McClain, F. L., Ebermon, K. M. Inpatient treatment of severe nicotine dependence. *Mayo Clinic Proceed* 67:823–828, 1992.

Hurt, R. D., Lauger, G. G., Offord, K. P., Kottke, T. E., Dale, L. C. Nicotine replacement therapy with use of a transdermal patch: A randomized double-blind, placebo-controlled trial. *Mayo Clin Proc* 65:1529–1537, 1990.

Janis, I. C. The role of social support in adherence to stressful decisions. *Am Psychol* 38:143–156, 1983.

Janz, N. K., Becker, M. H., Kirscht, J. P., Eraker, S. A., et al. Evaluation of a minimal-contact smoking cessation intervention in an outpatient setting. *Am J Public Health* 77:805–809, 1987.

Joseph, A. M., Nichol, K. L., Willenbring, M. L., Korn, J. E., Lysaght, L. S. Beneficial effects of treatment of nicotine dependence during an inpatient substance abuse treatment program. *JAMA* 263:3043–3046, 1990.

Kottke, T. E., Battista, R. N., DeFreise, G. H., Brekke, M. L. Attributes of successful smoking cessation interventions in medical practice: A meta-analysis of 39 controlled trials. *JAMA* 259:2883–2889, 1988.

Kottke, T. E., Brekke, M. L., Solberg, L. I., Hughes, J. R. A randomized trial to increase smoking intervention by physicians. *JAMA* 261:2101–2106, 1989.

Kristeller, J. L., and Ockene, J. K. Assessment and treatment of smoking on a consultation service. In Michels, R., ed. *Psychiatry: Volume 2.* Philadelphia: J.B. Lippincott, 1989, ch. 113, pp. 1–13.

Lam, W., Sze, P. C., Sacks, H. S., Chalmers, T. C. Meta-analysis of randomized controlled trials of nicotine chewing-gum. *Lancet* 4 July 1987, 27–29.

Lichtenstein, E., Glasgow, R. E., Abrams, D. B. Social support in smoking cessation: In search of effective interventions. *Behav Ther* 17:607–619, 1986.

Marlatt, A., and Gordon, J. R., eds. *Relapse Prevention.* New York: Guilford Press, 1985.

Mecklenburg, R. E., Christen, A. G., Gerbert, B., Gift, H. C., Glynn, T. J., Jones, R. B., Lindsey, E., Manley, M. W., Severson, H. *How to Help Your Patients Stop Using Tobacco: A National Cancer Institute Manual for the Oral Health Team.* Washington, D.C.: U.S. Department of Health and Human Services, National Cancer Institute. NIH Publication No. 91-3191, 1991.

Miller, W. R. and Rollnick, S. *Motivational Interviewing: Preparing People to Change Addictive Behavior.* New York: Guilford Press, 1991.

Nett, L. M. A new role for the respiratory therapist in smoking cessation. *Respiratory Care* 32:1009–1110, 1987.

Ockene, J. K. Clinical perspectives: Physician-delivered interventions for smoking cessation: Strategies for increasing effectiveness. *Prev Med* 16:723–737, 1987.

Ockene, J. K., Quirk, M. E., Goldberg, R. J., Kristeller, J. L., Donnell, G., Kalan, K. L., Williams, J. W. A residents' training program for the development of smoking intervention skills. *Arch Intern Med* 148:1039–1045, 1988.

Orleans, C. T. Helping your patients quit smoking. *PA Outlook* 2:4–7, 1984.

————. Smoking cessation in primary care settings. *J Med Soc NJ* 85:116–126, 1988.

————. Understanding and promoting smoking cessation: Overview and guidelines for physician intervention. *Annu Rev Med* 36:51–61, 1985.

Orleans, C. T., Kristeller, J., Gritz, E. R. Helping hospitalized smokers quit: New directions for treatment and research. *J Consult Clin Psychol*, in press.

Orleans, C. T., and Shipley, R. Assessment in smoking cessation research: Some practical guidelines. In Keefe, F. J., and Blumenthal, J., eds. *Assessment Strategies in Behavioral Medicine.* New York: Grune and Stratton, 1982, 216–321.

Orleans, C. T., George, L. K., Houpt, J. L., Brodie, H.K.H. Health promotion in primary care: A survey of U.S. family practitioners. *Prev Med* 14:636–647, 1985.

Orleans, C. T., Rotberg, H., Quade, D., Lees, P. A hospital quit-smoking consult service: Clinical report and intervention guidelines. *Prev Med* 19:198–212, 1990.

Orleans, C. T., Schoenbach, V. J., Wagner, E., Quade, D., Salmon, M.A.S., et al. Self-help quit smoking interventions: Effects of self-help materials, social support instructions and telephone counseling. *J Consult Clin Psychol* 59(3):439–448, 1991.

Orleans, C. T. and Slade, J. Smoking ban in U.S. presents new challenges. *Tobacco Control*, 1:46–47, 1992.

Pechacek, T. F., and Danaher, B. G. How and why people quit smoking: A cognitive–behavioral analysis. In Kendall, P. C., and Hollen, S. D., eds. *Cognitive–Behavioral Interventions: Theory Research and Practice.* New York: Academic Press, 1979.

Pederson, L. L., Baskerville, J. C., Wanklin, J. Multivariate statistical models for predicting change in smoking behavior following physician advice to quit smoking. *Prev Med* 11:536–549, 1982.

Pilgrim, J. What we're doing to help people quit smoking. *The Smoke-Free Pharmacy* 2:2–3, 1990.

Pomerleau, C. S., Pomerleau, O. F., Majchrzak, M. S., Kloska, D. D., Malakuti, R. Relationship between nicotine tolerance questionnaire scores and plasma cotinine. *Addict Behav* 15:73–81, 1990.

Prochaska, J. O., and DiClemente, C. C. Stages and processes of self-change of smoking: Toward an integrative model of change. *J Consult Clin Psychol* 51:390–395, 1983.

Prochaska, J. O., DiClemente, C. C., Norcross, J. C. In search of how people change: Applica-

tions to addictive behaviors. *Amer Psychol* 47:1102–1114, 1992.

Rossi, J. S. The hazards of sunlight: A report of the Consensus Development Conference on Sunlight, Ultraviolet Radiation and the Skin. *Health Psychologist* 11:2–3, 1989.

Russell, M. H., Wilson, C., Taylor, C., Baker, C. D. Effect of general practitioners' advice against smoking. *Br Med J* 2:231–235, 1979.

Schachter, S. Recidivism and self-cure of smoking and obesity. *Am Psychol* 37:436–444, 1982.

Schoenbach, V. J., Orleans, C. T., Wagner, E. H., Quade, D., Salmon, M.A.P., Porter, C. Characteristics of smokers who enroll and quit in self-help programs. *Health Educ Res,* 7:369–380, 1992.

Severson, H. H., Eakin, E. G., Stevens, V. J., Lichtenstein, E. Dental office practices for tobacco users: Independent practice and HMO clinics. *Am J Public Health* 80:1503–1505, 1990.

Severson, H. H., Stevens, V. J., Little, S. J., Lichtenstein, E. The teachable moment: Smokeless tobacco intervention in dental clinics. Paper presented at the Seventh World Conference on Tobacco and Health, Perth, Australia, 1–5 April 1990.

Taylor, C. B., Houston-Miller, N., Killen, J. D., DeBusk, R. F. Smoking cessation after acute myocardial infraction: Effects of a nurse-managed intervention. *Ann Intern Med* 113:118–123, 1990.

Transdermal Nicotine Study Group. Transdermal nicotine for smoking cessation: Six-month results from two multicenter controlled clinical trials. *JAMA* 266:3133–3139, 1991.

U.S. Department of Health and Human Services (USDHHS). *Helping Smokers Quit: A Guide for the Pharmacist.* Washington D.C.: Public Health Service, DHHS Publication No. 84-655, 1984.

————. *How You Can Help Patients Stop Smoking: Opportunities for Respiratory Care Practitioners.* Washington, D.C.: National Heart, Lung and Blood Institute. DHHS Publication No. 89-2961, 1989a.

————. *Reducing the Health Consequences of Smoking: 25 Years of Progress. A Report of the Surgeon General.* U.S. Department of Health and Human Services, Public Health Service, Centers for Disease Control, Center for Health Promotion and Education, Office on Smoking and Health. DHHS Publication No. (CDC) 89-8411, 1989b.

————. *The Health Benefits of Smoking Cessation: A Report of the Surgeon General.* Washington, D.C.: Public Health Service, Office on Smoking and Health. DHHS Publication No. 90-8416, 1990a.

————. *Nurses: Help Your Patients Stop Smoking.* Washington D.C. National Heart, Lung and Blood Institute. DHHS Publication No. 90-2962, 1990b.

Warner, K. E., Goldenhar, L. M., McLaughlin, C. G. Cigarette advertising and magazine coverage of the hazards of smoking. *N Engl J Med* 326:305–309, 1992.

Wechsler, H., Levin, S., Idelson, R. K., Rothman, M., Taylor, J. O. The physician's role in health promotion: A survey of primary care practitioners. *N Engl J Med* 308:97–100, 1983.

Wells, K. B., Ware, J. E., Newman, C. E. Physicians' attitudes in counseling patients about smoking. *Med Care* 22:360–365, 1984.

Wilcox, N. S., Prochaska, J. O., Velicer, W. F., DiClemente, C. C. Subject characteristics as predictors of self-change in smoking. *Addict Behav* 10:407–412, 1985.

9

Creating and Maintaining an Optimal Medical Practice Environment for the Treatment of Nicotine Addiction

THOMAS J. GLYNN, MARC W. MANLEY, LEIF I. SOLBERG, and JOHN SLADE

Involving the physician in the treatment of nicotine addiction, as outlined in Chapter 8, is an activity replete with anomalies. Most physicians want to reduce smoking prevalence among their patients and think that it is important to do so, but few physicians feel successful at actually helping patients stop (Rosen, Logsdon, Demak 1984). More than twice as many physicians *report* providing advice to their patients about smoking cessation, compared with patient reports of their *actually* having done so (Anda et al. 1987). Alternatively, as many as three-fourths of patients say they would stop smoking if their physician advised them to do so, but when they receive such advice, many fewer patients actually stop (Wechsler 1983; Wells, Ware, Lewis 1984; Wells et al. 1986).

There are, however, a number of positive aspects associated with these anomalies. Physicians *want* to treat their patients' nicotine addiction and think it is important to do so. Patients *want* advice from their physician about how to quit smoking and report that they would quit if given such advice. Further, there are data that clearly demonstrate that physicians *can* be successful at treating nicotine addiction (Russell et al. 1979, 1983; Kottke, Battista, DeFriese et al. 1988; Glynn, Manley, Pechacek 1990). The *opportunity* to reduce patient smoking prev-

alence therefore clearly exists, and the issue to address is how best to seize this opportunity and put it to use.

If it is possible to characterize and examine the "typical" medical practice, the activities of the physician and staff will more often than not appear to be *re*active—for example, the patient reports a problem and the physician asks relevant questions, examines the patient, and provides an appropriate response (Kottke, Solberg, Brekke 1990a,b). In other cases, the physician or staff provides a regularly scheduled medical procedure, whether it is a checkup, vaccination, Pap smear, or similar activity.

What is considerably more difficult, however, is to be *pro*active, that is, to treat a patient for, or discuss issues related to, symptoms, conditions, behaviors, and preventive procedures that the patient has *not* identified as a problem or concern. Obstacles to the proactive approach include time constraints, lack of appropriate experience, knowledge or skills, patient recalcitrance, and so on. Problems that might, therefore, be difficult to address are those such as screening for skin, breast, or colon cancers, nutrition issues, and—at issue here—nicotine addiction. Yet, these proactive, preventive activities can add significantly to patients' health and may be more important than any number of reactive behaviors.

Since most of the reinforcers of traditional clinical behavior of physicians and allied health care providers lie in the practice environment, it is essential to change that environment if we wish to expand these preventive activities.

INCREASING THE DELIVERY OF PREVENTIVE MEDICAL SERVICES

Table 9–1 outlines some of the barriers that physicians and patients have identified with regard to advice about smoking cessation. These same obstacles are also present, to a greater or lesser extent, for other preventive practices and procedures. Recently, however, a number of studies have begun to examine ways of overcoming the barriers. The studies have approached the issue of encouraging physicians to increase their preventive practices in a number of ways, as will now be discussed.

Screening/Counseling Reminders

Since there are strong indications that physicians believe most preventive practices are useful (Gemson and Elison 1986), a number of studies have examined how physicians can be reminded to use them. For instance, McPhee and associates (1989) investigated several methods of promoting routine cancer screening by randomly assigning internal medicine residents to receive cancer screening reminders (computer-generated lists of overdue tests at patient visits), audit with feedback (monthly seminars about screening, with feedback about their performance

Table 9–1   Barriers to Preventive Care in Medical Practice

Physicians' Perspective	Patients' Perspective
Lack of time	Cost of care
Lack of training	Visiting physician for
Lack of reimbursement	other purpose
Belief that patients are	Unaware of need for
not able to change	preventive care
relevant behavior	Unaware of
Belief that physician	physician's role in
preventive interventions	preventive care
are ineffective	Belief that physician's
Belief that intervention by	role in preventive care
referral sources is	is inappropriate
ineffective	

rates), or no intervention (controls). Half the patients in each resident group also were randomized to receive patient education (literature and notices of overdue tests). The medical records were assessed during a 9-month period before and after initiation of the interventions. Cancer screening reminders were found to increase performance in six of seven tests; audit with feedback, four of seven tests; patient education, one of two targeted breast cancer screening tests. These results suggest that the cancer screening reminder strategy is an effective method of promoting performance of routine cancer screening tests.

Providing reminders through a computerized system also was tested by Knight and colleagues (1987), who reported that their computerized prompting system was well accepted by physicians and appeared to improve attitudes toward health promotion, and by McDonald et al. (1984), who found a significant increase in preventive care activities among a group of physicians using computer-prompted reminders.

Finally, Cohen and co-workers (1987) investigated methods for improving and expanding the counseling of smokers by physicians and dentists by placing prominent reminder stickers on their patients' charts. Exit interviews of both medical and dental patients indicated that the presence of chart reminders increased the time spent counseling and altered the nature of the smoking cessation counseling provided by both physicians and dentists.

Use of Nurse Practitioners

Greater reliance on nurse practitioners to provide preventive health care has been discussed for some time, but it has not often been put into practice. Frame and colleagues (1978) reported that physicians will, on occasion, work with nurse practitioners to provide periodic health examinations and counseling at special visits; but, as reported by Berner et al. (1987), not all patients are willing to return for such health care delivery by nurse practitioners. Solberg and his colleagues (Solberg and Maxwell 1987; Solberg et al. 1990), however, have reported significant success with the use of nurse practitioners in providing smoking cessation counseling to patients after their physician has recommended that they see the specially trained nurse. Recognizing the great potential for the delivery of preventive services by nurse practitioners, Britain's National Health Service is now set to provide reimbursement to physicians who will use nurse practitioners to provide such services (G. Fowler, personal communication, 1991).

Feedback from Peers and Patients

Feedback and reinforcement from peers concerning levels of preventive care is another way in which these behaviors may be increased. Such feedback can be automatically generated at specific intervals or in response to specific actions or failures on the part of the physician, or to an individual practitioner or an entire group of practitioners (Winickoff et al. 1984). Although results of studies in which feedback is used to increase preventive practices are mixed, it appears that successful feedback requires prompt delivery and effective, practical suggestions for remedial action (Nelson 1976; Tierney, Siu, McDonald 1986) and that computer-based systems of performance evaluation and feedback also may be useful (Barnett et al. 1983; Goroll et al. 1985). Green and co-workers (1988), reviewing this area, concluded that feedback from colleagues and their support in providing preventive services is both reinforcing and predisposing to increases in the delivery of such services.

Physician Participation in Practice Change

Another area with promise, but which to date has produced mixed results, is the participation of physicians in planning and setting standards for preventive practice. In one study (Somers et al. 1984), in which physicians at four hospitals received feedback about patients whose hemoglobin levels were low, compliance with recommended standards over the next 4 months was no better for physicians who had helped set audit criteria than for those who had not.

Another study (Williams and Eisenberg 1986) made it clear that if standards are to be set concerning preventive practices, then they must neither be nor appear to be imposed from outside what the involved practitioners consider their peer group. Finally, Hulka and colleagues (1979) found that physicians who helped prepare management standards for four medical conditions performed better than uninvolved physicians regarding three of the four conditions studied.

Taken together, these data suggest that physician participation in planning and setting standards for preventive services may be a reasonable approach to increasing these services, but that recommended standards should originate with credible sources such as nationally convened and recognized groups and professional organizations.

Reimbursement

As Lurie and associates (1987), McPhee and Schroeder (1987), and others have pointed out, reimbursement is certainly *not* the single most important factor in determining whether physicians offer preventive services to their patients. McPhee and Schroeder, for example, noted that economic factors do not explain the low performance of sigmoidoscopic examinations, which are relatively well compensated (Schroeder and Showstack 1978). Nevertheless, there are data that indicate that physicians perform target preventive services more often when such services are covered by medical insurance (Rosen, Logsden, Demak 1984).

While this is a systemic issue, it can be dealt with also on the level of individual practice, hospital, or health maintenance organization (HMO) by encouraging (1) physicians to use those preventive practices for which reimbursement *is* usually available (e.g., sigmoidoscopy, mammography); (2) patients to ask for and use reimbursable preventive services and even those, such as nicotine addiction counseling, which are not currently reimbursable; and (3) health care administrators and physicians to lobby for an increase in the number of useful preventive services that *are* reimbursable. As employee groups and employers become more interested in these services, the insurance industry is likely to respond. In the meantime, strategies suitable for the present environment are discussed later in this chapter.

Patient Education

Educating patients about the importance of preventive services in maintaining and promoting their own health is seen by many as a key to increasing physician activity in this area. There are, however, a number of barriers to this concept. For example, many patients feel that it is the physician's role, rather than theirs, to raise issues of disease prevention. Also, physicians themselves may be uncomfortable when patients attempt to take an active role in their own treatment.

Nevertheless, there are ongoing studies on expanding the patients' role in suggesting appropriate preventive services. In one study (Bronson and O'Meara 1986), smokers given information from their medical records became more aware of the consequences of smoking and reported both a higher rate of quitting and a reduction in smoking. Other studies have investigated whether giving reminders directly to patients instead of to their physicians, as discussed earlier, improves their cooperation. The use of reminder letters and telephone calls has been associated with better rates of keeping clinic appointments (Gates and Colborn 1976), greater participation in influenza vaccination programs (Frank 1985; McDowell, Newell, Rosser 1986), and higher rates for performance of fecal occult blood tests (Thompson et al. 1986). Another strategy to increase patient participation in medical care has been to give the patients a mini-record of selected information to help them understand their current problems and consider future recommendations from their physicians (Giglio et al. 1978). In nearly all of these studies, however, it is the physician's attitude about the patient's role that is the critical factor in the patient's decision to accept more involvement (Giglio and Papazian 1986).

Except for the common thread of increasing the use of preventive services, the topics and studies summarized earlier may not, at first glance, have much in common. Nevertheless, further consideration will reveal a second thread woven throughout: tech-niques to increase preventive services need to involve changes and improvements in the practice environment of the physician if they are to be adopted and play a role in increasing the use of available preventive services.

DEFINING THE PROPER PRACTICE ENVIRONMENT FOR PREVENTIVE MEDICAL SERVICES

It may seem intuitive to say that a proper practice environment is required to deliver effective preventive medical services. The reality is, however, that the typical practice environment not only often fails to support the delivery of such services, but may also actively inhibit them. The many obstacles to delivery of preventive services require active efforts to overcome them, such as those already described. To be effective and sustained over time, these efforts must be integrated into a normal part of the operating procedures of a practice, that is, they must be systematized.

The remainder of this chapter focuses on the prevention and treatment of nicotine addiction as one such preventive service, and it discusses how minor but systematic modifications in the practice environment can both increase use of this service and reduce patient morbidity and mortality related to tobacco use. As a side benefit, understanding and applying these systems can facilitate similar approaches for all other preventive services.

The practice environment is defined broadly here as the physical surroundings, the management structure, and the operating procedures of a practice within which clinicians, staff, and patients come together. The environment thus includes waiting rooms, laboratories, examination rooms, and other parts of the physical plant; *all* staff, including receptionists, administrators, nurses, laboratory technicians, physicians, and others; and all aspects of the operation of the practice, including procedures, forms, appointments, billing, educational material, and so forth.

The *proper* practice environment for the treatment of nicotine addiction is one that not only enables physicians and staff to provide consistent advice and support for smoking cessation, but that actually makes doing so easier than avoiding it. The next section describes many ways in which the practice environment can be modified to encourage the delivery of treatment for nicotine addiction. Recommendations are based on a number of studies and reviews (e.g., Cohen et al. 1989; Cummings, Coates, Richard et al. 1989; Cummings, Richard, Duncan et al. 1989; Glynn, Manley, Pechacek 1990; Jamrozik and Fowler 1982; Kottke et al. 1987; Ramstrom, Raw, Wood 1988; Richmond, Austin, Webster 1986; Russell et al. 1979; Solberg and Maxwell 1987; Wilson et al. 1988) that have all examined ways in which this practice can be encouraged through modifications in the practice environment.

IMPLEMENTING AN ENVIRONMENT FOR PREVENTING AND TREATING NICOTINE ADDICTION

To successfully adopt the components of an office-based nicotine addiction treatment program, a specific, step-by-step approach, which initially will require some time and effort, is needed. The National Cancer Institute (NCI) has outlined such an approach in its manual for physicians, *How To Help Your Patients Stop Smoking* (Glynn and Manley 1989a), relying heavily on the studies cited earlier and, particularly, on the approaches to changing practice environment developed by Solberg and colleagues (1989). Establishment of an office smoking cessation program and facilitative practice environment requires that the office staff take these five steps:

1. Select an office smoking cessation coordinator;
2. Create a smoke-free office;
3. Identify all smoking patients;
4. Develop patient smoking cessation plans; and
5. Provide follow-up support.

Each step in the sequence can be integrated into a variety of practice settings.

Select an Office Smoking Cessation Coordinator

The first step in this program is to adopt the same administrative system that would be

necessary to successfully implement any program in an office practice.

1. The management must establish that there will be a systematic smoking cessation program as an official policy of the practice.
2. A staff smoking cessation coordinator must be named and given the authority and responsibility to develop and maintain the program. This person should be a staff member, usually a nurse. A physician coordinator also should be named to collaborate with and support the staff coordinator with the other physicians.
3. The coordinators should decide on the specifics of the program and develop an implementation plan, including a start date.
4. Other staff members and physicians should be oriented and trained for their roles in the program.
5. To maintain the program until it becomes a routine, permanent part of the practice, it will be necessary to audit its function, provide feedback and retraining, and conduct various activities to raise awareness of the program.

Create a Smoke-Free Office

Everything about the office environment should convey a consistent nonsmoking message and help set the stage for advising and counseling the patients. If the office is not smoke-free already, becoming so will be an essential next step in the program. NCI's *Manual for Physicians* recommends the following step-by-step strategy for becoming smoke free (Glynn and Manley 1989a):

1. *Select a date to make the office smoke free.* Establishing an office no smoking policy for both staff and patients is a necessary step in implementing this program. This action will emphasize a strong commitment to nonsmoking and the health of patients, including nonsmokers who are exposed to smoke produced by others. At this stage and at every step of this program, it is essential to empathize with patients who smoke, while providing all the assistance possible to help them stop. The selected date should leave

Table 9–2   Announcement of Smoke-Free Office
Policy

This Office Is Becoming Smoke Free

This office will become smoke free on [date].
We are doing this in recognition of the enormous
death toll of tobacco use: Tobacco is the chief avoidable cause of death among our patients, and tobacco
smoke is harmful even to people who do not smoke.
We welcome your questions about this policy and
about our reasons for becoming smoke free. We also
have information about quitting smoking, and we welcome the opportunity to discuss it with you.

adequate time to prepare staff and patients for the new policy.

2. *Advise all staff and patients of this plan.* It
   is critical that all physicians and administrators adhere to the policy if staff and
   patients are to accept it. A period of 4–6
   weeks should provide enough time to introduce the smoke-free office policy in
   most settings. Staff members who smoke
   will need reassurance that they will not
   lose their jobs or be stigmatized, but will
   be provided with cessation help if they
   wish it. It may help to prepare a sign that
   can be posted in the office. (An example
   is given in Table 9–2.)

   Larger institutions usually need to take
   additional steps before adopting a smoke-
   free policy. (For a discussion of these issues, see "Smoking and Hospitals Are a
   Bad Match" and "Clean Air Health
   Care," Appendix 9-A.)

3. *Post No Smoking signs in all office areas.*
   Once a no smoking policy has been established in the office, it will be important to
   remind people about it. Many offices
   have found it helpful to use several different no smoking signs and change them
   every 6–9 months to keep the smoke-free
   message fresh. Engaging, effective posters
   are available from a number of sources.

4. *Remove ashtrays from all office areas.* On
   the day set for the office to become smoke
   free, remove all ashtrays. This action will
   emphasize the commitment of the physician and staff to the smoke-free office.

5. *Prominently display smoking cessation
   materials and information.* Although the
   office may be working with a specific patient self-help manual or program, it is
   helpful also to make some materials and

information available in the office and to
keep an adequate supply of them on
hand. These materials should cover a variety of tobacco-related subjects, including overviews of the social, economic,
and policy issues that society at large
faces with regard to tobacco. Organizations from which such materials may be
ordered are listed in the following chapter.

6. *Eliminate all tobacco advertising from
   the waiting room.* To emphasize the commitment of the office to remain smoke
   free, eliminate all tobacco advertising
   from the waiting room. For additional
   emphasis, some offices have continued to
   order magazines that carry tobacco advertising but have crossed out the tobacco
   advertisements with bright markers.
   Other offices subscribe to magazines with
   no tobacco advertisements to show support of those publications, and they make
   that fact known to patients. The following list of magazines that do not carry tobacco advertising is extracted from the
   *Journal of the American Medical Associ-
   ation* (JAMA 1991):

   Accent on Living
   American Heritage
   Arizona Highways
   Audubon
   Bicycling
   Business Week
   Complete Woman
   Consumer Reports
   Golf Illustrated
   Good Housekeeping
   Men's Fitness
   Modern Maturity
   Modern Photography
   Mother Jones
   National Geographic
   National Wildlife
   New Yorker
   Old House Journal
   Parents Magazine
   PC World
   Popular Woodworking
   Ranger Rick
   Reader's Digest
   Runner's World
   Saturday Evening Post
   Science News

Name_____

Date_____

1. Do you now smoke cigarettes? ☐ yes   ☐ no
2. Does the person closest to you smoke cigarettes? ☐ yes   ☐ no
3. How many cigarettes do you smoke a day? _____ cigarettes
4. How soon after you wake up do you smoke your first cigarette?
   ☐ within 30 minutes   ☐ more than 30 minutes
5. How interested are you in stopping smoking?
   ☐ not at all   ☐ a little   ☐ some   ☐ a lot   ☐ very
6. If you decided to quit smoking completely during the next 2 weeks, how confident
   are you that you would succeed?
   ☐ not at all   ☐ a little   ☐ some   ☐ a lot   ☐ very

For Physicians Only

| | | Quit Date Established? | | Date of | |
Visit Date	Yes	No	When	Followup Visit	Comments
_____	____	____	_____	_____	_____
_____	____	____	_____	_____	_____
_____	____	____	_____	_____	_____
_____	____	____	_____	_____	_____

Fig. 9–1   Smoking assessment form. *Source:* Glynn and Manley 1991.

Scientific American
Sesame Street
Seventeen
Single Parent
Smithsonian
Southern Accents
Teen Magazine
Vegetarian Times
Westways
Yankee Magazine.

Identify All Smoking Patients

Identification of smokers should become a routine part of all patient visits. This can be institutionalized through the following actions.

Assess the Smoking Status of All Patients During Measurement of Vital Signs

Patients should be asked, "Do you smoke?" or "Are you still smoking?" while their vital signs are being measured. To help assess smoking patients, have all patients complete a brief patient smoking assessment form (Figure 9–1) or a more complete patient progress record, such as that used by Solberg et al. (1989) (see Figure 9–2). Additional examples are provided in Chapter 10.

Forms of this type will aid the physician in determining the most appropriate course of treatment for each patient. The completed form can be attached to the patient's chart for physician review and notes or kept in a file separate from the chart and clipped to the chart cover during visits as an obvious reminder to raise the topic.

Because relapse is common among former smokers, the status of patients who are initially identified as nonsmokers should be updated at least once a year. For example, the provider could say, "Your chart indicates that you don't smoke. Is this still true?" Nonsmokers should be congratulated for their healthful behavior. Patients who have

W	S	H	L	↓	?	N	O
Winner	Stop on Own	Stop with Help	Later	Decrease	Uncertain	No	Omitted

Name: _____ Phone: (H) _____ (W) _____

Address: _____ Birth Year: _____ Sex: _____

Smoke History: Type: _____ Years: _____ : _____ : _____ : Latest:

_____ _____ Quits _____ Longest: _____ _____

No. of Smokers at Home _____ Health Problems: _____

Date	Amount	Who	History	Cat.	Plans	Followup

Fig. 9–2 Patient's progress chart. *Source:* Glynn and Manley 1991.

relapsed and those who have begun to smoke should complete a new Patient Smoking Assessment Form.

Place a Mark on Every Chart to Identify Tobacco Use Status

It is just as important to label the charts of nonusers as those of users. Unmarked charts require that patients be asked at every visit, repeatedly, whether they are tobacco users. Various specific labels are available, but generic colored labels, available at any stationery store, can be used as effectively, provided the office staff knows what each color indicates. Several of the practice "quit kits" in Appendix 9-A contain such labels or stickers.

Use a Permanent Progress Card for Each Smoking Patient

Like smoking cessation itself, a cessation program is a process that requires maintenance. It is important to maintain program continuity by offering appropriate treatment at every visit by a smoking patient. A permanent progress card can be attached to the patient's chart or kept in a separate file and attached only for visits as an easy way to keep the physician informed of the patient's smoking progress and status. For example, this card will show whether a quit date was set and kept and whether congratulations and reinforcement are appropriate. It will also show whether a patient has relapsed and needs a reminder that relapse is common and encouragement or help to try again. A permanent progress card also will help the smoking cessation coordinator arrange suitable follow-up by showing what advice the physician has given.

Develop Patient Smoking Cessation Plans

The success of this type of smoking cessation program depends on the physician's commitment to implementing it. The physician's role is to motivate patients to stop, to increase confidence in their ability to do so, and to develop cessation plans. Smoking patients must believe that quitting is an issue of real concern to their physician. Guidelines for developing and implementing individualized smoking cessation plans (quitting methods, quit date, self-help materials, and so on) are presented in Chapter 10. They follow the four-step strategy of the NCI manual for physicians, *How To Help Your Patients Stop Smoking* (Glynn and Manley 1989a):

1. *Ask* about smoking at each visit;
2. *Advise* all smokers to stop;
3. *Assist* the patient in stopping by helping to set a quit date, providing self-help materials, and prescribing a nicotine replacement, if appropriate;
4. *Arrange* follow-up support (see following section).

Follow-up Activities

Follow-up support activities are valuable not only for the patient, but also for the physician and the office staff. When patients know their progress will be reviewed and the physician and staff care enough to help, their chances of quitting successfully improve substantially. For the physician and office staff, follow-up also may be the only way to track each patient's success. Cummings and co-workers (1986) found, for instance, that physicians who routinely schedule a follow-up appointment had a higher percentage of their patients quit smoking. Suggestions for various types of follow-up support are discussed in Chapter 10.

RESOURCES FOR THE PROPER PRACTICE ENVIRONMENT

There are a growing number of resources for the implementation and maintenance of a medical practice conducive to the successful treatment of nicotine addiction. These guides and resources are briefly described in Appendix 9-A. More and more, such resources are aimed not just at the physician, but also at other health care providers, including dentists, nurses, respiratory therapists, and pharmacists. Nor is such guidance limited to the primary care practice setting. Other health care settings are also being ad-

dressed, such as dental and obstetrical offices, pediatric clinics, and oncology practice sites. Of course, materials for patients also are essential, both cessation materials to help those who want to stop smoking and motivational/educational material to motivate others to try. Materials for patients are presented in Chapter 10.

Patient materials must be stocked in the office or practice setting. One study showed that having quit guides available in the office increased the likelihood of physicians' giving a clear quit smoking message (CA 1981).

Other sources of information that could be valuable to the development of a practice environment helpful to the prevention and cessation of nicotine addiction are listed in Appendix 9-B.

While following the steps outlined earlier in this chapter, becoming familiar with some of the material described here, and making motivational and self-help materials available to patients will certainly help provide the kind of office environment conducive to the successful treatment of nicotine addiction, there nevertheless remain a number of systemic barriers that preclude the universal treatment of nicotine addiction. Several of these barriers, and steps that might be taken to alleviate their effects, are discussed in the following section.

OVERCOMING BARRIERS IN THE SYSTEM

Table 9–1 outlines a number of barriers to preventive care in a medical practice, as perceived by both physicians and patients. Additional barriers, such as forgetfulness or a perceived inadequacy in behavioral skills, also have been suggested (e.g., Love 1988; Orleans et al. 1985). Some of these barriers, such as identifying those patients most likely to benefit from particular preventive measures or forgetting to either ask for or provide useful preventive measures, can be addressed and overcome in individual practices by instituting some of the relatively simple changes in the practice environment suggested earlier. Others, however, such as reimbursement for providing preventive care or training in the delivery of effective preventive practices such as the treatment of nicotine addiction, are systemic in nature and must be addressed not by individual practitioners, but in the context of the broader practice of clinical medicine.

Among the systemic barriers of particular relevance to the development of a proper practice environment for the treatment of nicotine addiction are (1) lack of training models and opportunities for physicians and appropriate staff; (2) inadequate reimbursement plans for the treatment of nicotine addiction; (3) physician perceptions of poor treatment outcome for nicotine addiction; and (4) resistance of many health care facilities, ranging from individual offices to large medical centers, to development of policies supporting a smoke-free environment.

Each of these obstacles, their importance in the development of a practice environment conducive to the treatment of nicotine addiction, and possible means of overcoming them, are discussed in the following paragraphs.

Training for Treatment of Nicotine Addiction

The teaching of preventive medicine has been termed one of the "orphan" areas of medical education (Somers 1987). More specific to nicotine addiction, a number of surveys (e.g., Orleans et al. 1985; Wechsler et al. 1983; Wells et al. 1984) have revealed that few physicians feel adequately trained to deliver effective treatment for nicotine addiction. Since it has been estimated that more than 1 million smokers can be helped to stop each year if only 20% of U.S. physicians are trained to deliver effective nicotine addiction treatment (Glynn 1988), this is clearly a barrier that should be immediately and forcefully addressed. Further, because of the obvious inadequacy of training physicians *individually* in how to deliver such treatment, the means of altering the *system* of medical education must be found.

Considering the three major systems involved in physician training—undergraduate medical school, residency training, and continuing medical education (CME)—it is obvious that medical schools offer the opportunity to reach the greatest number of physicians-to-be, that residency training provides access to those physicians who have chosen specialty areas most relevant to the treatment of nicotine addiction, and that CME can reach those physicians missed in the two other systems and provide updates to those exposed to training earlier.

While little emphasis has been placed on nicotine addiction treatment training in undergraduate medical education, effective training programs have been developed for both residency training and CME. Ockene and associates (1988), for example, have developed a brief (3-hour) training program for family practice residents that has shown itself effective in changing the behavior of both physicians and patients.

The NCI has developed a CME train-the-trainer program (Manley et al. 1991), based on a number of NCI-supported clinical trials (Glynn, Manley, Pechacek 1990), which is designed to reach 100,000 U.S. physicians by 1993. Through 50 1-day workshops, conducted from 1990 through 1993, 2,000 physicians will be trained to conduct short courses with their colleagues. The program strategy requires no new training institutions; rather, it incorporates a new course of 1–3 hours' length into established CME systems. NCI is collaborating with medical professional organizations, when possible, to help implement the program and optimize its impact (Manley et al., in press).

Finally, one important element that is often forgotten, in both the call for and the development of nicotine addiction treatment training efforts, is the need to include other health professionals and support staff associated with the physician, most importantly the nurse practitioner or physician assistant. As discussed earlier, the nurse and other support staff are often the key—after the physician has decided to offer such services—to the actual treatment of nicotine addiction treatment. As such they should be included in any training programs. Likewise, training should be offered to independent health care providers (e.g., dentists, pharmacists, respiratory therapists).

Reimbursement for Treatment

There is considerable controversy about the importance of reimbursement in the delivery of preventive medical services. While there is little argument about whether more preventive services *should* be covered by third-party payers, it is less evident that such coverage *must* be in place in order that preventive services be delivered. Certainly, the absence of third-party reimbursement cannot be used to justify the withholding of appropriate preventive care.

With regard to the specific issue of delivery of nicotine addiction treatment, the American Society of Addiction Medicine (ASAM) maintains that reimbursement mechanisms that promote the effective treatment of nicotine addiction are necessary (Eagle 1988). The society has developed four specific recommendations on which its position is based:

1. Third-party payers, whether private, nonprofit, government insurers, or plan administrators, are encouraged to make coverage for the treatment of nicotine dependence available to all group and individual enrollees. It should be viewed as coverage for treatment of a primary medical problem, not as preventive services.
2. Employers are encouraged to request coverage for the treatment of nicotine dependence among the health benefits they purchase for employees. Employers are further encouraged to consider on-site programs to help employees quit smoking.
3. Governments are encouraged to allow tax deductions for expenses for the treatment of nicotine dependence, whether the expenses be incurred by an individual or an employer.
4. Treatment providers are encouraged to set and adhere to standards on data collection with regard to patient characteristics, treatment methods, and treatment outcome.

Adoption of such approaches as the ASAM recommendations will provide a solid basis for reimbursement for a wide variety of preventive services, including treatment of nicotine addiction.

While health insurance policies usually do not cover treatment for nicotine addiction, they do cover many services necessary to the management of medical conditions that are caused or aggravated by tobacco use. If a patient has bronchitis, chronic obstructive pulmonary disease, coronary heart disease, or atherosclerotic peripheral vascular disease, for instance, part of the management of these conditions is abstinence from cigarettes. When a major goal of helping a patient stop smoking is improvement of an underlying medical condition, it is legitimate to document the circumstances and to bill for the underlying problem as the primary diagnosis, with nicotine dependence listed as secondary (Slade 1987; Eagle 1988). Similarly, in some situations, an emotional disturbance, such as an anxiety state or depression, can properly be treated through assistance with smoking cessation. In addition, insurance often will cover the cost of tests such as breath measurements of carbon monoxide, which can be used adjunctively in a management program (Chapter 10).

The need for appropriate reimbursement for treatment of nicotine dependence will come into sharper focus in coming years, because an even higher proportion of the decreasing number of smokers will be more heavily addicted to nicotine than is now seen (Chapters 7 and 18). Finally, the former secretary of the U.S. Department of Health and Human Services, Dr. Louis Sullivan, has called on private health insurers to cover effective treatments for nicotine dependence (USDHHS 1990) Health care reform schemes being considered by the Clinton administration also may have significant impact on plans for reimbursement for treatment of nicotine dependence.

Changing Perceptions of Treatment Outcome

Several trials have shown quit rates from two to six times as high for systematic quit smoking interventions in primary care as for "usual care"; however, a meta-analysis of 39 major physician-delivered smoking intervention trials showed that 12 months after a minimal intervention, the average difference in smoking cessation rates between intervention and control groups was only 5.8% (Kottke, Battista, DeFriese et al. 1988). These results are similar to those described in reviews by Ockene (1987) and Schwartz (1987), and several more recent trials have reported cessation rates of about 10% at 12 months after intervention (e.g., Wilson et al. 1988; Cohen et al. 1989).

The idea of a success rate of perhaps less than 1 patient in 10, however, may and should not appeal to many physicians. Most oncologists, for example, would find unacceptable anything less than a 75% survival rate for patients with testicular cancer; on the other hand, they would be elated to achieve consistent survival rates of 25% with lung cancer patients. These figures are reminders that success in medicine is relative. However, in comparison with the treatment of other conditions requiring behavior change—for instance, obesity—the long-term success rates documented in physician smoking intervention trials are quite good (Glynn and Manley 1989b).

The challenges are to change physicians' perceptions of what an acceptable "success" rate is in the treatment of nicotine dependence, and to improve the overall rates of success. Information that can help is available—for example, documentation of the public health effect of universal delivery of nicotine addiction treatment (Glynn and Manley 1989b), and of the cost-effectiveness of providing such treatment (Cummings, Rubin, Oster 1989)—but effective channels for *delivering* this information must be identified.

Nicotine dependence is a chronic disease, and patients often emerge from it gradually, over time. Relapses are common, but so are further attempts to quit. While any single quit attempt may have a relatively small chance of producing a stable abstinence, over a series of quit attempts, the chances for abstinence become better and better. Furthermore, patients learn from earlier quit attempts how to better organize subsequent ones.

Primary care physicians are in an especially favorable position to affect this process. Adopting the long view, that nicotine dependence is a treatable chronic disease

with periods of remission and exacerbation, chelps physicians remain sanguine and maintain their equanimity in managing this difficult condition.

Development of Smoke-Free Facilities

Development of smoke-free policies at all health care facilities is important not only for the health of the patients and staff at those facilities, but also to convey the importance that health care practitioners give to smoke-free environments.

While there is continuing progress in the institution of smoke-free health care facilities in individual settings, a broader, system-wide approach is needed. As outlined in the preceding section, descriptions of the methods involved in attaining such policy change in specific settings are available (e.g., Hurt et al. 1989; Knapp et al. 1986). Further, the continuing support for such policies by organizations such as the American Medical Association will be essential to winning the acceptance of smoke-free health care facilities as common practice rather than an aberration.

The recent (January 1992) requirement by the Joint Commission on Accreditation of Healthcare Organizations that all hospitals be smoke free to be accredited represents substantial progress. While the policy does not require hospitals to address nicotine addiction per se, it sets the stage for institutions to take an essential step.

CONCLUSION

The existence of a practice environment conducive to the treatment of nicotine addiction is essential if this preventive practice is to be brought into the mainstream of clinical medicine. This chapter reviews a number of ways in which the use of preventive practices may be increased, defines the elements of a proper practice environment for the delivery of nicotine addiction treatment services, suggests materials that may be used in the development of such an environment, and discusses current barriers to such development.

APPENDIX 9–A

Resources for the Health Professional

American Academy of Family Physicians (AAFP)
Health Education Department
8880 Ward Parkway
Kansas City, MO 64114-3246
1-800-274-2237

AAFP Stop Smoking Kit
This kit provides all instructions and materials necessary for the establishment of an office-based smoking cessation program for patients of family practice physicians. Included are a physician's handbook, patient self-help materials (including audiotapes, sample charts and chart reminders, and motivational information for patients not yet ready to stop). 1987. $50 for AAFP members, $80 for nonmembers. No quantity limit.

Family Physician's Guide to Smoking Cessation
This two-part videotape provides instruction on how to establish a smoking cessation program within a practice, techniques and strategies to motivate patients to stop smoking, and how to deal with problems of long-term management. Counseling skills and information on the addictive properties of nicotine are included. 1987. $49.

American Association for Respiratory Care
11030 Ables Lane
Dallas, TX 55229

Nicotine Intervention Kit
A complete package of resource materials was designed by the American Association for Respiratory Care to assist respiratory therapists in developing a service to help patients quit smoking. The kit contains a videotape to educate hospital administrators and physicians, a business and marketing plan, reproducible brochures, and other support materials.

American Cancer Society (ACS)
1599 Clifton Road, N.E.
Atlanta, GA 30329
404-320-3333

Tobacco-Free Young America: A Kit for the Busy Practitioner
This professional education packet provides materials to assist the smoking cessation efforts of physicians and their staffs. It contains the NCI/ACS booklet, *Quit for Good: A Practitioner's Stop-Smoking Guide;* the brochure, *Tobacco-Free Young America: Questions and Answers;* an ACS resource list; sample copies of the booklets *Smart Move* and *The Fifty Most Often Asked Questions About Smoking;* the professional brochure *Smokeless Tobacco: A Medical Perspective;* patient chart stickers; a physician-patient nonsmoking contract; and legislator's cards for use by the physician. ACS also offers a slide-tape program on smoking for health professionals. 1989. Materials available separately or as a kit from local ACS offices.

The American Health Foundation
320 E. 43rd Street
New York, NY 10017
212-953-1900

Stopping Smoking: A Nurse's Guide
This guide is designed to assist nurses in helping their clients to quit smoking and describes methods nurses can use to promote a smoke-free environment in health care facilities.

American Hospital Association
Order Services
840 N. Lake Shore Drive
Chicago, IL 60611
312-280-6000

Smoking and Hospitals Are a Bad Match
This kit suggests a sample strategy for developing a smoke-free or severely restrictive smoking policy. It also includes reproducible art for hospital communications, fact sheets, and resource lists. 1988. $18 for AHA members, $35 for nonmembers (discounts for more than 10 copies). No quantity limit.

*Smoke-free Hospital Patient
Communication and Staff Training
Resources*
The package includes smoking intervention guidelines and patient communication materials, staff training resources, and selected articles on smoke-free hospital policy implementation. Free.

American Lung Association (ALA)
1740 Broadway
New York, NY 10019
212-315-8700

*A Healthy Beginning: The Smoke-free
Family Guide for New Parents*
This kit for pediatricians and family physicians includes a guidebook on counseling patients about the effects of passive smoking on children, a waiting room poster and tent card, and a sample parent's packet. 1989. Consult local ALA chapters for price and ordering information.

ALA Pregnancy Kit
Smoking and Pregnancy, a handbook with flipchart and other materials for the health care professional on counseling pregnant women to quit. English and Spanish.

Center for Corporate Public Involvement
1001 Pennsylvania Avenue, N.W.
Washington, D.C. 20004-2599
202-624-2425

*Nonsmoking in the Workplace—A Guide
for Employers*
This comprehensive manual outlines procedures for developing cost-effective non-smoking program in the workplace, employee incentives to stop smoking, and methods to evaluate program results. $25. No quantity limit.

March of Dimes
Community Services Department
1275 Mamaroneck Ave.
White Plains, NY 10605
914-428-7100

*The Handbook to Plan, Implement and
Evaluate Smoking Cessation Programs for
Pregnant Women*
This 60-page guide is designed to provide practical, state-of-the-art information to help health professionals develop effective smoking cessation programs as part of an integrated prenatal care program. Numerous charts, tables, and forms are included. The handbook is a collaborative project of the Centers for Disease Control, the University of Alabama at Birmingham, the American Lung Association, and the National Office of the March of Dimes Birth Defects Foundation.

**Minnesota Coalition for a Smoke-Free
Society 2000**
Suite 400
2221 University Avenue, S.E.
Minneapolis, MN 55414
612-338-8193
612-378-0902 (FAX)

*Clean Air Health Care—A Guide to
Establish Smoke-Free Health Care
Facilities*
This guide is divided into two sections. The first section, "Setting the Agenda," demonstrates that a smoke-free hospital is legal, feasible, and desired by a majority of patients and employees. The second section, "Implementation," is a practical step-by-step guide to developing and adopting a smoke-free policy. $9.75. No quantity limit. "Clean Air Health Care for the Health of Our Patients," a poster suitable for framing, is $5.

*Making a Difference: The Occupational
Health Nurse's Smoking Cessation
Assistance Guide*
The guide provides recommendations from occupational nurses on how to work with and counsel smoking patients. The guide includes tips on tracking the individual smoker's response, dealing with patient fears about quitting smoking, a chart of common withdrawal symptoms, a questionnaire to determine nicotine dependency, stop-smoking patient checklists and tips, and recommended written and audiovisual resources to help smokers quit. $9.25 plus $2.00 postage and handling, $8.25 for two or more.

National Cancer Institute (NCI)
Office of Cancer Communications
Building 31, Room 10A24
9000 Rockville Pike
Bethesda, MD 20892
1-800-4-CANCER

How To Help Your Patients Stop Smoking: A National Cancer Institute Manual for Physicians
A step-by-step approach for the physician, with advice about office organization and involvement of support staff. Free. Limit of one at a time.

How To Help Your Patients Stop Using Tobacco: A National Cancer Institute Manual for the Oral Health Team
A step-by-step approach for both the dentist, the dental hygienist, and other members of the office oral health team. Free. Limit of one at a time.

Quit for Good Kit
This complete packet of materials is designed for physicians, dentists, and other health professionals to assist their smoking patients with cessation. Each kit contains enough materials for 50 patients. Includes "Quit For Good: A Practitioner's Stop-Smoking Guide," pamphlet, 1 copy; "Clearing the Air," pamphlet, 50 copies; patient stop-smoking contracts, pad of 50; patient chart stickers; tent cards, set of 2; waiting room poster; and "Thank You For Not Smoking" sign. 1988. Free. Limit of three kits may be ordered at one time.

Helping Smokers Quit: A Guide for the Pharmacist
January 1984. NIH Publication No. 84-655.

National Heart, Lung and Blood Institute
(in cooperation with the American Lung Association and the American Thoracic Society)
Order from:
Superintendent of Documents
U.S. Government Printing Office
Washington, D.C. 20402
202-783-3238

Clinical Opportunities for Smoking Intervention—A Guide for the Busy Physician
This guide discusses the important role physicians can play in helping their patients stop smoking and describes specific intervention strategies that can be integrated easily into the physician's clinical setting. A discussion of the biomedical consequences of smoking

is also provided. August 1986. NIH Publication No. 86-2178. Free. Limit of 25 copies.

National Heart, Lung and Blood Institute
Education Programs Information Center
Suite 530
4733 Bethesda Avenue
Bethesda, MD 20814-4820
301-951-3260

How You Can Help Patients Stop Smoking: Opportunities for Respiratory Care Practitioners
This guide contains practical information hospitals can use to provide smoking intervention activities for patients. Based on four levels of intervention, this publication discusses how to talk to smoking patients as part of usual respiratory care, how to set up a smoking intervention program within a respiratory care department, and how to reach out in the community with other smoking intervention activities. This monograph includes information about other private and public agencies and their specific smoking intervention activities, as well as a bibliography of relevant articles and resources. Free.

Making a Difference: Opportunities for Cessation Counseling
This video is designed to assist physicians in helping their patients quit smoking. The video demonstrates various approaches to cessation counseling and reviews the key points in each technique. 25 minutes. $10.

Nurses: Help Your Patients Stop Smoking
This is a practical smoking intervention guide for nurses to use in a variety of settings including hospitals, clinics, health department, schools, worksites, physicians' offices, and patients' homes. It contains background information about smoking cessation, an easy-to-use teaching guide, a pocket summary of the teaching guide, and two reproducible handouts for patients. The guide provides a simple four-step approach to smoking intervention—ask, advise, prepare, follow up—and describes techniques nurses can use to feel more comfortable in approaching the patient who smokes. October 1990. NIH Publication No. 90-2962. Free.

National High Blood Pressure Education Program
National Heart, Lung and Blood Institute
Building 31, Room 4A21
Bethesda, MD 20892
301-496-4236

The Physician's Guide—How To Help Your Hypertensive Patient Stop Smoking
Hypertensive patients who smoke greatly increase their probability of developing cardiovascular disease. This physician's guide describes the "minimal smoking cessation procedure" designed especially for this high-risk group—a simple, practical, step-by-step approach that can be integrated into every routine high blood pressure office visit. April 1983. NIH Publication No. 83-1271. Free. Limit of 25 copies.

U.S. Office on Smoking and Health
Centers for Disease Control
1600 Clifton Road, N.E.
Atlanta, GA 30333
(404) 488-5701

A Physician Talks About Smoking
This slide program is designed to meet the needs of physicians and other health care professionals who are called upon to speak to medical and lay audiences on smoking and health. The slides summarize cigarette smoking as a risk factor for premature morbidity and mortality; costs of smoking-related disease and death; how cigarettes cause disease; and who smokes, how much, and why. 1986. $35 (a booklet containing the text of the slides is available free).

APPENDIX 9-B

Other Sources of Information

Federal Government

National Cancer Institute
Office of Cancer Communications
Building 31, Room 10A24
9000 Rockville Pike
Bethesda, MD 20892
1-800-4-CANCER

National Heart, Lung and Blood Institute
Smoking Education Program
Building 31, Room 4A18
9000 Rockville Pike
Bethesda, MD 20892
301-496-1051

U.S. Office on Smoking and Health
Centers for Disease Control
1600 Clifton Road, N.E.
Atlanta, GA 30333
(404) 488-5701

Professional Organizations

American Academy of Family Physicians
Health Education Department
8880 Ward Parkway
Kansas City, MO 64114-3246
1-800-274-2237

American Association for Respiratory Care
11030 Ables Lane
Dallas, TX 55229

American Medical Association
Division of Communications
535 North Dearborn Street
Chicago, IL 60610
312-645-4419

Doctors Ought to Care (DOC)
Suite 235
5510 Greenbriar
Houston, TX 77005
713-798-7729
713-788-7775 (FAX)

Pharmacists for Non-Smoking Families
8 West Pacific Avenue
Henderson, NV 89015
702-564-3747

Voluntary Organizations

American Cancer Society
1599 Clifton Road, N.E.
Atlanta, GA 30329
404-320-3333

American Heart Association
7320 Greenville Avenue
Dallas, TX 75231
214-822-9380

American Lung Association
1740 Broadway
New York, NY 10019
212-315-8700

Smoke-free Educational Services
Suite 32F
375 South End Avenue
New York, NY 10280
212-912-0960
212-488-8911 (FAX)

Stop Teenage Addiction to Tobacco
Suite 210
121 Lyman Street
Springfield, MA 01103-1315
413-732-7828
413-732-4219 (FAX)

REFERENCES

Anda, R. F., Remington, P. L., Sienko, D. G., Davis, R. M. Are physicians advising smokers to quit? The patient's perspective. *JAMA* 257:1916–1919, 1987.

Barnett, G. O., Winickoff, R. N., Morgan, M. M., Zielstorff, R. D. A computer-based monitoring system for followup of elevated blood pressure. *Med Care* 21:400–409, 1983.

Berner, J. S., Frame, P. S., Dickinson, J. C. Ten years of screening for cancer in a family practice. *J Fam Pract* 24:249–252, 1987.

Bronson, D. L., and O'Meara, K. The impact of shared medical records on smoking awareness and behavior in ambulatory care. *J Gen Intern Med* 1:34–37, 1986.

CA—A Cancer Journal for Clinicians. The impact of providing physicians with quit-smoking materials for smoking patients. *CA* 31:75–78, 1981.

Cohen, S. J., Christian, A. G., Katz, B. P., Drook, C. A., Davis, B. J., Smith, D. M., Stookey, G. K. Counseling medical and dental patients about cigarette smoking: The impact of nicotine gum and chart reminders. *Am J Public Health* 77:313–316, 1987.

Cohen, S. J., Stookey, G. K., Katz, B. P., Drook, C. A., Smith, D. M. Encouraging primary care physicians to help smokers quit. *Ann Intern Med* 110:648–652, 1989.

Cummings, K. M., Giovino, G., Emont, S. L., Sciandra, R., Koenigsberg, R. Factors influencing success in counseling patients to stop smoking. *Patient Education and Counseling* 8:189–200, 1986.

Cummings, S. R., Coates, T. J., Richard, R. J., Hansen, B., Zahnd, E. G., Vander Martin, R., Duncan, C., Gerbert, B., Martin, A., Stein, M. J. Training physicians in counseling about smoking cessation: A randomized trial of the "Quit for Life" program. *Ann Intern Med* 110:640–647, 1989.

Cummings, S. R., Richard, R. J., Duncan, C. L., Hansen, B., Vander Martin, R., Gerbert, B., Coates, T. J. Training physicians about smoking cessation: A controlled trial in private practice. *J Gen Intern Med* 4:482–489, 1989.

Cummings, S. R., Rubin, S. M., Oster, G. The cost-effectiveness of counseling smokers to quit. *JAMA* 261:75–79, 1989.

Eagle, J. Reimbursement. Paper presented at the First National Conference on Nicotine Dependence, American Society of Addiction Medicine, Minneapolis, MN, 1988.

Frame, P. S., Wetterau, N. W., Parley, B. A model for the use of physicians' assistants in primary care. *J Fam Pract* 7:1195–1202, 1978.

Frank, J. W. Occult blood screening for colorectal carcinoma: The benefits. *Am J Prev Med* 1(3):3–9, 1985.

Gates, S. J., and Colborn, D. K. Lowering appointment failures in a neighborhood health center. *Med Care* 14:263–267, 1976.

Gemson, D. H., and Elinson, J. Prevention in primary care: Variability in physician practice patterns in New York City. *Am J Prev Med* 1:229–234, 1986.

Giglio, R. J., Spears, R. M., Rumpf, D. L., et al. Encouraging behavior changes by use of client-held records. *Med Care* 9:757, 1978.

Giglio, R. J., and Papazian, B. Acceptance and use of patient-carried health records. *Med Care* 24:1084–1092, 1986.

Glynn, T. J. Relative effectiveness of physician-initiated smoking cessation programs. *Cancer Bull* 40(6):359–364, 1988.

Glynn, T. J., and Manley, M. W. *How To Help Your Patients Stop Smoking: A National Cancer Institute Manual for Physicians.* U.S. Department of Health and Human Services, Public Health Service, National Institutes of Health. NIH Publication 89-3064, 1989a.

————. Physicians, cancer control and the treatment of nicotine dependence: Defining success. *Health Educ Res* 4(4):479–487, 1989b.

Glynn, T. J., Manley, M. W., Pechacek, T. F. Physician-initiated smoking cessation programs: The National Cancer Institute trials. In Engstrom, P., et al., eds. *Advances in Cancer Control.* New York: Alan R. Liss, 1990.

Goroll, A. H., Goodson, J. D., Piggins, J. L., et al. Evolution of computer-based supplement to the office medical record. *J Ambulat Care Manage* 8(2):39–65, 1985.

Green, L. W., Eriksen, M. P., Schoor, E. L. Preventive practices by physicians: Behavioral determinants and potential intervention. *Am J Prev Med* 4:S101–S107, 1988.

Hulka, B. S., Romm, F. J., Parkson, G. R., Jr., Russell, I. T., Clapp, N. E., Johnson, F. S. Peer review in ambulatory care: Use of explicit criteria and implicit judgments. *Med Care* 17(suppl. 3):i–vi, 1–73, 1979.

Hurt, R. D., Berge, K. G., Offord, U. P., Leonard, D. A., Gerlach, D. K., Renquist, C. L., O'Hara, M. R. The making of a smoke-free medical center. *JAMA* 261:95–97, 1989.

JAMA—Journal of the American Medical Association. Medical news and perspectives: Magazines without tobacco advertising. *JAMA* 226(22):3099–3102, 1991.

Jamrozik, K., and Fowler, G. Anti-smoking education in Oxfordshire general practices. *Coll Gen Pract* 32:179–183, 1982.

Knapp, J., Silvis, G., Sorenson, G., Kottke, T. E. *Clean Air Health Care. A Guide To Establish Smoke-Free Health Care Facilities.* Minneapolis: Minnesota Coalition for a Smoke-Free Society 2000, 1986.

Knight, B. P., O'Malley, M. S., Fletcher, S. W. Physician acceptance of a computerized health maintenance prompting program. *Am J Prev Med* 3:19–24, 1987.

Kottke, T. E., Blackburn, H., Brekke, M. L., Solberg, L. I. The systematic practice of preventive cardiology. *Am J Cardiol* 59:690–694, 1987.

Kottke, T. E., Battista, R. N., DeFriese, G. H., Brekke, M. L. Attributes of successful smoking cessation interventions in medical practice: A meta-analysis of 39 controlled trials. *JAMA* 259(19):2883–2889, 1988.

Kottke, T. E., Solberg, L. I., Brekke, M. L., Maxwell, P. Smoking cessation strategies and evaluation. *J Am Coll Cardiol* 12:1105–1110, 1988.

Kottke, T. E., Solberg, L. I., Brekke, M. L. Initiation and maintenance of patient behavioral change: What is the role of the physician? *J Gen Intern Med* 5(suppl.):S62–S67, 1990a.

————. Beyond efficacy testing: Introducing preventive cardiology into primary care. *Am J Prev Med* 6(suppl.):77–83, 1990b.

Love, R. R. The physician's role in cancer prevention and screening. *Cancer Bull* 40(6):380–383, 1988.

Lurie, N., Manning, W. G., Peterson, C., Goldberg, C. A., Phelps, C. A., Lillard, L. Preventive care: Do we practice what we preach? *Am J Public Health* 77:801–804, 1987.

McDonald, C. J., Hui, S., Smith, D. M., et al. Reminders to physicians from an introspective computer medical record system: A two-year randomized trial. *Ann Intern Med* 100:130–138, 1984.

McDowell, I., Newell, C., Rosser, W. Comparison of three methods of recalling patients for influenza vaccination. *Can Med Assoc J* 135:991–997, 1986.

McPhee, S. J., and Schroeder, S. A. Promoting preventive care: Changing reimbursement is not enough. *Am J Public Health* 77:780–781, 1987.

McPhee, S. J., Bird, J. A., Jenkins, C.N.H., Fordham, D. Promoting cancer screening: A randomized, controlled trial of three interventions. *Arch Intern Med* 149:1866–1872, 1989.

Manley, M., Epps, R. P., Husten, C., Glynn, T., Shopland, D. Clinical interventions in tobacco control. *JAMA* 266(22):3172–3173, 1991.

Manley, M., Epps, R. P., Mecklenburg, R., Husten, C. Clinical interventions in tobacco control: A National Cancer Institute training program for health care providers. In *Tobacco and the Clinician: Smoking Interventions in Medical and Dental Practice.* STCP Monograph 2. U.S. Department of Health and Human Services, Public Health Service, National Institutes of Health, National Cancer Institute, in press.

Nelson, A. R. Orphan data and the unclosed loop: A dilemma in PSRO and medical audit. *N Engl J Med* 295:617, 1976.

Ockene, J. K. Physician-delivered intervention for smoking cessation. Strategies for increasing effectiveness. *Prev Med* 16:723–737, 1987.

Ockene, J. K., Quirk, M. E., Goldberg, R. J., Kristeller, J. L., Donnelly, M., Kalkan, K. L., Gould, B., Greene, H. L., Harrison-Atlas, R., Pease, J., Pickens, S., Williams, J. A residents' training program for the development of smoking intervention skills. *Arch Intern Med* 148:1039–1045, 1988.

Orleans, C. T., George, L. K., Houpt, J. K., Brodie, H.K.H. Health promotion in primary care: A survey of U.S. family practitioners. *Prev Med* 14:636–647, 1985.

Ramstrom, L., Raw, M., Wood, M., eds. *Guidelines on Smoking Cessation for the Primary Health Care Team.* Geneva:WHO/UICC, 1988.

Richmond, R. L., Austin, A., Webster, I. W. Three year evaluation of a programme by general practitioners to help patients to stop smoking. *Br Med J* 292:803–806, 1986.

Rosen, M. A., Logsdon, D. N., Demak, M. N. Preventive and health promotion in primary care. *Prev Med* 13:535–548, 1984.

Russell, M.A.H., Wilson, C., Taylor, C., Baker, C. Effect of general practitioners' advice against smoking. *Br Med J* 2:231–235, 1979.

Russell, M.A.H., Merriman, R., Stapleton, J., Taylor, W. Effect of nicotine chewing gum as an adjunct to general practitioners' advice against smoking. *Br Med J* 287:1782–1785, 1983.

Schroeder, S. A., and Showstack, J. A. Financial incentives to perform medical procedures and laboratory tests: Illustrative models of office practice. *Med Care* 16:289–298, 1978.

Schwartz, J. L. *Review and Evaluation of Smoking Cessation Methods: The United States and Canada, 1978–1985.* Bethesda, MD: U.S. Department of Health and Human Services. NIH Publication No. 87-2940, 1987.

Slade, J. Using the medical office to prevent and treat nicotine dependence. Phamphlet, National Cancer Institute, COMMIT Project, Bethesda, May 1989.

Solberg, L. I., and Maxwell, P. L. A practical office-based smoking cessation program. *Patient Education Proceedings* 9:35–38, 1987.

Solberg, L. I., Maxwell, P. L., Kottke, T. E., Gepner, G., Brekke, M. L. A systematic primary care office-based smoking cessation program. *J Fam Pract* 6:647–654, 1990.

Solberg, L. I., Maxwell, P. L., Kottke, T. E., et al. *Doctors Helping Smokers: An Office Manual.* Minneapolis: University of Minnesota, 1989.

Somers, A. R. Four "orphan" areas in current medical education: What hope for adoption? *Fam Med* 19:137–140, 1987.

Somers, L. S., Scholts, R., Shepherd, R. M., et al. Physician involvement in quality assurance. *Med Care* 22:1115–1138, 1984.

Thompson, R. S., Michnich, M. E., Gray, J., et al. Maximizing compliance with hemoccult screening for colon cancer in clinical practice. *Med Care* 24:1084–1092, 1986.

Tierney, W. M., Siu, L. H., McDonald, C. J. Delayed feedback of physician performance versus immediate reminders to perform preventive care: Effect on physician compliance. *Med Care* 24:659–666, 1986.

U.S. Department of Health and Human Services (USDHHS). *The Health Benefits of Smoking Cessation: A Report of the Surgeon General.* U.S. Department of Health and Human Services, Public Health Service, Centers for Disease Control, Center for Chronic Disease Prevention and Health Promotion, Office on Smoking and Health. DHHS Publication No. (CDC) 90-8416, 1990.

Wechsler, H., Levine, S., Idelson, R. K., Rohman, M., Taylor, J. O. The physician's role in health promotion: A survey of primary care practitioners. *N Engl J Med* 308:97–100, 1983.

Wells, K. B., Lewis, C. E., Leake, B., Ware, J. E., Jr. Do physicians practice what they preach? A study of physicians' health habits and counseling practices. *JAMA* 252:2846–2848, 1984.

Wells, K. B., Ware, J. E., Lewis, C. E. Physicians' practices in counseling patients about health habits. *Med Care* 22:240–246, 1984.

Wells, K. B., Lewis, C. E., Leake, B., Schleiter, M. K., Brook, R. H. The practices of general and subspecialty internists in counseling about smoking and exercise. *Am J Public Health* 76:1009–1013, 1986.

Williams, S. V., and Eisenberg, J. M. A controlled trial to decrease the unnecessary use of diagnostic tests. *J Gen Intern Med* 1:8–13, 1986.

Wilson, D. M., Taylor, D. W., Gilbert, J. R., Best, J. A., Lindsay, E. A., Willms, D. G., Singer, J. A randomized trial of a family physician intervention for smoking cessation. *JAMA* 260:1570–1574, 1988.

Winickoff, R. N., Coltin, K. L., Morgan, M. M., et al. Improving physician performance through peer comparison feedback. *Med Care* 22:527–534, 1984.

10

Minimal-Contact Quit Smoking Strategies for Medical Settings

C. TRACY ORLEANS, THOMAS J. GLYNN, MARC W. MANLEY, and JOHN SLADE

Minimal-contact quit smoking treatment strategies are defined here as efforts to stop smoking not by participating in a formal treatment program, but with the help of brief instructions or advice on how to quit and/or by using self-help materials and quitting aids (e.g., self-help guide, instructional manual or video, adjunctive nicotine replacement) (Curry, in press; Glynn, Boyd, Gruman 1990). In medical settings, minimal-contact treatments generally involve brief smoking history assessment, personalized medical advice to quit, and a self-quitting guide, sometimes with the prescription of a pharmacologic adjunct. As discussed in Chapter 9, minimal-contact medical treatments require a practice environment that facilitates and reinforces smoking cessation (e.g., smoke-free facilities) (Glynn and Manley 1991).

EMPHASIS ON PHYSICIAN-INITIATED OFFICE-BASED INTERVENTIONS

This chapter fleshes out the stepped-care model introduced in Chapter 8 (see Figure 10–1) and builds on the "systems approach" introduced in Chapter 9 by describing physician-initiated minimal-contact strategies. The focus is on practical primary care smoking cessation interventions, exemplified by the National Cancer Institute four-step intervention model (Glynn and Manley 1991). However, the chapter also covers minimal-

contact *hospital-based treatments* and *interventions by nonphysician health care providers,* including nurses, respiratory therapists, physician assistants, chemical dependency counselors, psychologists, health educators, pharmacists, and dentists and oral hygienists. Similar minimal-contact strategies for *smokeless tobacco* users seen in medical and dental care settings are reviewed in Chapter 13. Subsequent chapters also give suggestions for how to tailor brief interventions for selected patient groups (Chapter 14), as well as for women (Chapter 17), minorities (Chapter 18), youth (Chapter 19), and older smokers (Chapter 20).

RATIONALE FOR SELF-HELP STRATEGIES

As outlined in Chapter 8, self-help strategies are a good starting point for most patients. Most smokers prefer "do-it-yourself" and minimal-contact strategies over formal treatment programs (Schwartz and Dubitsky 1967) and, in fact, 90% of U.S. ex-smokers have quit without the benefit of a formal treatment program (Fiore et al. 1990). Moreover, minimal-contact strategies can be easily integrated into routine patient care and readily applied to *all* smokers, regardless of their interest in quitting or motivational "stage" (Prochaska and DiClemente 1983). This stands in contrast to multisession clinics which typically are used by only a small percentage of eligible medical patients—

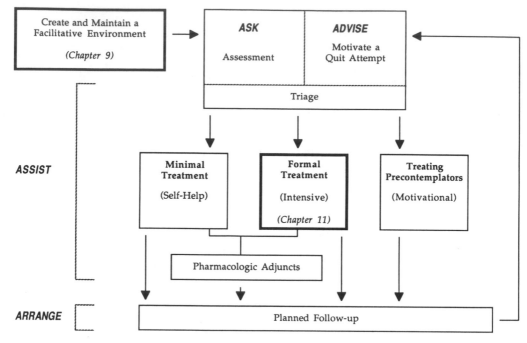

Fig. 10–1   Minimal-contact treatments in a stepped-care model. *Source:* Orleans 1988

usually only the most highly motivated (e.g., Hall et al. 1983; Hughes et al. 1982; Ockene, Kristeller, and Ockene 1990).

There are other reasons for recommending minimal-contact strategies as a starting point. The 8–15% 1-year quit rates typically achieved by smokers quitting without formal assistance (Fiore et al. 1990) or with self-help materials and aids (Cohen, Lichtenstein, Prochaska et al. 1989) are quite respectable when compared with typical 20–25% 1-year quit rates of formal treatment programs (USDHHS 1989a)—and even more impressive given that the self-quit rate climbs to 60% over a lifetime of repeated quit attempts (Schachter 1982). Moreover, there is an increasingly wide variety of self-help quitting guides and aids available to help the "solo" quitter—with long-term quit rates averaging 14–15%, and reaching 20–25% when guides are paired with low-contact add-on activities such as those recommended in this chapter to help smokers quit or stay quit (Cohen, Lichtenstein, Prochaska et al. 1989; Glynn, Boyd, Gruman 1990; USDHHS 1989a). Many of these add-on ac-

tivities are easily incorporated in primary care settings, including nicotine replacement therapy (Transdermal Nicotine Study Group 1991), brief telephone counseling calls (Orleans, Schoenbach, Wagner et al. 1991), access to a telephone quit smoking "hotline" (Ossip-Klein et al. 1991), personalized computer-generated progress reports (Prochaska, DiClemente, Velicer 1988), and serialized quit smoking materials or modules mailed in installments (Ershoff, Mullen, Quinn 1989).

There is one caveat. While minimal-contact self-help treatments represent the most practical, widely applicable, and potentially most cost-effective strategy for treating nicotine addiction in medical settings, emphasizing them does not preclude moving to more intensive or specialized treatments when they are indicated—either right at the start or after minimal-contact strategies have been tried. The minimal-contact treatments described in this chapter are recommended as part of the larger stepped-care model presented in Chapter 8 which includes triaging patients to intensive treatment programs when they are needed (see Figure 10–1). Chapter 11 describes these formal treatments in detail.

Beginning in the mid-1980s, the National Cancer Institute (NCI) funded five randomized, controlled clinical trials to evaluate the efficacy of minimal contact interventions in primary care medical and dental practices (Glynn and Manley 1989). Over 30,000 patients and 1,000 providers were involved (mostly physicians, also dentists). Patients in intervention groups had long-term quit rates two to six times as high as patients receiving usual care. The essential elements of these interventions were distilled into four steps:

1. *Ask* about smoking at every opportunity;
2. *Advise* all smokers to stop;
3. *Assist* the patient in stopping; and
4. *Arrange* follow-up support.

This four-step plan is incorporated into the treatment model presented in Figure 10–1. It is outlined in the guide *How to Help Your Patients Stop Smoking: A National Cancer Institute Manual for Physicians* (Glynn and Manley 1991) and in two similar guides— *How to Help Your Patients Stop Using Tobacco: A National Cancer Institute Manual for the Oral Health Team* (Mecklenburg et al. 1990) and *Nurses: Help Your Patients Stop Smoking* (USDHHS 1990b).

STEP 1. ASK ABOUT SMOKING AT EVERY OPPORTUNITY

Smoking Status as a Vital Sign

The importance of having a system in place to identify all smokers and to prompt asking about smoking at every opportunity was stressed in Chapter 9. The ideal is to institutionalize routine assessment of smoking status, elevating it to the priority of a "vital sign" (Fiore 1991). In fact, Fiore (1991, p. 3184) recommends using a vital signs stamp that includes all the following information: blood pressure, pulse, respiratory rate, temperature, weight, smoking status (current, former, never). As a reminder to the physician and office staff to discuss the smoker's status at each visit, a sticker, stamp, or other indicator should be placed prominently in or

on the charts of all patients who smoke (e.g., Cohen et al. 1987; Glynn and Manley 1991; Lindsay et al. 1989).

Assessing Nicotine Dependence and Smoking History

This first step, however, does not end with determining smoking status. It also includes collecting simple but sufficient data for a formal diagnosis of nicotine dependence and for an assessment of smoking history and related treatment needs.

Diagnosing "Nicotine Dependence"

The DSM-III-R *(Diagnostic and Statistical Manual of Mental Disorders)* classifies "nicotine dependence" as a psychoactive substance dependence disorder (305.10) (APA 1987). The essential feature of DSM-III-R substance use disorders is evidence that the person has "impaired control of psychoactive substance use and continues to use the substance despite adverse consequences" (APA 1987, p. 166). At least three of nine characteristic symptoms of dependence (over a month or more) are needed to make this diagnosis. These criteria can be easily judged through clinical interview. The symptoms most relevant for *nicotine* dependence are: (1) inability to reduce or abstain from substance use despite the desire to do so and recognition of its harms; (2) continued use despite the social, psychological, and physical problems that occur with heavy and prolonged substance use; (3) inability to participate in important social, occupational, or recreational activities because of substance use; (4) evidence of drug tolerance (markedly reduced effects with continued use of the same amount of the substance); (5) presence of characteristic withdrawal symptoms when substance use is discontinued or reduced; and (6) a return to substance use in order to alleviate unpleasant withdrawal symptoms after abstinence. DSM-III-R criteria for "nicotine withdrawal" (292.00) are the occurrence of at least four of the following symptoms when tobacco use is discontinued: craving for nicotine, irritability, frustration or anger, anxiety, difficulty concentrating, decreased heart rate, and increased appetite or weight gain.

Brief Clinical Assessment of Smoking Pattern/Quitting Needs

A brief assessment of the smoker's smoking pattern and quitting history will help the provider select the most appropriate minimal-contact nicotine addiction treatment (and/or identify patients who may need the extra help or support a formal quitting program can provide). A practical clinical smoking assessment will obtain only information bearing on the clinician's choice of treatment approach or method. Requesting too much information may overwhelm the patient and the busy practitioner.

Sample Questionnaire. Figure 10–2 presents an example of a practical smoking assessment form—one that takes only a few minutes for the patient to complete. Key items recommended by the NCI for studies of self-quitting are included (NCI 1986). (Figure 10–3 and the discussion of minimal-contact advice and assistance strategies describes how these items can be used to guide brief counseling and treatment choices.)

Assessing Degree of Dependence. Level of nicotine dependence or addiction is a critical determinant of withdrawal severity and quitting difficulty (USDHHS 1988). To assess it, this questionnaire asks both about *daily smoking rate* and *whether the smoker usually lights up within 30 minutes of awakening.*

Asking about daily smoking rate *in the past week* establishes a meaningful baseline against which to gauge changes in smoking rate at some future time (NCI 1986). If the past week has been anomalous (e.g., patient too ill to smoke or in a smoke-free hospital), this item can be restated to ask about *typical* daily smoking rate. A smoker who smokes 25 or more cigarettes a day is considered a "heavy smoker" (USDHHS 1988). Heavy smokers experience greater difficulty quitting smoking and staying off, are more troubled by withdrawal symptoms, and report stronger cravings and urges than "light"

smokers, who smoke 15 or fewer cigarettes a day (Killen et al. 1988).

As Henningfield (1988) notes, however, level of nicotine dependence for light and intermediate level smokers (16–24 cigarettes/ day) cannot be judged by cigarette count alone: assessment is aided by additional diagnostic tools, such as the Fagerström Tolerance Questionnaire (Fagerström 1978) or its recent revision, the Fagerström Test for Nicotine Dependence (Fagerström, Heatherton, Kozlowski 1992; Heatherton et al. 1991). This questionnaire is a widely used, validated index of physical nicotine dependency that can be administered and self-scored in just a few minutes (Appendix A, which follows Chapter 21). However, one item from this scale, time until first cigarette of the day, has been found to correlate highly with the overall scale score and has been recommended and adopted as a reliable, practical index of high nicotine dependence (Pomerleau et al. 1990). Smokers who report smoking within 30 minutes of awakening generally have more severe withdrawal reactions and greater difficulty quitting—even if they smoke relatively few cigarettes per day. As is the case with heavy smokers, such highly nicotine dependent smokers may benefit especially from adjunctive nicotine replacement therapies (Tonnesen 1988).

Analyses of biologic samples (e.g., measures of the nicotine-metabolite, cotinine, in urine, blood, or saliva) also can be used to judge addiction severity. In addition, they can be employed to monitor effectiveness of nicotine replacement if nicotine replacement is used (by assessing therapeutic levels of nicotine), or, as described in Chapter 11, to verify smoking abstinence (after the termination of nicotine replacement therapy) (e.g., Abrams et al. 1987; Henningfield 1988; Pomerleau et al. 1990).

Assessing Readiness to Quit. Items 3 and 4 in Figure 10–2 assess recent quit attempts and current readiness to quit. Together they identify a smoker's "stage of change" (Prochaska and DiClemente 1983; Prochaska et al. 1992).

Smokers with a serious quit attempt in the *past year* (i.e., where "serious" is defined as staying off 24 hours or more) can be re-

Name —————————————————————— Date ————————

1. **During the past 7 days,** how many cigarettes
   (not packs) did you smoke on a typical day?   ———— Cigarettes per day

2. Do you smoke your first cigarette within 30 minutes
   of waking up?   ☐ Yes   ☐ No

3. **In the past 12 months,** have you tried to quit and
   stayed off cigarettes for at least 24 hours?   ☐ Yes   ☐ No

4. Are you **seriously** thinking about quitting smoking
   in the next year?   ☐ Yes   ☐ No

5. **During the past 12 months,** have you had any of
   these conditions?
   a. Trouble breathing or shortness of
      breath... ☐ Yes   ☐ No
   b. Frequent coughing...................................... ☐ Yes   ☐ No
   c. Getting tired in a short time.................... ☐ Yes   ☐ No
   d. Pain or tightness in the chest................ ☐ Yes   ☐ No

6. How much of a problem do you think these might   None   Some   Very Much
   be for you when you quit smoking?
   a. Fear of failure.. ☐   ☐   ☐
   b. Being irritable, nervous or tense............. ☐   ☐   ☐
   c. Difficulty concentrating........................... ☐   ☐   ☐
   d. Missing or craving cigarettes................... ☐   ☐   ☐
   e. Losing a pleasure...................................... ☐   ☐   ☐
   f. Gaining weight... ☐   ☐   ☐
   g. Being around other smokers................... ☐   ☐   ☐

7. How much help & understanding would you expect   None   Some   Very Much
   from family & friends if you tried to quit smoking? ☐   ☐   ☐

8. How many times have you seriously tried to quit   ————   **Times tried to quit**
   smoking?

9. Have you **ever** tried these ways to quit smoking?
   a. A one-to-one program with personal counseling
      or advice.. ☐ Yes   ☐ No
   b. A group program or clinic......................... ☐ Yes   ☐ No
   c. A prescription for nicotine gum or patch................. ☐ Yes   ☐ No

Fig. 10–2 Smoking history assessment form. *Source:* Fox Chase Cancer Center, Philadelphia PA 19011,
1992.

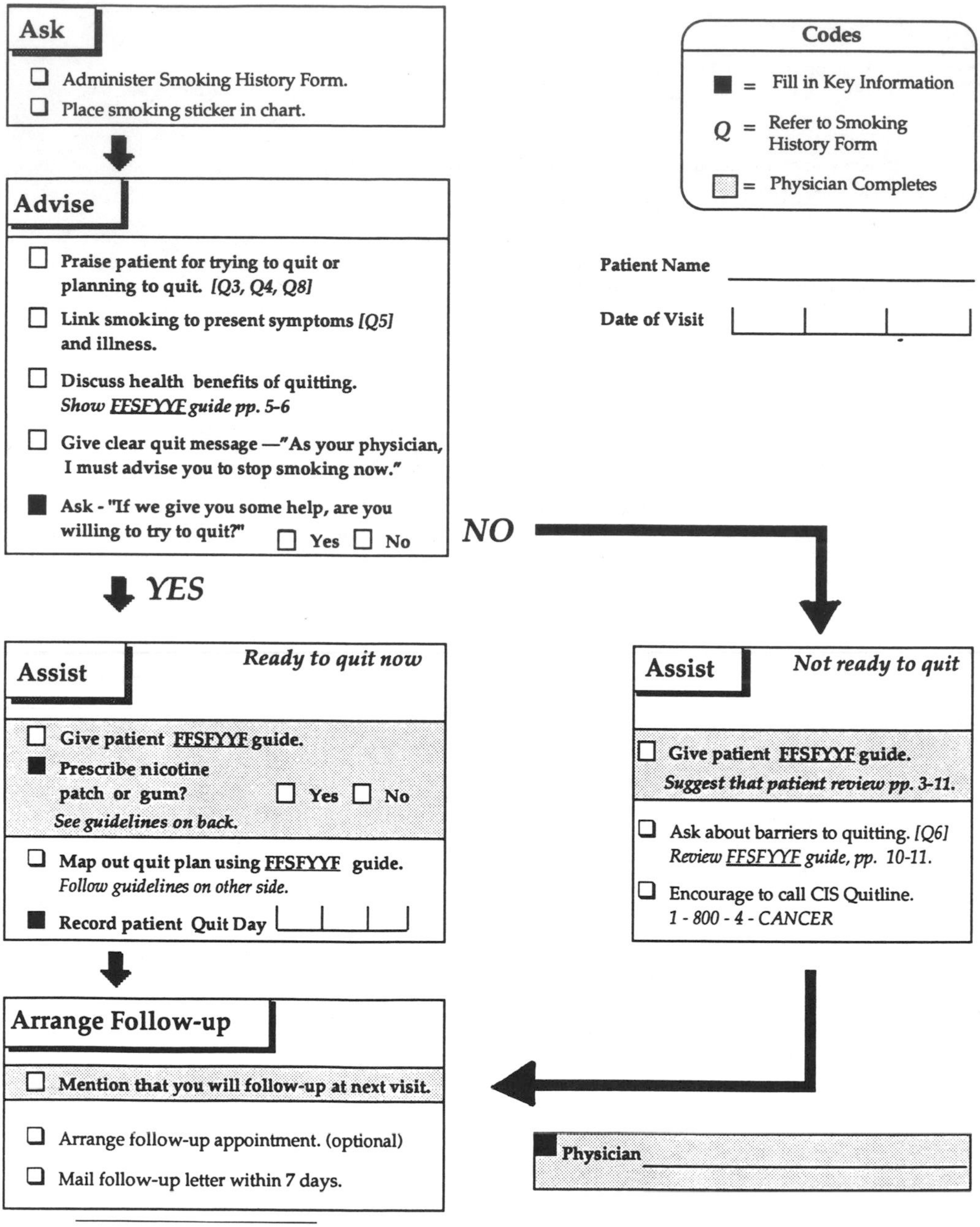

Ask
- ☐ Administer Smoking History Form.
- ☐ Place smoking sticker in chart.

↓

Advise
- ☐ Praise patient for trying to quit or planning to quit. *[Q3, Q4, Q8]*
- ☐ Link smoking to present symptoms *[Q5]* and illness.
- ☐ Discuss health benefits of quitting. *Show FFSFYYF guide pp. 5-6*
- ☐ Give clear quit message —"As your physician, I must advise you to stop smoking now."
- ■ Ask - "If we give you some help, are you willing to try to quit?" ☐ Yes ☐ No

NO →

↓ *YES*

Codes
- ■ = Fill in Key Information
- *Q* = Refer to Smoking History Form
- ☐ = Physician Completes

Patient Name _____

Date of Visit | | | . |

Assist — *Ready to quit now*
- ☐ Give patient **FFSFYYF** guide.
- ■ Prescribe nicotine patch or gum? ☐ Yes ☐ No *See guidelines on back.*
- ☐ Map out quit plan using **FFSFYYF** guide. *Follow guidelines on other side.*
- ■ Record patient Quit Day | | | |

↓

Assist — *Not ready to quit*
- ☐ Give patient **FFSFYYF** guide. *Suggest that patient review pp. 3-11.*
- ☐ Ask about barriers to quitting. *[Q6] Review FFSFYYF guide, pp. 10-11.*
- ☐ Encourage to call CIS Quitline. *1 - 800 - 4 - CANCER*

Arrange Follow-up
- ☐ Mention that you will follow-up at next visit.
- ☐ Arrange follow-up appointment. (optional)
- ☐ Mail follow-up letter within 7 days.

■ Physician _____

Fig. 10–3 Helping your patients stop smoking. *Source:* Fox Chase Cancer Center, Philadelphia PA 19011, 1992.

Guidelines for Prescribing Nicotine Replacement

Appropriate Candidate for Nicotine Gum or Patch

- ☐ Smokes 16 or more cigarettes per day. *[Q1]*
- ☐ Smokes within 30 minutes of waking. *[Q2]*
- ☐ Bothered by withdrawal symptoms in the past.
  (e.g., irritability, restlessness, difficulty concentrating)
- ☐ No medical contraindications. *(e.g., life-threatening arrhythmias, recent MI, severe or worsening angina, pregnancy/lactation)*

Recommended Gum Dose (2 mg gum)

- ☐ 1 pack/day = 12 pieces gum/day.
- ☐ 1- 1/2 packs/day = 16 pieces gum/day.
- ☐ 2 packs/day = 20 pieces gum/day.
- ☐ *Maximum = 30 pieces gum/day.*

Guidelines for Reviewing FFSFYYF Guide

1. **Describe 4 sections of FFSFYYF guide.**
   - ☐ Making The Decision *[pp. 3-17]*
   - ☐ Getting Ready *[pp. 19-31]*
   - ☐ Your First Two Weeks Off Cigarettes *[pp. 33-45]*
   - ☐ Going the Distance *[pp. 47-54]*

2. **Explain 3 different methods to get ready to quit.**
   - ☐ Nicotine Fading *[pp. 16-17]*
   - ☐ Pack Track *[pp. 20-23]*
   - ☐ Habit Breaking *[p. 24]*

3. **Ask if patient is ready to set a quit day.**
   - ☐ Fill in quit date on other side.

4. **Address relevant topics and quitting barriers.** *[Q6]*
   - ☐ Exercise *[p. 12]*
   - ☐ Deep Breathing *[p. 13]*
   - ☐ Coping with short-term withdrawal *[pp. 38-39]*
   - ☐ Diet Tips *[pp. 40-44]*

5. **Review nicotine gum or patch instructions, if prescribed.**
   - ☐ How to use gum *[p. 34]*
   - ☐ Weaning off gum *[p. 34]*
   - ☐ How to use patch *[see product guide]*

6. **Encourage to call CIS Quitline.**
   - ☐ 1 - 800 - 4 - CANCER

Progress Notes

Follow-up Date	Smoking Status	Notes *(including new quit date)*
_____	_____	_____
_____	_____	_____
_____	_____	_____

Congratulate if off cigarettes. Assess need for nicotine gum or patch refills/weaning. Encourage to "re-cycle " if quit but relapsed. Encourage to set a new quit date and quit plan if has not quit or tried to quit. Encourage to call 1 - 800 - 4 - CANCER for additional help.

Make sure form is completed. Staple to Smoking History Form. Place in patient chart for future reference.

FOX CHASE
CANCER CENTER

Fig. 10–3 (continued)

garded as being in a "relapse" stage—their past efforts suggest high potential openness to quitting assistance, and these efforts deserve praise as well as reassurance that multiple tries before achieving success are the norm. Rossi (1989) found that relapsers were two times more likely to quit permanently in the following year than smokers who had not made a serious (24-hour or more) quit attempt in the past year.

Smokers who say they are seriously thinking about stopping smoking in the *next year* are defined as *contemplators,* while those who answer "no" to this question fit the definition of *precontemplators. Contemplators* who report a serious quit attempt in the past year are defined as being in the determination or preparation stage. They are especially likely to take action to quit (Prochaska et al. 1992). One recent study of smokers aged 50 years and over found that being a contemplator, versus precontemplator, was associated with having smoking-related symptoms and illnesses, recent medical advice to stop smoking, stronger beliefs in smoking health harms and quitting benefits, fewer smokers in one's immediate social network, and greater interest in a variety of treatment options (Orleans, Rimer, Cristinzio et al. 1991). Contemplators also differ from precontemplators in how they evaluate the "pros and cons" of smoking (Velicer et al. 1985) and in their responsiveness to cessation-oriented, versus motivational, interventions (Prochaska 1991; Prochaska et al. 1992).

Hollis and associates (1991) found that contemplators were almost three times more likely than precontemplators to quit smoking in response to a brief office-based intervention. Similarly, Ockene, Kristeller, and Ockene (1992) evaluated an intensive inpatient quit smoking program for patients with serious cardiovascular disease and found that twice as many contemplators (44%) and precontemplators (22%) were abstinent at a 6-month follow-up. As discussed later in this chapter, smokers who are not ready to take action may benefit first from a motivational "primer"—with their progress measured by progress through the stages of change (Glynn and Manley 1989).

Ask about Smoking-related Symptoms. Item 5 in Figure 10–2 provides the clinician with self-appraised smoking-related symptoms. This self-assessment complements the objective review of the medical history and symptom profile that should be part of any medical nicotine addiction assessment. These self-reported symptoms give the physician additional evidence for personalizing smoking-related harms and likely quitting benefits (e.g., "Cough and fatigue are exacerbated by smoking and improve within a few weeks of quitting") (USDHHS 1990d).

Probe Quitting Barriers and Past Quit Attempts. Items 6–9 in Figure 10–2 pertain to common quitting barriers and past quit attempts and methods. They signal areas where the patient has had difficulty in the past and may indicate the need for specialized treatment programs. The withdrawal symptoms and problems listed include those most commonly rated as troublesome by quitters in self-help trials and national surveys (USDHHS 1990a). Fear of failure is another commonly cited quitting barrier—especially for those smokers who already have tried many times to quit. The presence of strong smoking norms and/or the absence of expected supports for quitting suggest the need for greater outside support. For all smokers, it is useful to review what went right and what went wrong in past quit attempts. Furthermore, a review of any formal treatments used in the past will help the clinician establish the extent to which the patient may or may not have acquired behavior change skills useful in future attempts and whether past treatments offered generally effective (or ineffective) treatment techniques.

More Comprehensive Clinical Assessments

More comprehensive smoking history questionnaires and test batteries will provide a much more complete smoking and quitting history. They also provide a much broader assessment of the motivations, social supports, quitting skills, and other life-style factors and addictive problems that may influence smoking cessation outcome or bear on treatment choice (e.g., stress management skills; type A behavior; weight and weight control strategies; use of other addictive substances including alcohol, drugs, and caffeine; or the presence of emotional problems or affective disorders that may complicate smoking cessation). More comprehensive questionnaires are presented elsewhere (e.g., Mayo Foundation 1991, Appendix B; Orleans and Shipley 1982). While not practical in most primary care settings, assessments such as these are advisable in medical programs organized expressly for the treatment of nicotine addiction, such as hospital-based consult services (Hurt et al. 1992).

Automated Assessment

An automated smoking history assessment can reduce the burden on the patient and provider in any practice setting. In one recent study, smokers on an inpatient chemical dependency unit completed a 25-item smoking history questionnaire that was rapidly analyzed by a portable computer programmed to provide instantaneous, parallel printouts of self-quitting instructions for the patient and for the physician (Orleans and Hutchinson, in press). The patient printout suggested a nicotine fading or brand switching program and steered patients to those sections of a self-help guide most relevant to their personal quitting needs and barriers. The physician printout indicated whether patients were ready for a motivational or a cessation-oriented treatment and whether they were good candidates for adjunctive nicotine replacement therapy. In addition, the printout provided advice for counseling on personal quitting barriers. Similar computerized assessment and feedback are described by Owen, Ewins, and Lee (1989) and by Schneider, Benya, and Singer (1984).

Laboratory Procedures and "Biofeedback"

Results of laboratory assessments to diagnose smoking-related disorders or conditions (i.e., pulmonary function testing, carboxyhemoglobin tests, and measures of alveolar carbon monoxide) can provide powerful feedback to the smoker. Results can heighten the sense of immediate personal vulnerability to smoking health harms. Furthermore, as Nett (1987) points out, these tests often are reimbursed by third-party payers—such as carbon monoxide testing, CPT Code 82375, billed at $15–$35 per test—helping to defray the costs of any additional equipment needed (e.g., instant alveolar carbon monoxide analyzers).

Risser and Belcher (1990) found that carbon monoxide feedback can have dramatic effects on long-term quit rates. They randomized 90 smokers seen in a general medical screening clinic to receive a standard, nurse-delivered, minimal-contact intervention either alone or with biofeedback. The standard intervention consisted of a 50-minute, one-to-one session with a nurse practitioner who reviewed smoking risks/quitting benefits, gave a clear quitting message, gave and reviewed a self-help quitting manual, urged the smoker to pick a quit date and quitting method, and invited smokers to attend a free, nine-session, one-to-one skills training and counseling program. The additional "biofeedback" included feedback and explanation of results of spirometry and carbon monoxide breath testing, as well as a review of a 10-item pulmonary symptom questionnaire. Self-reported 6-month quit rates were almost three times higher for smokers who received the intervention *with* (34%) than *without* (13%) motivational biofeedback.

Kilburn and Warshaw (1990) employed a similar approach using feedback of abnormal pulmonary function tests and elevated carbon monoxide levels to motivate asbestos-exposed shipyard workers to stop smoking. A physician–nurse team linked laboratory results to observed pulmonary symptoms, especially shortness of breath and limited endurance in climbing hills and stairs, pointed out that such symptoms would progress with continued smoking and stabilize with quitting. While not part of a controlled trial, the 1-year self-reported quit rate for workers receiving this smoking biofeedback was much higher than that estimated for a pretreatment baseline period.

Orleans and Hutchinson (1993) used carbon monoxide feedback to bolster quitting motivation among precontemplators hospitalized on an inpatient substance abuse treatment unit.

Linking Assessment and Advice— Using a Clinical Flowchart

It may be useful for the office to use a flowchart relating medical intervention to the smoking assessment results. The flowchart presented in Figure 10–3 presents detailed directions for each step in the four-step model referring the provider to relevant smoking history questionnaire items and to relevant sections of the widely available American Lung Association (ALA) self-help guide *Freedom from Smoking for You and Your Family,* available from the ALA (see Table 10–1).

This flowchart can be modified for any smoking history, self-help guide, or office intervention plan. It can serve as a clinical tool both to guide and to record office-based interventions. By attaching this flowchart to the charts of all patients identified as smokers by the smoking history assessment form, it can cue physician quitting advice. Once completed, the flowchart provides a permanent record for the patient's chart—serving both as a summary of the intervention and as a reminder to check progress on follow-up visits.

The flowchart in Figure 10–3 was designed to facilitate a *team* approach—involving both the physician and nonphysician office staff: steps in the shaded portions of the flowchart are recommended for the physician; steps in the unshaded portions can be carried out either by the physician or by an allied staff member (i.e., nurse, physician assistant, medical technologist). Involving nonphysician office staff in more time-consuming counseling is likely to enhance adherence to the counseling protocol by shifting the burden from the physician (Hollis et al. 1991). In addition, Kottke and co-workers (1988) found that medical interventions involving physicians *and* nonphysician counselors were more effective than those that used either alone.

The time required to perform the shaded

physician steps is as little as 2–3 minutes. The rest of the intervention could be completed in as little as 5 minutes. As Cummings, Rubin, and Oster (1989) have demonstrated, limited physician quit smoking counseling on this scale is likely to be at least as cost-effective as treating mild to moderate hypertension or hypercholesterolemia.

STEP 2: ADVISE ALL SMOKERS TO STOP

The purpose of this step is to raise quitting motivation among all smokers, contemplators and precontemplators alike, setting the stage for a serious quit attempt (Figure 10–1). At a minimum, the physician should personalize the risks of smoking and the benefits of quitting and give a strong quitting message. Health risk information should be conveyed matter-of-factly, without scare tactics that can boomerang—creating high levels of anxiety that may lead to *increased* smoking. Since medical advice is likely to carry the greatest weight coming from a physician, the physician probably should play the key role in this brief "motivating" intervention. Hence, these steps are shaded in the flowchart presented in Figure 10–3. Effective medical advice can take as little as 1–2 minutes and often is given at the end of the medical visit.

Praise Quitting Efforts and Plans

The flowchart in Figure 10–3 suggests beginning this step by praising the patient for trying, or planning, to quit—based on a quick review of the smoking history questionnaire (Figure 10–2). As noted in Chapter 8, about 15% of smokers are likely to be in the action stage at any given time, with an additional 50% in the contemplation stage, and only 35% in the precontemplation stage (Glynn, Boyd, Grumman 1990). Hence, most smokers can be praised at least for "contemplating" quitting. This step can help reduce patient defensiveness and foster a positive alliance between the physician and the patient.

Personalize the Risks and Benefits

The single most important reason people have for quitting smoking is concern over

Table 10–1 Self-Help Smoking Cessation Materials

AMERICAN CANCER SOCIETY
1599 Clifton Rd. NE
Atlanta, GA 30329
404-320-3333

How to Stay Quit Over the Holidays
This self-help pamphlet gives hints on how to "stay quit" after the Great American Smokeout and through the holiday season. It briefly gives ideas on using exercise and diet plans to help curb the urge to begin smoking again. 1985 (12 pp), free. No quantity limit. Order from local ACS offices.

Smart Move
This booklet presents a variety of tips for quitting plus "how I did it" testimonials from former smokers. 1988 (21 pp), free. No quantity limit. Order from local ACS offices.

AMERICAN HEART ASSOCIATION
7320 Greenville Avenue
Dallas, TX 75231
214-822-9380

Calling It Quits
This folder contains two pamphlets with tips on how to stop smoking and remain a nonsmoker. *How to Quit* includes points to think about such as reasons for quitting, setting a target date, and conditioning oneself physically and emotionally not to smoke cigarettes. *The Good Life* discusses the temptation to begin smoking again and provides examples of situations that will be difficult and ways to cope with them. 1984, single copies free (bulk orders available in orders of 25 folders at $16.20 per 25). Two pamphlets (15 and 23 pp). No quantity limit. Order from local AHA chapters.

AMERICAN LUNG ASSOCIATION
1740 Broadway
New York, NY 10019
212-315-8700

Freedom From Smoking for You and Your Family
This booklet gives suggestions on preparing to quit smoking, picking a day to quit, quitting for good, and benefits of quitting. Includes quitting calendar and exercise/diet tips to be used during the attempt to stop smoking. Daily tally sheets and charts are included to help track quitting smoking. This booklet is a simplified, condensed version of "Freedom From Smoking in 20 Days." 1987. (50 pp) $3.50. Consult local offices of the American Lung Association.

Freedom From Smoking for You and Your Baby (kit)
This is a 10-day stop-smoking program specifically for pregnant women. It assists in analyzing what determines smoking patterns, reasons for wanting to quit, ways to break the smoking pattern, and methods to reinforce the new habit of not smoking. 1987 (32 pp). No quantity limit. Consult local ALA chapters for price and ordering information.

A Lifetime of Freedom From Smoking: Maintenance Program for Ex-Smokers
This maintenance manual was designed to help former smokers maintain their nonsmoking behavior.

A daily routine is included, with examples of situations that produce strong cravings for a cigarette and how to develop ways to cope with them. The plan emphasizes staying off cigarettes permanently. 1986 (27 pp). No quantity limit. Consult local ALA chapters for price and ordering information.

Stop Smoking, Stay Trim
This pamphlet addresses the problem of weight gain after stopping smoking. It discusses how stopping smoking affects metabolism, weight, and food cravings. It gives 10 tips on how to control weight after stopping smoking. 1985 (10 pp). No quantity limit. Consult local ALA chapters for price and ordering information.

A Healthy Beginning: The Smoke-Free Family Guide for New Parents (kit)
This packet of information explains how to create smoke-free environments for babies and children. It includes a brochure, tent card, worksheet, and discount coupon for ordering an "I'm A Born Nonsmoker" bib. 1989. Consult local ALA chapters for price and ordering information.

BLOOMINGTON HEART AND HEALTH PROGRAM
1900 West Old Shakopee Road
Bloomington, MN 55431
612-887-9603
612-887-9684 FAX

Quit and Win
Contains two booklets, one to help the smoker quit and the other "to win the war" against starting to smoke again. "The Quit Book" contains the problems test, which highlights problems that are likely to occur when one initially quits smoking. "The Win Book" includes discussions of smoking urges and temptations, tension and restlessness, withdrawal problems, weight gain, and relapse. Suggestions are made on how to deal with each of these common problems encountered by ex-smokers. 1982 (90 pp), $10.

FOX CHASE CANCER CENTER
510 Township Line Road
Cheltenham, PA 19012
215-728-2715

Clear Horizons
This magazine-style guide is designed for long-term heavy smokers who are 50 years or older. Written at an eighth-grade reading level, it is divided into four sections designed for smokers who are at various stages of quitting. Special sections explain nicotine addiction and outline two quitting strategies— nicotine fading and nicotine gum. The guide gives explicit messages about the health consequences of continued smoking and the health benefits of quitting for older, long-term smokers. The guide also contains photovignettes, inspirational quotes, cartoons, and a puzzle. 1989 (49 pp). Call for distribution information.

Pathways to Freedom
This magazine-style guide is aimed at African American smokers. A motivational section covers

continued

Table 10–1 Self-Help Cessation Materials (continued)

health risks for African American smokers and deglamorizes tobacco advertising. Quitting methods are tailored to low-rate smokers. Support tips for the quitter's family and friends and a section on community action to control tobacco make the guide appropriate for nonsmokers and smokers alike. 1992 (36 pp). Call for distribution information.

Quitting Times
This guide is targeted to mothers of preschool-age children, using a four-color, magazine-style format to present articles and stories appealing to women at all stages of quitting. Topics include the hazards of passive smoking on infants and young children, immediate and intermediate benefits of quitting, as well as controlling withdrawal symptoms and weight gain. The guide is written at a sixth-grade reading level. 1987 (65 pp). Call for distribution information.

Stop Now for Your Baby
This guide focuses on the concerns of pregnant smokers and gives an explicit message about the health consequences of maternal smoking. Designed for women at various stages of quitting, it uses a four-color magazine style and is written at the fifth-grade reading level. It addresses both prenatal and postpartum smoking cessation issues. 1989 (29 pp). Call for distribution information.

GROUP HEALTH COOPERATIVE OF PUGET SOUND
521 Wall Street
Seattle, WA 98121
1-800-437-6668

Free & Clear
This is a guide to help smokers stop smoking on their own. It uses the theme of planning and going on a trip as an analogy to quitting smoking. The guide includes charts to be filled out during the four phases of becoming a nonsmoker: making the decision, preparing to stop, stopping, and remaining a nonsmoker. The kit contains a guide to stopping smoking, two copies of the *Helping a Smoker Quit* social support booklet, a "Thank You For Not Smoking" table tent, a "Cigarette Savings" bank, and a relaxation tape and manual. All participants are free to use the toll-free "Free & Clear" telephone counseling Quitline for 1 year after beginning the program. 1985 (36 pp), $35. Volume discounts available.

HAZELDEN EDUCATIONAL MATERIALS
Pleasant Valley Road
Box 176
Center City, MN 55012-0176
1-800-328-9000

If Only I Could Quit: Recovering From Nicotine Addiction
This book contains 24 stories of personal recovery from nicotine addiction told in a way that invites readers to identify with the experiences, difficulties, and successes others have had in stopping smoking. It includes inspirational meditations for the first 90 days of tobacco abstinence. 1987 (290 pp), $9. Quantity discounts available.

The Twelve Steps for Tobacco Users
A recovering smoker shares her interpretation of the Twelve Steps that, applied to nicotine addiction, helped her stop smoking. 1984 (24 pp), $9. Quantity discounts available.

HEALTH PROMOTION RESOURCE CENTER
Stanford Center for Research in Disease Prevention
1000 Welch Road
Palo Alto, CA 94304-1885
415-723-1000

Quit Smoking Kit
This self-paced kit includes a how-to-use guide and *Get Ready to Quit, Tomorrow's the Day, You've Quit,* and *Staying Free* sections. A heart magnet is included to use in posting tips on staying free from cigarette smoking. 1986 (9 pp), $2.95. Quantity discounts for orders of 1,000 or more.

Como Dejar de Fumar en Tres Pasos
This program in Spanish outlines a three-step quit-smoking program. Printed on brightly colored flyers. (16 pp), $2.

MINNESOTA HEART HEALTH PROGRAM
Stadium Gate 20
611 Beacon Street
University of Minnesota
Minneapolis, MN 55455
612-624-1818

Quit and Win
One of these two booklets helps the smoker quit; the other aids in "winning the war" against starting to smoke again. *The Quit Book* contains the Problems Test, which highlights problems that are likely to occur when one initially stops smoking. *The Win Book* discusses smoking urges and temptations, tension and restlessness, withdrawal problems, weight gain, and relapse. Suggestions are made on how to deal with each of these common problems encountered by former smokers. 1982 (90 pp), $12.75. Quantity discounts for orders of 15 or more.

NATIONAL CANCER INSTITUTE
Office of Cancer Communications
Building 31, Room 10A24
9000 Rockville Pike
Bethesda, MD 20892
1-800-4-CANCER

Clearing the Air—How To Quit Smoking and Quit for Keeps
This is a guide to help the individual think about why he or she smokes, the benefits of stopping, preparing to stop, knowing what to expect, and handling relapse. Fifty copies are included as patient handouts in the *Quit for Good* kit for professionals (see appendix E). 1988 (24 pp), free. Limit of 200 ordered at one time.

Guia para Dejar de Fumar
This full-color Spanish-language booklet addresses smoking cessation and relapse. 1988 (36 pp), free. Limit of 200 ordered at one time.

Table 10-1   (continued)

UNIVERSITY OF CALIFORNIA	NORTH CAROLINA MUTUAL LIFE
Division of General Internal Medicine	INSURANCE COMPANY
400 Parnassus Avenue, Room A-405	411 West Chapel Hill Street
San Francisco, CA 94143-0320	Durham, NC 27701
408-476-2151	919-682-9201, ext. 316
Quit For Life	**Quit for Life** (kit)
This is a three-step smoking cessation guide that outlines reasons for stopping, preparation for stopping, and an explanation of withdrawal symptoms and common complaints. It includes a smoking monitor and a daily inventory chart to record the number of cigarettes smoked, time, need, place of activity, with whom, and mood or reason for smoking. 1985 (16 pp), $1. No quantity limit.	This kit is specifically aimed at helping African Americans stop smoking. It gives suggestions on getting ready to stop, steps to take before stopping, and tips on staying smoke free and maintaining weight control after stopping smoking. 1987. Call for distribution information.

Source: Based on the National Cancer Institute publication *How to Help Your Patients Stop Smoking: A National Cancer Institute Manual for Physicians* (Glynn and Manley 1989) and *Self-Guided Strategies for Smoking Cessation: A Program Planners Guide* (Glynn, Boyd, Gruman 1991).

their health, and smokers who quit for health reasons are more likely to succeed (Orleans 1985). Feeling personally vulnerable to smoking health risks and being troubled by reversible smoking-related symptoms (e.g., coughing, wheezing, shortness of breath, poor endurance, tiring easily) are especially likely to trigger quit attempts (e.g., Dudley, Aicken, Martin 1977).

The 1986 Adult Use of Tobacco Survey (USDHHS 1990b) found that only 43% of current U.S. smokers aged 21-74 years were "fairly" or "very" concerned about the personal health effects of smoking, and that even fewer (32%) agreed that there was a "very strong" connection between smoking and illness in general. Another recent survey (Orleans, Rimer, Cristinzio et al. 1991) suggests that even long-term smokers who report smoking-related symptoms may not recognize these symptoms as caused by their smoking.

Therefore, the physician must be certain to clearly link smoking to the patient's medical history, current illness and symptoms, and to any smoking-related symptoms reported in the smoking assessment form (Figure 10-2). Patients regularly taking beta-blocking drugs, theophylline, insulin, or phenylbutazone should be informed that smoking interferes with the effects of these medications (USDHHS 1984). Links between a parent's smoking and children's symptoms or illnesses also should be made clear (Chilmonczyk et al. 1990).

After reviewing the hazards of continuing to smoke, the physician should briefly describe the *quitting benefits* this patient is likely to experience. These benefits are cataloged in the 1990 Surgeon General's Report (USDHHS 1990d). For instance, lung function and circulation show improvement within days of quitting; the excess risk of heart disease is reduced to half within a year of quitting; risks for respiratory infections also decline quickly; and risks of stroke and lung cancer decline over 5-15 years to almost the level of never-smokers. Smokers already suffering from chronic obstructive pulmonary disease should be advised that their conditions will stabilize, and that the rate of further decline in lung function may return to that of never-smokers. Long-term smokers who fear that "the damage is done" should be reassured that "it's never too late to quit" (USDHHS 1990d, p. vii).

If spirometry, carbon monoxide feedback or other laboratory tests are used in the initial assessment, their results should be discussed—again with an emphasis on the benefits of stopping smoking. Examples of such feedback are provided by Emmons et al (1992), Kilburn and Warshaw (1990) and Risser and Belcher (1990). This strategy is consistent with the "drinker's check-up" found to be highly effective in motivating problem drinkers to take action to control their drinking (Miller and Rollnick 1991).

Explore the Patient's Quitting Motives and Attempts

Time permitting, the physician may want to briefly review (and reinforce) *the patient's* reasons for quitting. The NCI *How to Help Your Patients Stop Smoking Manual for Physicians* (Glynn and Manley 1991, p. 23) suggests "How do you think quitting smoking would improve your life?" and "How does your family feel about your smoking?" as good questions to start with. Likewise, reviewing past attempts provides an opportunity to assess and bolster quitting motivation, and will help indicate the most appropriate treatment plan. For instance, even brief probing will reveal whether past difficulties chiefly involved initial acute withdrawal difficulties, longer-term negative side effects (e.g., weight gain, stress), a lack of social support, and/or reliance on ineffective quitting strategies or programs.

Give a Clear, Strong, Quitting Message—Tied to an Offer of Help

For instance, the physician might say: "I strongly recommend that you stop smoking as soon as possible. It's the single most important thing you can do for your health. If we can give you some help, are you willing to give it a try?" Most smokers will accept this offer—leading directly to the step of selecting an appropriate treatment, setting a quit date, and arranging for follow-up. However, a specific intervention is recommended even for smokers who do not. The following section presents suggestions both for smokers ready for action, and for those in the precontemplation stage.

STEP 3: ASSIST THE PATIENT IN STOPPING

As the flowchart in Figure 10–3 shows, a team approach—involving both physician and nonphysician office staff—can be used to deliver the quitting assistance required in this step. The physician can readily supply the patient with quitting or motivational materials and the physician will typically be the one to provide a prescription for nicotine replacement or other pharmacologic aids. However, further counseling in how to use self-help materials or pharmacologic aids may be more efficiently handled by a nonphysician provider—still all in one visit. Therefore, the physician may end the previ-

ous step with a statement like the following, based on a sample script recommended by Hollis and colleagues (1991, p. 499): "Whether or not you're ready to set a stop date now, I want you to check with our health counselor who has some tips to make stopping smoking easier when the time is right." A decision about the use of formal treatment in addition to self-help materials can be made by the physician or by the nonphysician counselor at any point in the intervention outlined during this step.

Innovative Team Approaches

Hollis and his colleagues (1991) evaluated several innovative approaches involving the physician (who gave a 30-second quitting message) and a nurse (who provided brief one-to-one video-assisted counseling). The interventions they evaluated exemplify the four-step NCI model. Smokers were identified through a brief "Health Habits Survey" administered to all health maintenance organization (HMO) outpatient clinic patients when they checked in. When patients reported smoking, a colored form was attached to their charts, alerting the physician to give a 30-second quitting message at the end of their medical visit.

On a random basis, one-quarter of the 2,700 smokers in this study received only physician advice; the rest were randomized equally to one of three different nurse-delivered interventions. Each nurse counseling protocol lasted 15 minutes and included (1) alveolar carbon monoxide assessment and feedback, (2) a 10-minute videotape, and (3) brief counseling encouraging smokers to commit to a specific quitting plan and describing office follow-up procedures. The focus of the counseling varied with the focus of the videotapes. One videotape encouraged smokers to quit on their own, with the aid of *self-help* materials. Smokers in this condition were offered a choice of three different quitting guides, assisted to select a quit date and a quitting method, and notified that they would receive a follow-up call in 4–6 weeks. Smokers were mailed stop-smoking tip sheets and six bimonthly quit smoking newsletters, and were invited to call an HMO quit smoking hotline, and to come in for a free 90-minute counseling session (though very few did). The second videotape encouraged patients to enroll in a free nine-session quit smoking *clinic* offered by the HMO. Nurse counseling and follow-up focused on encouraging enrollment. The third videotape presented the *self-help and clinic* options, with some suggestions to help patients self-triage into the most suitable treatment for them. These smokers received the same self-help materials and follow-up mailings that the self-help only smokers were offered. Smokers who got any of these nurse-assisted interventions were over 1.5 times as likely as those receiving physician advice only to have stopped smoking at the time of a 3-month follow-up (13–14% vs. 8%) (Hollis et al. 1991).

Assisting Smokers Ready for Action

Give a Self-Help Quitting Guide

Table 10–1 lists a number of self-quitting guides available to help smokers quitting on their own. Basically, they convert effective behavioral clinic treatments (described in Chapter 11) into self-help formats. In general, they meet the following criteria set forth by Glynn, Boyd, and Gruman (1990): they include information about the health and social consequences of quitting, specific strategies and exercises for quitting, maintaining nonsmoking, avoiding relapse or recycling in the event of a return to smoking. Most take quitters through three stages of quitting:

1. *Contemplation and determination (or preparation):* recording smoking behavior, identifying smoking triggers, listing quitting motives, setting a quit date;
2. *Action:* preparing to quit by switching to lower nicotine brands or cutting down smoking rate or circumstances, quitting abruptly, practicing nonsmoking skills, coping with withdrawal reactions, using nicotine patches or gum; and
3. *Maintenance* of nonsmoking: avoiding high-risk relapse situations, recovering from slips, weight control guidance, using exercise as a new stress coping strategy, recycling in the event of a relapse.

Many contain motivational material appropriate for smokers in the precontemplation stage (information on smoking hazards and quitting benefits and overcoming quitting barriers). Most include support tips for the quitter's friends and family.

The majority of the self-help guides in Table 10–1 are free or low cost—the exceptions being those tied to ongoing support services for quitters. Most are written at or below a 9th–10th grade reading level. However, reading levels are coming down to the 6th–7th grade level as program designers recognize that the population of U.S. smokers increasingly is made up of those with less education (Strecher, Rimer, Monaco 1989).

Consider Tailored Guides and Materials

The collective evaluation of existing self-help materials indicates that smokers will achieve fairly similar long-term quit rates using *any* of these guides (Glynn, Boyd, Grumman 1990; Cohen, Lichtenstein, Prochaska et al. 1989). However, guides tailored to special populations (e.g., women, pregnant women, African Americans, Hispanics, older smokers, blue-collar smokers) may have special appeal and efficacy.

Windsor et al. (1985), for instance, found that pregnant smokers who received brief quitting advice in the course of routine prenatal care achieved higher quit rates with a guide geared to the unique quitting motives of the pregnant smoker than with a "generic" quitting guide. Older smokers who received the *Clear Horizons* quitting guide for smokers aged 50 years and over—featuring older smokers as quitting models and emphasizing quitting methods geared to the concerns and life-styles of older Americans—rated this guide as more appealing than a standard quitting guide and had higher 12-month quit rates (Rimer, Orleans, Fleisher et al. in press). Materials designed for smokers with other chemical dependencies may be more appealing because they incorporate 12-step techniques familiar from conventional chemical dependency treatment programs, like Alcoholics Anonymous (Casey 1987). The Spanish-language guide *Guia para Dejar de Fumar*—extensively pretested with Latino smokers—employs testimonials from Latino smokers to convey main points and stresses themes that resonate with the Latino culture (e.g., an emphasis on how smoking affects family relationships, suggestions for saying "no" to cigarettes in a culturally polite way) (Perez-Stable et al. 1991). The *Quit for Life* and *Pathways to Freedom* guides developed for African Americans not only use exclusively African American quitting models, but also emphasize quitting strategies appropriate to the distinctive low-rate, high tar/nicotine menthol smoking pattern common among African American smokers (Orleans et al. 1989, Robinson et al. 1992).

Quit Rates with Self-Help Guides

Patients using guides like those in Table 10–1 along with minimal-contact medical treatments generally achieve higher long-term quit rates (22–26%) than smokers using self-help guides on their own, without quit smoking advice or counseling from a physician (14–15%) (Glynn et al. 1990; Cohen, Lichtenstein, Prochaska et al. 1989). This is true even though smokers quitting "on their own" are, by definition, already motivated to quit or try to quit while smokers receiving physician-initiated, minimal-contact interventions include many who are not even thinking about quitting smoking.

Similarly, quit rates for patients who receive self-help materials along with physician advice/counseling achieve higher quit rates than patients who receive medical quit advice alone—*without* self-help materials. Usual 1-year quit rates for medical quitting advice *alone* are 5–10% for predominantly healthy patients, 10–30% for high-risk patients (e.g., pregnant, at risk for myocardial infarction, or MI) and those with chronic smoking-related illnesses (e.g., coronary heart disease, chronic obstructive pulmonary disease), and 40–60% for recent MI victims (e.g., Orleans 1985; Gritz 1988). But rates are higher in every patient group when the medical intervention includes self-help materials. For instance, Janz and associates (1987) randomly assigned patients seen in two outpatient medical clinics to receive: (1) usual care; (2) a quit smoking message from the physician followed by brief nurse counseling addressing the patient's personal quitting barriers; or (3) health provider advice/counseling plus a self-help manual. Six-month self-reported quit rates were significantly higher for patients receiving medical quitting advice/counseling *plus* the guide (approximately 26%) than for patients receiving usual care or medical advice/counseling alone (10–15%).

Prescribe Adjunctive Pharmacologic Therapy

Nicotine replacement is the most effective pharmacologic adjunct to smoking cessation treatment and should be considered for smokers who appear highly physically dependent (e.g., heavy smokers, those smoking within 30 minutes of awakening) and those who have suffered severe withdrawal problems in previous quit attempts (e.g., Benowitz 1991; Tonnesen 1988). Therefore, suggestions for nicotine replacement are built into the flowchart in Figure 10–3. Other pharmacologic aids are reviewed in Chapter 12—including oral or transdermal clonidine for patients troubled by strong cravings (Franks, Harp, Bell 1989) and antidepressants for patients at risk for significant depression after quitting (Glassman et al. 1990).

Nicotine Replacement as an Adjunct

Nicotine polacrilex (gum) helps to alleviate nicotine-related withdrawal—especially irritability, restlessness, anxiety, and difficulty concentrating—and significantly boosts the quit rates of minimal-contact or intensive quit smoking treatments, with greatest benefits for more highly nicotine-dependent smokers (e.g., Fagerström 1982; Fortmann et al. 1988; Tonnesen 1988). However, when used alone or with only brief medical advice to stop smoking, 2 mg gum has no advantage over a placebo (Lam et al. 1987). Therefore, nicotine gum therapy must include useful patient instructions and be embedded in a broader minimal-contact intervention. Physicians' misconceptions about proper gum use (Cummings et al. 1988) and patients' difficulties adhering to recommended gum use protocols have contributed to widespread misuse of the gum—chiefly involving patients taking too little gum for too short a time (Fortmann et al. 1988). In addition, possible problems of long-term dependence on the gum by quitters indicate the need for careful follow-up to monitor gum use and weaning (Hajek, Jackson, Belcher 1988).

Transdermal patches represent a promising alternative to gum as a nicotine delivery system because of more reliable nicotine replacement, better defined dosing and weaning schedules, and fewer troubling side effects (Fiore, Jorenby, Baker, Kenford, 1992; Transdermal Nicotine Study Group 1991). The early outcome trials have evaluated transdermal nicotine as an adjunct to intensive behavioral treatments. In one of these large, double-blind, placebo-controlled trials, 6-month biochemically verified quit rates were 26% with nicotine patches as an adjunct to a behavioral cessation and support group program versus 12% with placebo patches (Transdermal Nicotine Study Group 1991). A similar 26% 12-month quit rate was reported by Hurt et al. (1990) in a study evaluating nicotine patches among smokers who met with a nurse coordinator for six individual counseling sessions. Future trials will clarify the impact of transdermal nicotine in context of the minimal treatments outlined in this chapter. However, given the experience with nicotine gum, it is unlikely that any form of nicotine replacement would prove effective with medical advice *alone* (Fiore et al. 1992).

Nicotine replacement by gum or patch should be carefully weighed against the likelihood of continued smoking in the presence of several conditions (e.g., pregnancy, lactation, recent MI, arrythmias, severe angina) or some complications (e.g., hypertension, peptic ulcer, cardiovascular disease, insulin-dependent diabetes) (Christen and McDonald 1988). Benowitz (1991) argues that the relative risks of cigarette smoking and nicotine replacement must be considered on a case-by-case basis—suggesting that there are circumstances where nicotine replacement would be a reasonable choice in the management of the highly dependent pregnant smoker. Federal Drug Administration-approved labeling for nicotine patches sug-

gests that nicotine be prescribed for pregnant women who smoke only after an unsuccessful attempt to stop using behavioral supports alone, and then only after a discussion with the patient of the potential adverse effects of nicotine on the fetus. Similar counseling is advised in the prescription of nicotine to a nursing mother. A lower initial dose of nicotine (i.e., a 14 mg patch instead of a 21 mg patch) may be advisable for patients with cardiovascular disease.

Brief Quitting Counseling: Essential Elements

Brief counseling is defined here as reviewing self-help materials to assist patients to map out a quit plan and set a quit date. Two counseling practices appear especially important: advising patients to set a specific quit date and scheduling definite follow-up contacts (Cummings et al. 1986). Either physicians or nonphysician office staff may furnish this counseling. Counseling also may be provided through follow-up phone contacts, videotaped presentations, or personalized quitting tips sent through the mail. This is where the greatest variation in intensity and modality of intervention is seen in minimal-contact programs, with counseling ranging from as little as 5 minutes to as much as an hour and a half.

Review Self-Help Materials to Map Out a Quitting Plan

Stocking quitting guides in the medical office ensures that patients receive them and increases the likelihood that physicians will give strong quit smoking advice (CA 1971). For best results, the physician or allied staff should not do more than simply hand the patient a quitting guide (Orleans et al. 1990; Risser and Belcher 1990; Windsor et al. 1985). Ideally, a few minutes should be spent introducing the patient to the guide, pointing out how it is organized, and helping the patient select a quitting method using the guide. The flowchart in Figure 10–3 suggests briefly explaining the various quit methods described in a guide, pointing out where they are described, helping the smoker pick one or two that fit their smoking pattern and personal preference, and indicating sections of the guide that present tips for getting through withdrawal or overcoming personal quitting barriers. If the physician has prescribed a pharmacological adjunct but not explained how it is to be used, an explanation should be given at this time.

Reviewing the self-help guide reduces the burden on the physician and allied staff to come up with a *de novo* counseling approach for each patient—and communicates to the patient that the guide is a truly useful resource. Brief counseling engages the smoker immediately in the quitting process which may raise their involvement and commitment. In fact, smokers who received similar brief quitting instructions through two short phone counseling calls reported at an 8-month follow-up that they had used more of the quitting methods in the guide than those who only received the guide (Orleans, Schoenbach, Wagner et al. 1991). They also were significantly more likely to have quit smoking (23 vs. 15%).

Telephone follow-up calls (see "Arrange Follow-up Support" section) provide an especially attractive option for brief counseling in hospital and HMO settings where phone contacts can be handled by a centralized counseling staff (e.g., Ershoff et al. 1983; Hurt et al, 1992; Orleans, Schoenbach, Wagner et al. 1991). Computer-generated personalized counseling advice is another option also described in the next section on follow-up strategies. Videotapes that can be seen in the office help to simplify and standardize counseling and reduce the time required by office staff. Videotapes have shown promise in outpatient (Hollis et al. 1991) as well as hospital (Stevens et al. 1990) settings.

Set a Quit Date

Patient should be encouraged to set a quit date—preferably within the next 6 weeks. Cummings and colleagues (1986) found that advising patients to select a definite quit date was associated with higher quit rates. Patients may be more willing and able to set a quit date once they have mapped out a quitting plan. If they are hesitant, it may be helpful to present the quit date as a "goal to work

towards" and to point out that there is no "ideal" time to quit, but that avoiding high-stress times is best. Patients should record the quit date in their self-help materials. The quit date also should be recorded on the patient flowchart or in whatever progress notes the office staff will be using.

Notify of Follow-Up Plans

Just making arrangements for continued contact through follow-up calls, visits, or letters itself appears to enhance the effectiveness of physician advice. Such arrangements express ongoing commitment and help to encourage compliance with quitting plans. Russell and co-workers (1979), in a now classic study, found that 1–2 minutes of medical quit smoking advice to unselected smokers resulted in a 3.3% self-reported continuous quit rate, but that a significantly higher 5.1% quit rate occurred among smokers who also received four pages of quit tips and warning that they would be followed up by the practice. Similarly, Cummings et al. (1986) found that a higher percentage of patients quit smoking after brief office-based counseling when physicians routinely scheduled a follow-up appointment to monitor quitting progress.

Counsel about Personal Quitting Barriers

The purpose of "barriers counseling" is to address the patient's quitting concerns and obstacles by acknowledging them, correcting any misconceptions, and pointing out ways they can be overcome, with reference to coping strategies and treatment methods outlined in the take-home self-help materials. The sample smoking history assessment form in Figure 10–2 asks about a number of the quitting barriers commonly reported by self-quitters (Orleans, Rimer, Cristinzio et al. 1991; Orleans, Schoenbach, Wagner et al. 1991) and by smokers who have tried to quit (USDHHS 1990a). Barriers counseling can be done as part of the initial brief counseling and/or later through follow-up contacts. Moreover, it may be especially helpful with smokers who are not yet ready to quit. Next, some suggestions for brief counseling are given.

Fear of Failure. Almost two-thirds of current U.S. smokers have tried to quit, many more than once (USDHHS 1990d). Smokers who have tried to quit before, especially those with repeated quit attempts, are likely to have given up to some extent on their ability to succeed (Pechacek and Danaher 1979) or on the value of outside help—often based on experiences with cessation products and programs having no demonstrated effectiveness such as one-shot hypnosis, acupuncture, untested over-the-counter aids (Fiore et al. 1990; Orleans 1988).

To counteract pessimism and a fear of failure, these patients need to know that quitting *usually* involves "trial and error" learning over repeated attempts, that *most* successful ex-smokers made more than one attempt before succeeding, and that most smokers who try to eventually do succeed (Schachter 1982). Past quitting efforts can be reframed as evidence of determination and as learning experiences, and *not* as "failures." A review of past quitting methods and treatments, to identify what worked and what did not work, will help to clarify future treatment needs (i.e., severe withdrawal reaction, too few coping skills or alternative to smoking, too much social pressure to smoke).

Withdrawal Effects. Many smokers, especially long-term smokers, wonder what life will be like without cigarettes, fearing that withdrawal symptoms will last forever. The most common troubling withdrawal symptoms include cravings, irritability/anger, anxiety, restlessness, difficulty concentrating, and increased appetite (APA 1987). Other symptoms include dysphoria, disturbed sleep, increased productive coughing, and impaired productivity or performance on rapid information processing tasks (USDHHS 1990d).

As the 1990 Surgeon General's Report reviews, most symptoms appear within 24 hours of quitting, peak in the first 1–2 days after quitting, and last for 2–4 weeks. Smokers therefore need reassurance that these reactions are normal and temporary—and that they can be eased with behavioral coping tactics (e.g., deep breathing, exercise) and pharmacological treatments, especially

nicotine replacement (Tonnesen 1988; Transdermal Nicotine Study Group 1991), but possibly also clonidine (Franks, Harp, Bell 1989).

Negative Long-Term Emotional Effects. Many smokers also are concerned about losing their all-purpose coping tactic or about losing a pleasure, or worry that they will not be able to relax without cigarettes. These concerns are normal, and often reflect their experiences with severe withdrawal effects in short-term quit attempts.

However, besides their being no evidence for a prolonged nicotine withdrawal syndrome (with the possible exception of increased hunger or smoking urges), there also is no evidence for prolonged impairment of mood, psychological functioning or emotional well-being among former smokers (USDHHS 1990d). In fact, the weight of the evidence, summarized in the 1990 Surgeon General's Report, points to the opposite conclusion; that is, that quitting smoking leads to *improved* well-being and *reduced* stress. For example, in one study, ex-smokers (abstinent for an average of 7 months) reported less anxiety and depression, better control over their health, and less frequent use of drugs or alcohol to relax than when they smoked.

Most self-help guides recommend alternative ways to relax, and introduce exercise as a stress management aid. Self-quitters with clear deficits in healthy *alternative* stress coping skills may require a more intensive nicotine addiction treatment, or stress management treatment, emphasizing these skills. Since clinically depressed smokers and those with a past history of major depression have been found to have a harder time quitting, treatment for them may need to include greater attention to the social and assertive skills required for quitting and to the development of alternative rewards and reinforcers to replace smoking, in addition to independent treatment for the depression itself (e.g., Glassman et al. 1990; Hughes 1988).

Having another substance use problem (drug/alcohol use) may create more of an intervention barrier for the *provider* than for the *smoker*. Smokers with other substance use problems have *not,* until recently, been considered good candidates for nicotine addiction treatment. However, growing empirical evidence challenges the clinical lore that smokers in treatment for, or recovery from, other chemical dependencies are not interested in quitting smoking, or not able to maintain their drug or alcohol sobriety in the face of the stress of quitting smoking.

Two recent surveys of smokers in treatment for drug or alcohol problems found that about half indicated a strong desire to stop smoking, and that very few (10%) thought stopping smoking would seriously jeopardize their drug or alcohol sobriety (Kozlowski et al. 1989; Orleans and Hutchinson, in press). Another study found better short- and long-term quit rates among smokers who took part in brief three-session group nicotine addiction program during their hospitalization for drug or alcohol dependency—with no evidence of impaired drug/alcohol treatment outcomes as a result (Joseph et al. 1990). Nicotine addiction treatment for these patients may even reinforce and/or benefit from the self-management skills and cognitive-behavioral and 12-step strategies introduced to treat other chemical dependencies (Orleans and Hutchinson, in press).

Fear of Weight Gain. Fear of weight gain is one of the most commonly reported quitting barriers, among both men and women, and among both older and younger smokers (e.g, Orleans, Rimer, Cristinzio et al. 1991; Orleans, Schoenbach, Wagner et al. 1991). Moreover, the 1985 national Adult Use of Tobacco Survey (AUTS) found weight gain, or possible weight gain, cited as a reason for returning to smoking by over a fifth of the current male smokers, and by over a third of the current female smokers, who had a history of having quit in the past (USDHHS 1990a). According to the AUTS, older smokers (age 50–74 years) are no less concerned about weight gain than younger smokers (age 21–49 years). In fact, the AUTS indicated that more older than younger smokers agreed that smoking was less harmful than being 20 lbs overweight (47 vs. 28%).

Smokers who fear weight gain need to know that the average quitter will gain only 4–10 lbs (2–4 kg), that half of those who quit will gain less, and that fewer than one in 10 smokers will gain as much as 25–30 lbs or more (Williamson et al. 1991). The 1990 Surgeon General's Report (USDHHS 1990d) reviewed studies of over 20,000 persons followed for a median of 2 years and concluded that: the average weight gain after quitting smoking is only 5 lbs; that only a small percentage (3.5%) of former smokers gain 20 lbs or more; and that quitting-related weight gain usually poses minimal health risks, especially relative to smoking risks. Williamson and co-workers (1991) examined weight change in a national cohort of over 9,000 U.S. adults followed over a longer 10-year period. The average weight gain among smokers who had quit in this study (median abstinence = 5 years) was 6 lbs (2.8 kg) in men and 8 lbs (3.8 kg) in women, with major weight gain (greater than 25 lbs) occurring in 9.8% of the men and 13.4% of the women. Still, however, by the end of the study, the mean body weight of those who had quit smoking increased only to that of persons who had never smoked.

Weight-concerned smokers will benefit from insight into the reasons for weight gain (metabolic changes, increased caloric intake, increased appetite for sweets), as well as from advice about small adjustments in diet and exercise that may help to limit weight gain (see USDHHS 1990d). Most of the self-help guides in Table 10–1 include a section on weight gain and strategies for limiting or preventing it (e.g., low-calorie snacks, dietary restraint, increased exercise).

Smokers worried that weight gain might pose a greater risk than smoking need reassurance that this is rarely the case. Smokers have almost twice the mortality risk of non-smokers at most weight levels, while each 1% increase in weight (up to 30% excess weight) is associated with only about a 1% increase in premature mortality (Kristeller 1990; USDHHS 1989a). Hence, for most smokers, a 5–10 lb weight gain will pose a minimal risk—especially compared to the benefit gained from stopping smoking. However, there are some exceptions. Individuals who are more than 40% overweight have twice the mortality risk of normal weight individuals in the general population and among cardiac patients (Kristeller 1990). And for diabetics, excess weight can pose significantly greater risks (Fisher et al. 1990; Kristeller 1990). Diabetic smokers and other patients at risk for serious medical complications of excess weight may require special help to control or prevent weight gain after quitting. This same help should be considered when fears about the cosmetic effects of weight gain interfere with quit attempts or maintenance (Williamson et al. 1991).

Social Pressure to Smoke/Lack of Quitting Support. Having a greater number of smokers in one's immediate environment has been linked to poorer quitting maintenance. Conversely, high levels of social support for quitting helps smokers quit and stay quit (Lichtenstein, Glasgow, Abrams 1986). Smokers who report strong smoking norms or weak quitting supports in their social environment therefore should get help to fortify themselves to resist social pressures to smoke and to engineer support from others, even when they are smokers. These patients may benefit from more frequent follow-up contacts or from referral to a formal treatment or support group.

Refer Patients Needing/Requesting Extra Help

More intensive face-to-face (one-to-one or group) treatment may be recommended to complement self-help strategies when the patient has many prior self-quitting and/or formal treatment failures; has very little confidence in his or her self-quitting ability; lacks adequate social support for quitting at home and work (e.g., lives or works primarily with smokers); or has other emotional or behavioral problems (e.g., Type A behavior, depression, other psychoactive substance use disorder), or coping skill deficits likely to substantially interfere with quitting. Some patients also may express a preference for the structure and support a clinic, group, or counselor can provide. Finally, some patients who have tried self-quitting *and* effective formal treatment programs in the past may be good candidates for new inpatient nicotine addiction treatment programs like those described in Chapter 14 (see also Hurt et al. 1992).

It is just as important to be specific in making a referral as in introducing a self-help program. Suggesting that patients "look into a local treatment program" is very different from providing a list of screened, reputable programs with descriptions, costs, locations, phone numbers, contact persons, and so forth and then following up with the patient about the success of the referral. The medical office should maintain and annually update a list of local quitting programs. Regional American Cancer Society, American Lung Association, and Cancer Information Service (1-800-4-CANCER) offices can provide details of local programs. The Nicotine Anonymous (formerly Smokers Anonymous) offers free 12-step support (vs. treatment) groups. Though this program has not been formally tested as a support strategy, it may be especially helpful for quitters with a history of 12-step chemical dependency treatment.

Assisting Smokers Not Ready to Quit (Precontemplators)

Patients who say they are *not* willing or ready to try quitting should be treated and followed up no less diligently than those who *are.* The initial goal with these precontemplators is to move them into contemplation and action stages, since they may not be ready for cessation-oriented strategies (Prochaska 1991). Again, a two-part strategy— involving physician and nonphysician staff—should be considered. It is important at the same time, however, not to underestimate the precontemplator's receptivity to nonjudgmental medical advice and assistance. In one study, 43% of precontemplators who declined to set a quit date or commit to a definite quitting plan had made a serious quit attempt within 6 months of receiving motivational counseling and self-help materials, and 13% had quit (Orleans et al. 1990). Likewise, Hollis et al. (1991), who found contemplators less likely than precontemplators to quit, still found that a minimal-contact intervention doubled contemplators' quit rates. As Glynn and Manley (1989) point out, a legitimate goal for precontemplators is simply to move them closer to quitting readiness.

Provide Motivational and/or Self-Help Materials

Precontemplators should be given take-home motivational or self-help materials containing information to raise awareness of smoking health risks and quitting benefits, to bolster quitting confidence, and to address common quitting barriers. Many of the self-help *quitting* guides listed in Table 10–1 contain such information. In addition, there are a number of resources designed specifically to *motivate* quitting—some tailored to specific patient or sociodemographic groups. Several are described in Table 10–2.

Provide Brief Motivational Counseling

A low-key, nonjudgmental approach is best for helping these smokers since their resistance to quitting may be, in part, a reaction against coercive or unsympathetic social pressures to quit at home or at work. Prochaska and colleagues (1987) include a section on "Coping with Pressures to Quit" in their guide for precontemplators. This section acknowledges that it is natural to feel defensive, resentful, or even defiant in the face of growing social pressures to quit, but it points out that these reactions can cloud the smoker's *personal* decision about what's best for him or her. Practical tips for dealing with excess pressure from family and friends are included. Along these lines, Kristeller and Ockene (1989) recommend that the clinician explore, in a nonthreatening manner, the precontemplator's beliefs, attitudes, and misconceptions about smoking and quitting. Similar empirically-tested motivational interviewing techniques are described by Miller and Rollnick (1991) for precontemplators with a variety of substance abuse disorders.

Address Quitting Barriers. Barriers counseling is particularly important for precontemplators—since barriers undermine quitting motivation and perceived self-efficacy. However, the challenge with many precontemplators is to bolster their confidence that

they can *overcome* common quitting difficulties while at the same time undermining their misconceptions about the *ease* of quitting. In one study, precontemplators rated withdrawal difficulties and fear of failure to be less important quitting barriers than did contemplators (Orleans, Rimer, Cristinzio et al. 1991). Prochaska et al. (1987) note that precontemplators and chronic contemplators (who fail to progress into quitting stages) often exhibit unrealistic expectations of the quitting process, telling themselves that quitting is an easy task, and that therefore they can quit "any time."

Notify of Follow-Up

Precontemplators should be followed no less diligently than smokers who are ready to set a quit date. In most cases, this follow-up will occur in the course of routine care, and the physician should tell the patient that she or he will bring up the issue of smoking again in the next visit. However, in cases where there is an urgent or serious medical need to stop smoking soon, a follow-up "smoking only" visit specifically to address nicotine dependence should be scheduled.

STEP 4. ARRANGE FOLLOW-UP

Continued support and encouragement to stop smoking are crucial for all patients who smoke—precontemplators, contemplators and those in action, maintenance, and relapse stages. As Kottke et al. (1988) and Ockene (1987) found in their reviews of smoking cessation interventions in medical practice, the greater the number of contacts, and the longer the period of intervention, the better the results.

The NCI guide strongly recommends two follow-up strategies: (1) sending a letter to (or calling) the patient reinforcing the decision to stop smoking (or "to think about stopping smoking" in the case of a precontemplator) and (2) scheduling a visit with the physician or a designated staff member 1–2 weeks after the patient's quit date (Glynn and Manley 1991). Figure 10–3 incorporates both of these recommendations. All patients should be invited to return for follow-up help at any time. But actually scheduling a

Table 10–2 Motivational Materials for Smoking Cessation

AMERICAN CANCER SOCIETY
1599 Clifton Rd., NE
Atlanta, GA 30029
404-320-3333

The Fifty Most Often Asked Questions About Smoking and Health and the Answers
This booklet gives brief explanations about harmful effects of cigarette smoking and other related common questions on lung cancer, addictive properties of cigarettes, and chewing tobacco. There are a total of 50 questions with brief answers. 1982, free from local ACS offices.

How Can We Reach You?
This pamphlet highlights the major health risks of smoking cigarettes for women. It outlines six steps to take instead of reaching for a cigarette. 1981 (4 pp.), from local ACS offices. No quantity limit.

I'm in Charge Now . . . What's My Secret?
This pamphlet is designed for young women who want to take charge of their lives and end their smoking habit. It lists six true or false statements that summarize common beliefs about smoking cigarettes. 1986, free from local ACS offices (4 pp). No quantity limit.

Why Start a Life Under a Cloud?
This pamphlet gives three reasons why pregnant women should stop smoking. Data are accompanied by a graph depicting lower birth weight babies among smoking women and the higher incidence of perinatal mortality if the mother smokes during pregnancy. 1985 (4 pp.), free from local ACS offices. No quantity limit.

AMERICAN DENTAL ASSOCIATION
Bureau of Health Education and Audiovisual Services
211 East Chicago Avenue
Chicago, IL 60611
312-440-2500

38 Million People Have Quit Smoking, You Can Too
This pamphlet lists health risks of smoking, particularly to the teeth and gums. It briefly discusses reasons people smoke and tips on how to stop. 1985 (6 pp.), $4.75 for 25 copies for ADA members, $5.94 for 25 copies for nonmembers. No quantity limit; order in quantities of 25.

FOX CHASE CANCER CENTER
520 Township Line Road
Cheltenham, PA 19012
1-215-728-2715

Pathways to Freedom (videotape)
This 11-minute videotape was designed to raise knowledge of smoking health risks and heighten quitting motivation among African American smokers. It deglamorizes advertising targeted at African Americans and introduces antitobacco action strategies for the African American community. 1991. Call for distribution information.

NATIONAL CANCER INSTITUTE
Office of Cancer Communications
Building 31, Room 10A24
9000 Rockville Pike
Bethesda, MD 20892
1-800-4-CANCER

Why Do You Smoke?
This pamphlet includes a short questionnaire that addresses questions on cigarette stimulation, handling, accentuation of pleasure, reduction of negative feelings, and psychological addiction and habit. A self-scoring method is included for self-evaluation to determine reasons for smoking and suggestions on how to stop smoking. 1985 (15 pp.), free. Limit of 200 ordered at one time.

UNIVERSITY OF RHODE ISLAND
Cancer Prevention Research Unit
Self-Change Laboratory
Flagg Road
Kingston, RI 02881
401-792-2830

Understanding Yourself As A Smoker
This guide was developed especially for precontemplators, with exercises and personalized feedback to impart "a more balanced view about smoking" and help move smokers into the contemplation stage. 1987 (11 pp.). Call for distribution information.

Source: Based on the National Cancer Institute publication *How to Help Your Patients Stop Smoking: A National Cancer Institute Manual for Physicians* (Glynn and Manley 1989) and *Self-Guided Strategies for Smoking Cessation: A Program Planners Guide* (Glynn, Boyd, Gruman 1991).

follow-up visit for patients who set a quit date may help by providing a short-term goal (e.g., 2 weeks) that appears more manageable than "forever." For smokers who do not set a quit date, the physician should tell the patient that he or she will continue the discussion at the next medical visit, which might be organized around any significant smoking-related illness or condition.

Content of Follow-Up Counseling

Contacts with quitters should praise their efforts and success, help them identify which behavior change strategies and nonsmoking are working best for them, and assist with any unwanted quitting side effects (e.g., withdrawal reactions, weight gain). The use of biofeedback, such as breath carbon monoxide level, to tangibly demonstrate health gains adds powerful reinforcement. It may be helpful in later maintenance stages to discuss referral to other life-style change programs offered in the practice or in the community (e.g., exercise, weight control, stress management) to help the new ex-smoker better adjust to a new nonsmoking life-style.

Nonquitters should receive praise for any steps taken towards quitting, be helped to identify and overcome quitting obstacles, and be encouraged to set up a new quitting plan, including a new quit date. Precontemplators should be encouraged to continue to reevaluate their smoking habits and overcome motivational or practical quitting barriers. Contemplators and those in action stages who have not begun or completed their quitting plan should be encouraged to set a definite quit date. A future follow-up contact should be scheduled.

Relapsers should be helped to analyze the circumstances leading to the setback, and to make a new quitting plan which includes a way to deal with these circumstances in the future. Relapsers should be clued into the so-called abstinence violation effect—whereby unnecessary guilt and self-blame after a slip can actually help pave the way to full-blown relapse (Marlatt and Gordon 1985), for example, "Well, now that I've slipped and smoked one cigarette, I've really blown it. I guess I just don't have what it takes to succeed. I may as well throw in the towel." Upbeat messages normalizing "trial-and-error learning over repeated quit attempts" should be given (or repeated). "Recyclers" should be encouraged to maintain any gains they have made (e.g., using deep breathing instead of smoking, getting more exercise, smoking fewer cigarettes or a lower nicotine brand) and assisted to select a new quitting strategy and quit date, no matter how far off.

Depending on the relapser's experience with the initial treatment, and analysis of factors contributing to the relapse, the patient can be advised to try the same approach again, or to switch to another approach. For instance, if withdrawal symptoms were the major problem, the next attempt might include nicotine replacement. If a lack of structure or social support for a solo quit attempt was a problem, then more intensive treatment may be helpful. If high levels of anxiety led the smoker back to cigarettes, then more attention should be given to anxiety management strategies. In short, the triage decisions made at this point would be informed by the patient's immediate quitting experiences. As before, a definite follow-up contact should be scheduled. And, as before, it should be clear to the patient that each attempt brings him or her that much closer to permanent nonsmoking, and that different timing, and/or a new approach, may be all that is needed to succeed.

Follow-Up Formats and Methods

Minimal-contact programs can select from a variety of follow-up strategies, including follow-up visits and several effective self-help treatment adjuncts that Glynn, Boyd, and Gruman (1991) have labeled *add-on activities* because they significantly boost quit rates among smokers using self-help methods. Visits and telephone follow-up strategies that are interactive provide the best opportunities for personalized counseling. However, mailed tip sheets and personalized feedback also can address individual quitting needs and concerns. The choice will depend on what is feasible for each practice setting. Kottke and associates (1988) found that the most effective medical smoking cessation interventions employed a mix of providers (physician and nonphysician) and modalities (face-to-face, interactive, print, pharmacologic). Follow-up strategies could be selected to enhance this mix.

Follow-Up Visits

For the patient who sets a quit date, the NCI recommends a follow-up visit within 1–2 weeks of the quit date, and a second follow-up visit 1–2 months later. If pharmacologic aids have been prescribed, follow-up visits should be scheduled to allow for timely monitoring of drug treatment effects.

Several studies have shown that follow-up visits boost adherence to the prescribed quitting plan and quit rates (Kottke et al. 1988; Ockene 1987). Wilson et al. (1982), for instance, found that 3–5 minutes of physician advice to quit combined with brief cessation counseling but *without* follow-up resulted in

10.5% self-reported long-term (6–14 month) quit rates. Higher 19.8% quit rates were observed among patients randomly assigned to receive follow-up appointments at 1, 3, and 6 months to review their progress and provide additional counseling.

Telephone Follow-Up

Telephone contacts afford a practical and effective alternative to follow-up visits and can be used alone or in conjunction with other follow-up strategies. The most effective contacts are those initiated by the provider (proactive calls), if staff are available. A variation on this approach is to have trained counselors available for smokers to call at their discretion (such as through the NCI's Cancer Information Service (CIS) number, 1-800-4-CANCER). Some self-help guides also include a quitline service for users (Table 10–1).

Proactive Calls. In a randomized clinical trial of self-quitting in an HMO, two to four brief calls from a telephone counselor boosted long-term, biochemically verified quit rates for a self-help guide by more than 50%, from 14–15% to 23% (Orleans, Schoenbach, Wagner et al. 1991). Subjects were highly addicted smokers who had volunteered for a free self-help quitting program (rather than smokers identified by their physicians). They received calls 6, 18, 34, and 60 weeks after receiving their self-help materials. Calls focused on facilitating adherence to the behavioral self-change strategies recommended in the guide, barriers counseling, and bolstering quitting confidence and motivation. Smokers who received these calls also reported greater adherence to the quitting methods outlined in their self-help materials. Interestingly, additional print interventions (mailed social support tips for family/friends and a 1-year reinforcement mailing) did not benefit these smokers—perhaps because they did not add a new treatment *modality* to the mix.

Smokers in the Orleans, Schoenbach, Wagner et al. (1991) study who appeared to benefit most from brief proactive phone counseling were those who lived alone or lived with other smokers, and those who had

not taken part in a formal clinic program in the past (who presumably had never before received personalized counseling) (Schoenbach et al., 1992). Smokers in precontemplation stages may not benefit as much from such follow-up calls. Lando and associates (1992) studied a similar telephone outreach and support strategy as part of a community quit smoking program. They found better results with smokers who had enrolled in a community quit smoking contest than with smokers identified through a community survey (who presumably were less motivated to stop smoking).

Telephone "Quitlines." In one of the first studies of telephone support services, Dubren (1977) offered prerecorded nonsmoking telephone messages to a random half of the participants in a televised stop smoking clinic. At a 1-month follow-up, self-reported quit rates were twice as high for quitters who had access to this "quitline" as for those who did not (66 vs. 34%). Shiffman (1982) used telephone hotline counselors to counsel new quitters who were tempted to smoke or who had recently lapsed ("crisis callers") with self-reported 6-month quit rates of 63%, and Giovino and co-workers (1986) reported informant-corroborated quit rates of 34% and 26% at 6- and 12-month follow-up contacts with similar crisis callers.

Recently, Ossip-Klein and colleagues (1991) found that providing a regional smokers' hot line as an adjunct to self-help materials boosted cotinine-verified overall 12-month quit rates by 50%, from 8–12%. However, only 36% of smokers made one or more calls to the hot line. Other studies of smokers recruited from medical settings have reported similarly disappointing minimal use of so-called passive quit lines (Glasgow et al. 1993; Hollis et al. 1991; Orleans, et al. 1991). Simple interventions to increase quit line utilization would enhance their efficacy as a follow-up strategy.

Counselors at the NCI's CIS telephone help line all have been trained to provide behavioral quit smoking counseling for callers in various stages of change, and are able to send free self-help and educational materials that address the smoker's concerns and needs (Anderson et al. 1992). In 1989, the

CIS received more than 38,000 calls nation-wide for smoking-related information. Health professionals can rely on the counseling available through the CIS to supplement their own expertise in smoking cessation counseling, deferring questions about different quit smoking strategies and programs to the experts at this number. Therefore, the flowchart in Figure 10–3 suggests CIS calls (1-800-4-CANCER).

Mail Follow-Up

There are a number of different types of mail follow-up strategies. Mail follow-up includes a follow-up letter reiterating physician quitting advice, tip sheets or newsletters reiterating or expanding the counseling provided in the office, and even personalized feedback based on a computerized analysis of individual quitting needs. Selection of a strategy will depend on available resources.

Follow-up Letter. As noted earlier, the NCI *Manual for Physicians* recommends that a follow-up letter be sent within 7 days of the smoking cessation message and intervention. A simple follow-up letter can serve as a timely "cue to action," fostering compliance with antismoking advice, and conveying the seriousness of the provider's concern about smoking. It should be sent soon after the visit, repeating quitting advice and congratulating the smoker on having set a quit date, started a treatment or, in the case of precontemplators, having taken *any* steps toward reevaluating or changing their smoking habits. The NCI *Manual for Physicians* (Glynn and Manley 1991) and the parallel *Manual for the Oral Health Care Team* (Mecklenburg et al. 1990) provide sample letters. However, it is best if such follow-up letters can be sent as personal communications from the physician to the patient, so they do not seem like impersonal form letters simply signed by the physician.

Mailed Self-Help Quitting Materials. Quitting materials sent through the mail provide another option for follow-up. Hollis et al. (1991), for instance, sent a number of tip sheets and a bimonthly quitters newsletter to smokers who received a physician quitting

message and brief nurse-delivered counseling plus self-help quitting methods. Fleisher et al. (1989) sent monthly newsletters to briefly counseled smokers identified in Women, Infants, Children (WIC) clinics. A single mailing may not be effective (Orleans, Schoenbach, Wagner et al. 1991), but multiple mailings may serve as "cues to action," helping patients to stay actively involved in their efforts to quit.

For instance, Ershoff, Mullen, and Quinn (1989) evaluated a quit smoking intervention for pregnant women which consisted predominantly of follow-up print materials sent through the mail. Pregnant smokers (n = 323) at five HMO clinics received 2 minutes of medical risk information and quitting advice from a health educator at their initial prenatal visit along with a two-page pamphlet on the hazards of smoking during pregnancy and the benefits of quitting. Patients then were randomly assigned to usual care (referral to an HMO quit smoking clinic), or to a minimal-contact intervention involving an additional 3 minutes of quitting advice based on the first of eight serialized pregnancy-tailored quit smoking modules also distributed to the patient at the intake prenatal visit. Participants were asked to read the first booklet and to complete the initial exercise it recommended (i.e., listing personal quitting motives). The remaining seven booklets presented a step-by-step quitting program and were sent in weekly installments over the next 7 weeks. Biochemically confirmed continuous abstinence (from the 20th week of pregnancy through delivery) indicated a 22% quit rate for women in the intervention group versus a 9% quit rate in the usual care condition.

Personalized computerized progress reports (Velicer et al. 1988) or letters (Curry et al. 1991) provide another avenue for improving patient outcomes. With a computerized progress report, the smoker completes a brief questionnaire and then receives from a centralized service or an intermediary organization an individualized report describing how to proceed in quitting (Glynn, Boyd, Gruman 1991). Velicer et al. (1988) geared reports to each individual's stage of change and recommended specific strategies for advancing to the next desirable stage.

Owens et al. (1989) and Schneider et al. (1984) used microcomputers to tailor correspondence course mailings to quitters' smoking patterns, quitting motives, progress with homework assignments, and high-risk relapse situations. Orleans and Hutchinson (in press) used a similar approach with chemical dependency patients. And Hurt and associates (1992) used personalized computer-generated follow-up letters for hospital patients receiving a minimal contact nicotine addiction treatment while they were in the hospital.

In sum, follow-up can fortify any minimal contact primary care physician-initiated intervention. As the next section of this chapter will show, the NCI four-step strategy that includes systematic follow-up also has value in hospitals in targeting and in treatment initiated by nonphysician health professionals.

Hospital-Based Treatments

Unique Potential of Hospital-Based Programs

The hospital setting offers unique opportunities for minimal-contact nicotine addiction interventions. Hospitalization represents a critical health care incident and "teachable moment"—when perceived vulnerability to smoking-related health harms and responsiveness to medical stop smoking advice are probably at their peak. The prevalence of smoking in hospitalized patients is not known. However, there were more than 25 million short-term hospital admissions among adults in the United States in 1989 (AHA, 1992). Since the national adult smoking prevalence is estimated at 27% (USDHHS 1990D), well over 5 million smokers might be reached each year through hospital-based programs (Nett 1987; Orleans and Slade 1992).

Many hospitalized patients cut down or abstain from smoking in preparation for inpatient diagnostic or treatment procedures (e.g., cardiac catheterization, pre- or postoperative care, oxygen therapy). Glasgow and associate (1991) recently surveyed more than 500 HMO members who smoked and were hospitalized for nonpregnancy-related, nonterminal conditions 1 year after hospi-

talization and found that 51% had abstained from smoking while hospitalized, 37% had attempted to stop smoking after discharge, and 16% were abstinent.

Increasingly, patients in U.S. hospitals will be required to abstain from smoking while in the hospital (Hurt et al. 1989). A 1987 American Hospital Association survey found that 16% of the over 50% of its member institutions responding had enacted total smoking bans affecting all patients, visitors, and staff (AHA 1988). By 1990, four states had passed legislation prohibiting smoking in hospitals (Maine, Maryland, Michigan, and Minnesota) and Hospital Association resolutions or state resolutions accomplished a similar end in seven other states (Alabama, Florida, Massachusetts, New Jersey, New Mexico, South Carolina, and Virginia) (AHA 1991). In January 1992, the Joint Commission on Accreditation of Healthcare Organizations (JCAHO) mandated that hospitals applying for accreditation become smoke-free within 24 months (JCAHO 1991). The JCAHO ban applies to patients, visitors, employees, volunteers, and medical staff in approximately 80% of all U.S. hospitals (some 5,000 hospitals and 560 psychiatric institutions) allowing exceptions only for patients on a physician's order. The ban has the potential to foster important changes in employee and patient smoking.

The JCAHO recommends that an implementation plan "may include the offering of a smoking cessation support program to those staff members and employees who wish to stop smoking" (JCAHO 1991). A hospital smoking ban introduced with such services can result in significant reductions in employee smoking prevalence and daily smoking rate in all employee groups (Stillman et al. 1990). Unfortunately, the new JCAHO standard does not require hospitals to help patients stop smoking. However, minimal-contact nicotine addiction treatment programs during hospitalization can help these patients turn enforced, short-term abstinence into permanent cessation. Increasingly, the primary-care based strategies reviewed earlier are being adapted for hospital settings. The results presented later suggest benefits even for patients not initially disposed to quitting permanently.

Offering a nicotine addiction treatment program in the hospital obviates problems of the patient's not having time for, or access to, expert quit smoking assistance. Moreover, as the examples given later suggest, a variety of health care providers can be involved—physicians, nurses, respiratory care practitioners, psychologists, physician assistants, addiction counselors, and health educators. (Emmons and Goldstein 1992; Orleans, Kristeller, Gritz in press).

Bedside Consultation Models

Bedside nicotine addiction treatments are becoming increasingly popular. Several such programs are described here. When run by independent health professionals, hospital-based quit smoking programs such as these may be self-supporting (Orleans, Rotberg, Quade et al. 1990; Nett 1987). If state or federal regulatory authorities decide that this is a worthwhile service to make available to inpatients, they can permit hospitals to include the cost of this service in their rates for reimbursement. This step would represent significant progress toward achieving health insurance coverage for nicotine addiction in the United States (Institute for the Study of Smoking Behavior and Policy 1990).

One bedside treatment program, organized as a smoking cessation consultation service, was staffed by masters- and PhD-level psychologists and administered through the hospital's Department of Psychiatry (Orleans et al. 1990). The intervention was congruent with the NCI four-step model (Ask, Advise, Assist, Arrange). Physician-referred patients first completed a detailed smoking and quitting history which included assessment of current anxiety and depression levels. Consultation took place in one session (30–75 minutes), and patients were billed for this service as for any other inpatient psychological/psychiatric consultation. A brief review of assessment results provided the context for initial motivational counseling for all patients. Then, smokers were triaged to one of three different interventions: (1) smokers with evidence of high nicotine dependence and/or a preference for delayed quitting received behavioral counseling and materials to set up a 4-week nicotine fading plan, and advice to stay off smoking during the acute withdrawal period and beyond (nicotine replacement medication had not been marketed yet); (2) smokers ready to quit immediately received behavioral abstinence and relapse prevention counseling and materials; and (3) smokers unwilling to quit received self-help materials for future reference. All smokers, even those who were not yet ready to quit, received follow-up calls at 6 weeks and 6 months and had access to a open telephone "quit line."

Referrals to this hospital consult service were predominantly middle-aged chronic, heavy smokers (n = 62). Most (58%) had chronic cardiovascular and pulmonary diseases. Results of the single consultation with follow-up were comparable to those of more intensive programs: at 6 months, the informant-verified quit rate was 27%. The highest 6-month quit rate (38%) was observed among patients triaged to immediate abstinence counseling: they were significantly less nicotine dependent and more anxious than patients receiving nicotine fading counseling. Smokers receiving only assessment and motivational counseling had the lowest quit rate (13%)—but a substantial 43% of them reported serious quit attempts.

Whether or not the physician had provided a clear quitting message along with the referral proved a strong predictor of outcome: none of the patients who did not recall physician advice to stop smoking had made any substantial changes in their smoking behavior at follow-up. Physician messages must be incorporated into inpatient programs directed by other health professionals. Ideally, some follow-up contact with the patient's primary care physician, especially if this person is different from the admitting physician, should also be built into the treatment protocol.

Similar bedside nicotine addiction programs described by Stevens and colleagues (1993) and by Hurt and colleagues (1992; Hurt et al., in press) have used innovative videotape counseling and follow-up procedures. Stevens and colleagues (1993) recently reported results of a brief, inexpensive smoking cessation and relapse prevention program for over 1,000 hospitalized smokers. The intervention included a 15-minute bedside counseling session accompanied by a 10-minute counseling videotape and the offer of a variety of self-help materials. Intervention patients received a telephone call from the interventionist a week after leaving the hospital, bimonthly quitting newsletters, and access to a 24-hour telephone quit line. Results showed 9.2% of usual care control patients, and 13.5% of intervention patients, not smoking at 3 and 12 months after treatment.

In a nicotine addiction consult program at the Mayo Clinic in Rochester, Minnesota, physician-referred patients receive a 45- to 60-minute initial consultation from a specially trained nicotine addiction counselor (Hurt et al., in press). Consultations are preceded by physician referral and stop smoking advice, and by a thorough assessment of smoking and quitting history and stage of change (see Appendix B, which follows Chapter 21). Counselors provide brief cessation counseling and self-help materials and, if indicated, suggest the prescription of pharmacologic therapy. Assessment and feedback of alveolar carbon monoxide levels is included to help motivate smokers in all stages of change. Referral to more intensive treatment is automatic for smokers needing or wanting the extra help. Follow-up support and motivation are provided throughout the year following discharge via three phone counseling calls (3, 6, and 9 months) and eight personalized, computer-generated letters. Counselors are health educators and chemical dependency counselors who receive brief training in integrating behavioral, traditional 12-step (chemical dependency) and pharmacologic treatment methods. The self-reported 1-year quit rate for patients initially seen as inpatients was 30% (Hurt 1992).

New Roles for Hospital Respiratory Therapists

Nett (1987) has developed a physician-referred, bedside nicotine dependency program directed and conducted by hospital respiratory therapists. This program is out-lined in the National Heart, Lung and Blood Institute (NHLBI) guide *How You Can Help Your Patients Stop Smoking: Opportunities for Respiratory Care Practitioners* (USDHHS 1989b). Brief (2–5 minutes) quitting advice and assistance are recommended for all hospitalized smokers receiving respiratory care. This advice is tied to feedback of results of biologic tests already ordered to diagnose a condition (e.g., spirometry, expired air carbon monoxide or carboxyhemoglobin levels) and to an explanation of personal smoking health risks. A step-by-step, individualized counseling plan is outlined for smokers who want to quit: after an initial assessment of smoking history and degree of nicotine dependence, the respiratory care practitioner works with the patient to set up an appropriate behavioral quitting plan and quit date, provides counseling to address quitting barriers and impart nonsmoking/relapse prevention skills, and obtains a prescription for nicotine replacement therapy, if indicated. The NHLBI guide includes suggestions for how such a hospital consult service can be organized and financed. In 1990 the American Medical Association adopted Resolution number 80: that such a respiratory care hospital intervention be reimbursed by third-party payers: "Whereas, respiratory therapists are being trained to conduct a comprehensive (smoking intervention) program focused on hospital inpatients which costs about $120 and is reimbursable by Medicare, therefore be it resolved that the American Medical Association supports the concept of inpatient smoking cessation programs which are conducted by appropriately trained health care personnel under the supervision of a physician" (AMA 1990, p. 1).

A Model Nurse-Managed Hospital Program. A recently reported program for post-MI patients provides an example of a *nurse-managed* hospital intervention (Taylor et al. 1990). The emphasis of treatment was on relapse prevention since all patients were abstinent from smoking during the hospitalization. Participating nurses took part in three 4-hour training workshops prior to delivering the intervention. Consistent with the four-step strategy outlined in this chapter, this hospital intervention included an assessment of high-risk relapse situations, quit smoking advice, assistance, and follow-up.

Physicians treating the patients who took part in this study (in intervention and usual care groups) were asked to give a firm quit smoking message in the coronary care unit. Then, the day after transfer from the coronary care unit, these smokers received the nurse-managed intervention, beginning with the nurse reviewing the benefits of not smoking and the dangers of returning to smoking after an infraction. Nurses provided brochures and a workbook introducing effective nonsmoking maintenance strategies plus supporting audiotapes for review at home. High-risk relapse situations were assessed using a short questionnaire: individualized barriers counseling reviewed strategies for dealing with the individual's particular high-risk relapse situations or triggers. Follow-up was provided in nurse-initiated telephone contacts—weekly calls for the first 2–3 weeks, followed by monthly calls for the next 4 months. Patients who continued to smoke were scheduled for additional face-to-face counseling and, if appropriate, nicotine gum. The average time spent per patient in this intervention was 3.5 hours.

Smokers treated in this way (n = 86) were compared to those receiving usual hospital care (n = 87), which included no systematic treatment for nicotine addiction. The intervention almost doubled long-term (biochemically verified) quit rates in this high-risk patient population: 61% of intervention patients were abstinent at 12 months compared with 32% of patients in the usual care group. Quit rates in both groups were highest for patients with greater stated intention to quit at the time of initial intervention—but the treatment effect documented here was apparent even for those patients who initially said they had little or no intention to stay off cigarettes (33% intervention vs. 11% usual care). The authors suggest ways in which a triage system could be used to reduce average patient contact time to 2 hours in order to improve cost-effectiveness.

Hospital-Based Treatments for Chemical Dependency Patients

Finally, there are several examples of hospital-based nicotine addiction treatments for chemical dependency patients. Joseph and co-workers (1990) evaluated a three-session smoking cessation program for chemically dependent patients on a 21-day residential unit. The program consisted of three weekly didactic lectures on nicotine dependence and cessation strategies, including nicotine replacement. Hospital policy prohibited patient smoking inside hospital buildings during the program; and clonidine was made available to abstaining smokers troubled by strong cravings and withdrawal reactions. This treatment reduced smoking prevalence during hospitalization and increased interest in future quitting without compromising drug and alcohol treatment outcomes. Orleans and Hutchinson (in press) describe a similar program for hospitalized chemical dependency patients, with the explicit goals of boosting quitting motivation and confidence among precontemplators and contemplators. Addiction counselors were the key interventionists in both programs, integrating standard cognitive-behavioral smoking cessation techniques and self-help materials with traditional 12-step chemical dependency treatment strategies.

Minimal-Contact Interventions by Nonphysician Providers

The meta-analysis of 108 interventions used in 39 controlled trials of medical smoking cessation interventions found the best results when both physician *and* nonphysician providers were involved, and when interventions took place on several occasions (Kottke et al. 1988). Nonphysician practitioners have a critical role to play, both working with the physician as part of the health care team, and acting independently in a variety of health care settings.

Nurses

Nurses represent the single largest health professional group and thus potentially could reach and assist the most smokers (Royce et al. 1989). Moreover, in many health care settings, the nurse spends the most time with the patient and has the greatest involvement in patient education (Goldstein et al. 1987; Haughley, O'Shean, Dittmar 1986). Within primary care settings, nurses can reduce the burden on the primary care physician by taking part in a team approach to quit smoking advice and nicotine addiction counseling, like the one advocated in this chapter and elsewhere (Blair 1989; Hollis et al. 1991; Janz et al. 1987; Kilburn and Warshaw 1990). Within hospital settings, nurses also can play a critical role (Goldstein et al. 1987). Finally, the occupational health nurse is uniquely situated to provide quit smoking advice and assistance to employees through worksite-based programs (Hourigan, Knapp, Kottke 1989).

The relatively high rate of smoking among nurses in the United States—essentially the same rate as U.S. women in general (Feldman and Richard 1986; Garfinkel and Stellman 1986)—represents a stumbling block to nurse involvement. Several investigators have developed and evaluated quit smoking programs for nurses (e.g., Gritz et al. 1988), and nursing school curricula are increasingly likely to train nurses to intervene with nicotine addiction in patients and to overcome their own addiction (Royce et al. 1989).

The NHLBI's (1990) guide, *Nurses: Help Your Patients Stop Smoking,* outlines a practical, four-step intervention plan for nurses that is quite similar to the plan outlined in the NCI manual for physicians (Glynn and Manley 1989): (1) *Ask* all patients if they smoke; (2) *Advise* all smokers to quit; (3) *Prepare* smokers to quit with brief counseling, self-help materials, and/or referral to local treatment programs; and (4) *Follow up* through follow-up visits, cards, or phone calls.

Studies by Hollis et al. (1991), Risser and Belcher (1990), and Taylor et al. (1990), reviewed earlier in this chapter, illustrate such nurse-managed interventions in primary care and hospital-based minimal-contact treatments. Nurses have another critical role in public health clinic settings as illustrated

in studies by Fleisher et al. (1989) and Sexton and Hebel (1984).

Fleisher et al. (1989) designed and evaluated a nurse-managed smoking cessation intervention for mothers of young children seen in WIC clinic settings. Nurses followed a brief three-step counseling protocol, including a brief smoking history survey (assessing degree of dependency as well as readiness to quit), 3–5 minutes of medical quit smoking advice, and the offer of the *Quitting Times* self-help quit smoking guide tailored to the concerns of mothers with young children (Table 10–1). Follow-up took the form of reinforcement tip sheets sent in the mail. Women also were encouraged to call the CIS for additional help. Over 2,700 low-income smokers at 14 WIC sites were counseled in a 2-month period, the vast majority of whom expressed only limited interest in stopping smoking. Of the 72% reached for a 3-month telephone follow-up, 39% had cut down their smoking, 30% had tried to quit, and 5% had quit. In a follow-up study, the program was tested in 49 clinics as part of ongoing services over a 2½ year period: 19,322 women were queried about smoking, and 4,408 smokers received counseling. The self-reported 12-month quit rate was 12.4%, about twice as high as the baseline quit rate of 5.8% in these clinics.

Sexton and Hebel (1984) achieved a 27% biochemically verified quit rate in 388 pregnant smokers in private prenatal care who were randomized to receive a minimal-contact quit smoking intervention from public health nurses. This now classic intervention included medical advice to quit tied to education about the risks of smoking in pregnancy, behavioral cessation counseling—both in the clinic and through home visits—and follow-up mailings and telephone calls over the course of the pregnancy. Patients who received usual care had only a 3% end-of-pregnancy quit rate. Moreover, mothers in the intervention group had babies with significantly higher birth weights than mothers in the control group.

Physician Assistants

There are almost 20,000 practicing physician assistants (PAs) in the United States.

PAs practice medicine with the supervision of a licensed physician and provide patients with services ranging from primary medicine to surgery: 56% report a primary care specialty, with 31% in family/general practice, and 28% practice in public or private hospital settings (American Academy of Physician Assistants 1991). Over 80% of PAs practice in states that allow them to prescribe drugs (30 states and the District of Columbia). In 1990, PAs logged over 147 million patient contacts, and wrote 112 million prescriptions. These statistics indicate that PAs can take an active role in quit smoking counseling and pharmacologic treatment for nicotine addiction. Several smoking cessation interventions for physician assistants have been outlined (e.g., Cox 1990; Orleans 1984), but, to date, there are no published studies evaluating the results of interventions managed by this important group of health care providers.

Respiratory Care Practitioners

As Nett (1987) has outlined, respiratory therapists represent a group of health professionals in an ideal position to establish and staff hospital-based nicotine addiction treatment programs:

1. There are approximately 100,000 respiratory therapists working in 5,700 hospitals in the United States;
2. The majority (64%) of respiratory care departments already deliver health promotion services, many related to smoking cessation;
3. The patient education skills required for pulmonary rehabilitation and nicotine addiction treatment are similar;
4. Respiratory care departments have a close relationship with a physician; and
5. Respiratory therapists can charge for nicotine dependency treatments using existing billing codes and procedures.

The American Association for Respiratory Care (AARC) has developed a protocol and training package to assist respiratory therapists in treating nicotine addiction. Much of this is presented in the 1989 NHLBI guide for respiratory care practitioners (USDHHS 1989b). This guide outlines four levels of in-

tervention for hospital-based respiratory therapists. The major focus is on Level II interventions which parallel the four-step Ask, Advise, Assist, Arrange model promulgated by the NCI (Glynn and Manley 1989). To date, there are no published reports of program effectiveness, but research is now underway.

Dentists and the Oral Health Care Team

As summarized in Chapter 8, an estimated 39 million U.S. smokers receive routine dental care from the nation's 140,000 dentists each year (Christen 1990). As is true for U.S. physicians, only about 15% of U.S. dentists are smokers and more than a third are ex-smokers, making them good role models for quitting (Garfinkel and Stellman 1986). A recent Oregon survey of dentists, dental hygienists, and their male patients showed that more dentists reported routinely discussing the health hazards of smokeless/spitting tobacco use (77–88%) than smoking (47–55%)—but that fewer than 33% offered advice to quit smokeless *or* smoking, or even stocked information about quitting or about tobacco health effects in the office (Severson, Eakin, Stevens et al. 1990). The oral health care providers and hygienists in this survey acknowledged the same barriers to intervention that primary care physicians report (Orleans et al. 1985)—with fully one-third to one-half reporting a lack of time and training.

To address these barriers, the NCI has outlined a brief minimal-contact intervention plan for dentists and hygienists in the guide *How to Help Your Patients Stop Using Tobacco Products: A National Cancer Institute Manual for the Oral Health Care Team* (Mecklenburg et al. 1990). This guide introduces the office procedures and four-step action plan promulgated for physicians, but it also includes more detailed information about the effects of smoking on oral health and hygiene, and about *smokeless* tobacco hazards and cessation resources.

Brief, office-based dental interventions following these general guidelines have proven highly effective. In an NCI-funded randomized, controlled trial with 50 dentists, Cohen and colleagues (1987, p. 313) offered a 1-hour lecture to 50 dentists outlining the four-step strategy: "Step (1) Ask your patients about smoking; Step (2) Deliver a firm quit smoking message; Step (3) Mutually agree on a quit date; and Step (4) Check up on your patients' progress at each regularly scheduled visit." Dentists were then randomly assigned to one of four groups: in the advice only group, dentists received a booklet summarizing these four steps; in the reminder group, dentists were instructed in the use of two chart labels ("Did you talk to the patient today about smoking?" and "The patient has agreed to the following quit date."); in the gum group, dentists were offered a free 10-box supply of nicotine gum for eligible quitters; and a reminder plus gum group combined both experimental interventions.

The presence of chart stickers and/or the availability of nicotine gum significantly increased the percentage of dental patients reporting that their dentist had counseled them about cigarette smoking and the number of minutes of smoking counseling patients reportedly received. The best results occurred in the reminder plus gum group. For instance, only 37% of patients in the advice only group reported that their dentists had "asked them about smoking" and only 18% said they had been advised to quit. In contrast, 85% of the patients in the reminder plus gum group reported having been asked about smoking, and 54% reported dental advice to quit. Patients in this group estimated that smoking counseling, including gum use advice, took only 7 minutes in the first visit, and only 3 minutes in a second follow-up visit. This 10-minute intervention strikingly increased quit rates. The percentage of patients who had quit smoking a year later was 16.9% (biochemically verified) in the reminder plus gum group, about twice as high as the 7.7% reported in the advice only group (Cohen, Stookey, Katz et al. 1989). Nicotine gum availability and use appeared to account for most of this effect—a comparable 16.3% quit rate was found in the gum only group.

Severson, Stevens, Little et al. (1990) employed a videotape to facilitate and standardize a minimal-contact dental intervention for smokeless tobacco users. Preliminary results of a randomized trial with more than 400 smokeless tobacco users found short-term quit rates twice as high among patients who received a strong quitting message from the dentist along with self-help materials and a 10-minute videotape (25%) than among "usual care" patients (12%).

Pharmacists

Pharmacists represent another group of health professionals ideally situated to provide advice and assistance about tobacco use and cessation. As the NCI guide *Helping Smokers Quit: A Guide for the Pharmacist* (USDHHS 1984) points out:

1. Pharmacists are uniquely qualified to inform smokers on how nicotine (smoking) reduces the therapeutic effectiveness of other prescription drug regimens (e.g., oral contraceptives, insulin, bronchodilators, antidepressants);
2. Patients have easy access to pharmacists—with many pharmacies open 7 days a week and no appointment required for pharmacist consultation;
3. Most pharmacists are nonsmokers and therefore qualify as role models.

Moreover, two new developments give pharmacists an even more important role— the growing use of pharmacologic aids to treat nicotine addiction and recent state and federal legislation mandating that pharmacists provide medication counseling for Medicaid and other patients (Kessler 1991). The pharmacist is in a unique position to counsel the patient on proper use of nicotine replacement and other pharmacologic treatments. Computers now in use (primarily for billing) in 90% of the nation's 56,000 pharmacies (Kessler 1991) provide the potential to generate personalized mailings to assist smokers quitting with pharmacologic aids. Since older Americans are the major consumers of prescription medication, pharmacists represent a particularly important source of information for older smokers (Rimer et al. 1990).

In addition, the American Pharmaceutical Association encourages its members not to sell tobacco products and to prohibit smoking in pharmacies (Pilgrim 1990). Tobacco-free pharmacies also represent an ideal location for the placement and distribution of quit smoking materials and products.

Davidson and colleagues (1988) surveyed pharmacies which did not sell tobacco products and a control group of pharmacies which sold these products. The owners or managers of tobacco-free pharmacies had a much more realistic understanding of the magnitude of harm tobacco causes, and they felt far more empowered to help their customers stop smoking than did their peers in control stores. In recent years, there have been a number of organized efforts at the local, state, and provincial levels in the United States and Canada encouraging pharmacies to stop selling tobacco products. Independent pharmacies are the most likely to make the change, and those which take this step demonstrate their commitment to the ethical precept, *primum no nocene.* In many cases, the local medical society or voluntary health association affiliates can offer pharmacies support, advice, and publicity for this change.

The NCI guide for pharmacists contains posters and counter cards, a program guide for the pharmacist, and patient quitting materials. Consistent with the four-step model presented in this chapter, the program guide for pharmacists recommends a clear health message about quitting and quitting benefits, and recommends that self-help materials be given in addition to brief barriers counseling. A formal evaluation of pharmacist-assisted quitting is greatly needed.

CONCLUSION

The minimal-contact treatments reviewed in this chapter provide models and resources for a wide variety of medical settings and health care professionals—making it possible for the systematic treatment of nicotine dependence to truly become part of routine health care in the United States. While minimal-contact treatments will not be sufficient for all smokers, they are widely preferred by smokers and constitute a potentially highly cost-effective intervention strategy.

If treatment of nicotine dependence were broadly used by physicians alone, the public health impact would be enormous. If only half of office-based physicians in the United States delivered a brief intervention to each of their smoking patients, and achieved only a 10% sustained quit rate, the national cessation rate would more than double—jumping from 2 million to 4.5 million new ex-smokers each year (Glynn and Manley 1991). Therefore, every opportunity to motivate and assist medical and dental patients to stop smoking should be seized.

ACKNOWLEGDGMENTS

The writing of this chapter was supported in part by National Cancer Institute grant CA 34856. The authors are grateful to Janet Telepchak, BS and Martha K. Keintz, ScM of the Fox Chase Cancer Center for assistance with the design and format of Figures 10–1, 10–2, and 10–3 and to Joan Magee and Siobhan LaCreta for clerical assistance.

REFERENCES

Abrams, D. B., Follic, M. J., Biener, L., Carey, K. B., Hitti, J. Saliva cotinine as a measure of smoking status in field settings. *Am J Public Health* 77:846–848, 1987.

American Academy of Physician Assistants. *Physician Assistants.* Virginia: American Academy of Physician Assistants, 1991.

American Hospital Association (AHA). *Final Report: Census of Hospital-Based Health Promotion and Patient Education Programs.* Chicago: American Hospital Association, 1988.

———. *Smokefree Hospital Patient Communication and Staff Training Resources.* Chicago: American Hospital Association, 1991.

———. *Hospital Statistics: 1991–1992 Edition.* Chicago: American Hospital Association, 1992.

American Medical Association (AMA). *American Medical Association House of Delegates: Resolution 80,* 1990.

American Psychiatric Association (APA). *Diagnostic and Statistical Manual of Mental Disorders—DSM-III-R,* 3d. ed., rev., Washington, D.C.: American Psychiatric Association, 1987.

Anderson, D. M., Duffy, K., Hallett, C. D., Marcus, A. C. Proactive health education and patient counseling through telephone helplines.

Unpublished manuscript, National Cancer Institute, Bethesda, MD, January 1992.

Benowitz, N. L. Nicotine replacement therapy during pregnancy. *JAMA* 22:3174–3177, 1991.

Blair, J. E. Smoking intervention: Opportunities for office nurses. *Office Nurse* 2:2–7, 1989.

CA—A Cancer Journal for Clinicians. The impact of providing physicans with quit-smoking materials for smoking patients. *CA* 31:75–78, 1971.

Casey, K. *If Only I Could Quit: Recovery from Nicotine Addiction.* Center City, MN: Hazelden Educational Materials, 1987.

Chilmonczyk, B. R., Knight, G. J., Palomaki, G. E., Pulkkinen, A. J., Williams, J., Haddow, J. E. Environmental tobacco smoke exposure during infancy. *Am J Public Health* 80:1205–1209, 1990.

Christen, A. G. The dental team: If teeth could talk. Paper presented at the Marion Merrell Dow Meetings, Palm Desert, CA, December 1990.

Christen, A. G., and McDonald, J. Safety of nicotine-containing gum. In Pomerleau, O. F., and Pomerleau, C. S., eds. *Nicotine Replacement. A Critical Evaluation.* New York: Alan R. Liss, 1988, 219–235.

Cohen, S. J., Christen, A. G., Katz, B. P., Drook, C. A., et al. Counseling medical and dental patients about cigarette smoking: The impact of nicotine gum and chart reminders. *Am J Public Health* 77:313–316, 1987.

Cohen, S., Lichtenstein, E., Prochaska, J. O., Rossi, J. S., et al. Debunking myths about self-quitting. *Am Psychol* 44(11):1355–1365, 1989.

Cohen, S. J., Stookey, G. K., Katz, B. P., Drook, C. A., Christen, A. G. Helping smokers quit: A randomized controlled trial with private practice dentists. *J Am Dent Assoc* 118:41–45, 1989.

Cohen, S. J., Stookey, G. K., Katz, B. P., Drook, C. A., Smith, D. M. Encouraging primary care physicians to help smokers quit. *Ann Intern Med* 110(8):648–652, 1989.

Cohen, S., and Lichtenstein, E. Perceived stress, quitting smoking and smoking relapse. *Health Psychol* 9:466–478, 1990.

Cox, J. L. How to help your patients stop smoking. *J Am Acad of Physician Assistants* 3:600–606, 1990.

Cummings, K. M., Giovino, G., Emont, S. L., Sciandra, R., Koenigsberg, M. Factors influencing success in counseling patients to stop smoking. *Patient Education and Counseling* 8:189–200, 1986.

Cummings, S. R., Hansen, B., Richard, R. J.,

Stein, M. J., Coates, T. J. Internists and nicotine gum. *JAMA* 260(11):1565–1569, 1988.

Cummings, S. R., Rubin, S. M., Oster, G. The cost-effectiveness of counseling smokers to quit. *JAMA* 261(1):75–79, 1989.

Curry, S. J. Self-help strategies for smoking cessation. *J Consult Clin Psychol*, in press.

Curry, S. J., Wagner, E. H., Grothaus, L. C. Evaluation of intrinsic and extrinsic motivation interventions with a self-help smoking cessation program. *J Consult Clin Psychol* 59:318–324, 1991.

Davidson, L., Slade, J., Stang, C. L. Knowledge and attitudes about tobacco among pharmacists who do and who do not sell tobacco. In Aok, M., Hisamichi, S., Tominaga, S., eds. *Smoking and Health 1987.* Amsterdam: Excerpta Medica, 1988, 343–345.

Dubren, R. Self-management by recorded telephone messages to maintain nonsmoking behavior. *J Consult Clin Psychol* 45:358–360, 1977.

Dudley, D. L., Aickin, M., Martin, C. J. Cigarette smoking in a chest clinic population—psychophysiological variables. *J Psychosom Res* 21:367–375, 1977.

Emmons, K. M., Goldstein, M. G. Smokers who are hospitalized: A window of opportunity for cessation interventions. *Prev Med* 21:262–269, 1992.

Emmons, K. M., Weidner, G., Foster, W. M., Collins, R. L. Improvement in pulmonary function following smoking cessation. *Addic Beh* 17:301–306, 1992.

Ershoff, D., Aaronson, N., Danaher, B., Wasserman, F. Behavioral, health and cost outcomes of an HMO-based prenatal health education program. *Public Health Rep* 98:536–547, 1983.

Ershoff, D. H., Mullen, P. D., Quinn, V. P. A randomized trial of serialized self-help smoking cessation program for pregnant women in an HMO. *Am J Public Health* 79(2):182–187, 1989.

Fagerström, K. O. Measuring degree of physical dependence on tobacco smoking with reference to individualization of treatment. *Addict Behav* 3:235–241, 1978.

————. A comparison of psychological and pharmacological approaches in smoking cessation. *J Behav Med* 5:343–351, 1982.

————. Effects of nicotine chewing gum and follow-up appointments in physician-based smoking cessation. *Prev Med* 13:517–527, 1984.

Fagerström, K. O., Heatherton, T. F., Kozlowski, L. T. Nicotine addiction and its assessment. *Ear Nose Throat J* 69(11):763–767, 1992.

Feldman, B. M., and Richard E. Prevalence of nurse smokers and variables identified with successful and unsuccessful smoking cessation. *Res Nurs Health* 9:131–138, 1986.

Fiore, M. C. The new vital sign: Assessing and documenting smoking status. *JAMA* 266(22):3183–3184, 1991.

Fiore, M. C. Jorenby, D. E., Baker, T. B., Kenford, S. L. Tobacco dependence and the nicotine patch: Clinical guidelines for effective use. *JAMA* 268:2687–2694, 1992.

Fiore, M. C., Novotny, T. E., Pierce, J. P., Giovino, G. A., Hatziandreu, E. J., Newcomb, P. A., Surawicz, T. S., Davis, R. M. Methods used to quit smoking in the United States: Do cessation programs help? *JAMA* 263:2760–2765, 1990.

Fisher, E. B., Haire-Joshue, D., Morgan, G. D., Rehberg, H., Rost, K. Smoking and smoking cessation. *Am Rev Respir Dis* 142:702–720, 1990.

Fleisher, L. F., Keintz, M., Rimer, B., Utt, M., Workman, S., Engstrom, P. Process evaluation of a minimal-contact smoking cessation program in an urban nutritional assistance (WIC) program. In Engstrom, P., Rimer, B., Mortensen, L. E., eds. *Advances in Cancer Control: Screening and Prevention Research.* New York: Wiley-Liss, 1989, 95–106.

Fortmann, S. P., Killen, J. D., Telch, M. J., Newman, B. Minimal contact treatment for smoking cessation: A placebo controlled trial of nicotine polacrilex and self-directed relapse prevention: Initial results of the Stanford Stop Smoking Project. *JAMA* 260(11):1575–1580, 1988.

Frank, E., Winkleby, M. A., Altman, D. G., Rockhill, B., Fortmann, S. P. Predictors of physicians' smoking cessation advice. *JAMA* 266(22):3139–3144, 1991.

Franks, P. O., Harp, J., Bell, B. Randomized, controlled trial of clonidine for smoking cessation in a primary care setting. *JAMA* 262(21):3011–3013, 1989.

Garfinkel, L., and Stellman, S. D. Cigarette smoking among physicians, dentists and nurses. *CA* 36:2–9, 1986.

Giovino, G. A., Ossip-Klein, D. J., Shulman, E., Black, P., Lurier, A., Sementilli, E., Bonnani, A. M., Seidman, R., LaVigne, M., Megahed, N., Webster, S., Stiggins, J. Determinants of relapse and predictors of outcome for callers to a smoking relapse prevention hotline. Paper presented at the annual convention of the Association for Advancement of Behavior Therapy, Chicago, IL, 1986.

Glasgow, R., Lando, H., Hollis, J., McRae, S. G., LaChonce, P. A stop-smoking telephone helpline that nobody called. *Amer J Pub Health* 83:252–253, 1993.

Glasgow, R. E., Stevens, V. J., Vogt, T. M., Mullooly, J. P., Lichtenstein, E. Changes in smoking associated with hospitalization: Quit rates, predictive variables, and intervention implications. *Am J Health Promotion* 6:24–29, 1991.

Glassman, A. H., Helzer, J. E., Covey, L. S., Cottler, L. B., Stetner, F., Tipp, J. E., Johnson, J. Smoking, smoking cessation and major depression. *JAMA* 264:1546–1549, 1990.

Glynn, T. J., Boyd, G. M., Gruman, J. C. Essential elements of self-help/minimal intervention strategies for smoking cessation. *Health Educ Q* 17(3):329–345, 1990.

Glynn, T. J., and Manley, M. *How to Help Your Patients Stop Smoking: A National Cancer Institute Manual for Physicians.* U.S. Department of Health and Human Services, Public Health Service, National Institutes of Health. NIH Publication No. 92-3064, 1991.

Glynn, T. J., and Manley, M. Physicians, cancer control and the treatment of nicotine dependence: Defining success. *Health Educ Res* 4(4):479–487, 1989.

Goldstein, A. O., Hellier, A., Fitzgerald, S., Stegall, T. S., Fischer, P. M. Hospital nurse counseling of patients who smoke. *Am J Public Health* 77:1333–1334, 1987.

Gritz, E. R. Cigarette smoking: The need for action by health professionals. *CA* 38(4):194–212, 1988.

Gritz, E. R., Marcus, A. C., Berman, B. A., Read, L. L., Kanim, L. E., Reeder, S. J. Evaluation of a worksite self-help smoking cessation program for registered nurses. *Am J Health Promotion* 3:26–35, 1988.

Hajek, P., Jackson, P., Belcher, M. Long-term use of nicotine chewing gum. *JAMA* 260(11):1593–1596, 1988.

Hall, S. M., Bachman, J., Henderson, J. M., Barstow, R., et al. Smoking cessation in patients with cardiopulmonary disease: An initial study. *Addict Behav* 8:33–42, 1983.

Haughley, B. P., O'Shean, R. M., Dittmar, S. Smoking behavior among student nurses: A survey. *Public Health Rep* 101:652–657, 1986.

Heatherton, T. F., Kozlowski, L. T., Frecker, R. C., Fagerström, K. O. The Fagerstrom Test for nicotine dependence: A revision of the Fagerström Tolerance Questionnaire. *Br J Addict* 86:1119–1127, 1991.

Henningfield, J. E. Improving the diagnosis and treatment of nicotine dependence. *JAMA* 260:1613, 1988.

Hollis, J. F., Lichtenstein, E., Mount, K., Vogt, T. M., Stevens, V. J. Nurse-assisted smoking counseling in medical settings: Minimizing demands on physicians. *Prev Med* 20.497–507, 1991.

Hourigan, M., Knapp, J., Kottke, T. E. *Making a Difference: The Occupational Health Nurse's Smoking Cessation Assistance Guide*. Minneapolis: Minnesota Coalition for a Smoke-Free Society 2000, 1989.

Hughes, J. Clonidine, depression and smoking cessation. *JAMA* 259.2901–2902, 1988.

Hughes, J. R., Epstein, L. H., Andrasik, F., Neff, D., et al. Smoking and carbon monoxide levels during pregnancy. *Addict Behav* 7:271–276, 1982.

Hughes, J. R., Gust, S. W., Keenan, R. M., Fenwick, J. W., Healey, M. L. Nicotine vs. placebo gum in general medical practice. *JAMA* 261(9):1300–1305, 1989.

Hurt, R. D., Berge, K. G., Offord, K. P., Leonard, D. A., Gerlach, D. K., Renquist, C. L., O'Hara, M. R. The making of a smoking-free medical center. *JAMA* 261:95–97, 1989.

Hurt, R. D., Dale, L. C., McClain, F. L., Eberman, K. M., Offord, K. P., Bruce, B. K., Lauger, G. G. A comprehensive model for the treatment of nicotine dependence in a medical setting. *Med Clin North Am* 76:495–515, 1992.

Hurt, R. D., Lauger, G. G., Offord, K. P. Nicotine-replacement therapy with use of a transdermal nicotine patch—a randomized double-blind placebo-controlled trial. *Mayo Clin Proc* 65:1529–1537, 1990.

Hurt, R. D., Lauger, G. G., Offord, K. P., Bruce, B. K., Dale, L. C., McClain, F. L., Eberman, K. M. An integrated approach to the treatment of nicotine dependence in a medical center setting: Description of the initial experience. *J Gen Int Med* January–February 1992.

Institute for the Study of Smoking Behavior and Policy. *Smoking Cessation—The Organization, Delivery and Financing of Services*. Hollis, NH: Puritan Press, 1990.

Jackson, P. H., Stapleton, J. A., Russell, M.A.H., et al. Predictors of outcome in a general practitioner intervention against smoking. *Prev Med* 15:244–253, 1986.

Jackson, P. H., Stapleton, J. A., Russell, M.A.H., Merriman, R. J. Nicotine gum use and outcome in a general practitioner intervention against smoking. *Addict Behav* 14:335–341, 1989.

Janz, N. K., Becker, M. H., Kirscht, J. P., Eraker, S. A., Billi, J. E., Woolliscroft, J. O. Evaluation of a minimal-contact smoking cessation intervention in an outpatient setting. *Am J Public Health* 77(7):805–809, 1987.

Joint Commission on the Accreditation of Healthcare Organizations (JCAHO). *Hospital Standards—1992*. Chicago: Joint Commission on the Accreditation of Healthcare Organizations, 1991.

Joseph, A. M., Nichol, K. L., Willenbring, M. L., Korn, J. E., Lysaght, L. S. Beneficial effects of treatment for nicotine dependence during an inpatient substance abuse treatment program. *JAMA* 263.1581–1583, 1990.

Kessler, D. A. Communicating with patients about their medications. *N Engl J Med* 325:1650–1652, 1991.

Kilburn, K. II., and Warshaw, R. II. Effects of individually motivating smoking cessation in male blue collar workers. *Am J Public Health* 80:1334–1337, 1990.

Killen, J. D., Fortmann, S. P., Telch, M. J., Newman, B. Are heavy smokers different from light smokers? *JAMA* 260:1581–1585, 1988.

Kottke, T. E., Battista, R. N., DeFriese, G. H., Brekke, M. L. Attributes of successful smoking cessation interventions in medical practice. *JAMA* 259(19):2882–2889, 1988.

Kozlowski, L. T., Skinner, W., Kent, C., Pope, M. A. Prospects for smoking treatment in individuals seeking treatment for alcohol and other drug problems. *Addict Behav* 14:273–278, 1989.

Kristeller, J. L. Individuals at high medical risk for weight gain. Paper presented at the National Heart, Lung and Blood Institute Conference on Smoking Cessation and Weight Gain, Memphis, TN, September 1990.

Kristeller, J. L., and Ockene, J. K. Assessment and treatment of smoking on a consultation service. In Michels, R., ed. *Psychiatry: Volume 2*. Philadelphia: J. B. Lippincott, 1989, ch. 113, pp. 1–13.

Lam, W., Sze, P. C., Sacks, H. S., Chalmers, T. C. Meta-analysis of randomized controlled use of nicotine chewing gum. *Lancet* 4 July 1987, 27–30.

Lando, H. A., Hellerstedt, W. L., Pirie, P. L., McGovern, P. G. Brief supportive telephone outreach as a recruitment and intervention strategy for smoking cessation. *Am J Public Health* 82(1):41–46, 1992.

Lichtenstein, E., Glasgow, R. E., Abrams, D. B. Social support in smoking cessation: In search of effective interventions. *Behav Ther* 17:607–619, 1986.

Lindsay, E. A., Wilson, D. M., Best, A. J., Willms, D. G., Singer, J., Gilbert, J. R., Taylor, D. W. A randomized trial of physician training for smoking cessation. *Am J Health Promotion* 3:11–18, 1989.

Marlatt, G. A., and Gordon, J. R., eds. *Relapse Prevention.* New York: Guilford Press, 1985.

Mayo Foundation. Mayo Foundation Nicotine Dependence Center Patient Questionnaire. Rochester, MN: Mayo Foundation, 1991.

Mecklenburg, R. E., Christen, A. G., Gerbert, B., Gift, H. C., Glynn, T. J., Jones, R. B., Lindsay, E., Manley, M. W., Severson, H. *How to Help Your Patients Stop Using Tobacco: A National Cancer Institute Manual for the Oral Health Team.* Washington D.C.: U.S. Department of Health and Human Services, National Cancer Institute. NIH Publication No. 91-3191, December 1990.

Miller, W. R. and Rollnick, S. *Motivational Interviewing: Preparing People to Change Addictive Behavior.* New York: Guilford Press, 1991.

National Cancer Institute (NCI). *Smoking Tobacco and Cancer Program: 1985 Report.* Bethesda, MD: National Cancer Institute. NIH Publication No. 86-2687, 1986.

Nett, L. M. A new role for the respiratory therapist in smoking cessation. *Respiratory Care* 32:1009–1110, 1987.

————. Respiratory therapists' nicotine dependency intervention program for hospital patients. Unpublished manuscript, PSL Center for Health Sciences Education, Denver, CO, 1990.

Ockene, J. K. Clinical perspectives: Physician-delivered interventions for smoking cessation: Strategies for increasing effectiveness. *Prev Med* 16:723–737, 1987.

Ockene, J., Kristeller, J., Goldberg, R., Ockene, I., Merriam, P., Barrett, S., Pekow, P., Hosmer, D., Gianelly, R. Smoking cessation and severity of disease: The coronary artery smoking intervention study. *Health Psychol* 11:119–126, 1992.

Orleans, C. T. Helping your patients quit smoking. *PA Outlook* 2:4–7, 1984.

————. Understanding and promoting smoking cessation: Overview and guidelines for physician intervention. *Annu Rev Med* 36:51–61, 1985.

Orleans, C. T., and Shipley, R. H. Assessment in smoking cessation research: Some practical guidelines. In Keefe, F. J., and Blumenthal, J., eds. *Assessment Strategies in Behavioral Medicine.* New York: Grune and Stratton, 1982, 216–321.

Orleans, C. T., Shipley, R. H., Wilbur, C., Piserchia, P., Whitehurst, D. Wide-ranging improvements in employee health life-style and well-being accompanying smoking cessation

in the Live for Life program. Paper presented at the annual meeting of the Society of Behavioral Medicine, Baltimore, MD, 1983.

Orleans, C. T., George, L. K., Houpt, J. L., Brodie, H.K.H. Health promotion in primary care: A survey of U.S. family practitioners. *Prev Med* 14:636–647, 1985.

Orleans, C. T., Strecher, V. J., Schoenbach, V. J., Salmon, M. A., Blackmon, C. Smoking cessation initiatives for Black Americans: Recommendations for research and intervention. *Health Educ Res* 4:13–25, 1989.

Orleans, C. T., Rotberg, H., Quade, D., Lees, P. A hospital quit-smoking consult service: Clinical report and intervention guidelines. *Prev Med* 19:198–212, 1990.

Orleans, C. T., Rimer, B. K., Cristinzio, S., Keintz, M. K., Fleisher, L. A national survey of older smokers: Treatment needs of a growing population. *Health Psychol* 110:343–351, 1991.

Orleans, C. T., Schoenbach, V. J., Wagner, E., Quade, D., Salmon, M. A., Pearson, D. C., Fiedler, J., Porter, C. Q., Kaplan, B. H. Self-help quit smoking interventions: Effects of self-help materials, social support instructions and telephone counseling. *J Consult Clin Psychol* 59(3):439–448, 1991.

Orleans, C. T., and Hutchinson, D. Tailoring nicotine addiction treatments for chemical dependency patients. *J Subs Abuse Treat,* 10:197–208, 1993.

Orleans, C. T., Kristeller, J. L., Gritz, E. R. Helping hospitalized smokers quit: New directions for treatment and research. *J Consult Clin Psychol,* in press.

Ossip-Klein, D. J., Giovino, G. A., Megahed, N., Black, P. M., Emont, S. L., Stiggins, J., Shulman, E., Moore, L. Effects of a smokers' hotline: Results of a 10-county self-help trial. *J Consult Clin Psychol* 59(2):325–332, 1991.

Owen, N., Ewins, A. L., Lee, C. Smoking cessation by mail: A comparison of standard and personalized correspondence course formats. *Addict Behav* 14:355–363, 1989.

Pechacek, T. F., and Danaher, B. G. How and why people quit smoking: A cognitive–behavioral analysis. In Kendall, P. C., and Hollen, S. D. eds. *Cognitive–Behavioral Interventions: Theory Research and Practice.* New York: Academic Press, 1979.

Perez-Stable, E. J., Sabogal, F., Marin, G., Marin, B. V., Otero-Sabogal, R. Evaluation of "Guia para Dejar de Fumar," a self-help guide in Spanish to quit smoking. *Public Health Rep* 05:564–570, 1991.

Pilgrim, J. What we're doing to help people quit

smoking. *Smoke-Free Pharmacy* 2:2–4, 1990.

Pomerleau, C. S., Pomerleau, O. F., Majchrzak, M. J., Kloska, D., Malakuti, R. Relationship between nicotine tolerance and questionnaire scores and plasma cotinine. *Addict Behav* 15:73–81, 1990.

Prochaska, J. O. Assessing how people change. *Cancer* 67 (1 February suppl.):805–807, 1991.

Prochaska, J. O., and DiClemente, C. C. Stages and processes of self-change of smoking: Toward an integrative model of change. *J Consult Clin Psychol* 51:390–395, 1983.

Prochaska, J. O., DiClemente, C. C., Norcross, J. In search of how people change: Applications to addictive behavior. *Amer Psychol* 47:1102–1114, 1992.

Prochaska, J. O., DiClemente, C. C., Verdi, M., Grossman, A. *Understanding Yourself as a Smoker.* East Greenwich, RI: Mancini Press, 1987.

Prochaska, J. O., DiClemente, C. C., Velicer, W. Personalized computer-generated progress reports for smoking cessation. Unpublished paper, Kingston, RI, University of Rhode Island, 1988.

Prue, D. M., Davis, C. J., Martin, J. E., Moss, R. A. An investigation of a minimal contact brand fading program for smoking treatment. *Addict Behav* 8:307–310, 1983.

Rimer, B. K., Orleans, C. T., Keintz, M. K., Cristinzio, S., Fleisher, L. The older smoker: Status, challenges and opportunities for intervention. *Chest* 97:547–553, 1990.

Rimer, B. K., Orleans, C. T., Fleisher, L., Cristinzio, S., Telepchak, J., Keintz, M. K. Does tailoring matter? The impact of a tailored guide on ratings and short-term smoking-related outcomes for older smokers. *Health Educ Q,* in press.

Risser, N. L., and Belcher, D. W. Adding spirometry, carbon monoxide, and pulmonary symptom results to smoking cessation counseling: A randomized trial. *J Gen Intern Med* 5:16–22, 1990.

Robinson, R., Orleans, C. T., James, D., Sutton, C. *Pathways to Freedom: Winning the Fight Against Tobacco.* Philadelphia: Fox Chase Cancer Center, 1992.

Rossi, J. S. The hazards of sunlight: A report of the Consensus Development Conference on Sunlight, Ultraviolet Radiation and the Skin. *Health Psychologist* 11:2–3, 1989.

Royce, J. M., Gorin, S. S., Edelman, B., Rendino-Perrone, R., Orlandi, M. Student nurses and smoking cessation. In Engstrom, P., Rimer, B., Mortensen, L. E., eds. *Advances in Cancer Control: Screening and Prevention Research.* New York: Wiley-Liss, 1989, 49–72.

Russell, M. H., Wilson, C., Taylor, C., Baker, C. D. Effect of general practitioners' advice against smoking. *Br Med J* 2:231–235, 1979.

Schacter, S. Recidivism and self-cure of smoking and obesity. *Am Psychol* 37(4):436–444, 1982.

Schneider, S. J., Benya, A., Singer, H. Computerized direct mail to treat smokers who avoid treatment. *Comput Biomed Res* 17:409–418, 1984.

Schoenbach, V. J., Orleans, C. T., Wagner, E. H., Quade, D., Salmon, M.A.P., Porter, C. Characteristics of smokers who enroll and quit in self-help programs. *Health Educ Res,* 7:369–380, 1992.

Schwartz, J. L., and Dubitzky, M. Expressed willingness of smokers to try 10 smoking withdrawal methods. *Public Health Rep* 82(10):855–861, 1967.

Severson, H. H., Eakin, E. G., Stevens, V. J., Lichtenstein, E. Dental office practices for tobacco users: Independent practice and HMO clinics. *Am J Public Health* 80:1503–1505, 1990.

Severson, H. H., Stevens, V. J., Little, S. J., Lichtenstein, E. The teachable moment: Smokeless tobacco intervention in dental clinics. Paper presented at the Seventh World Conference on Tobacco and Health, Perth Australia, April 1990.

Sexton, M., and Hebel, J. A clinical trial of change in maternal smoking and its effect on birth weight. *JAMA* 251:911–935, 1984.

Shiffman, S. A relapse-prevention hotline. *Bulletin of the Society of Psychologists in Substance Abuse* 1:50–54, 1982.

Stevens, V. J., Glasgow, R. E., Lichtenstein, E., Hollis, J., Vogt, T. M. A Smoking intervention for hospital patients. *Medical Care* 31(1):65–72, 1993.

Stillman, F. A., Becker, D. M., Swank, R. T., Hantula, D., Moses, H., Glantz, S., Waranch, R. Ending smoking at the Johns Hopkins medical institutions. *JAMA* 264:1565–1569, 1990.

Strecher, V. J., Rimer, B., Monaco, K. Development of a new self-help guide—Freedom From Smoking For You And Your Family. *Health Educ Q* 1:101–112, 1989.

Taylor, C. B., Houston-Miller, N., Killen, J. D., DeBusk, R. F. Smoking cessation after acute myocardial infarction: Effects of a nurse-managed intervention. *Ann Intern Med* 113:118–123, 1990.

Tonnesen, P. Dose and nicotine dependence as determinants of nicotine gum efficacy. In

Pomerleau, O.F., and Pomerleau, C. S. eds. *Nicotine Replacement: A Critical Evaluation.* New York: Alan R. Liss, 1988, 129–144.

Tonnesen, P., Norregaard, J., Simonsen, K., Sawe, U. A double-blind trial of a 16-hour transdermal nicotine patch in smoking cessation. *N Engl J Med* 325:311–315, 1991.

Transdermal Nicotine Study Group. Transdermal nicotine for smoking cessation: Six-month results from two multicenter controlled clinical trials. *JAMA* 266:3133–3138, 1991.

United States Department of Health and Human Services (USDHHS). *Helping Smokers Quit: A Guide for the Pharmacist.* Washington, D.C.: National Cancer Institute. NIH Publication No. 84-655, 1984.

———. *The Health Consequences of Smoking: Nicotine Addiction. A Report of the Surgeon General.* United States Department of Health and Human Services, Public Health Service, Centers for Disease Control, Center for Health Promotion and Education, Office on Smoking and Health. DHHS Publication No. (CDC) 88-8406, 1988.

———. *The Health Consequences of Smoking: 25 Years of Progress.* United States Department of Health and Human Services, Public Health Service, Centers for Disease Control, Center for Health Promotion and Education, Office on Smoking and Health. DHHS Publication No. (CDC) 89-8411, 1989a.

———. *How You Can Help Patients Stop Smoking: Opportunities for Respiratory Care Practitioners.* Washington, D.C.: National Heart, Lung and Blood Institute. NIH Publication No. 89-2961, October 1989b.

———. *The Health Benefits of Smoking Cessation: A Report of the Surgeon General.* United States Department of Health and Human Services, Public Health Service, Centers for Disease Control, Center for Health Promotion and Education, Office on Smoking and Health. DHHS Publication No. (CDC) 90-8416, 1990a.

———. *Nurses: Help Your Patients Stop Smoking.* Washington, D.C.: National Heart, Lung and Blood Institute. NIH Publication No. 90-2962, October 1990b.

———. *Self-Guided Strategies for Smoking Cessation.* United States Department of Health and Human Services, Public Health Service, Centers for Disease Control. DHHS Publication No. 93-3104, 1990c.

———. *Smoking and Health: A National Status Report.* United States Department of Health and Human Services, Public Health Service, Center for Chronic Disease Prevention and Health Promotion, DHHS Publication No. (CDC) 87-8396, 1990d.

Williamson, D. F., Madans, J., Anda, R. F., Kleinman, J. C., Giovino, G. A., Byers, T. Smoking cessation and severity of weight gain in a national cohort. *N Engl J Med* 324:739–745, 1991.

Wilson, D., Wood, G., Johnston, N., Sicurella, J. Randomized clinical trial of supportive follow-up for cigarette smokers in a family practice. *CMA* 126:127–129, 1982.

Wilson, D. M., Taylor, D. W., Gilbert, J. R., Best, A. J., Lindsay, E. A., Willms, D. G., Singer, J. A randomized trial of a family physician intervention for smoking cessation. *JAMA* 260:1570–1574, 1988.

Windsor, R. A., Cutter, G., Morris, J., Reese, Y., Manzella, B., et al. The effectiveness of smoking cessation methods for smokers in public health maternity clinics: A randomized trial. *Am J Public Health* 75:1389–1392, 1985.

11

Formal Quit Smoking Treatments

HARRY A. LANDO

Smoking cessation treatments have evolved considerably over the 25 years since the release of the landmark 1964 Report of the Surgeon General on Smoking and Health (US Public Health Service 1964). It is well known that smokers prefer self-help and minimal-contact treatments over more intensive face-to-face or individual treatment programs (Schwartz 1987). However, formal treatment programs provide a critical backup to self-help and minimal-contact approaches. Formal treatments are more intensive; they offer structured assistance, important group and therapist support during the quitting phase, and the opportunity for individual counseling and program tailoring often not possible with self-help programs.

The stepped-care treatment model in Chapter 8 recommends that smokers be referred to increasingly more intensive or specialized treatments over repeated quit attempts. Referral to a formal treatment should be considered for smokers who have already tried repeatedly to quit on their own and lack confidence in repeated self-quit attempts, as well as for highly addicted, chronic heavy smokers who have tried minimal-contact or formal treatment programs in the past. Even on first quit attempts, however, smokers may prefer the additional help, support, and structure that a formal treatment can offer, especially if their social networks provide little support for quitting and/or include a majority of smokers. Smokers who seek formal treatments on their own may do so because they see themselves as less likely to succeed without outside help or with self-help approaches.

This chapter provides a detailed review of the variety of quit smoking programs and techniques currently available in the United States. Treatment methods are described and typical long-term results (quit rates) are presented. The chapter includes advice on how to evaluate a formal treatment program before making a referral. The emphasis is on state-of-the-art cognitive–behavioral treatments developed, evaluated, and refined over the past 25 years, since the release of the landmark 1964 Report of the Surgeon General on Smoking and Health. Widely available voluntary health organization and commercial clinics are given special attention. Quit smoking aids (filters, lozenges) are reviewed, and unproven treatments (hypnosis, acupuncture, adrenocorticotrophic hormone, or ACTH, injections) are considered briefly. Pharmacologic treatments are covered in Chapter 12. Treatments for other forms of nicotine dependence besides cigarette smoking are not covered. Although not yet extensively tested, pipe and cigar smokers may benefit from approaches similar to those developed for cigarette smokers. Smokeless tobacco treatments are reviewed in detail in Chapter 13.

HISTORICAL PERSPECTIVE

One of the earliest formal programs to assist smokers in quitting was initiated in the late 1950s by the Seventh Day Adventist Church. This program, referred to as the "Five-Day Plan to Stop Smoking" emphasized education about smoking health harms and a public pledge to quit, changes in diet and increases in physical activity, and a buddy system (updated Five-Day Plans are reviewed later in this chapter).

Programs offered during the 1960s tended to emphasize behavior modification strategies. Conditioning techniques, including the widespread use of aversion, were quite popular. Content of treatment was geared primarily to initial quitting, with relatively little emphasis on long-term maintenance. Results of these early programs tended to be disappointing, not surprising given the lack of attention to maintenance and relapse prevention (Bernstein 1969; Hunt and Bespalec 1974). In the 1970s emphasis shifted somewhat to include cognitive as well as behavioral treatment components. Programs became more complex and multifactorial. Increasing attention was given to techniques aimed at long-term maintenance.

In the 1980s emphasis was placed on developing effective relapse prevention strategies (Marlatt and Gordon 1985) and pharmacologic adjuncts to behavioral and cognitive approaches. At the same time, there was recognition that quitting smoking represented a process usually involving multiple quit attempts rather than a discrete act. Prochaska and DiClemente (1985) identified several stages in the quitting process including precontemplation, contemplation, action, and maintenance or relapse (see Chapters 4 and 8). These investigators argue that treatment must be responsive to smokers' readiness to change. Ongoing research is evaluating the effectiveness of relapse prevention strategies and the results of tailoring treatment to smokers' quitting stages.

Treatment outcomes have improved significantly since the late 1960s (Bernstein 1969; Schwartz 1987; USDHHS 1988). However, even with these improvements, the majority of smokers return to smoking within 1 year. Perhaps too much effort has been placed into treatment programs designed to produce permanent abstinence with a one-time intervention and not enough into programs designed to elicit renewed quit attempts in those who have returned to smoking (Schachter 1982; Cohen et al. 1989, Prochaska et al. 1992).

WHAT TO EXPECT FROM FORMAL TREATMENTS

Quit smoking treatments are generally evaluated on the basis of the long-term quit rates they produce. End-of-treatment quit rates and the impact of treatment on withdrawal reactions are important. But because 70% of smokers enrolled in formal treatment programs who quit have relapsed by the time of a 6–12 month follow-up (Hunt and Bespalec 1974), long-term (6- to 12-month) quit rates must be evaluated.

As is discussed later in this chapter, long-term quit rates are usually based on abstinence for at least 1 week prior to the follow-up date, though in some cases continuous abstinence (since the quit date) is assessed. Validation of self-reported quit status is required for the rigorous evaluation of any quit smoking treatment and may involve informant or biochemical verification methods (see later).

The majority of formal treatment programs produce 20–25% 1-year quit rates when subjected to an objective, rigorous evaluation (USDHHS 1989; Glasgow and Lichtenstein 1987; Schwartz 1987). It should not be surprising that outcomes are similar to those achieved by self-quitters—smokers who enroll in formal treatment programs may do so because they lack the motivations, skills, or supports that are needed to quit successfully on their own (see Chapter 8). However, some multicomponent treatments have produced 40–50% 1-year quit rates. As will be discussed in the final section of this chapter, programs claiming long-term quit rates of 40% or higher must be carefully scrutinized.

To date, no *single* treatment suitable for all smokers has emerged. Given the multiplicity of smoking determinants reviewed in Chapter 4—pharmacologic and conditioning, cognitive, psychological and social—it would be unrealistic to expect any single "magic bullet" solution to the smoking problem. Single component and single modality programs have *not* been found effective to promote abstinence over the long run. Multicomponent programs are required. As is discussed later, we hope to improve long-term quit rates from the best state-of-the-art multicomponent interventions through pharmacologic adjuncts, better matching of treatments to individual quitting needs, and improved relapse prevention strategies (Lichtenstein and Glasgow 1992).

BEHAVIORAL TREATMENT TECHNIQUES

Behavioral treatment approaches have been widely used for many years. In the 1960s smoking was viewed, along with many other behaviors, as essentially a learned activity. Conditioning principles were seen as extremely important in producing a habit that was resistant to elimination. Smoking was in fact regarded as highly *overlearned* behavior. It was noted that heavy smokers might have taken literally millions of puffs in association with numerous cues which might now elicit conditioned cravings for a cigarette.

Although smoking is now regarded as a function of both pharmacologic and psychologic determinants, behavioral aspects of smoking are still seen as critical. Behavioral treatment techniques are an essential part of any "state-of-the-art" treatment for nicotine addiction. Behavioral techniques are generally taught using such methods as verbal instruction, modeling of desired behaviors, behavioral rehearsal, feedback with respect to quality of performance, and coaching in specific coping skills. This chapter will review a number of behavioral approaches including (1) aversive counterconditioning techniques; (2) standard nonaversive behavioral and cognitive quit smoking techniques; and (3) multicomponent cognitive–behavioral treatments that combine several treatment methods. Additional detailed information on behavioral treatments is available elsewhere (Schwartz 1987; USDHHS 1988, 1989).

Aversive Procedures

Aversive procedures involve pairing smoking with unpleasant stimuli. The original purpose of aversion was to establish a negative conditioned response to cigarettes. It is unclear, however, that such a conditioned response is typically established through the use of aversive procedures. Aversive techniques may reduce the level of pleasure experienced from smoking or increase the level of unpleasantness on at least a short-term basis. These techniques may also be effective in increasing smokers' commitment to quitting by emphasizing unpleasant aspects of smoking.

Several types of aversive techniques have been used, including electric shock, rapid smoking, satiation (or oversmoking), and covert sensitization (a conditioning technique in which smoking is paired with unpleasant images rather than actual aversive events). As the following review shows, the most effective are those intrinsically linked with smoking (e.g., satiation, rapid smoking).

Electric Shock

A number of reports of use of electric shock appeared in the literature in the late 1960s and early 1970s. The rationale for use of electric shock generally follows from conditioned aversion. It is assumed that systematic pairing of aversive shock with smoking will cause smoking itself to become aversive. There is little evidence to support this assumption. Electric shock represents an artificial stimulus with no intrinsic relation to the act of smoking. Smokers can readily distinguish between laboratory conditions under which electric shock is administered and the natural environment in which shock administration is absent. Furthermore, use of electric shock actually can be counterproductive in that this stimulus tends to produce anxiety and therefore may increase subjective desire to smoke. Few reports of electric shock treatment have appeared in the literature in recent years, although this procedure remains in use in the commercial program offered by Schick.

Satiation

In this procedure subjects dramatically increase their cigarette consumption prior to attempting abstinence. Typically smokers are requested to double or even triple their usual smoking intake for a specified interval (e.g., 1 week). Early results with the satiation technique appeared quite promising (Resnick 1968). Unfortunately, replications of the satiation method generally produced disappointing outcomes (Claiborn, Lewis, Humble 1972; Lando 1975).

More recently, satiation has been incorporated into multicomponent treatment programs (Best, Owen, Trentadue 1978; Lando 1977). Lando and colleagues (Lando 1982; Lando and McGovern 1985) attempted to isolate the specific role of satiation in the context of multicomponent treatment methods. By itself, satiation produced disappointing 15% 1-year follow-up quit rates. When combined with other components in a multicomponent treatment, however, 1-year quit rates approached 50%. Although satiation appears to represent a plausible preparation strategy for quitting (Lando 1986), there is little evidence that this procedure leads to an aversion for cigarettes (Tiffany, Martin, Baker 1986).

Rapid Smoking

Rapid smoking, like satiation, uses cigarettes as their own aversive agent: smokers are instructed to greatly accelerate their rate of puffing on each cigarette. A typical procedure requires smokers to take a puff every 6 seconds for as long as they can tolerate rapid smoking (Lichtenstein et al. 1973). Variations of this procedure employ standardized rapid smoking trials (e.g., rapid smoking trials are limited to 3 minutes each; Lando 1975, 1977).

As with satiation, good early results were obtained with rapid smoking as the primary intervention technique. More recent results with rapid smoking alone have been variable. But results for this procedure in the context of multicomponent intervention have been encouraging. Studies have found that outcome is improved when rapid smoking is incorporated within the context of a warm client–therapist relationship and strategies to boost expectations of success (Hall, Sachs, Hall et al. 1984; Lichtenstein et al. 1973).

Overall, it appears that rapid smoking by itself has a substantial impact on immediate quit rates (Poole, Sanson-Fisher, German

1981). However, rapid smoking procedures fare best in producing good long-term quit rates when combined with nonaversive cognitive behavioral strategies.

Limitations of Standard Aversive Techniques

Despite some good outcomes with standard aversive techniques, these methods are less widely used at present than they were in the 1970s. Concerns about possible medical effects have been expressed, especially with respect to the potentially stressful rapid smoking technique. Horan and his colleagues (1977) found that rapid smoking produced increased heart rate, blood pressure, and carboxyhemoglobin levels as well as electrocardiographic abnormalities. Lichtenstein and Glasgow (1977) provided recommendations for screening and subject selection. Most researchers and clinicians exclude older adults and those with such conditions as hypertension, chronic obstructive pulmonary disease, and cardiovascular disease. Although rapid smoking has been used safely with cardiac and pulmonary patients under close medical supervision (Hall, Sachs, Hall et al. 1984), this has not been a common practice.

The unpleasantness of aversive procedures limits their appeal to smokers and program sponsors. Moreover, conservative practice dictates medical screening prior to electric shock, satiation or rapid smoking, which presents an additional burden and cost to program enrollees.

Reduced Aversion Techniques

Because of the limitations of standard aversive procedures, considerable effort has been devoted to establishing effective procedures that are less aversive and that do not require medical screening or supervision. Focused smoking is one alternative in which the patient smokes at a regulated but slower rate. Smoke holding techniques have required patients to hold cigarette smoke in the mouth and throat while breathing through the nose. These procedures are physiologically less stressful than satiation or rapid smoking and yet can produce a relatively high level of subjective discomfort. Research indicates that these reduced aversion techniques produce long-term outcomes comparable to, or only moderately lower than, those obtained with rapid smoking (Powell and McCann 1981; Tiffany, Martin, Baker 1986).

Nonaversive Cognitive–Behavioral Techniques

Nonaversive cognitive and behavioral techniques are widely used in current research and clinical practice. This section reviews nonaversive reinforcement and stimulus control procedures, self-management strategies, and training to shape behaviors to replace smoking and/or assist the quitter to cope with difficulties in abstaining. Specific techniques reviewed include contingency contracting, social support, stimulus control, relaxation training, coping skills, and nicotine fading. Although these approaches are described individually in this section, they are typically used in combination in multicomponent treatment programs.

Contingency Contracting

Contracted rewards and punishment have been used to bolster commitment to abstinence. Several studies have required participants to submit monetary deposits that are refunded contingent upon maintained abstinence. In an early study, Elliott and Tighe (1968) returned portions of an initial deposit in regular installments over a period of 16 weeks. Lando (1976) combined contracts with preparation for quitting. Subjects who maintained abstinence not only received their own deposits, but shared in any deposits forfeited by nonabstinent participants. As in most other studies, contracting improved short-term abstinence, but long-term results were disappointing.

The relatively small financial incentives used in most of these studies may have been inadequate to maintain commitment in the face of strong temptations to smoke. Combining contingency contracts with other intervention strategies in multicomponent programs appears more promising (Lando 1977). Even if contracts are not formally in-

corporated into treatment, results may be enhanced if participants are encouraged to reward themselves for progressively increasing periods of abstinence. Worksite and community competitions and contests are positive outgrowths of early work on contingency contracting (see Chapter 21).

To date no studies have been conducted assessing the effects of differential payments for treatment upon abstinence outcome. Providing treatment at no cost may lead to recruitment of less committed participants. Lando and colleagues offered the American Lung Association *Freedom from Smoking* as part of two separate studies. Participants were drawn from a similar population and the studies were conducted concurrently. One of these studies required a $35 treatment fee; clinics in the other study were free. One-year abstinence prevalence with the $35 fee was 31.5% as opposed to 24.8% for the free program. Although charging a modest fee may be useful in screening out less committed smokers, imposition of higher fees could preclude applicability of treatment to disadvantaged smokers.

Social Support

Although social support from friends and family is strongly related to successful outcomes in smoking cessation treatments, efforts to systematically enhance natural social support as part of treatment intervention generally have proven unsuccessful (Lichtenstein, Glasgow, Abrams 1986). Interventions which have been tested include support training and materials for friends and spouses of smokers and worksite buddy systems.

Perhaps these negative findings should not be surprising. It is extremely difficult in short-term intervention to change established interactions among family members or co-workers. Some treatment participants have a far greater portion of smokers in their social network than do others. These smokers may not be supportive of their behavior change. Still, most programs do, and probably should continue to, include guidelines for gathering social support from family, friends, and co-workers. One reason for triaging smokers into formal treatment programs is to provide them with support from a therapist or group members—particularly if their natural social environment provides little support.

Lando and colleagues (Etringer, Gregory, Lando 1984; Lando and McGovern 1991) have attempted to build social support into the treatment program itself by enhancing group cohesiveness. Although initial results were promising, a larger-scale replication failed to achieve significant effects in favor of an enhanced cohesion condition.

Ongoing social support has been incorporated into some self-help programs. One example is Smokers' Anonymous (also Nicotine Anonymous) which follows a 12-step approach based on that used for alcohol and other drug dependencies. Smokers' Anonymous is described in more detail in Chapter 15.

Stimulus Control and Cue Extinction

Chronic smokers have been exposed to a huge number of environmental cues in association with smoking (see Chapter 4). These cues come to serve as triggers to a smoking episode. The work of Abrams and colleagues (Abrams 1986; Abrams et al., in press) indicates that conditioned reactivity to smoking cues may be an important predictor of relapse. In theory, if some of the cues governing smoking can be weakened or extinguished, quitting should be facilitated. New cue extinction techniques appear to hold promise as preparation strategies for quitting (Orleans, Rimer, Fleisher et al. 1989).

Several studies have attempted to reduce the number of cues associated with smoking prior to abstinence. One strategy has been to gradually reduce smoking consumption by progressively restricting the types of situations in which smoking is permitted. A participant may smoke only at certain times and in certain locations (e.g., smoking might not be permitted during the first hour after awakening and might not be permitted in the car). Eventually smoking might be restricted only to a designated smoking chair at home (which may be in an unattractive lo-

cation such as an unfinished basement or a garage).

Another type of stimulus control strategy permits smoking only at set times (e.g., every hour on the half hour) regardless of the individual's desire to smoke (Shapiro et al. 1971). The LifeSign computer schedules smoking in this manner (see later). Theoretically, this procedure should weaken the association of smoking with internal and external cues except for time.

Stimulus control techniques when used in isolation have tended to produce weak results. Even when combined with other techniques in multicomponent programs, the effectiveness of stimulus control has either been disappointing or impossible to ascertain (Best, Owen, Trentadue 1978; Colletti, Supnick, Rizzo 1982).

Relaxation Training

Progressive relaxation has been employed as a treatment for smoking cessation, although rarely in isolation. A major rationale for the use of relaxation training is that smoking relapses are very likely to occur during negative emotional states (Brandon, Tiffany, Baker 1986; Shiffman 1982). Relaxation training allows an alternative response for coping with negative emotions or stressful situations and with the stress of quitting smoking and nicotine withdrawal effects. There is little evidence to support the efficacy of relaxation training by itself. Instead, relaxation is commonly incorporated into multicomponent treatment programs as only one of a number of behavioral and cognitive coping skills taught to participants.

Coping Skills and Behavioral Rehearsal

Several studies have investigated the efficacy of specific training in coping skills. These studies have indicated that individuals who actively cope with tempting situations are more successful in resisting slips. Shiffman's work has been especially influential in this area (e.g., Shiffman 1982). He has found that a combination of cognitive and behavioral coping responses provides maximum protection against smoking in a potential crisis situation. Behavioral coping responses include physical activity or exercise, relaxation, food consumption, leaving a tempting situation, and so forth. Cognitive coping strategies include mentally reviewing benefits of quitting or negative consequences of continued smoking and mentally rehearsing coping techniques for high-risk situations. Some former smokers simply tell themselves that smoking is not an option.

Hall and colleagues (Hall, Rugg, Tunstall et al. 1984; Hall et al. 1985) improved outcomes by incorporating specific training in coping skills into multicomponent treatment programs. However, in one of their studies, differences in favor of the coping skills conditions were evident only in lighter smokers (20 or fewer cigarettes/day). Although coping skills training has been effective in improving short-term outcomes, long-term benefits have been less apparent (Glasgow and Lichtenstein 1987). However, it is unclear from much of the research either that training has been effective in increasing coping skill proficiency or that participants continue to practice coping skills following the conclusion of treatment.

Behavioral rehearsal has been an important element of coping skills training. Participants identify both common smoking situations and situations in which temptations to smoke may be especially severe. They develop a repertoire of activities to replace smoking in these situations. Activities may include exercise, doodling, crossword puzzles, reading, hobbies, and more concrete substitutes such as gum, hard candy, or swizzle sticks. Self-management skill training is often included as well. Participants are instructed to reward themselves for periods of abstinence or for practicing nonsmoking skills. They may also learn cognitive strategies to resist urges, such as focusing on the negative aspects of smoking or the benefits of quitting.

Reduced Smoking and Nicotine Fading

Nicotine fading is a nonaversive preparation technique for quitting designed to address the pharmacological basis of smoking and addiction. This procedure is based on the logical premise that withdrawal discomfort might be ameliorated if nicotine consumption is progressively reduced prior to abstinence. This premise may appear to be in conflict with the results of gradual reduction or cigarette "tapering" procedures. Strategies that have emphasized cutting down the numbers of cigarettes smoked have been almost uniformly unsuccessful (Flaxman 1978). Smokers appear to reach a "stuck point," often at approximately 10–12 cigarettes per day, the number needed to maintain steady-state blood nicotine levels (Russell 1988). Attempts to reduce consumption further have led to substantial withdrawal effects that may persist considerably longer than would be the case for total abstinence. Most smokers who continue gradual reduction strategies beyond 10–12 cigarettes per day resume previous levels of consumption.

More promising have been procedures that have adopted gradual reduction strategies to a point (e.g., 50% of initial cigarette consumption) followed by abrupt cessation (Flaxman 1978). In nicotine fading, numbers of cigarettes typically are not reduced. Rather smokers switch in a series of progressive steps to cigarettes rated lower in tar and nicotine (Foxx and Brown 1979). Smokers using any reduction or fading technique must be cautioned that there is no "safe" smoking, and that these methods are recommended only as pre-*quitting* strategies.

Lando and his colleagues have incorporated nicotine fading into multicomponent treatment as a specific preparation strategy for quitting (Lando and McGovern 1985; Lando, McGovern, Sipfle 1989). The nicotine fading procedure was far more acceptable to participants than aversive smoking and did not require medical screening. Participants experienced a series of apparent successes in reducing nicotine intake prior to quitting. Following Nicki and associates (1984), these apparent successes translated into substantial increases in perceived self-efficacy to quit smoking. Self-efficacy is in turn an important predictor of successful outcome.

In fact, tar and nicotine ratings of cigarettes are obtained through the use of standardized smoking machines using a method approved by the Federal Trade Commission. These standardized machines may not approximate nicotine deliveries to human smokers. Smokers can compensate for reduced nicotine yields by altering their style of inhalation to take deeper, longer, and more frequent puffs and by covering the small air holes around the filter (Kozlowski et al. 1988). Although the "ultra-low" tar and nicotine cigarettes lead to reduced nicotine intake, nicotine reduction does not necessarily occur with cigarettes above this ultra-low category (Benowitz et al. 1983).

Until recently, there were few data on physiological effects of nicotine fading. In a laboratory study, West and colleagues (1984) documented substantial (64%) reductions in plasma nicotine among smokers who switched to brands with estimated nicotine yields 92% lower. These smokers experienced no significant withdrawal effects during nicotine fading. McGovern and Lando (1991) were the first to assess nicotine deliveries obtained during nicotine fading by participants in a smoking cessation clinic. Results indicated substantial reductions in nicotine (as measured by cotinine, a metabolite of nicotine), although considerably less than would have been expected from machine-derived yields of the cigarettes. Surprisingly, the biggest reduction in intake occurred during the first week of the nicotine fading procedure, prior to the assignment of ultra-low brands for the vast majority of subjects. Thus in clinical practice, nicotine fading does reduce actual nicotine intake. More research is needed to evaluate the impact of this technique on self-efficacy and on withdrawal severity after quitting.

Outcomes for nicotine fading have been mixed. The initial study of Foxx and Brown (1979) produced encouraging results (40% abstinence at 18-month follow-up), but these results were based on a very small number of subjects. Several other investigators have reported less favorable findings (Beaver, Brown, Lichtenstein 1981; Nicki, Remington, MacDonald 1984). Lando and McGovern (1985) incorporated nicotine fading into a standard multicomponent treatment program including 6 weeks of

maintenance following an assigned quit date (Lando 1982). Results were disappointing: 19% of subjects were abstinent at 1-year follow-up. But Lando (1987) obtained more positive outcomes in a second study combining nicotine fading and multicomponent treatment (35% abstinence at 1-year follow-up) in which subjects self-selected either nicotine fading or aversive smoking. And Lando and colleagues (1989) have obtained good outcomes with nicotine fading as part of a multicomponent intervention in community settings. Participants were given a choice of preparation strategy (satiation or nicotine fading). More than 80% elected nicotine fading. Results for nicotine fading have been comparable to those for satiation. Three- to five-year follow-up data indicate a stable quit rate of approximately 32%.

Burling, Lovett, and Frederiksen (1989) found that smoking behavior during nicotine fading treatment predicted outcome. Subjects who continued to smoke after the quit date or who relapsed immediately following treatment smoked significantly more cigarettes per day during the program than did abstainers. Unsuccessful participants also increased their cumulative puff duration as they switched to progressively lower tar and nicotine cigarettes, whereas cumulative puff duration did not change for successful participants. However, number of cigarettes per day and puff duration were related only to short-term and not to long-term success.

Multicomponent Treatment Programs

The most effective behavioral programs have encompassed multiple interventions. Attention has been devoted both to initial preparation for quitting and to longer-term maintenance. Specific training in nonsmoking and coping skills has commonly been incorporated into these programs. Many of the techniques described earlier are included, along with attention to life-style changes that support abstinence (e.g., exercise, prudent diet tips to prevent or limit weight gain).

The most effective multicomponent treatments have yielded long-term abstinence rates approaching 50% (Elliott and Denney 1978; Hall et al. 1985; Lando 1977; Tiffany, Martin, Baker 1986). This section reviews some of the most successful multicomponent intervention programs.

Lando (1977) compared a multicomponent intervention procedure (satiation, group support, contingency contracts) against a treatment limited to satiation. All subjects attended six sessions in small groups for 1 week prior to an assigned quit date. Those assigned to the multicomponent intervention also attended seven maintenance sessions over a 2-month period following the quit date. Results at 6-month follow-up were extremely encouraging: 76% abstinence for the multicomponent intervention and 35% for satiation. It should be noted, however, that these results were based on a total of only 17 subjects (two small groups) per condition.

Elliott and Denney (1978) developed a somewhat more structured method than that reported by Lando (1977). Their method incorporated a number of cognitive and behavioral techniques, including covert sensitization, rapid smoking, self-reward and punishment, applied relaxation, emotional role playing, systematic desensitization, behavioral rehearsal, and cognitive restructuring. Covert sensitization is an aversive imagery procedure. Participants imagined starting to smoke a cigarette in a particular setting, becoming nauseous and vomiting. In a subsequent relief scene, participants visualized themselves turning away from cigarettes and immediately starting to feel better. Behavioral rehearsal included substitute activities (e.g., rubbing two coins together) for combatting cravings and practice in refusing cigarettes in a variety of social situations. In cognitive restructuring, participants listed typical rationalizations for why it was difficult for them to quit. They were then taught to formulate counters to each rationalization and to use these when tempted to smoke.

Results favored this comprehensive intervention over either rapid smoking alone or two control conditions. The comprehensive procedure yielded 45% abstinence at 6-month follow-up as opposed to no more than 17% abstinence in any of the other three conditions (total n = 60).

Best, Owen, and Trentadue (1978) incorporated aversive smoking (satiation and rapid smoking) into the context of training in self-management skills. Emphasis was placed on identifying possible alternatives or coping strategies for anticipated problem situations. Recommended strategies included social support, contingency contracting, stimulus control, relaxation, and behavioral rehearsal. Overall 6-month abstinence (n = 60) was 47%.

Powell and McCann (1981) supplemented aversive smoking with lectures and self-management techniques. The stress of aversive smoking was reduced by prescribing rapid puffing without inhalation. Subjects were also instructed to hold their cigarettes in an awkward position. The unpleasantness of the procedure was enhanced by dipping cigarettes in a bitter-tasting solution, requiring subjects to use ashtrays that were full of cigarette butts, and showing slides of diseased organs. The contribution of maintenance to this intervention was unclear, however. No differences were found between either of two maintenance conditions (a 4-week support group, 4 weeks of assigned telephone calls between subjects) and a no-contact control. Overall results for the 51 subjects at 1-year follow-up exceeded 60% abstinence.

Ericksen and colleagues (1983) found that a combination of behavioral counseling and rapid smoking produced 70% abstinence at 1-year follow-up. A less aversive rapid puffing procedure in combination with behavioral counseling was considerably less successful as was behavioral counseling alone. However, these findings are considerably limited by the fact that a total of only 26 subjects participated in the study.

Hall, Rugg, Tunstall, and Jones (1984) examined the effectiveness of behavioral skills training and aversive smoking in a multicomponent treatment program. A total of 135 subjects entered the study and 123 completed treatment. The program included 14 sessions of which 8 involved aversive smoking and 6 were devoted to skills training in relapse prevention. Aversive smoking consisted of puffing on either a 6- or a 30-second schedule. Behavioral skills training included relapse prevention skills (e.g., rehearsal of common relapse situations), cue-produced relaxation (e.g., pairing a cue word such as calm with deep breathing and feelings of relaxation), and strengthening of commitment to abstinence. Results favored skills training over a discussion control. At 1 year, abstinence for the 6-second inhalation/skills training condition was 52% as compared to less than 40% in any of the other conditions. Differences between the 6- and 30-second aversive smoking procedures were not significant.

Tiffany, Martin, and Baker (1986) assessed several levels of aversive smoking together with variations in behavioral counseling. Aversive smoking consisted of either full-scale rapid smoking, truncated rapid smoking, or rapid puffing. Counseling consisted of either behavioral counseling (anticipation of potential problem situations, rehearsing of coping strategies) or discussion emphasizing support and encouragement rather than specific behavioral skills. A total of 82 subjects completed treatment. Results at 6-month follow-up supported the combination of behavioral counseling and either rapid smoking or rapid puffing (59 and 55% abstinence, respectively). Outcomes for procedures including reduced counseling or truncated rapid smoking were less encouraging (35% of subjects were abstinent at 6 months in each of these conditions).

Thus, a number of multicomponent treatments have achieved relatively high levels of long-term abstinence. Most of these positive results are based on biochemically confirmed self-report data. In reviewing the results of these studies, practitioners may be tempted to add additional elements to effective multicomponent programs. Yielding to this temptation is often a mistake, however (Lando 1981). More is not always better. Participants may be overwhelmed by treatment techniques that are too complex or that include excessive content. Furthermore, extensive didactic material may detract from the spontaneous group discussion that is very important to successful cohesive groups (Etringer et al. 1984; Lando and McGovern 1991). Lando (1984) has suggested

that a few key elements are responsible for the success of his clinic program: small group support, target date for quitting, and specific preparation techniques and coping strategies.

These core treatment components may be essential to success. These components must impart the motivations, skills, and supports for both quitting and maintenance (see Chapters 8, 10). The clinic facilitator is also likely to play a critical role. This person can dramatically affect individual adherence to recommended treatment procedures as well as the overall level of group support. Interestingly, it does not appear that the clinic leader must be a highly trained professional. Lando (1987) found that lay facilitators fared at least as well as advanced doctoral students in counseling psychology.

An important benefit of multicomponent treatments may be the ability of participants to tailor such treatments to their own needs. Participants may choose from a menu of options in selecting personally relevant coping strategies, for example. Anxious smokers may be more likely to benefit from relaxation training, addicted smokers may be more responsive to nicotine fading, and so forth. Studies assessing the benefits of individually tailored versus standardized treatments have been rare. Yet in some of the most successful multicomponent programs (e.g., Best et al. 1978; Lando, McGovern, Sipfle 1989), smokers have been encouraged to choose those techniques that are most personally relevant.

Relapse Prevention Strategies and Recycling

Maintenance or relapse prevention techniques are often included in multicomponent treatments. These components are intended to reduce relapse by extending treatment beyond the quit date and/or by providing specific coping skills to foster continued abstinence. In even the most successful multicomponent programs, the majority of participants relapse within 1 year of intervention. Unfortunately, maintenance treatments have not always significantly enhanced long-term outcomes (Lichtenstein and Glasgow 1992). Booster treatment ses-

sions, for example, generally have been ineffective, perhaps because they largely dupli-
cate the content of the original treatment
program or because they are sometimes
offered too late, that is, only after a
relapse.

Marlatt and Gordon (1985) proposed that
training in relapse prevention may be effective in sustaining higher levels of abstinence.
They noted similarities in relapse situations
across a number of behaviors including
smoking, alcohol consumption, overeating,
gambling, and use of narcotics, and suggested that an "absolute abstinence" model
might be counterproductive. If a single
"slip" is viewed as a relapse, this can create
a self-fulfilling prophecy. A predictable result of a slip is the "abstinence violation effect" which includes both feelings of guilt
and a loss of confidence in one's ability to
avoid further lapses that pave the way to a
full-blown relapse.

Instead of an absolute abstinence approach, Marlatt and Gordon have suggested
preparing the quitter to face temptations and
recover from slips, should they occur. Relapse prevention typically has included
training in identifying and coping with situations in which relapse is likely to occur and
confronting potentially self-defeating beliefs
and expectations about quitting (Curry et al.
1988). Slips are viewed as a natural part of
the learning process in quitting rather than
as precursors to renewed addiction.

Results for relapse prevention strategies
have been mixed, although as noted earlier,
coping skills training has improved outcome
(Hall, Rugg, Tunstall et al. 1984). Stevens
and Hollis (1989) assessed the effectiveness
of individually tailored relapse prevention
training on long-term abstinence. Subjects
(n = 744) who stopped smoking during an
intensive four-session cessation program
were randomly assigned to relapse prevention skills training, a nonspecific discussion
control, or to a control which received no
further treatment. Results favored relapse
prevention training over either of the control
conditions. One-year biochemically verified
sustained abstinence levels (no tobacco use
in the previous 6 *months*) were 41% for relapse prevention skills training, 34% for the
discussion control, and 33% for the no treat-

ment control. The relatively high quit rates
for the control conditions suggest that the
initial cessation procedure was itself a relatively powerful intervention.

Curry and colleagues (1988) compared a
traditional absolute abstinence program
against a relapse prevention treatment that
stressed gradual acquisition of nonsmoking
skills. Each approach was evaluated in both
a group and a self-help format (n = 139).
One-year verified abstinence rates indicated
no significant differences either for relapse
prevention versus absolute abstinence or for
group versus self-help. Outcomes for group
and self-help were very similar in the relapse
prevention condition (25 vs. 26% abstinence
for group and self-help procedures, respectively), whereas group participants were
more than twice as successful in the absolute
abstinence approach (38% abstinent vs. 17%
abstinent for self-help). Again, however, this
latter difference was not statistically significant.

Davis and Glaros (1986) evaluated the effectiveness of a multicomponent relapse prevention treatment based on the Marlatt and
Gordon model. All participants attended six
sessions which lasted from one and one-half
to two hours. One control group (n = 16)
was assigned a basic treatment package
which did not include consideration of specific high-risk situations. A second control (n
= 14) was assigned discussion of 11 high-
risk situations. The experimental group (n
= 15) underwent an active cognitive–behavioral skills training program designed to
prevent relapse. This group used the same
situations provided to the discussion control. However, in this case, participants were
given instruction, modeling, behavioral rehearsal, feedback, and coaching of coping
skills derived from responses of successful
exsmokers. Results failed to indicate significant differences in abstinence between treatment conditions. However, only subjects in
the experimental condition improved problem-solving and social skills needed to cope
with high-risk situations. These subjects
tended to take longer to relapse and to
smoke fewer cigarettes at the time of
relapse.

Overall results for relapse prevention
training are mixed. It is not clear that appli-

cation of a relapse prevention model significantly improves long-term abstinence, although some studies have found a correlation between competency on relapse prevention skills and length of time abstinent.

Surprisingly little attention has been paid to recycling of those who return to smoking (see the discussion of the stepped-care cyclical model in Chapter 10). This is especially puzzling when it is considered that even the most effective multicomponent treatment programs fail to achieve 50% long-term abstinence. Schachter (1982) in a provocative article observed that spontaneous recycling occurs for both smoking and obesity. Cohen and associates (1989) found the number of past quit attempts unrelated to outcome in several large-scale studies of minimally aided quitters. These authors agreed that quitting is a dynamic and continuing process, rather than a discrete event (Prochaska et al. 1992).

Little research has been done to assess the effect of further intervention on spontaneous recycling rates. Further intervention may be especially indicated for the increasingly hardcore smokers who enter intensive treatment programs. In assessing outcome data for several hundred of our clinic subjects, we found that 4.8% of individuals who reported smoking at 1-year follow-up were abstinent 1 year later. Although this is approximately twice the national average spontaneous quit rate for U.S. smokers, it does leave substantial room for improvement.

In a preliminary study, Lando and colleagues assessed the effectiveness of a telephone outreach campaign in smokers recruited from Bloomington, one of the education communities for the Minnesota Heart Health Program (Murray et al. 1986). This telephone campaign was based on encouraging results obtained for minimal telephone intervention by Orleans and colleagues (1988). Participants were randomly assigned either to receive one to two brief supportive telephone calls intended to elicit *renewed* quit attempts or to a nonintervention control. Although overall results significantly favored the telephone intervention,

of greatest interest was the subgroup (n = 447) of smokers who had previously participated in classes or contests offered as part of the Minnesota Heart Health Program. Based on self-reports, 13.2% of this subgroup assigned to telephone intervention were abstinent at 6-month follow-up compared to only 5.7% for the controls. Cotinine-validated 6-month abstinence rates were 9 and 2.1%, respectively. These preliminary findings indicate that even brief supportive telephone calls may improve rates of recycling among chronic smokers.

Other Treatment Strategies

Hypnosis

Hypnosis has been the most widely advertised of all commercial smoking cessation treatments, accounting for 31% of Yellow Pages listings for 1984–85 (Schwartz 1987). Although many hypnotists are very cautious in their claims, hypnosis is often seen by smokers as a "magic bullet" treatment.

Hypnosis is applied to increase participant motivation or commitment to smoking cessation. Posthypnotic suggestions often stress both the negative aspects of smoking and techniques of problem-solving. The suggestions formulated by Spiegel (1970) are common: (1) smoking is a poison to your body; (2) you need your body to live; and (3) you owe your body this respect and protection (Hyman et al. 1986). Unfortunately, most outcome studies fail to adequately describe treatment procedures, to include long-term follow-up, or to verify self-reported quit rates (Schwartz 1987). Better controlled studies have found no significant effects for posthypnotic suggestions when compared to suggestions without hypnosis (Javel 1980) or to either focused smoking or an attention placebo control condition (Hyman et al. 1986). Overall, hypnosis in isolation has not been demonstrated to be an effective treatment for nicotine dependency. It may be of value when combined with other procedures such as behavioral skills training, although it is not established that hypnosis per se is a key element of treatment. And, unfortunately, hypnotists are not required to be certified, and commercial programs vary enormously in focus and content.

Acupuncture

Acupuncture has gained in appeal as an intervention technique for smoking cessation and like hypnosis, often is viewed by smokers as a "magic bullet." Commercial treatment involves the use of needles or staplelike attachments most often administered to the ear. Most reports of acupuncture have not employed controlled evaluations: Many have failed to include long-term follow-up or biochemical validation of self-reported quitters (Schwartz 1987). Five of six studies that systematically compared the use of acupuncture at the "correct" site versus an "incorrect" or sham site for smoking cessation yielded negative results. Currently there is no scientific evidence for the efficacy of acupuncture either in relieving withdrawal symptoms or in aiding smoking cessation.

In evaluating techniques such as hypnosis and acupuncture, an additional concern should be noted. Smokers using ineffective methods, especially those they believe to be of proven efficacy, may be at greater risk of attributing failure to personal rather than treatment limitations. This in turn undermines self-efficacy for future quit attempts.

Pharmacologic Adjuncts

Pharmacologic adjuncts to treatment are discussed in detail in Chapter 12. Some multicomponent programs have systematically combined behavioral and pharmacologic treatment (e.g., Hall et al. 1985; Cooper and Clayton 1989). Unfortuntely, this is not true of the vast majority of interventions. Behavioral programs in the mid- to late 1980's included nicotine gum as an option, for example, but usually failed to provide essential information concerning appropriate use and limitations of the gum. Recent placebo-controlled studies combining transdermal nicotine with comprehensive cognitive-behavior treatments have in many cases doubled the quit rates achieved with cognitive-behavioral treatments alone (Fiore et al. 1992; Hughes

in press). Neither nicotine gum nor transdermal nicotine have shown benefits over placebo when used on their own; transdermal nicotine, but not nicotine gum, has shown benefit when used in concert with minimal-contact treatments (Fiore et al. 1992; Hughes, in press; Hughes et al. 1989).

The possibility of strengthening behavioral programs through the systematic use of pharmacologic agents appears much stronger today given the number and diversity of such agents currently under study. However, more systematic evaluations of pharmacologic adjuncts in combination with state-of-the-art cognitive–behavioral treatments are needed. Currently there is *no* evidence that drug treatments are effective on their own.

Voluntary Health Organizations and Commercial Clinics

Voluntary Health Organizations

The American Cancer Society and the American Lung Association have offered nonprofit smoking cessation clinics for a number of years and increasingly make use of standard cognitive behavior strategies. These clinics are typically available to the general public at a nominal fee.

The American Cancer Society FreshStart program consists of four, 1-hour group sessions. Sessions cover why people smoke and effects of smoking, methods of quitting, withdrawal symptoms and coping strategies, barriers to cessation, and suggestions for maintaining abstinence. Emphasis is placed on individualization of program content by the facilitator and eliciting the active involvement of group members. Participants are informed that smokers who take 2 weeks to quit smoking are as likely to be successful as are smokers who take 2 months to quit. Quitting is described as a two-part process: (1) stopping and (2) staying stopped. Unlike most clinic programs there is not a set target date for abstinence, although participants are strongly encouraged to quit cold turkey during the program.

The American Lung Association has developed a more extensive clinic program that also incorporates behavioral techniques. Smoking is viewed as a learned behavior and emphasis is placed on methods of unlearning the behavior. Healthy alternatives to smoking (or "positive addictions") are also presented. The clinics include a total of seven 90-minute to 2-hour sessions plus an initial orientation over a 7-week period. The first session provides an in-depth discussion of the general health effects of smoking. Emphasis is placed on the fact that participants can quit and that help and encouragement to do so are available in the clinic program. The second session introduces coping strategies for confronting urges to smoke. Quit Day occurs at the third session. A fourth session held 2 days later focuses on benefits of quitting and possible withdrawal symptoms. The remaining sessions stress maintenance and include recommendations for healthier more enjoyable nonsmoking life-styles. Discussion covers relaxation techniques, exercise or physical fitness programs, avoiding weight gain, and coping with tension. The final session is a celebration in which participants elect options such as a wine and cheese party. A modified American Lung Association clinic format is also available. This format, originally developed for worksite settings, includes 10 1-hour sessions.

Lando and colleagues (1990) undertook a comparative evaluation of the American Cancer Society and American Lung Association smoking clinics. Smokers (n = 1,041) in three Iowa communities were randomly assigned to American Cancer Society clinics, American Lung Association clinics, or to an intensive multicomponent cognitive–behavioral laboratory clinic derived from a systematic program of research. The laboratory clinic consisted of 16 sessions over a 9-week period. Techniques included nicotine fading, smoke-holding, target date for quitting, identification of alternatives to smoking, self-rewards for nonsmoking, and life-style changes conducive to maintained abstinence. Emphasis was also placed on informal group discussion and support (Lando 1982; Lando and McGovern 1985).

Results through 3-month follow-up favored the laboratory method over either of the voluntary organization clinics. At 6-month and 1-year follow-ups, differences between the laboratory program and the American Lung Association clinics were no longer significant. The American Cancer Society clinics fared least well at all follow-up intervals. One-year point prevalence abstinence rates were 28.5% for the laboratory method, 24.8% for the American Lung Association clinics, and 22.4% for the American Cancer Society clinics. Sustained abstinence rates were 22.2, 19.0, and 12.1% for the laboratory, American Lung Association, and American Cancer Society clinics, respectively.

The American Cancer Society FreshStart method fared less well than the others, but it is a considerably briefer program. The absence of a target date for quitting also may have detracted from its effectiveness.

The oldest of the nonprofit programs is the Five-Day Plan sponsored by the Seventh-Day Adventist Church (McFarland 1986). This program considers both physical and psychological aspects of cigarette dependence, but uses few cognitive–behavioral strategies. Over 14 million smokers in more than 150 countries are estimated to have entered Five-Day Plans. Treatment consists of five 90-minute to 2-hour sessions on consecutive days. In addition, several weekly follow-up meetings are available.

Participants are instructed to abstain at the outset. Emphasis is placed on consumption of healthy foods and considerable intake of liquids. Warm baths and hot and cold showers are strongly recommended. Scare tactics are typically used, including a film depicting surgery on a cancerous lung at the first session. Physical fitness is strongly advocated and participants are encouraged to maintain regular exercise programs. A "buddy system" is recommended in which participants draw support from another group member. Lectures are presented by clergy, physicians, and psychologists. Schlegel and Kunetsky (1977) reported strong immediate effects for the Five-Day-Plan (68% of participants reported abstinence 3 days after the last session). Longer-term effects were somewhat disappointing, however: 6-month abstinence was 11%. Other evaluations of the Five-Day-Plan have generally reported somewhat more positive findings. A review of 14 evaluations of the Five-Day-Plan that included 1-year follow-up indicated a median 1-year abstinence rate of 26% (Schwartz 1987). It should be noted, however, that these quit rates are based on unverified self-reports.

The Five-Day Plan has recently been revised and renamed. The new program, "The Breathe-Free Plan to Stop Smoking," includes eight sessions over a 3-week period. An increased emphasis is placed on motivation and life-style modification strategies, with specific attention to self-rewards (Schwartz 1987). In addition to formal sessions, participants receive supportive telephone calls 1 week, 3, 6, and 12 months after completion of the program. Outcome data on the revised program currently are not available.

Commercial Clinics

In addition to the programs offered by voluntary agencies and nonprofit organizations, a large number of commercial programs also are in place. Many of these programs operate in a single metropolitan area; a few are offered nationally. Schwartz (1987) compiled an informative review of listings of stop-smoking programs in the yellow pages of telephone directories in 47 U.S. cities of 300,000 or more population. He found that the number of listings for "Smokers' Information and Treatment Centers" increased from 112 in 1976–77 to 385 in 1984–85.

Perhaps the best known of the commercial programs is Smokenders which was established by Jacquelyn Rogers in 1969. Smokenders describes itself as an adult education program with the objective not only of producing smoking cessation but also of achieving enjoyment of a nonsmoking lifestyle. Smokenders currently includes a series of six weekly meetings of approximately 2 hours each. Sessions tend to be didactic. Content includes information with respect to addiction, effects of nicotine, and nature of the smoking habit. Group participation is encouraged. Participants are given assignments between sessions such as delaying lighting up or changing brands to increase awareness and to facilitate practice at ab-

staining. Sessions are supplemented by other materials, including written informational packets.

Smokenders *reports* extremely high success rates. Their literature indicates that among a random sample of 95,000 smokers who started the program, 81% successfully completed the program and stopped smoking. Their literature also states that of 4,000 "graduates" who recently responded to a survey, 84% indicated that they were still abstinent 12 months after completing treatment. Schwartz reported that the 4,000 graduates who responded to the survey represented only 16% of a random sample of 25,000 graduates who had been sent a follow-up questionnaire. He views this response rate as so low as to preclude any conclusions about the effectiveness of the Smokenders method.

Kanzler, Jaffe, and Zeidenberg (1976) published an evaluation of the Smokenders program. Records of 553 participants of the program in 1971 were assessed and 3½- to 4-year follow-up was attempted on the 385 (70%) who were not smoking at end of treatment. Only 167 were successfully contacted, and of these, 57% of the males and 30% of the females were abstinent. However, even if it is assumed that the smoking rates of those located at follow-up provide an accurate representation of the overall successful sample, the long-term success rates based on all participants (including treatment dropouts) is approximately 27%. Smokers seen in the early 1970s may have been significantly more responsive to treatment than the current smoker population.

The Schick Smoking Centers were established in 1971 and currently operate in only four states. The Schick program had been offered more widely, but centers in the eastern United States were closed due to lack of a response from the public. Smith (1988) published a follow-up study of a sample of 327 participants treated at Schick Centers during the year 1985. This sample was randomly selected from the total number of 832 participants treated in that year. The treatment program included 5 days of "countercondi-tioning" consisting of both a level of shock determined to be aversive to the individual participant and a rapid puffing technique.

Educational and counseling components were also presented both during the counter-conditioning phase of treatment and during a 6-week support phase. The support phase included six weekly support group sessions plus an additional counterconditioning treatment during the second week. Smith noted that participants are entitled to a refund of all treatment fees if they are unable to stop smoking by the end of the initial counterconditioning phase of treatment.

Follow-up telephone interviews were conducted by a professional research firm a minimum of 13 months (mean of 13.7 months) after program completion. Only those 91% who completed the initial 5 days of treatment without requesting a refund were included in follow-up. Of those participants contacted at follow-up, 52.0% claimed not to have smoked at all since "graduation." These results would be extremely impressive if based on all respondents and if some type of self-report validation were incorporated. However, this continuous quit rate is two to four times higher than those observed in carefully controlled, objective studies and therefore should be viewed with skepticism. Furthermore, the use of aversive electric shock and rapid puffing may limit the generalizability of the treatment. Rapid puffing, although not clearly described, may involve potential risk. Conservative practice would dictate that participants undergo medical screening before being assigned to these procedures.

Smokeless is the name of a proprietary multicomponent cognitive–behavioral program that licenses its smoking cessation programs to hospitals and corporations.[1] This program is currently being offered by more than 500 hospitals and 1,000 corporations nationwide. Behavioral nonsmoking skill development is covered in five consecutive 1-hour sessions or four consecutive 1½ hour sessions. Three additional relapse prevention sessions are held during a maintenance phase. Content of sessions includes stimulus control, relaxation training, stress management, positive rewards and reinforcements,

attitude change, dietary management, behavioral rehearsal (e.g., imagining desired nonsmoking behavior), cognitive coping strategies, and reduced aversion smoking.

A study by Powell and McCann (1981) provided an initial evaluation of the essential Smokeless method. This study showed very encouraging 12-month quit rates (63% overall) in a sample of 51 medically high-risk subjects. These results are based on unconfirmed self-reports. Powell and Arnold (1982) applied this method to 22 men, aged 42 to 61 years, also with elevated risk for coronary heart disease (CHD). Participants were drawn from the Multiple Risk Factor Intervention Trial (MRFIT), a 6-year project intended to reduce CHD mortality in men aged 35 to 57 years who were estimated to be in the upper 10% of risk for CHD. These individuals had failed to quit in 5 years of prior MRFIT intervention. At the end of treatment, 19 of the 22 men (86%) reported total smoking abstinence. Biochemically validated abstinence at 1-year follow-up was 50%. Despite the use of motivated high-risk smokers, the limited number of participants and the absence of a comparison condition, these results are quite encouraging.

Smoke Stoppers is a commercial program that is in many respects similar to Smokeless and was also designed by Don Powell.[2] The Powell and McCann (1981) study is cited by both Smoke Stoppers and Smokeless as evidence for the effectiveness of their methods. Smoke Stoppers has been offered at more than 250 hospitals and more than 200 companies. Like Smokeless, Smoke Stoppers licenses hospitals to use their method. The multicomponent cognitive–behavioral Smoke Stoppers treatment includes weight management, relaxation techniques, stress management, nutritional awareness, group support, and reduced aversion techniques. More recently, Smoke Stoppers has begun to incorporate nicotine replacement therapy (i.e., nicotine polacrilex gum) into treatment as an option.

Smoke Stoppers claims success rates av-

[1]Smokeless program. American Institute for Preventive Medicine, 24450 Evergreen Road, Suite 200, Southfield, MI 48075 (313) 352-7666.

[2]Smoke Stoppers program. The National Center for Health Promotion, 3920 Varsity Drive, Ann Arbor, MI 48108 1-800-843-6247.

eraging 51–53% at 1 year based on reports from their hospital affiliates. These reports are apparently unconfirmed by biochemical validation. Kramer (1982) in a published report obtained 1 year self-reported abstinence of 32% using the Smoke Stoppers method. Smoke Stoppers describes itself as "the most successful cessation intervention strategy in North America."

Other commercial programs have been marketed primarily through physicians. Nix-O-Tine Pharmaceuticals, for example, has developed a program described as a comprehensive treatment that addresses both physical and behavioral aspects of nicotine withdrawal. A key component of the intervention involves intramuscular injections of ACTH. In an article describing the use of ACTH injection in smoking cessation treatment, McElhaney (1989) cites an association between tobacco withdrawal and a rebound underproduction of cortisol. He noted a suggestive study in which ACTH injections led to significant relief of tobacco withdrawal symptoms (Bourne 1985). McElhaney stated that patients were provided with support to reinforce their motivation and to assist in long-term behavior modification. A single evaluation based on a 1-month follow-up of 15 patients indicated a 47% self-reported quit rate (McElhaney 1989). Despite the absence of any controlled evaluations, Nix-O-Tine appears to be marketing quite aggressively. Their materials place a good deal of emphasis on the profit-making potential for physicians who use their program of smoking cessation. The program includes an untested patient kit that contains a "behavioral modification" videotape, an audiotape, packages of vitamins, cytology testing materials, medical questionnaires, and "behavioral modification" aids.

In evaluating smoking cessation clinics and commercial programs, it can be concluded that the most successful clinics are those that incorporate multicomponent cognitive–behavioral techniques. There is no evidence that commercial clinics are any more effective than those offered by voluntary health organizations. However, commercial programs cost more and may therefore attract more motivated and/or advantaged smokers. Furthermore, a substantial clinic fee may provide an additional incentive for quitting.

Smoking Cessation Products and Aids

Although this chapter focuses on intensive smoking cessation treatments, it is appropriate to briefly review several smoking cessation products recommended for hardcore smokers. Several recent products include CigArrest, LifeSign, and Kick the Habit filters.

CigArrest was extensively advertised as a smoking cessation system. Included in the CigArrest package were 2 mg lobeline sulfate tablets or gums, vitamin pills, a motivational audiotape, and written instructions and suggestions for smoking cessation. CigArrest recently had been marketed as a temporary support for smokers undergoing nicotine withdrawal in circumstances where smoking was not allowed (e.g., plane trips). No published data were available on the effectiveness of this product. Similar lobeline sulfate tablets had been sold over the counter for a number of years under such trade names as Nikoban and Bantron. Lobeline is chemically similar to nicotine and was thought to provide a potential substitute. But controlled studies showed it to have no efficacy in alleviating withdrawal or promoting cessation (Hunt and Bespalec 1974; USDHHS 1988). In June 1993, the Food and Drug Administration therefore banned its sale as a cessation aid.

Silver acetate preparations are available under such trade names as Healthbreak or Tabmit. These preparations are supposed to produce a distinctly unpleasant taste when combined with cigarettes. Such preparations are analogous to the use of disulfiram (Antabuse) with alcoholics. There is little published research on silver acetate products. At this point there is no evidence that such preparations can aid cessation (Malcolm et al. 1986).

Nicotine reduction filters were sold widely in the 1970s and remain available today. These filters were intended to allow smokers to progressively reduce their nicotine intake in preparation for quitting. Early results for filters were mixed. Miller (1980) reported that only 3% of a sample of purchasers (n = 67) of One Step at a Time (Waterpik) or other similar products had stopped smoking within a month or two of their scheduled quit dates. Hymowitz, Lasser, and Safirstein (1982) were somewhat more encouraging, at least as far as absolute abstinence levels. In a controlled study, 130 subjects were randomly assigned to graduated filters, placebo filters, or self-quitting. Self-reported abstinence results at 1-year follow-up were 22% for graduated filters and 12% for placebo filters. However, 33% of those attempting cessation on their own were abstinent at 1 year.

A new generation of filters has recently been marketed (e.g., Kick the Habit, Vipont Pharmaceuticals). These filberts have been redesigned to reduce the likelihood and extent of compensatory increases in nicotine intake. Furthermore, the preparation period for quitting has been reduced from 8 to 3 weeks to minimize continuing dependency on the filters. Behavioral coping strategies and suggestions have been incorporated with the filters in an effort to develop a more complete smoking cessation system. It is unlikely that the filters used alone would be an effective aid to quitting. McGovern and Lando (1991) assessed nicotine intake in smokers (n = 110) assigned either to nicotine fading or to the nicotine reduction filters in preparation for quitting. Substantial reductions in nicotine intake did occur as reflected in reduced cotinine levels. Cotinine reductions with the final type III reduction filters exceeded 50%. However, significant compensation also appears to have taken place. The machine rated yields of the type III filters would have led to nicotine reductions of approximately 80%.

Another aid to cessation that has been widely marketed is LifeSign, a small credit card-sized computer unit that signals smokers when to smoke. The computer is programmed to consider individual smoking patterns in leading to progressive reduction in number of cigarettes. LifeSign includes a treatment manual presenting cognitive–behavioral treatment techniques such as stimulus control, self-monitoring, and reinforcement. An instructional video is also included. In addition to reductions in cigarette intake, LifeSign can lead to disassociation of smoking episodes from normal environmental cues. This may be useful in weakening some of the habitual aspects of smoking, although there is little research evidence to support this point. It is unclear that the use of the computer is superior to simply establishing a schedule of progressively increased intervals without cigarettes.

A pilot assessment of two cohorts totaling 77 smokers yielded an overall 1-year abstinence rate of 21% (Prue et al., in press). Self-reported abstinence was validated by carbon monoxide assessment. These subjects may not have been fully representative of those quitting on their own, however. Smokers in the first cohort were seen weekly in individual assessment sessions until they completed the program. Although smokers in the second cohort completed the program essentially on their own with minimal supervision, they were drawn from participants in formal intervention programs in worksites and a community smoking cessation clinic. A second unpublished study (n = 71) evaluated the LifeSign procedure in both a self-administered and therapist assisted format. A wait list control group was also included. A $100 refundable deposit was required for participation in the study, undoubtedly attracting more highly motivated or advantaged smokers. The wait list control was followed for 3 months and then offered treatment. As might be expected for a wait list-delayed treatment condition, none of those assigned to the wait list control were abstinent at 1-week posttreatment. Subjects in the therapist-assisted condition met weekly with a therapist for 60- to 90-minute sessions over a 6-week period. Subjects in the self-administered format attended weekly assessment sessions over a 6-week period during which they met with a research assistant to complete questionnaires and to provide carbon monoxide samples. Results at 18-month follow-up, validated by carbon monoxide assessment or telephone contact with significant others, indicated 36% abstinence for the therapist-assisted condition and 24% abstinence for the self-administered condition. Continuous abstinence rates in these two treatments were 22 and 12%, respectively. These differences were not significant. Again it is unclear that the self-administered condition was truly representative of those quitting on their own given the amount of time spent in weekly assessment meetings. At this point there are no data indicating that the computer adds to the effectiveness of the core behavioral program.

Inpatient Treatment Programs

Inpatient treatment is sometimes available to smokers on chemical dependency units. The trend to include services to smokers as part of inpatient chemical dependency treatment accelerated once nicotine was defined as an addicting drug (USDHHS 1988). Inpatient smoking cessation treatments offered as part of chemical dependency services are described in more detail in Chapter 18.

A few inpatient programs have operated independently of chemical dependency programs. Unfortunately, published data on the effectiveness of these methods is difficult to locate. One of the oldest of these programs is offered at the St. Helena Hospital Health Center in Deer Park, California. This program is affiliated with the Seventh Day Adventist Church. The St. Helena 7-day program includes general health education emphasizing improved overall life-style. Individualized medical assessment and counseling are also incorporated. Consistent with the Seventh Day Adventist philosophy, the diet is vegetarian and treatment includes physical therapy, exercise, relaxation training, and nutritional advice. Supportive newsletters are mailed to participants following the conclusion of treatment and follow-up staff telephone support is available. A similar 5-day residential treatment program is offered by the Portland Adventist Medical Center. This program is conducted under the supervision of physicians, health educators, and other health professionals. Stress management sessions, coronary risk screening, computerized health appraisal, and weight control instruction are included along with smoking cessation techniques.

Controlled evaluations of other types of intensive treatments, such as extended individual treatment sessions (by psychologists,

psychiatrists, health educators, or other trained smoking cessation personnel) have not appeared in the literature. Likewise, though tailoring of treatment programs to individual needs has often been recommended, there is very limited evidence on the effectiveness of individual tailoring in improving treatment outcomes. More research is needed to evaluate a range of individualized treatment options.

Referral Resources

It is increasingly important that health professionals be informed consumers of smoking cessation services and products. Health professionals should also be aware of the types of smoking cessation programs that exist in their communities. An excellent guide to programs entitled *State and Local Programs on Smoking and Health* is available from the Office on Smoking and Health.[3] The most recent edition was published in 1988. Unfortunately, this guide is no longer being published. Current plans are to provide a database listing smoking cessation programs through the Association of State and Territorial Health Officials.[4] The Cancer Information Service (1-800-4-CANCER) in your area will provide referrals to reputable treatments. Local voluntary organizations (the American Lung Association, the American Cancer Society) will provide information about the many programs they offer. State and county health departments also may be a useful source of information. Unfortunately, information from the Office on Smoking and Health does not include objective evaluation of programs included in their directory. Objective evaluations also may be unavailable from voluntary organizations, which may be unaware of outcome data for a particular approach or which may have a vested interest in promoting their own programs.

There has been a rapid increase in the number and variety of formal treatment programs available for addicted smokers.

[3]Office on Smoking and Health, Center for Disease Control, 1600 Clifton Road, N.E., Atlanta, GA 30333. (404) 488-5701.
[4]Association of State and Territorial Health Officials, Washington, D.C. (202) 467-5085.

State-of-the-art multicomponent treatments are available in many communities, especially in larger cities, through both voluntary and commercial providers. Such treatments are often offered through hospitals, especially major medical centers.

Evaluation Standards

Standards for the evaluation of smoking cessation programs have been recommended by several advisory groups (Shumaker and Grunberg 1986). Although there is some inconsistency in exactly how treatment success is defined, the accepted outcome criterion is long-term abstinence rather than reduced smoking. Treatment evaluations should be based on a *minimum* of 6-month and preferably 12-month follow-up. Current smoking status (point prevalence) should be based on at least a 7-day interval. It is also useful to report on the entire follow-up period. Sustained abstinence is a somewhat flexible criterion which distinguishes between slips and relapse (Lando 1989; Shumaker and Grunberg 1986). Participants may have smoked during follow-up and still be classified as abstinent. Continuous abstinence is a more rigid standard in which the requirement for success is complete continuous abstention from all forms of tobacco throughout follow-up.

Even when stringent evaluation criteria are rigorously applied, self-reports from participants are likely to overestimate actual abstinence, perhaps by a substantial amount. The main purpose in using biochemical measures is validation of self-reports. The most commonly used biochemical measures have included carboxyhemoglobin estimates from breath samples and assessment of thiocyanate in plasma, saliva, or urine and of cotinine in serum and saliva (Lando 1989; USDHHS 1988). Cotinine in particular has been shown to have excellent sensitivity and specificity in discriminating smokers from nonsmokers. However, the alveolar carbon monoxide measure, as estimated in breath samples, may be more practical for most clinical purposes. This measure is inexpensive and easily administered and provides immediate feedback to participants who may respond very positively to objective indications of reduced smoke exposure.

Products and programs that make claims of effectiveness should include biochemical assessment of abstinence among at least a portion of their self-reported abstainers. Informant validation represents another, although less satisfactory, alternative. Individuals who know the smoker can be queried about the smoker's smoking status. Unfortunately, there is no guarantee that informants will be accurate or honest in their reporting. Biochemical assessment or informant validation is done only rarely. The cost of validating self-reports is not prohibitive especially when carbon monoxide is used and when the technique is applied to random samples of abstainers. A program such as that offered by the American Lung Association, the American Cancer Society, or one of the major commercial providers is likely to enroll thousands of participants each year. Assume, for example, a total of 4,000 smokers in treatment of whom 1,600 report abstinence at 1-year follow-up. In this case, a random sample of 160 claimed abstainers (10% of the total) should be quite adequate to allow calculation of a confirmed quit rate for all treatment participants.

The consumer of smoking cessation products and services must be especially vigilant in evaluating claims of effectiveness. The major providers may not deliberately distort their outcome data, but they may present very misleading data. Although the generally accepted outcome criterion is abstinence at 1-year follow-up, some programs publicize end-of-treatment success, which is seldom more than a few days or weeks after an assigned quit date. End-of-treatment results might indicate 60% abstinence, whereas 1-year outcome figures might be as low as 5–10%.

Participant attrition can also dramatically affect reported outcome (Glasgow and Lichtenstein 1987). Too many programs inflate their outcomes by failing to count nonrespondents to follow-up. Assume, for example, that a program attracts 100 individuals of whom 50 complete the treatment, 30 respond to the follow-up, and 20 report abstinence. Reported cessation outcomes based on these results could range from 20 to 67%.

Research specialists who deal with smoking cessation programs would recognize 20% as the appropriate outcome figure because the vast majority of nonrespondents are likely to be recidivists who do not wish to report their failure. This may be especially true for evaluations of formal treatment programs that involve face-to-face contact with a therapist or facilitator.

Consumers should be especially skeptical in evaluating treatment programs that claim 1-year abstinence appreciably higher than 40%. It is important to determine on what number and percentage of participants outcome figures are based. Are these participants representative of all those who enrolled in treatment? Are dropouts included or excluded from the reported outcome figures? Has biochemical validation been used in confirming self-reported abstinence rates? Are "successes" those who report abstinence 1 year after treatment, 1 month, 1 day? Is it necessary to be continuously abstinent to be counted as a success? If so, for how long?

Thus in summary, an informed skepticism is very important in evaluating formal quit smoking treatment programs. Claimed cure rates should be supported by all of the following: (1) biochemical validation, (2) at least 6 months and preferably a 1-year follow-up period in evaluating success and inclusion of all participants (not just treatment completers) in calculating outcome, (3) counting of dropouts and those who cannot be reached at follow-up as treatment failures.

CONCLUSION

Formal quit smoking treatments have made remarkable progress in the past 25 years. Many of the best programs are based on and profit from extensive laboratory research. Biochemical measures are available to validate self-reported abstinence. Multicomponent treatments sometimes yield 40% long-term abstinence rates in hardcore smokers undertaking a single quit attempt. As concluded in the 1988 Report of the Surgeon General (USDHHS 1988), tobacco dependence can be successfully treated.

Health professionals must continue to recognize, however, that smoking cessation can be quite difficult for many individuals. They should encourage smokers who encounter relapses to keep trying to quit. Although the prospects for any single quit attempt sometimes appear discouraging, those who do initiate repeated attempts have an excellent chance of ultimately being successful. The combination of personal interest and concern, advice and counseling from the health professional, and intelligent referrals to appropriate products and programs can be extremely powerful. Health professionals can play a vital role in encouraging smoking cessation for their patients, thereby enabling them to live longer and healthier lives.

REFERENCES

Abrams, D. B. Roles of psychosocial stress, smoking cues and coping in smoking-relapse prevention. *Health Psychol* 5(suppl):91–92, 1986.

Abrams, D., Monti, P., Carey, K., Pinto, P., Jacobus, S. Reactivity to smoking cues and relapse: Two studies of discriminator validity. *Behav Res Ther,* in press.

Beaver, C., Brown, R. A., Lichtenstein, E. Effects of monitored nicotine fading and anxiety management training on smoking reduction. *Addict Behav* 6(4):301–305, 1981.

Benowitz, N. L., Hall, S. M., Herning, R. I., Jacob, P., III, Jones, R. T., Osman, A. L. Smokers of low-yield cigarettes do not consume less nicotine. *N Engl J Med* 309(3):129–142, 1983.

Bernstein, D. A. Modification of smoking behavior: An evaluative review. *Psychol Bull* 71(6):418–440, 1969.

Best, J. A., Owen, L. E., Trentadue, L. Comparison of satiation and rapid smoking in self-managed smoking cessation. *Addict Behav* 3(2):71–78, 1978.

Bourne, S. Treatment of cigarette smoking with short-term high-dosage corticotropin therapy: Preliminary communication. *J Royal Soc Med* 78:649–650, 1985.

Brandon, T. H., Tiffany, S. T., Baker, T. B. The process of smoking relapse. In Tims, F. M., and Leukefeld, C. G., eds. *Relapse and Recovery in Drug Abuse.* NIDA Research Monograph 72. U.S. Department of Health and Human Services, Public Health Service, Alcohol, Drug Abuse, and Mental Health Administration, National Institute on Drug Abuse. DHHS Publication No. (ADM) 86-1473, 1986.

Burling, T. A., Lovett, S. B., Frederiksen, L. W. Can across-treatment changes in cumulative puff duration predict treatment outcome during nicotine fading? *Addict Behav* 14:75–82, 1989.

Claiborn, F., Lewis, P., Humble, S. Stimulus satiation and smoking: A revisit. *J Clin Psychol* 28(7):416–419, 1972.

Cohen, S., Lichtenstein, E., Prochaska, J. O., Rossi, J. S., Gritz, E. R., Carr, C. R., Orleans, C. T., Schoenbach, V. J., Biener, L., Abrams, D., DiClemente, C., Curry, S., Marlatt, G. A., Cummings, K. M., Emont, S. L., Giovino, G., Ossip-Klein, D. Debunking myths about self-quitting. *Am Psychologist* 44(11):1355–1365, 1989.

Colletti, G., Supnick, J. A., Rizzo, A. A. Long-term follow-up (3–4 years) of treatment for smoking reduction. *Addict Behav* 7(4):429–433, 1982.

Cooper, T. M., and Clayton, R. R. Stop-smoking program using nicotine reduction therapy and behavior modification for heavy smokers. *J Am Dent Assoc* 118:47–51, 1989.

Curry, S. J., Marlatt, G. A., Gordon, J., Baer, J. S. A comparison of alternative theoretical approaches to smoking cessation and relapse. *Health Psychol* 7(6):545–556, 1988.

Davis, J. R., and Glaros, A. G. Relapse prevention and smoking cessation. *Addict Behav* 11:105–114, 1986.

Elliott, C. H., and Denney, D. R. A multiple-component treatment approach to smoking reduction. *J Consult Clin Psychol* 46(6):1330–1339, 1978.

Elliott, R., and Tighe, T. Breaking the cigarette habit: Effects of a technique involving threatened loss of money. *Psychological Record* 18:503–513, 1968.

Ericksen, L. M., Tiffany, S. T., Martin, E. M., Baker, T. B. Aversive smoking therapies: A conditioning analysis of therapeutic effectiveness. *Behav Res Ther* 21(6):595–611, 1983.

Etringer, B. D., Gregory, V. R., Lando, H. A. The influence of group cohesion on the behavioral treatment of smoking. *J Consult Clin Psychol* 52(6):1080–1086, 1984.

Fiore, M. C., Jorenby, D. E., Baker, T. B., Kenford, S. Tobacco dependence and the nicotine patch: Clinical guidelines for effective use. *JAMA* 268:2687–2694, 1992.

Flaxman, J. Quitting smoking now or later: Gradual, abrupt, immediate, and delayed quitting. *Behav Res Ther* 9:260–270, 1978.

Foxx, R. M., and Brown, R. A. A nicotine fading and self-monitoring program to produce cigarette abstinence or controlled smoking. *J Appl Behav Anal* 12(1):111–125, 1979.

Glasgow, R. E., and Lichtenstein, E. Long-term effects of behavioral smoking cessation interventions. *Behav Res Ther* 18:297–324, 1987.

Hall, R. G., Sachs, D.P.L., Hall, S. M., Benowitz, N. L. Two-year efficacy and safety of rapid smoking therapy in patients with cardiac and pulmonary disease. *J Consult Clin Psychol* 52(4):574–581, 1984.

Hall, S. M., Rugg, D., Tunstall, C., Jones, R. T. Preventing relapse to cigarette smoking by behavioral skill training. *J Consult Clin Psychol* 52(3):372–382, 1984.

Hall, S. M., Tunstall, C., Rugg, D., Jones, R. T., Benowitz, N. Nicotine gum and behavioral treatment in smoking cessation. *J Consult Clin Psychol* 53(2):256–258, 1985.

Horan, J. J., Hackett, G., Nicholas, W. C., Linberg, S. E., Stone, C. I., Lukaski, H. C. Rapid smoking: A cautionary note. *J Consult Clin Psychol* 45(3):341–343, 1977.

Hughes, J. R. Pharmacotherapy for smoking cessation: Unvalidated assumptions, anomalies, and suggestions for future research. *J Consult Clin Psychol*, in press.

Hughes, J. R., Gust, S. W., Keenan, R. M., Fenwick, J. W., Healey, M. L. Nicotine vs. placebo gum in general medical practice. *JAMA* 261:1300–1305, 1989.

Hunt, W. A., and Bespalec, D. A. An evaluation of current methods of modifying smoking behavior. *J Clin Psychol* 30(4):431–438, October 1974.

Hyman, G. J., Stanley, R. D., Burrows, G. D., Horne, D. J. Treatment effectiveness of hypnosis and behavior therapy in smoking cessation: A methodological refinement. *Addict Behav* 11:355–365, 1986.

Hymowitz, N., Lasser, N. L., Safirstein, B. H. Effects of graduated external filters on smoking cessation. *Prev Med* 11:85–95, 1982.

Javel, A. F. One-session hypnotherapy for smoking: A controlled study. *Psychol Rep* 46(pt. 1):895–899, 1980.

Kanzler, M., Jaffc, J. H., Zeidenberg, P. Long- and short-term effectiveness of a large-scale proprietary smoking cessation program—a four-year follow-up of Smokenders participants. *J Clin Psychol* 32(3):661–669, July 1976.

Kozlowski, L. T., Pope, M. A., Lux, J. E. Prevalence of the misuse of ultra-low tar cigarettes by blocking filter vents. *Am J Public Health* 78(6):694–695, 1988.

Kramer, J. F. A one-year follow-up of participants in a smoke stoppers program. *Patient*

Counselling and Health Education 4(2):89–94, 1982.

Lando, H. A. A comparison of excessive and rapid smoking in the modification of chronic smoking behavior. *J Consult Clin Psychol* 43(3)350–355, 1975.

———. Aversive conditioning and contingency management in the treatment of smoking. *J Consult Clin Psychol* 44:312, 1976.

———. Successful treatment of smokers with a broad-spectrum behavioral approach. *J Consult Clin Psychol* 45:361–366, 1977.

———. Toward effective long-term strategies in the maintenance of nonsmoking. *Behav Res Ther* 9:666–668, 1978.

———. Effects of preparation, experimenter contact, and a maintained reduction alternative on a broad-spectrum program for eliminating smoking. *Addict Behav* 6:123–133, 1981.

———. A factorial analysis of preparation, aversion, and maintenance in the elimination of smoking. *Addict Behav* 7:143–154, 1982a.

———. A revised manual for a broad-spectrum behavioral approach to cigarette smoking. *Catalog of Selected Documents in Psychology* 12:22–23, 1982b.

———. Treatment and prevention of smoking. In Keller, P. A., ed. *Innovations in Clinical Practice,* vol. 3. Sarasota, FL: Professional Resource Exchange, 1984.

———. Long-term modification of chronic smoking behavior: A paradigmatic approach. *Bulletin of Society of Psychologists in Addictive Behaviors* 5:5–17, 1986.

———. Lay facilitators as effective smoking cessation counselors. *Addict Behav* 12:69–72, 1987.

Lando, H., and McGovern, P. Nicotine fading as a nonrisky alternative in a broad-spectrum treatment for eliminating smoking. *Addict Behav* 10:153–161, 1985.

Lando, H., McGovern, P., Sipfle, C. Public service application of an effective clinic approach to smoking cessation. *Health Educ Res* 4:103–109, 1989.

Lando, H., McGovern, P., Barrios, F., Etringer, B. Comparative evaluation of American Cancer Society and American Lung Association smoking cessation clinics. *Am J Public Health* 80:554–559, 1990.

Lando, H., and McGovern, P. The influence of group cohesion on the behavioral treatment of smoking: A failure to replicate. *Addict Behav* 16:111–121, 1991.

Lichtenstein, E., Harris, D. E., Birchler, G. R., Wahl, J. M., Schmahl, D. P. Comparison of rapid smoking, warm, smoky air, and attention placebo in the modification of smoking behavior. *J Consult Clin Psychol* 40(1):92–98, 1973.

Lichtenstein, E., and Glasgow, R. E. Rapid smoking: Side effects and safeguards. *J Consult Clin Psychol* 45(5):815–821, 1977.

Lichtenstein, E. and Glasgow, R. E. Smoking cessation: What have we learned over the past decade? *J Consult Clin Psychol* 60:518–527, 1992.

Lichtenstein, E., Glasgow, R. E., Abrams, D. B. Social support in smoking cessation: In search of effective interventions. *Behav Res Ther* 17:607–619, 1986.

McElhaney, J. L. Repository corticotropin injection as an adjunct to smoking cessation during the initial nicotine withdrawal period: Results from a family practice clinic. *Clin Ther* 11:854–860, 1989.

McFarland, M. I. When five became twenty-five. A silver anniversary of the five-day plan to stop smoking. *Adventist Heritage* 11(1):57–64, 1986.

McGovern, P. G., and Lando, H. A. Reduced nicotine exposure and abstinence outcome in two nicotine fading methods. *Addict Behav* 16:11–20, 1991.

Malcolm, R., Currey, H.S., Mitchell, M. A., Keil, J. E. Silver acetate gum as a deterrent to smoking. *Chest* 90(1):107–111, 1986.

Marlatt, G. A., and Gordon, J. R., eds. *Relapse Prevention. Maintenance Strategies in the Treatment of Addictive Behaviors.* New York: Guilford Press, 1985.

Miller, G. H. Devices to help smokers stop don't. *Am Pharm* 11:669, 1980.

Murray, D. M., Luepker, R. V., Pirie, P. L., Grimm, R. H., Bloom, E., Davis, M. A., Blackburn, H. Systematic risk factor screening and education: A community-wide approach to prevention of coronary heart disease. *Prev Med* 15:661–672, 1986.

National Center for Health Education. *Standards for the Evaluation of Group Smoking Cessation Programs.* New York: National Center for Health Education, 1981.

Nicki, R. M., Remington, R. E., MacDonald, G. A. Self-efficacy, nicotine-fading-self-monitoring and cigarette-smoking behavior. *Behav Res Ther* 22:477–485, 1984.

Orleans, C., Schoenbach, V., Salmon, M., Wagner, E., Pearson, D., Fiedler, J., Quade, D., Porter, C., Kaplan, B. Effectiveness of self-help quit smoking strategies: Long-term results of a randomized controlled trial. Paper presented at the annual meeting of the American Public Health Association, Boston, November 1988.

Orleans, C. T., Rimer, B., Fleisher, L., Keintz, M. K., Telepchak, J., Robinson, R. *Clear Horizons*. Philadelphia: Fox Chase Cancer Center, 1989.

Poole, A. D., Sanson-Fisher, R. W., German, G. A. The rapid-smoking technique. Therapeutic effectiveness. *Behav Res Ther* 19(5):389–397, 1981.

Powell, D. R., and McCann, B. S. The effects of a multiple treatment program and maintenance procedures on smoking cessation. *Prev Med* 10:94–104, 1981.

Powell, D. R., and Arnold, C. B. Antismoking program for coronary-prone men. *NY State J Med* 82(10):1435–1438, 1982.

Prochaska, J. O., and Diclemente, C. C. Common processes of self-change in smoking, weight control, and psychological distress. In Shiffman, S., and Wills, T. A., eds. *Coping and Substance Use.* Orlando: Academic Press, 1985, 367–386.

Prochaska J. O., DiClemente, C. C., Norcross, J. C. In search of how people change: Applications to addictive behaviors. *Amer Psychol* 47:1102–1114, 1992.

Prue, D. M., Riley, A. W., Orlandi, M. A., Jerome, A. Development of a computer-assisted smoking cessation program: A preliminary report. *Journal of Advancement in Medicine.* 3(2):131–139, 1990.

Resnick, J. H. Effects of stimulus satiation on the overlearned maladaptive response of cigarette smoking. *J Consult Clin Psychol* 32(5):501–505, 1968.

Russell, M.A.H. Nicotine replacement: The role of blood nicotine levels, their rate of change and nicotine tolerance. In Pomerleau, O. F, and Pomerleau, C. S., ed. *Nicotine Replacement: A critical evaluation.* New York: Alan R. Liss, Inc., 1988, 63–94.

Schachter, S. Recidivism and self-cure of smoking and obesity. *Am Psychol* 37:436–444, 1982.

Schlegel, R. P., and Kunetsky, M. Immediate and delayed effects of the "five-day plan to stop smoking" including factors affecting recidivism. *Prev Med* 6(3):454–461, September 1977.

Schwartz, J. L. *Review and Evaluation of Smoking Cessation Methods: the United States and Canada 1978–1985.* U.S. Department of Health and Human Services. NIH Publication No. 87-2940, 1987.

Shapiro, D., Tursky, B., Schwartz, G. E., Shnid-man, S. R. Smoking on cue: A behavioral approach to smoking reduction. *J Health Soc Behav* 12(2):108–113, 1971.

Shiffman, S. Relapse following smoking cessation: A situational analysis. *J Consult Clin Psychol* 50(1):71–86, 1982.

Shumaker, S., and Grunberg, N. Proceedings of the National Working Conference on Smoking Relapse. *Health Psychol* 5:1–99, 1986.

Smith, J. W. Long term outcome of clients treated in a commercial stop smoking program. *J Subst Abuse Treat* 5:33–36, 1988.

Speigel, H. A single-treatment method to stop smoking using ancillary self-hypnosis. *International Journal of Clinical and Experimental Hypnosis* 18(4):235–250, 1970.

Stevens, V. J., and Hollis, J. F. Preventing smoking relapse, using an individually tailored skills-training technique. *J Consult Clin Psychol* 57(3):420–424, 1989.

Tiffany, S. T., Martin, E. M. Baker, T. B. Treatments for cigarette smoking: An evaluation of the contributions of aversion and counseling procedures. *Behav Res Ther* 24(4)437–452, 1986.

U.S. Department of Health and Human Services (USDHHS). *The Health Consequences of Smoking: Nicotine Addicition. A Report of the Surgeon General, 1988.* U.S. Department of Health and Human Services, Public Health Service, Centers for Disease Control, Center for Health Promotion and Education, Office on Smoking and Health. DHHS Publication No. (CDC) 88–8406, 1988.

————. *Reducing the Health Consequences of Smoking: 25 Years of Progress. A Report of the Surgeon General.* U.S. Department of Health and Human Services, Public Health Service, Centers for Disease Control, Center for Chronic Disease Prevention and Health Promotion, Office on Smoking and Health. DHHS Publication No. (CDC) 89-8411, 1989.

U.S. Public Health Service (USPHS). *Smoking and Health. Report of the Advisory Committee to the Surgeon General of the Public Health Service.* U.S. Department of Health, Education, and Welfare, Public Health Service, Center for Disease Control. PHS Publication No. 1103, 1964.

West, R. J., Russell, M.A.H., Jarvis, M. J., Feyerabend, C. Does switching to an ultra-low nicotine cigarette induce nicotine withdrawal effects? *Psychopharmacology* 84:120–123, 1984.

12

Pharmacological Adjuncts for the Tre| Tobacco Dependence

MURRAY E. JARVIK and JACK E. HENNINGFIELD

The vast majority of current tobacco users are interested in quitting smoking and have tried to quit at some point (USDHHS 1989). Although approximately one-third of all cigarette smokers attempt to quit each year, most quickly relapse in the first week or two (USDHHS 1989). For many, pharmacologic aids may make the transition from nicotine addiction to a stable abstinence more tolerable, and this may make the difference between premature death due to tobacco exposure and the improved health achieved by abstinence from tobacco. The advent of a medication approved by the Food and Drug Administration (FDA) for assisting in the maintenance of tobacco abstinence—nicotine polacrilex (gum)—was one of the important biomedical breakthroughs in the 1970s. Understanding both the known benefits of this medication and the limits of its use provides a useful perspective for the evaluation of other putatively effective medications.

In this chapter, after briefly reviewing the salient features of tobacco use that may yield to pharmacologic treatment, we shall review theory and data concerning the adjunctive use of nicotine polacrilex and other medications. Other chapters in this volume describe in detail the diagnosis and prognosis of tobacco dependence and the minimal-contact and formal treatments that may be supplemented by proper use of medications. We will describe the general theory and data underlying the actual or potential use of four categories of medications to assist in achieving or maintaining abstinence from tobacco: (1) replacement, (2) blockade, (3) nonspecific pharmacotherapy, and (4) deterrent therapies.

NICOTINE DEPENDENCE AND WITHDRAWAL

According to the revised third edition of the American Psychiatric Association's *Diagnostic and Statistical Manual of Mental Disorders* (DSM III-R) (APA 1987), repeated use of tobacco products can lead to two disorders: (1) psychoactive substance use disorder, nicotine dependence and (2) nicotine-induced organic mental disorder, nicotine withdrawal.

According to these criteria, nicotine withdrawal is deemed present when (1) there has been daily use of nicotine for at least several weeks and (2) abrupt cessation of nicotine use, or reduction in the amount of nicotine used, is followed within 24 hours by at least four of the following signs:

1. craving for nicotine;
2. irritability, frustration, or anger;
3. anxiety;
4. difficulty concentrating;
5. restlessness;
6. decreased appetite;
7. increased appetite or weight gain.

As described in the DSM III-R, the course of nicotine dependence is also variable in duration and severity. People at lower levels of dependence find quitting easier and with-symptoms less severe (Henningfield, USDHHS 1988). In nicotine dependence, the drug has come to control a significant portion of the person's behavior. General principles of treatment for both of these disorders are similar to those for other forms of drug dependence and drug withdrawal syndromes (USDHHA 1988).

The effects of nicotine are dose-related, but tolerance occurs such that the daily dose levels that most users achieve after several years of use are much higher than levels that would produce aversive or toxic effects on initial exposure. This process underlies the development of tolerance to the dose that produces nausea and dizziness. Even within a single day, a considerable degree of tolerance may be lost and gained. For instance, tolerance decreases as the smoker sleeps through the night such that the first cigarettes of the day provide the strongest effects on behavioral and physiological responses. Throughout the day of smoking, tolerance increases and the smoker may report little effect from cigarettes (USDHHS 1988; Swedberg, Henningfield, Goldberg, 1980). Repeated tobacco use is not only accompanied by the development of tolerance to nicotine, but physical dependence may develop as well. Physical dependence can complicate efforts to achieve and maintain tobacco abstinence because of the occurrence of tobacco withdrawal symptoms which may range from a mild nuisance to an incapacitating level of severity. In fact, most smokers who quit relapse within the first 2 weeks, the time when nicotine withdrawal symptoms are most severe (USDHHS 1988; Kottke et al. 1989).

In addition to tolerance and physical dependence, nicotine itself can serve as a primary reinforcer by virtue of its actions in the central nervous system of humans, and also in nonhuman species (USDHHS 1988). Although definitive evidence of this action was obtained only in the past few decades, the critical role of nicotine in tobacco use was generally understood by pharmacologists such as Lewin in the beginning of the twentieth century, and was most succinctly described by Johnston, who wrote in 1942 that "smokers show the same attitude to tobacco as addicts to their drug."

Nicotine also produces a wide range of other effects which serve to strengthen the behavior of tobacco use, for example, control of weight and appetite, alleviation of stress and anxiety, and maintenance of concentration and cognitive performance in nicotine-dependent individuals. Finally, tobacco use, like other drug dependencies, is a multidetermined behavior in which the psychoactive drug is only one of the many factors to be addressed in treatment (Chapter 4). Analogously, because the patterns of relapse and the situations in which they tend to occur are similar for tobacco, opioids, and alcohol, similar strategies of treatment and relapse prevention have been applied (USDHHS 1988).

Pharmacologic treatments of chemical dependence may be classified as follows: (1) *replacement* or *substitution* therapies (e.g., methadone for opiate dependence), in which a safer, more manageable and, ideally, less behaviorally addicting form of the drug—an agonist—is provided according to a prearranged maintenance protocol; (2) *blockade* therapies (e.g., naltrexone for opiate dependence), in which the behavior-controlling effects of the abused drug are blocked by pretreatment with an antagonist; (3) *nonspecific pharmacotherapies* (e.g., use of clonidine during opioid detoxification), in which the patient is treated symptomatically; (4) *deterrent* therapies (e.g., the use of disulfiram to treat alcoholism; Jaffe, 1985, in which a treatment drug is administered that produces aversive effects when the abused drug is subsequently taken. All four approaches may have applications in the treatment of cigarette smoking (USDHHS 1988; Jarvik and Henningfield 1988).

NICOTINE REPLACEMENT THERAPIES

Theory

The general principle of replacement therapy is to provide the patient with a safer and more manageable form of drug that mimics the symptom-alleviating effect of the substance on which the patient is dependent. The replacement drug should also be of lower abuse liability so that its use may be more readily discontinued. The replacement agent should possess some degree of cross-tolerance and cross-dependence with the abused substance. It may be an alternate formulation of the same chemical or a distinct chemical that is characterized by common effects. Thus, methadone has been given to the opioid-dependent person, and benzodiazapines have been used to stabilize the alcoholic patient (Newsom and Seymour 1983; Sellers et al. 1983). Similarly, a nicotine-delivery preparation can be administered to cigarette smokers.

Nicotine replacement can alleviate withdrawal signs and symptoms and may reduce the psychological desire to use tobacco. Even in people not attempting to quit, cigarette smoking can be modified or reduced through the surreptitious administration of nicotine (see reviews by Gritz 1980; Henningfield 1987). In fact, cigarette smoking has been decreased across all tested forms of supplemental nicotine administration (USDHHS 1988). For instance, cigarette smoking was decreased by administration of intravenous nicotine (Henningfield and Goldberg 1983; Lucchesi, Schuster, Emley 1967), by oral administration of nicotine in capsule form (Jarvik, Glick, Nakamura 1970), by buccal administration of nicotine in the form of chewing gum (Nemeth-Coslett et al. 1987), and by nasal administration of nicotine in liquid form (Jarvis 1986). Additionally, transdermal nicotine administration reduced the preferred concentration of nicotine in smoke by smokers (Rose et al. 1986).

Reduction of nicotine withdrawal symptoms by nicotine replacement has been demonstrated in both laboratory and clinical settings, and the magnitude of the effect is directly related to the administered nicotine dose (e.g. Pickworth, Herning, Henningfield 1989; Snyder and Henningfield 1988; Henningfield and Nemeth-Coslett 1988). Difficulty concentrating, irritability, and restlessness are each reliably attenuated by nicotine replacement in acute nicotine withdrawal. The desire to smoke can be decreased by increasing the nicotine content of cigarettes smoked or by pretreatment of smokers with nicotine gum (Frith 1971; Nemeth-Coslett et al. 1987); however, the effect on desire to smoke is not as reliable as are other effects of

nicotine administration and appears more subject to environmental factors (Nemeth-Coslett et al. 1987).

Nicotine Replacement Medications

Lobeline and Other Nonnicotine Agonists

One putative tobacco substitute that is present in several aids for quitting smoking (such as CigArrest, Bantron, and Nicoban) is *lobeline*. Although described as a weak nicotinic receptor agonist (Taylor 1985), lobeline is of unproven efficacy for the treatment of tobacco dependence (USDHHS 1988; Schwartz 1987; and Sachs 1986 for an interesting discussion). In fact, it now appears that lobeline does not act via the same cholinergic receptor sites that appear important in mediating the discriminative effects of nicotine (Rosecrans and Chance 1977). Consistent with the reported inefficacy of lobeline (Schwartz 1969) is the observation that lobeline will not substitute for nicotine in animal drug discrimination studies (Rosecrans and Chance 1977). It is conceivable that higher doses of lobeline would help, but informative studies have yet to be conducted (Sachs 1986). The Food and Drug Administration recently removed these products from the market (FDA 1993).

Substitution of psychomotor stimulants for nicotine has also been attempted, but there is a little evidence that these approaches are effective in the treatment of tobacco dependence (Gritz et al. 1977; Jarvik 1977; USDHHS 1988). In fact, giving *d*-amphetamine to smokers enhances the pleasure gained by smoking and increases the rate of smoking (Henningfield and Griffiths 1984). Caffeine has little consistent direct effect on rate of smoking.

Nicotine

Nicotine replacement has been demonstrated helpful in a variety of formulations and routes of administration. Two are presently available. Nicotine polacrilex (Nicorette) was the first commercially available formulation. More recently, several brands of nicotine transdermal patch have received

FDA approval. A brief review of potential routes of nicotine administration may be useful.

Enteral or oral administration of nicotine is limited by the high acidity of the stomach, which inhibits absorption; furthermore, most of the nicotine is metabolized in its first pass through the liver (USDHHS 1988). The fortunate aspect of this pharmacokinetic characteristic is that despite the several potentially lethal doses of nicotine contained in a single package of cigarettes (each cigarette may contain more than 10 mg of nicotine; Benowitz et al. 1983), nicotine poisoning of children through swallowing cigarettes or cigars has been rare. In fact, despite widespread availability of tobacco products, the American Association of Poison Control Centers cited no nicotine poisoning deaths due to tobacco ingestion in 1985 (Litovitz et al. 1986).

Nicotine could be administered in suppositories because absorption from the rectum and distal colon should be quite efficient. However, there are no reports of rectal administration, and aesthetic considerations might militate against their use.

Another method of nicotine administration, inhalation of a nicotine aerosol, appears to resemble that of inhaled cigarette smoke. For instance, nicotine inhalers modeled after the popular medihalers were successfully used to investigate various physiological actions of nicotine (Domino 1979; Herxheimer et al. 1967). Jarvik and his colleagues (1970) also attempted to use these inhalers as cigarette substitutes in smoking experiments, but discovered what Domino (1979) had previously reported, namely, that human subjects found nicotine delivered in this fashion so irritating as to limit their use. The particle size was so large that the nicotine was deposited in the sensitive upper airway rather than being delivered to the alveoli as it is with cigarette smoke which has an aerosol particle size of less than 1 μ in diameter.

A more recent variant on the aerosol procedure is possibly adaptable for treatment applications. The nasally inhaled aerosol preparation of Perkins and Epstein and their co-workers (1986) appears to have the advantages of reasonable subject acceptance and excellent control over dose as measured by plasma nicotine level, cardiovascular effects, and self-reported responses.

A variation on the inhaler technology is the nicotine-delivering rod or "smokeless cigarette" first described by Jacobson and his co-workers (Jacobson 1979) and then markteed by Advanced Tobacco Products under the trade name Favor. Even though the FDA decided that this nicotine vapor inhaler fell within its jurisdiction and was subject to its regulatory powers, it was initially marketed as a nontherapeutic cigarette substitute. In some studies (Schumaker and Grunberg 1986; Russell and Jarvis 1987), puffing on this inhaler created several effects that mimicked those of nicotine delivered by tobacco, including acute heart rate increase and some of the sensations of tobacco smoke inhalation. In fact, in a study by Henningfield (personal communication), use of the vapor inhaler produced reliable decreases in self-reported desire to smoke cigarettes, although it was not determined whether or not such effects would persist if abstinence from cigarette smoking were prolonged. Interestingly, use of the vapor inhalers in these two studies did not produce detectable elevations in plasma nicotine levels. Russell and colleagues (1987) found that measurable nicotine plasma levels could be produced by use of the vapor inhaler, but only following extremely active inhalation. These findings suggest that the vapor inhaler, as currently designed, is not a practically effective means of nicotine delivery, and that the apparently nicotinic effects are actually conditioned responses elicited by the peripheral stimulation provided by the vapor inhaler. In fact, Rose and Hickman (1987) have demonstrated that the oral inhalation of a citric acid spray can mimic certain properties of tobacco smoke and reduce self-reported "craving" for cigarettes. Despite their current limitations, future versions of vapor inhalers might possibly provide a useful adjunct to other forms of replacement therapy and to behaviorally oriented tobacco treatment strategies.

Another explanation for the occurrence of nicotinic effects produced by the nicotine vapor inhaler in the absence of measurable plasma nicotine levels is the possibility that nicotine delivery by this route produces effects mediated by the peripheral nervous system. Ginzel (1987) has reported that regional administration of nicotine to the lungs of animals results in a variety of nicotinic effects often considered to be due primarily to central actions of nicotine, perhaps as a result of vagal stimulation.

Such peripherally mediated actions of nicotine could result from a mode of nicotine delivery in which there was a higher ratio of peripheral to central nicotinic stimulation than that obtained when nicotine is delivered via tobacco use. Nicotine carried by cigarette smoke is in the form of a nicotine salt which adheres to solid and liquid particles. These particles are an ideal size (about 1 μ in diameter) for deep airway penetration to the alveolar membranes of the lungs where absorption into the plasma is extremely efficient. In contrast, the nicotine vapor delivered by the inhaler is a free base and a gas. It is possible that this mode of nicotine delivery results in a higher ratio of upper to lower airway nicotine absorption where systemic absorption may be less efficient. This might account for the rather high ratings of "harshness," and "irritation of the throat," as well as the cigarette-like effects produced by the nicotine vapor inhaler that were observed in the Henningfield study. Thus, this device might provide a tobacco-like sensation with relatively little absorption of nicotine into the blood stream. It remains to be determined if such effects would be efficacious as a tobacco replacement formulation in the nicotine tolerant and dependent tobacco user.

An interesting mode of delivery using sublingual nicotine tablets has been described by Wesnes and Warburton (1978). Though not available for therapeutic application, this sublingual-oral mode of delivery proved useful as a research tool. Nicotine was added to buffered dextrose tablets which were then held in the mouth for 5 minutes, producing fairly efficient and quick nicotine delivery; the tablets were than swallowed and continued to deliver a small but apparently significant amount of nicotine to the plasma (cf. Wesnes and Warburton 1984). The 1–2 mg of nicotine delivered and some of the effects produced via this modality appear to roughly correspond to the nicotine delivered and effects produced by the smoking of cigarettes.

A nicotine-delivering formulation that holds considerable promise as an aid in treating nicotine dependence is the transdermal patch, first investigated by Rose and Jarvik (Rose, Jarvik, Rose 1984). The development of practical methods of transdermal nicotine administration has been driven by the need for nicotine replacement modalities to address the apparently diverse range of patient requirements and preferences. Nicotine is an ideal candidate for transdermal administration because it is lipophilic and potent. Nicotine dose may not be as readily controllable by this route of administration, but nicotine's relatively short half-life (about 2 hours), the pharmacodynamic characteristics of rapid initial tolerance to many of its effects, and the rapid decline in plasma levels that should follow removal of the patch enhances the safety of transdermal nicotine administration.

Three features of transdermal nicotine administration that should be addressed in formulating a patch are: (1) factors affecting control of the rate and magnitude of nicotine dose administration; (2) possible local irritation; and (3) the degree to which transdermal nicotine application reduces nicotine-mediated signs and symptoms of tobacco withdrawal (e.g., impairment of mood and performance and weight gain).

The following three benefits of transdermal administration over the use of nicotine polacrilex seem noteworthy: (1) persons who are physically unable to obtain adequate amounts of nicotine by chewing the gum (e.g., those with dental problems) might be able to use the patch; (2) any embarrassment resulting from frequent medication administrations should be obviated by the infrequency and privacy of transdermal administration; (3) finally and most importantly, patient compliance with the required dosing regimen should be more readily obtainable and verifiable.

A patch could also be used in conjunction with nicotine gum or with a variety of the nicotine-free components of cigarette smoking. These could include the sight and feel of cigarettes; the sight and smell of tobacco smoke or some substitute; and the taste and the sensations in the mouth, nose, throat, and trachea produced by normal smoking but reproduced with as few components of smoke as possible.

Transdermal nicotine patches have been tested clinically in the United States. Rose and colleagues (1990) tested 65 subjects with one type of patch and found continuous abstinence at the end of 3 weeks was 18% for the experimental group and 6% for the placebo. These results are consistent with those of European investigators, all of whom found a facilitation of smoking cessation with a nicotine patch. Another study by Mulligan and associates (1990), found that plasma concentrations comparable to that seen with nicotine gum were achieved with the patch that they used. In addition, they found that in a 6-week, placebo-controlled, double blind study, there was a significant reduction of smoking activity in those using the active patch. By the end of the study, 20 subjects, or 50% in the nicotine group, had stopped smoking, compared with 7 subjects or 17% in the placebo group. Tonnesen and colleagues (1991) have described a clinical trial of a nicotine patch delivered with a low intensity intervention which demonstrated a sustained abstinence rate of 17% compared to 4% in the placebo group. Other workers have published similarly promising results (Daughton et al. 1991; Transdermal Nicotine Study Group 1991), and a review of the English language clinical trials has been published (Fiore et al. 1992).

Of all the possible types of nicotine delivery systems, nicotine polacrilex or gum (Nicorette) was the first to be approved by the FDA and, accordingly, is associated with the largest store of clinical experience. Use of nicotine polacrilex has been shown to increase the rates of success of a variety of cigarette smoking treatment programs. Under a wide range of conditions, rates of smoking have diminished and abstinence-associated discomfort ("withdrawal") has been alleviated (USDHHS 1988). Desire to smoke may also be lessened as well, although this effect is not as reliable as effects of nicotine polacrilex on other withdrawal symptoms. General strategies for using nicotine polacrilex as an aid to smoking cessation have been described in detail elsewhere (Schneider 1988; Cooper and Clayton 1988).

Nicotine Replacement Guidelines, with Special Refernce to Using Nicotine Gum

Formulation

Nicotine gum (Nicorette) delivers nearly 1 mg of nicotine from the 2 mg contained in the pressure-sensitive resin of a single dose. The resin matrix minimizes the risk of accidental poisoning since nicotine is only released slowly and some chewing is necessary for activation. Patients often find the taste mildly unpleasant. This is deliberate to further reduce the risk of accidental poisoning of a child. Some practice and patience is required to obtain an adequate dose of nicotine. The drug is delivered across the buccal mucosa over about 30 minutes. The venous nicotine level after a dose of nicotine gum rises much more gradually than following a cigarette.

Efficacy

Nicotine gum has repeatedly been shown to substantially increase the efficacy of a variety of behavioral interventions for nicotine dependence. It also has been convincingly shown that, for all practical purposes, the drug does not help people stop smoking if it is used by itself (Hughes et al. 1989). If the drug can be provided at little or no cost, it is more likely to be used (Hughes et al. 1991). The drug relieves irritability, restlessness, tension, and difficulty concentrating, but not urges, thoughts, or cravings about smoking.

Patient Selection

The people who benefit most from adjunctive nicotine replacement are those who experience more withdrawal symptoms when nicotine intake is abruptly curtailed. In general, patients have high Fagerström Tolerance Questionnaire (FTQ) scores and patients smoking greater numbers of cigarettes daily benefit from adjunctive nicotine gum while patients having low scores and patients smoking fewer cigarettes each day do not.

The Fagerström Test for Nicotine Dependence (FTND), a refinement of the FTQ, is presented in Appendix A, which follows Chapter 21 (Heatherton et al. 1991).

Contraindications

Nicotine replacement, whether delivered as gum, patch, or some other form, is contraindicated in people not actively addicted to nicotine and in people who intermix the use of tobacco products with nicotine gum(e.g., using nicotine gum to temporarily ameliorate nicotine withdrawal when in a place where smoking is not permitted). The gum formulation may be difficult or impossible for some patients to use because of dental appliances or concomitant dental or other oral pathology.

Nicotine replacement is relatively contraindicated in situations where vascular compromise or arrhythmia may be induced or worsened by nicotine. These situations include the immediate postmyocardial infarction period, life-threatening arrhythmias, and worsening angina pectoris. The use of nicotine replacement is also discouraged in pregnant patients, and the labeling for nicotine gum also cautions about prescribing it in patients who might become pregnant. At the same time, nicotine replacement may be an essential part of helping a patient who has vascular disease or who is pregnant to stop smoking or to be comfortable not smoking at a critical time. The toxicity of cigarettes is greater in nearly every respect than that of either nicotine gum or patch, including the rate of nicotine delivery to the tissues and the levels of peak and steady-state blood nicotine concentrations (Benowitz 1991).

Dosing Concentrations

The 4 mg dose of gum is more efficacious than the 2 mg dosage. The 4 mg formulation can be approximated by instructing the patient to use two, 2 mg doses at once, holding one in each cheek.

Instructions to Patients

The drug is an adjunct to a treatment program for nicotine dependence. It will pre-

vent or ameliorate nicotine withdrawal symptoms, but it will not keep a patient from thinking about smoking or from having urges to smoke. Since the nicotine level does not rise as rapidly in the blood with nicotine gum as it does with a cigarette, it is best to take nicotine gum on a schedule, every hour or two for instance, ahead of symptoms (Fortmann et al. 1988). Additional doses can be used ad lib in addition to the scheduled dose to relieve discomfort.

As a starting schedule, use 10–14 doses spaced out over the day if the smoking rate had been about 20 cigarettes per day, 14–18 doses for 30 cigarettes, and 18–22 doses to replace 40 cigarettes (Henningfield et al. 1990). Substantially higher doses may be necessary in some situations. Lower doses are usually not particularly helpful.

For the most part, the gum should stay in the cheek after an initial few chews render the gum malleable. It should be worked around with the tongue and teeth for a few seconds every few minutes, but it should not be chewed constantly. If it is chewed like chewing gum, most of the nicotine will be swallowed instead of absorbed across the buccal mucosa. This may result in an upset stomach, nausea, gas, jaw ache, or throat irritation along with reduced amounts of nicotine getting to the brain because of first pass metabolism. A single dose is used up in about 30 minutes.

Nicotine absorption in the mouth requires a mildly alkaline environment (pH about 8.0). Therefore, consumption of foods or beverages which lower the pH will reduce or block nicotine absorption. This includes most beverages, such as coffee, tea, carbonated beverages, and fruit juices, as well as chewing gums containing sugar (Henningfield et al. 1990). A period of 10–15 minutes should elapse after eating or drinking before the next dose of nicotine gum.

Schneider (1988) has written an excellent patient guide for stopping smoking which highlights how to use nicotine gum.

Duration of Therapy

Optimally, nicotine gum should be used for several months. Regular use in the first month is the most important. Most patients can comfortably reduce their use gradually after this interval. Longer periods, up to a year or so, may benefit some patients. To wean off the gum, some patients will benefit from a weaning plan. Schneider (1988) suggests several useful weaning strategies (i.e., cutting daily dose by one piece per week, cutting gum pieces in half, breaking up gum rituals). Another approach is to slowly increase the drug-free interval that begins with each night's sleep, extending this into the morning hours, then the afternoon hours, and finally into the evening over a period of weeks (Cooper and Clayton 1988).

Rarely, patients may be encountered who cannot be weaned from nicotine gum without a prompt relapse to tobacco use. Management options in this instance include dealing with nicotine gum use as a primary drug dependence or simply continuing to maintain the patient on nicotine gum indefinitely after appropriate counseling.

NICOTINE BLOCKADE THERAPIES

Theory

A pharmacologic alternative to replacement therapy is pharmacologic blockade of receptors which mediate the reinforcing as well as the toxic effects of the abused substance (Jaffe 1985). In the case of opioid agonists, such as morphine and heroin, the short-acting antagonist, naloxone, can be used to reverse the effects of an overdose of the opioid agonist. The longer-acting antagonist, naltrexone, can be given on a daily basis to opioid abusers to prevent them from experiencing the reinforcing and toxic effects of opioid agonists. Unfortunately, few patients dependent on opiates remain on a therapeutic regimen which prevents the possibility of experiencing pleasurable opioid agonist effects. For the highly motivated patients that do take the medication, however, the antagonist is invaluable in preventing "experimentation" and in preventing "slips" from developing into relapses. Unfortunately, the nicotine blockers that have been studied either have little effect on smoking (e.g., pentolinium) or have a range of undesirable actions (e.g., mecamylamine produces sedation and orthostatic hyperten-

sion). Nonetheless, preliminary experimental data suggest that this approach may warrant further investigation.

Nicotine Blockade Medications

Drugs which diminish a variety of responses to nicotine (antagonists) have been recognized for many decades (Domino 1979). Those antagonists which act both centrally and peripherally (mecamylamine), but not those which only act peripherally (e.g., pentolinium and hexamethonium), have functional effects on patterns of cigarette smoking in humans and behavioral effects of nicotine (including self-administration) in animals (USDHHS 1988). Preliminary data suggest the possibility that mecamylamine could be used as an antagonist to block the nicotine-mediated reinforcing consequences of cigarette smoking.

The following findings seems of particular relevance:

1. Mecamylamine pretreatment produces a dose-related blockade of the ability of animals and humans to discriminate nicotine from placebo (USDHHS 1988);
2. Mecamylamine pretreatment diminishes the reinforcing efficacy of intravenous nicotine administration in animals (Goldberg et al. 1983), and possibly in humans (see preliminary data in Henningfield and Goldberg 1983);
3. Acute mecamylamine pretreatment increases the preference for high nicotine-delivering cigarette smoke (apparently by reducing its nicotinic effects) when subjects are tested using a device that blends smoke from high and low nicotine-delivering cigarettes (Rose et al. 1985);
4. Acute mecamylamine pretreatment increases a variety of measures of cigarette smoking behavior and/or tobacco smoke intake when subjects are allowed to freely smoke (Nemeth-Coslett et al. 1986; Pomerleau, Pomerleau, Majchrzak 1987). Interestingly, results from the Pomerleau study also suggested that the toxicity of nicotine exposure was substantially reduced by mecamylamine pretreatment.

In addition, a preliminary clinical trial was conducted by Tennant and colleagues

(1984) to determine if mecamylamine could be used to treat cigarette smoking. Mecamylamine was given to a population of heavy cigarette smokers in conjunction with counseling to quit smoking. It was found that mecamylamine reduced tobacco craving in 13 of 14 subjects, and half of the subjects quit smoking within 2 weeks of initiation of mecamylamine treatment. The mean dose level of mecamylamine, at the time of quitting, was 26.7 mg per 24-hour day. A rather curious aspect of this application of mecamylamine is that it was not used in a fashion analogous to naltrexone used for opioid dependence: that is, it was used as an aid to detoxification and as a means to alleviate withdrawal. In theory, a blocker should precipitate withdrawal, and, therefore, would ordinarily not be used in detoxification. Rather, it would be expected to be used as a means to prevent relapse once acute detoxification had been achieved. Perhaps the apparently beneficial effects of mecamylamine were due to its sedating side effect or some as yet unreported nicotine-mecamylamine interaction. Despite these curiosities and the fact that the trial was not placebo-controlled, the data suggest that this treatment approach warrants further exploration.

NONSPECIFIC PHARMACOTHERAPIES—SYMPTOMATIC TREATMENT

Theory

The pharmacologic intervention approaches just described are specifically aimed at nicotine-receptor mediated responses, either by agonist administration (e.g., nicotine replacement), or by antagonist administration (e.g., mecamylamine pretreatment). However, administration of and withdrawal from nicotine produces a cascade of effects that involve a variety of neurohormones.

It has been hypothesized that certain neurohormonal effects of nicotine enhance the reinforcing efficacy of nicotine by providing therapeutic benefit or useful effect; such effects may vary across individuals (Pomerleau and Pomerleau (1984). Consequently, it should be possible to achieve some of these same effects using pharmacologic intervention-

tions that do not directly involve activation or blockade of nicotinic receptors at the ganglia. Moreover, it should be possible to target treatment approaches to meet individual needs. For instance, if stress precipitates smoking in certain individuals (discussed later), it should be possible to develop specific pharmacologic and behavioral treatments to replace nicotine (see Pomerleau and Pomerleau 1984; Jarvik and Henningfield 1988, for a more thorough discussion of these issues).

Nicotine administration can produce a variety of useful pharmacologic effects (e.g., relief of somnolence, fatigue and anxiety, or weight control) which could be considered clinically therapeutic, and which probably contribute to the abuse liability of the drug. Thus, it appears likely that some individuals may have specific needs which they attempt to treat by using nicotine. In such individuals, prevention of a relapse to tobacco may require specific intervention (pharmacologic or behavioral) for that need. It is in this context that supportive, nonspecific pharmacologic therapies are explored.

Nonspecific Pharmacotherapy Medications

Several effects of nicotine may be regarded as anxiolytic and might be mimicked either by use of behavioral relaxation techniques and/or selective anxiolytic medications (e.g., benzodiazapines). For example, laboratory studies with human subjects have shown that nicotine administration can reduce reported dysphoric responses to stressful stimuli and enhance mood. Other investigations have demonstrated that stressful situations may lead to increased nicotine self-administration (i.e., increased cigarette intake). Conversely, relapse to cigarette smoking often occurs in response to stressful situations (USDHHS 1988). Such observations suggest the possibility that targeted use of relatively specific anxiolytics, such as benzodiazepines, may be useful for some persons in the achievement of stable abstinence. It appears plausible that certain therapeutic drugs could be highly useful as adjuncts in specific subpopulations, even though their possible benefit would not be evident when administered indiscriminately. Some of the newer serotonin reuptake inhibitors, such as fluoxetine and buspirone, could be useful in individuals for whom depression or anxiety are prominent symptoms. For selected individuals, the situational use of an anxiolytic for a brief period such as benzodiazepene might be of benefit.

Nicotine may also be useful as a general mood regulator, in part by virtue of its stimulation of release of catecholamines, as well as its modulation of a variety of other neuroregulatory hormones (USDHHS 1988). Catecholamine release both peripherally and centrally is also stimulated by excitement, exercise, sex, antidepressant drugs, and other drugs of abuse, suggesting that cigarette smoking may pharmacologically function to alleviate depression, boredom, and stress. Both animal and human data suggest that an elevated ratio of norepinephrine to epinephrine release is associated with pleasurable states of arousal (e.g., sex, cocaine or amphetamine administration, electrical brain self-stimulation), whereas the reverse (increased epinephrine) is thought to be associated with certain dysphoric mood states (e.g., boredom, stress, and electric shock administration) (USDHHS 1988). Interestingly, both animal and human data also suggest that nicotine administration results in an increased ratio of norepinephrine to epinephrine release (Cryer et al. 1976). These observations suggest that for certain persons, selective use of antidepressants, or even psychomotor stimulants, may be beneficial in preventing relapse.

People who have a history of depression or who have high scores on a depression scale are more likely to smoke than control groups. Such people also have a more difficult time achieving abstinence (Anda et al. 1990; Glassman et al. 1990) (See Chapters 10 and 16). An antidepressant, begun several weeks prior to a quit attempt and adjusted to full antidepressant dosage, may be a useful adjunct for such patients. If abstinence is achieved, the drug should be continued for at least several months. An antidepressant can be used in conjunction with nicotine replacement.

Nicotine administration or deprivation can also affect body weight. Smokers weigh less than nonsmokers, although the relation is not simple; moderate smokers weigh the least, light and heavy smokers somewhat more, and nonsmokers weigh the most (USDHHS 1988). As an anorectant or weight reducer, smoking and/or nicotine itself functions in at least three ways: (1) by increasing resting metabolic rates; (2) by specifically reducing the appetite for foods containing simple carbohydrates; (3) by nonspecifically reducing the eating that may occur in times of stress, although these relations are confounded by observations that some smokers eat more than nonsmokers (USDHHS 1990).

Among persons who have quit smoking, those treated with nicotine gum gain less weight than those treated with placebo gum, and it appears that the magnitude of the effect is directly related to nicotine intake via the gum (Stitzer and Gross 1988). Quitting smoking is associated with a mean weight gain of 2.8 kg in men and 3.8 kg in women, which brings former smokers nearly up to the weight of people who have never smoked (Williamson et al. 1991 and USDHHS 1990). People tend to eat somewhat more when they quit smoking, and some may even increase their food intake as an adjunctive strategy to quitting smoking (USDHHS 1988). If potential or actual weight gain seriously interferes with stopping smoking, a weight control program is indicated. Dietary counseling, especially the avoidance of sweet-tasting, high carbohydrate food, and an exercise program are the major recommended maneuvers (Grunberg 1991). A selective anorectant such as fenfluramine may have an adjunctive role.

Nicotine can also reverse decrements in performance induced by acute tobacco deprivation. The findings that the nicotine withdrawal syndrome includes performance impairments on a variety of measures of cognitive function, and conversely, that nicotine administration can reverse such deficits have now been fairly well established (cf. USDHHS 1988). Since a variety of attentional, motivational, memory, and even mood-related factors can contribute to measured performance, it may not be possible to completely compensate for the loss of these effects by nicotine replacement strategies.

Development of selective cognitive-enhancing medications, or at least medications to reverse cognitive deficits is still in its infancy, but this approach could ultimately offer much needed help to individuals who are unable to perform adequately when they quit smoking.

Finally, supportive pharmacotherapies to treat tobacco withdrawal symptoms offer some promise. In one of the few recent controlled studies of treating tobacco dependence with a supportive form of pharmacotherapy, Glassman and colleagues (1984) compared alprazolam and clonidine to placebo, in heavy cigarette smokers on days during which they abstained from tobacco. Clonidine is an alpha-adrenergic agonist used as an antihypertensive agent. The subjects were exposed to one of the medication conditions on 3 separate study days, which were separated by at least 3 days of normal smoking. Alprazolam, a benzodiazepine, was included as a "sedative placebo" because of the known sedative effects of clonidine. Both clonidine and alprazolam were more effective than placebo in reducing anxiety, irritability, restlessness, and tension. Only clonidine, however, successfully reduced thoughts about smoking. Since desire to smoke tended to increase during the day, the difference between clonidine and the other two conditions became more evident as the day progressed. This important observation of the possible utility of a nonnicotine-based pharmacologic treatment strategy has been extended in subsequent investigations.

Published studies on clonidine in the management of nicotine dependence suggest a modest benefit from clonidine when it is used as an adjunct to standard behavioral therapies (Covey and Glassman 1991).

Adjunctive clonidine might be considered for patients in whom adjunctive pharmacotherapy is desired, but who are not candidates for nicotine replacement or who have not been able to achieve a stable abstinence with nicotine replacement alone. Clonidine patches are more convenient, and there is suggestive evidence in the literature of higher quit rates using the patch (Covey and Glassman 1991). However, tablets are less expensive and permit more precise dose adjustments. The drug may be begun 2–5 days before the quit attempt begins with a total daily dose of 0.2 mg. The dose can be decreased if there is intolerance (most often somnolence or hypotension) or increased to achieve better supression of symptoms. Used as part of an active treatment program, the drug should be continued for a period of weeks to months. It can be used in conjunction with nicotine gum or an antidepressant.

It is interesting to compare the utility of clonidine in the treatment of tobacco withdrawal to its utility in the treatment of opioid withdrawal. When assessed in an analogous paradigm, clonidine was just as effective as morphine in the reduction of certain selected physiologic signs of the opioid withdrawal syndrome (Jasinski, Johnson, Kocher 1985); however, in the Jasinski study, clonidine did not reduce the self-reported "discomfort" as effectively as morphine. Measures of "desire to use narcotics" or narcotic seeking behavior were not collected. However, observation of the subjects suggested to the investigators that clonidine was not as effective as morphine in suppressing the desire to take a narcotic (D.R. Jasinski, personal communication).

PHARMACOLOGIC DETERRENT THERAPIES

Theory

The last category of pharmacologic aids to treat tobacco dependence are the deterrents. The rational basis for the use of pharmacologic deterrents is aversive conditioning. There are reports that drug taking can sometimes be reduced or eliminated if the consequences are severe enough (e.g., use of punishment for drug use). For example, Elliott and Tighe (1968) found that loss of money, and/or even "threatened" loss of money, substantially reduced expected relapse to cigarette smoking following treatment.

Perhaps the best exmple of a form of drug self-administration in which pharmacologic pretreatment has such a consequence is the treatment of alcoholism by daily administration of disulfiram (Antabuse). Disulfiram inhibits the further degradation of a toxic ethanol metabolite, acetaldehyde, and therefore leads to a toxic accumulation of acetalde-hyde (Jaffe and Ciraulo 1984). Thus, a small amount of alcohol will often produce severe discomfort and acute illness. The severity of the reaction is a function of the dose of di-sulfiram, the dose of ethanol, and individual variability. A few observations about the use of disulfiram therapy may illustrate some of the problems and issues that may arise when such approaches are applied to tobacco de-pendence.

The main difficulty with disulfiram ther-apy is in maintaining adequate levels of use of the medication itself. It appears to be most effectively employed when circumstances can be arranged so that the drug is taken when the motivation to drink is relatively low, such as upon daily attendance to a treat-ment clinic or when patients are under a court order to comply with the therapeutic protocol. The same issues might be relevant to the development of effective deterrents for cigarette smoking. That is, they should be able to be administered when the motivation to smoke is relatively low; then the medica-tion can provide a "crutch" for subsequent instances of high motivation to smoke. Un-fortunately, a characteristic of nicotine-de-pendent tobacco users is that one of the most consistent periods of high motivation to smoke is immediately upon awakening after a night of sleep (Fagerström 1982). There-fore, upon waking, the immediate motiva-tion to smoke may preclude the taking of a medication which will facilitate abstinence later in the day. Alternately, very long-acting (at least 24 hours) deterrents might be devel-oped which would permit the person to take them later in the day and ensure that smok-ing the next morning would be accompanied by aversive consequences.

Deterrent Medications

The only analogues to a "disulfiram" treat-ment for smoking that have been widely marketed are silver acetate-based formula-tions. The physiological basis of the ap-proach is that sulfides are produced when sil-ver ion contacts the sulfides in tobacco smoke. The resulting sulfides are extremely distasteful for most people. However, they have the danger of inducing argyria. The ap-proach is not specific to nicotine intake, but rather to sulfide-containing smoke. Variants on this procedure have been reviewed (Schwartz 1987; USDHHS 1988). Most re-cently, a gum preparation of silver acetate has been tested as a means to maintain ab-stinence from tobacco (Malcolm et al. 1986) and seems promising.

CONCLUSION

This chapter summarized the theoretical basis for the use of pharmacological adjuncts to achieving abstinence from tobacco use. Similar approaches are used to treat other substance abuse disorders. Such approaches are limited by the same kinds of factors that limit the efficacy of using pharmacologic ad-juncts for treating other kinds of drug depen-dence and related disorders. One implica-tion of these observations is that evaluation of the utility of specific medications in the al-leviation of certain signs and symptoms should not be confused with the evaluation of programs that are aimed at reducing the prevalence of tobacco use and its associated morbidity and mortality. For example, a medication that provides relief of acute nic-otine withdrawal symptoms or selectively prevents cognitive deficits could be useful in a program to help people quit smoking. However, motivating patients to attempt to quit, to take their medications, and provid-ing them with strategies for avoiding relapse (including possible long-term maintenance on medications) is the responsibility of the health care professional and the patient. Long-term outcomes, in turn, will be a re-flection of the overall strength of the entire treatment program, and not the efficacy of a particular pharmacologic adjunct alone.

The diversity of factors which appear rel-evant to the control and treatment of to-bacco use across individuals implies the need for a diversity of treatment approaches. Development of either new medications or more effective ways of using existing medi-cations will probably be required to ade-quately address diverse patient needs in this important area of medicine and public health.

In summary, the prominent role of nico-tine itself in the mediation of tobacco dependence suggests that replacement therapies might be the most useful form of pharmacotherapy. Nicotine polacrilex was the first approved formulation in the United States for clinical use, and it has a clearly demonstrable efficacy in both laboratory and clinical settings. However, its efficacy appears to be related to the rate and efficiency with which nicotine is extracted and absorbed; patients need very specific instructions on the use of this drug, and clinical follow-up is important. Alternate replacement formulations are needed for those who cannot use the gum for dental and other reasons. Recently, nicotine transdermal patches have largely supplanted nicotine polacrilex as the initial choice for nicotine replacement therapy. Other nicotine replacement approaches under active development include a nasal spray or droplet form, and a nicotine vapor inhaler.

Blockade approaches (e.g., naltrexone) have not been acceptable for more than a few highly compliant chemically dependent persons. However, such approaches would still seem important to pursue since the potential absolute numbers of persons who could benefit from such approaches is considerable (e.g., if 5% of the estimated 50 million people who smoke could be helped, this would be 2.5 million individuals). Mecamylamine is available at present, but its use will probably be constrained by its unpleasant ganglionic-blocking actions. A more selective, centrally acting blocker, which could be analogous to naltrexone for opiate dependence, would be highly desirable.

Another potentially useful but not widely used approach is nonspecific pharmacotherapy. This is the use of agents that do not act upon nicotine or nicotinic receptors but that produce symptomatic relief from the various sequelae of tobacco abstinence, which range from the specific nicotine abstinence effects described in DSM III-R to the occasional severe affective symptoms and other disorders that may occur. The symptoms may be part of the short-term withdrawal syndrome from nicotine, the more protracted phase of nicotine withdrawal, or emergent symptoms which had been suppressed by the chronic use of tobacco. Fortunately, therapeutic strategies are available

for many such symptoms (e.g., anxiety, depression, and weight control problems) which can occur independently of nicotine dependence and withdrawal. Therefore, it is plausible that medications that do not provide significant benefit for unselected groups of smokers may still be appropriately used on an individual case basis. For instance, the use of benzodiazepines and anorectants should not be ruled out simply because such drugs may increase smoking in persons not trying to quit. There seems to be modest benefit from the adjunctive use of clonidine, although it is unclear whether there are particular subpopulations for which this drug might be especially helpful. Similarly, even though there is still little evidence for the use of antidepressants to treat tobacco dependence, it is plausible that they could facilitate abstinence in selected individuals. Such pharmacologic approaches would probably benefit from concurrent behavioral treatment.

Deterrent approaches, in principle, could be of enormous potential utility. However, a satisfactory nicotine deterrent has yet to be developed and marketed. The problem for development is to produce a product which reliably leads to consequences that are both sufficiently severe and immediate to discourage smoking, and be without side effects that would act to inhibit its use (e.g., the staining of gums caused by silver salts).

As the preceding review has shown, there is a strong rational basis, and even some direct evidence, that pharmacologic intervention for the treatment of cigarette smoking could be of significant therapeutic value. The efficacy of pharmacologic intervention may be limited by the extent to which the substance seeking behavior, and the derived rewards, have become functionally autonomous from the drug itself. However, this problem is not unique to tobacco. It is well known that effective programs for assisting opiate users in achieving long-term abstinence, for instance, involves considerably more means of intervention than simply blocking physiologic withdrawal symptoms. An entire "life-style" may require change (Bigelow, Stitzer, Liebson 1985; Grabowski and Hall 1984). By the time the dependent cigarette smoker attempts to quit, there have usually been hundreds of thousands of pairings of various effects of nicotine with the stimuli provided by the use of the tobacco product. These stimuli are certainly not replaced by any pharmacologic agent, and much time may be required until their absence no longer contributes to the discomfort of withdrawal and the occurrence of relapse. Perhaps the most that adjunctive pharmacologic intervention can provide is a means to alleviate the physiologically mediated components of withdrawal and their contribution to relapse. The rest will be up to intervention programs and the contingencies set by the individuals themselves.

ACKNOWLEDGMENTS

Supported by U.C. Tobacco Related Disease Program grant #RT87, NIDA Grant #DA5111, and a grant from the John D. and Catherine T. MacArthur Foundation.

REFERENCES

American Psychiatric Association (APA). *Diagnostic and Statistical Manual of Mental Disorders—DSM-III-R, 3rd ed.,* rev. Washington, D.C.: American Psychiatric Association, 1987.

Anda, R. F., Williamson, D. F., Escobedo, L. G., et al. Depression and the dynamics of smoking. *JAMA* 264:1541–1545, 1990.

Benowitz, N. L. Nicotine replacement therapy during pregnancy. *JAMA* 266:3174–3177, 1991.

Benowitz, N. L., Hall, S. M., Herning, R. I., Jacob, P., III, Jones, R. T., Osman, A. L. Smokers of low-yield cigarettes do not consume less nicotine. *N Engl J Med* 309:139–142, 1983.

Bigelow, G. E., Stitzer, M. L., Liebson, I. A. Substance abuse. In Hersen, M., ed. *Pharmacological and Behavioral Treatment: An Integrative Approach.* New York: John Wiley & Sons, 1985, 289–311.

Covey, L. S., and Glassman, A. H. A meta-analysis of double-blind placebo-controlled trials of clonidine for smoking cessation. *Br J Addict* 86:991–998, 1991.

Cooper, T. M., and Clayton, R. R. Help your patients stop smoking; A great practice builder. *Dental Management* 28(5):46–49, 1988.

Cryer, P. E., Haymond, M. W., Santiago, J. V., Shah, S. D. Norephinephrine and epinephrine release and adrenergic mediation of smoking-associated hemodynamic and metabolic events. *N Engl J Med* 295:573–577, 1976.

Daughton, D. M., Heatley, S. A., Prendergast, J. J., et al. Effect of transdermal nicotine delivery as an adjunct to low-intervention smoking cessation therapy. A randomized, placebo-controlled, double-blind study. *Arch Intern Med* 151:749–752, 1991.

Domino, E. F. Behavioral, electrophysiological, endocrine and skeletal muscle actions of nicotine and tobacco smoking. In Remond, A., and Izard, C., eds. *Electrophysiological Effects of Nicotine.* Amsterdam: Elsevier, 1979, 133–146.

Elliott, R., and Tighe, T. Breaking the cigarette habit: Effects of a technique involving threatened loss of money. *Psychol Rec* 18:503–513, 1968.

Fagerström, K. A comparison of psychological and pharmacological treatment in smoking cessation. *J Behav Med* 5:343–351, 1982.

Fiore, M. C., Jorenby, D. E., Baker, T. B., Kenford, S. L. Tobacco dependence and the nicotine patch: clinical guidelines for effective use. *JAMA* 268:2687–2694, 1992.

Food and Drug Administration (FDA). Smoking deterrent drug products for over-the-counter human use; Rule. *Federal Register* 58(103):31236–31241, 1993.

Fortmann, S. P., Killen, J. D., Telch, M. J., Newman, B. Minimal contact treatment for smoking cessation. A placebo controlled trial of nicotine polacrilex and self-directed relapse prevention: initial results of the Stanford Stop Smoking Project. *JAMA* 260(11):1575–1580, 1988.

Frith, C. D. The effect of varying the nicotine content of cigarettes on human smoking behavior. *Psychopharmacologia* 19:188–192, 1971.

Ginzel, K. H., Watanabe, S., Eldred, E. Drug-induced depression of gamma efferent activityii. Central action of nicotine. *Neuropharmacology* 9:369–379, 1970.

Ginzel, K. H. The lungs as sites of origin of nicotine-induced skeletomotor relaxation and behavioral and electrocortical arousal in the cat. *Proc. Int. Symp. on Nicotine.* Goldcoast, Australia: ICSU Press, 1987.

Glassman, A. H., Jackson, W. K., Walsh, T., Roose, S. P., Rosenfeld, B. Cigarette craving, smoking withdrawal, and clonidine. *Science* 226:864–866, 1984.

Glassman, A. H., Helzer, J. E., Covey, L. S., Cottler, L. B., et al. Smoking, smoking cessation, and major depression. *JAMA* 264:1546–1549, 1990.

Goldberg, S. R., Spealman, R. D., Risner, M. E., Henningfield, J. E. Control of behavior by intravenous nicotine injections in laboratory animals. *Pharmacol Biochem Behav* 19:1011–1020, 1983.

Grabowski, J., Stitzer, M. L., Henningfield, J. E., eds. *Behavioral Intervention Techniques in Drug Abuse Treatment.* National Institute on Drug Abuse Research Monograph Series No. 46. Washington, D.C.: U.S. Government Printing Office, 1984.

Gritz, E. R., and Jarvik, M. E. Pharmacological aids for the cessation of smoking. In Steinfeld, J., Griffiths, W., Ball, K., Taylor, R. M., eds. *Proceedings of the Third World Conference—Smoking and Health,* vol. 2. Washington, D.C.: U.S. Government Printing Office, 1977.

Gritz, M. E. Smoking behavior and tobacco abuse. In Mello, N. K., ed. *Advances in Substance Abuse: Behavioral and Biological Research.* Greenwich, CT: JAI Press, 1980, 91–158.

Gross, J., and Stitzer, M. L. Nicotine replacement: Ten-week effects on tobacco withdrawal symptoms. *Psychopharmacology* 98:334–341, 1989.

Grunberg, N. E. Smoking cessation and weight gain. *N Engl J Med* 324:768–769, 1991.

Heatherton, T. F., Kozlowski, L. T., Frecker, R. C., Fagerström, K. O. The Fagerstrom Test for nicotine dependence: A revision of the Fagerström Tolerance Questionnaire. *Br J Addict* 86:1119–1127, 1991.

Henningfield, J. E. Pharmacologic basis and treatment of cigarette smoking. *J Clin Psychiatry* 45:24–34, 1984.

Henningfield, J. E., and Goldberg, S. R. Control of behavior by intravenous nicotine injections in human subjects. *Pharmacol Biochem Behav* 19:1021–1026, 1983.

Henningfield, J. E., Chait, L. D., Griffiths, R. R. Effects of ethanol on cigarette smoking by volunteers without histories of alcoholism. *Psychopharmacology* 82:1–5, 1984.

Henningfield, J. E., and Brown, B. S. Do replacement therapies treat craving? *NIDA Notes* 2(1):8–9, 1987.

Henningfield, J. E., and Nemeth-Coslett, R. Nicotine dependence: Interface between tobacco and tobacco-related disease. *Chest* 98(suppl.)37S–55S, 1988.

Henningfield, J. E., Radzius, A., Cooper, T. M., Clayton, R. R. Drinking coffee and carbonated beverages blocks absorption of nicotine from nicotine polacrilex gum. *JAMA* 264:1560–1564, 1990.

Herxheimer, A., Lond, M. B., Griffiths, R. L., Hamilton, B., Wakefield, M. Circulatory effects of nicotine aerosol inhalations and cigarette smoking in man. *Lancet* 2:754–755, 1967.

Hughes, J. R., Gust, S. W., Keenan, R. M., Fenwick, J. W., Healey, M. L. Nicotine vs. placebo gum in general medical practice. *JAMA* 261:1300–1305, 1989.

Hughes, J. R., Wadland, W. C., Fenwick, J. W., Lewis, J., Bickel, W. K. Effects of cost on the self-administration and efficacy of nicotine gum: A preliminary study. *Prev Med* 20:486–496, 1991.

Jacobson, N. L., Jacobson, A. A., Ray, J. P. Noncombustible cigarette: Alternative method nicotine delivery. *Chest* 76:355–356, 1979.

Jaffe, J. H. Drug addiction and drug abuse. In Gilman, A. G., Goodman, L. S., Rall, T. W., Murad, F., eds. *Goodman and Gilman's Pharmacological Basis of Therapeutics.* New York: Macmillan, 1985, 532–581.

Jaffe, J. H., and Ciraulo, D. A. Drugs used in the treatment of alcoholism. In Mendelson, J. H., and Mello, N. K., eds. *The Diagnosis and Treatment of Alcoholism,* New York: McGraw-Hill, 1984, 355–389.

Jarvik, M. E. Can drug treatment help smokers? In Steinfeld, J., Griffiths, W., Ball, K., Taylor, R. M., eds. *Proceedings of the Third World Conference—Smoking and Health,* vol. 2. Washington, D.C.: U.S. Government Printing Office, 1977, 509–514.

Jarvik, M. E., Glick, S. D., Nakamura, R. K. Inhibition of cigarette smoking by orally administered nicotine. *Clin Pharmacol Ther* 11:574–576, 1970.

Jarvik, M. E., and Henningfield, J. E. Pharmacologic approaches to smoking cessation. In Lynn, W. R., Lando, H. A., Davis, R. M., Henningfield, J. E., eds. *Nicotine Addiction. The Health Consequences of Smoking. A Report of the Surgeon General.* U.S. Department of Health and Human Services, Public Health Service, Office on Smoking and Health, Rockville, MD, 1988.

Jarvis, M. Nasal nicotine solution: Its potential in smoking cessation and as a research tool. In Ockene J. K., ed. *The Pharmacologic Treatment of Tobacco Dependence: Proceedings of the World Congress.* Cambridge, MA: Harvard Institute for the Study of Smoking Behavior and Policy, 1986, 167–173.

Jasinski, D. R., Johnson, R. E., Kocher, T. R. Clonidine in morphine withdrawal: Differential effects on signs and symptoms. *Arch Gen Psychiatry* 42:1063–1066, 1985.

Johnston, L. M. Tobacco smoking and nicotine. *Lancet* 2:742, 1942.

Klesges, R. C., Meyers, A. W., Klesges, L. M., La Vasque, M. E. Smoking, body weight, and their effects on smoking behavior: A comprehensive review of the literature. *Psychol Bull* 106(2):204–230, 1989.

Kottke, T. E., Brekke, M. L., Solberg, L. I., Hughes, J. R. A randomized trial to increase smoking intervention by physicians: Doctors helping smokers, Round 1. *JAMA* 261:2101–2106, 1989.

Litovitz, T. L., Normann, S. A., Veltri, J. C. 1985 annual report of the American Association of Poison Control Centers National Data Collection System. *Amer J Emergency Med* 4(5):427, 1986.

Lucchesi, B. R., Schuster, C. R., Emley, G. S. The role of nicotine as a determinant of cigarette smoking frequency in many with observations of certain cardiovascular effects associated with the tobacco alkaloid. *Clin Pharmacol Ther* 8(6):789–796, 1967.

Malcolm, R., Currey, H. S., Mitchell, M. A., Keil, J. E. Silver acetate gum as a deterrent to smoking. *Chest* 90:107–111, 1986.

Mulligan, S. C., Masterson, J. G., Devane, J. G., Kelly, J. G. Clinical and pharmacokinetic properties of a transdermal nicotine patch. *Clin Pharmacol Ther* 47:331–337, 1990.

Nemeth-Coslett, R., Henningfield, J. E., O'Keeff, M. K., Griffiths, R. R. Nicotine Gum: Dose-related effects on cigarette smoking and subjective ratings. *Psychopharmacology* 92:424–430, 1987.

Newsom, J. A., and Seymour, R. B. Benzodiazepines and the treatment of alcohol abuse. *J Psychoactive Drugs* 15(1–2):97–98, 1983.

Perkins, K. A., Epstein, L. H., Stiller, R., Jennings, J. R., Christiansen, C., McCarthy, T. An aerosol spray alternative to cigarette smoking in the study of the behavioral and physiological effects of nicotine. *Behav Res Methods* 18:420–426, 1986.

Pickworth, W. B., Herning, R. I., Henningfield, J. E. Spontaneous EEG changes during tobacco abstinence and nicotine substitution in human volunteers. *J Pharmacol Exp Ther* 251(3):976–982, 1989.

Pomerleau, C. S., Pomerleau, O. F., Majchrzak, M. J. Mecamylamine pretreatment increases subsequent nicotine self-administration as indicated by changes in plasma nicotine level. *Psychopharmacology* 9(3):391–393, 1987.

Pomerleau, O. F., and Pomerleau, C. S. Neuro-

regulators and the reinforcement of smoking: Towards a biobehavioral explanation. *Neurosci Biobehav Rev* 8:503–513, 1984.

Rose, J. E., Jarvik, M. E., Rose, K. D. Transdermal administration of nicotine. *Drug Alcohol Depend* 13:209–213, 1984.

Rose, J. E., Sampson, A., Henningfield, J. E. Blockage of smoking satisfaction with mecamylamine. Paper presented to the American Psychological Association, Los Angeles, California, August 26, 1985.

Rose, J. E., Herskovic, J. E., Trilling, Y., Jarvik, M. E. Transdermal nicotine reduces cigarette craving and nicotine preference. *Clin Pharmacol Ther* 38:450–456, 1986.

Rose, J. E., and Hickman, C. S. Citric acid aerosol as a potential smoking cessation aid. *Chest* 1987.

Rose, J. E., Levin, E. D., Behm, F. M., Adivi, C., Schur, C. Transdermal nicotine facilitates smoking cessation. *Clin Pharmacol Ther* 47:323–330, 1990.

Rosecrans, J. A., and Chance, W. T. Cholinergic and non-cholinergic aspects of the discriminative stimulus properties of nicotine. In Lal, H., ed. *Discriminative Stimulus Properties of Drugs.* New York: Plenum, 1977, 155–185.

Russell, M.A.H., Jarvis, M. J., Sunderland, G., Feyerabend, C. Nicotine replacement in smoking cessation: Absorption of nicotine vapor from smoke-free cigarettes. *JAMA* 257:3262–3265, 1987.

Sachs, D.P.L. Cigarette smoking health effects and cessation strategies. *Clin Geriatr Med* 2:337–362, 1986.

Schneider, N. G. *How to Use Nicotine Gum & Other Strategies to Quit Smoking.* New York: Simon & Schuster, 1988.

Schwartz, J. L. Critical review and evaluation of smoking control methods. *Public Health Rep* 84:483–506, 1969.

———. *Review and Evaluation of Smoking Cessation Methods: The United States and Canada, 1978–1985.* Bethesda, MD: U.S. Department of Health and Human Services. NIH Publication No. 87-2940, 1987.

Sellers, E. M., Naranjo, C. A., Harrison, M., Devenyi, P., Roach, C., Sykora, K. Diazepam loading: Simplified treatment of alcohol withdrawal. *Clin Pharmacol Ther* 34(6):822–826, 1983.

Shumaker, S. A., and Grunberg, N. E., eds. Proceedings of the National Working Conference on Smoking Relapse. *Health Psychol* 5(suppl.):1–99, 1986.

Snyder, F. R., and Henningfield, J. E. Effects of nicotine administration following 12 h of tobacco deprivation: Assessment on computerized performance tasks. *Psychopharmacology* 97:17–22, 1989.

Stitzer, M. and Gross, J. Nicotine replacement effects on post-cessation withdrawal symptoms and weight gain. *NIDA Research Monograph* 81:53–58, 1988.

Swedberg, M.B.D., Henningfield, J. E., Goldberg, S. R. Evidence of nicotine dependence from animal studies: Self-administration, tolerance and withdrawal. In Russell, M.A.H., Stolerman, I. P., Wanacott, S., eds. *Nicotine: Action and Medical Implications* Oxford University Press, Oxford, 1990.

Taylor, P. Ganglionic stimulating and blocking agents. In Gilman, A. G., Goodman, L. S., Rall, R. W., Murad, F., eds. *The Pharmacological Basis of Therapeutics.* New York: Macmillan, 1985, 215–221.

Tennant, F. S., Tarver, A. L., Rawson, R. A. Clinical evaluation of mecamylamine for withdrawal from nicotine dependence. In Harris, L. S., ed. *Problems of Drug Dependence, 1983.* National Institute on Drug Abuse Research Monograph Series No. 49. Washington, D.C.: U.S. Government Printing Office, 1984, 239–246.

Tonnesen, P., Norregaard, J., Simonsen, K., Sawe, U. A double-blind trial of a 16-hour transdermal nicotine patch in smoking cessation. *N Engl J Med* 325:311–315, 1991.

Transdermal Nicotine Study Group. Transdermal nicotine for smoking cessation. Six-month results from two multicenter controlled clinical trials. *JAMA* 266:3133–3138, 1991.

U.S. Department of Health and Human Services (USDHHS). *The Health Consequences of Smoking: Nicotine Addiction. A Report of the Surgeon General.* U.S. Department of Health and Human Services, Public Health Service,

Centers for Disease Control, Center for Health Promotion and Education, Office on Smoking and Health. DHHS Publication No. (CDC) 88-8406, 1988.

U.S. Department of Health and Human Servcies (USDHHS). *Reducing the Health Consequences of Smoking: 25 Years of Progress, A Report of the Surgeon General.* U.S. Department of Health and Human Services, Public Health Service, Centers for Disease Control, Center for Chronic Disease Prevention and Health Promotion, Office on Smoking and Health. DHHS Publication No. (CDC) 89-8411, 1989.

U.S. Department of Health and Human Services. *The Health Benefits of Smoking Cessation, A Report of the Surgeon General.* U.S. Department of Health and Human Services, Public Health Service, Centers for Disease Control, Center for Chronic Disease Prevention and Health Promotion, Office on Smoking and Health. DHHS Publication No. (CDC) 90-8416, 1990.

Wesnes, K., and Warburton, D. M. Smoking, nicotine and human performance. In Balfour, D.J.K., ed. *Nicotine and the Tobacco Smoking Habit* Pergamon Press, Oxford, 1984, 133–151.

————. The effects of cigarette smoking and nicotine tablets upon human attention. In: Thornton, R. E., ed. *Smoking Behavior: Physiological and Psychological Influences.* Churchill-Livingston, London, 1978. pp 131–147.

Williamson, D. F., Madans, J., Anda, R. F., Kleinman, J. C., Giovino, G. A., Byers, T. Smoking cessation and severity of weight gain in a national cohort. *N Engl J Med* 324:739–745, 1991.

13

Smokeless Tobacco: Risks, Epidemiology, and Cessation

HERBERT H. SEVERSON

While cigarette smoking has long been called the number one preventable cause of cardiovascular disease and cancer, the hazards of smokeless tobacco use only have recently come under scrutiny. Statements by the Surgeon General and the National Institutes of Health have now warned Americans about the potential health dangers of regular use of snuff or chewing tobacco. In 1986, a special report of the Surgeon General concluded that "oral use of smokeless tobacco represents a significant health risk and is not a safe substitute for smoking cigarettes" (USDHHS 1986).

Smokeless tobacco (SLT) is a term which encompasses two general types of tobacco: oral snuff and chewing tobacco. Snuff is a cured, finely ground tobacco that comes in three forms: (1) dry snuff, (2) moist snuff, and (3) fine cut tobacco. Chewing tobacco also is produced in three forms: (1) loose leaf tobacco, (2) plug tobacco, and (3) twist chewing tobacco. Users of moist snuff put a "dip" (pinch) of snuff between the lower lip or cheek and the gum and let it rest there. Users of chewing tobacco put a "chew" (wad or quid) of tobacco in the cheek pouch and chew the tobacco to mix with saliva. While the increasing use of SLT products has only recently received a great deal of publicity, the use of SLT has a long history in the United States.

SLT use originated with the American Indians and was transferred to English and European cultures through the travels of Christopher Columbus and other early explorers (Christen and Glover 1987). The practice of sniffing or inhaling dry tobacco through the nostrils was the most popular form of tobacco use for many years. Dipping (oral snuff use) and chewing (leaf or plug tobacco use) became more popular during the 1800s. While snuffing was quite popular in Britain, the colonists in America preferred to break with the English tradition and dipped or chewed tobacco instead. Dipping and chewing were common habits in the American culture until the discovery of the bacillus tuberculosis organism in 1882, which raised a concern for the unsanitary practice of tobacco spitting and the use of cuspidors. This concern, combined with the invention of cigarette-making machines, caused a dramatic decrease in the use of SLT products over the following several decades (Christen et al. 1982).

In the 1970s, SLT use gained new momentum in America, with the strongest resurgence in the use of moist snuff. Currently, the majority of new SLT users use moist snuff products and this product has shown the strongest increase in sales (Gritz, Ksir, McCarthy 1985). The 1986 Surgeon General's Report estimated that 12 million American men were users of SLT, and that half of these were regular users (USDHHS 1986).

Four recent surveys provide data on SLT use by adults. Data collected in 1985 and 1986 by the Office on Smoking and Health included questions on SLT use in the Current Population Survey (CPS). The other two surveys, conducted in 1970 and 1987 by the National Center for Health Statistics in the National Health Interview Survey (NHIS), also are shown in Table 13-1. As one can see from Table 13-1, statistics on snuff and chewing tobacco use have been collected in four surveys having comparable questions; point-prevalence use is generally in the 6% range.

A recent survey by the national Institute of Drug Abuse (NIDA) included a question on SLT use in their National Household Interview Survey conducted in 1985. This survey involved interviewing persons age 12 years and older and provides the only national probability data currently available on SLT use by persons under 17 years of age. There are no national data on use by children under age 12 years. Estimates from the NIDA survey indicate that 20% of males age 12–17 years used SLT sometime in 1985 (Rouse 1989). Overall, 11% of the general population has tried chewing tobacco, snuff, or other SLT. Of these, 5% were former users and 3% used SLT daily in the past year (Rouse 1989). All surveys report that SLT use is predominantly a male activity. Although a substantial number of females reportedly have tried SLT, only approximately 1% of females report any use in the past year (Marcus et al. 1989). Additionally, all national surveys indicate that the highest rates of use occur among adolescent and young adult males (Orlandi and Boyd 1989).

Regional and local prevalence often is much higher than national prevalence of SLT use. Its use is more common in rural areas, small communities, and in areas where regular use is traditional. Current daily use was over four times higher in nonmetropolitan areas than in metropolitan areas (9 vs. 2%) (Rouse 1989).

One exception to the pattern of male-only SLT use appears among native Americans, among whom substantial use is reported for females. Native American males have higher rates than other ethnic groups, and use by females often is similar to use by younger male children and adolescents (Hall and Dexter 1988). Schinke and colleagues (1989) surveyed native Americans living on reservations in Washington State and reported that nearly half of the students (aged 8–16 years) had used SLT 11 to 20 or more times. Al-

Table 13–1 Prevalence (%) of Smokeless Tobacco (SLT) Current Use By Males in the U.S.—Four National Surveys

SLT	NHIS (1970)[a]	CPS (1985)[b]	1986[c]	NHIS (1987)[d]
Snuff	1.4	1.9	2.4	3.2
Chewing tobacco	3.8	3.9	3.3	4.1
Any form	—	5.5	5.2	6.2

Source: Orlandi and Boyd 1989.

[a]Males were ≥ 17 yrs old. Survey was by household interview with extensive use of proxy respondents (3).

[b]Males were ≥ 16 yrs old. Survey was by household interview with extensive use of proxy respondents (13).

[c]Adult Use of Tobacco Survey (AUTS) was done of males ≥ 17 yrs old by telephone survey (14).

[d]Males were ≥ 18 yrs old. Survey was done by household interview (15).

Note: Current use is point-prevalence (i.e., Do you currently use snuff or chewing tobacco?).

CPS = Current Population Survey; NHIS = National Health Interview Survey.

most one-third of females reported regular use. They concluded that there was exceptionally high usage by both male and female native American youth, with an early age of initial use and regular use. SLT use, with the exception of native Americans, is generally more predominant in white populations than in other ethnic groups. Blacks, Asians, and other minority groups usually report much lower use (Severson 1990). Rates for other ethnic groups may be increasing, however, as Dent and colleagues (1987) reported 53% of white, 35% of Hispanic, 36% of black, and 23% of Asian ninth graders in the Los Angeles area had at least tried SLT.

In sum, there is clear evidence for widespread use of moist snuff and other SLT, especially among young males. Its use is most prevalent in rural areas and among young white males. Marcus et al. (1989) concluded that of all users of chewing tobacco in the United States, 90% were male, and of these, 90% were white and 50% reside in the South. In addition, SLT use is two to three times more prevalent among blue-collar than among white-collar workers (Marcus et al. 1989). The age group of most concern is the young male (16–19 years old). This group has shown a tenfold increase in reported moist snuff use between 1970 and 1985, and a twofold increase in chewing tobacco use (Marcus et al. 1989).

Table 13–2   Health Effects of Smokeless Tobacco Use

Cancerous and Noncancerous Conditions

Pre-cancerous soft tissue effects:
  Leukoplakia
Noncancerous soft tissue effects:
  Gingival recession
  Gingivitis/inflammation
  Periodontal degeneration
  Salivary gland inflammation/degeneration
Hard tissue effects (noncancerous):
  Tooth abrasion
  Dental caries
  Bone loss
  Stained teeth

Carcinogenesis and Carcinogens

Location/sites
  Oral-buccal or labial mucosa, gums, tongue, lips
  Nasal
  Esophagus/larynx
  Stomach
  Urinary tract
  Other (e.g., pancreas, colon)
By types:
  Carcinoma in situ
  Squamous cell carcinoma
  Verrucous carcinoma
Carcinogens:
  N-nitrosamines (NNN,NNK)
  Polycyclic aromatic hydrocarbons
  Polonium 210
  Volatile aldehydes

HEALTH EFFECTS OF SLT USE

Regular SLT usage is a major concern because of the addictive qualities of nicotine and the detrimental effects on health. The addictive qualities of nicotine are well documented and are covered in depth in other chapters of this volume (Chapters 2 and 4). The detrimental effects of SLT use on health are less well known, both to the user and to the general public. These effects include halitosis, discoloration of teeth, destruction of periodontal bone and soft tissue, slow healing of cuts and sores in the mouth, dental caries, tooth abrasion, gum recession, tooth destruction, and leukoplakia (Glover et al. 1988). Leukoplakia is usually defined as a white patch or plaque that cannot be clinically or pathologically associated with another disease. Additionally, SLT has been implicated in cancers of the gum, mouth, pharynx, larynx, esophagus, stomach, nasal cavity, pancreas, kidney, and bladder (Schroeder 1989; USHDDS 1986). Table

13–2 summarizes the health effects of SLT use. The most frequently reported health effect for SLT users is oral lesions. There are many reports of the relationship between SLT use and the development of premalignant lesions, including leukoplakia in the oral mucosa (Greer and Poulson 1983; Schroeder 1989; Glover et al. 1989).

The preponderance of scientific and clinical evidence is that SLT can produce oral soft tissue responses such as gingival recession and leukoplakia, especially in long-term users (Schroeder 1987; USDHHS 1986). It is believed that 3–6% of leukoplakia lesions have the potential to convert to squamous cell carcinomas (Silverman 1981; Axel, Mornstead, Sundstrom 1976). It is estimated that over 50% of regular users have at least a degree I (early-stage) leukoplakia lesion (Glover et al. 1989). Other studies have shown that almost half of adolescent snuff dippers exhibited oral soft tissue lesions after using SLT for an average of only 3.3 years (Greer and Poulson 1983). Our own data on SLT users coming into dental clinics showed that 78% had a clinically identifiable oral lesion where they held their snuff or chew in their mouth. Ernster et al. (1990) assessed major and minor league professional baseball players and compared 412 current SLT users to 493 nonusers. Oral leukoplakia was present in 46% (196/423) current-week SLT users and only 1.4% (7/493) of nonusers. The use of snuff resulted in much higher prevalence of leukoplakia than chewing tobacco. Dental caries, gingivitis, and plaque did not differ between SLT users and nonusers. There was evidence, however, for SLT-related gingival recession and tooth attachment loss at the facial surfaces of the mandibular incisor tooth, where most SLT users held the tobacco in their mouth (Ernster et al. 1990).

A growing body of evidence points to a causal relationship between cancers of the oral cavity and pharynx and the use of chewing tobacco and snuff. The products contain potent carcinogens (see later), and epidemiologic studies show significant increased risks of oral cancer due to SLT use. Among the clearest such studies is that of Winn and co-workers (1981). They reported a case control study conducted to identify risk factors for cancers in the oral cavity among women in North Carolina. Results indicated that white SLT users were 4.76 times more likely to develop oral cancers than nonusers and that black SLT users were only 1.5 times more likely to do so than nonusers. The odds ratio was consistently higher among snuff dippers who did not smoke than among smokers. Mattson and Winn (1989) concluded that cancer risks increase with length of exposure, and risks are greatest for anatomic sites where the product has been held in contact for the longest time. In some studies, other organs such as the esophagus, larynx, and stomach, have been shown to be at increased risk for cancer from the use of SLT (Roed-Peterson and Pindborg 1973; Schroeder 1987; USDHHS 1986). Additionally, synergistic actions with other oral cancer risk factors, such as smoking and alcohol use, show an increase in cancer risks for SLT users who engage in multiple high-risk behaviors (Mattson and Winn 1989).

TOBACCO-SPECIFIC NITROSAMINE AND CARCINOGENESIS

Chemical analyses of SLT have shown it to include four classes of carcinogens: certain volatile aldehydes, radioactive polonium 210, polycyclic aromatic hydrocarbons, and N-nitrosamines (USDHHS 1986).

The prime carcinogenic ingredients in SLT are the tobacco-specific nitrosamines (TSNA), such as NNN and NNK. These are already present in the product as it is purchased, but they are also thought to form in the mouth through a reaction of salivary nitrites with nicotine from the SLT (Hoffman, Brunnemann, Adams et al. 1986; Hoffman, Harley, Fisenne et al. 1986). Both NNN and NNK are mutagenic and carcinogenic. They are found in SLT in quantities between 10 and 1,400 times greater than the allowable amounts for food and beverages (USDHHS 1986).

NICOTINE ABSORPTION/ADDICTION

Studies of nicotine absorption by snuff and chewing tobacco users conclude that venous plasma nicotine levels are similar in users of SLT and cigarette smokers (Benowitz 1986).

Data suggest that SLT users develop a dependency similar to that of cigarette smokers.

Benowitz, Porchet, and Sheiner (1988) compared the venous nicotine levels in men who smoked cigarettes, took oral snuff, used chewing tobacco, or chewed 4 mg nicotine gum for 30 minutes. The results showed that within 20 minutes, plasma nicotine levels for cigarettes, snuff, and chewing tobacco are approximately equal; nicotine gum provided less plasma nicotine than the other products. Gritz and associates (1981) found that plasma nicotine and cotinine levels in habitual users of SLT, after ad lib consumption, rose to levels typically reached in regular cigarette smokers. Russell and colleagues (1981) report that plasma nicotine concentrations for daily snuffers are comparable to those for a group of heavy smokers. Multiple-dose snuff use resulted in increases in plasma nicotine to concentrations that exceeded levels recorded in smokers. Russell et al. concluded that the similarity in concentrations produced by regular snuff use and regular daily smokers suggests that the plasma nicotine concentrations have a controlling influence over the self-regulation of these quite different forms of tobacco use.

Nicotine is absorbed more slowly from SLT than from cigarettes, but the peak venous blood levels are similar (Benowitz 1988; Russell et al. 1981). Full nicotine absorption from snuff takes approximately 20 minutes. The absorption of nicotine per dose is greater with the use of chewing tobacco (average 4.5 mg nicotine) or snuff (average 3.6 mg. nicotine) than with smoking cigarettes (average 1.0 mg. nicotine).

There is no evidence that the route by which nicotine is administered (e.g., smoke inhalation, SLT, intravenous administration, or nicotine gum) makes any difference to the titrated plasma nicotine levels for the user. Henningfield (1984) concluded that nicotine meets the criteria of being an addictive drug and that nicotine produces tolerance and an addictive pattern following regular use. In an analogue series of studies, Hughes and Hatsukami (1986) studied the physiological dependence that can develop when nicotine is taken in the form of cigarette smoke, SLT, or nicotine polacrilex (nicotine gum). Their main conclusions are that (1) an orderly syndrome of physiologic and subjective responses follow abrupt termination of nicotine administration, and (2) withdrawal from nicotine is qualitatively similar regardless of the vehicle employed (Hatsukami et al. 1984; Hughes and Hatsukami 1986). Brief withdrawal from regular SLT use (mean of two tins/week) results in the same withdrawal symptoms and subjective discomfort as observed in heavy cigarette smokers attempting to quit (mean of 26 cigarettes/day) (Hatsukami, Gust, Keenan 1987).

MARKETING AND AVAILABILITY OF SLT

Given the increasing prevalence of SLT use among young males in recent years, there has been an increasing concern about the role of advertising and promotional efforts that encourage this use. Between 1970 and 1985, the domestic production of all forms of SLT increased by 42%, and the production of fine-snuff cut tobacco used in moist snuff tripled. It appears that from 1980 on, the increase in sales was largely a function of an increasing use of moist snuff and, in particular, its use by young males. (All other categories of tobacco, such as plug, moist plug, dry snuff, twist, roll, or loose leaf, declined over the same period of time.) Recent reports in the *Wall Street Journal* (Deveny, 3 May 1990) indicate a significant increase in moist snuff sales to new record levels, with a 4.6% increase in sales for 1989.

Snuff and chew are widely available in convenience stores, gas stations, and grocery stores (Braverman, D'Onofrio, Moskowitz 1990). Although the laws are not uniform, sale to minors is illegal in many states. However, these laws seldom are enforced and adolescents report easy access. While firm data on advertising expenditures for SLT are not readily available, various estimates have been published. In 1984, $8–$10 million was spent on advertising by the U.S. Tobacco Company alone, which commands nearly 90% of the domestic moist snuff market, and estimates of industrywide advertising expenditures for that same year ranged from $20 to $31 million (Ernster 1989).

Companies producing SLT use promotional efforts similar to those used success-fully for cigarettes. Advertisements offer free samples and encourage participation in contests and competitions, as well as promoting clothing and other items bearing product logos. Offers of free merchandise or gift catalogs commonly are included. Underwriting sporting events, particularly auto racing, has been a major form of promotion. Exposure of cars bearing Skoal Bandits and Copenhagen logos on each televised broadcast of a race has an estimated value of over a half million dollars in advertising coverage, not including promotional benefits derived from the appearance of logos in related stories and magazines (Ernster 1989). It was estimated that the publicity of obtaining the pole position in the Indianapolis 500, for a car in which the logo is prominently displayed, is worth approximately $3 million (Ernster, 1989).

SLT products have long been particularly associated with the sport of baseball. Use is prominent among both major and minor league baseball teams, and SLT product manufacturers have traditionally provided cases of free samples to professional baseball teams. The prevalence of use by baseball players is very high, with one study reporting 39% of 1,109 baseball team members using SLT in the past week (Ernster et al. 1990). A second survey reported that 34% of 265 players were current users (Connolly, Orleans, Kogan 1988), and a small study found 17 of 25 minor league players were current users (Cummings et al. 1989). Concern by management for the health of their players is evidenced by several teams now banning the availability of free smokeless products in the clubhouse, some teams providing information on the health risks of SLT use, and 1991–92 bans on the use of smokeless products on the field in Rookie and Single A minor league teams. Recently, Major League Baseball joined forces with the National Cancer Institute (NCI) to produce and distribute a smokeless cessation guide to all major and minor league players, coaches, and trainers (Orleans, Connolly, Workman 1991).

For a time, professional athletes served as the spokesmen for SLT products, a practice barred by Public Law 99-252 (The Comprehensive Smokeless Tobacco Act of 1986). This law also bans the use of electronic media (television and radio) in advertising SLT products, and requires that rotating health warnings be placed on SLT products and displayed in all print advertisements. Official policy notwithstanding, industry activities appear to be youth oriented, and company representatives have handed out free samples of "Frisbee"-like toys, t-shirts, hats, and other products that are attractive to young males. Recent testimony from documents and testimony delivered under oath in the Sean Marsee vs. U.S. Tobacco Company suit in U.S. District Court, documented that companies had encouraged, via marketing and promotional techniques, the use of starter products that have low nicotine absorption levels in order to accelerate nicotine delivery gradually with the change to higher nicotine products (Glover et al. 1989b). U.S. Tobacco's major moist snuff products follow a graduation strategy both in nicotine available (nicotine content and pH of product determine nicotine absorption) and taste. Products such as Happy Days and Skoal Bandits are designed as "starter" products and it is expected that as a person becomes more addicted, he will move up to Skoal and finally to Copenhagen. Reports from adolescents confirm this pattern of use (Ary, Lichtenstein, Severson 1987).

Countering the promotional efforts by tobacco companies are articles in the popular press that describe some of the health risks of SLT use. An article in *Readers' Digest* in October 1985 described the death (from oral cancer) of Sean Marsee, a 19-year-old Oklahoma track star who had used snuff from ages 12–18 years. The media attention to this case of oral cancer appeared to increase public awareness of the potential risks involved in regular snuff use.

Prevention strategies emerging from a consideration of marketing and availability issues include reduced availability, enforcement of age-of-sale laws, higher excise taxes, and countering the "macho" imagery used in SLT marketing efforts (USDHHS 1989).

PSYCHOSOCIAL VARIABLES IN SLT USE

A number of studies have examined the individual psychosocial variables associated with adolescent SLT use. The factors that appear most correlated with SLT use for adolescents are having friends who also chew or dip; experimentation and early use of cigarettes, alcohol, marijuana; and a willingness to take risks. Broader contextual variables, such as the effects of price, availability, advertising and promotion, and free samples on use are not assessed in studies such as this.

Ary and colleagues (1987, 1989) investigated variables thought to discriminate between male adolescents reporting using SLT and those who did not. Peer use of SLT and experience with cigarettes were both related to chewing status. Peer influence seemed to be an important variable, not just in trying SLT, but also in the development of a daily use pattern. Additional factors related to daily use of SLT included the number of times marijuana and alcohol were used in the last week. Ary also studied the onset of SLT use and found that this was related to offers to use alcohol, cigarettes, and marijuana. In sum, peer use was the best single predictor of onset and continued daily use (Ary 1989).

The importance of peer usage of SLT has been confirmed in a number of studies (Chassin et al. 1985; Ary et al. 1987; Dent et al. 1987; Hunter et al. 1986; Marty et al. 1986; Severson et al. 1987). Dent and colleagues (1987) reported that the onset of SLT use was related to higher levels of cigarette smoking and use of cigarettes by significant others. Additionally, they reported that the onset of SLT use was related to beer, wine, and other alcohol use; to having been drunk on liquor; to marijuana use; and was more probable in individuals who enjoyed taking risks. Sussman and associates (1990) found a strong relationship between self-identified peer group membership and tobacco use. A group of "skaters" (skateboarders) who had a distinctive group centered around risky, individual, outdoor-oriented activities were the most likely to be current SLT users. Tobacco use was related to problem-prone attributes (Jessor and Jessor 1977), such as poor school performance, low self-esteem, and risk taking (Sussman et al. 1990). Dent and co-workers (1987) concluded that SLT users were engaged in higher levels of drug experimentation prior to and concurrent with their SLT use.

The relationship between a father's use of

chewing tobacco and an adolescent son's use is reported as marginally significant (Severson 1985; Botvin et al. 1989) or nonsignificant (Ary et al. 1987). Bauman and colleagues (1989) found an inverse relationship between use of smokeless tobacco and parents' education. They also reported a significant association between fathers' and children's use of SLT. Ary and associates (1989) found that the father's use of SLT was significantly higher among current users (29.4%) than among experimenters (11.5%). Father's use may not be clearly related to son's use unless other variables, such as parental education and acceptance of the son's usage, are considered.

The general acceptability of adolescent SLT use by parents also may be related to its increasing use. Chassin and colleagues (1985) found that while 41% of smokers report that their parents were aware of their smoking, 71% of SLT users report that their parents knew of their use of snuff. The implication is that parents are more accepting of their sons' use of SLT than of cigarettes. Bonaguro and co-workers (1986) reported that the fathers' and mothers' approval of SLT usage was positively correlated with use by boys in grades 4–12. Parental acceptance may be based on a perception that chewing and snuff use is a safe alternative to smoking cigarettes.

Other investigators also have reported a relationship between smoking cigarettes and the use of chewing tobacco (Severson et al. 1991). Among males who reported using SLT in the past week, 33% reported also smoking cigarettes, while among nonusers of SLT, only 8% reported smoking in the past week. This is consistent with Newman and Duryea (1981), who found that 36% of male users of SLT were smokers, but the base rate of smoking prevalence was only 13.5%.

Of particular interest is analyzing the sequence of trying cigarettes and smoking SLT to determine which precedes the regular use of the other. Some authors have cited the earlier age of onset with SLT use as evidence that it is the initial product of use (Ary et al. 1987; Hunter et al. 1986; Lichtenstein et al. 1984). As examples of early age of initiation, Young and Williamson (1985) reported that

21.4% of a sample of 112 kindergarten children in Arkansas had used SLT; among boys in Oregon, the mean age for first use is reported to be 11.2 years (Ary et al. 1987). The Office of the Inspector General Monograph (1986) on SLT reported that the overall age of initiation was 10.4 years, or in the fifth grade. Dent and associates (1987) reported that at each level of initial smoking, SLT users reported higher rates of onset to regular smoking than did nonusers. Current smoking was related to the onset of SLT use, with subjects in transition from experimental to regular smoking showing the highest SLT onset. This underscores the potential for SLT use to contribute to the onset of cigarette smoking. Peterson et al. (1989) reported a consistently strong relationship between the onset of SLT and smoking among adolescents.

In sum, it appears that peer use of SLT, early experiences with cigarettes, alcohol, and marijuana, and parental acceptance of use, are all related to the onset and use of SLT for adolescents. Prevention programs should emphasize peer refusal skills, increased awareness of detrimental health effects of SLT use, and the frequent transition from SLT to cigarette addiction as a strategy for deterring or reducing SLT use.

Other Factors and Their Relationship to SLT Use

In addition to the adolescent's use or his peer's use of chew, cigarettes, and other drugs, variables such as perceived health risk, sibling use of chew, and social image variables have been examined in relationship to the use of SLT. Chassin and colleagues (1985) reported that chewing is perceived as less dangerous by users of SLT than by subjects that smoked or did neither. Some authors have also reported that chewers perceived chewing to be less harmful than smoking, while most nonchewers disagree (Bauman 1990; Lichtenstein 1984). Chassin et al. (1985) reported that among nonusers, the intention to chew in the future was negatively related to the perceived health risks of chewing.

A report by the Office of Inspector General on Youth's Use of Smokeless Tobacco

(1986) indicated that 59% of youth are very or somewhat unaware of health risks associated with dipping and chewing. Eighty-six percent of youth regard SLT as a safe alternative to cigarette smoking. About 6 of 10 junior high school users and 4 of 10 senior high school users see no risk or even slight risk of regular use. Eighty-one percent of users see SLT as *much safer than cigarettes.* Recent studies have reported that 77% of school-age children believe that cigarette smoking is very harmful to one's health, where only 40% believe that SLT is harmful (Schaefer et al. 1985).

Chassin (1985) reported that the image of a chewer was more positive than that of a smoker. Compared to a smoker, a chewer is seen as more self-confident, happier, more popular, healthier, more relaxed, liking the country more, using drugs less, and more athletic. A study by Edmundson (1987) reported that on a personality test, dippers were described as more socially outgoing, enthusiastic, imaginative, and group-dependent than chewers.

In sum, the research shows that many of the psychosocial variables related to onset and use of cigarettes also are related to the use of SLT by adolescents. However, there are specific positive social images attributed to SLT users that are different than for smokers: namely, the relationship to risk-taking and perception that use involves low risk, general parental acceptance of use, as well as the relationship of chewing to specific desirable activities, such as playing baseball or football, horseback riding, auto racing, rodeo competition, and outdoor "macho" activities. The implications of these findings are that treatment programs need to emphasize the health risks of SLT use, the addictive nature of nicotine, and the level of addiction one reaches with SLT use. Since boys may use it to project a masculine image, showing females' negative reaction to snuff and chewing tobacco also could be used effectively in prevention programs.

DIAGNOSIS AND ASSESSMENT OF SLT ADDICTION

There are no standard self-report measures of SLT consumption, such as those for smoking (i.e., number of cigarettes/day). There are emerging standards for assessing SLT use, although the varied packaging and use of snuff and loose leaf chew make this difficult. Surveys of adolescent SLT users have benefited from having research groups agree on a "standard" set of questions. These questions were chosen to provide a direct comparison to the use of cigarettes for the same samples. These questions include asking the individual if he or she used one or more dips or chews in the past 7 days, one or more dips or chews in the past 24 hours (or day), and whether he or she uses dip or chew daily.

Recent studies have focused on the topography of SLT use and on the relationship between different measures of use. In a study of 94 daily SLT users, Severson and associates (1990a) reported that snuff users reported a mean level of 10 dips per day while chewers reported a mean of 6 pinches of loose leaf tobacco per day. A heavy snuff user typically reported buying a tin every other day, with some using as much as a tin per day. The average user reported a mean level of 5 days per tin.

In a study of male college-aged SLT users, Hatsukami, Keenan, and Anton (1988) reported an average of six dips per day, with a mean of 103 minutes between dips, an average dip duration of 40 minutes and a mean total daily dip duration of approximately 4 and ¼ hours. There were approximately 2 g of tobacco in an average dip or chew, with a total of 12 g of tobacco per day on an average. In an interview study of adolescent male SLT users, Ary and colleagues (1987) reported that an average can lasted 5 days and that the boys used an average of five dips of snuff per day. An estimate of the dip size was obtained by dividing the net weight of the can by the number of dips per can. This yields a reported dip size of 1.3 g. When asked how long they kept the tobacco in their mouths, 58% reported 10–20 minutes, 22.7% reported more than 20 minutes, and 8% reported less than 10 minutes (Ary, Lichtenstein, Severson 1987).

Severson et al. (1990a) assessed the intercorrelation of four self-report measures of SLT use and weight of the actual dip and assessment of saliva nicotine for 94 daily smokeless users. The measures included: number of dips per day, number of minutes the dip or chew is kept in the mouth, the number of days a tin or pouch lasts, and the number of tins or pouches per week. All four measures of SLT intercorrelated significantly with saliva cotinine assays; the weight of the dip and the number of dips per day showed the highest correlations (Severson et al. 1990a). The measure most users felt confident in reporting was the number of days a tin or pouch lasts, and this would appear adequate as a rough guide to level of use.

Schroeder and colleagues (1988) suggest categorizing the SLT user as a "light," "moderate," or "heavy" user according to the potential amount of nicotine consumed per week from chewing tobacco and snuff products. By analyzing the nicotine levels of the most frequently reported brands of snuff and chewing tobacco and by using self-reported consumption patterns, the authors were able to define three levels of nicotine exposure from SLT. In this scheme, light users consume up to one-half tin or pouch per week (up to 88 mg of nicotine), moderate users one-half to two and one-half cans or packages per week (88–388 mg nicotine), and heavy users were classified on the basis of their consumption of more than two and one-half cans or over 388 mg of nicotine per week.

Recent laboratory analysis of popular snuff brands revealed large differences in available nicotine content based on nicotine level and pH. Nicotine varied by brand from 5.7 mg/g for Hawken, to 14.6 mg/g for Kodiak, 10.7 mg/g for Skoal, and up to 30.7 mg/g for Copenhagen (Hoffman et al. 1986a,b). The pH values also varied, with higher values associated with greater nicotine absorption. Skoal and Copenhagen brands account for the vast majority of moist snuff sales and are among the highest levels of nicotine bioavailability. Ernster et al. (1990) and Connolly, Orleans, and Kogan (1988) found evidence for higher addiction levels and greater oral pathology among Copenhagen users.

Unfortunately, the nicotine content of specific smokeless products is not always available, and manufacturers reformulate their products from time to time, so one has to assess addiction level solely on the basis of the number of tins or packets per week. It is suggested that less than one pouch or tin of SLT per week represents light use, one or two tins per week represents moderate use, and that any use in excess of two pouches or tins per week be regarded as heavy use. This proposed definition of SLT usage provides a clinically useful index of whether nicotine replacement (i.e., nicotine gum or transdermal patches) may be an appropriate adjunct to treatment (see Chapter 12).

An alternative measure of addiction was reported by Eakin, Severson, and Glasgow (1989), who adapted the Fagerström Tolerance Questionnaire (Fagerström 1978) for use with smokeless tobacco users. Cigarette-based items were simply converted to SLT-use items; "I chew or dip first thing in the morning or within 30 minutes of waking up in the morning." Additional questions have to do with chewing or using SLT in situations where spitting is not allowed and choosing to swallow rather than not taking a chew or dip. Subjects who succeeded in quitting had somewhat lower scores on this scale than subjects who were not successful, but the scale has not yet been validated as a predictor of SLT cessation or severity of nicotine withdrawal.

In assessing a SLT user, it is also important to ask whether the person wants to quit their use and whether the person has made any serious attempts to quit in the past 12 months. Questions were adapted from the Prochaska and DiClemente (1983) stages of change model to inquire about their readiness for change. These questions cover whether they are seriously considering quitting their use of SLT in the next 6 months (contemplation) and whether they are considering quitting in the next month (determination or preparation) (see Chapters 6 and 10).

The measures of SLT use and addiction have been adapted from the clinical cigarette cessation literature. Further refinements are needed to accurately measure use and stages of change to provide information to guide the intervention.

POTENTIAL FOR MEDICAL–DENTAL INTERVENTION

A majority of men who use SLT report being interested in quitting. In an interview with 94 snuff users, 68% reported attempting to quit, with an average of four quit attempts each. When the snuff users quit, they reported remaining abstinent from tobacco from an average of 1–3 months (Severson et al. 1990a). The majority of these men (77%) quit cold turkey and used substitutes such as gum and sunflower seeds while quitting. From a list of eight potential withdrawal symptoms, the three cited most often were irritability, tension, and hunger. It appears that the withdrawal symptoms experienced in an SLT cessation effort are similar, if not identical, to the smokers experience (Hatsukami, Gust, Keenan 1987). Unfortunately, 36% of snuff users reported smoking cigarettes during attempts to quit chewing. Interestingly, over half (54%) of all snuff users said they would try to quit their use of chewing tobacco within the next year, while 12% were unsure, and 35% said they did not plan to quit. Sixty-two percent of SLT users in dental clinics reported that they seriously considered quitting in the next 6 months (Severson 1990a).

Subjects in the Severson et al. (1990a) study reported that they would be motivated to quit if they experienced smokeless-related health problems (54%), if their significant others encouraged them to quit (25%), or if their concern about the risk of SLT use increased through education about health risks (19%). Ninety-six percent of the snuff users interviewed acknowledged that there are health risks associated with SLT use and many of the men had experienced these symptoms directly. Sixty-three percent of the men interviewed reported soreness of gums, lips, or tongue, and 41% experienced leukoplakia. Additional symptoms included stomach upset (38%), receding gums (37%), and open sores in the mouth (10%) (Severson et al. 1990a).

Fifty-seven percent of snuff users see their dentists at least once per year (Severson et al. 1990a). Among subjects who had seen their dentists in the past year, 57% reported that their dentists had noticed their use of SLT.

Thirty-three percent of the men reported that their dentists had advised them to quit use of SLT; 63% of those advised to quit by their doctors said they actually appreciated this advice. Only 11% reported actually attempting to quit. However, the majority of SLT users interviewed said they would be interested in receiving self-help materials or direct advice from their dentists on how to quit (Severson et al. 1990a).

SELF-HELP AND FORMAL TREATMENTS

It appears that adult SLT users are aware of health risks and often are interested in quitting. However, the use of self-help guides and formal treatment for SLT dependence have been largely unexplored. Whereas there is a large body of literature on prevalence and consequences of use, little effort has been devoted to assisting SLT users in recovering from nicotine dependence. Because of the steady rise and prevalent use of SLT, and because of the severe health consequences of use, there is a dire need for successful treatments to be developed.

Self-help and Minimal-Contact Intervention

Self-help smokeless cessation materials have not been widely available, and health professionals have had few resources to offer. Voluntary health organizations, such as the American Lung Association and American Cancer Society have few educational or self-help materials available on SLT (see Table 13–3). However, the American Cancer Society recently published a cessation pamphlet for SLT users (see Table 13–3). The materials have shown promise when pretested in a behavioral group treatment program with adolescent SLT users (Glover et al., in press). The NCI's recent smokeless cessation guide for baseball players will soon be evaluated with college and junior college baseball players (Orleans, Connolly, Workman 1991). A self-help manual for smokeless users has recently been published (Severson 1992) which provides comprehensive self-guided cessation for SLT users. This manual is being used in current studies of nicotine replacement, but no efficacy

Table 13–3 Selected Smokeless Tobacco-related Education Resources

Federal Government Reports (Available from the U.S. Government Printing Office or specific agency noted)

National Cancer Institute. *Smokeless Programs for Youth*. Washington, D.C., 1986.

————. *State and Local Programs on Smoking and Health*. Washington, D.C., 1986.

————. *Chew or Snuff is Real Bad Stuff*. Washington, D.C. Publication No. 88-2976, 1988.

National Institutes of Health. *Health Implications of Smokeless Tobacco Use: Consensus Development Conference*, 1986 (105 pp).

————. *Chew or Snuff is Real Bad Stuff*. NIH Publication No. 88-2976, February 1988.

U.S. Dept. of Health and Human Services (1986). *The Health Consequences of Smokeless Tobacco. A Report from the Surgeon General*. Washington, D.C.: U.S. Government Printing Office. NIH Publication No. 86-2874.

Pamphlets—Private Organizations (Available from local office unless otherwise noted)

American Cancer Society. *If You're Dipping Snuff You Should Know the Truth*. 1987.

American Dental Association. *Smokeless Tobacco*. 1988.

American Lung Association. *A Guide to Smokeless Tobacco*. 1983.

————. *Is There a Safe Tobacco?* 1986.

Channing L. Bete Co., Deerfield, MA. *What Everyone Should Know About Smokeless Tobacco*. 1986.

Reader's Digest Reprint: *Sean Marsee's Smokeless Death*. 1985.

Audiovisuals Resources

Alfred Higgins Productions, Los Angeles, CA. *Smokeless Tobacco: It Can Snuff You Out*. Film. 1985.

American Cancer Society. *Smokeless Doesn't Mean Harmless*. Video.

————. *Smokeless Tobacco: Is It Really Safe*. Video.

American Dental Association and American Cancer Society. *Smokeless Tobacco*. (Video). 1986.

Idaho Cancer Coordinating Committee and Idaho Department of Health and Welfare, Boise, ID. *Are You Up to Snuff?* Film. 1984.

Independent Video Services and Oregon Research Institute, Eugene, OR. *The Big Dipper*. Film and video. 1986.

Wisconsin Department of Health and Social Services. 40 slides. 1985.

Curriculum Guides and Resources for Teachers

American Academy of Otalaryngology—Head & Neck Surgery Inc. *Through With Chew*. One Prince St., Alexandria, VA 22314. 1988.

American Cancer Society, Wisconsin Division, Inc., Madison, WI 53708. *S.O.S.: Snuff Out Snuff: A Guide to School and Community Smokeless Tobacco Intervention*. 1988.

Glover, E.D., Schroeder, K.L., and Scott, L. *Curriculum Guide and Tape: Teacher's Written Supplements on Smokeless Tobacco*. Balance Productions, 27 Wellstone Dr., Portland, MA 04103. 1987.

Indiana State Board of Health, Division of Health Education, Indianapolis, IN 46206. *Smokeless Tobacco Resource Materials*. 1986.

Oregon Research Institute. *Project PATH Tobacco Prevention Program for Grades 6–12*. Independent Video Services, 401 East Tenth Ave., Eugene, OR 97401.

Severson, H., James, L., LaChance, P.A., Eakin, E. *Up To Snuff: A Handbook on Smokeless Tobacco*. Independent Video Services, 401 East Tenth Ave., Eugene, OR 97401.

Self-help Cessation Materials

American Cancer Society: *Smokeless Tobacco, Check it Out, Think it Out. Take it Out, Throw it Out, Snuff it Out, Keep it Out*. (91-10M-No. 2090) 1991.

————. *Beat The Smokeless Habit: Game Plan for Success*, by C. Tracy Orleans, Greg Connelly, Stephen Workman. Washington, D.C., 1991. NIH Publication No. 92-3270.

Severson, H. *Enough Snuff: A Manual for Quitting Smokeless Tobacco on Your Own*. Rainbow Productions, 4080 Hilyard St., Eugene, OR, 97405. 1992.

data is available on the use of this manual alone.

Health care providers, particularly oral health providers (dentists and hygienists), can play a critical role in helping SLT users to become more aware of potential health effects and to become more interested in quitting. SLT users who receive direct advice to quit by oral health professionals and are shown oral lesions directly attributable to their SLT use, would appear especially responsive or receptive to help with quitting. Pointing out the user's oral lesion is particularly relevant, since we found that 78% of regular SLT users coming to health maintenance organization (HMO) dental clinics for a hygiene visit had clinically detectable oral lesions. These lesions varied in severity or stage; 28% degree I; 27% degree II; and 23% degree III (Severson 1990).

An ongoing study of SLT cessation in dental clinics confirms that brief, direct advice from the dental hygienist and dentist, when provided in the context of regular oral health care, can help a significant number of SLT users quit (Severson et al. 1990b). This randomized clinical trial involves identifying SLT use through a brief questionnaire given to all patients in HMO dental clinics and then randomizing users to receive usual care or the minimal intervention. Preliminary data on 450 subjects, with a 3-month follow-up on self-reported quitting, indicate that approximately 25% of regular users are able to quit when provided with direct advice to quit, a brief self-help manual, and a 10-minute videotape in the dental clinic. The usual care group had a self-reported quit rate of 12% during the same time. The self-help manual and videotape were developed specifically for the project. The manual *(Enough Snuff)* focused on specific cognitive–behavioral tips for making a decision to stop using SLT, quitting tips, and dealing with urges and slips. The videotape presented information on oral health effects of SLT and brief motivational interviews with men who had successfully quit. A 1-year follow-up will assess whether these cessation efforts are maintained. This approach of providing a brief intervention in the context of routine health care shows great promise (Little et al. 1992).

Formal Treatment Programs

In an early report on SLT cessation for young adults, Glover et al. (1986) adapted the American Cancer Society's FreshStart Adult Smoking Cessation Program for use with 41 SLT users. He reported a 6-month abstinence rate of only 2.3%. However, these subjects were mandated to attend the program, as they had been found in violation of school rules which prohibited the use of tobacco products. Given the nonvoluntary nature of the subject sample, this low success rate is not surprising. Subsequent studies by Eakin, Severson, and Glasgow (1989) and DiLorenzo et al. (1991) provide a more optimistic view of the potential cessation rates that can be achieved by formal SLT cessation treatments.

Eakin, Severson, and Glasgow (1989) reported an intervention with adolescent daily users, aged 14 to 18 years, who were recruited from Eugene, Oregon high schools. The study involved 25 subjects with a quasi-experimental design in which a comparison group of 11 subjects received delayed treatment. This behavioral treatment consisted of three small-group meetings with counselors, lasting approximately 1 hour. The multiple component treatment was cognitive–behavioral in nature and focused on encouraging subjects to use coping skills for cessation (e.g., "The 4-A's": Avoid, Alter, Alternatives, and Activities). Of the 21 subjects completing treatment, 9 were successful in quitting their SLT use at the end of treatment. Self-reported quitting was confirmed with saliva cotinine assessment and subjects were followed up at 6 months posttreatment. Long-term cessation rates were reduced to 12% at 6-month follow-up; however, subjects not achieving abstinence had a self-reported reduction of 45% in their daily use of SLT from baseline levels. The participants in this study reported that in addition to the group sessions, the ongoing telephone calls and support by the counselor were key elements in their successful quitting.

DiLorenzo et al. (1991) reported a multiple baseline design intervention on nine adult males recruited to a behavioral SLT cessation program. Mean age of the subjects was 32 years and the average length of use of SLT was 9.3 years. Subjects were involved in eight, 1-hour behavioral treatment sessions over a period of 7 weeks in small groups of three subjects each. Cue extinction, setting a target date for quitting, the use of a buddy system, and relapse prevention were the primary components of the intervention. Cue extinction involved identifying two or three situations most strongly associated with SLT use and breaking these associations by refraining from taking a dip for 30 minutes or more. Of the seven subjects who completed the program, six remained abstinent through the second treatment phase, and a 9-month follow-up showed all six subjects still abstinent. These data were confirmed by collateral sources. The program appears quite successful, although the modest number of subjects dictates caution in interpretation.

By and large, formal SLT treatment programs have simply adapted standard cognitive–behavioral techniques used in formal *smoking* cessation programs (see Chapter 14). Likewise, personal communication with SLT cessation counselors indicates that self-help *smoking* cessation materials can be readily adapted and used by SLT users. In our study of adolescent users, we depended heavily on the adaptation of smoking cessation materials for each of the group sessions (Eakin, Severson, Glasgow 1989). However, further research is needed to determine how SLT cessation differs from smoking cessation. For instance, the use of oral substitutes may be more important for SLT users, and there may be differences in the impact of nicotine gum.

Persons going through treatment for SLT addiction often request an oral substitute. Products such as cinnamon sticks, gum, sunflower seeds, finely ground mint leaves, or other chewed foodstuff appear to be useful substitutes for SLT. Unpublished case reports and ongoing cessation studies report the successful ad lib use of a mint snuff (non-tobacco) product as an SLT substitute. This product (Mint Snuff), which contains finely ground mint in snuff-like tins, is used in the same way as snuff, but provides no nicotine or carcinogenic compounds. Focus on self-examination of oral lesions is, of course, a treatment component uniquely suited to SLT treatments.

SLT cessation programs to date have focused on using a "cold turkey" procedure. However, one guide suggests a "nicotine fading" approach involving switching to lower nicotine snuff products before quitting (Orleans, Connolly, Workman 1991). Larger-scale experimental SLT treatments are sorely needed. Future studies should employ objective verifications of SLT cessation rates.

PHARMACOLOGIC ADJUNCTS

To date, there are no published reports of using nicotine replacement therapy as an adjunct to a behavioral SLT cessation program. The use of nicotine gum appears attractive for SLT cessation, since the topography of the behavior, route of administration, and rate of absorption are similar to SLT. Dorothy Hatsukami (personal communication 1990) and her colleagues report promising preliminary results using nicotine gum as part of a behavioral group treatment program for SLT users. They found no difference between the use of the gum ad lib or on a fixed schedule, or between the 2 and 4 mg doses, in initial or 6-month quit rates. The use of the gum consistently resulted in higher quit rates than use of a placebo adjunct. Randomized clinical trials are underway which compare 2 mg nicotine gum with 0 mg gum (placebo) to test the incremental cessation effect of providing this pharmacologic adjunct to patients. Similarly, ongoing research is comparing transdermal nicotine to nicotine gum as an adjunct.

PUBLIC HEALTH PERSEPCTIVE

There is growing interest in public health approaches to treating SLT use and addiction. The public health approach moves away from individual, "clinical" approaches to more economic and broader scale interventions that focus on public education and awareness. Making individuals increasingly aware of the health risks via media or print presentations, integrating SLT into standard smoking prevention curricula in schools, and providing educational and self-help materials in the context of routine health care are examples of public health efforts. These approaches reach users who are not motivated to seek treatment, as well as those who are (Hollis et al. 1992).

An excellent example of a public health intervention was a recent randomized clinical trial which reported that at 3-month follow-up 23% of SLT users receiving direct advice from the dentist and hygienist quit their use of SLT (Little et al. 1992). The intervention was conducted in seven HMO dental clinics and was supplemented by supportive materials from the hygienist (self-help manual and brief videotape) and feedback on the patients' soft tissue oral health status. Patients in the usual care condition reported a 14% cessation rate at 3-month follow-up. The intervention was conducted in the context of routine dental hygiene visits and did not slow patient flow in the busy clinics.

PREVENTION OF SLT USE

Educational Material

Examples of available video and print materials on SLT are shown in Table 13–3. These materials can assist in providing the user with a better understanding of the health risks of regular SLT use. Additionally, providing materials, either in health education classes (for adolescents), or to users in the context of medical/dental health care delivery, has the potential to significantly decrease the use of these products. However, as noted, most available print and video resources focus on increasing knowledge of the health risks of SLT use, very few provide cessation advice.

School Prevention Programs

Recently, interest has increased in adding SLT prevention programs to school-based prevention curricula. A recent randomized trial found that a brief, five- to seven-session program in the seventh and ninth grades led to a significant decrease in SLT use in males (Severson, Glasgow, Wirt et al. 1990). Current ongoing NCI-funded studies also have incorporated a SLT focus into existing *smoking* prevention programs in San Diego, Los Angeles, Washington state, and Kansas City. Special curriculum materials have been developed for native American youth in an effort to impact this high-risk group. Other NCI-funded programs have targeted Little League Baseball and 4-H Clubs as groups that provide an opportunity to provide information on the health risks involved in SLT use. In 1986, 20 states already reported offering SLT education programs. This has likely grown to encompass most

states. However, the extent to which these programs are actually implemented in the schools is unknown and the effectiveness of these interventions has not been evaluated to date.

Environmental Strategies

Controls on availability, price, and marketing, along with adequate warnings and countermarketing are additional available public health approaches. These approaches are expected to have similar impacts on SLT use and initiation to those that they have with cigarette use and initiation (see Chapter 19).

CONCLUSION

SLT use and popularity has risen dramatically over the past decade, and represents a significant form of tobacco addiction. Over 12 million males use SLT regularly, and their addiction to this tobacco product represents a serious public health risk. The serious health consequences of regular SLT use have been well established. The nicotine addiction associated with SLT use appears equivalent to that for cigarette smoking. Recent publication of the Surgeon General's Report on the Health Consequences of Using Smokeless Tobacco (USDHHS 1986) has led to increased research on treatment, health effects, and prevention of SLT use. An increasing awareness of the detrimental effects of smokeless tobacco use has led to recent legislative efforts, such as Public Law 99-252, to ban media advertising of SLT products, and provide rotating health warnings on product packages. Significant progress has been made in targeting SLT as an addictive substance that requires special consideration in clinical and public health tobacco control efforts. However, to date, the increased awareness of detrimental health effects of SLT use has not resulted in providing assistance to SLT users to quit. The development, evaluation, and dissemination of effective SLT prevention and treatment programs is critical in reducing the national use of these oral tobacco products. It is time to focus our attention on SLT use in our continuing battle to control tobacco addiction.

REFERENCES

Ary, D. V. Use of smokeless tobacco among male adolescents: Concurrent and prospective relationships. *Natl Cancer Inst Monogr* 8:49–55, 1989.

Ary, D. V., Lichtenstein, E., Severson, H. H. Smokeless tobacco use among male adolescents: Patterns, correlates, predictors, and the use of other drugs. *Prev Med* 16:385–401, 1987.

Axell, T., Mornstad, H., Sundstrom, B. The relation of the clinical picture to the histopathology of snuff dipper's lesions in a Swedish population. *J Oral Pathol* 5:229–236, 1976.

Bauman, K. E. Effect of parental smoking classifications on the association between parental and adolescent smoking. *Addict Behav,* 15(5):413–422, 1990.

Bauman, K. E., Koch, G. C., Fisher, L. A., Bryan, E. Use of smokeless tobacco by age, race, and gender in ten Standard Metropolitan Statistical Areas of the Southeast United States. *Natl Cancer Inst Monogr* 8:35–37, 1989.

Benowitz, N. L. Nicotine and smokeless tobacco. *CA* 38(4):244–247, 1988.

Benowitz, N. L., Porchet, H., Sheiner, L., Jacob, P. Nicotine absorption and cardiovascular effects with smokeless tobacco use: Comparison with cigarettes and nicotine gum. *Clin Pharmacol Ther* 44:23–28, 1988.

Bonaguro, J. A., Pugh, M., Bonaguro, E. W. Multivariate analysis of smokeless tobacco use by adolescents in grades four through twelve. *Health Educ* April/May 1986, 17.

Botvin, G. L., Baker, E., Tortu, E., Dusenburg, L., Gessula, J. Smokeless tobacco use among adolescents: Correlates and concurrent predictors. *Dev Behav Pediatr* 10(4):181–186, 1989.

Braverman, M. T., D'Onofrio, C. N., Moskowitz, J. M. Marketing smokeless tobacco in California communities: Implications for health education. *NCI Monographs.* 8:79–85, 1989.

Chassin, L., Presson, C. C., Sherman, C. J., McGlaughlin, L., Giolia, D. Psychological correlates of adolescent smokeless tobacco use. *Addict Behav* 10:431–435, 1985.

Christen, A. G., Swanson, B. Z., Glover, E. D., Henderson, A. H. Smokeless tobacco: The folklore and social history of snuffing, sneezing, dipping, and chewing. *J Am Dent Assoc* 105:821, 1982.

Christen, A. G., and Glover, E. D. History of smokeless tobacco use in the United States. *Health Educ* June/July 1987, 6–13.

Connolly, G. N. Reemergence of smokeless to-

bacco. *New Engl J Med* 314:1026–1027, 1986.

Connolly, G. N., Orleans, C. T., Kogan, M. Use of smokeless tobacco in major-league baseball. *New Engl J Med* 318:1281–1284, 1988.

Cummings, K. M., Michalek, A. M., Carl, W., Wood, R., Haley, N. J. Use of smokeless tobacco in a group of professional baseball players. *J Behav Med* 12(6):559–567, 1989.

Dent, C. W., Sussman, S., Johnson, A., Hansen, W., Flay, B. R. Adolescent smokeless tobacco incidence: Relations with other drugs and psychosocial variables. *Prev Med* 16:422–431, 1987.

Deveny, K. With help of teens, snuff sales revive. *Wall Street Journal* 3 May 1990, B1.

DiLorenzo, T. M., Kern, T. G., Pieper, R. M. Treatment of smokeless tobacco use through a formalized cessation program. *Behav Ther* 22(1):41–46, 1991.

Eakin, E., Severson, H. H., Glasgow, R. E. Development and evaluation of a smokeless tobacco cessation program: A pilot study. *Natl Cancer Inst Monogr* 8:95–100, 1989.

Edmundson, E. W., Glover, E. D., Alston, P. P., Holbert, D. H. Personality traits of smokeless tobacco users and nonusers: A comparison. *Int J Addict* 22(7):671–683, 1987.

Ernster, V. L. Advertising and promotion of smokeless tobacco products. *Natl Cancer Inst Monogr* 8:87–94, 1989.

Ernster, V. L., Grady, D. C., Greene, B., Hauck, W. W. Smokeless tobacco use and health effects among baseball players. *JAMA* 264(2):218–224, 1990.

Fagerström, K. O. Measuring the degree of dependence in tobacco smoking with reference to individualization of treatment. *Addict Behav* 3:235–241, 1978.

Glover, E. D., Edmundson, M. A., Edwards, S. W., Schroeder, K. L. Implications of smokeless tobacco use among athletes. *The Physician and Sports Medicine.* 14(12):94–105, 1986.

Glover, E. D., Schroeder, K. L., Henningfield, J. E., Severson, H. H., Chrksten, A. G. An interpretive review of smokeless tobacco research in the United States: Part I. *Drug Educ* 18(4):305–330, 1988.

———. An interpretive review of smokeless tobacco research in the United States: Part II. *Drug Educ* 19(1):1–19, 1989b.

Glover, E. D., Wang, M. O., Glover, P. N. (in press). Development of a high school smokeless tobacco cessation manual. *Health Values.*

Greer, R. O., and Poulson, T. C. Oral tissue alternations associated with the use of smokeless tobacco by teen-agers. *Oral Surg* 56:275–284, 1983.

Gritz, E. R., Baer-Weiss, V., Benowitz, N. L., Van Vinakos, H., Jarvik, M. E. Plasma nicotine and cotinine concentrations in habitual smokeless tobacco users. *Clin Pharmacol Ther* 30(2):201–209, August 1981.

Gritz, E. R., Ksir, C., McCarthy, W. J. Smokeless tobacco use in the United States: past and future trends. *Ann Behav Med* 7:24–27, 1985.

Hall, R. L., and Dexter, D. Smokeless tobacco use and attitudes toward smokeless tobacco among Native American and other adolescents in the northwest. *Am J Public Health* 78(12):1586, 1988.

Hatsukami, D. K. Personal communciation, 1990.

Hatsukami, D. K., Gust, S. W., Keenan, R. M. Physiological and subjective changes from smokeless tobacco withdrawal. *Clin Pharmacol Ther* 41:103–107, 1987.

Hatsukami, D. K., Hughes, J. R., Pickens, R. W., Svikis, D. Tobacco withdrawal symptoms: An experimental analysis. *Psychopharmacology.* 84:231–236, 1984.

Henningfield, J. E. Behavioral pharmacology of cigarette smoking. In Thompson, T., Dew, P. B., Barrett, J. E., eds. *Advances in Behavioral Pharmacology,* vol. 4. New York: Academic Press, 1984, 131–220.

Hoffman, D., Brunnemann, K. D., Adams, J. D., Hecht, S. Laboratory studies on snuff-dipping and oral cancer. *Cancer J* 1(1):9, 1986.

Hoffman, D., Harley, N. H., Fisenne, I., Adams, J. D., Brunnemann, K. D. Carcinogenic agents in snuff. *J Natl Cancer Inst* 76(3):9, 1986.

Hollis, J. F., Lichtenstein, E., Vogt, T. M., Stevens, V. J., Biglan, A. A practical nurse-assisted tobacco intervention program for primary care. Annals of Internal Medicine (in press).

Hughes, J. R., and Hatsukami, D. K. Signs and symptoms of tobacco withdrawal. *Arch Gen Psychiatry* 43:289–294, 1986.

Hunter, S. M., Croft, J. B., Burke, G. L., Parker, F. C., Webber, L. S., Beremson, G. S. Longitudinal patterns of cigarette smoking and smokeless tobacco use in youth. *Am J Public Health* 76:193–195, 1986.

Jessor, R., Jessor, S. L. *Problem Behavior and Psychosocial Development: A Longitudinal Study of Youth.* New York, NY: Academic Press, 1977.

Lichtenstein, E., Severson, H. H., Friedman, L. S., Ary, D. V. Chewing tobacco use by adolescents: Prevalence and relation to cigarette smoking. *Addict Behav* 9:351–355, 1984.

Little, S. J., Stevens, U., Severson, H., Lichtenstein, E. An effective smokeless tobacco intervention for dental hygiene patients. *J Dental Hygiene* 66:185–190, 1992.

Marcus, A. C., Crane, L. A., Shopland, D. R., Lynn, W. L. Use of smokeless tobacco in the United States: Recent estimates from the Current Population Survey. *Natl Cancer Inst Monogr* 8:17–23, 1989.

Marty, P. J., McDermott, R. J., Williams, T. Patterns of smokeless tobacco use in a population of high school students. *Am J Public Health* 76(2):190–192, 1986.

Mattson, M. E., and Winn, D. M. Smokeless tobacco: Association with increased cancer risk. *Natl Cancer Inst Monogr* 8:13–16, 1989.

Newman, I. M., and Duryea, E. J. Adolescent cigarette smoking and tobacco chewing in Nebraska. *Nebr Med J* October 243–244, 1981.

Office of the Inspector General. Youth use of smokeless tobacco: More than a pinch of trouble. *Office of Analysis and Inspections; Region VI.* Washington, DC 1986.

Orlandi, M. A., and Boyd, G. Smokeless tobacco use among adolescents: A theoretical overview. *Natl Cancer Inst Monogr* 8:6, 1989

Orleans, C. T., Connolly, G., Workman, S. *Beat the smokeless habit.* Washington, D.C.: National Cancer Institute, 1991. NIH Publication No. 92-3270.

Peterson, A. V., Marek, P. M., Mann, S. L. Initiation and use of smokeless tobacco in relation to smoking. *Natl Cancer Inst Monogr* 8:63–69, 1989.

Pindborg, J. J., Reibel, J., Roed-Pedersen, B., Mehta, F. S. Tobacco induced changes in oral leukoplakic epithelium. *Cancer* 45:2330–2336, 1980.

Reader's Digest. *Sean Marsee's Smokeless Death.* October 1985.

Roed-Pedersen, B., and Pindborg, J. J. A study of Danish snuff induced oral leukoplakia. *J Oral Pathol* 2:301–313, 1973.

Rouse, B. A. Epidemiology of smokeless tobacco use: A national study. *Natl Cancer Inst Monogr* 8:29–33, 1989.

Russell, M.A.H., Jarvis, M. J., Devitt, G., Feyerabend, C. Nicotine intake by snuff users. *Br Med J* 283:814–817, 1981.

Schaefer, S. P., Henderson, A. H., Glover, E. D., Christen, A. G. Patterns of use and incidence of smokeless tobacco consumption in school aged children. *Arch Otolaryngol* 111:639–642, 1985.

Schinke, S. P., Shilling, R. F., II, Gilchrist, L. D., Ashby, M. R., Kitajima, E. Native youth and smokeless tobacco: Prevalence rates, gender differences, and descriptive characteristics. *Natl Cancer Inst Monogr* 8:39–42, 1989.

Schroeder, K. L. Oral and systemic concerns with smokeless tobacco. *Clarks Clin Dent* 2(9):1–27, 1987.

Schroeder, K. L., Chen, M. S., Jr., Iaderosa, G. R., Glover, E. D., Edmundson, E. W. Proposed definition of a smokeless tobacco user based on "potential" nicotine consumption. *Addict Behav* 13:395–400, 1988.

Severson, H. *Enough Snuff: A Manual for Quitting Smokeless Tobacco on Your Own.* Eugene, OR: Rainbow Productions, 1992.

Severson, H. H. Psychosocial factors in the use of smokeless tobacco and their implications for P.L. 99-252. *J Public Health Dent* 50(1):90–97, 1990.

Severson, H. H., Lichtenstein, E., Gallison, C. A pinch or a pouch instead of a puff? Implications of chewing tobacco for addictive process. *Bull Psychologists Addict Behav* 4:85–92, 1985.

Severson, H. H., Glasgow, R., Wirt, T., Brozovsky, P., Eakin, E. Evaluation of a school based prevention program to reduce smokeless tobacco use by teen males. In Aoki, M., Hisamichi, S., Tominaga, S., eds. *Smoking and Health.* New York: Excerpta Medica, International Congress Series 780, 1987, 575–579.

Severson, H. H., Eakin, E. G., Lichtenstein, E., Stevens, V. J. The inside scoop on the stuff called snuff: An interview study of 94 adult male smokeless tobacco users. *J Substance Abuse* 2:77–85, 1990a.

Severson, H. H., Eakin, E. G., Stevens, V. J., Lichtenstein, E. Dental office practices for tobacco users: Independent practice and HMO clinics. *Am J Public Health* 80(12):1503–1505, 1990b.

Severson, H. H., Glasgow, R., Wirt, R., Brozovsky, P., Zoref, L., Black, C., Biglan, A., Ary, D., Weissman, W. Preventing the use of smokeless tobacco and cigarettes by teens:

Results of a classroom intervention. *Health Educ Res* 6(1):109–120, 1991.

Severson, H. H., Stevens, V. J., Little, S. J., Lichtenstein, E. The teachable moment: Smokeless tobacco intervention in dental clinics. Paper presented at the Seventh World Conference on Tobacco and Health, Perth, Australia, 1–5 April 1990.

Silverman, S. *Oral cancer.* NY: *Am Cancer Soc* 6–35, 1981.

Sussman, S., Holt, L., Dent, C. W., Flay, B. R., Graham, J. W., Hansen, W. B., Johnson, C. A. Activity involvement, risk-taking, demographic variables, and other drug use: Prediction of trying smokeless tobacco. *Natl Cancer Inst Monogr* 8:57–62, 1989.

Sussman, S., Dent, C. W., Stacy, A. W., Burciaga, C., Raynor, A., Turner, G. E., Charlin, V., Craig, S., Hansen, W. B., Burton, D., Flay, B. R. Peer-group association and adolescent tobacco use. *J Abnorm Psychol* 99(4):349–352, 1990.

U.S. Department of Health and Human Services. (USDHHS). *The Health Consequences of Using Smokeless Tobacco. A Report to the Advisory Committee to the Surgeon General.* Public Health Service. NIH Publication No. 86-2874, 1986.

U.S. Department of Health and Human Services (USDHHS). *The Health Consequences of Smoking: 25 Years of Progress.* Public Health Service, Publication No. (CDC) 89-8411, 1989.

———. *How to Help Your Patients Stop Using Tobacco.* Public Health Service. NIH Publication No. 91-3191, 1990.

Winn, D. M., Blot, W. J., Shy, C. M., Pickle, L. W., Toledo, A., Fraumeni, J. F., Jr. Snuff dipping and oral cancer among women in the southern United States. *N Engl J Med* 304–745–749, 1981.

Young, M., and Williamson, D. Correlates of use and expected use of smokeless tobacco among kindergarten children. *Psychol Rep* 56:63–66, 1985.

14

Treating Nicotine Addiction in High-Risk Groups and Patients with Medical Co-Morbidity

ELLEN R. GRITZ, JEAN L. KRISTELLER, and DAVID M. BURNS

Opportunities for smoking cessation intervention represented by patient–physician and patient–health care delivery system interactions have generated a substantial body of research that defines the content and effectiveness of physician-based smoking cessation programs. Many of these programs are appropriately designed for use in routine office visits by a patient, and the content of the intervention is not focused on a specific disease or condition. However, many patient interactions occur as the result of specific health problems or conditions that may increase the patient's motivation and interest in cessation assistance. Cessation programs delivered in conjunction with initiation of other therapy for a newly diagnosed major illness or as part of prenatal care have generally had higher cessation rates than have interventions delivered to healthy patients as part of a routine office visit.

The reasons for the greater efficacy of interventions delivered as part of the treatment of a specific disease or condition include a greater intensity of the intervention effort and higher motivation of the patient. An additional reason, however, may be that the intervention can be customized to match the predictable psychologic and emotional response of the patient to the change in their health status and to the nature of the ongoing interactions with the health care delivery

system that result from their disease or condition.

CONDITION-SPECIFIC DIFFERENCES IN THE INTERACTION OF PATIENTS WITH THE HEALTH CARE SYSTEM

This chapter presents the results of smoking cessation interventions delivered to patients with four separate and quite distinct medical conditions: pregnancy, cardiovascular disease, chronic obstructive pulmonary disease (COPD), and cancer. These conditions are all linked by a common concern about present and potential future damage due to cigarette smoking, and by the hope that future adverse health outcomes can be avoided through cessation of smoking. However, the style and context of the patient's interactions with the health care system are vastly different. One needs to view the information presented on these interventions with an appreciation of the differences in the nature of the health care interaction that is occurring in order to fully understand the differences in program design and cessation results.

Pregnancy is a time limited condition commonly viewed as an exciting and positive experience by the women who are pregnant. Interactions with the health care delivery system are frequent and the frequency accelerates as the pregnancy progresses, but often abruptly stop with the last postpartum visit. The focus of a large part of the care being delivered is preventing injury to the fetus and optimizing the pregnancy outcome. Major life-style changes are accepted as a part of the pregnancy, including changes in diet, activity, alcohol use, and smoking; but these life-style changes are also often viewed as time limited changes that are required only for the duration of the pregnancy. Smoking cessation advice fits easily into the other care that is being delivered and is readily accepted as an intrinsic part of the care by both the patient and the health care practitioner. However, this acceptance also means that both the patient and the health care practitioner are less motivated to sustain the cessation effort once the pregnancy has been successfully completed. The resumption of normal dietary, activity, and alcohol consumption patterns is a legitimate expectation of women upon completion of the pregnancy, and it is perhaps not surprising that resumption of smoking occurs in the same context.

Cardiovascular disease is often first manifest as a major catastrophic life event, commonly a myocardial infarction. A rapid, intense, and often invasive interaction with the health care system ensues leaving the patient overwhelmed and dependent. Once the initial stage of therapeutic intervention is over, the focus rapidly shifts from survival and preservation of myocardial tissue to prevention of future events through a series of life-style changes: diet, exercise, control of blood pressure, and smoking cessation. Discharge from the hospital is accompanied by a period of rehabilitation focused on life-style adjustment. There is frequent, but decelerating over time, interaction with the health care system. The motivation and enthusiasm for smoking cessation of both the patient and the health care provider is high during the initial stages of recovery. However, the patient's motivation lessens with time, and this waning motivation occurs at the same time that the frequency of interaction with the health care system is diminishing.

The initial diagnosis of COPD can be a catastrophic hospitalization, but is more commonly the onset of shortness of breath.

Early in the course of the disease the motivation of the patient to stop smoking may be low, but the steady progression of symptoms usually provides a continually increasing stimulus to quit. Both the patient and providers of care are focused on the moderation of the symptoms of the disease, and cigarette smoking has a major influence on these symptoms. The motivation of the patient to quit and to stay quit is sustained by the immediate reinforcement of their symptoms and is not dependent on the hope of avoiding some poorly defined future disease state. As the disease progresses, the frequency and intensity of interaction with the health care system commonly increases, as does the frequency and intensity of the cessation advice and assistance. In contrast with the other states described, the opportunity to deliver cessation advice and the efficacy of that advice slowly and steadily increases over the often prolonged course of COPD.

The diagnosis of a cancer is a sudden and emotionally devastating life event that usually occurs in the absence of the drama and sense of short-term crisis that characterize a myocardial infarction. Hospitalization and invasive therapy may not occur for days or weeks following diagnosis, if at all. Just as with a myocardial infarction, the focus of the patient and the care giver rapidly shifts to those factors that will influence longevity. However, the factors that influence longevity with cancer are largely either present at the time of diagnosis (tumor type, extent of invasion, and presence of metastatic spread) or beyond the patient's control (response to therapy). Early in the course of the illness the support for life-style changes is usually focused on coping with the psychologic and emotional response to the diagnosis and adjusting to the consequences of the treatment. There is often a prolonged and highly stressful interaction with the health care system, but there is usually little interest on the part of either the patient or the providers of care in smoking cessation until the factors that cloud the prognosis are resolved. A shift in the focus of the patient and the care delivery process from defining how long the patient is likely to live to what life-style changes can alter future health and survival usually does not occur until weeks to months after the initial diagnosis and treatment. Both patient and physician may be very fatalistic about the benefits of cessation. When cessation assistance is provided, it is usually timed to occur late rather than early in the course of treatment. For cessation assistance to be maximally effective, it may be necessary to access patients when they are most vulnerable and motivated for change; however, there may be substantial provider-based barriers to considering or implementing cessation programs at this point in the patient's illness. This chapter outlines a far more aggressive and acutely initiated approach to smoking cessation advice and assistance for cancer patients.

These brief descriptions of the interactions with the health care system that occur with each of the conditions will help provide the context for understanding the differences in the cessation approaches described in the remainder of this chapter.

SPECIAL ISSUES IN TREATING THE PREGNANT SMOKER

A great deal is known about the adverse consequences of cigarette smoking during pregnancy—to the mother, fetus and, following delivery, to the infant and young child. This body of knowledge is widely disseminated in the medical and public health communities. However, the large research literature on treating nicotine dependence, in general, contains relatively few studies targeting the pregnant woman. Even less attention has been devoted to preventing relapse to smoking following delivery for women who succeed in abstaining until term. This section will address health consequences, smoking prevalence estimates during pregnancy, research on cessation during pregnancy and on relapse following delivery. In addition, ongoing efforts to develop and test innovative interventions targeted to high-risk pregnant smokers will be described.

Health Consequences of Smoking During Pregnancy

The 1989 and 1990 Reports of the Surgeon General on Smoking and Health (USDHHS 1989, 1990) synthesize the scientific litera-

ture on the effects of smoking on reproduction and pregnancy. The brief review presented here is drawn primarily from those documents and from earlier Surgeon General's reports.

Cigarette smoking has adverse effects on the major functions of the female reproductive system, beginning with fertility. The possible mechanisms for the reduced fertility associated with smoking include "hormonal effects, impaired tubal motility, impaired implantation, oocyte depletion, and altered immunity leading to pelvic inflammatory disease" (USDHHS 1990, Table 1, p. 372). Stopping smoking prior to attempting to conceive eliminates certain factors producing delays in conception, and returns fertility to a level comparable to never-smokers.

The major adverse consequence of smoking during pregnancy is reduction in infant birth weight, by an average of 200 g (USDHEW 1980). The proportion of low birth weight babies is also approximately doubled. Reduction in infant birth weight occurs primarily through intrauterine growth retardation (IUGR). Intrauterine hypoxia is believed to be the major mechanism for IUGR. The oxygen supply to the fetus is reduced due to the increased levels of carbon monoxide (and carboxyhemoglobin) in mother and fetus, and to vasoconstriction of the umbilical arteries, decreasing placental blood flow (USDHHS 1990).

The number of cigarettes smoked per day bears a dose-response relationship to the magnitude of the birth weight deficit (USDHHS 1990). Research has shown no apparent birth weight benefit to reductions in cigarettes smoked, short of complete cessation. Quitting prior to pregnancy prevents any birth weight deficits entirely, as does stopping by the third or fourth month and continuing to abstain. Cessation of smoking up to the 30th week of gestation produces a birth weight benefit. Parenthetically, stopping smoking even several days before delivery may provide some benefit during the birth process, because of increased availability of oxygen to the fetus (USDHHS 1990).

In addition to reduced birth weight, there are other serious medical consequences to smoking during pregnancy. Direct links have been identified between smoking and spontaneous abortion, abruptio placenta, bleeding during pregnancy, premature rupture of the membranes, and preterm delivery. Risks of fetal, neonatal, and perinatal mortality also are increased (USDHEW 1980; USDHHS 1989, 1990). Furthermore, there is evidence linking maternal smoking to a low or depressed 1 and 5 minute Apgar score (Garn et al. 1981). A fetal nicotine syndrome has been defined, which involves symmetrical growth retardation in the infant at term that cannot be attributed to other causes (Nieburg et al. 1985; USDHHS 1989).

The 1990 Surgeon General's Report cites Kramer (1987) in stating that "smoking is probably the most important modifiable cause of poor pregnancy outcome among women in the United States" (USDHHS 1990, p. 395). Given the figure that approximately 25% of U.S. women smoke during pregnancy (NCHS 1988), the report estimates that 5–6% of perinatal deaths, 17–26% of low birth weight births, and 7–10% of preterm deliveries are attributable to smoking during pregnancy. In higher prevalence subgroups, such as non-high school graduates among whom the prevalence of smoking may reach 50%, the estimates of adverse pregnancy outcomes attributable to smoking increase to 10–11% of perinatal deaths, 29–42% of low birth weight births, and 14–18% of preterm deliveries. These adverse outcomes would be eliminated with cessation of smoking during pregnancy (USDHHS 1990).

Adverse effects of smoking, both during pregnancy and following delivery, also have been documented for the infant and growing child. A major conclusion of the 1986 Report of the Surgeon General was that, "The children of parents who smoke compared with the children of nonsmoking parents have an increased frequency of respiratory infections, increased respiratory symptoms, and slightly smaller rates of increase in lung function as the lung matures" (USDHHS 1986, p. 7). The landmark EPA Report (USEPA 1992) expands and further documents the effects of ETS on infants and children. Infants are exposed to nicotine through breast milk and children are passively exposed to the smoke of their parents'

cigarettes. Long-term behavioral, intellectual, and emotional deficits in children of women who smoked during pregnancy have been reported (USDHEW 1980; USDHHS 1989).

Given the extraordinary burden of adverse health sequelae imposed by cigarette smoking upon the child, and the documented benefits of cessation, abstinence from smoking during pregnancy and thereafter is clearly a critical priority. It is worth stating that smoking-related burdens in pregnancy are both physical and emotional. No documentation is needed to substantiate the distress of losing a fetus, bearing a child with major health problems, or raising a child with chronic or recurrent disease or behavioral problems. Yet it has proved surprisingly difficult to reduce women's smoking during pregnancy. Even more challenging is the effort to sustain abstinence beyond delivery.

Smoking Prevalence During Pregnancy

National surveys undertaken between 1967 and 1988 reveal that smoking rates during pregnancy have decreased, but remain unacceptably high. Data from the 1967 and 1980 National Natality Surveys, national probability samples of live births to white and black mothers married at the time of delivery, showed different smoking patterns among women under 20 years of age and those 20 years and older (Kleinman and Kopstein 1987). Smoking during pregnancy showed little change in married teenagers of either race between surveys, 38–39% of whites and 27% of blacks. In the 20 years and older group, smoking rates declined: 40% of whites smoked in 1967 compared to only 25% in 1980; and 33% of blacks smoked in 1967 compared to 23% in 1980. Among white women, educational status bore a negative relationship to smoking prevalence prior to pregnancy and a positive relationship to the likelihood of cessation. (The sample size of black women was too small for similar analyses.)

Almost 40% of the white smokers who had been pregnant or delivered within the preceding 5 years and who participated in the 1985 National Health Inverview Survey (NHIS)/1986 Linked Telephone Survey quit during pregnancy (Fingerhut, Kleinman, Kendrick 1990). Education was directly related, and amount smoked inversely related, to the likelihood of cessation. Physician advice to quit was reported by 75.6%. Unfortunately, 70.5% of women who quit while pregnant relapsed in the first year postpartum. Ninety-three percent of all relapses occurred within 6 months. Heavier smokers were more likely to relapse, as were younger women (age 20–29 years) and those who quit later in pregnancy.

A third survey, the Center for Disease Control's Pregnancy Nutrition Surveillance System (PNSS), "monitors the prevalence of various risk factors for adverse pregnancy outcomes among low-income pregnant women who participate in publicly funded programs" (such as the Women, Infants, Children, or WIC supplemental nutrition program) (Fichtner et al. 1990, p. 14). Combining data from 1978 to 1988, the prevalence of smoking by race/ethnicity was highest among whites (42.3%), followed by blacks (19.8%), and next by Hispanics (12.8%). Asians (7.8%) and American Indians (6.1%) had the lowest smoking prevalence. For all groups, risk of low birth weight (LBW) was greater among smokers (9.9%) than nonsmokers (5.7%). For the three major ethnic groups, the rate of LBW was highest among black women smokers (14.3%) and lowest among white nonsmokers (4.1%). The mean LBW deficit was 178 g.

Finally, comparisons of smoking patterns of pregnant and nonpregnant women were taken from the Behavioral Risk Factor Surveillance System, which conducted interviews in 26 states in 1985 and 1986 (Williamson et al. 1989). Pregnant women had lower smoking prevalence (21 vs. 30%) and were lighter smokers (12 vs. 20 cigarettes/day) than women who were not pregnant. These results suggest that the quit rate during pregnancy was 30% and that those smokers who continued to smoke reduced their consumption (Williamson et al. 1989).

Interventions During Pregnancy

Smoking cessation interventions have been delivered in a variety of settings in which prenatal and related services are provided to pregnant women. These include the private physician's office, health maintenance organizations (HMO), and other prepaid medical plans, and increasingly in public health maternity clinics and the WIC supplemental nutrition program. Health care providers have included physicians, nurses, health educators, and nutrition counselors.

Both the American Lung Association (ALA) and the American Cancer Society (ACS) have nationally distributed programs with physician and patient intervention materials for pregnant smokers. The ALA intervention, designed for health care providers and for the pregnant woman, involves office restrictions on smoking, physician counseling at each visit, a review of the *Because You Love Your Baby* flip chart, staff follow-up of patient smoking, a slide-tape presentation, and take-home self-help materials tailored to pregnancy. *Special Delivery . . . Smoke Free* (ACS) is designed specifically to reach low-income pregnant women in the agencies in which they receive prenatal health, education, or social services, with the intermediary facilitating efforts of ACS volunteers. Supporting materials provide direction for ACS volunteers and agency personnel. The self-help information and activity booklet for pregnant women is designed to make minimal reading demands on recipients.

Intervention studies demonstrate that smoking cessation rates of pregnant women can be successfully boosted, but that relapse rates remain high (Ershoff, Mullen, Quinn 1989; McBride and Pirie 1990; Mullen, Quinn, Ershoff 1990; Mayer, Hawkins, Todd 1990; Sexton and Hebel 1984; Sexton, Hebel, Fox 1987; Windsor et al. 1985, 1990b, 1993). Most of the interventions that have been evaluated with pregnant smokers have been intensive minimal-contact interventions offered during routine prenatal care and consisting of physician quitting advice and brief risk education, self-help materials (usually tailored to pregnancy) with or without brief office-based counseling, and follow-up via office visits, home visits, mailings, and/or telephone calls throughout the pregnancy. In general, end-of-pregnancy quit rates have been two to four times higher for such interventions than with usual care. As has been found with all physician-initiated quit smoking interventions (Kottke et al. 1988), the best results have occurred for those involving a greater number of contacts and more face-to-face contact, and results have varied with patient population and treatment setting. However, postpartum follow-ups generally show end-of-pregnancy treatment advantages to be short-lived, dissipating in the absence of postpartum relapse prevention treatment.

This problem underscores the need to reach all pregnant women who smoke both during their pregnancies and afterwards, when the stressors of infant care, physical fatigue, termination of breast feeding, return to work, desire to lose weight gained during pregnancy, and resumption of alcohol and caffeine use all may provide cues to smoke (McBride and Pirie 1990; Mullen, Quinn, Ershoff 1990). Postpartum stressors may be exacerbated in low-income women, who are also less likely to receive support for quitting and remaining abstinent. Selected intervention studies will be briefly mentioned to provide examples from the various U.S. health care settings in which research has been conducted to indicate the impact treatment can have and to suggest new directions for interventions.

One of the most effective interventions was that studied in the private medical sector in a large randomized trial by Sexton and Hebel (1984); 935 women smoking at least 10 cigarettes per day at the start of pregnancy and who had not passed the 18th week of gestation were recruited through private obstetricians and a university obstetric clinic. The control condition consisted of routine obstetrical advice, and the intervention group received ongoing contacts throughout pregnancy, including at least one personal visit with a health educator, monthly telephone calls and mailings. At the 8-month assessment, 43% of the treatment group had stopped smoking compared to 20% of the control group. However, postpartum treatment was not provided and by 3 months after delivery, 81% of the treatment group and 88% of the control group were smoking (Sexton et al. 1987).

An HMO setting was successfully utilized in a prospective randomized controlled trial conducted with a population of socioeconomically and ethnically diverse pregnant women (n = 242). The study compared a minimal contact intervention consisting of eight self-help, mailed smoking cessation booklets plus individualized advice delivered by a health educator, to health educator advice alone (Ershoff, Mullen, Quinn 1989). Twenty-three percent of the women who were less than 18 weeks pregnant at intake were current smokers. The study was restricted to those who were still smoking seven or more cigarettes per week. In the experimental condition, the first booklet was delivered by the health educator along with a brief overview of the program and a commitment to read the booklet was sought. There was no further contact with the health educator. Overall, the verified quit rate by the end of pregnancy was 26.2% in the experimental group and 17.2% in the control group; early quitters (sustained quit prior to the 20th week of pregnancy) comprised 22.2% of the experimental and 8.6% of the control subjects. The intervention appeared to be most effective among light smokers and women with high self-efficacy. The effects were only partially sustained, with 63% of abstinent subjects relapsing by 6 months postpartum (Mullen, Quinn, Ershoff 1990).

The relapse rates observed in this study are lower than reported by Sexton, Hebel, and Fox (1987) at 3 months postpartum and similar to those documented 6 months postpartum among mostly untreated smokers in the NHIS follow-up study (Fingerhut, Kleinman, Kendrick 1990). Another parallel finding comes from a telephone interview study of a random sample of births in the Midwest, in which 43% of smokers reported being off cigarettes during most of their pregnancy, and 65% of quitters had relapsed by 6 months postpartum (McBride and Pirie 1990). Predictors of postpartum relapse included concern about weight gained during pregnancy, duration of breastfeeding, and prepregnancy smoking rate.

Federal agencies are seeking to operationalize and diffuse the state-of-the-art minimal-contact programs found to be effective in pregnancy. The National Institute of Child Health and Human Development (NICHD) has developed a comprehensive team-based smoking cessation program to be implemented by obstetricians and their staffs (Leslie Cooper, personal communication, 9 April 1993). In addition to advice delivered by physicians, nurses, or office staff, other components of the educational intervention include: a self-help booklet; an ALA audiotape on relaxation techniques; a brochure designed to encourage the social support of family and friends; four reminder cards to be mailed between physician office visits; and a 15-minute videotape for home viewing designed as a companion to the self-help booklet and as a stimulus for social support by significant others.

Interventions also have been conducted with low-income smokers in public health maternity clinics and WIC settings. Windsor and his colleagues (1985, 1990b, 1993) have conducted two trials in the public health maternity clinics in the state of Alabama. In the first study, a randomized pretest, posttest trial, quit rates were significantly higher in the group receiving the tailored manual, *A Pregnant Womans' Self-Help Guide to Quit Smoking* (14%) compared to an ALA self-help booklet (6%) or usual care control (2%) (Windsor et al. 1985). In the second study (Windsor et al. 1990b; 1993), which enrolled almost 1,000 women in four clinics, the overall end-of-pregnancy quit rate in the intervention group *(Guide)* was 14.3%, compared to 8.5% among usual care controls. A fascinating finding is that the cessation rate among black women in this biracial population was approximately double that of the white women. A dissemination manual, designed to facilitate the planning, implementation, and evaluation of smoking cessation programs in public health settings nationwide has been published (Windsor et al. 1990a).

Mayer and colleagues (1990) conducted a randomized trial in a Michigan local health department WIC clinic with 219 volunteer pregnant smokers. Clinic smoking rates were high (42% of attendees), concurrent with other WIC estimates. Usual care (printed advice) was compared to a minimal-contact risk information intervention which consisted of a 10-minute face-to-face session in which a health educator dispensed factual information, and to a more intensive multiple component intervention. In the intensive condition, the health educator gave extended counseling (20 minutes), including behavior change advice and a self-help manual adapted from Windsor's *Guide* and the ALA *Freedom From Smoking* program. The multiple component program achieved predelivery quit rates of 11% compared to 3% in usual care, and postpartum quit rates of 7% compared to 0%. These initial results are quite promising and not dissimilar from Windsor's.

A number of additional efforts in the public health arena are in progress. Several studies featuring materials and interventions tailored for low-literacy populations including new mothers attending WIC centers and pregnant smokers seen in public health maternity clinics are being carried out by researchers at the Fox Chase Cancer Center (Fleisher et al. 1990). Interventions include brief training and written counseling guidelines for public health nurses. Centers for Disease Control (CDC) is sponsoring the development of similar smoking cessation interventions designed to reach pregnant smokers through public prenatal and WIC programs (Zahniser et al. 1993). Three research and demonstration projects conducted in Colorado, Maryland, and Missouri evaluated prenatal smoking cessation/maintenance interventions uniquely developed by each state in collaboration with the CDC. Nurses or WIC educators provided standard minimal-contact interventions, consisting of assessment of smoking behavior and appropriate advice at each prenatal visit, supportive written or audiovisual materials, and pregnancy-tailored quit kits with coping aids. Evaluations conducted at end of pregnancy did not show an increase in cotinine-verified quit rates, perhaps because intensive data collection efforts interfered with delivery of the intervention (Zahniser et al. 1993).

Pursuit of the development of such programs designed for use in the public sector and their implementation is an important public health priority for socioeconomically disadvantaged women in our society. They have the least access to prenatal care and are at the greatest risk for complications of pregnancy, low birth weight infants, and excess infant mortality.

Essential Elements of Quit Smoking Treatment Programs for Pregnant Women

There are several similarities between tailoring smoking cessation advice to a patient with a medical condition and the pregnant smoker. These involve the delivery of individualized (usually) advice at the first visit to the health care provider, supportive printed or audiovisual quit smoking materials, usually tailored to pregnancy and repetitive, sustained counseling throughout the provider–client relationship. However, while the pregnant woman may be considered a patient, in the great majority of cases, she is a healthy woman whose smoking places her and her unborn child at special risk. Of course, any concurrent smoking-related disorder increases the risk to the mother and, potentially, to the fetus as well.

The key issues in smoking cessation interventions for pregnant women are the following:

1. Creating and sustaining motivation based on benefits to mother and fetus, capitalizing on the fact that pregnancy truly is a "critical period" for smoking cessation;
2. Capitalizing on the "teachable moment" as early as possible in pregnancy;
3. Tailoring materials to be appropriate to the racial/ethnic group, literacy level, and culture of the pregnant woman;
4. Preventing relapse late in pregnancy or postpartum.

The following elements are present in most minimal-contact quit smoking interventions during pregnancy. Typically, the personal counseling that occurs on the initial prenatal visit involves assessing smoking behavior, describing the health risks for the fetus and the mother, contracting for a quit date, and offering self-help materials, and providing support or encouragement. Providers must avoid focusing exclusively on LBW per se, since for many women having a smaller baby may be desirable. The implications of LBW need to be presented, and the other serious problems associated with smoking during pregnancy must be noted (e.g., abruptio placenta, preterm delivery, spontaneous abortion). The emphasis should be on "sicker babies," not just "smaller babies." Any myths about smoking during pregnancy also should be explored (e.g., "dealing with my smoking will make my baby tougher, stronger"). Multiparous women who delivered healthy babies in previous pregnancies despite smoking will require special risk education. On the other hand, past harmful effects of smoking during and after pregnancy on their infants and children need to be discussed in a way that heightens quitting motivation without engendering unhelpful guilt. On repeated visits, often the same general schema is followed, with the nature of the advice tailored to the current smoking status of the client (abstainer, relapser, or continuing smoker).

Special problems also should be discussed, including concern about weight gain in pregnancy, the presence of other smokers in the woman's family and social environment, high-risk situations for relapse, ongoing stressors that promote smoking, and so forth. It is important to avoid blaming a woman for being unable to attain or maintain cessation, and to deliver support and encouragement. Smoking cessation must be placed in the context of the other changes needed to reduce health threats to the pregnancy, including the clearly more serious risks posed by alcohol, cocaine, and other drug use. Considering the damage and disability wreaked upon the fetus by these forms of drug abuse, cocaine and alcohol should have first priority. On the other hand, for most women, smoking cessation is probably *more* important to a positive pregnancy outcome than limiting weight gain to an arbitrary amount, for instance, 30 pounds. Furthermore, there are no data which indicate it is harmful to stop smoking at the same time as one stops drinking or using cocaine (see Chapter 15).

A variety of creative materials to supplement the provider-delivered verbal advice are likely to be helpful. Many available self-help booklets contain the state-of-the-art smoking cessation motivational and "how-to" messages, tailored to pregnancy (e.g., ACS, ALA materials; Ershoff, Mullen, Quinn 1989; Windsor et al. 1985, 1990a). Essential quitting and maintenance information is provided. High-risk situations are described and coping behaviors suggested. These usually include relaxation and stress reduction techniques. Relapse prevention strategies are outlined. Special postpartum triggers, such as those referred to earlier, may be discussed. Counseling concerning weight gain in pregnancy is extremely important. In one study, concern about weight gained during pregnancy was the best predictor of postpartum relapse (McBride and Pirie 1990). Finally, techniques for seeking out and encouraging social support for cessation and maintenance from partner, family, and friends are commonly described, often with accompanying materials for distribution to such persons.

Additional audiovisual aids to cessation provide multiple channels of reinforcement (ACS, ALA, CDC). Videotapes have been designed for home or clinic viewing. Audiotapes can teach relaxation and temptation resistance skills. Slide/cassette programs can be delivered in a clinic or office setting. The ALA *Flip Chart for Health Care Providers* is designed to facilitate the delivery of health information. Between-visit reminders can be sent on mailed postcards and take-home quit kits and posters also provide sustaining reminders of the nonsmoking message.

All of these are meant to be delivered in minimal-contact interventions which appear to be the most acceptable to pregnant smokers. Group or clinic-based programs have been unable to attract substantial attendance (Ershoff, Mullen, Quinn 1989; Hughes, et al. 1982; Sexton and Hebel 1984; Windsor et al. 1985). However, pregnant smokers who do not succeed with minimal-contact treatments should be referred to more intensive and/or specialized formal treatments (see Chapters 11 and 17).

A few of the effective intensive treatment techniques, namely, those involving rapid smoking are contraindicated for pregnant women. No objections should be raised to the use of normal-paced aversive smoking (focused smoking), in which a woman smokes a cigarette at her usual puffing rate and depth of inhalation while concentrating on the negative sensory feedback which accompanies smoking (smell, taste, burning sensation in mouth, scratchy throat, etc.).

This technique is often used in conjunction with an audiotape which contains a suggestive monologue on the dysphoric sensations in smoking, and is meant to be used daily in the preparatory phase of cessation.

Likewise, adjunctive nicotine replacement is generally considered contraindicated for pregnant or lactating women—although recently Benowitz (1991) has discussed circumstances where its use should be considered. Likewise, most other pharmacologic aids should also be avoided during pregnancy (e.g., clonidine, antidepressants). Other obvious proscriptions would involve beginning new vigorous exercise programs, dramatic restrictions or changes in diet, or other changes that might pose a risk to pregnancy.

Postpartum relapse is a problem of such magnitude that it is likely that special interventions will need to be developed. The opportunities to implement relapse prevention protocols are just beginning to be explored. Optimally, these interventions should be administered in the context of routine postnatal care, including well-baby and pediatric care, WIC programs, early child development classes, family planning clinics, and so forth. Programs should be provided by medical, nursing, nutrition, psychology, social work, or education professional or paraprofessional staff. Intervention content is a logical extension of the cessation approach, in that the benefits to *both* infant and mother are pointed out (as well as other family members). Special emphasis, however, needs to be placed on: (1) the risks of environmental tobacco smoke (ETS) exposure for the infant, perhaps using new portable nicotine dosimeters to monitor the infant's exposure to household ETS (Hammond and Leaderer 1987); and (2) the particular stressors of the postpartum period, described earlier, as they may provide triggers to relapse (McBride and Pirie 1990; Mullen, Quinn, Ershoff 1990). In addition, any degree of postpartum depression may further predispose a woman to a slip or relapse. Analyzing relapse triggers, designing coping strategies, developing alternate behaviors and reinforcers, and forming support systems are all part of relapse prevention approaches. A temporal analysis of triggers may be particularly helpful, as different stressors emerge over time. For example, fatigue and the desire to lose extra weight gained during pregnancy may tempt a mother to resume smoking immediately postpartum. Several months later, the primary triggers might be weaning the infant and returning to the work force where others may be smoking. This analysis suggests an ongoing need for relapse prevention support for perhaps up to a year, similar to the general high-risk period for long-term maintenance of abstinence.

In conclusion, the special risks of smoking during pregnancy, and the demonstrated benefits of cessation, underscore the need for intensifying national efforts to increase and maintain abstinence in this period of women's lives. Particular attention must be paid to socioeconomically disadvantaged women, those with low educational attainment, and those at risk for LBW infants for multiple reasons, and to new interventions designed to prevent relapse.

SPECIAL ISSUES IN TREATING PATIENTS WITH CARDIOVASCULAR DISEASE

This section will address issues of smoking and smoking cessation in patients with coronary artery disease, those who have suffered or are at high risk for a myocardial infarction, and those with peripheral vascular disease or who are at high risk for cerebrovascular disease. Although the disease context is different for each of these syndromes, there is shared pathophysiology and shared attributable risk from smoking. A more comprehensive review of pathophysiological processes and their relationship to smoking is provided in the Surgeon General's Report on *The Health Benefits of Smoking Cessation* (USDHHS 1990).

One of the major advances in the last three decades in understanding the dangers of smoking is recognizing and establishing the relationship between smoking and cardiovascular disease. The Framingham Study (cf. Doyle et al. 1964), designed to follow men at high risk for cardiac disease, did not originally propose to collect information on smoking status, as it was not considered to be a major factor in etiology. Because of the higher prevalence of cardiovascular disease in the U.S. population compared to COPD and lung cancer, smoking causes a greater number of cardiovascular deaths than deaths due to lung cancer or COPD, although the fraction of cardiovascular disease attributable to smoking is closer to 30% than to 90% for pulmonary disease.

Effects of Smoking on Cardiac Function

It is now well established that smoking increases the risk of myocardial infarction (MI) (USDHHS 1990). Smokers may also experience a first MI at a younger age, may be more likely to have an MI in the absence of coronary artery disease, and may experience different patterns of infarct than a nonsmoker, both in location and size (Robinson, Conroy, Mulcahy 1988). The association has been well established in numerous prospective studies (USDHHS 1983, 1990). Recent evidence suggests that the long-term benefits of angioplasty are greatly decreased for patients who continue to smoke (Galan et al. 1988). The same may be true for coronary bypass surgery.

Smoking appears to affect cardiac functioning in several ways: nicotine and perhaps other components appear to accelerate the development of atherosclerosis, both by damaging the arterial walls and by facilitating aggregation of platelets to endothelium; smoking may also promote development of thrombi, or the clots which block narrowed arteries, thereby causing MIs; smokers may be more likely than nonsmokers to have higher levels of triglycerides and lower levels of HDL cholesterol; smoking decreases oxygen supply and increases carbon monoxide; nicotine may lead to arterial spasming, promote arrhythmias, and increase cardiac load by leading to peripheral vascular constriction. Increased risk for peripheral artery disease and cerebrovascular disease in smokers is related to similar processes. Of note, smoking has not been shown to be clearly related to hypertension, although as co-factors for coronary artery disease, their effects are multiplicative, rather than additive. Smoking also interferes with the efficacy of pharmacological treatments for angina

(Deanfield et al. 1984) and hypertension (Greenberg, Thompson, Brennan 1987).

Benefits of Quitting for Cardiac Function

Prospective studies (Mulcahy et al. 1977; Hallstrom, Cobb, Ray 1986; USDHHS 1990) have shown that post-MI patients who stop smoking reduce the likelihood of a second MI by as much as 50% and to that of a nonsmoker within several years. The recurrence of a heart attack and the likelihood of death (Salonen 1980) are both decreased. Some of the effects of smoking—in particular, arterial spasming, platelet aggregation, increased arrhythmias and effect on oxygenation—are rapidly reversible. Effects on atherosclerotic processes may take much longer to reverse. The same processes would likely be true for cerebrovascular and peripheral vascular processes.

Although most patients stop smoking at the time of an MI, if only because of the trauma of the event and restrictions on smoking imposed by the hospitalization, fewer remain abstinent than might be expected. A review of the literature (Perkins 1988) found that the proportion of post-MI patients reporting abstinence at 3 months was approximately one-half. When appropriate validation techniques were employed, the proportion may be one-third or less (Burling et al. 1984). Perkins notes that this proportion is similar to relapse rates observed with other addictions (Brownell et al. 1986). These spontaneous cessation rates appear to have not improved in more recent investigations (Ockene et al. 1991; Taylor et al. 1990), which is discouraging, given the increased awareness of the dangers of smoking in relation to heart disease. Although relatively few studies address this issue, cessation rates among women cardiac patients appear to be even lower.

Relatively sophisticated and methodologically sound research has been conducted in the area of smoking intervention with cardiac patients. In general, the methodological issues important in smoking abstinence research (Perkins 1988) have been better addressed in this area than with other types of high risk patients, due to the substantial commitment to supporting prospective research made by the National Heart, Lung and Blood Institute (NHLBI) over the last 20 years. Most recently, a program of intervention studies with subgroups of cardiovascular populations have been carried out (cf. Ockene et al. 1991; Taylor et al. 1990) and will be summarized later.

Intervention in Cardiovascular Disease

Prevention in High-Risk Populations

The focus of most primary and secondary prevention efforts has been on community and individually oriented screening and educational programs (e.g., Farquhar et al. 1977; WHO 1982); however, several studies, notably the Multiple Risk Factor Intervention Trial (MRFIT 1982; Jarvis et al. 1984) and the Stanford Three Community Study (Farquhar et al. 1977), have also added behavioral intervention components, directed at smoking, among other risk factors. In general, these studies have shown relatively consistent effects regarding the potential for both educational and behavioral intervention components in decreasing smoking rates and prevalence (Langeluddecke 1986) in individuals at high risk for coronary heart disease. Changes in smoking rates in the range of 15–50% have been obtained, depending on the intensity of the intervention, length of follow-up, and selection of study participants.

Intervention in Diseased Populations

Intervention studies with cardiac patients have more generally investigated formal intervention programs, rather than physician advice to stop smoking, although Perkins (1988) points out that the rates of observational investigations involving physician advice have been similar to those in naturalistic studies. Studies of more intensive interventions report higher rates, generally over 50% (Perkins 1988), than do naturalistic studies, but earlier investigations often lacked appropriate validation techniques. A series of recent studies (Ockene, Kristeller, Goldberg et al. 1992; Taylor et al. 1990) supports the role of such interventions for patients with more severe disease, but raises questions concerning the effectiveness of current techniques with less diseased and/or motivated populations (Orleans, Kristeller, Gritz in press).

Ockene and colleagues (1992) compared an individually delivered behavioral smoking intervention to a control condition consisting of brief advice to stop smoking to 267 patients who had just undergone coronary arteriography with documented coronary artery disease (CAD). As documented by other investigators (Gross et al. 1987), cardiac patients were unreceptive to joining a formal group treatment program. Treatment, delivered by health educators experienced in smoking intervention, consisted of inpatient counseling oriented toward self-management and relapse prevention, an outpatient visit (attended by approximately half of the eligible patients), telephone counseling at weekly and then monthly intervals, and self-help materials geared toward the needs of an older, more disabled population. An audiotape contained instruction in relaxation techniques. After 6 months, validated cessation rates were 34 versus 45% for the control and intervention groups, respectively, and at 12 months 28 and 35%, respectively, for the two groups. However, cessation rates were substantially higher for patients who were immediately post-MI and for those with two or more occluded arteries versus only one. Of note, the impact of the intervention was largely limited to those patients with more serious disease, which was counter to the original hypothesis that intervention might allow less motivated patients to improve their cessation rates. Instead, it appeared that the intervention was most successful in providing support and preventing relapse in patients who had the strongest desire and motivation to remain abstinent.

Taylor and associates (1990) provided a similar intervention approach to that used by Ockene and associates (1992). Intervention was intiated in the hospital, consisting of an unequivocal message from the physician that the patient should stop smoking, followed by structured counseling from a nurse based on social learning theory, in particular improvement of self-efficacy, and supported by a manual, workbook, and re-laxation tape. Training time for nurses was approximately 12 hours, plus monthly supervision. Contact was then maintained through weekly telephone calls for 3 weeks and monthly calls for 4 months, with a focus on relapse prevention. Patients who continued or returned to smoking were asked to return for outpatient visits. Five such patients were provided with a prescription for nicotine gum to assist with withdrawal symptoms. Average contact time was approximately 2 hours. Probably because the population in this study was limited to post-MI patients, the smoking cessation rate at 1 year in those patients receiving intervention was very high: 71%, as compared to 45% in the usual care condition. Of note, there was no difference in the proportion of patients smoking at 3 weeks postdischarge between the intervention and usual care groups (25 vs. 24%, respectively) nor in the amount smoked by patients at 12-month follow-up (16 vs. 17 cigarettes, respectively), although that amount had decreased significantly in both groups. Of the 34 patients smoking at 3 weeks, only 5 were abstinent at 1 year. Intention to quit was strongly related to likelihood of maintained abstinence, as was self-efficacy. At each level of intention to quit, abstinence rates were higher in the intervention condition, although at low levels of intent to quit, this difference was marginal, consistent with the results found by Ockene and colleagues (1992). Increased effort directed toward less motivated patients did not appear to improve likelihood of abstinence.

It is evident that one of the variables that most affects the likelihood of smoking cessation in cardiovascular disease is the seriousness of the disease, both among post-MI patients (Baile, Bigelow, Gottlieb 1982; Burling et al. 1984) and among patients with documented CAD (Ockene et al. 1992; Cutter et al. 1985). Cutter and associates (1985) reported a range of abstinence from only 7% in individuals with no disease to 30% in patients with one or two vessel disease to 47% in those with three vessel disease. It also appears that severity of disease affects response to intervention (Ockene et al. 1992). Given the value of smoking cessation, this pattern deserves further exploration, as it may result from several factors. One possibility is that healthier patients are given reassuring messages that their heart disease is relatively less serious; although such a message is consistent with encouraging cardiac patients to return to as active a life-style as is feasible, it may translate into denial of risk for some individuals. Conversely, patients with more serious disease may be receiving stronger medical advice to quit. Ockene and colleagues (1987) found evidence for this among medical outpatients, who were twice as likely to report receiving advice to quit if they already had diagnosable cardiac disease than if they only were experiencing cardiac-related symptoms. Such a difference may also occur among diseased patients in relation to disease severity. Another possibility is that patients with more serious disease experience greater disability and therefore find it less physically comfortable to continue smoking. Conversely, Scott and Lamparski (1985) found that regardless of disease severity, continuing smokers were less likely to believe that smoking was related to their heart disease. In any case, stronger messages from health care professionals concerning the dangers of smoking may be needed. Perkins (1988) posits several other intervening factors, particularly increased social support for sustained abstinence, in the more seriously ill patient.

Smoking Intervention in Cardiac Patients: Essential Elements

One of the important conclusions to be drawn from the recent research is the opportunity offered for initiating intervention during hospitalization. Considerable benefit is then derived from offering follow-up support oriented toward relapse prevention in the form of both personal counseling and self-help materials to cardiac patients who have already stopped smoking and are highly motivated to remain abstinent. Addressing issues of stress-related relapse and providing training in relaxation techniques may be particularly important components (Epstein and Perkins 1988; Havik and Maeland 1988). Another important element appears to be a strong and consistent message

from the physician concerning the critical importance of stopping smoking and remaining abstinent; however, other health care professionals, including nursing staff or health educators, may be in a better position to provide consistent counseling regarding relapse prevention. The availability of other supports such as formal treatment groups, hot lines (Ossip-Klein et al. 1990), or outpatient visits may be important for certain individuals but have limited value overall. However, continued outpatient contact in the context of a cardiac rehabilitation program might be efficient, as these programs often attract the more motivated patient (Comoss 1988). Pharmacological aids, such as nicotine-containing gum or transdermal patches, have not been fully evaluated with cardiac patients. Treatment protocols have been outlined by a number of investigators (Orleans, Rotberg, Quade et al. 1990; Kristeller and Ockene 1989) and are adaptable to a variety of settings. Nicotine gum is contraindicated immediately following a MI, but may play a role for the post-MI patient who has relapsed or who desires to stop at some other point in the course of his or her illness.

Both clinical and cost-effectiveness appears to be improved by providing individually oriented counseling by telephone. Although group treatment programs have been recognized for their high levels of effectiveness for a self-selected group of smokers in the general population, it appears that they are less appropriate for providing treatment to the post-MI patient. This is due to both clinical and logistical reasons: clinically, most post-MI patients who are going to benefit from intervention have already stopped smoking at the time of hospital discharge, and the effectiveness of group intervention has only been evaluated for current smokers; logistically, groups require substantial staff time to organize and lead, and are unlikely to attract sufficient participants to offset the benefits from providing group intervention. Taylor et al. (1990) estimates that at a time commitment of 2 hours per patient (the average time provided to most patients in his study), a single nurse working quarter-time could provide effective intervention for 120 post-MI patients in a 6-month period. This time commitment is similar to that provided to post cardiac catheterization patients by Ockene and colleagues. Orleans and associates (Orleans, Rotberg, Quade et al. 1990) provided approximately 1½ hours of contact to a less medically ill population. Taylor et al. also suggest that scheduling and managing of content of follow-up contacts could be facilitated by use of computer-based algorithms, although this is not necessary.

Less understood is how to intervene effectively with patients who continue to deny or minimize the impact of smoking on their medical illness and who are less motivated to quit or remain abstinent. Most treatments evaluated to date appear to be effective in improving self-management skills for those individuals who are highly motivated. Such motivation appears strongly related to severity of illness. It may be that the physician needs to be more aggressive in the role of motivating the patient with less severe disease to quit, communicating strongly the benefit to future health of remaining abstinent, while simultaneously conveying the good news that the cardiac disease is still relatively limited.

SPECIAL ISSUES IN TREATING PATIENTS WITH PULMONARY DISEASE

Among debilitating diseases, the COPDs occur only rarely among nonsmoking individuals and exacerbations of the symptoms of these diseases are most clearly linked to continued smoking. In addition to chronic bronchitis and emphysema, for which smoking is the primary causal factor, asthma is exacerbated by smoking, and infectious respiratory disorders increase in frequency and duration among smokers. In 1986 more than 71,000 individuals died from COPD in the United States, and over 164,000 died with COPD as the underlying or contributing cause (CDC 1989). Through 1985, mortality rates from COPD have been increasing in the United States (USDHHS 1989). In 1985, 82% of COPD deaths were attributed to smoking. Air pollution, industrial exposure, lung damage in childhood, and genetic influences (Holland 1988) are important cofactors with smoking.

Public awareness of the relationship be-tween smoking and COPD has increased substantially, from about 50% in 1964 to more than 80% in 1986. However, over 25% of smokers still deny that smoking causes chronic bronchitis and about 15% do not believe that it causes emphysema (USDHHS 1989).

Although substantial efforts directed at smoking prevention and early cessation have been initiated out of a concern for preventing lung disease, relatively less attention has been paid in the research literature to smoking interventions among individuals who already have pulmonary symptoms. Consequently, much of what is understood concerning the special treatment needs of pulmonary patients at different levels of morbidity is based on observational studies or clinical lore.

Effects of Smoking on Lung Function

There is tremendous individual variability in the extent to which tobacco intake affects pulmonary functioning. Only a relatively small proportion (15%) of smokers develop clinically significant COPD, characterized by reductions in the rate of expiratory airflow. Approximately three times as many smokers compared to nonsmokers develop chronic bronchitis, defined by chronic cough and/or sputum production for at least 3 months per year for 2 consecutive years. In a study of over 4,000 individuals drawn from the general population (Foxman et al. 1986), approximately 16.5% of smokers reported the presence of chronic bronchitis, increasing to as high as 32% among males over age 54 years. Even exposure to the lower levels of tobacco smoke found in environmental tobacco smoke is sufficient to cause morbidity in some individuals. It is now well documented that children of smokers are much more likely to suffer respiratory ailments; for asthmatics, even small amounts of smoke inhalation can exacerbate airway hyperresponsivity. (USDHHS 1986; USEPA, 1992).

The exact mechanisms by which smoking causes COPD are still not clearly understood (USDHHS 1989), but the deposition of particulates and exposure to the gaseous substances in tobacco smoke are the primary culprits in the development of lung disease. Although machine-measured tar levels have decreased substantially, largely as part of an effort on the part of the tobacco industry to make cigarettes appear safer, it is not clear that such reductions actually decrease exposure or affect morbidity and mortality (Peach et al. 1986). Regardless of actual presence of diagnosable disease, sensitive tests of pulmonary functioning detect deficiencies in many smokers: the level of ventilatory function (as measured by 1-second forced expiratory, volume, or FEV_1) decreases as amount of smoking increases.

Benefits of Quitting for Lung Function

The 1990 Report of the Surgeon General (USDHHS 1990), which summarized the health benefits of smoking cessation, helped to clarify some of the confusion concerning benefits of quitting for patients with different levels of disease severity or impairment. Stopping smoking reduces many symptoms in patients without overt COPD, including cough, sputum production, and wheezing, and it improves pulmonary function approximately 5% within a few months of quitting. (See also Emmons, Weidner, Foster et al. 1992.) Respiratory infections, including bronchitis, pneumonia, and the common cold, decline in prevalence after quitting. With sustained abstinence, the *rate of decline* in pulmonary functioning returns to that of a nonsmoker—although the actual level of functioning usually remains poorer than that of a nonsmoker unless cessation occurs after relatively few years of smoking. Also with sustained abstinence, patients already diagnosed with COPD will show decreased mortality rates compared to continued smokers. Although mortality rates from COPD are reduced by as much as 50% over continued smokers, they still remain very high relative to those of nonsmokers, even after 5 to 10 years.

Changes in pulmonary status for asthmatics are less consistent. Although reduction in smoking should decrease airway hyperresponsivity, asthmatics sometimes complain that their symptoms worsen temporarily after smoking cessation; this may be due to increased secretions as the airways clear.

Smoking Cessation and Pulmonary Disease

The 1984 Surgeon General's Report on COPD summarized 17 studies examining smoking cessation in pulmonary patients. Most studies were cross-sectional and did not specify or control for the severity of disease. However, much of the data reported was collected 15 to 20 years ago (USDHHS 1984), and may no longer represent current status among respiratory patients. As noted elsewhere in this book, today's smokers, especially those with known chronic smoking-related diseases, may represent an especially highly addicted ("hard core") group. Nevertheless, the quit rates reported were generally comparable to those observed in other medical populations, varying, for example, from 20% in an outpatient clinic to 63% in a hospitalized population.

One unanswered question is whether individuals with lung disease have unusual difficulty in stopping smoking. The perception that this is true may arise from the frustration of observing anyone with severe COPD continuing to smoke despite disability, use of oxygen, or even through a tracheostomy. However, it is not known whether COPD patients in general are less likely to stop smoking than are individuals with comparable morbidity from heart disease or other smoking-exacerbated medical problems, if offered equivalent support or treatment. As with cardiac disease, the likelihood of cessation appears to increase with severity of symptoms (which may in turn provoke strong physician advice to quit and subsequent abstinence). Pederson, Williams, and Lefcoe (1980) found a cessation rate of 62% among COPD patients receiving physician-delivered intervention as compared to a 26% rate among patients with bronchitis or asthma. In a study with a small sample, Ward and associates (1990) found that COPD patients quit smoking at a similar rate to patients with other medical diagnoses (who were generally comparable on baseline characteristics), but were far more likely to have relapsed at follow-up. They speculate that this may be due to the lack of perceived benefit following smoking when lung function failed to improve noticeably or to a greater need to smoke to deal with the frustrations of poorer quality of life due to the COPD.

Tashkin and colleagues (1984) found a 5-year cessation rate of 27% among the smokers enrolled in the UCLA population study of respiratory disease. Unfortunately, there was no comparison group of smokers with other smoking-related disorders or from the general population. In a study of individuals with chronic bronchitis (Foxman et al. 1986), about half of those patients reporting associated pain or activity restriction also reported having quit or decreased smoking, as compared to only about one-quarter of those without such symptoms. Kulpa (1990) reports an 82% quit rate after initiation of home-based oxygen therapy in a group of 237 smokers with severe chronic bronchitis, and a relapse rate of 12% among 1,527 ex-smokers in the same study.

Much of the intervention research with COPD patients has been focused on physician-delivered smoking intervention. Findings suggest that physicians can have a significant effect and that better results occur with more intensive intervention. A review (Pederson 1982) of observational studies in which pulmonary patients had received physician advice to stop smoking reported abstinence rates at 3–12 months varying from 12.5 to 51%. Two prospective studies by Pederson and colleagues (Pederson, Baskerville, Wanklin 1982; Pederson and Baskerville 1983) of newly diagnosed pulmonary patients who were heavy smokers found abstinence rates of only about 15% at 6 months following *brief* physician-delivered advice to quit. But in the UCLA study by Tashkin, the likelihood of changing smoking patterns greatly increased among those who had seen a physician about their chronic bronchitis. Although only about 64% of patients reported receiving advice from their physicians to stop smoking, many more of those patients reported having changed their smoking habits than did those not receiving advice. In a well controlled study by Rose and Hamilton (1978) of 1,445 men at high risk for cardiorespiratory disease, 51% of the intervention group reported not smoking cigarettes at 1 year following four appointments focused on smoking cessation with

their physicians, compared to 10% of the usual care control group. The abstinence rate was still 36% at 3 years follow-up in the intervention group.

The NHLBI is close to completing the Lung Health Study (Anthonisen, 1989; Connett et al. 1993, O'Hara et al. 1993), a five-year multicenter clinical trial of early intervention with COPD, incorporating both smoking cessation efforts and use of an inhaled bronchodilator in individuals with mild to moderate airflow obstruction. The smoking cessation program included a strong physician message, educational efforts; behaviorally biochemically validated point-prevalence quit rates were 34% for the 3,923 Special Intervention Participants and 9% for the 1,964 Usual Care participants (Rigdon, 1990). Quit rates were computed using the conservative method of classifying non-attenders at the 12-month visit as smokers. Endpoint data should be available toward the end of 1994. Although several prior investigations (Hall et al. 1983; Ward et al. 1990) had evaluated the effect of behavioral or group treatment programs on smoking in pulmonary patients, the results have been inconclusive or difficult to interpret because the sample sizes were too small to detect intervention effects that may have occurred.

Another problem in interpreting results and predicting the likelihood of cessation among pulmonary patients is a failure to specify severity of illness in most studies. As lung disease is gradually progressive with many early signs and symptoms (i.e., cough, shortness of breath), individuals more motivated or able to stop smoking may do so well before their symptoms progress into further disability, leaving an increasingly addicted group of smokers as disease progresses. This problem of an "eroding" baseline may be more of an issue in understanding probability of cessation in pulmonary patients than, for example, in cardiac patients for whom symptoms are often relatively absent until the occurrence of an MI, which serves as a clear "trigger" for the decision to quit and an easily and reliably identifiable point from which to investigate cessation rates. Few studies have attempted to address this issue systematically; at the least, outcome studies must carefully define the range of severity of disease in pulmonary population to which the results apply, in order for them to be accurately interpreted.

Smoking Intervention in Pulmonary Patients: Essential Elements

Treatment of smoking in the pulmonary patient is moving into the realm of usual care (Nett 1986). Quitting smoking is of most benefit prior to the development of serious disease or disability, and that message can be effectively and appropriately delivered by the primary care physician within the context of usual medical treatment. As discussed elsewhere in more detail, smoking intervention is most effective when brief counseling, prescription of nicotine-containing gum or transdermal patches, provision of self-help materials and follow-up appointments are offered, in addition to giving advice to quit (See Chapter 10).

For the more seriously disabled COPD patient, hospitalization provides an opportunity to initiate intervention; intervention must also be included in any comprehensive respiratory care treatment program (Orleans, Rotberg, Quade et al. 1990). The American Association for Respiratory Care (AARC) has recently initiated a nicotine-dependency treatment program to instruct and support all hopsital-based respiratory therapists in providing smoking intervention (Nett 1990). Not only is smoking cessation important in symptom relief and possible reduction of mortality, but continued smoking will contraindicate use of oxygen and will limit participation in rehabilitative exercise and the action of therapeutic medication (e.g., Theodur). As reviewed in Chapter 20, the effects of continued smoking should be presented to patients as, at the least, impairing *quality* of life by contributing to yet further limitations in activity and to more discomfort.

The environment of the patient care facility should reflect the concern for smoking as a risk factor. Even if the medical facility is not yet smoke-free, it is important that all efforts be made to ensure the the respiratory care area is smoke-free. Smoke-free areas should extend to staff rooms that are visible or that share ventilation space with patient care areas. This is important not only out of respect for those patients who no longer smoke, but to provide environmental support to those patients desiring to quit (see Chapter 9).

The physician's office or hospital also can be a ready source of self-help materials for the smokers considering stopping smoking or their own or actively making an attempt. Providing a patient with self-help materials alone plus advice to quit has not been shown to be particularly effective (Pederson, Wood, Lefcoe 1983), but materials that reinforce behavioral self-management are important to supplement more extensive counseling. The NHLBI also has developed a set of brief video vignettes entitled "We Can't Go On Like This" (USDHHS 1986), illustrating particular aspects of the frustrations and rewards associated with smoking cessation. Viewing these in the waiting room or hospital room can further motivate quit attempts.

As with any smoker, careful evaluation of the history of previous quit attempts, of current situational factors maintaining smoking, and sensitivity to the patient's sense of low self-confidence are critical in attempting to promote progress through the stages of quitting from precontemplation to contemplation to action (Prochaska and DiClemente 1983). Patients with pulmonary disease may feel particularly caught in an emotionally conflicting situation; unlike most diseases, the etiological connection with smoking is so clear that denial is virtually impossible, so that self-blame in the continued smoker is usually evident. Unlike cardiac disease, which can express itself with little warning and for which the connection to smoking is less apparent, virtually all COPD patients have given serious consideration to stopping smoking and have usually tried numerous times. They may consequently feel resignation, guilt, frustration, and helplessness from being unsuccessful with yet one more attempt. One response to such a constellation of feelings is defiance; another is avoidance of further "contemplation" of the issue. Both reactions may lead to very poor receptivity to smoking cessation advice.

It is therefore especially important to assuage guilt by pointing out to the smoker with COPD that he or she began to smoke long before recognizing the dangers of cigarette smoking and was lured by pervasive cigarette advertising to continue to view smoking as "acceptable." Likewise, past quit attempts must be reframed not as "failures," but as evidence of determination and as useful *practice*. Nicotine addiction must be carefully explained as an obstacle to quitting. And excess spousal pressure to quit must be "defused" to help reduce resistance and defiance.

The adjunctive use of nicotine replacement therapy (e.g., transdermal nicotine, nicotine gum) should be given serious consideration in a smoking intervention program with any pulmonary patient. Inpatients with pulmonary disease are particularly good candidates for prescription of nicotine replacement, as they generally have few or no medical contraindications for its use. If other diagnoses are present, guidelines relevant to those disorders should be followed. The hospital pharmacy should be encouraged to stock nicotine gum, and other nicotine replacements as they become available. Appropriate medical staff, including residents, nurses, and attending physicians, can benefit from training in appropriate use and prescribing practices. A nicotine fading program, involving reduction in number of cigarettes smoked and/or brand switching, can also help to minimize withdrawal symptoms, and is an alternative during outpatient treatment. However, patients should not be led to believe that changing to a lower tar cigarette will be of much therapeutic value as an end in itself (Warner and Slade 1992).

The usual tools of the pulmonary clinic also may be utilized to provide objective feedback to pulmonary patients, for example by using spirometry findings to motivate patients (Hale 1983; Risser and Belcher 1990). However, because spirometric values do not necessarily improve much or at all after smoking cessation occurs, they are not likely to be of much value in following the patient's progress after smoking cessation. Furthermore, for patients with only mild pulmonary symptoms, spirometry findings may be normal and caution must be taken to prevent patients from viewing normal results as a "clean bill of health." Rather, if spirometric values are normal, the patient can be advised to stop smoking in order to avoid future lung damage. Another tool is the measurement and feedback of heightened alveolar carbon monoxide levels, which drop within several hours of the last cigarette, providing immediate reinforcement for abstinence (Sirota, Curran, Habif 1985).

Referral to more intensive or more specialized formal treatment programs is indicated for patients who lack confidence they can quit without such help. Such clinics can be customized for the COPD patient (e.g., Hall et al. 1983) to bolster their quitting motivation and success.

Although the process of smoking cessation and the barriers to cessation for pulmonary patients are not fully understood, it is apparent that many of the resources to motivate and assist other patient groups to stop smoking are applicable. Furthermore, medical personnel working with pulmonary patients have additional tools specific to lung functioning which may be utilized. Most critical, however, is taking advantage of the earliest symptoms and signs of lung disease to educate and counsel patients as to the risks of continued smoking and means by which to stop. Substantially more work needs to be done to encourage both health care professionals and patients to take very seriously any early signs of pulmonary distress associated with smoking as the primary means to combat more serious lung disease.

SPECIAL ISSUES IN TREATING PATIENTS WITH CANCER

Until recently, cancer patients have been overlooked as a target population for smoking cessation intervention, perhaps because of expectations that quitting would yield little benefit and might compromise quality of life. In 1993, approximately 1,170,000 individuals will be diagnosed with malignant disease in the United States and 85 million living Americans (about 33%) will eventually have cancer (ACS, 1993). Some three of four families in the United States will be affected over time. One out of every five deaths from all causes in this country will be from cancer, striking down some 526,000 individuals this year (ACS, 1993). The long-term survival for persons diagnosed with a malignancy has risen steadily since the 1930s, with the 5-year relative survival rate for all cancers currently standing at 52% in the United States (ACS, 1993). This improved survival rate and the size of the population affected compel examination of the affects of continued cigarette smoking upon the general well-being of persons with cancer. Moreover, a special window of opportunity for intervention is introduced by the diagnosis and commencement of treatment for cancer.

Harmful Effects of Smoking and Benefits of Quitting Among Persons with Cancer

Tobacco has long been established as a causal or contributing agent in the development of cancers of the lung, upper aerodigestive tract, pancreas, bladder, and kidney, and has been associated with cancers of the uterine cervix and stomach (USDHHS 1989). Tobacco use has been considered an independent and synergistic risk factor along with alcohol intake for oral cancer (Mashberg, Garfinkel, Harris 1981). Persons diagnosed with a smoking-related malignancy face increased risks of a second malignancy at the same or another smoking-related site, especially if they continue to smoke (Wynder, Mushinski, Spivak 1977). Moreover, for all cancer patients, smoking compounds and heightens vulnerability to additional malignancies which may result from altered host immunity, radiation, or chemotherapy (DeVita, Hellman, Rosenberg 1989).

In addition, smoking cessation appears to confer many benefits for cancer patients. Longer survival and fewer second primary cancers have been reported for persons with cancers of the lung and upper aerodigestive tract who stopped smoking (Browman et al. 1993; Johnson et al. 1986; Johnston-Early et al. 1980; Moore 1971; Silverman, Gorsky, Greenspan 1983; Stevens et al. 1983) with some exceptions (Castigliano 1968; Schottenfeld, Gantt, Wynder 1974; Bergman and Sorenson 1988). Poorer survival has been reported for current smokers at diagnosis, compared to nonsmokers, with cancer of the prostate (Bako et al. 1982) and invasive cervical cancer (Kucera et al. 1987). Further benefits of quitting include reduced risks of other serious smoking-related diseases (COPD, coronary and vascular diseases) and improvement in well-being (self-control, self-esteem, etc.) (Knudsen et al. 1984; USDHHS 1990).

The treatment of cancer by surgery, radiation, and chemotherapy is likely to be associated with greater morbidity and higher rates of complications among smokers than nonsmokers. Patients undergoing general anesthesia are advised to stop smoking in order to benefit the cardiovascular system, via carbon monoxide and nicotine elimination, and the respiratory system, via improved ciliary beating and reduced sputum volume (Pearce and Jones 1984; USDHHS 1983). Similarly, excess sputum production resulting from chronic bronchitis and reduced airflow rates associated with emphysema may compromise or prohibit surgical approaches to speech rehabilitation in head and neck cancer patients (Ariyan 1987; Miller 1990). Finally, periodontal and wound healing are adversely affected in smokers via the actions of nicotine and carbon monoxide: vasoconstriction, inhibition of epithelization, damage to blood cellular components, and creation of a cellular hypoxia (Preber and Bergstrom 1990; Sherwin and Gastwirth 1990; Siana, Rex, Gottrup 1989; USDHHS 1983).

Many radiation side effects may be exacerbated or further complicated by cigarette smoking. Radiation to the head and neck produces oral mucositis, loss of taste, and xerostomia (dry mouth). These sequelae, and long-term complications such as soft tissue and bone necrosis, are likely to occur more frequently in smokers and to be exacerbated by smoking (Million and Cassisi 1984; Whittet et al. 1991; Wang 1990). Following radiotherapy for laryngeal carcinoma, continuing smokers are significantly less likely to regain satisfactory voice quality (Karim et al. 1983). Finally, an elevated relative risk of lung cancer has been observed among patients successfully treated with radiation therapy for Hodgkin's disease; all patients who developed lung cancer were smokers (Tucker, Coleman, Cox et al. 1988).

Cancer chemotherapy exerts toxic effects

on normal cells as well as tumors. A number of these overall toxicities might potentially be exacerbated by cigarette smoking: increased susceptibility to infection; disturbances of the gastrointestinal tract, such as ulcerations, dysphagia, and diarrhea; pneumonitis and pulmonary fibrosis; and congestive heart failure (Renneker 1988; DeVita, Hellmann, Rosenberg 1989). In addition, abnormalities in the airway mucociliary system produced by smoking (USDHHS 1984) likely further predispose the patient to respiratory complications such as bacterial pneumonia and other postoperative complications.

The metabolism of a variety of pharmacologic agents is accelerated in smokers, presumably through the mechanism of enhanced hepatic enzyme induction (Beckett and Triggs 1967). Increased clearance or inadequate bioavailability (Benowitz 1988) of chemotherapeutic agents, potentially resulting in subtherapeutic blood concentrations, could adversely affect antineoplastic potency in smokers. Such an interaction has not been examined to date. Another potential consequence is a change in the toxicity of these agents or their metabolic by-products.

Suppression of the immune system in cancer patients may result from an underlying malignancy or from antineoplastic therapy, especially when the latter includes corticosteroids, cytotoxic chemotherapy, or irradiation (DeVita, Hellman, Rosenberg 1989). In healthy individuals, cigarette smoking has been associated with a decrease in the number of circulating natural killer cells and an increase in the number of chromosomal abnormalities in circulating lymphocytes (Tucker, Ashworth, Johnston et al. 1988; Tollerud et al. 1989). Whether such overall changes might further compromise an immune-suppressed patient has yet to be determined. In the perioperative period, smoking could adversely affect host defenses when superimposed on immune suppression arising from anesthesia and surgery (Pearce and Jones 1984).

Malnutrition and cachexia in the cancer patient contribute to morbidity and may accelerate the end of life (DeVita, Hellman, Rosenberg 1989). Smoking affects eating behavior, body weight, and nutrition in several ways: decreasing appetite and serving as a substitute for eating (Gritz, Klesges, Meyers 1989); decreasing the hedonic value of food (Perkins, et al. 1990); affecting specific food consumption and taste preferences (Grunberg 1985); delaying gastric emptying, and thus perhaps increasing feelings of satiety (Gritz et al. 1988); elevating metabolic rate (USDHHS 1988; Klesges 1989); and decreasing body stores of vital nutrients, such as vitamin C (Smith and Hodges 1987). Clearly, in the face of poor weight gain and appetite, none of these effects are desirable in the cancer patient.

This brief review underscores the severe and potentially life-threatening consequences of cigarette smoking in persons with both smoking- and nonsmoking-related malignancies. Smoking cessation should be a high priority and has far more benefits than potential costs.

Smoking Prevalence in Cancer Patient Samples

Except for individuals with smoking-related tumors, smoking prevalence in cancer patient samples should not differ from age- and sex-matched national cohorts. Since cancer is predominantly a disease of the middle and later years, population comparisons are often difficult to make.

In a sample of 5,998 cancer patients with mixed diagnoses including smoking-related tumors admitted to the M.D. Anderson Hospital from 1986 to 1988, current and recent (abstinent less than 1 year) smoking prevalence was 30% for males and 29% for females (Spitz, Fueger, Eriksen et al. 1990). Response rate was not reported. In a second recent study, only 18% of 688 consenting patients sampled in six cancer clinics between 1989 and 1990 were current smokers; smokers were likely overrepresented among patients not consenting to the survey (Orleans, Lindblad, Davis et al. 1990). Eligible patients included all Stage I–II cancers and Stage III–IV breast, prostate, or testicular cancers, or lymphoma; breast cancer was the most frequent diagnosis (45%). In both studies, the smokers were likely to be moderate to heavy chronic users. Two-thirds of the clinic sample expressed a strong belief in the personal health benefits of quitting, had a strong desire to quit, and/or were interested in self-help quitting materials. The authors of both reports call for systematic quit smoking programs for cancer patients as part of their treatment regimens.

Samples of patients with smoking-related malignancies obviously have much larger proportions of current (and former) smokers at diagnosis. For example, in two lung cancer clinical trials, ever-smokers comprised 94.5% and 99% of patients at diagnosis (Gail et al. 1984; Johnston-Early et al. 1980). Approximately 51% of each sample were current smokers. This figure underestimates the proportion of recent smokers, since a large group of patients who quit at diagnosis or shortly before were counted as former smokers (over 31% in Johnston-Early's study). In two other studies, self-reported quit rates among lung cancer survivors were 52 and 60% 3 months or 5 or more years past surgery (Davison and Duffy 1982; Knudsen et al. 1985). Similarly, among survivors of head and neck cancer, quit rates of 40% to more than 60% have been reported (Castigliano 1968; Moore 1971; Stevens et al. 1983). In the most recent report of head and neck cancer survivors (30 months or longer), 62.5% were smoking at initial interview and quit rates were 70.6% among males and 61.1% among females (Spitz, Fueger, Chamberlain et al. 1990).

High cessation rates have been reported in a prospective analysis of patterns of smoking behavior among 840 patients with resected Stage I nonsmall cell lung cancer participating in clincial trials (Gritz et al. 1991). Lung cancer patients were heavier smokers at diagnosis than age- and sex-comparable cancer patients with non-lower respiratory tract diagnoses and the general population. At 1 year, only 16.8% of the subsample of 317 current smokers followed for 2 or more years were still smoking, while 83.2% either quit permanently (53%) or temporarily (30.2%). By 2 years, permanent cessation stabilized at over 40%. This analysis reveals both the potential for success to be realized from encouraging cessation among such a chronic heavy smoking population as well as the problem of maintaining that abstinence for a large segment of patients.

The limitations of the estimates of smoking at diagnosis and distant follow-ups reported here are substantial. All are based on self-reported smoking status. An underreporting bias would be expected, given the undesirability of continued smoking and likelihood that physician advice to stop has been delivered. Several samples were quite small, follow-ups are limited to surviving patients, and at least one had a sizeable non-response rate (Spitz, Feuger, Chamberlain et al. 1990). More prospective surveys of smoking behavior on representative samples of cancer patients are clearly indicated, taking diagnostic and demographic variables into account. The likelihood of cessation and long-term abstinence will be affected by cancer site and stage, prognosis and treatment-related sequelae, and on the advice and assistance given by the health professionals providing patient care. Whenever feasible, self-reports of smoking cessation should be accompanied by objective validation or the use of a *bogus pipeline* (i.e., a warning that objective validation may occur, which is given to improve the veracity of self-report).

Helping Patients with Cancer Stop Smoking

Until the present, there have been no published reports of controlled trials of smoking cessation interventions with cancer patients. One such study with head and neck cancer patients (Gritz et al. 1993; Gritz et al. 1991) was recently completed, and the other with a general population of primarily early stage cancer patients mentioned earlier is in progress (Orleans, Linblad, Davis et al. 1990). Both of these studies employ a randomized, controlled trial design, comparing usual care to the specialized intervention. Both feature health care provider advice to quit smoking and materials appropriately tailored to individuals being treated for cancer, and both evaluate smoking cessation over 12 months or longer. Results should provide guidelines to oncologic medical, dental, nursing, and psychology/social work professionals, as well as to primary care providers, for assisting their cancer patients in stopping smoking.

The head and neck study evaluated an extended physician intervention with several novel features (Gritz et al. 1993). Participants were current or recent smokers with a first primary squamous cell carcinoma of the upper aerodigestive tract. Baseline descriptive data showed these persons to be older (mean age = 58.5 years) and more likely to be male (73.7%), with a long history of heavy smoking (mean = 23.0 cigarettes/day for 39.7 years). Patients reported being highly addicted to nicotine, having a strong desire to quit, and confident in their ability to remain abstinent. A forceful quitting message was delivered by the head and neck surgeon or maxillofacial prosthodontist caring for the patient. For patients in the Intervention Group, initial advice to stop smoking and/or remain abstinent was delivered during routine care at the end of the postsurgical hospitalization or at the beginning of radiation therapy (for nonsurgical patients). Cessation benefits were emphasized and patients were encouraged to sign a contract designating a target quit date, which was also signed by the provider. All patients received a copy of the self-help guides *Team Up to Stop Smoking* and *Team Up to Stay Off,* written by project staff especially for head and neck cancer patients. Family members received *Team Up to Help a Friend.* These booklets depict the physiological relationships between smoking and upper aerodigestive tract tumors and provide standard smoking cessation, abstinence, and social support advice in the context of these tumors. For example, since difficulties with eating may pose special problems during and following cessation and withdrawal, appropriate dietary suggestions are provided. Also, normal behavioral routines are disrupted during extended treatment and recuperation. Thus, suggestions are made to family members for helping patients cope with depression, physical disfigurement, and functional disabilities without returning to smoking.

Six monthly booster sessions were delivered during routine medical or dental follow-up visits to reinforce the message and provide additional support according to whether the patient successfully abstained, relapsed, or never stopped. These brief counseling sessions were followed by mailed postcards that contained general, helpful hints. While the self-help booklets did not produce an incremental effect over provider-delivered smoking cessation advice, most smoking cessation occurred during hospitalization for initial surgery and treatment. High continuous abstinence rates were observed (up to 70%). Predictors of cessation included stage of change, medical treatment, nicotine dependence, age, and race.

The intervention trial with a mixed population of cancer patients (Orleans, Lindblad, Davis et al. 1990) is unique in that it draws from the National Cancer Institute (NCI)-sponsored Community Clinical Oncology Program (CCOP), a network of community oncologists collaborating in clinical trials research. In this study, the four-step physician smoking cessation intervention promoted by the NCI (Glynn and Manley 1989) will be compared to usual care (see Chapter 10). Oncologists will give quitting advice, discussing the health benefits for their early stage cancer patients, and attempt to set a quit date. All patients will receive a copy of the ALA self-help guide, *Freedom From Smoking for You and Your Family,* along with handouts addressing the benefits of quitting and interactions of smoking with cancer treatment, and nicotine gum prescriptions, if appropriate. CCOP nurses will provide brief counseling in how to use the guide and nicotine gum. Patients will be asked to call specially-trained NCI Cancer Information Service (CIS) counselors for additional, more expert, cessation advice. Patients will receive follow-up letters from their physicians and be asked about smoking at subsequent visits.

Results of these and similar trials will help to inform the routine treatment of cancer patients who smoke. In the interim, however, practical advice about how to intervene can be extrapolated from what is already known.

Critical Clinical Issues

Which Patients Should Be Counseled?

As demonstrated by the medical evidence offered earlier in this chapter, all smokers are likely to benefit from smoking cessation. The exception might be those with end-stage disease, for whom benefits would be minimal. Since, even among cancer patients, the risk of relapse remains high for at least 6 months to 1 year (Davison and Duffy 1982; Gritz et al. 1991), recent quitters also should be counseled to maintain abstinence. The greatest risk for additional smoking-related disease exists for patients with smoking-related cancers. The following list broadly covers other groups who might benefit especially from counseling because of specific risk factors:

1. Heavy drinkers;
2. Those with cancer-linked occupational exposures;
3. Those with smoking-related pre-neoplastic conditions, such as leukoplakia, erythroplakia, or severe cervical dysplasia;
4. Members of ethnic minorities or lower socioeconomic status, who have poorer overall cancer survival.

In addition, extremes of age should not be a deterrent from counseling. Both adolescent cancer survivors, who may benefit from prevention and/or cessation messages, and geriatric patients, for whom cessation can still have substantial benefits (USDDHS 1990), deserve attention. Finally, the families and other relatives of cancer patients are also good candidates for smoking cessation advice.

Counseling—by Whom, When, and How Much?

Personalizing the risks of continued smoking and highlighting the benefits of cessation may be especially important for cancer patients, particularly when delivered by the primary medical care provider. Physicians, nurses, dentists, dietitians, rehabilitation specialists, psychologists and social workers, and so forth are all powerful carriers and supporters of the message. Working as a team, each can provide a special tailoring of advice and information, according to the type of care delivered.

Advice given at the time of diagnosis if often overwhelmed by the emotional and cognitive impact of the concept of cancer, its treatment, and the fear of death. Many physicians will discuss smoking as part of the explanation of the causes of a patient's smoking-related cancer, but detailed advice is best left until later. Great sensitivity is required by the medical care provider in discussing the etiology of a patient's smoking-related cancer. Patients may express denial and anger about the relationship of smoking to their disease, or claim that the benefits of cessation are "too late" in their case. They may also claim that smoking is the only pleasure they have left to them. Facts should be presented in a way that avoids "blaming the victim." This can be done by acknowledging that smoking initiation most likely occurred in adolescence, before personal knowledge of the adverse health effects, and that addictive smoking was the result. The opportunity to break loose from this form of substance dependence should be framed to the patient as a means of gaining a sense of personal control over recovery.

The key element in counseling interventions, as exemplified in the ongoing head and neck and CCOP trials, is the repetitive, supportive content of the message (Kottke et al. 1988). The acute phases of many cancer treatments may have already involved an enforced nonsmoking hospitalization and/or period of treatment-related morbidity during which smoking is impossible or unlikely. Ongoing care can further be expanded to include patient and family support groups, telephone counseling, survivor programs, and, of course, following a stepped-care model (Chapter 8), referral to more intensive treatments for patients unsuccessful with self-help, minimal-contact treatments. Also, many difficult psychological issues arise in the diagnosis and treatment periods which affect smoking cessation attempts. These include disease-and prognosis-related anxiety, guilt and depression, and the stress of adjusting to a modified life-style. Psychological counseling or patient support groups may be appropriate for this transitional period. These are often available at hospitals or in the community, led by mental health professionals. The entire oncology treatment support team should become part of the intervention, with the recognition that quitting often will require repeated attempts for these high-risk, highly addicted patients.

Tailoring of Smoking Cessation Advice and Material

The techniques, coping behaviors, and activities recommended to promote cessation and prevent relapse must be sensitive to the physical limitations accompanying cancer and its various forms of treatment. Many widely available self-help materials written for healthy populations have inappropriate content (e.g., emphasizing preventive avoidance of illness) or approach. The most obvious tailoring would involve suggestions about exercise regimens and changes in diet, and awareness that some cancer patients may be too ill to seek out nonsmokers, situate themselves in nonsmoking external environments (e.g., restaurants with nonsmoking sections), or take up new and challenging hobbies.

The precise nature of tailoring varies according to the primary cancer site. For example, head and neck cancer patients often have problems with excessive weight loss, while breast cancer patients tend to gain, especially when receiving adjuvant chemotherapy. For the head and neck cancer population, we felt it necessary to develop tailored materials (described earlier) which were designed for the special physical and psychological needs and concerns of this patient group. A similar approach is being used in the CCOP cancer patient antismoking intervention (Orleans, Lindblad, Davis et al. 1990). Special cancer-focused tip sheets and CIS-telephone counseling supplement physician-delivered advice to quit. This general approach is more relevant to the majority of cancer patients than most other publicly available materials.

The Role of Pharmacotherapy

Nicotine replacement has not been formally tested in clinical populations of cancer patients. However, given that many cancer patients are long-term, heavy, dependent smokers, the gum is an appropriate therapeutic medium for many of these patients

when accompanied by a sound behavioral program (USDHHS 1988). With regard to use by head and neck cancer patients, it is noted that nicotine polacrilex (gum) does not appear to produce adverse effects on the gingiva for up to 6 months of daily use (Silver, Sachs, Hottel 1989). However, patients with surgically produced oral defects, edentulous patients, radiated patients, and the like are better candidates for transdermal nicotine. Likewise, many surgeons are hesitant for patients to continue to use oral nicotine with any oral cavity cancer. For these and other cancer patients, other nicotine delivery systems (transdermal patch, nasal spray, aerosol) and other pharmacotherapeutic agents (e.g., clonidine, fluoxetine) remain to be investigated. Of course, as with any medication, the pharmacologic actions of the adjunctive drug must be considered in conjunction with the patient's medical condition (neoplastic and non-neoplastic diseases) as well as other medications being concurrently administered.

In conclusion, individuals with malignant disease have been a neglected population for smoking cessation therapy. The increasing numbers of long-term cancer survivors and the complications induced by other smoking-related diseases mandate that the nicotine dependence be addressed in these persons. The biological, biomedical, and behavioral aspects of this therapy will be challenging, but ultimately rewarding, potentially yielding the highest quit rates of any chronic disease patient group. Optimally, ongoing physician, nursing, and allied health professional support for cessation, as well as salient issues in patient health and well-being, will reinforce motivation to quit. These forces will combine with the assistance of significant others to provide broad social support for long-lasting valuable behavioral change.

CONCLUSION

Individuals who are pregnant or who have developed a major tobacco-related illness are more likely than the general population to quit smoking and to remain abstinent. It is likely that a part of this increased cessation is due to the greater motivation provided by their health condition and that a part is due to the increased intensity of intervention efforts delivered by the health care system because of their condition. However, it remains a remarkable observation that, even among these patients who have the greatest reason to quit and who have access to state-of-the-art cessation assistance, a substantial fraction do not quit smoking.

It is perhaps too limiting to view smoking cessation in these high-risk populations only within the context of the patient–provider interaction. Like all other smokers, these individuals live in an environment that is saturated with messages and cues to smoke, and it may be unreasonable to expect that any individual cessation intervention could enable enough change for all smokers to resist these influences. Interventions delivered to these high-risk populations may define the limits of current smoking cessation technology for producing behavior change in individual smokers.

Changes in the environment within which the smoker lives and works, such as restrictions on where smoking is allowed, are currently thought to be a substantial reason why smoking prevalence is declining. It is likely that these general environmental changes may also influence cessation among high-risk smokers, and they may interact with the cessation interventions delivered to these smokers to increase the rate of successful cessation.

REFERENCES

American Cancer Society (ACS). *1993 Cancer Facts and Figures.* Atlanta: American Cancer Society, Inc., 93-400M-No. 5008.93, 1993.

Anthonisen, N. R. Lung health study (editorial). *Am Rev Respir Dis* 140:871–872, 1989.

Ariyan, S., ed. *Cancer of the Head and Neck.* St. Louis: C. V. Mosby, 1987.

Baile, W. F., Bigelow, G. E., Gottlieb, S. H., Stitzer, M. L., Sacktor, J. D. Rapid resumption of cigarette smoking following myocardial infarction: Inverse relation to MI severity. *Addict Behav* 7:377–380, 1982.

Bako, G., Dewar, R., Hanson, J., Hill, G. Factors influencing the survival of patients with cancer of the prostate. *Can Med Assoc J* 127:727–729, 1982.

Beckett, A. H., and Triggs, E. J. Enzyme induction in man caused by smoking. *Nature* 216:587, 1967.

Benowitz, N. L. Pharmacologic aspects of cigarette smoking and nicotine addiction. *N Engl J Med* 319:1318–1330, 1988.

———. Nicotine replacement therapy during pregnancy. *JAMA* 266:3174–3177, 1992.

Bergman, S., and Sorenson, S. Smoking and effect of chemotherapy in small cell lung cancer. *Eur J Respir Dis* 1:932–937, 1988.

Browman, G. P., Wong, G., Hodson, I., Sathaya, J., Russel, R. McAlpine, L., Skingley, P., Levine, M. N. Influence of cigarette smoking on the efficacy of radiation therapy in head and neck cancer. *N Engl J Med* 328(3):159–163, 1993.

Brownell, K. D., Marlatt, G. A., Lichtenstein, E., Wilson G. T. Understanding and preventing relapse. *Am Psychol* 41:765–782, 1986.

Burling, T. A., Singleton, E. G., Bigelow, G. E., Baile, W. F., Gottlieb, S. Smoking following myocardial infarction: A critical review of the literature. *Health Psychol* 3:83–96, 1984.

Castigliano, S. G. Influence of continued smoking on the incidence of second primary cancers involving mouth, pharynx and larynx. *J Am Den Assoc* 77:580–585, 1968.

Centers for Disease Control (CDC). Chronic disease reports: Chronic obstructive pulmonary disease mortality—United States, 1986. *MMWR* 38:549–552, 1989.

Comoss, P. M. Nursing strategies to improve compliance with life-style changes in a cardiac rehabilitation population. *J Cardiovasc Nurs* 2(3):23–36, 1988.

Connett, J. E., Kusek, J. W., Bailey, W. C., O'Hara, P., Wu, M. Design of the Lung Health Study: A randomized clinical trial of early intervention for chronic obstructive pulmonary disease. *Controlled Clinical Trials* 14(Suppl.):35–195, 1993.

Cutter, G., Oberman, M. K., Kimmerling, R., Oberman, A. The natural history of smoking cessation among patients undergoing coronary arteriography. *J Cardiovasc Rehab* 5:332–340, 1985.

Davison, G., and Duffy, M. Smoking habits of long-term survivors of surgery for lung cancer. *Thorax* 37:331–333, 1982.

Deanfield, J., Wright, C., Krikler, S., Ribeiro, P., Fox, K. Cigarette smoking and the treatment of angina with propranolol, antenolol, and nifedipine. *N Engl J Med* 310:951–954, 1984.

Devita, V. T., Jr., Hellman, S., Rosenberg, S. A., eds. *Cancer—Principles and Practice of On-*

cology, 3d ed. Philadelphia: JB Lippincott, 1989.

Doyle, J. T., Dawber, T. R., Kannel, W. B., Kinch, S. H., Kahn, H. A. The relationship of cigarette smoking to coronary heart disease. *JAMA* 190:108–112, 1964.

Emmons, K. M., Weidner, G., Foster, W. M., Collins, R. L. Improvement in pulmonary function following smoking cessation. *Addic Beh* 17:301–306, 1992.

Epstein, L. H., and Perkins, K. A. Smoking, stress, and coronary heart disease. *J Consult Clin Psychol* 56:342–349, 1988.

Ershoff, D. H., Mullen, P. D., Quinn, V. P. A randomized trial of a serialized self-help smoking cessation program for pregnant women in an HMO. *Am J Public Health* 79(2):182–187, 1989.

Farquhar, J. W., Wood, P. D., Brietrose, H., Haskell, W. L., Meyer, A. J., Maccoby, N., Alexander, J. K., Brown, B. W., Acalister, A. L., Nash, J. D., Stern, M. P. Community education for cardiovascular health. *Lancet* 1:1192–1995, 1977.

Fichtner, R. R., Sullivan, K. M., Zyrkowski, C. L., Trowbridge, F. L. Racial/ethnic differences in smoking, other risk factors, and low birth weight among low-income pregnant women, 1978–1988. *MMWR* 39(SS-3):13–21. U.S. Department of Health and Human Services, Public Health Service, Centers for Disease Control, Altanta, Georgia, July 1990.

Fielding, J. E. Smoking: Health effects and control. Part 1. *N Engl J Med* 313:491–498, 1985.

Fingerhut, L. A., Kleinman, M. C., Kendrick, J. S. Smoking before, during and after pregnancy. *Am J Public Health* 80(5):541–544, 1990.

Fleisher, L. F., Keintz, M., Rimer, B., Utt, M., Workman, S., Engstrom, P. Process evaluation of a minimal-contact smoking cessation program in an urban nutritional assistance (WIC) program. In Engstrom, P., Rimer, B., Mortensen, L. E., eds. *Advances in Cancer Control: Screening and Prevention Research.* New York: Wiley-Liss, 1990, 95–107.

Foxman, B., Sloss, E. M., Lohr, K. N., Brook, R. H. Chronic bronchitis: Prevalence, smoking habits, impact, and antismoking advice. *Prev Med* 15:624–631, 1986.

Gadek, J. E., Fells, G. A., Crystal, R. G. Cigarette smoking induces functional anti-protease deficiency in the lower respiratory tract of humans. *Science* 206:1315–1316, 1979.

Gail, M. H., Eegan, R. T., Feld, R., Ginsberg, R., Goodell, B., Hill, L., Holmes, E. C., Luke-man, J. M., Mountain C. F., Oldham, R. K., Pearson, F. G., Wright, P. W., Lake, W. H., The Lung Study Group. Prognostic factors in patients with resected Stage I non-small cell lung cancer. A report from the Lung Cancer Study Group. *Cancer* 54:1802–1813, 1984.

Garn, S. M., Jonston, M., Ridella, S. A., Petzold, A. S. Effects of maternal cigarette smoking on Apgar scores. *Am J Dis Child* 135:503–506, 1981.

Glezen, W. P., Decker, M., Perrota, D. M. Survey of underlying conditions of persons hospitalized with acute respiratory disease during influenza epidemics in Houston, 1978–1981. *Am Rev Respir Dis* 126:265–269, 1987.

Glynn, T. J., and Manley, M. W. *How to Help Your Patients Stop Smoking. A National Cancer Institute Manual for Physicians.* Smoking, Tobacco and Cancer Program, Division of Cancer Prevention and Control, National Cancer Institute. NIH Publication No. 89-3064, 1989.

Greenberg, G., Thompson, S. G., Brennan, P. J. The relationship between smoking and the response to anti-hypertensive treatment in mild hypertensives in the Medical Research Council's trial of treatment. *Inter J Epidemiol* 16:25–30, 1987.

Gritz, E. R., Carr, C. R., Rapkin, D. A., Chang, C., Buemer, J., Ward, P. H. A smoking cessation intervention for head and neck cancer patients: Trial design, patient accrual and characteristics. *Cancer Epidemiology. Biomarkers and Prevention* 1:67–73, 1991.

Gritz, E. R., Ippoliti, A., Jarvik, M. E., Rose, J. E., Shiffman, S. M., Harrison, A., Van Vunakis, H. The effect of nicotine on the delay of gastric emptying. *Alimentary Pharmacology and Therapeutics* 2:173–178, 1988.

Gritz, E. R., Klesges, R. C., Meyers, A. W. The smoking and body weight relationship: Implications for intervention and postcessation weight control. *Ann Behav Med* 11(4):144–153, 1989.

Gritz, E. R., Carr, C. R., Rapkin, D., Abemayor, E. A., Chang, L.-J., Wong, W.-K., Belin, T. R., Calcaterra, T., Robbins, K. T., Chonkich, G., Beumer J. Ward, P. H. Predictors of long-term smoking cessation in head and neck cancer patients. *Cancer Epidemiology, Biomarkers and Prevention* 2(3):261–269, 1993.

Gritz, E. R., Nisenbaum, R., Elashoff, R. E., Holmes, E. C, The Lung Cancer Study Group. Smoking behavior following diagnosis in patients with stage I non-small cell lung cancer. *Cancer Causes and Control* 2(2):105–112, 1991.

Gross, J., Bigelow, G., Rand, C., Stewart, K., Gottlieb, S. Smoking cessation in cardiac patients. Paper presented at the Society of Behavioral Medicine Annual Meeting, Washington, D.C., 20 March 1987.

Grunberg, N. E. Specific taste preferences: An alternative explanation for eating changes in cancer patients. In Burish, T. G., Levy, S. M., Meyerowitz, B. E., eds. *Cancer, Nutrition, and Eating Behavior: A Biobehavioral Perspective.* Hillsdale, NJ: Lawrence Earlbaum Associates, 1985, 43–61.

Hale, K. A. Chronic airflow obstruction: A two-pronged approach to outpatient management. *Postgrad Med* 73(6):259–265, 1983.

Hall, S. M., Bachman, J., Henderson, J. B., Barstow, R., Jones, R. T. Smoking cessation in patients with cardiopulmonary disease: An initial study. *Addict Behav* 8:33–42, 1983.

Hallstrom, A. P., Cobb, L. A., Ray, R. Smoking as a risk factor for recurrence of sudden cardiac arrest. *N Engl J Med* 314(5):271–275, 1986.

Hammond, S. K., and Leaderer, B. P. A diffusion monitor to measure exposure to passive smoking. *Environ Sci Technol* 21:494–497, 1987.

Havik, O. E., and Maeland, J. G. Changes in smoking behavior after a myocardial infarction. *Health Psychol* 7:403–420, 1988.

Holland, W. W. Chronic obstructive lung disease prevention. *Br J Dis Chest* 82:32–44, 1988.

Hughes, J. R., Epstein, L. H., Andrasik, F., Neff, D. F., Thompson, D. S. Smoking and carbon monoxide levels during pregnancy. *Addict Behav* 7:271–276, 1982.

Jarvis, M., West, R., Tunstall-Perdoe, H., Vesey, C. An evaluation of the intervention against smoking in the Multiple Risk Factor Intervention Trial. *Prev Med* 13:501–509, 1984.

Johnson, B. E., Ihde, D. C., Matthews, M. J., Bunn, P. A., Zabell, A., Makuck, R. W., Johnston-Early, A., Cohen, M., Glatstein, E., Minna, J. D. Non-small-cell lung cancer: Major cause of late mortality in patients with small cell lung cancer. *Am J Med* 80(6):1103–1110, 1986.

Johnston-Early, A., Cohen, M. H., Minna, J. D., Paxton, L. M., Fossick, B. E., Jr., Ihde, D. C., Bunn, P. A., Matthews, M. J., Makuch, M. Smoking abstinence and small cell lung cancer survival. *JAMA* 244:2175–2179, 1980.

Karim, A. B., Snow, G. B., Siek, H. T., Njo, K. H. The quality of voice in patients irradiated for laryngeal carcinoma. *Cancer* 51:47–49, 1983.

Kleinman, J. C., and Kopstein, A. Smoking during pregnancy, 1967–80. *Am J Public Health* 77(7):823–825, 1987.

Klesges, R. C., Meyers, A. W., Winders, S. E., French, S. N. Determining the reasons for weight gain following smoking cessation: Current findings, methodological issues, and future directions for research. *Ann Behav Med* 11(4):134–143, 1989.

Knudsen, N., Schulman, S., Fowler, R., van den Hoek, J. Why bother with stop-smoking education for lung cancer patients? *Oncol Nurs Forum* 11:30–33, 1984.

Knudsen, N., Schulman, S., van den Hoek, J., Fowler, R. Insights on how to quit smoking: A survey of patients with lung cancer. *Cancer Nurs* 8(3):145–150, 1985.

Kottke, T. E., Battista, R. N., DeFriese, G. H., Brekke, M. L. Attributes of successful smoking cessation interventions in medical practice. A meta-analysis of 39 controlled trials. *JAMA* 259(19):2883–2889, 1988.

Kramer, M. S. Determinants of low birth weight: Methodological assessment and meta-analysis. *Bull WHO* 65(5):663–737, 1987.

Kristeller, J. L., and Ockene, J. K. Assessment and treatment of smoking on a consultation liaison service. In Cavenar, ed. *Consultation Liaison Psychiatry and Behavioral Medicine, Vol. 3, Psychiatry.* Philadelphia: J. B. Lippincott, 1989, ch. 113, pp. 1–13.

Kucera, H., Enzelsberger, H. Eppel, W., Weghaupt, K. The influence of nicotine abuse and diabetes mellitus on the results of primary irradiation in the treatment of carcinoma of the cervix. *Cancer* 60(1):1–4, 1987.

Kulpa, M. Smoking habit of respiratory care patients. *Am Rev Respir Dis* (Abstr), A776, 1990.

Langeluddecke, P. M. The role of behavioral change procedures in multifactorial coronary heart disease prevention programs. *Prog Behav Mod* 20:199–225, 1986.

McBride, C. M., and Pirie, P. L. Brief report—postpartum smoking relapse. *Addict Behav* 15:165–168, 1990.

Mashberg, A., Garfinkel, L., Harris, S. Alcohol as a primary risk factor in oral squamous carcinoma. *CA* 31(3):146–155, 1981.

Mayer, J. P., Hawkins, B., Todd, R. A randomized evaluation of smoking cessation interventions for pregnant women at a WIC clinic. *Am J Public Health* 80(1):76–78, 1990.

Miller, S. The role of the speech-language pathologist in voice restoration after total laryngectomy. *CA* 40(3):174–182, 1990.

Million, R. R., and Cassisi, N. J., eds. *Management of Head and Neck Cancer: A Multidis-*

ciplinary Approach. Philadelphia: J. B. Lippincott, 1984.

Moore, C. Cigarette smoking and cancer of the mouth, pharynx and larynx. *JAMA* 218(4):553–558, 1971.

Mulcahy, R., Hickey, N., Graham, I., Macairt, J. Factors affecting the 5 year survival rate of men following acute coronary heart disease. *Am Heart J* 93(5):556–559, 1977.

Mullen, P. D., Quinn, V. P., Ershoff, D. H. Maintenance of nonsmoking postpartum by women who stopped smoking during pregnancy. *Am J Public Health* 80(8):992–994, 1990.

Multiple Risk Factor Trial Research Group (MRFTRG). Multiple risk intervention trial—risk factor changes and mortality results. *JAMA* 248:1465–1467, 1982.

National Center for Health Statistics (NCHS). Health promotion and disease prevention: United States, 1985. *Vital and Health Statistics,* ser. 10, no. 163. Public Health Service. DHHS Publication No. (PHS) 88-1591, 1988.

Nett, L. The physician and smoking cessation as part of usual care. *Respir Times* December 1986, 9–10.

———. Respiratory therapists' nicotine dependency intervention program for hospital patients. Paper presented at the Nicotine Reduction Therapy in the 90's Symposium. Palm Springs, CA, November 1990.

Nieburg, P., Marks, J. S., McLaren, N. M., Remington, P. L. The fetal tobacco syndrome. *JAMA* 253(20):2998–2999, 1985.

Ockene, J. K., Hosmer, D., Rippe, J., Williams, J., Goldberg, R. J., Decosimo, D., Maher, P. M., Dalen, J. E. Factors affecting cigarette smoking status in patients with ischemic heart disease. *J Chronic Dis* 12:985–994, 1985.

Ockene, J. K., Hosmer, D., Williams, J., Goldberg, R. J., Ockene, I., Bilouris, T., Dalen, J. E. The relationship of patient characteristics to physician delivery of advice to stop smoking. *J Gen Int Med* 2:337–340, 1987.

Ockene, J. K., Kristeller, J., Goldberg, R., Ockene, I., Merriam, P., Barrett, S., Pekow, P., Hosmer, D., Gianelly, R. Smoking cessation and severity of disease: The Coronary Artery Smoking Intervention Study. *Health Psychol* 11:119–126, 1992.

O'Hara, P., Grill, J., Rigdon, M. A., Connett, J. E., Lauger, G., Johnston, J. J. Design and results of the initial intervention program for The Lung Health Study. *Prev Med* (In press).

Orleans, C. T., Kristeller, J., Gritz, E. R. Helping hospitalized smokers quit: New directions for treatment and research. *J Consult Clin Psychol* (In press).

Orleans, C. T., Lindblad, A., Davis, S., Rose, M., James, J., Engstrom, P., Robinson, R., Brody, D., Angel, I., Gritz, E. R. The need for brief physician-initiated quit smoking strategies in CCOP settings. Paper presented at the 14th Annual Meeting of the American Society of Preventive Oncology/Advances in Cancer Control III, Bethesda, MD, 19–21 March 1990.

Orleans, C. T., Rotberg, H. L., Quade, D., Lees, P. A hospital quit-smoking consult service: Clinical report and intervention guidelines. *Prev Med* 19:198–212, 1990.

Ossip-Klein, D. J., Giovino, G. A., Megahed, N., Black, P. M., Emont, S. L., Stiggins, J., Shulman, E., Moore, L. Effects of a smokers' hotline: Results of a 10-county self-help trial. *J Consult Clin Psychol* 59:325–332, 1991.

Peach, H., Hayward, D. M., Ellard, D. R., Morris, R. W., Shah, D. Phlegm production and lung function among cigarette smokers changing tar groups during the 1970s. *J Epidemiol Community Health* 40:110–116, 1986.

Pearce, A. C., and Jones, R. M. Smoking and anesthesia: Preoperative abstinence and perioperative morbidity. *Anesthesiology* 61:576–584, 1984.

Pederson, L. L. Compliance with physician advice to quit smoking: A review of the literature. *Prev Med* 11:71–84, 1982.

Pederson, L. L., and Baskerville, J. C. Multivariate prediction of smoking cessation following physician advice to quit smoking: A validation study. *Prev Med* 12:430–436, 1983.

Pederson, L. L., Baskerville, J. C., Wanklin, J. M. Multivirate statistical models for predicting change in smoking behavior following physician advice to quit smoking. *Prev Med* 11(5):536–649, 1982.

Pederson, L. L., Williams, J. I., Lefcoe, N. M. Smoking cessation among pulmonary patients as related to type of respiratory disease and demographic variables. *Can J Public Health* 71:191–194, 1980.

Pederson, L. L., Wood, T., Lefcoe, N. M. Use of a self-help smoking cessation manual as an adjunct to advice from a respiratory specialist. *Int J Addict,* 18:777–789, 1983.

Perkins, K. A. Maintaining smoking abstinence after myocardial infarction. *J Substance Abuse* 1:91–107, 1988.

———. Interactions among coronary heart disease risk factors. *Ann Behav Med* 11:3–11, 1989.

Perkins, K. A., Epstein, L. H., Stiller, R. L., Fernstrom, M. H., Sexton, J. E., Jacob, R. G. Perception and hedonics of sweet and fat taste in smokers and nonsmokers following nicotine intake. *Pharmacol Biochem Behav* 35(3):671–676, 1990.

Preber, H., and Bergstrom, J. Effect of cigarette smoking on periodontal healing following surgical therapy. *J Clin Periodontol* 17(5):324–328, 1990.

Prochaska, J. O., and DiClemente, C. C. Stages and processes of self-change of smoking: Toward an integrative model of change. *J Consult Clin Psychol* 51:390–395, 1983.

Puska, P., Tuomilehto, J., Salomen, J., Nissinen, A., Virtamo, J., et al. *Community Control of Cardiovascular Diseases: The North Karelia Project.* Report published on behalf of the National Public Health Laboratory of Finland by the Regional Office for Europe. World Health Organization, Copenhagen, 1981.

Renneker, M., ed. *Understanding Cancer,* 3d ed. Palo Alto, CA: Bull Publishing, 1988.

Rigdon, M. Intervention goals and results of the first annual visit in the Lung Health Study. American Thoracic Society. Annual meeting, Boston, MA, May 20, 1990.

Risser, N. L., and Belcher, D. W. Adding spirometry, carbon monoxide, and pulmonary symptom results to smoking cessation counseling: A randomized trial. *J Gen Intern Med* 5:16–22, 1990.

Robinson, K., Conroy, R. M., Mulcahy, R. Smoking and acute coronary heart disease: A comparative study. *Br Heart J* 60:465–469, 1988.

Rose, G., and Hamilton, P.J.S. A randomized controlled trial of the effect on middle-aged men of advice to stop smoking. *J Epidemiol Community Health* 32:275–281, 1978.

Salonen, J. T. Stopping smoking and long-term mortality after acute myocardial infarction. *Br Heart J* 43(4):463–469, 1980.

Schottenfeld, D., Gantt, R. C., Wynder, E. L. The role of alcohol and tobacco in multiple primary cancers of the upper digestive system, larynx and lung: A prospective study. *Prev Med* 3:277–293, 1974.

Scott, R. R., and Lamparski, D. Variables related to long-term smoking status following cardiac events. *Addict Behav* 10:257–264, 1985.

Sexton, M., and Hebel, J. R. A clinical trial of change in maternal smoking and its effect on birth weight. *JAMA* 251(7):911–915, 1984.

Sexton, M., Hebel, J. R., Fox, N. L. Postpartum smoking. In Rosenberg, M. J., ed. *Smoking and Reproductive Health.* Littleton, MA: PSG, 1987, 222–226.

Sherwin, M. A., and Gastwirth, C. M. Detrimental effects of cigarette smoking on lower extremity wound healing. *J Foot Surg* 29(1):84–87, 1990.

Siana, J. E., Rex, S., Gottrup, F. The effect of cigarette smoking on wound healing. *Scand J Plast Reconstr Surg* 23(3):207–209, 1989.

Silver, K. J., Sachs, D. P., Hottel, T. L. Gingival response to nicotine polacrilex. *J Am Dent Assoc* 188:53–56, 1989.

Silverman, S., Gorsky, M., Greenspan, D. Tobacco usage in patients with head and neck carcinomas: A follow-up study on habit changes and second primary oral/oropharyngeal cancers. *J Am Dent Assoc* 106:33–35, 1983.

Sirota, A. D., Curran, J. P., Habif, V. Smoking cessation in chronically ill medical patients. *J Clin Psychol* 41:575–579, 1985.

Smith, J. L., and Hodges, R. E. Serum levels of vitamin C in relation to dietary supplemental intake of vitamin C in smokers and nonsmokers. *Ann NY Acad Sci* 498:144–151, 1987.

Spitz, M. R., Fueger, J. J., Chamberlain, R. M., Goepfert, H., Newell, G. R. Cigarette smoking patterns after treatment of upper aerodigestive tract cancers. *J Cancer Ed* 5:109–113, 1990.

Spitz, M. R., Fueger, J. J., Eriksen, M. P., Newell, G. R. Cigarette smoking patterns of cancer patients. In Engstrom P., Rimer, B., Mortensen, L. E., eds. *Advances in Cancer Control: Screening and Prevention Research,* New York: Wiley-Liss, 1990, 73–82.

Stevens, M. H., Gardner, J. W. Parkin, J. L., Johnson, L. P. Head and neck cancer survival and lifestyle change. *Arch Otolaryngol* 109:746–749, 1983.

Tashkin, D. P., Clark, V. A., Coulson, A. H., Simmons, M., Bourque, L. B., Reems, C., Detels, R., Sayre, J. W., Rokaw, S. N. The UCLA population studies of chronic obstructive respiratory disease. VIII. Effects of smoking cessation on lung function: A prospective study of a free-living population. *Am Rev Respir Dis* 130:707–715, 1984.

Taylor, C. B., Houston-Miller, N., Killen, J. D., Debusk, R. F. Smoking cessation after acute myocardial infarction: Effects of a nurse-managed intervention. *Ann Intern Med* 113:118–123, 1990.

Tollerud, D. J., Clark, J. W., Bronn, L. M., Neuland, C. Y., Mann, D. L., Pankiw-Trost, L. K., Blattner, W. A., Hoover, R. N. Association of cigarette smoking with decreased numbers of circulating natural killer cells. *Am Rev Respir Dis* 139:194–198, 1989.

Tucker, J. D., Ashworth, L. K., Johnston, D. R.,

Allen, N. A., Carrano, A. V. Variation in the human lymphocyte sister chromatid exchange frequency: Results of a long term longitudinal study. *Mutat Res* 204:435–444, 1988.

Tucker, M. A., Coleman, C. N., Cox, R. S., Varghese, A., Rosenberg, S. A. Risk of second cancers after treatment for Hodgkin's disease. *N Engl J Med* 318(2):76–80, 1988.

Turner, S. A., Daniels, J. L., Hollandsworth, J. G. The effects of a multicomponent smoking cessation program with chronic obstructive pulmonary disease patients. *Addict Behav* 10:87–90, 1985.

U.S. Department of Health, Education and Welfare (USDHEW). *The Health Consequences of Smoking for Women. A Report of the Surgeon General.* U.S. Department of Health and Human Services, Public Health Service, Office of the Assistant Secretary for Health, Office on Smoking and Health, 1980.

U.S. Department of Health and Human Services (USDHHS). *The Health Consequences of Smoking: Cardiovascular Disease. A Report of the Surgeon General.* U.S. Department of Health and Human Services, Public Health Service, Office on Smoking and Health. DHHS Publication No. (PHS) 84-50204, 1983.

———. *The Health Consequences of Smoking: Chronic Obstructive Lung Disease. A Report of the Surgeon General.* U.S. Department of Health and Human Services, Public Health Service, Office on Smoking and Health. DHHS Publication No. (PHS) 84-50205, 1984.

———. *The Health Consequences of Involuntary Smoking. A Report of the Surgeon General.* U.S. Department of Health and Human Services, Public Health Service, Centers for Disease Control, Office on Smoking and Health. DHHS Publication No. (CDC) 87-8398, 1986.

———. *The Health Consequences of Involuntary Smoking. A Report of the Surgeon General.* U.S. Department of Health and Human Services, Public Health Service, Centers for Disease Control, Office on Smoking and Health. DHHS Publication No. (CDC) 87-8398, 1987.

———. *The Health Consequences of Smoking: Nicotine Addiction. A Report of the Surgeon General.* U.S. Department of Health and Human Services, Public Health Service, Centers for Disease Control, Center for Chronic Disease Prevention and Health Promotion, Office on Smoking and Health. DHHS Publication No. (CDC) 88-8406, 1988.

———. *Reducing the Health Consequences of Smoking: 25 Years of Progress. A Report of the Surgeon General.* U.S. Department of Health and Human Services, Public Health Service, Centers for Disease Control, Center for Chronic Disease Prevention and Health Promotion, Office on Smoking and Health. DHHS Publication No. (CDC) 89-8411, 1989.

———. *The Health Benefits of Smoking Cessation. A Report of the Surgeon General.* U.S. Department of Health and Human Services, Public Health Service, Centers for Disease Control, Center for Chronic Disease Prevention and Health Promotion, Office on Smoking and Health. DHHS Publication No. (CDC) 90-8416, 1990.

U.S. Environmental Protection Agency (USEPA). *Respiratory Health Effects of Passive Smoking: Lung Cancer and Other Disorders.* U. S. Environmental Assessment, Office of Research and Development. EPA/600/6-90/006F, Washington D. C., 1992.

Wang, C. C., ed. *Radiation Therapy for Head and Neck Neoplasms: Indications, Techniques, and Results.* Chicago: Year Book Medical Publishers, 1990.

Ward, C. H., Graybar, S., Rallof, D., Antonuccio, D. O., Boutilier, L. R. Smoking cessation and relapse in chronic obstructive pulmonary disease patients. Paper presented at the American Psychological Association, Boston, MA, August 1990.

Warner, K. L., and Slade, J. Low tar, high toll. *Am J Public Health* 82:17–19, 1992.

Whittet, H. B., Lund, J. V., Brockbank, M., Feyerbend, C. Serum cotinine as an objective marker for smoking habit in head and neck malignancy. *J Laryngology and Otology* 105:1036–1039, 1991.

Williamson, D. F., Serdula, M. K., Kendrick, J. S., Binkin, N. J. Comparing the prevalence of smoking in pregnant and nonpregnant women, 1985 to 1986. *JAMA* 261(1):70–74, 1989.

Windsor, R. A., Green, L. A., Roseman, J. M. Health promotion and maintenance for patients with chronic obstructive pulmonary disease: A review. *J Chronic Dis* 33:5–12, 1980.

Windsor, R. A., Cutter, G., Morris, J., Reese, Y., Manzella, B., Bartlett, E. E., Samuelson, C., Spanos, D. The effectiveness of smoking cessation methods for smokers in public health maternity clinics: A randomized trial. *Am J Public Health* 75:1389–1392, 1985.

Windsor, R. A., Dalmat, M., Orleans, C. T., Gritz, E. R. *The Handbook to Plan, Implement, and Evaluate Smoking Cessation Pro-*

grams for Pregnant Women. White Plains, NY: March of Dimes Birth Defect Foundation, 1990a.

Windsor, R. A., Lowe, J. B., Artz, L., Contreras, L. Smoking cessation and pregnancy intervention trial: Preliminary mid-trial results. In Engstrom, P., Rimer, B., Mortensen, L. E., eds. *Advances in Cancer Control Screening and Prevention Research.* New York: Wiley-Liss, 1990b, 107–117.

Windsor, R. A., Lowe, J. B., Perkins, L. L., Smith-Yoder, D., Artz, L., Crawford, M., Amburgy, K., Boyd, N. R. Health education for pregnant smokers: Its behavioral impact and cost benefit. *Am J Public Health* 83:201–206, 1993.

World Health Organization European Collaborative Group (WHO). Multifactorial trial in the prevention of coronary heart disease. II. Risk factor changes at two and four years. *Euro J Cardiol* 3:184–190, 1982.

Wynder, E. L., Mushinski, M. H., Spivak, J. C. Tobacco and alcohol consumption in relation to the development of multiple primary cancers. *Cancer* 40:1872–1878, 1977.

Zahniser, S. C. and The SCIP Working Group. Integrating smoking cessation into public prenatal clinics: Results of the Smoking Cessation in Pregnancy (SCIP) Project. Unpublished report, Centers for Disease Control and Prevention, Atlanta, Georgia, February, 1993.

15

Treating Nicotine Addiction in Patients with Other Addictive Disorders

RICHARD D. HURT, KAY M. EBERMAN, JOHN SLADE, and LORI KARAN

The modern era of treatment for alcoholism has its origins in the founding of Alcoholics Anonymous (AA) over 50 years ago. Formal treatment of alcoholism became more widely available in the 1960s, and the chemical dependence (CD) field now encompasses a full range of treatment services provided by tens of thousands of experts. In most CD treatment settings, the "pure alcoholic" has become a less frequent occurrence as more and more patients present with dependence on more than one drug. The special challenge of treating patients with multiple addictions has required introspection and change on the part of treatment providers who have met this challenge with the flexibility, understanding, and vigor necessary to provide effective treatment.

Although nicotine has been and continues to be one of the most common drugs of dependence among CD patients, treatment centers have traditionally ignored it. This apparent paradox and the surrounding intellectual conflict are beginning to change as smoking becomes more widely accepted as an addictive behavior responsible for substantial death and disability among CD patients. There are growing signs of a paradigm shift in the field which involves diagnosing and addressing nicotine dependence in the context of treating other addictions (Hoffman and Slade 1993). This chapter explores the origins of the current treatment paradigm, reviews the extent of the problem of nicotine dependence in the special popula-

tion of CD patients, and presents a clinical framework for working with these patients.

At the outset, it should be acknowledged that the development and successful implementation of nicotine-dependence treatment in CD treatment units is a process that may take considerable time and effort. Part of the resistance to the changes discussed in this chapter is based on the realistic perception that they are difficult to implement. Until recently, there has been little hope of sufficient external or internal support to provide the CD unit with the infrastructure necessary to make these changes. The external environment is rapidly changing in this regard, however, and this places substantial pressure on the health care community to provide a smoke-free environment and to put more emphasis on healthier life-styles. It is ironic that CD units have often been excluded from smoke-free hospital policies despite the observations that, of all health care professionals, the CD staff should have the best understanding of nicotine as a drug of dependence (Hurt et al. 1989, Hurt 1990). Implementing nicotine-dependence treatment in the CD setting presents some unique but surmountable problems that will require planning and diligence to overcome.

EPIDEMIOLOGY

An association between smoking and drinking behaviors has been known for many years, with those who are the heaviest smokers also being the heaviest drinkers and vice versa (Craig and Vannatta 1977). Among alcoholic patients, this association is much greater, not only in the rate of smoking among alcoholics compared to nonalcoholics, but also in the amount smoked, with alcoholic patients smoking more heavily than their smoking, nonalcoholic counterparts (Maletzky and Kottler 1974). The rate of smoking among alcoholics (83%) continues to be about three times that of the adult population. Alcoholic smokers smoke 10 more cigarettes per day on average than nonalcoholic smoking controls (DiFranza and Guerrera 1990). Alcoholic smokers are also less likely to achieve abstinence from cigarettes, even though the number of attempts to stop is the same in both groups. An equally high prevalence of smoking has been observed among drug and mixed substance abuse groups (Burling and Ziff 1988).

Regular smoking typically precedes the development of alcoholism by many years. Although alcoholics and nonalcoholics report similar levels of childhood experimentation with smoking, once smoking is tried, the future alcoholics are much more likely to become regular smokers. The relative risk of alcoholism among smokers is estimated to be 10 times that of nonsmokers. This relationship is so strong that intractable heavy smoking has been identified as a strong predictor of unrecognized alcohol abuse or alcoholism (Valliant 1991).

The relationship between smoking and other drug use has deep roots. Tobacco use usually precedes the use of illicit drugs, and patterns of its use often predict the extent of use of other psychoactive drugs (Clayton and Ritter 1985). Some have speculated that efforts to discourage alcohol and other drug abuse may benefit from prevention efforts focused on tobacco (Henningfield, Clayton, Pollin 1990). Tobacco, alcohol, and marijuana have been implicated as "gateway drugs," linked to more acutely severe drug problems by a fairly stereotypic developmental sequence (Kandel 1975). More recent research has confirmed the key role cigarettes play in predicting risk for other drug problems even though only a minority of all smokers are affected (Fleming et al. 1989;

USDHHS 1988). The majority of people who have ever used drugs such as marijuana and cocaine have previously used cigarettes and alcohol.

Conversely, people who have never smoked rarely abuse illicit drugs or alcohol (Kandel 1975). Fewer than 10% of adolescent nonsmokers in Canada reported using one or more nonmedical drugs, whereas 80% of the heaviest smokers reported using at least one nonmedical drug and 20% used five or more (Kozlowski, Coambs, Ferrence et al. 1989). Thus, adolescents who smoke heavily are at very high risk for multiple drug use. In a large study of students in Milwaukee, cigarettes were the drug with the youngest mean age of onset of use, and students who had tried only cigarettes or marijuana were significantly more likely to be using other drugs 2 years later (Fleming et al. 1989).

NICOTINE USE IN CD UNITS

Although some efforts have recently been made to treat nicotine as a drug of dependence in the CD setting (Delaney 1988; Joseph 1990; Goldsmith, Hurt, Slade 1992; Hoffman and Slade 1993), standard practice in most alcoholism- and drug dependence-treatment facilities has been to let patients continue to smoke while undergoing treatment for other addictive disorders. A common rationale has been that efforts to stop smoking might jeopardize successful long-term recovery from dependence on alcohol and other drugs. Another perception is that nicotine dependence is very different from other chemical dependencies since the consequences experienced from smoking are less severe and less immediate. It is also argued that successful smoking cessation is not necessary for recovery from alcoholism. Many treatment professionals contend that stopping smoking is harder than stopping drinking and adds unnecessary stress to individuals in the midst of the treatment crisis.

These explanations are based on clinical lore, and only recently has this been seriously questioned. Since nicotine is a prototypic drug of dependence, acceptance of it by the treatment community has a direct bearing on the treatment process itself. The cues to the use of other drugs are frequently related to smoking, so stopping smoking may actually contribute to the establishment and maintenance of abstinence from other drugs. In fact, when abstinence from alcohol is attained without formal treatment, smoking often stops at or about the same time (Sobell, Sobell, Toneatto 1991).

Many patients undergoing treatment for alcohol and other drug problems have the perception that stopping smoking is harder than giving up alcohol or other drugs (Kozlowski, Wilkinson, Skinner et al. 1989). Many elements undoubtedly contribute to this perception, including the widespread availability of nicotine and the way it insinuates itself into all activities. However, part of this perception arises from the attitudes of treatment program staff. Denial and rationalization play such a large role in everyday coping for these patients, that, if they are overtly or covertly given the message that doing both (i.e., stopping smoking and stopping drinking) at the same time is too hard, only the few, very insightful patients will question this reasoning. Despite this treatment bias, when CD patients were asked whether they had an interest in receiving treatment for nicotine dependence, 46% indicated that they were interested in such treatment if it were available, and a somewhat smaller percentage wanted simultaneous treatment for all their addictive disorders (Kozlowski, Skinner, Kent et al. 1989).

In a survey of alcoholism treatment professionals in 23 inpatient facilities in Washington state, 45% of those surveyed indicated that they would *never* personally encourage their alcoholic patients to attempt to stop smoking (Bobo and Gilchrist 1983). In this study, the clinical staff who described themselves as recovering alcoholics but current smokers were significantly less likely than nonalcoholic, nonsmoking staff to urge attention to nicotine dependence. The fear of relapse to drinking was the most commonly cited reason for this approach. No controlled data currently exist concerning the risk of relapse to alcohol use because of relapse to smoking. However, alcohol consumption frequently accompanies relapse to use of nicotine (Lichenstein 1982; Henningfield, Clayton, Pollin 1990). It has been spec-

ulated that alcohol may reduce the ability of a person to cope with relapse crises; thus, the actual relapse rate for a person experiencing a relapse crisis increases from 33 to 61% when the ex-smoker is drinking (Shiffman 1982). The risk may also increase simply because of the close pairing of the two behaviors or perhaps because of complementary actions of the drugs.

Stopping smoking has been associated with successful outcome for alcoholism treatment. Smoking cessation may actually improve the chances of maintaining sobriety, or it may reflect a degree of commitment to sustained recovery that positively influences recovery from nicotine as well as alcohol and other drug dependencies (Miller, Hedrick, Taylor 1983). Over the long-term, men who remained continuously abstinent from alcohol had a stop smoking rate of 58%, and continuously abstinent women had a rate of 48%. Smoking cessation rates were much lower for subjects who relapsed to alcohol (0% for men and 33% for women) (DeSoto, O'Donnell, DeSoto 1989).

Many recovering alcoholics state that stopping smoking was much more difficult than stopping drinking. Though widely believed, this information is not only anecdotal but may be misleading. The recovering alcoholic has often been through a formal treatment program lasting several weeks followed by an outpatient counseling program or involvement in AA. Their efforts to stop smoking have usually been self-motivated and, of necessity, have utilized ad hoc minimal intervention strategies. It should come as no surprise that the patient perceives the two as having such different levels of difficulty. If this perception is accurate, special treatment strategies will be needed to address nicotine dependence in CD patients.

The conflicts that arise when nicotine-dependence treatment is brought closer to the CD unit can be quite emotional and divisive. Sound argument for including nicotine treatment can be displaced by denial, rationalization, and fear. For example, the premise that it is "too hard" to stop smoking at the same time does not hold up to scrutiny when it is observed that the patient in treatment is expected to address and abstain from all other mood-altering substances. That *is* hard to do, but it is recognized and accepted that there is an integral relationship between all other drugs of dependence that necessitates abstinence from all. The argument that the patient should focus on "the primary" dependence drug is clouded by the fact that the first drug of dependence used by most alcoholics is nicotine (Henningfield, Clayton, Pollin 1990). Which drug, then, is primary?

Treating nicotine dependence along with other chemical dependencies may actually enhance the treatment process. When CD patients in treatment continue to smoke, they use smoking as an outlet which hides or suppresses feelings that otherwise would surface to be dealt with in the treatment milieu. A smoke-free unit can potentially provide a more productive treatment environment, yet there are remarkably few data which explore this possibility.

There is concern that implementing a tobacco-free policy and treating nicotine dependence in the CD unit can have a negative effect on patient census and referral. On the other hand, some treatment facilities have perceived that there could be a marketing advantage by providing more complete treatment. As more treatment centers incorporate nicotine-dependence treatment into their programs, the census and referral bias problems will subside.

Finally, the fact that the consequences of smoking are usually not as immediate as those of other drugs gives the patient and staff a false sense of security that, by ignoring nicotine, no harm will come. However, it is unusual for a treatment program to have no recent or current examples of serious harm from smoking among staff or patients who could serve as examples to make seemingly distant consequences feel more immediate. The presence of even one patient on an inpatient CD unit who has obvious chronic obstructive pulmonary disease (COPD) and is primarily trying to stop smoking has changed the atmosphere on the unit as a whole to one which addresses nicotine far more seriously (Kotz 1993).

COMPLICATIONS OF SMOKING AMONG PATIENTS WITH ALCOHOLISM

The health risk is but one of the many compelling reasons to address the problem of nicotine dependence in CD patients. Overall tobacco-related mortality in alcoholics has not been well studied. The synergistic effect of tobacco use and alcohol intake in the risk of developing oropharyngeal and esophageal cancers is well established (USDHHS 1982; Blot et al. 1988; Tuyns et al. 1988). Alcoholics show a high mortality rate from cirrhosis, pneumonia, violent death, lung cancer, and cancers of the upper digestive and respiratory tracts. When compared with veterans whose smoking behavior was similar to that of alcoholics, similar rates of death for lung cancer were observed (Schmidt and Poplan 1981). In this study, there was excess mortality among the alcoholics from cancer of the upper digestive and respiratory tracts, but there was no difference in overall cancer mortality. However, mortality from heart disease accounted for 32% of the deaths in this group, an observation not fully explored by the authors.

In another study of alcoholics, coronary artery disease accounted for 25.3% of deaths. This was considered to be no different than that in the general population for similar age groups, although smoking was not taken into account as a factor in either study (Gillis 1969). Among 133 Irish alcoholics with an extend follow-up, 28% of the cohort died from myocardial infarction while three patients died from each of the following: lung cancer, cirrhosis, respiratory disease, and stroke (O'Connor and Daly 1985). Finally, in a study in Japan, cirrhosis and heart failure ranked high among the causes of death in alcoholics, and though cancer occurred more frequently in alcoholics, no details are given as to the types of cancer nor was any information provided about the smoking behavior of the more than 1,000 patients who were studied (O'Hara et al. 1989).

Pancreatitis is increased 10-fold among alcoholics who smoke compared to those who do not (Pitchumoni et al. 1988). It is hypothesized that cyanide from cigarette smoke is toxic to the pancreas and that alcohol ingestion interferes with its detoxification. Cirrhosis is three times more common among alcoholics who smoke (Klatsky and Armstrong, 1992).

Given the frequency with which smoking causes a wide spectrum of diseases, illnesses caused by smoking must be an important factor in the mortality of a patient popula-

Table 15–1 Making the Transition to a Tobacco-Free Unit

Accept that nicotine dependence can no longer be ignored during the prevention, diagnosis, and treatment of chemical dependencies.

Develop a policy with clear goals, objectives, and consequences for breaches (the consequences must be ones the staff feels comfortable enforcing).

Obtain support of administration and staff.

Train staff in diagnosis and treatment of nicotine dependence.

Develop a tobacco-free staff.

Provide a tobacco-free milieu.

Communicate policy changes to referral sources.

Obtain support of self-help groups.

Develop and implement an approach to education about and treatment of nicotine dependence which fits the treatment philosophy of the program.

Develop and encourage smoke-free aftercare settings as part of recovery. Have patients only attend smoke-free 12-step meetings.

Maintain the policy through active review and attention.

Patience and perseverance.

Source: Adapted from Hoffman and Slade 1993.

tion that smokes at approximately three times the rate of the general population. Most experienced clinicians in addiction medicine have cared for patients who, although successfully recovering from their presenting chemical dependency, died prematurely as a consequence of nicotine dependence (Twerski 1990).

PROVIDING NICOTINE-DEPENDENCE TREATMENT IN THE SETTING OF OTHER ADDICTIVE DISORDERS TREATMENT

There is a growing experience with integrating the diagnosis and treatment of nicotine dependence with that of other chemical dependencies. Little Hill-Alina Lodge was the first to pioneer this integration in 1985 (Delaney 1988). Other programs, available in centers such as the Veterans Medical Center in Minneapolis, the Halterman Center in London, Ohio; Parkwood Hospital in Atlanta; Gateway Rehabilitation Center in Aliquippa, Pennsylvania; the Cleveland Clinic; the Medical College of Virginia; and the University of Texas Medical School at Houston, have attempted this integration

with varying degrees of success (Hoffman and Slade 1993). Unique aspects of each program's leadership, staffing, patient population, treatment philosophy, and treatment modalities have contributed to the successes that have been observed. Although similar issues and themes have emerged from these pioneering efforts, there is not one infallible method to achieve this change. Table 15–1 outlines the basic steps involved in incorporating nicotine-dependence diagnosis and treatment with the treatment of other chemical dependencies. Key topics include developing a nonsmoking staff, providing a smoke-free milieu, developing and enforcing clear consequences for breaches in the policy, and obtaining assistance and cooperation from referral resources, including 12-step support groups. These topics including points of controversy, will now be examined in more detail.

RECOGNIZE THAT NICOTINE DEPENDENCE CAN NO LONGER BE IGNORED DURING THE PREVENTION, DIAGNOSIS, AND TREATMENT OF CHEMICAL DEPENDENCIES

Staffs will need special training to learn about the pharmacology of nicotine, its many effects, and the nicotine withdrawal syndrome. Its unique inhalation delivery form allows smokers to receive rapid drug boluses and to carefully regulate their nicotine intake. Patterns of tobacco use are regular and compulsive, tolerance occurs, and tobacco abstinence is often accompanied by withdrawal symptoms. Tolerance and escalation to dependent patterns of use occur more often with tobacco than with other dependence-producing drugs. Nicotine dependence is associated not only with medical problems, but also with increasingly adverse psychological and social consequences. Similar to other addictions, persons who have nicotine dependence frequently relapse during attempts to attain abstinence. The application of the *Diagnostic and Statistical Manual of Mental Disorders* (DSM-III-R) diagnostic criteria for substance use disorders to nicotine dependence is a critical tool in fostering the staffs' acceptance of nicotine as a drug of dependence (APA 1987).

If the program requires or encourages persons to become totally abstinent from nicotine, it needs to allow for the emergence of nicotine withdrawal symptoms (Chapter 2). Initially, concentration ability may be impaired and patients may be anxious and irritable. This may affect the attention span in educational groups and emotional expressions in group therapy. In addition, there is increasing documentation of depressive comorbidity in patients with nicotine dependence, and clinicians need to be aware of this as a potential problem (Chapter 16) (Glassman 1990).

The best methods for addressing nicotine addiction in traditional CD diagnosis and treatment are not yet known. The difficulties encountered in treating chemically dependent persons for nicotine dependence may be attributed to the severity of their nicotine dependence, the highly reinforcing qualities of nicotine, the lower motivation for stopping use of a drug that has caused them few immediate problems, and the absence of an environment which facilitates abstinence from nicotine. Nonetheless, there have been successful programs. Planning, clarity, consistency, patience, and perseverance have been important in enabling programs to achieve this end.

DEVELOP A POLICY WITH CLEAR GOALS AND OBJECTIVES

It is essential that the policy fit the treatment philosophy of the individual program. In accordance with the goal of providing sound clinical practice, programs need to develop specific goals for addressing the diagnosis and treatment of nicotine dependence. Academic centers have additional missions of research and education.

As part of the development of the policy, it is important to establish a firm base of support from both top management and staff. To gain administrative support, it is necessary to set specific goals and objectives as managers need to fully comprehend the overall objective of the diagnosis and treatment of nicotine dependence. With this understanding, they may provide critical input into the planning, budget for this endeavor, and support program development. They

may develop plans for employee training and, when needed, facilitate treatment for nicotine-dependent employees.

Staff support for this new dimension will emerge from training and program development that provide worthwhile skills and functions. Although the staff may be hesitant to actively address nicotine dependence, they are usually aware of examples of serious harm from smoking among their colleagues and/or patients in recovery. Involving staff in problem-solving in the implementation of the policy will help them to more actively achieve support of the program.

DEVELOP A 100% TOBACCO-FREE STAFF

Appropriate staff attitudes are essential for recognizing nicotine as a drug of dependence and for providing effective therapy in a CD treatment setting. Current relaxed attitudes about nicotine addiction is influenced by the fact that the staffs of most CD units, until recently, were predominantly recovering alcoholics with a very high prevalence of smoking. Their attitude has been, until now, actively supportive of allowing staff and patients to smoke. As more nonalcoholic and nonsmoking professionals have entered the field, and as smokers in recovery from alcoholism and other chemical dependencies have quit smoking, questions have arisen about this prevailing attitude. The smoking status of the staff clearly predicts whether a patient is advised to attempt to stop smoking (Bobo and Gilchrist 1983). As the prevalence of smoking among staff declines, the resistance may also decline. The majority of CD staff with a history of smoking have tried to quit, and for those who were successful, stopping "cold turkey" and relying on the 12-step principles were important factors (Bobo and Davis 1993). Preliminary reports from pioneering programs requiring tobacco abstinence indicate that there must be a zero tolerance for tobacco use among staff (Fishman and Earley 1993; Pletcher 1993). This observation is directly analogous to the accepted notion about staff members not using illicit drugs or actively drinking in an alcoholic manner.

However, since staff are allowed to have a social drink if it does not interfere with their work, many contend that this should be the same of nicotine since it too is a legal drug. The differences between social alcohol and social nicotine use soon become apparent, however. Some smoking staff may claim that it is their "right" to take their smoke breaks and to have smoke on their breath during contact with patients, even though they uniformly believe that having alcohol on their breath during similar contact with patients would be inappropriate. Converting to a tobacco-free staff is a gradual process usually involving the provision of treatment and support for existing staff and selectively hiring new employees who are nonsmokers or nonusers of other tobacco products (Capretto 1993). Employers must insist that persons treating nicotine dependence do not have smoke on their breath or evidence of being a tobacco user during patient contacts. New labor legislation was passed in New Jersey in 1991 which guarantees job-bias protection for smokers except in cases where reasons related to employment exist. Such legislation can be helpful in supporting the achievement of CD treatment staffs that are tobacco-free (Slade 1993), but the law in many states interferes with this goal (Malouff et al., 1993). It is optimal if employers help current staff quit smoking, transfer those who continue to smoke to other jobs, and refrain from hiring people who have a history of nicotine dependence unless they have at least 6 months of solid recovery.

PROVIDE A SMOKE-FREE MILIEU

Providing a smoke-free milieu is also important. Exposure to environmental tobacco smoke is not only an issue of comfort, but it is known to be a cause of disease as well (USDHHS 1986; see also Chapter 7). For those smokers who are in the precontemplative phase of stopping (DiClemente and Prochaska 1991), providing a smoke-free milieu gives a clear message and places a proper emphasis on smoking as an important issue, both as an addiction and as a threat to health. The simple provision of a smoke-free environment in the CD unit moves some pa-

tients into the contemplative phase of stopping smoking (Joseph et al. 1990).

There is a significant disruption to the treatment milieu when a "smoking room" is provided, even if the hours of use are restricted. Patients who want to stop smoking at the same time they address other addictive disorders find this very difficult to do if smoking is allowed within the treatment setting. One patient's observation has been that allowing an area for smoking is like "trying to quit drinking and then opening the bar every day." A smoking room becomes a social gathering spot where patients can retreat from staff and participate in unsupervised group activity. Such smoking rooms can even attract nonsmokers who otherwise feel left out of the group where the "real action" occurs. In fact, some nonsmokers and ex-smokers admitted to CD units where smoking is allowed start smoking or relapse. Furthermore, in adolescent units it is usually against the letter and/or spirit of the law to provide tobacco products, and as with adults, exposure to the use of such products while in treatment increases the risk that the nonuser may start.

Eliminating smoking on the unit and enforcing abstinence may create a new set of problems which will require persistent staff attention. There may be dramatic differences in behavior between patients who are restricted in the time and places they are allowed to smoke and those who are forced to become abstinent. When no smoking was allowed in some pioneering CD programs, underground enterprises, including ingenious hiding areas for supplies, black markets, cover-up activities, and risk-taking behaviors to acquire and use tobacco were observed (Kotz 1993). Whether or not nicotine is completely disallowed, CD treatment programs should actively diagnose nicotine addiction and motivate patients for future or continued cessation. This must be accomplished, however, without the program becoming either too chaotic because of a lack of consistency between policy rules and action or too increasingly restrictive.

One option is to limit smoking to outside the building; however, facilities that treat acutely ill patients may find it difficult to transport patients outdoors to smoke. The amount of staff time needed to escort patients offsite to smoke several times a day is significant. It also provides a reward of sorts to the smokers, and there is not usually enough staff time to provide outside activities for all nonsmokers. The number of nonsmokers on the unit at any one time is few, and they tend to be less demanding of time outside than smokers.

DEVELOP AND IMPLEMENT AN APPROACH TO TREATMENT WHICH FITS THE TREATMENT PHILOSOPHY OF THE PROGRAM

When and how should CD patients be treated for nicotine dependence? In the absence of prospective studies, this question will continue to be asked. It can confidently be said that all CD patients should, at a minimum, be given education about nicotine dependence and be advised by the treatment staff to quit. Unfortunately, the question of when and how to treat these patients beyond these straightforward measures is difficult to answer with clinical research. Besides the usual difficulties of treatment outcome research, this issue is undergoing rapid shifts in norms in the culture at large. Is the role of the CD program to enforce tobacco abstinence and then to work on motivational factors so that maintenance of this action might be continued after treatment? Alternatively, might a program educate patients about the addictive, psychoactive, and physically harmful aspects of nicotine and the benefits of quitting and help patients design a personalized treatment plan for a specific time in the future?

Programs may find individual solutions to this dilemma based on their structure, intensity, treatment goals, treatment modalities, and patient population. Some treatment programs feel that patients should become nicotine-free at the same time they become abstinent from all other nonprescribed, mood-altering drugs so that patients can abstain from nicotine while support is maximal (Fishman and Earley 1993). There is reason to suspect that patients do not feel a great deal worse when nicotine withdrawal occurs simultaneously with alcohol and drug withdrawal. Also, synchronous withdrawal might lessen substance cravings and other relapse factors for all of the addictive drugs.

Other programs that required nicotine abstinence upon admission often had to confront surreptitious smoking by the patients, thus alienating many of them, and losing the therapeutic alliance with them (Kotz 1993; Karan 1993). These programs are now researching ways of actively addressing nicotine dependence while patients have designated times and places to smoke outdoors. These programs still want to motivate patients for future cessation. Unfortunately, these are only descriptive case reports; virtually no well-researched outcome data are available at this time. The only report of substance is from the VA Medical Center in Minneapolis, which shows that a smoke-free unit policy can be implemented and nicotine-dependence treatment incorporated into the overall treatment program without having an adverse impact on recovery from alcohol or other drug dependence (Joseph 1990, 1993).

For some, providing a treatment plan for nicotine dependence after other addictive disorders are addressed may still be a reasonable option, especially for patients who are not yet motivated to stop. Specific, individualized cessation plans should be developed during treatment with a tentative quit date and mechanism for follow-up. If the patient cannot be assured of adequate treatment for nicotine dependence after discharge, however, this should be provided at the time of treatment of the other drug dependencies. Since a growing number of treatment programs are offering nicotine-dependence treatment as either an optional or required part of their program (Pletcher, Lysaght, Hyman 1990; Joseph 1990; Fishman and Earley 1993), it may soon no longer be acceptable to ignore or postpone the issue.

TREATMENT APPROACHES

If treatment for nicotine dependence should be offered along with that for other addictive disorders, what services should be provided?

On average, patients with other addictive disorders who are also nicotine dependent have a higher level of nicotine dependence than their nonalcoholic and nondrug-dependent counterparts. Thus, treatment measures should probably be at a similar intensity as for those other drugs. The very same mechanisms that are in play for other addictive drugs (denial, defensiveness, rationalization, etc.) are present in patients with nicotine dependence. Educational efforts should be undertaken to provide the patient with a better understanding of nicotine as a drug of dependence and to try to break through this denial and defensiveness. The effort can begin at the intake interview by the counselor and/or physician. The time after arising in the morning until the first cigarette is smoked is used by many clinicians as a sign of severity of dependence. The Fagerström Tolerance Questionnaire (Fagerström 1978) or the more refined Fagerström Test for Nicotine Dependence (Appendix A, which follows Chapter 21; Fagerström, Heatherton, Kozlowski 1992) can also be used in the evaluation of the smoking patient. Personalizing the risk of continued smoking for the individual patient helps to focus the problem while the benefits of stopping smoking can be used to motivate the patient. A detailed tobacco use history should be taken on each patient, including age of onset of use, frequency, and patterns used (see Chapter 10). Adverse social or medical consequences to smoking should be highlighted to provide better understanding for the patient. Reviewing previous quit attempts and factors associated with relapse provide insight into developing a more effective treatment plan.

Regular lectures on nicotine dependence and the adverse health consequences caused by smoking provide a foundation on which the staff can build better understanding and acceptance among the patients. A wide range of self-help and other educational materials can be used to motivate a patient. All of this requires an enlightened and supportive staff who have a thorough understanding of these issues. A more comprehensive approach should also include elements of behavioral medicine, principles of CD treatment, adjunctive pharmacologic therapy, and relapse prevention (Hurt 1992).

Knowledge of the behavioral aspects of smoking and smoking cessation can be used effectively in the CD setting. This includes important elements such as learning about the cues for nicotine use and, in particular, how these relate to the use of other drugs. Stress management training should be included, particularly since smoking has been viewed as a socially acceptable means of relieving stress. The patient also needs to understand that the calming effect of nicotine may be, in reality, the relief of withdrawal symptoms. Changes in diet and exercise may be needed to address the weight gain that frequently occurs with stopping smoking. Substitute activities should be structured for use at times when the cues to smoke are the strongest, that is, upon arising in the morning or after meals. The use of carbon monoxide breath testing and spirometry as a motivational intervention to help people stop smoking has been shown to be effective (Risser and Belcher 1990) and can be incorporated into the treatment regimen in much the same way that medical testing is used to demonstrate abnormalities in alcoholic patients.

The principles of therapy for chemical dependency that have developed over the last several decades are directly relevant to the patient with nicotine dependence. Table 15–2 lists some resources that approach nicotine dependence from the perspective of the chemical-dependence field.

The recognition that nicotine is a drug of dependence and the fact that the DSM-III-R criteria used to diagnose psychoactive substance use disorders are applicable to nicotine dependence are important concepts for the patient and staff to understand and accept. Providing a protected drug- and tobacco-free milieu is important because it allows the patient to focus efforts on recovery rather than be constantly distracted by the opportunity to use. The group support provided in a traditional CD treatment program can easily be expanded to deal with issues surrounding nicotine use, and the incorporation of the 12-step approach has direct application to nicotine. Many units may prefer to have a regular group specifically dedicated to nicotine and smoking cessation while others may incorporate nicotine into their regular groups.

The term *self-help* is used by two traditions which converge in the field of nicotine dependence. Behavioral clinicians have used the term to denote self-instruction and minimal-contact materials such as the ALA's "Lifetime of Freedom from Smoking." The CD field has used the term to refer to 12-step programs (Alcoholics Anonymous, Nicotine Anonymous, etc.) (see Table 15–3). These programs serve as a cornerstone for many CD treatment programs and are central to their postdischarge planning. The basis of the 12-step philosophy is for individual patients to recognize their powerlessness over the drugs to which they are addicted followed by working through specific steps of personal growth to achieve recovery. This structured program takes place in a fellowship of other recovering people which provides a network of nurturing and support for the process. Table 15–3 lists the 12 steps for tobacco users.

Since the 12-step approach is commonly used in CD units, using the same approach for nicotine dependence seems particularly applicable to patients who have other addictive disorders. The number of smoke-free AA meetings and Nicotine Anonymous activities throughout the country is increasing. Since smoking by others is such a powerful cue to smoke, not only should the CD unit itself be smoke-free, but patients should *only* attend smoke-free 12-step meetings while in treatment and after discharge.

The issue of relapse prevention carries with it a multiplicity of behavioral connotations that are important for abstinence from nicotine and alcohol. Regular attendance at the programs described earlier are an important element in preventing relapse for many CD patients. This traditional aftercare approach can now incorporate Nicotine Anonymous in addition to other ongoing support groups. A more structured relapse prevention program might include a 1-year followup with regular office visits, telephone calls, and mailings.

The emerging area of adjunctive phar-

Table 15–2 Resources that Approach the Management of Nicotine Dependence from the Perspective of Traditional Chemical-Dependence Treatment

Casey, Karen. *If Only I Could Quit.* Center City, MN: Hazelden, 1987.

E, Jeanne. *Twelve Steps for Tobacco Users.* Center City, MN; Hazelden, 1989.

Nicotine Anonymous World Services. *Nicotine Anonymous: The Book.* 2118 Greenwich St., San Francisco, CA 94123. 415–922–8575. 1992.

Seven Minutes: The Newsletter of Nicotine Anonymous.

O'Connell, Tom. *Up in Smoke: The Nicotine Challenge in Recovery.* Center City, MN: Hazelden, 1990.

Pletcher, Vincent C., Lysaght, Linda S., Hyman, Vincent L. *Treating Nicotine Addiction: A Challenge for the Recovery Professional.* Center City, MN: Hazelden, 1990.

Rustin, Terry. *Quit and Stay Quit.* Center City, MN: Hazelden, 1991.

Schneider, Max. *Medical Aspects of Tobacco.* Video. FMS Productions, 1990. For information call 800–421–4609.

Table 15–3 The 12 Steps for Tobacco Users

1. We admitted we were powerless over nicotine—that our lives had become unmanageable.
2. Came to believe that a Power greater than ourselves could restore us to sanity.
3. Made a decision to turn our will and our lives over to the care of God as we understood Him.
4. Made a searching and fearless moral inventory of ourselves.
5. Admitted to God, to ourselves, and to another human being the exact nature of our wrongs.
6. Were entirely ready to have God remove all these defects of character.
7. Humbly asked Him to remove our shortcomings.
8. Made a list of all persons we had harmed, and became willing to make amends to them all.
9. Made direct amends to such people wherever possible, except when to do so would injure them or others.
10. Continued to take personal inventory and when we were wrong promptly admitted it.
11. Sought through prayer and meditation to improve our conscious contact with God as we understood Him, praying only for knowledge of His will for us and the power to carry that out.
12. Having had a spiritual awakening as the result of these steps, we tried to carry this message and to practice these principles in all our affairs.

Source: E., Jeanne. *Twelve Steps for Tobacco Users.* Center City, MN: Hazelden, 1989.

macologic therapy is becoming increasingly important in the treatment of nicotine dependence (see Chapter 12). Nicotine-replacement therapy using nicotine polacrilex in conjunction with smoking cessation treatment enhances the potential for success. Higher-dose nicotine-replacement therapy is more beneficial for smokers with more severe nicotine dependence as measured by the Fagerström Tolerance Questionnaire (Tonneson 1988). Since alcholics are more likely to have severe nicotine dependence, it can be speculated that they may need more aggressive nicotine-replacement therapy. Transdermal nicotine therapy is also effective and has the added benefit of promoting better patient compliance (Hurt 1990; Abelin 1989; Daughton 1991; Tonneson 1992). Clonidine has been shown to be of benefit when used in conjunction with other treatment strategies but, as with other pharmacologic adjuncts, is ineffective when used alone (Covey and Glassman 1991). Drugs such as bupropion, doxepin, fluoxetine, and buspirone, among many others, are also being evaluated. Though pharmacologic therapy offers great promise, it is not a stand-alone treatment and should only be presented as an adjunct to other forms of therapy. Tested protocols for using adjunctive pharmacologic therapy have thus far been based on outpatient treatment models. Trials specific for patients with alcoholism and/or other drug dependencies have not been performed.

CD programs may or may not choose to use pharmacologic adjuncts based on their overall program philosophy and future research about the effectiveness of such medication in this special patient population. Although smoking cessation programs frequently use nicotine-replacement therapy, its use poses philosophical problems for some CD professionals. Many are reluctant to use a cross-tolerant drug for withdrawal. Others may approve of its use in withdrawal but fear substitution dependency by using nicotine replacement as maintenance therapy. Others regard long-term nicotine-replacement therapy as being a better alternative for some patients than risking relapse to smoking with all of its attendant health risks. Short-term nicotine-withdrawal therapy has

not been studied. There simply have been no smoke-free, protected milieu programs where such traditional CD withdrawal therapy can be evaluated. Prospective clinical trials are needed to better evaluate this question, and how these issues will be addressed and resolved in the CD treatment community is an important topic for ongoing discussion.

Behavioral skills, CD therapy, pharmacologic therapy, and relapse prevention should all be included in a treatment plan. This plan can be individualized based on the patient's needs and stage of readiness to stop smoking (DiClemente and Prochaska 1991). For the precontemplative patient, the goal may be only to move forward to contemplative. Moving the patient to the action stage may require more motivation and depend on the patient's resistance to change as well as on the staff's objectives.

Table 15–4 summarizes the relationships between the stages of readiness model and the CD treatment model that have been outlined in this chapter.

The table allows the reader to see how these components can be integrated to provide a more comprehensive approach to nicotine-dependent patients. The stages of readiness have been modified for use in a medical setting from the readiness to change definitions used by DiClemente and Prochaska (1991).

Some CD programs have developed such strong nicotine-dependence treatment components that they accept patients for primary treatment of nicotine dependence (Fishman and Earley 1993). As discussed earlier, such a treatment milieu requires substantial changes in treatment center philosophy and staff attitudes for most CD units. Earlier reports of two intensive residential treatment programs for patients with severe nicotine dependence have appeared (Docherty 1991; Hurt 1992). In the latter report, a significant percentage of patients admitted for nicotine-dependence treatment were recovering from alcoholism and other addictive disorders. In addition to the programs at Brookside Hospital (Docherty 1991) and Mayo Clinic (Hurt *et al.* 1992), residential programs for primary nicotine-dependence treatment are also found at St. Helena Hos-

Table 15–4 Mayo Nicotine-Dependence Center Treatment Plan Components

Stages of Readiness	Behavioral	Chemical Dependence	Pharmacologic	Aftercare/Relapse Prevention
Precontemplative (Smoking, not motivated to change)	Attempt to control use/delay use Keep a log of tobacco use Talk to an ex-smoker/chewer Read literature, view films Become more conscious of negative aspects (health, social, image) Learn benefits of abstinence Identify reasons for tobacco use	Recognize defenses (denial, rationalization) Identify importance of tobacco use Identify powerlessness in controlling use	Review use of: 1. Nicotine gum 2. Transdermal nicotine patch 3. Clonidine	Receive routine 1-year follow-up
Contemplative (Smoking, motivated to quit, no quit date)	Practice situational quitting List harmful effects of tobacco use List all triggers List coping skills/try new ones Develop exercise program Review diet Keep a log of tobacco use Change trigger situations Identify/practice positive self messages Delay/distract Identify reasons for stopping/not stopping Study information on stress management Become familiar with experiences of ex-smokers/chewers Discuss benefits of quitting/obstacles	Use the 12 steps Identify unmanageability/consequences Plan for withdrawal Identify fears of quitting Recognize life centers around use Confront and work through defenses Increase understanding of addiction process Accept need to quit Be willing to change Clarify values and role of smoking Plan for recovery Acknowledge that will power is not enough Ask for help Attend Nicotine Anonymous/support group	Determine appropriate medication: 1. Nicotine gum 2. Transdermal nicotine patch 3. Clonidine Learn the physically addictive nature of nicotine Learn and understand the significance of physiologic changes in withdrawal	Receive routine 1-year follow-up Contact counselor to set quit date and review plans Attend Nicotine Anonymous/support group
Action (Motivated to quit	Select quit date Plan for quit day, follow plan	Plan and use a daily program Accept need for recovery	Use medications if appropriate:	Receive routine 1-year follow-up Contact counselor close to stop date

continued

Table 15–4 Mayo Nicotine-Dependence Center Treatment Plan Components (Continued)

Stages of Readiness	Behavioral	Chemical Dependence	Pharmacologic	Aftercare/Relapse Prevention
within one month, or having quit for one month or less)	Exercise/diet/rest Destroy tobacco Follow relaxation plan/techniques Avoid triggers associated with use Change environment/routines Avoid stress as much as possible Clean car, house, clothes Escape high-risk situations Talk to ex-smokers/chewers Reward yourself/self-talk List positive effects of not smoking Distract yourself Review reasons for quitting Review fears Contract with someone Use oral and handling substitutes	Arrange specific support Develop an emergency list of persons and actions Remember abstinence is necessary/primary Live one moment/one day at a time Focus on progress Attend Nicotine Anonymous/support group Attend group therapy Be willing to be uncomfortable for now Act "as if" you don't use tobacco Recognize the loss, related feelings Find a sponsor	1. Nicotine gum: up to 6 months 2. Transdermal nicotine patch: 4–8 weeks 3. Clonidine: up to 6 weeks Understand expected effect and limitations of medications	Contact counselor to identify high risks Attend organized cessation program Attend aftercare sessions Attend Nicotine Anonymous/support group Set follow-up counseling appointments to deal with withdrawal, behavioral changes, etc.
Maintenance (Not smoking for at least one month)	Get counseling as needed Continue to reward yourself Use HALT (Hungry, Angry, Lonely, Tired) Find and use social support List potential relapse situations and review coping skills Expand coping skills Practice positive thinking Practice self-affirmation Review progress Build stress management skills	Identify mood states and emotions Use the 12 steps Attend Nicotine Anonymous/support group Write good-bye letter to your cigarettes/chew/pipe, etc. Accept lapse as part of the process Make necessary amends Address personal defenses Use the Serenity Prayer Help others quit	Adjust Nicotine gum, transdermal nicotine patch, and/or clonidine as recovery requires	Receive routine 1-year follow-up Attend aftercare sessions Set follow-up appointments to deal with maintenance issues Examine overall wellness/life-style Attend Nicotine Anonymous/support group

pital in Deer Park, California and Hazelden in Center City, Minnesota. For the more severely nicotine-dependent patient, a smoke-free milieu with intensive treatment may be needed to produce initial abstinence and make longer-term abstinence possible. Only a small percentage of patients need this level of treatment. Patients most likely to benefit already have serious tobacco-related health problems and/or have been unsuccessful at stopping smoking with structured, well-designed outpatient therapy. An intensive residential treatment program can be modeled after a traditional CD treatment program, but will likely need more behavioral treatment components.

OTHER ISSUES IN MAKING THE TRANSITION TO A TOBACCO-FREE UNIT

The policy statement itself should be clearly written, and there should be well-understood consequences for any breaches. These consequences must be ones that the staff will feel comfortable enforcing, otherwise the policy will not stand. In order to obtain support of referral resources, the rationale and particulars of the policy must be clearly articulated. Even with a clear understanding of a unit's treatment philosophy, some referral sources may react negatively while others will react positively. The program's goals must be communicated clearly to prospective patients so that they know what to expect before arrival at the treatment facility. Finally, the policy itself should be actively reviewed and altered to meet the needs of the staff and patients.

CONCLUSION

Nicotine dependence is a common, serious and, usually unaddressed problem among patients who present with other chemical dependencies. In recent years, a number of pioneering programs have made the transition to becoming tobacco-free (or nearly so) and have begun to deal with nicotine in a direct manner. Regional approaches to this problem are beginning to emerge and offer the potential for a cooperative and coordinated effort among treatment units. Just as some regions have implemented community-wide smoke-free hospital policies, so the competition between CD units can also be eliminated if they band together to simultaneously implement nicotine treatment programs. As the cultural norms about smoking continue to change, it will become easier for CD units to approach nicotine as an important and often primary addiction. This trend has enormous potential for improving the health and well-being of CD patients.

The model in medicine is that until there are data affirming the need to sequence or limit therapy, the whole patient should be treated. All other serious drug problems have been routinely approached together in CD treatment units despite the absence of data demonstrating the appropriateness of this strategy. Patients are now expected to become abstinent from all mood-altering drugs at the same time. Thus, in the absence of data demonstrating that the practice is harmful, the presumption should be that nicotine dependence should be treated along with other chemical dependencies. Though difficult to accomplish, providing nicotine-dependence treatment at the same time has historical and rational support. Such efforts need to be well-planned. Furthermore, they must have the unqualified commitment of a smoke-free staff in order to succeed. The sooner the treatment community accepts and embraces these changes, the more patients will be spared the risk of premature death and disability caused by nicotine dependence.

REFERENCES

Abelin, T., Buehler, A., Möller, P., Vesanen, K., Imhof, P. R. Controlled trial of transdermal nicotine patch in tobacco withdrawal. *Lancet* 1:7–10, 1989.

American Psychiatric Association (APA). *Diagnostic and Statistical Manual of Mental Disorders—DSM-III-R,* 3d ed., rev. Washington, D.C.: American Psychiatric Association, 1987.

Blot, W. J., McLaughlin, J. K., Winn, D. M., Austin, D. F., Greenberg, R. S., Preston-Martin, S., Bernstein, L., Schoenberg, J. B., Stemhagen, A., Fraumeni, J. F. Smoking and drinking in relation to oral and pharyngeal cancer. *Cancer Res* 48:3283–3287, 1988.

Bobo, J. K., Gilchrist, L. D. Urging the alcoholic client to quit smoking cigarettes. *Addict Behav* 8:297–305, 1983.

Bobo, J. K., Gilchrist, L. D., Schilling H., Noach, B., Schinke, S. P. Cigarette smoking cessation attempts by recovering alcoholics. *Addict Behav* 12:209–215, 1987.

Bobo, J. K., and Davis, C. M. Recovering staff and smoking in chemical dependency programs in rural Nebraska. *J Substance Abuse Treat* 10(2):221–228, 1993.

Burling, T. A., and Ziff, D. C. Tobacco smoking: A comparison between alcohol and drug abuse inpatients. *Addict Behav* 13:185–190, 1988.

Capretto, N. Confronting nicotine dependency at the Gateway Rehabilitation Center. *J Substance Abuse Treat* 10(2)113–116,1993.

Clayton, R. R., and Ritter, C. The epidemiology of alcohol and drug abuse among adolescents. *Adv Alcohol Subst Abuse* 4:69–97, 1985.

Covey, L. S., and Glassman, A. H. A meta-analysis of double-blind placebo-controlled trials of clonidine for smoking cessation. *Br J Addict* 86(8):991–998, 1991.

Craig, T. J., and Vannatta, P. A. The association of smoking and drinking habits in a community sample. *J Stud Alcohol* 38:1434–1439, 1977.

Daughton, D. M., Heatley, S. A., Prendergast, J. J., et al. Effect of transdermal nicotine delivery as an adjunct to low-intervention smoking cessation therapy. A randomized, placebo-controlled, double-blind study. *Arch Intern Med* 151:749–752, 1991.

Delaney, G. O. Tobacco dependence in treating alcoholism. *NJ Med* 85:131–134, 1988.

DeSoto, C. B., O'Donnell, W. E., DeSoto, J. L. Long-term recovery in alcoholics. *Alcoholism: Clin Exper Res* 13:693–697, 1989.

DiClemente, C. L., Prochaska, J. O., Fairhurst, S. K., et al. The process of smoking cessation: An analysis of precontemplation, contemplation, and preparation stages of change. *J Consult Clin Psychol* 59:295–304, 1991.

DiFranza, J. R., and Guerrera, M. P. Alcoholism and smoking. *J Stud Alcohol* 51:130–135, 1990.

Docherty, J. P. Residential treatment. In Cocores, J. A., ed. *The Clinical Management of Nicotine Dependence.* New York, Springer-Verlag, 1991, 266–279.

Fagerström, K. O. Measuring degree of physical dependence on tobacco smoking with reference to individualization of treatment. *Addict Behav* 3:235–241, 1978.

Fagerström, K. O., Heatherton, T. F., Kozlowski, L. T. Nicotine addiction and its assessment. *Ear Nose Throat J* 69(11):763–767, 1992.

Fishman, M. L., and Earley, P. H. Treatment centers—the next challenge. *J Substance Abuse Treat* 10(2):133–138, 1993.

Fleming, R., Leventhal, H., Glynn, K., Ershler, J. The role of cigarettes in the initiation and progression of early substance use. *Addict Behav* 14:261–272, 1989.

Gillis, L. S. The mortality rate and causes of death of treated chronic alcoholics. *S Afr Med J* 43:230–232, 1969.

Glassman, A. H., Helzer, J. E., Covey, L. S. et al. Smoking, smoking cessation and major depression. *JAMA* 264:1546–1555, 1990.

Goldsmith, R. J., Hurt, R. D., Slade, J. Development of smoke-free chemical dependency units. *J Addict Dis* 11(2):67–77, 1991.

Henningfield, J. E., Clayton, R., Pollin, W. The involvement of tobacco in alcoholism and illicit drug use. *Br J Addict* 85:279–292, 1990.

Hoffman, A. L., and Slade, J. Following the pioneers: Addressing tobacco in chemical dependency treatment. *J Substance Abuse Treat* 10(2):153–160, 1993.

Hurt, R. D. Toward smoke-free medical facilities (editorial). *Chest* 97:1027–1028, 1990.

Hurt, R. D., Berge, K. G., Offord, K. P., Leonard, D. A., Gerlach D. K., Larson Renquist, C., O'Hara, M. R. The making of a smoke-free medical center. *JAMA* 261:95–97, 1989.

Hurt, R. D., Lauger, G. G., Offord, K. P., Kottke, T. E., Dale, L. C. Nicotine replacement therapy with use of a transdermal patch: A randomized double-blind placebo-controlled trial. *Mayo Clin Proc* 65:1529–1537, 1990.

Hurt, R. D., Dale, L. C., McClain, F. L., Eberman, K. M., Offord, K. P., Bruce, B. K., Lauger, G. G. A comprehensive model for the treatment of nicotine dependence in a medical setting. In Fiore, M., ed. *Medical Clinics of North America.* Philadelphia: W. B. Saunders, 76:495–514, 1992.

Joseph, A. M. Inpatient treatment of nicotine dependence in inpatient substance use disorder patients. *J Substance Abuse Treat* 10(2):147–152, 1993.

Joseph, A. M., Nichol, K. L., Willenbring, M. L., Korn, J. E., Lysaght, L. S. Beneficial effects of treatment of nicotine dependence during an inpatient substance abuse treatment program. *JAMA* 263:3043–3046, 1990.

Kandel, D. B. Stages in adolescent involvement in drug use. *Science* 190:912–914, 1975.

Karan, L. D. Initial encounters with tobacco on the inpatient substance abuse unit of the Medical College of Virginia. *J Substance Abuse Treat* 10(2):117–124, 1993.

Klatsky, A. L. and Armstrong, M. A. Alcohol, smoking, coffee, and cirrhosis. *Amer J Epidemiology.* 136(10):1248–1257, 1992.

Kotz, M. M. A smoke-free chemical dependency unit: The Cleveland Clinic experience. *J Substance Abuse Treat* 10(2):125–132, 1993.

Kozlowski, L. T., Coambs, R. B., Ferrence, R. G., Adlaf, E. M. Preventing smoking and other drug use: Let the buyers beware and the interventions be apt. *Can J Public Health* 80:452–456, 1989.

Kozlowski, L. T., Skinner, W., Kent, C., Pope, M. A. Prospects for smoking treatment in individuals seeking treatment for alcohol and other drug problems. *Addict Behav* 14:273–278, 1989.

Kozlowski, L. T., Wilkinson, A., Skinner, W., Kent, C., Franklin, T., Pope, M. Comparing tobacco cigarette dependence with other drug dependencies. *JAMA* 261:898–901, 1989.

Lichenstein, E. The smoking problem: A behavioral perspective. *J Consult Clin Psychol* 50:804–819, 1982.

Maletzky, B. M., and Klotter, J. Smoking and alcoholism. *Am J Psychiatry* 131:4, 1974.

Malouff, J., Slade, J., Nielsen, C., Schutte, N., Lawson, E. U. S. laws that protect tobacco users from employment discrimination. *Tobacco Control* 2: 1993, (in press).

Miller, W. R., Hedrick, K. E., Taylor, C. A. Addictive behaviors and life problems before and after behavioral treatment of problem drinkers. *Addict Behav* 8:403–412, 1983.

O'Donnor, A., and Daly, J. Alcoholics: A twenty year follow-up study. *Br J Psychiatry* 146:645–647, 1985.

O'Hara, K., Suzuki, Y., Sugita, T., Kobayashi, K., Tamefusa, K., Hattori, S., O'Hara, K. Mortality among alcoholics discharged from a Japanese hospital. *Br J Addict* 84:287–291, 1989.

Pitchumoni, C. S., Jain, N. K., Lowenfels, A. B., DiMagno, E. P. Chronic cyanide poisoning: Unifying concept for alcoholic and tropical pancreatitis. *Pancreas* 3(2):220–222, 1988.

Pletcher, V. C. Integration of nicotine addiction and chemical dependency treatment. *J Substance Abuse Treat* 10(2)139–146, 1993.

Pletcher, V. C., Lysaght, L. S., Hyman, V. L. *Treating Nicotine Addiction.* Center City, MN: Hazelden Foundation, 1990.

Risser, N. L., and Belcher, D. W. Adding spirometry, carbon monoxide, and pulmonary symptom results to smoking cessation counseling: A randomized trial. *J Gen Intern Med* 5:16–22, 1990.

Schmidt, W., and Poplan, R. E. The role of drinking and smoking in mortality from cancer and other causes in male alcoholics. *Cancer* 47:1031–1041, 1981.

Shiffman, S. Relapse following smoking cessation: A situational analysis. *J Consult Clin Psychol* 50:71–86, 1982.

Slade, J. Protection from job bias for people who smoke. *J Substance Abuse Treat* 10(2)229–232, 1993.

Sobell, L. C., Sobell, M. B., Toneatto, T. Recovery from alcohol problems without treatment. In Heather, N., Miller, W. R., Greeley, J., eds. *Self-Control and Addictive Behaviors.* New York: Pergamon Press, 1991.

Tonneson, P., Fryd, V., Hansen, M., Helsted, J., Gunnersen, A. B., Forchammer, H., Stockner, M. A smoking cessation study with 0, 2 and 4 mg nicotine chewing gum plus group counseling with a 2 year follow-up period. *N Engl J Med* 318:15–18, 1988.

Tonneson, P., Norregaard, J., Simonsen, K. A double-blind trial of a 16-hour transdermal nicotine patch in smoking cessation. *N Engl J Med* 325:311–315, 1991.

Tuyns, A. J., Estève, J., Raymond, L., Berrino, F., Benhamou, E., Blanchet, F., Boffetta, P., Crosignani, P., del Moral, A., Lehmann, W., Merletti, F., Pèquignot, G., Riboli, E., Sancho-Garnier, H., Terracini, B., Zubiri, A., Zubiri, L. Cancer of the larynx/hypopharynx, tobacco and alcohol. *Inter J Cancer* 41:483–491, 1988.

Twerski, A. J. Nicotine in chemical dependency units. *Professional Counselor* 4(4):15, 1990.

U.S. Department of Health and Human Services (USDHHS). *The Health Consequence of Smoking: Cancer. A Report of the Surgeon General.* U.S. Department of Health and Human Services, Public Health Service, Office on Smoking and Health. DHHS Publication No. (PHS) 82-50179, 1982.

———. *The Health Consequences of Involuntary Smoking. A Report of the Surgeon General.* U.S. Department of Health and Human Services, Public Health Service, Centers for Disease Control, Office on Smoking and Health. DHHS Publication No. (CDC) 87-8398, 1986.

————. *The Health Consequences of Smoking: Nicotine Addiction. A Report of the Surgeon General.* U.S. Department of Health and Human Services, Public Health Service, Centers for Disease Control, Center for Health Promotion and Education, Office on Smoking and Health. DHHS Publication No. (CDC) 88-8406, 1988.

Vaillant, G. E., Schnurr, P. P., Baron, J. A., Gerber, P. D. A prospective study of the effect of cigarette smoking and alcohol abuse on mortality. *J Gen Intern Med* 6:299–304, 1991.

16

Treating Nicotine Addiction in Patients with Psychiatric Co-morbidity

MICHAEL P. RESNICK

Psychiatric patients deserve to be at the forefront of efforts to treat nicotine addiction. While historically there has been little interest in this population, as well as considerable denial and avoidance, these patients are as likely as others to benefit from quitting. Psychiatry is belatedly awakening to the seriousness of nicotine addiction (Gralnick 1988; Cohen 1988). This chapter will explore the unique circumstances of psychiatric patients, the relationship between psychiatric disorder and nicotine addiction, and special problems in psychiatric institutions. Recent research on the interaction between smoking cessation, relapse, and mood disorder is reviewed. In addition, this chapter discusses interactions between psychotropic medications and smoking. A special challenge arises from the traditional, permissive attitude much of psychiatry has had toward tobacco use by psychiatric patients.

Progress in providing a smoke-free treatment environment for psychiatric patients has lagged behind efforts to make the general hospital smoke-free (Catford and Nutbeam 1983; Hay 1986; Orleans and Slade 1992). This neglect has been rationalized with several questionable litanies. Psychiatric patients are seen as too fragile to attempt treatment. The field has been ambivalent toward all addictive diseases and has been slow to acknowledge the usefulness of the 12-step model (see Table 15–2). Patients are often considered unready for chemical-dependence (CD) treatment until they have insight. In the seriously mentally ill, achieving

this "primary" goal is often impossible, so addiction has been ignored. Psychodynamic interpretations of addiction have contributed little to the understanding or treatment of nicotine dependence. Psychiatric residency education has also failed to deal adequately with the addictions, but nowhere has neglect been more evident than in the case of nicotine dependence. Another rationalization for smoking by psychiatric patients has been that "staff smoking along with patients served to break-down communication barriers" (Feldman 1984 p 14). Contributing to the problem is the use of tobacco products as a reward for desired behavior. A recent article raises the plea that smoking may be the only pleasurable, socially reinforcing activity for the chronically mentally ill (Greeman and McClellen 1991). The problem of tobacco smoke pollution in psychiatric settings is compounded by the risk of introducing smoking to nonsmokers and the risk of relapse by recovering smokers in a milieu where smoking is the social norm. Confounding factors of mood disorder and cognitive impairments interact with nicotine withdrawal and pose special problems in psychiatric patients.

In 1980, the *Diagnostic and Statistical Manual of Mental Disorders* (DSM-III-R) (APA 1980) established a diagnosis for tobacco dependence, but this condition has not been a focus for the specialty. The epidemiologic catchment area survey neglected to include nicotine abuse as a subcategory of drug abuse and dependence (Regier et al.

1984). In addition, nicotine dependence was not included in a recent survey of substance abuse among emergency psychiatric patients (Barbee et al. 1989). Despite recent interest in the co-morbidity of psychiatric disorder and chemical dependence, and a rapidly expanding literature on dual diagnosis, nicotine dependence has usually been ignored.

SMOKING IN PSYCHIATRIC PATIENTS

While nicotine addiction commonly occurs in individuals without evidence of psychiatric disorders, it has long been known that psychiatric patients are more likely to be smokers (Lawton and Phillips 1956). This is especially true of patients who have a history of being psychiatrically hospitalized. Psychiatric inpatients were much more likely to smoke than medical inpatients at the same VA facility; they also smoked significantly more cigarettes per day (Gritz et al. 1985). Smoking is clearly the most common addictive behavior among psychiatric patients. Prevalence in various studies has ranged from 50 to 84%, and in each case, the rate was higher than in the control population (Connors, O'Farrell, Upper 1983). In a period where smoking has declined dramatically in the United States, prevalence among psychiatric patients has successfully resisted the trend. In the best controlled study (Hughes et al. 1986), psychiatric patients had a higher rate of smoking than the population at large when controlled for age, sex, marital status, socioeconomic status, alcohol, and caffeine use. In addition, smoking was more common among patients who had a previous psychiatric hospitalization and who had the diagnosis of schizophrenia (88%) or mania (70%) and was strongly correlated with severity of illness.

In our unpublished series of 132 consecutive admissions to an urban, acute care psychiatric unit in a university hospital, 95 (72%) were current smokers. Fourteen (10%) had successfully quit smoking, all without formal treatment. In this severely ill population, there was a high rate of abuse of other drugs. The mean age of onset for smoking was 16.6 years, and the amount smoked averaged slightly less than one pack a day.

Table 16–1   Reasons for Smoking Reported by 95 Consecutive Patients Currently Smoking in an Acute Psychiatric Unit

Reason	% of Patients
Pleasurable	71
Relaxing	67
Psychologically addicted	60
When upset	50
When angry	43
To perk up	29
To help with psychiatric medication	14

Those currently smoking reported having tried to stop smoking an average of 2.3 times. Most of the current smokers had successfully been abstinent from nicotine for at least one 6-month period since establishing their habit. Patients were queried about their reasons for smoking. These self-reports are listed in Table 16–1.

In nonhospitalized individuals (Glassman et al. 1990), an association exists between smoking and having experienced a major depression. Importantly, this history predicted a marked reduction in ability to stop or significantly cut down on cigarette smoking. Anda and colleagues (1990) also found smokers with symptoms of depression 40% less likely to quit. An accompanying editorial (Glass 1990) emphasizes that depression may often underlie continued, active nicotine dependence despite negative health effects and declining social acceptance.

As early as 1834 (Woodward as cited in Geller and Kaye 1990), an attempt was made to ban smoking at the Worcester State Hospital with mixed success. A severely ill community mental health center patient group (Maiuro et al. 1989) was surveyed about a change in smoking policy. Eighty percent smoked, 64% of these reported that smoking made it easier to talk to others, and 78% percent reported having tried unsuccessfully to quit smoking. Smokers and nonsmokers viewed the proposed policy change differently. Smokers expected negative mental effects and few positive physical effects, nonsmokers the reverse. They also disagreed on satisfaction in coming to the center and on their sense of personal control. Smokers reported greater anxiety, depression, and anger/hostility. After the policy change, clinicians did not notice significant mental health or social consequences. The report that the center was viewed less positively raised concerns over treatment acceptance and compliance, but the reaction appeared short-lived.

The reasons for psychiatric patient smoking are probably multiple. They include the presence of excessive negative affect such as depression and anxiety which can lead to "self-treatment" with nicotine. Psychiatric impairment almost presupposes a paucity of successful coping skills, especially in interpersonal settings which can be dealt with by smoking (Abrams, Monti, Pinto 1987). The failure of the smoking rate to fall in this population in parallel with that of the general population can be partly explained by the greater risk of relapse experienced by patients with depression (Glassman et al. 1988). The inherently stressful nature of early abstinence, the lack of social support and positive coping strategies, and the high levels of other coexisting substance abuse problems undoubtedly contribute to the risk of relapse.

In summary, psychiatric patients are more likely to be smokers. Few successfully quit smoking on their own. Most wish they could stop and have made attempts, though they are highly prone to relapse. At the same time, patients report that they would participate in smoking cessation activities if available (Table 16–2). Nicotine, a drug that aids affect regulation, diminishes negative affect (Chapter 2), and whose continued use is associated with depression, especially in women (Glassman et al. 1988), is overused in psychiatric patients.

SMOKING POLICIES ON PSYCHIATRIC UNITS

Anyone who has been involved in psychiatric institutions will recognize the following scene:

Twenty-five patients chain-smoked in the day room and hallways. When the cigarettes were consumed, stolen, taken or given away, they smoked butts scavenged from the floors, garbage barrels, or ashtrays. They often burned their lips and noses. . . . The patients showered themselves with sparks as they smoked. Shirts and pants were dotted

Table 16–2 Opinions about Stopping Smoking and Hospital Policy among 95 Consecutive Currently Smoking Patients in an Acute Psychiatric Unit

Reason	% of Patients
Hospital should offer stop smoking programs	77
Would attend a stop smoking program	60
Would try to quit if hospital enforced a no smoking policy	27

with burn holes. Occasionally, a patient set himself on fire. . . . The aides . . . constantly carried two to three packs of cigarettes with them to dispense over the day. They found cigarettes quick and effective tools for managing patients. Some patients got belligerent if they ran out of their own cigarettes. Others who got agitated could be quieted with a smoke. The aides also dispensed cigarettes to reward cooperative behavior and to promote alliances and goodwill. In short, the milieu was utterly dominated by the procurement and consumption of cigarettes.

(Gaston 1982)

Prompted by a lethal fire, Gaston, after considerable effort to change staff attitudes and revamp the management of the ward, found that smoking problems could be diminished. Most important, he reported, "The riot that the staff expected when the program began, did not occur." This observation applies to outpatient settings as well (Barmann et al. 1980; Maiuro et al. 1989).

Some facilities have focused on smoking control (Dawley et al. 1989) to limit where people can smoke. There may have been early attempts at creating nonsmoking psychiatric inpatient wards (Riffer 1982). There are no publications reporting this early experiment except a personal communication that the program was "working."

In 1986, Resnick and Bosworth surveyed smoking policies at psychiatric facilities in Oregon—a state with active environmental and clean air legislation—and found that all facilities had restricted smoking to particular areas and hours, and many controlled the numbers of cigarettes (Resnick and Bosworth 1988). All wards had specific areas in which smoking was permitted. All respondents believed it unlikely that smoking could be banned in psychiatric facilities. Half of the respondents indicated that cigarettes were used informally as reinforcers or rewards for patient compliance and behavior modification.

Actual experience with smoke-free inpatient psychiatric units has been far more positive than initially predicted (Grant and Smith 1989; Resnick and Bosworth 1989; Joseph and O'Neil 1992). A psychiatric unit was used to test the feasibility of an institution-wide smoke-free policy at the Oregon Health Sciences University (Barker, Mosely, Glidewell 1989). This was the reverse of most hospital situations where psychiatry has often been exempt when smoke-free policies are instituted. In the more typical sequence, after the rest of the facility becomes smoke-free, special administrative and clinical planning occurs to bring the psychiatry services into line (Hurt et al. 1989). Ten years of preparation had preceded this *total* ban on smoking (virtually no patient passes were allowed; the average length of stay was 6 days). Over these 10 years, the distribution of free tobacco materials was halted, on ward smoking by staff stopped, and times and places where patients could smoke were gradually restricted. Nicotine was eliminated as a positive reinforcer. One month after the ban, a survey showed no significant changes in antipsychotic drug administration and no increase in seclusion, restraints, or discharges against medical advice. No greater number of patients had to be placed on involuntary holds. Campus security was not called any more frequently for backup. Of all medications, only nicotine gum use was increased as a result of this total no smoking policy. Prior to the ban, nursing staff had reservations about the unit becoming tobacco-free: Only one-fourth of the nurses supported a total ban prior to its initiation. Afterwards, however, the staff overwhelmingly supported (95%) a total ban on smoking (Dingman et al. 1988).

A private, nonprofit hospital was able to initiate a no smoking policy on its psychiatric service (Grant and Smith 1989). Patients at appropriate privilege levels could be granted brief passes to leave the building to smoke. Patients reported some benefits from successfully restraining from or reducing their smoking during their stay, and 54% indicated they expected to reduce their smoking after discharge. This report notes that few patients refused admission. No instances of patient–patient injury, staff–patient injury, elopement, medication refusal, or verbal threats occurred. There were two premature discharges believed related to smoking as well as four discharges against medical advice (AMA). Medical consultants commented on the improved working environment. Smoking and nonsmoking nursing staff viewed the ban more favorably after the policy took effect than before it was instituted. In summary, smoking can be eliminated in psychiatric inpatient services.

Gralnick has written (1989; 1990) excellent discussions of the process of creating a smoke-free environment. The emphasis is on preparation of staff by education, banning sales of cigarettes, limiting hours and places for smoking, encouraging staff to become abstinent, and not allowing staff to smoke around patients. A year after the preliminary ban on smoking at the psychiatric facilities in Oregon (Resnick, Gordon, Bosworth, 1989), other hospitals in the area dramatically restricted their smoking policies. This included the remainder of the university hospital, private psychiatric facilities in the area, and two of the three state hospitals in Oregon. A survey demonstrated remarkable attitudinal changes among staff at these facilities after the change in policy. Sixty percent believed a smoking ban was likely or very likely or that their wards were already smoke-free. All respondents said that it was likely or very likely that staff smoking would be prohibited. Facilities began to use nicotine gum for nicotine withdrawal and had initiated policies to help patients cope nonpharmacologically with stopping smoking. There has been little resistance from the "smoker's rights" movement (Lavin 1989).

Patients' advocates in Oregon objected when a state hospital banned smoking on hospital grounds (Coleman 1990). They demanded a covered outdoor area for patients to smoke. It is hoped that advocacy groups will mobilize around the issue of providing treatment to CD individuals in institutions and support smoke-free facilities (Resnick 1990). In dissent, a recent report (Greeman and McClellen 1991) claims 20–25% of patients have difficulties adjusting to a smoke-free psychiatric environment and provides four case histories that purport to show negative outcomes. The authors suggest that problems going smoke-free may be underreported, but provide no concrete evidence that problems at their facility have increased. They agree that problems have been less than anticipated. The process at their hospital successfully took an institution with a lenient policy on cigarettes (providing free nicotine and extensive use of cigarettes as reinforcers) abruptly to a no smoking policy. These findings have been replicated for a community mental health center (Maiuro, Michael, Vitaliano 1989) where banning smoking led to transient negative reactions from smokers, but positive responses from nonsmokers.

It is likely that providing tobacco at state expense, using cigarettes as reinforcers, and exposing patients and staff to smoke in hospitals will soon end. The Joint Commission on Accreditation of Healthcare Organizations (JCAHO) has made having a smoke-free facility a requirement for accreditation (JCAHO 1991). Although this policy has a loophole which permits smoking by a patient on physician order, it is apparent that psychiatry will be confronting nicotine dependence more directly than in the past.

TREATMENT OF THE NICOTINE-DEPENDENT PSYCHIATRICALLY ILL

Although there is a growing interest in the treatment of dual diagnosis patients (coexisting substance abuse and serious mental illness), the published experience about the treatment of nicotine dependence among severely ill psychiatric patients is limited. Twenty-three older schizophrenic, nicotine-dependent veterans were treated with combined nicotine polacrilex and behavioral management in an outpatient setting (Breckenridge 1990). The 1-year abstinence rate was 21.8%, which is comparable to results in other populations using this treatment (Chapter 12).

Some basic principles for managing the dually diagnosed patient are important for addressing nicotine dependence among the psychiatrically ill. Assessment and treatment planning must be done by people comfortable in the fields of both addiction treatment *and* psychiatric disorder. Treatment providers must be aware of vulnerability to relapse during periods of worsening mental symptoms (Lehman, Myers, Corty 1989) and that treatment of such patients must be coordinated by one service provider (Osher and Kofoed 1989). Engagement in treatment may be especially difficult in nicotine dependence where external consequences are delayed and family interventions are of unknown utility. Persuasion of the patient to accept treatment and abstinence is crucial. This is difficult where nicotine dependence is excused or reinforced by the social milieu. Active treatment of nicotine dependence and relapse prevention are unstudied in this population. Consistent, effective treatment of the psychiatric disorder is doubtlessly important to maintaining abstinence. If treatment of the psychiatric disorder requires medication, it should be chosen with consideration of nicotine interactions (discussed later), and new data about medications possibly helpful at diminishing withdrawal symptoms should be considered carefully.

A number of positive factors aid in treatment planning for patients with coexisting psychiatric and nicotine dependence problems. These patients are seen repeatedly over long periods of time, which creates multiple opportunities to engage, motivate, and assist them. Many psychiatric patients want to quit smoking (Maiuro et al. 1989). Techniques and methodologies must be developed which facilitate abstinence; providing smoke-free treatment facilities is clearly a step in the right direction. A few patients are self-motivated and are able to quit without formal assistance. Identifying characteristics of these patients and factors that aided in their quitting is a promising area for research. The best time to intervene has yet to be defined, but this is likely dependent on numerous environmental factors and the availability of support. A variety of treatment models adjusted to patient characteristics will need to be developed.

PHARMACOLOGICAL INTERACTIONS

The pharmacology of nicotine is complex (Chapter 2). In psychiatric patients, the number of cigarettes smoked appears to be related to the severity of illness and the amount of tension or agitation experienced (Hall and Hennings 1980). Hyponatremia may be an additional deleterious health effect of smoking in psychiatric patients (Blum 1984). Nicotine induces hepatic microsomal enzymes and smoking appears to alter psychotropic drug effects (Beckett and Triggs 1967; Stimmel and Falloon 1983). Smokers exhibit less drowsiness and hypotension in response to taking chlorpromazine (Swett 1974). The drowsiness associated with diazepam and chlordiazepoxide diminishes as the numbers of cigarettes smoked increases (Miller 1977). Other benzodiazepines metabolized by conjugation may be differently affected (Dawson, Vestal, Jusko 1984). The antidepressants are variably affected. Imipramine metabolism is accelerated (Perel, Hurwic, Kanzler 1975), while blood levels of nortriptyline do not vary with smoking (Benowitz 1988). Cigarette smoking is highly correlated with both coffee consumption and alcohol use. The metabolism of psychotropic agents may be variably affected by this combination (Downing and Rickels 1981).

Smokers appear to need higher doses of neuroleptic drugs (Vinarova, Vinar, Kalvach 1984), and dyskinetic movements are more prevalent in medicated, chronic psychiatric outpatients who smoke (Yassa et al. 1987). This may be due to an increase in the synthesis and release of dopamine stimulated by nicotine. Smokers in this study were on significantly higher doses of neuroleptics; smoking as few as 10 cigarettes a day was a risk factor for developing dyskinetic movements. Of 154 patients (mostly schizophrenic), 54% (46/85) of smokers had a movement disorder compared to 26.1% (18/69) of nonsmokers. The disorder was more severe in smokers, and smokers were prescribed higher doses of neuroleptics. In contrast, a study of mortality in 101 psychiatric inpatients (Youssef and Waddington 1987) did not find a significant relationship between smoking and movement disorders. These authors observed that smokers with movement disorders had a higher mortality than nonsmokers with movement disorder and postulated that patients with such

movements are more sensitive to the deleterious effects of smoking. The differences between these two studies are unexplained, but the combination of neuroleptics and smoking is consistently associated with morbidity.

The interaction between smoking and psychotropic agents may be especially problematic if patients start and stop smoking. If psychotropic drugs are adjusted in smoke-free hospitals and patients relapse back to smoking, they are theoretically at a higher risk for decompensation after enzyme induction by smoking. The practical significance of this is unknown, but it would probably be mitigated by the common practice of discharging patients on relatively high doses of antipsychotic agents. Data about effects of smoking on blood levels of other psychotropic drugs is limited and requires further study.

PSYCHOTROPIC AGENTS AND THE TREATMENT OF NICOTINE DEPENDENCE IN THE PSYCHIATRICALLY ILL

Several pharmacologic agents are available to aid in nicotine withdrawal and in the management of nicotine addiction. The best studied of these is nicotine polacrilex (Chapter 12). On a nonsmoking psychiatric ward (Resnick, Pasley, Siemsen et al. 1989), 60 consecutive admissions were asked to complete a questionnaire. Fifty-three were completed and 68% of these 53 patients smoked. Nicotine polacrilex was made available to each patient (one to two pieces every hour, as needed) and each was instructed in its proper use. These patients were highly addicted to nicotine. Their mean score on the Fagerström Tolerance Questionnaire (Fagerström 1978) was 7.6 (mode 9.0). Despite this high level of nicotine dependence, the patients used little gum. Some refused to try it (7/53). Those who did averaged 1.9 pieces per day, and the heaviest use was only 6.6 pieces a day. This population may have not used the gum properly or may have become discouraged because they did not get expected nicotine effects. Some patients disliked the taste of the gum. An entirely smoke-free ward markedly reduces cues to smoke. It is possible that antipsychotics may reduce the withdrawal syndrome or craving. Transdermal nicotine was used in paid volunteers receiving psychiatric services (Hartman 1989, 1991) and it was effective in reducing the number of cigarettes smoked. This may be a useful approach for alleviating withdrawal among addicted smokers in smoke-free settings since it does not require motivation or a high level of cognitive functioning and demands little nursing time (Chapter 12).

Clonidine was used in a group of highly dependent smokers (Glassman et al. 1988). This study revealed a high prevalence of a past history of major depression among this population. While this study demonstrated that clonidine was a modestly helpful adjunct in quitting smoking, a history of major depression was a negative prognostic sign. The depressed group believed they had a "moral weakness," a perception that may be associated with cognitive aspects of depression. These data are consistent with a report (Downs et al. 1989) of a small number of patients treated with the antidepressant doxepin. Although the sample was small, there was significant improvement in abstinence from nicotine among treated patients at 2-month follow-up. The association of depression and depressive symptoms with smoking and with difficulty quitting make antidepressants attractive drugs to consider as adjunctive therapy in selected patients (Glassman et al. 1990; Anda et al. 1990). A preliminary, uncontrolled report (Byck, Compton, Gawin 1989) reported positive results with buspirone in heavy smokers who had previous failed attempts to quit. None of the subjects in the latter study met criteria for an anxiety disorder. The patients were able to cut down their smoking, and they experienced both less craving and diminished subjective withdrawal symptoms.

There is limited information on the psychologic impact of stopping smoking in psychiatric patients. In a volunteer group of 24 patients finishing a cessation program, 12 had a history of psychotherapy (Pertschuk et al. 1979). These patients did not increase their use of medications or mental health services during the cessation program. The authors believed smoking cessation was accomplished without noticeable stress.

IMPLICATIONS FOR THE TREATMENT MODEL

The nicotine-addicted patient with psychopathology requires assessment of both disorders. Often little attention is paid to assessing the addiction, the role it serves, and its relationship to psychiatric symptoms. For example, occasional patients only smoke when depressed or manic and may easily stop once the psychiatric disorder is treated. This assessment must also emphasize other addictive substances. It is worth asking the patient if nicotine is used to combat adverse effects of medications such as sedation or akathesia. An inventory of the patient's usual and successful coping strategies, the results of previous attempts, and the identification of relapse factors is often neglected due to the bias that psychiatric patients cannot or will not quit smoking. The clinician must assess the timing of motivating or confronting interventions based on psychiatric symptoms, medications, environmental stresses, and the availability of personal and treatment resources. It is worth remembering that these may often become rationalizations. At the least, consistent advice, education, and encouragement for smoking cessation and a smoke-free environment should be maintained.

There is no literature on minimal-contact treatment in this population. Since this population has not experienced the reduction in smoking observed in the population at large, minimal-contact treatments will probably be less useful in this group. These individuals have less self-esteem and confidence, more external locus of control, more primitive coping strategies, and less environmental support; all of these features predict greater difficulty quitting. Given this setting, it is reasonable to proceed directly with intensive interventions. Individualization based on psychopathology would seem appropriate. Patients with a history of depression may need antidepressants and formal cognitive treatment to prevent self-defeating behavior. Support and help with grief over the loss of a valued coping strategy could be a focus as well.

Patients with anxiety disorders will require special techniques to deal with increased symptoms. Stress reduction tapes, relaxation training, and cognitive skills may be helpful. Many patients with psychopathology will require increased assertiveness skills. Finally, relapse will need to be addressed in the light of the individual's psychopathology. Psychiatric patients are more prone to black and white thinking which makes the abstinence violation effect (Marlatt and Gordon 1985) more likely to occur and to be increased in severity.

CONCLUSION

Nicotine dependence in the psychiatric patient has not received attention commensurate with its risks and prevalence. It is not surprising that current rates of addiction are so high in this population. In the last few years, published reports on the problem have appeared at an increasing rate and will stimulate further research interest. The work on smoke-free psychiatric facilities and dual diagnosis programs brings focus to the field. Adjunctive psychopharmacologic interventions and new data about special populations at high risk for relapse (such as depression) are important contributions. Also important is societal progress on reducing acceptance of smoking and addiction. More and more professionals working with psychiatric patients will recognize the denial that has pervaded the field. Additional resources can be developed and methodologies researched to extend effective treatment for nicotine addiction to this population.

REFERENCES

Abrams, D. B., Monti, P. M., Pinto, R. P. Psychosocial stress and coping in smokers who relapse or quit. *Health Psychol* 6(4):289–303, 1987.

Anda, R. F., Williamson, D. F., Escobedo, L. G., Mast, E. E., Giovino, G. A., Remington, P. L. Depression and the dynamics of smoking. *JAMA* 264(12):1541–1545, 1990.

American Psychiatric Association (APA). *Diagnostic and Statistical Manual of Mental Disorders—DSM-III,* 3d ed. Washington, D.C.: American Psychiatric Association, 1980.

Barbee, J. G., Clark, P. D., Crapanzano, M. S., Heintz, G. C., Kehoe, C. E. Alcohol and substance abuse among schizophrenic patients presenting to an emergency psychiatric service. *J Nerv Ment Dis* 177(7):400–407, 1989.

Barker, A. F, Mosely, J. R., Glidewell, B. L. Components of a smoke-free hospital program. *Arch Intern Med* 149(6):1357–1359, 1989.

Barmann, B. C., Burnett, G. F., Malde, S. R., Zinik, G. Token reinforcement procedures for reduction of cigarette smoking in a psychiatric outpatient clinic. *Psychol Rep* 47:1245–1246, 1980.

Beckett, A. H., and Triggs, E. J. Enzyme induction in man caused by smoking. *Nature* 216:587, 11 November 1967.

Benowitz, N. L. Pharmacologic aspects of cigarette smoking and nicotine addiction. *N Engl J Med* 319(20):1318–1330, 1988.

Blum, A. The possible role of tobacco cigarette smoking in hyponatremia of long-term psychiatric patients. *JAMA* 252(20):2864–2865, 23/30 November 1984.

Breckenridge, J. S. Smoking by outpatients. *Hosp Community Psychiatry* 41(4):454–455, 1990.

Byck, R., Compton, M., Gawin, F. Buspirone reduces smoking. *Arch Gen Psychiatry* 46:288–289, March 1989.

Catford, J. C., and Nutbeam, D. Smoking in hospitals. *Lancet* 2:94–96, 1983.

Cohen, S. B. Tobacco addiction as a psychiatric disease. *South Med J* 81(9):1083–1088, 1988.

Coleman, T. Letter to the editor: Smokers' civil rights. *Hosp Community Psychiatry* 41(2):198–199, 1990.

Connors, G. J., O'Farrell, T. J., Upper, D. Addictive behaviors among hospitalized psychiatric patients. *Addict Behav* 8:329–33, 1983.

Dawley, H. H., Williams, J. L., Guidry, L. S., Dawley, L. T. Smoking control in a psychiatric setting. *Hosp Community Psychiatry* 40(12):1299–1301, 1989.

Dawson, G. W., Vestal, R. E., Jusko, W. J. Smoking and drug metabolism. In Balfour, D.J.K., ed. *Nicotine and the Tobacco Smoking Habit.* Oxford: Pergamon Press, 1984, ch. 12.

Dingman, P., Resnick, M., Bosworth, E. E., Kamada, D. A non-smoking policy on an acute psychiatric unit. *J Psychosoc Nurs Ment Health Serv* 26(12):11–14, 1988.

Downing, R. W., and Rickels, K. Coffee consumption, cigarette smoking and reporting of drowsiness in anxious patients treated with benzodiazepines or placebo. *Acta Psychiatr Scand* 64:398–408, 1981.

Downs, A. D., Edwards, N. B., Murphy, J. K. Doxepin as an adjunct to smoking cessation: a double-blind pilot study. *Am J Psychiatry* 146(3):373–376, 1989.

Fagerström, K. O. Measuring degree of physical dependence to tobacco with reference to individualization of treatment. *Addict Behav* 3:235–241, 1978.

Feldman, R. Smoking and the psych nurse. *J Psychosoc Nurs Ment Health Serv* 22(8):13–16, 1984.

Gaston, E. H. Solving the smoking problem on a chronic ward. *J Psychiatr Treat Eval* 4:397–401, 1982.

Geller, J. L., and Kaye, N. Smoking in psychiatric hospitals: A historical view of a hot topic. *Hosp Community Psychiatry* 141(12):1349–1350, 1990.

Glass, R. M. Blue mood, blackened lungs: Depression and smoking. *JAMA* 264(12):1583–1584, 1990.

Glassman, A. H., Stetner, F., Walsh, T., Raizman, P. S., Fleiss, J. L., Cooper, T. B., Covey, L. S. Heavy smokers, smoking cessation, and clonidine. *JAMA* 259(19):2863–2866, 1988.

Glassman, A. H., Helzer, J. E., Covey, L. S., Cottler, L. B., Stetner, F., Tipp, J. E., Johnson, J. Smoking, smoking cessation and major depression. *JAMA* 264(12):1546–1549, 1990.

Gralnick, A. A. Nicotine addiction in the psychiatric hospital: A preliminary report. *Psychiatr J Univ Ottawa* 13(1):25–27, 1988.

———. Commentary: Coping with nicotine addiction in the psychiatric hospital. *Psychiatr Hosp* 19(2):85–88, 1989.

———. Nicotine addiction in the psychiatric hospital: final report. *Psychiatr J Univ Ottawa* 15(3):165–168, 1990.

Grant, B. L., and Smith, W. S. Effects of a smoking ban on a general hospital psychiatric service. *Hosp Community Psychiatry* 40(5):497–502, 1989.

Greeman, M., and McClellen, T. A. Negative effects of a smoking ban on an inpatient psychiatry service. *Hosp Community Psychiatry* 42(4):408–412, 1991.

Gritz, E. R., Hill, M. A., Stapleton, J. M., Jarvik, M. E. Prevalence of cigarette smoking in VA and psychiatric hospitals. *Bull Soc Psychologists Addict Behav* 4(3):151–165, 1985.

Hall, G. H., and Hennings, N. G. *Biochemistry of Schizophrenia and Addiction.* Lancaster, England: MTP Press, 1980.

Hartman, N., Jarvik, M., Wilkins, J. Reduction of cigarette smoking by use of a nicotine patch. *Arch Gen Psychiatry* 46:289, March 1989.

Hartman, N., Leong, G. B., Glynn, S. M., Wilkins, J. N., Jarvik, M. E. Transdermal nicotine and smoking behavior in psychiatric patients. *Am J Psychiatry* 148(3):374–375, 1991.

Hay, D. R. A policy for the control of smoking in hospitals. *New Zealand Med J* 99:505–507, 9 July 1986.

Hughes, J. R., Hatsukami, D. K., Mitchell, J. E., Dahlgren, L. A. Prevalence of smoking among psychiatric outpatients. *Am J Psychiatry* 143(8):993–997, 1986.

Hurt, R. D., Berge, K. G., Offord, K. P., Leonard, D. A., Gerlach, D. K., Renquist, C. L., O'Hara, M. R. The making of a smoke-free medical center. *JAMA* 261(1):95–97, 1989.

Joint Commission on Accreditation of Healthcare Organizations (JCAHO). *Hospital Standards, 1992* Chicago: Joint Commission on Accreditation of Healthcare Organizations, 1991.

Joseph, A. M., and O'Neil, P. J. The Department of Veterans Affairs' smoke-free policy. *JAMA* 267:87–90, 1992.

Lavin, M. Letter to the editor: Let the patient smoke. *Hosp Community Psychiatry* 40(12):1301–1302, 1989.

Lawton, M. P. and Phillips, R. W. The relationship between excessive cigarette smoking and psychological tension. *Am J Med Sci* 232:397–402, 1956.

Lehman, A. F., Myers, C. P., Corty, E. Assessment and classifications of patients with psychiatric and substance abuse syndromes. *Hosp Community Psychiatry* 40(10):1019–1025, 1989.

Maiuro, R. D., Michael, M. C., Vitaliano, P. P., Chiles, J. A., Davis, P. M. Patient reactions to a no smoking policy in a community mental health center. *Community Ment Health J* 25(1):71–77, 1989.

Marlatt, G. A., and Gordon, J. R. *Relapse Prevention.* New York: Guilford, 1985.

Miller, R. R. Effects of smoking on drug action. *Clin Pharmacol Ther* 22(5):749–756, 1977.

Niskanen, P., Saiki, P., Tamminen, T. Smoking in psychiatric inpatients. *Psychiatr Fenn* 163–168, 1978.

Orleans, C. T., and Slade, J. Smoking ban in US hospitals presents new challenges. *Tobacco Control* 1:46–47, 1992.

Osher, F. C. and Kofoed, L. L. Treatment of patients with psychiatric and psychoactive substance abuse disorders. *Hosp Community Psychiatry* 40(10);1025–1030, 1989.

Perel, J. M., Hurwic, M. J., Kanzler, M. B. Pharmacodynamics of imipramine in depressed patients. *Psychopharmacol Bull* 11:16–18, 1975.

Pertschuk, M. J., Pomerleau, O. F., Adkins, D., Hirsch, C. Smoking cessation: The psychological costs. *Addict Behav* 4:345–348, 1979.

Regier, D. A., Myers, J. K., Kramer, M., Robins, L. N., Blazer, D. G., Hough, R. L., Easton, W. W., Locke, B. Z. The NIMH epidemiologic catchment program. *Arch Gen Psychiatry* 41(10):934–941, 1984.

Resnick, M. P. Reply to letter to the editor: Smokers' civil rights. *Hosp Community Psychiatry* 41(2):199, 1990.

Resnick, M., and Bosworth, E. E. A survey of smoking policies in Oregon psychiatric facilities. *Hosp Community Psychiatry* 39(3):313–315, 1988.

———. A smoke-free psychiatric unit. *Hosp Community Psychiatry* 40(5):515–527, 1989.

Resnick, M. P., Gordon, R., Bosworth, E. E. Evolution of smoking policies in Oregon psychiatric facilities. *Hosp Community Psychiatry* 40(5):527–529, 1989.

Resnick, M. P., Pasley, D. R., Siemsen, F. K., Yok, L. Nicotine gum use with nicotine addiction. *J Clin Psychiatry* 50(8):310, 1989.

Riffer, J. Hospitals challenged to restrict smoking. *Hospitals Headlines* 16 March 1982.

Stimmel, G. L., and Falloon, I.R.H. Chlorpromazine plasma levels, adverse effects, and tobacco smoking: Case report. *J Clin Psychiatry* 44(11):420–422, 1983.

Swett, C. Drowsiness due to chlorpromazine in relation to cigarette smoking. *Arch Gen Psychiatry* 31:211–213, August 1974.

Vinarova, E., Vinar, O., Kalvach, Z. Smokers need higher doses of neuroleptic drugs. *Biol Psychiatry* 19(8):1265–1268, 1984.

Yassa, R., Lal, S., Korpassy, A., Ally, J. Nicotine exposure and tardive dyskinesia. *Biol Psychiatry* 22:67–72, 1987.

Youssef, H. A., and Waddington, J. L. Morbidity and mortality in tardive dyskinesia: Associations in chronic schizophrenia. *Acta Psychiatr Scand* 75:74–77, 1987.

PART III

PUBLIC HEALTH AND PREVENTION

17

Women Who Smoke

LAURA J. SOLOMON and BRIAN S. FLYNN

In this chapter we will review changing knowledge of the impact of cigarette smoking on women's health, smoking patterns among women, special factors influencing smoking among women, and the application of this knowledge to more effective approaches to help women quit smoking. Our discussion of health impact and smoking patterns reflect what now seems a simple and easily understood phenomenon: smoking has increased among women in the past several decades and the health impact of this increased exposure is now being seen in women's rates of smoking-related diseases.

HEALTH CHARACTERISTICS OF WOMEN WHO SMOKE

Women who smoke, like men who smoke, experience higher death rates in all age categories. Excess mortality for women who smoke has increased sharply. The relative risk of death for women aged 36 years or older who were smokers was 1.2 in a mortality follow-up study conducted from 1956 to 1965 and 1.9 in a similar follow-up study conducted from 1982 to 1986; comparable ratios for male smokers were 1.8 and 2.3, respectively (USDHHS 1989). Although these overall ratios remain somewhat lower for women, the rate of increase in relative risk of death for women smokers has increased much more sharply than it has for men. This change reflects more similar patterns of smoking among women and men in recent decades than in decades past. Women who have patterns of exposure to cigarettes similar to men experience similar mortality rates (USDHHS 1980). In plainer language, women who smoke like men die like men. About 106,000 women died from the 10 major causes of death from cigarette smoking in 1985; adjusted for age, about 2.2 times more women died from smoking in 1985 than in 1965.

Estimates of the percentages of deaths of women from specific causes which could have been avoided in the absence of cigarette smoking have been calculated from mortality follow-up studies (USDHHS 1989). Table 17–1 shows that the percentage for most of the major causes of death related to cigarette smoking has increased in the past 20 years, and is now similar to smoking attributable risks for men, except for the oldest age groups. In 1985, among both men and women under 65 years of age, smoking caused more than 40% of coronary heart disease (CHD) deaths and more than 50% of cerebrovascular deaths. Among women, smoking now caused almost 80% of deaths from both chronic obstructive pulmonary diseases (COPD) and from lung cancer; according to American Cancer Society data, lung cancer now exceeds breast cancer as the leading cause of cancer death for women.

In addition to these health consequences of smoking which women share equally with men, women are subject to several additional ill effects. Smoking and oral contraceptive use interact to dramatically increase the risk of cardiovascular disease. The multiple impacts of smoking on pregnancy and birth outcomes are reviewed in Chapter 14. Recent evidence also suggests that smoking is associated with increased risk of cervical cancer.

Table 17–1 Estimated Attributable Risk for 10 Selected Causes of Death from Smoking, Males and Females, U.S., 1965 and 1985

Cause of Death	Males		Females	
	1965 (%)	1985 (%)	1965 (%)	1985 (%)
CHD, age <65 yrs.	42	45	26	41
CHD, age ≥65 yrs.	11	21	3	12
COPD	84	84	67	79
Cancer of lip, oral cavity, and pharynx	74	92	27	61
Cancer of larynx	84	81	47	87
Cancer of esophagus	57	78	14	75
Cancer of lung	86	90	40	79
Cancer of pancreas	41	29	14	34
Cancer of bladder	53	47	36	37
Cancer of kidney	36	48	17	12
Cerebrovascular disease, age <65 yrs.	28	51	28	55
Cerebrovascular disease, age ≥65 yrs.	2	24	1	6

Source: Adapted from USDHHS 1989.

CHD = coronary heart disease; COPD = chronic obstructive pulmonary disease.

SMOKING PATTERNS AMONG WOMEN

The direct cause of increases in smoking-related deaths among women is, of course, vast changes in smoking behavior. A half century ago about 20% of women and more than 50% of men were regular smokers (USDHHS 1980). While male smoking declined beginning in the mid-1960s, around the time of the first Surgeon General's Report on Smoking and Health, smoking among women increased steadily until it peaked in the early 1970s at about 32%. From 1965 to 1987, the prevalence of regular smoking among women declined from about 32% to about 27%, while among men rates declined from about 50% to about 32%. Between 1965 and 1985, smoking prevalence overall declined in the United States adult population at a rate of about 0.5% per year, but among women the average decline during this period was approximately 0.2%. As a result of these marked relative differences in behavior change, recent projections indicate that smoking rates will be nearly equal among men and women in the mid-1990s, after which women may smoke at a higher rate than men (Fiore, Novotny, Pierce 1989; Pierce, Fiore, Novotny et al. 1989b).

Underlying these changes is the increased initiation of smoking by less well-educated adolescent women (Pierce, Fiore, Novotny et al. 1989a), while initiation rates are falling in other groups (USDHHS 1989). National survey data suggest also that less long-term quitting by women also contributes to these stagnating rates of decline in smoking among women (USDHHS 1989).

For both women and men, educational attainment is an increasingly valuable sociodemographic predictor of cigarette smoking status. Pierce and colleagues (1989a) have pointed out the increasing gap in prevalence of cigarette smoking between those with greater and lesser amounts of educational attainment. Between 1965 and 1985, the rate of decline in cigarette smoking was 12 times greater in the best-educated, as compared to the least well-educated sectors of our population. Similar differences are seen between white-collar workers and blue-collar and service workers, although these differences are not as great for women as they are for men (USDHHS 1985, 1989).

African-American women have higher rates of smoking than other American women and suffer from higher rates of morbidity and mortality from smoking-related diseases. Although they tend to smoke fewer cigarettes per day, African-American women are more likely to smoke high-nicotine brands. It also is possible that the menthol-flavored cigarettes used by more than half of these smokers facilitate deeper and longer inhalations because of their anesthetic effects, thus increasing exposure, dependency, and risk (Orleans et al. 1989). Smoking rates for women of Hispanic origin are lower than those for non-Hispanics, but still reflect a substantial prevalence of about 21% in 1985. Recent reports indicate that cigarette smoking among Hispanic women may be increasing (Escobedo and Remington 1989).

Basic smoking patterns among women have changed little in the past two decades. Nearly all women smoke filtered cigarettes, and women are more likely than men to smoke cigarettes rated as having lower tar yields (≤ 15 mg). Women are less likely than men to be heavy smokers (≥ 25 cigarettes/day). Use of other forms of tobacco by women, including pipes, cigars, cigarillos, and smokeless tobacco is rare (USDHHS 1989). It has not been shown that women smokers are less dependent on cigarettes than men, as suggested by these patterns of lower exposure to nicotine. It is possible that women require a lower exposure to achieve an equivalent level of dependency because of their lower body weight, as with other psychoactive drugs.

Although women who smoke suffer consequences from smoking similar to those suffered by men who smoke, women who quit smoking benefit as much as men who quit. This evidence has been reviewed in a recent report of the Surgeon General (USDHHS 1990). Illustrative of general health quitting benefits for women, a recent report (Rosenberg, Palmer, Shapiro 1990) demonstrated that among women, as for men, most of the increased risk of suffering an initial myocardial infarction dissipated within 2 to 3 years of stopping smoking. Benefits of quitting for pregnant women are reviewed in Chapter 14. The discussion now turns to factors that appear to be especially important in determining successful outcomes of quit attempts among women.

HELPING WOMEN SMOKERS QUIT

Three issues emerge from the literature on treating nicotine dependence in women that warrant special attention. These three salient concerns for women who are quitting smoking include: (1) dealing with negative affect; (2) eliciting social support; and (3) handling weight gain. Each of these issues will be discussed in turn.

Dealing with Negative Affect

Numerous studies suggest that women are more likely than men to smoke and relapse back into smoking in response to psychological stress and/or negative affect (USDHHS 1980). Negative affect can include a broad range of emotional feelings, including high energy negative emotions (e.g., anger, stress, anxiety, frustration) and low-energy negative emotions (e.g., sadness, loneliness, boredom, depression).

When examined within the context of the stress and coping literature, these gender differences in smoking in response to negative affect are not surprising. For example, Solomon and Rothblum (1986) reviewed the research literature on gender differences in coping with stress. Of the four studies that examined differences by gender, two (Folkman and Lazarus 1980; Pearlin and Schooler 1978) found that women compared to men use *fewer* active coping strategies (i.e., strategies that attempt to alter the stressful situation directly), particularly in the occupational domain, but also in the domains of marriage and parenting. The other two studies (Billings and Moos 1981; Stone and Neale 1984) found that women compared to men use *more* palliative coping strategies (i.e., strategies that serve to alter their level of emotional arousal but leave the stressful situation intact).

Taken together, these studies suggest that women tend to cope with stress in more passive ways than do men. The reasons why are not clear. Differences between men and women in perceptions of control and/or in actual control over stressors in numerous domains may help account for the differences in coping behaviors; however, research evidence is not yet available to address this issue. Nevertheless, within the context of the stress and coping literature, the smoking differences between men and women make sense. Women are more likely to use palliative coping strategies in response to stressful circumstances, and smoking is a readily available palliative coping behavior. Thus, smoking may serve an important coping function for women by abating negative affect. The cigarette does not completely alleviate the negative feelings; however, it tempers the aversive experience somewhat, making it a powerful reinforcer to women. Quitting smoking takes away this convenient coping behavior. In light of this, it is not surprising that women frequently relapse back into smoking in the presence of negative affective states.

The question of how to help women cope with negative affective states in the absence of smoking is an important one. Research on coping with relapse crises reveals that using some form of active coping strategy, whether it is behavioral or cognitive, results in greater success in resisting the urge to smoke compared to doing nothing to resist the urge for a cigarette (Curry and Marlatt 1985; Shiffman 1984). However, this research speaks primarily to coping with the desire for a cigarette. If negative affect is a frequent precursor to a woman's urge to smoke, particularly after she has quit, then how to handle the negative affect might best be the focus of our intervention efforts. Because women are more likely to use palliative strategies than are men, perhaps women should be encouraged to identify other palliative techniques already in their coping repertoires as a substitute for smoking in the presence of negative affect. Care should be taken to ensure that the alternative palliative strategies do not have harmful side effects, as is often the case with eating, drinking alcohol, or taking medication. Active coping also should be stressed.

The identification and rehearsal of other palliative coping responses such as positive imagery and self-talk, relaxation techniques, venting of emotions (e.g., talking with a friend, crying), and physical activity may provide women with the resources needed to better handle negative affect in the absence of smoking. Some women may also find it helpful to strengthen their active coping strategies through assertiveness-training and assistance with problem-solving in the interpersonal domain. Clinical observations suggest that alternative strategies are more easily identified for high energy negative emotions (e.g., anger, anxiety, frustration, stress) than for low energy negative emotions (e.g., loneliness, boredom, depression). Physical activity (e.g., walking, cleaning, gardening, shoveling snow) and relaxation strategies (e.g., deep breathing, taking a bubble bath, listening to soothing music) appear helpful in tempering high energy emotion; however, low energy emotions seem less responsive to these approaches. Cognitive strategies (e.g., positive self-talk) as well as social support may be useful to women experiencing dysphoric affect. Of particular concern is the small subset of women who may have used nicotine as self-medication for depression. These women are likely to have difficulty maintaining abstinence, and formal treatment for depression may be indicated (Glass 1990).

Eliciting Social Support

The provision of social support refers to the exchange of information leading a person to believe that he or she is cared for and loved, esteemed and valued, or part of a network having mutual obligations (Cobb 1976). In general, women more than men use social support as a means of coping with stress and changing life-style behaviors (Belle 1982; Hobfoll 1986).

In the literature on quit smoking treatments, there is abundant evidence to suggest that social support is an important ingredient in the mix of aids offered to women who are attempting to quit and stay quit (Guilford 1972; Schwartz and Dubitsky 1968; Chapter 4). For example, women were less successful at quitting smoking following pharmacotherapy and educational treatments compared to psychotherapy and group behavioral interventions (USDHHS 1980). Guilford (1972) found that while women and men had the same success rates in group cessation programs, women showed lower maintenance of cessation than did men when not participating in a group program. All women (gender homogeneous) groups appear to be more effective for women than mixed gender groups (Delarue 1973), and women appear to be more likely than men to participate in formal group smoking cessation programs (Shiffman 1982).

Numerous correlational studies indicate that support for smoking cessation from significant others enhances cessation maintenance (Coppotelli and Orleans 1985; Mermelstein, Lichtenstein, McIntyre 1983; Ockene et al. 1982). For example, Coppotelli and Orleans (1985) found that their measure of partner facilitation taken immediately postcessation was the primary predictor of abstinence for women at 6–8 weeks following quitting, accounting for 31% of the variance in relapse, and correctly classifying 85% of the subjects into abstinent and nonabstinent categories at follow-up. Their partner facilitation factor assessed the women's perceptions of partner support behaviors in general as well as those specific to quitting smoking. Supportive partner behaviors included encouraging self-reward; minimizing the woman's stress by avoiding interpersonal conflict and by taking over some of the woman's usual responsibilities; offering general problem-solving assistance; offering specific help with cravings; showing empathy and tolerance for moodiness; and showing concern about quitting. Copotelli and Orleans (1985) also found that women who remained abstinent 8 weeks following cessation were more likely than their nonabstinent counterparts to have ex-smoking partners or partners who successfully quit with them. Other studies suggest that women may be more responsive than men to the smoking status of others around them, as more women tend to quit smoking if no one in their environment is a regular smoker (Warnecke et al. 1978; West et al. 1977). This is a particularly noteworthy finding, as women are more likely than men to have a smoking spouse in the household since more men than women currently smoke.

Thus, social support in the form of individual or group assistance with quitting and significant other support for maintenance of cessation appear to be particularly important for women. Interventions to help women quit smoking and remain abstinent should include the provision of ongoing social support through either informal or formal networks. While group cessation programs have become widely available, ongoing group support for staying quit, perhaps based on the Alcoholics Anonymous model, might strengthen the resolve to remain abstinent while rallying support from understanding peers. In Vermont, Solomon and Flynn are currently testing a one-to-one support network in which women who are ex-smokers volunteer to be trained in telephone support skills and are then matched with women attempting to quit whom they call on a weekly basis to provide encouragement and assistance in staying quit. This proactive approach to the provision of support bypasses the problem of the woman having to ask for help, a common barrier to the use of smoking cessation hot lines.

Concerns about Weight Gain

Fear of weight gain and actual weight gain after quitting are salient concerns among many women who smoke. Survey data reveal that women are more concerned about weight gain related to smoking cessation than are men (Camp et al. 1993; Sorensen and Pechacek 1987). In a 1986 unpublished survey of 879 women in four communities in Vermont, 46% reported that they were moderately or very concerned about their weight. Of the women who smoked, 55% stated that they had little or no confidence that they could control their weight if they quit smoking.

It appears that women's concerns about weight gain following quitting are well-founded. Although women smokers tend to weigh less than women nonsmokers (Blitzer, Rimm, Giffer 1977), weight gain often follows quitting in both females and males (Albanes et al. 1987; Blitzer, Rimm, Giffer 1977; Hall et al. 1989). A recent review of longitudinal studies of postcessation weight gain revealed that 79% of smokers who quit smoking experienced some weight gain; the average weight gain for smokers who quit was 4.6 pounds (range = 1.6–11.2 pounds) compared to an average of .90 pounds (range = 0–3.5 pounds) gained by smokers who continued to smoke (USDHHS 1990). There is some evidence to suggest that the total weight gain postcessation may be slightly greater for women than for men (Hall et al. 1989; Klesges et al., 1990), and that the total weight gain may be closer to 10 pounds when ex-smokers are followed to 12 months postcessation (Pirie 1990). These findings are exacerbated by the fact that the social consequences of weight gain may be more negative for women due to the cultural value placed on their thinness (Orleans 1986).

The mechanisms for weight gain following smoking cessation are not entirely clear. Indirect evidence suggests that a reduction in metabolic rate following cessation is responsible for some of the weight change (USDHHS 1990). However, most of the evidence supporting this relationship comes from studies showing increases in metabolic rate as a function of nicotine administration, not from observations of metabolic rate decreases as a function of smoking cessation (Klesges, Meyers, Winders 1989). Dietary changes following cessation have been well-documented, but many of these changes tend to support shifts in components of the diet (e.g., toward higher fat and higher sugar foods) rather than increases in total caloric intake (Rodin 1987). It is an increase in total caloric intake relative to total caloric expenditure that would need to occur to explain the weight gain phenomenon postcessation (Klesges, Meyers, Winders 1989). To date, no study has demonstrated that postcessation weight gain can be attributed to decreases in physical activity (Klesges et al. 1989); however, Rodin (1987) observed that smokers who quit smoking and did not gain weight had higher precessation and postcessation physical activity levels than did smokers who quit smoking and gained weight. Thus, the mechanisms accounting for postcessation weight gain may be a complex interaction of variables. The most promising explanations include decreases in metabolic rate coupled with increases in caloric intake.

Four controlled studies have attempted to test behavioral intervention strategies to prevent weight gain following smoking cessation (Grinstead 1981; Hall 1990; Mermelstein 1987; Pirie 1990). None of these studies successfully prevented weight gain, none showed a positive effect for the weight management intervention on smoking cessation rate, and only one (Mermelstein 1987) found a significant difference between the groups in the amount of weight gained. In fact, two of the studies (Hall 1990; Pirie 1990) suggest that the inclusion of a weight management program within a smoking cessation intervention may be counterproduc-

tive to the goal of accomplishing abstinence as measured at a 12-month follow-up.

More promising results have been observed in studies examining the effects of nicotine replacement on postcessation weight gain. Two studies (Emont and Cummings 1987; Fagerstrom 1987) found that a higher level of nictoine gum use was related to a reduced level of postcessation weight gain. A third study (Gross, Stitzer, Maldonado 1989) examined the relationship between nicotine gum and body weight using a randomized, double-blind procedure in which subjects received either nicotine gum or placebo. During the 10 weeks of cigarette abstinence, abstinent subjects in the placebo condition gained an average of 4 pounds more than abstinent nicotine gum users. A nicotine dose effect on weight gain was also observed, with less frequent gum users gaining more weight. At a 6-month assessment after the gum was discontinued, however, the total weight gain in abstinent subjects was comparable in the two conditions, indicating that the nicotine gum delayed, but did not prevent, postcessation weight gain. It should be noted, however, that a study by Pirie (1990) failed to find the delay of weight gain effect in women smokers who smoked at least a pack of cigarettes a day at baseline and who demonstrated good adherence to the nicotine gum postcessation. Thus, the few studies on the use of nicotine gum on postcessation weight gain showed mixed, yet encouraging, results.

Other pharmacologic agents are under examination for their possible postcessation weight prevention benefits. It is important to consider, however, that these medications may be useful only to the extent that they increase smoking abstinence rates and do so without harmful side effects. To date, none have met these criteria. It is also worth noting that for most women who quit smoking, the 5–10 pound weight gain that occurs is not a health risk. Were it not for the negative feelings and possible social consequences associated with postcessation weight gain in women, this issue would be of little concern. In fact, two studies suggest that people who are most likely to remain abstinent appear to be the people who gain *more* weight early on in the quitting process (Hall, Ginsberg, Jones 1986; Streater, Sargent, Ward 1989).

Given the concerns expressed by many women about postcessation weight gain, however, it seems advisable to address the issue with those women who are seriously contemplating quitting. Because weight management programs delivered simultaneously with smoking cessation programs have uniformly failed, this approach does not appear advisable. Instead, several other options might be offered to women. These options are as follows: (1) recognize that gaining some weight postcessation is normal and may be, in part, due to changes in metabolic rate; accept the small amount of weight gain and deal with it later after smoking is under control; (2) decrease the likelihood of gaining large amounts of weight by holding caloric intake constant; avoid snacking on foods high in fat and sugar content; (3) consider the use of nicotine gum as a way to delay the onset of weight gain until smoking is under control.

Perhaps most importantly, the issue of weight gain after smoking cessation warrants serious attention because it highlights cultural norms that lead women to conclude that it is more desirable to smoke than it is to gain some weight after quitting. These norms are not inevitable; in other eras, other body images were viewed as desirable. Efforts to change rigid cultural notions about acceptable body images might help to eliminate this barrier to quitting smoking.

RECOMMENDATIONS FOR HEALTH CARE PROVIDERS

Women who smoke are a population deserving special attention by the health care community for several reasons: (1) medical findings document serious health risks in addition to those experienced by male smokers in women who smoke (e.g., pregnancy complications, stroke risk associated with oral birth control, infertility, early menopause); (2) epidemiological data indicate that women of lower income and education are likely to be the largest group of smokers in the future; and (3) women are prime users of health care services, both for themselves and for their children. For these reasons, health care providers, particularly those who serve low-income women of childbearing age, are urged to give high priority to the smoking issue with female patients who smoke. The model for clinical management of cigarette smoking outlined in Chapters 8 and 10 serves as an appropriate guide for counseling women who smoke.

Motivating a Quit Attempt

Depending on the specific population of women seen, motivational messages might include information about the personal health consequences of smoking, the health and behavioral consequences for her pregnancy and/or her children, cosmetic consequences (e.g., staining of teeth, wrinkling of skin, offensive odor of smoke), and/or financial consequences (i.e., the ongoing costs of smoking). Because women view physicians as the most credible sources of health information, delivery of a clear health risk message coupled with an unambiguous quit message is likely to be the best way to motivate a woman to quit. Such a message could be very brief. An example to a pregnant women would be: "I'm concerned about your smoking because we know that smoking during preganancy can be harmful to you and your baby. Therefore, as your physician, I strongly recommend that you quit smoking during your pregnancy." This brief message serves to legitimize the smoking concern for each individual woman, and includes a clear directive to quit. While that message, heard in isolation, may not result in a quit attempt each time it is delivered, research indicates that its repeated delivery by multiple health care providers is the most effective way to motivate quit attempts in medical practices (Kottke et al. 1988).

Minimal Counseling

After legitimizing concern about smoking and delivering an unambiguous quit message, the health care provider might acknowledge the predictable barriers to quitting and difficulties associated with staying quit experienced by women (e.g., coping with negative emotions without smoking, managing weight gain, trying to quit in the presence of other smokers). These issues cannot be addressed easily in the context of a brief clinical encounter; therefore, it is reasonable to consider supplemental support that could be provided to women contemplating quitting. Mention the availability of such support through in-house counselors, community organizations, and/or self-help materials.

Probably the most important step in smoking cessation counseling is the elicitation of a quit date. Over 80% of successful exsmokers quit "cold turkey"; therefore, encouraging the women to pick a day when she will no longer smoke is a realistic strategy to promote. Be sure to write the date in her chart and tell her you will ask her about it at her next visit (or in a telephone call if you or your office staff can do so). For women who are unwilling to commit to a quit date, encourage either quitting for a short time or cutting down to half the number of cigarettes she currently smokes as an interim step to quitting.

Self-instructional materials specifically developed for women smokers may be useful to motivate women who need additional information. The voluntary organizations (e.g., American Lung Association, American Cancer Society, American Heart Association) as well as the federal government (e.g., National Heart, Lung and Blood Institute; National Cancer Institute) have self-help materials for women who smoke and for pregnant women. Look for guides that specifically address ways to handle negative emotions, elicit social support, and deal with weight gain concerns as these may be useful adjuncts to your direct advice.

Formal Treatment

Because we know that social support is an important factor in the way women make health behavior changes, one potentially powerful adjunct to your quit smoking advice and assistance is direct contact with others who are quitting smoking or who have successfully quit. Thus, community smoking cessation groups, one-to-one support networks, drop-in support groups, and telephone buddy systems may provide women with the opportunity to problem-solve difficulties in quitting with credible others and to receive the kind of ongoing encouragement that can result in a successful outcome. It is unlikely that the level of ongoing support helpful to women who are quitting smoking can be provided in the context of a busy medical practice; therefore, referral resources should be identified and/or developed at the community level to ensure that women who are motivated to quit smoking receive the support needed to be successful. These referral resources should be prepared to address difficulties managing negative emotions without smoking, concerns about weight gain, and problems associated with trying to quit smoking in the context of a smoking culture.

Pharmacologic Adjuncts

Nicotine replacement therapies hold promise for some women who are contemplating quitting (Chapter 12). Appropriate candidates for nicotine gum or transdermal nicotine include women who are not pregnant, not breast-feeding, have no history of heart disease or ulcers, and have no problems associated with chewing gum. Nicotine replacement may be particularly appropriate for women who smoke at least a pack of cigarettes a day and are greatly concerned about postcessation weight gain. Outcome studies indicate that nicotine replacement in conjunction with behavioral counseling results in some of the most successful quit rates ever observed. As discussed in Chapter 12, the prescription of nicotine gum or patches without behavioral counseling, however, is no better than placebo. Therefore, health care providers should prescribe nicotine replacement only in conjunction with in-house counseling or referral to community-based support options like those mentioned earlier. Because nicotine gum and transdermal nicotine are prescription medications, some insurance plans and some state Medicaid policies cover the cost of the medication. It is helpful to know about these policies when prescribing nicotine replacement.

PUBLIC HEALTH STRATEGIES

Many of the components of a comprehensive public health approach to reduction of smoking by women have been addressed in this and other chapters. Here we have been concerned with delivery of cessation messages by health care providers and with the identification or creation of sources of support to help women deal with the particular problems they encounter when trying to quit. Other chapters address strategies focusing on schools, worksites, and public policy. These service-focused strategies have been shown to be individually strong, and more powerful when used in combination, but their impact can be enhanced by strategies that directly address social norms related to women's smoking.

Women have been targeted as a special market by the tobacco industry for many decades (Whelan 1984). During this time, enormous resources have been devoted to creating appealing images of women smokers; the importance of this effort to the domestic cigarette industry has been magnified by the relatively greater importance of women cigarette purchasers in the past two decades. It is apparent from earlier experiences with counteradvertising and from our own current research with mass media approaches to smoking prevention (Worden et al. 1988), that these strategies can have substantial impact on adoption and continuance of cigarette smoking. Further testimony to the strength of these approaches can be obtained through analyses of the behavior of the tobacco industry, which uses its economic power to project positive images of women smokers through the print media and sponsorship of highly visible athletic and cultural events, while suppressing the projection of images that emphasize the health consequences of smoking and quitting techniques (Ernster 1985). These intensive efforts to control public images of smoking may be a major factor accounting for the continued increases in cigarette smoking prevalence among younger, less-educated women.

The development and testing of mass media approaches is recommended to counteract the efforts of the tobacco industry to maintain a positive image of women smokers. In addition, support by concerned citizens of organized efforts is needed to restrict the projection of images that promote the use of this deadly product. The power of organized citizen action was recently demonstrated by a successful effort protesting the introduction of a new cigarette brand targeted to African-Americans. Unfortunately, a similar effort concerned with the introduction of a new brand targeted to young, less-educated women has not been as successful; the Dakota brand cigarette is now being marketed in several U.S. test cities.

CONCLUSIONS

Health care providers play an important role in encouraging women to stop smoking. By addressing the smoking issue repeatedly in the context of routine medical care, they can legitimize the concern about smoking and strive for a commitment to change. But women smokers face predictable difficulties when considering and attempting to quit smoking. The challenge lies in creating ways to address these special needs either within the practice setting or through resources in the community.

REFERENCES

Albanes, D. M., Jones, Y., Micozzi, M. S., Mattson, M. E. Associations between smoking and body weight in the US population: Analysis of NHANES II. *Am J Public Health* 77:439–444, 1987.

Belle, D. Social ties and social support. In Belle, D., ed. *Lives in Stress.* Beverly Hills, CA: Sage, 1982.

Billings, A. G., and Moos, R. H. The role of coping responses and social resources in attenuating the stress of life events. *J Behav Med* 4:139–157, 1981.

Blitzer, P. H., Rimm, A., Giffer, E. E. The effect of cessation of smoking on body weight in 57,032 women: Cross-sectional and longitudinal analyses. *J Chronic Dis* 30:415–429, 1977.

Camp, D. E., Klesges, R. C., Relyea, G. The relationship between body weight concerns and adolescent smoking. *Health Psychol* 12:24–32, 1993.

Cobb, S. Social support as a moderator of life stress. *Psychosom Med* 38:300–314, 1976.

Coppotelli, H., and Orleans, C. Partner support and other determinants of smoking cessation maintenance among women. *J Clin Psychol* 53:455–460, 1985.

Curry, S. G., and Marlatt, G. A. Unaided quitters' strategies for coping with temptations to smoke. In Shiffman, S., and Wills, T. A., eds. *Coping and Substance Use.* New York: Academic Press, 1985, 243–265.

Delarue, N. C. A study in smoking withdrawal. The Toronto Smoking Withdrawal Study Centre: description of activities. *Can J Public Health Smoking and Health Suppl.* 64:S5–S19, 1973.

Emont, S. L., and Cummings, K. M. Weight gain following smoking cessation: A possible role for nicotine replacement in weight management. *Addict Behav* 12:151–155, 1987.

Ernster, V. L. Mixed messages for women—a social history of cigarette smoking and advertising. *NY State J Med* 85:335–340, 1985.

Escobedo, L. B., and Remington, P. L. Birth cohort analysis of prevalence of cigarette smoking among Hispanics in the United States. *JAMA* 261:66–69, 1989.

Fagerström, K. O. Reducing the weight gain after stopping smoking. *Addict Behav* 12:91–93, 1987.

Fiore, M. C., Novotny, T. E., Pierce, J. P., Hatziandreu, E. J., Patel, K. M., Davis, R. M. Trends in cigarette smoking in the United States—the changing influence of gender and race. *JAMA* 261:49–55, 1989.

Folkman, S., and Lazarus, R. S. An analysis of coping in a middle-aged community sample. *J Health Soc Behav* 21:219–239, 1980.

Glass, R. M. Blue mood, blackened lungs: Depression and smoking. *JAMA* 264:1583–1584, 1990.

Grinstead, O. A. Preventing weight gain following smoking cessation: A comparison of behavioral treatment approaches. Dissertation, University of California, Los Angeles, 1981.

Gross, J. Stitzer, M. L., Maldonado, J. Nicotine replacement: Effects on post-cessation weight gain. *J Consult Clin Psychol* 57:87–92, 1989.

Guilford, J. Group treatment versus individual initiative in the cessation of smoking. *J Appl Psychol* 56:162–167, 1972.

Hall, S. M. Weight gain prevention after smoking cessation: A cautionary note. Paper presented at National Heart, Lung and Blood Institute Smoking and Body Weight Conference, Memphis, TN, 1990.

Hall, S. M., Ginsberg, D., Jones, J. T. Smoking cessation and weight gain. *J Consult Clin Psychol* 54:342–346, 1986.

Hall, S. M., McGee, R., Tunstall, C., Duffy, J., Benowitz, N. Changes in food intake and activity after quitting smoking. *J Consult Clin Psychol* 57:81–86, 1989.

Hobfall, S. E. The ecology of stress and social support among women. In Hobfoll, S. E., ed. *Stress, Social Support, and Women.* Washington, D.C.: Hemisphere Publishing Corporation, 1986, 3–14.

Klesges, R. C., Eck, L. H., Clark, E., Meyers, A. W., Hanson, C. L. The effects of smoking cessation and gender on dietary intake, physical activity, and weight gain. *Inter J Eating Dis* 9:435–445, 1990.

Klesges, R. C., Meyers, A. W., Winders, S. E., French, S. N. Determining the reasons for weight gain following smoking cessation: Current findings, methodological issues, and future directions for research. *Ann Behav Med* 11:134–143, 1989.

Kottke, T. E., Battista, R. N., DeFriese, G. H., Brekke, M. L. Attributes of successful smoking cessation interventions in medical practice. *JAMA* 259:2883–2889, 1988.

Mermelstein, R. J. Preventing weight gain following smoking cessation. Paper presented at the Society of Behavioral Medicine Eighth Annual Scientific Session, Washington, D. C., 1987.

Mermelstein, R. J., Lichtenstein, E., McIntyre, K. O. Partner support and relapse in smoking cessation programs. *J Consult Clin Psychol* 51:465–466, 1983.

Ockene, J. K., Benfari, R. C., Nuttall, R. L., Hurwitz, I., Ockene, I. S. Relationship of psychosocial factors to smoking behavior change in an intervention program. *Prev Med* 11:13–28, 1982.

Orleans, C. T. Reaching and supporting women quitters: overcoming the obstacles to smoking cessation. Paper presented at the annual meeting of the Association for the Advancement of Behavior Therapy, Chicago, IL, 1986.

Orleans, C. T., Strecher, V. J., Schoenbach, V. J., Salmon, M. A., Blackmon, C. Smoking cessation initiatives for Black Americans: Recommendations for research and intervention. *Health Educ Res* 4:13–25, 1989.

Pearlin, L. I., Schooler, C. The structure of coping. *J Health Soc Behav* 19:2–21, 1978.

Pierce, J. P., Fiore, M. C. Novotny, T. E., Hatziandreu, E. J., Davis, R. M. Trends in cigarette smoking in the United States—educational differences are increasing. *JAMA* 261:56–60, 1989a.

————. Trends in cigarette smoking in the United States—projections to the year 2000. *JAMA* 261:56–60, 1989b.

Pirie, P. Effect of nicotine gum on postcessation weight gain in a randomized intervention study. Paper presented at National Heart, Lung and Blood Institute Smoking and Body Weight Conference, Memphis, TN, 1990.

Rodin, J. Weight change following smoking cessation: The role of food intake and exercise. *Addict Behav* 12:303–317, 1987.

Rosenberg, L., Palmer, J. R., Shapiro, S. Decline in the risk of myocardial infarction among women who stop smoking. *New Eng J Med* 322(4):213–217, 1990.

Schwartz, J. D., and Dubitsky, M. One-year follow-up results of a smoking cessation program. *Can J Public Health* 59:161–165, 1968.

Shiffman, S. Relapse following smoking cessation: A situational analysis. *J Consult Clin Psychol* 50:71–86, 1982.

————. Coping with temptations to smoke. *J Consult Clin Psychol* 52:261–267, 1984.

Solomon, L. J., Rothblum, E. D. Stress, coping and social support in women. *Behav Ther* 9:199–204, 1986.

Sorensen, G., and Pechacek, T. F. Attitudes toward smoking cessation among men and women. *J Behav Med* 10:129–137, 1987.

Stone, A. A. and Neale, J. M. New measure of daily coping: Development and preliminary results. *J Pers Soc Psychol* 46:892–906, 1984.

Streater, J. A., Sargent, R. G., Ward, D. S. A Study of factors associated with weight change in women who attempt smoking cessation. *Addict Behav* 14:523–530, 1989.

U.S. Department of Health and Human Services (USDHHS). *The Health Consequences of Smoking for Women. A Report of the Surgeon General.* U.S. Department of Health and Human Services, Public Health Service, Office of the Assistant Secretary for Health, Office on Smoking and Health, 1980.

————. *The Health Consequences of Smoking. Cancer and Chronic Lung Disease in the Workplace. A Report of the Surgeon General.* U.S. Department of Health and Human Services, Public Health Service, Office on Smoking and Health. DHHS Publication No. (PHS) 85-50207, 1985.

————. *Reducing the Health Consequences of Smoking: 25 Years of Progress. A Report of the Surgeon General* U.S. Department of Health and Human Services, Public Health Service, Centers for Disease Control, Office on Smoking and Health. DHHS Publication No. (CDC) 89-8411, 1989.

————. *The Health Benefits of Smoking Cessation. A Report of the Surgeon General.* U.S. Department of Health and Human Services, Public Health Service, Centers for Disease Control, Office on Smoking and Health. DHHS Publication No. (CDC) 90-8416, 1990.

Warnecke, R. B., Rosenthal, S., Graham, S., Manfredi, C. Social and psychological correlates of smoking behavior among black women. *J Health Soc Behav* 19:397–410, 1978.

West, D. W., Graham, S., Swanson, M., Wilkinson, G. Five year follow-up of a smoking withdrawal clinic population. *Am J Public Health* 67:536–544, 1977.

Whelan, E. M. *A Smoking Gun—How the Tobacco Industry Gets Away With Murder.* Philadelphia: Stickley, 1984.

Worden, J. K., Flynn, B. S., Geller, B. M., Chen, M., Shelton, L. G., Secker-Walker, R. S., Solomon, D. S., Solomon, L. J., Couchey, S., Costanza, M. Development of a smoking prevention mass media program using diagnostic and formative research. *Prev Med* 17:551–558, 1988.

18

Nicotine Dependence Among Blacks and Hispanics

AMELIE G. RAMIREZ and KIPLING J. GALLION

Increasingly, minority populations are edging ahead of their white counterparts in prevalence of adult tobacco use and overall risk of tobacco-related disease. Improved smoking cessation and prevention programs aimed at the dominant segments of United States society need to be made more accessible, relevant, and appealing to these minority populations at risk (Cooper and Simmons 1985; Glynn, Boyd, Gruman 1990; Orleans et al. 1989, 1993).

African Americans are currently the largest minority, representing 12% of the U.S. population. At 9%, or 24 million, Hispanics are the second largest population and growing at a rate that should see their number triple in 30 years (U.S. Department of Commerce, Bureau of Census 1993). African Americans include a wide diversity of socioeconomic and cultural subgroups. There is also great heterogeneity among Hispanic populations in the United States, based on country of origin (see Table 18–1). For this reason, researchers and clinicians face special challenges in designing programs and materials with wide appeal and relevance. While this chapter seeks to identify the distinctive smoking patterns, quitting motivations, and quitting barriers of black and Hispanic Americans, it does not assume that minority populations are homogeneous.

Both blacks and Hispanics suffer from long-standing disparities in knowledge of smoking health risks and access to health care when compared to the white majority (Andersen, Giachello, Aday 1986; Blendon et al. 1989). A discriminatory job market, educational inequalities, residential isolation, and persistent prejudices have created oppressed minority populations. Smoking prevention and treatment programs must address this reality.

SMOKING PREVALENCE AND TOBACCO-RELATED DISEASES IN BLACKS AND HISPANICS

The reduction of cigarette smoking would be one of the most crucial and effective means of decreasing the disparities in health status between majority and minority Americans. After several decades of public education concerning the dangerous consequences of smoking, whites have begun to show significant declines in their rate of smoking. While overall trends are similar for blacks, studies reveal they are still less likely to quit than whites (Novotny et al. 1988). Among Hispanics, however, recent analysis of Hispanic Health and Nutrition Examination Survey

Table 18–1 Origin of Hispanic Population in U.S.

	Millions	% of all U.S. Hispanics
Mexico	12.1	62.3
Puerto Rico	2.5	12.7
Central and South America	2.2	11.5
Cuba	1.0	5.2
Other	1.6	8.1
Total	19.4	99.8

Source: U.S. Department of Commerce, Bureau of Census 1988.

Table 18-2 Adult Smoking Status (%) by Race/Ethnicity and Sex

	Blacks		NonHispanic Whites		Hispanics	
	Males	Females	Males	Females	Males	Females
Current smokers	35.5	24.5	27.5	24.6	25.2	15.5
Former smokers	18.5	11.7	32.5	21.4	21.6	12.5
Never-smokers	46.0	63.8	39.9	54.2	53.3	72.0

Source: Estimates from 1991 NHIS, adults 18+ years of age (Giovino, 1993).

(HHANES)[1] data still the most complete recent survey data examining smoking rates among U.S. Hispanic populations, indicate an upward surge in smoking prevalence for both males and females (Haynes et al. 1990). Compounding these findings is mounting evidence of underreporting of cigarette consumption by significant portions of this population (Perez-Stable et al. 1990).

Nonminority whites once had the highest rates of smoking, but this is no longer so. The 1991 National Health Interview Survey (NHIS) showed that 35.5% of black males and 24.5% of black females over 18 years of age smoked, compared to 27.5% of non-Hispanic white males and 24.6% of non-Hispanic white females (Giovino 1993) (Table 18-2). Rates of frequent smoking (smoking on 20 of the past 30 days) are currently lower among black high school students (3.1%) than among their Hispanic (6.8%) of white counterparts (15.4%) (CDC 1992), but adult prevalence remains higher, perhaps because African American teens who smoke are under-represented in high school samples, and perhaps because African American youth are protected from smoking onset by cultural factors that remain in operation until their transition to

the adult workforce. NHIS data have long shown lower daily smoking rates for black men and women than for nonHispanic whites (Table 18-2).

Adult smoking prevalence among Hispanics also is increasing. The 1991 NHIS showed smoking rates of 25.2% for adult Hispanic males and 15.5% for adult Hispanic females (Giovino, 1993) (Table 18-2). The latest analysis of HHANES data, based on a larger and more representative samples of Hispanic adults with varied national origins (e.g., Central and South America, Cuba, Mexico, Puerto Rico) indicates a *higher* smoking prevalence among Hispanic men than nonHispanic white men (Haynes et al. 1990) (Table 18-3). While NHIS data have shown that Hispanic males and females smoke fewer cigarettes per day than non-Hispanic whites (Table 18-4) (e.g., Giovino 1993; Marcus and Crane 1987), the latest trends reported in HHANES run contrary to this conclusion (Table 18-5).

Rates of smoking-related disease are also on the increase for minorities. Fifty-five percent of all deaths among blacks are caused by the major smoking-related diseases: lung cancer, chronic obstructive pulmonary disease, emphysema, and coronary heart disease (NCHS 1987). Rates of lung cancer,

[1]The Hispanic Health and Nutrition Examination Survey (HHANES) surveyed Mexican-Americans throughout the Southwest United States, Cuban Americans from Dade County, Florida, and Puerto Ricans from the New York City area. The results reported here are adjusted to reflect those values that might occur if the entire Hispanic population had been studied. These figures have been extracted from Haynes et al. (1990). It should be noted both English and Spanish instruments were used and interviews were bilingual. Only Mexican-American, Puerto Rican, and Cuban Hispanics participated. Included in the interview was a free 3-hour medical examination performed in specially designed mobile examination centers situated within Hispanic communities. The age range was 20–74 years.

Table 18-3 Comparison of Current Smoking Prevalence (%) Rates Among Whites, Blacks, and Hispanics

Ages 25–74 yrs.	Males	Females
Hispanics	17.7–57.7	9.7–41.1
Whites	21.2–37.1	17.8–32.9
Blacks	31.0–47.4	18.6–40.2

Source: Hispanic Health and Nutrition Examination Survey (HHANES) (Haynes et al. 1990).

Ranges are used, as rates were weighted in original analyses, to approximate the entire Hispanic population.

Table 18–4 Cigarettes Smoked Per Day by Race and Sex

Cigarettes/Day	Blacks		NonHispanic Whites		Hispanics	
	Males (%)	Females (%)	Males (%)	Females (%)	Males (%)	Females (%)
≤ 10	52.8	62.1	21.8	32.3	61.2	66.3
11–20	35.6	31.5	45.7	49.2	32.1	29.4
21–30	7.9	3.7	17.1	11.5	4.0	1.6
31+	3.7	2.7	15.4	7.1	2.7	2.7

Source: Estimates from 1991 National Health Interview Survey (NHIS), adults 18+ years of age (Giovino 1993).

first recognized in the 1930s as increasing among blacks, have risen dramatically since 1950. Compared to whites, blacks have higher rates of several tobacco-related illnesses, including cancer, cardiovascular disease, and infant mortality. Heart disease rates among black males are 20% higher, and lung cancer is 58% more prevalent than among white males (*MMWR* 1987; TUAC 1989). Blacks experience a 45% higher mortality for lung cancer than whites (USDHHS 1989). Black females experience 50% more heart disease, and higher rates of infant mortality and low birth weight than whites (*MMWR* 1987).

Although in the past, Hispanics have experienced lower cancer rates than the total population, increases in prevalence of smoking-related diseases are evident and expected to rise as smoking prevalence increases. A survey in New Mexico (Pathak et al. 1986) revealed lung cancer rates had tripled from 1958 to 1982 for Hispanic males, yet only doubled for white males. Further analysis found that chronic obstructive pulmonary disease increased sixfold for Hispanic males compared to a fourfold increase for white

Table 18–5 Cigarettes Smoked Per Day (by Gender and Sub-Hispanic Ethnicity)

Men Who Smoke	<10	10–19	20+
Mexican-American	41%	25%	34%
Puerto Rican	21%	27%	52%
Cuban-American	17%	19%	64%
Range	17–41%	19–25%	34–64%

Women Who Smoke	<10	10–19	20+
Mexican-American	27%	29%	19%
Puerto Rican	33%	33%	35%
Cuban-American	33%	18%	49%
Range	27–33%	18–29%	19–49%

Source: Hispanic Health and Nutrition Examination Survey (HHANES) (Haynes et al. 1990).

males. Other smoking-related cancers (head, neck, and bladder) are expected to increase among Hispanic Americans. The same New Mexico study found esophageal cancer rates 20% higher among Hispanic females than among nonminority white females (Pathak et al. 1986).

SMOKING PATTERNS

Prior to the latest HHANES data, the number of cigarettes smoked per day was thought to be lower for Hispanics and blacks than for white smokers (Marcus and Crane 1987; USDHHS 1986). Even 1991 NHIS data (Table 18–4) showed 32.5% of nonHispanic white male smokers reported smoking 21 or more cigarettes a day, compared to only 11.6% of black men and 6.7% of Hispanic men. Among females, 6.4% of black and 4.3% of Hispanic women smoked at this rate, while 18.6% of nonHispanic white women did so (Giovino 1993).

Analysis of latest HHANES data (Table 18–5) show startling increases in daily level of cigarette consumption by Hispanic men and women. Some underreporting is suspected in the HHANES data, which employed cotinine levels to validate self-reported cigarette consumption. Cotinine is a metabolite of nicotine and considered a good indicator of exposure to tobacco. The study revealed that one in five reportedly light smokers were indeed heavy smokers. Compared to the 1985 NHIS data, HHANES reveals that among Hispanic male smokers 34% of Mexican-Americans, 52% of Puerto Ricans, and 64% of Cuban Americans consume 20 or more cigarettes daily. For Hispanic women the numbers are 19, 35, and 49%, respectively. Both groups show decreases in the less than 10 cigarette categories.

The lower rate of cigarette consumption among blacks is offset by a predilection for high tar/nicotine (greater than 1.0 mg nicotine/cigarette), mentholated cigarettes. Seventy-six percent of all black smokers smoke menthol brands. Newport, Salem, and Kool represent 60% of all cigarettes purchased by blacks (Cummings, Giovino, Mendicino 1987). Cummings, Giovino, and Mendicino (1987) report that blacks are twice as likely to smoke menthol cigarettes as whites. The preference for high nicotine menthol cigarettes may lead to greater dependency on nicotine among black smokers and potentially to more difficulty in severing addiction (Orleans et al. 1989). Royce et al. (1993) found that compared with whites, African Americans who smoked less than 25 cigarettes per day were 1.6 times more likely to smoke within 10 minutes of awakening, a reliable index of high physical nicotine dependency. The inclusion of chemical additives, which produce the cigarette's menthol flavor and serve to anesthetize the throat and lungs, may encourage deeper and more frequent inhalation of the cigarette, thereby intensifying smoking health risks (Orleans et al. 1989; Novotny et al. 1988). Menthol-related carcinogenic compounds, such as benzo[a]pyrenes, also may raise cancer risks (Sidney, Tekawa, Friedman 1989).

A recent clinical study (Wagenknecht et al. 1990) of black smokers examined cotinine levels. After thorough controls, researchers still found higher levels of cotinine in blacks than in white smokers, suggesting differences in nicotine metabolism and cotinine excretion which may help to explain the lower quit rates and higher cancer rates of black smokers.

Based on HHANES data, Hispanics smoke more cigarettes per day than blacks or whites. They tend to smoke more on weekends, during social activities, and less when by themselves (McGraw et al., in press; Castro et al. 1989). Hispanics are characterized as very brand loyal. Brands of choice among Mexican American males are Marlboro (males 47%, females 30%) and Winston (males and females 20% each). Tobacco company promotional campaigns for two new brands of cigarettes, Dorado and Rio, are aimed exclusively at the Hispanic. Established brands such as Camel are also attempting to increase their market share (TUAC 1989) through a vigorous Hispanic-targeted print and outdoor advertising campaign featuring "a smooth talking camel" *(un tipo suave)* posing in masculine attire with an attractive woman in the background (TUAC 1989).

DETERMINANTS OF SMOKING

Sociodemographic Factors and Reduced Access to Smoking Health Risk Information and Medical Care

Sociodemographic factors associated with smoking among blacks are similar to those for the U.S. population as a whole—lower income, education level and occupational status, higher unemployment, being male and being single (Marcus and Crane 1987; Orleans et al. 1987). Novotny and colleagues (1988) suggest that when sociodemographic conditions are controlled, blacks are no more likely than whites to be smokers. On the other hand, even with these factors controlled, blacks are less likely to quit smoking.

Likewise, the demographic factors associated with smoking status are similar for Hispanic populations (Haynes et al. 1990). But, in addition, smoking status among Hispanics varies with ethnic subgroup and level of acculturation, defined as the degree of social integration of a subordinate culture or tradition into the dominant social order. Puerto Ricans, Mexican Americans, Cubans and Central and South Americans have different smoking prevalences which may be due in part to their different levels of acculturation. For instance, the cultural protectors which help Hispanic groups to resist pressures to smoke (and drink) are weakened as the degree of acculturation increases (Markides et al. 1988). Paradoxically, the weakening of strong ethnic cultural traditions restricting smoking by women could account for the later-in-life smoking initiation recently observed among Hispanic women in the United States (McGraw et al. 1989). Reviewing HHANES data, Scribner and Dwyer (1989) found that measures of increased acculturation also were associated with a smoking-related rise in prevalence of low birth weight babies among mothers of Mexican descent. Another effect of acculturation within the Puerto Rican community may have been to lower the age of experimentation with tobacco (McGraw et al. 1990). Researchers hypothesize that as Hispanics continue to acculturate, higher rates of smoking and smoking-related disease may follow (Sorlie et al. 1982).

The possible effects of acculturation just mentioned are tempered with recent HHANES data (Haynes et al. 1990) that looked only at Mexican Americans. It found that when education and income levels were controlled (two items unrelated to acculturation), the association between acculturation and smoking for women was low. For Mexican-American men there was no significant correlation (Haynes et al. 1990). Further, when the three dominant Hispanic subgroups are combined, the HHANES data reveals an inverse relationship between socioeconomic status and smoking prevalence for both men and women.

The 1985 Cancer Prevention Awareness Survey (U.S. Dept. of Commerce, Bureau of the Census 1986) found that blacks are less likely to have received information about cancer prevention and less likely to associate tobacco use with cancer risk. Moreover, blacks are less likely than whites to report a physician's office as their usual source of health care (54 vs. 70%), and rely more on public health clinics and emergency rooms, which cannot provide preventive health care as effectively (USDHHS 1985). Ramirez and Fletcher (1987) report that Hispanics also show a significant lack of knowledge about health issues and an underestimation of the value of early detection for disease risk reduction. Likewise, Hispanics tend less to seek advice from physicians. This may be attributed to cultural barriers, greater use of public clinic settings, the lack of funds or insurance for personal physician care, and so on. Still, both ethnic groups rank the information provided by a physician as having a strong influence on their health-related behaviors (Orleans et al. 1989; Wittenberg 1983).

Targeted Tobacco Marketing

Extensive tobacco marketing campaigns targeting minorities create formidable barriers to cessation and prevention efforts (Blum 1989; Cooper and Simmons 1985; Cummings, Giovino, Mendicino 1987; Davis 1987; Robinson, Barry, Block et al. 1992). It is clear that the tobacco industry has set its sights on both the Hispanic and black populations as two consumer groups crucial to its future commercial survival. Social pressures and regulatory legislation have restrained some marketing activities, but advertising tobacco products to minorities is still big business. Adept advertising campaigns target minorities via important channels for blue-collar workers (i.e., transit shelters, blue-collar magazines such as *Popular Mechanics,* sports publications, and the urban and inner-city landscapes) where the highest percentage of minority smokers live and work. And tobacco products are heavily promoted to blacks and Hispanics in ethnic publications, during ethnic cultural and sporting events, and through a host of organizations that accept sponsorship from the tobacco industry (Blum 1989).

Many Hispanic and black publications depend heavily on hefty advertising budgets from cigarette and alcohol companies. In 1987, Philip Morris was ranked first in American magazine advertising, fifth in newspaper advertising, and as one of the top five billboard advertisers (with all of the five top advertisers being cigarette companies). R.J. Reynolds was fourth and third, respectively, in magazine advertisements and also a top billboard advertiser. The year 1989 saw Philip Morris in second place among the top 50 Hispanic market advertisers, spending $8.6 million.

Black magazines (e.g., *Ebony, Jet,* and *Essence*) rely heavily on tobacco advertising with the brands Kool, Winston, More, Salem, Newport, and Virginia Slims receiving the most exposure (Cummings, Giovino, Mendicino 1987; TUAC 1989). For instance, *Essence,* the "magazine for today's Black woman," garners 12% of its annual advertising revenue from cigarette advertisements. Magazines are also a source of coupons redeemable for free or discounted cigarettes (TUAC 1989).

Magazines that depend on cigarette ad revenues are reluctant to include articles which specifically delineate the risks of cigarette smoking to health. The two major black periodicals, *Essence* and *Ebony,* have avoided publishing critical articles on explicit effects of tobacco. As advertising of cigarettes increases in a magazine, the number of instances where smoking is criticized decreases (Williams 1986).

Major sporting, cultural, and other events have found sponsorship through tobacco companies (Blum 1990; TUAC 1989). Since 1981, Philip Morris has published annually "A Guide to Black Organizations" that is filled with cigarette advertising featuring black models and widely distributed to black politicians and other black leaders (TUAC 1989). Ironically, educational institutions are benefactors of tobacco promotion, too. Educational funding for the United Negro College Fund, which in turn provides support to 43% of the predominantly black colleges in the United States, receives substantial contributions from tobacco companies. *Ebony* has featured an annual nationally touring "More" Fashion Show, underwritten by R.J. Reynolds for more than 29 years, which has raised $23 million for charity. The fashion circuit, which features models who are smoking, makes well over a hundred stops across the nation and internationally. Funds are distributed to educational, religious, and community organizations along the travel schedule of the fashion show.

Outdoor Media Campaigns

Perhaps the most insidious tobacco advertising campaigns are waged on the streets of minority neighborhoods in the form of billboards. In 1985, cigarette advertising accounted for $945 million, or 22.3%, of total outdoor media expenses (TUAC 1989). This powerful form of advertising is used in low-income neighborhoods, where signs are nearer to eye level, more numerous, in a variety of sizes, and appear literally everywhere within the community (Coalition for Scenic Beauty 1988).

In 1985, cigarette advertisements accounted for 14.6% of all transit shelter advertisements and 50% ($7.8 million) of all "eight sheet" (5 × 11 ft) billboard content (Davis 1987). Smaller and closer to street level, such advertising format is widely used in minority and inner-city neighborhoods. Advertisements associate smoking with glamour, sexuality, independence, and escape—themes to which those of lower socioeconomic status and those with lower self-esteem may be especially susceptible (TUAC 1989).

Thirty-five percent of all spending for urban billboards is in black neighborhoods (Davis 1987). A street survey in St. Louis found three times as many billboards in black neighborhoods than in white neighborhoods. Sixty-two percent of all billboards featured tobacco advertising compared to only 36% in predominately white neighborhoods. Other surveys yield similar results (McMahon 1988). Billboard advertisements often include older adults and blacks of lighter complexion, and portray a higher socioeconomic status life-style than the neighborhood in which the advertising is located. Slogans imply success, pleasure and increased liveliness, vitality, and sexual attractiveness (Blum 1989).

The Rise of Hispanic Consumers

The 1980s have seen the emergence of a multibillion dollar Hispanic market. Increased attention from the advertising industry has not excluded purveyors of tobacco products. A *Business Week* article suggests that advertising executives consider the Hispanic market naive and easily swayed: "These people haven't been Ralph Naderized" (Engardio 1988, p. 100). As with the Black print media, Hispanic magazine tobacco advertising revenues support many fledgling Hispanic-targeted publications.

The Specific Vulnerability of Youth to Targeted Advertising

Among adolescents smoking often is interpreted as a rite of passage to adulthood (McGraw, in press; Sussman 1989). Advertisements promoting freedom, new opportunity, and the glamour of early adulthood would seem to mirror these precocious expectations. Likewise, as peer groups grow developmentally in importance, the likelihood of tobacco use by youth increases. The effects of peer and family modeling are similar for Hispanics to those found within other ethnic groups in the United States (Dusenbury et al. 1992). However, minority youth seeking to identify with the mainstream culture are likely to be especially vulnerable to ethnic-targeted advertising.

Cigarette companies must target youth to replenish those tobacco consumers who have quit or died (Tuckson 1989). Minority youth are less equipped than whites to resist advertising because of their lower education, more limited knowledge of health risks, greater life stress, and reduced access to anti-cigarette advertising and health promotion programs.

QUITTING MOTIVATIONS

Determinants of quitting among blacks and Hispanics are not unlike those observed within the general population. Most smokers want to quit, and many have tried (McAlister et al. 1989).

Among black smokers and ex-smokers, the health risks of smoking are fairly widely recognized, yet may not always be the prime motivators of cessation—perhaps because of blacks' relatively restricted health care access. Affective issues, such as the changing image of the smoker in society and growing constraints on smoking habits, are increasingly common quitting motives. In four focus groups for black smokers in Philadelphia (n = 44 participants), the social costs of smoking (e.g., "smoking reduces a smoker's circle of friends"), concerns to set a good example for one's children, increasing restrictions on where one can smoke, the rising cost of tobacco products, and factors related to personal appearance (e.g., breath odor, burns in clothes, negative sex appeal) were the most frequently cited motivations for quitting (American Lung Association 1990). Other factors related to quitting motivation among black smokers include the expectation of health and psychosocial benefits, number of sources of support for, and communication about, smoking health risks and

quitting benefits, and medical advice to quit (Orleans et al. 1989; Royce et al. 1993).

New data show, in fact, a stronger desire to quit and greater readiness to do so among African American than white smokers. Royce et al. (1993) analyzed baseline data from eight U.S. Community Intervention Trial for Smoking Cessation (COMMT) sites, comparing white and African American respondents (see Chapter 21). Compared with whites, African Americans reported a stronger desire to quit smoking, were more in favor of tobacco restrictions, and were more likely to view smoking as a serious public health problem in their community. Pierce et al. (1992) found African American smokers in California more likely to be in contemplation and action stages of smoking cessation than whites, and to agree that smoking was harming their health.

Hispanics, like blacks, cite personal information about smoking risks, personal medical advice to quit, self-motivation, past efforts to quit or cut back, degree of tobacco dependence, and primary group social supports for quitting and nonsmoking as important factors in the decision to initiate a quit attempt.

QUITTING BARRIERS

Socioeconomic status and occupational stress have been negatively associated with smoking status in blacks (Feigelman and Gorman 1989). However, a recent secondary analysis of the NHIS for persons aged 25–64 years found that blacks were less likely than whites to quit smoking regardless of socioeconomic status or demographic factors (Novotny et al. 1988).

Similar to other studies (Hoffman et al. 1989), a recent survey of black life insurance policyholders (Orleans et al. 1989) who were current smokers reported an average of 3.8 quit attempts. Most smokers showed a strong desire to quit, but few reported any past experience with formal treatment programs. Quitting barriers included low income, employment status, limited access to health care, weaker social support to quit, and stronger environmental influences to relapse once quit. The study concluded that blacks would benefit from targeted health education emphasizing the benefits of quitting and the harms of tobacco use. Data from the 1990 California survey showed that African American smokers, especially men, were more likely to quit smoking, but had very low short-term success rates (Pierce et al. 1992). Both mass media and interpersonal channels of communication are seen as necessary avenues for information dissemination. Since effective information on quitting smoking aimed at minorities still is either minimal (Hoffman et al. 1989) or underutilized by these populations (Manfredi 1992), more ethnoculturally appropriate information and methods of distribution should be part of any health promotion effort targeting minorities.

Stress related to employment status and family relationships has been found to have a greater impact on smoking prevalence than race (Feigelman and Gorman 1989). Similarly, a study of family roles and smoking (Waldron and Lye 1989b) found that those who were separated, divorced, or widowed were less likely to have quit smoking than currently married individuals. Blacks and Hispanics have proportionally higher rates of unemployment, single-parent households, and divorce than do nonminority whites—all important barriers to adopting nonsmoking (Waldron and Lye 1989a).

Intensive marketing aimed at minorities presents an ominous quitting obstacle within black and Hispanic communities. Although the tobacco industry claims that its advertising campaigns aim at reestablishing brand loyalty among current smokers, others correctly see it as perpetuating or increasing cigarette consumption, making smoking acceptable, recruiting new smokers, and inducing former smokers to relapse, making quitting even harder while acting as a cue to smoke (Blum 1989; TUAC 1989). Lack of counteradvertising on billboards, lack of critical health articles in minority-based populations, low or limited volume of antismoking and smoking cessation information, and a shortage of skill development programs aimed exclusively at blacks and Hispanics represent unique barriers facing minority smokers in the United States.

Marketing low tar and special filter cigarettes as somehow "safer" is misleading and may further contribute to misconceptions about the magnitude of health risk associated with smoking. Brands that are discounted and generic products appeal particularly to low-income smokers. Price-sensitive consumers, especially teenagers, also are likely to be especially influenced by this pricing strategy (Davis 1987). Cigarette producers are beginning to increase cigarette pack size from 20 to 25 as a marketing ploy. Minorities who typically smoke at a lower rate may increase their intake if increased availability leads to increased consumption (Davis 1987; Gloede 1986).

The U.S. military, whose enlisted ranks are disproportionately black and Hispanic, has one of the highest rates of smoking of any U.S. institution or organization. Military publications feature extensive tobacco advertising aimed exclusively at the military life-style. In 1985, 47% of military servicemen used tobacco (USDD 1986), although the armed forces are now attempting to reduce this health risk.

Defending targeted advertising as a civil rights issue is another insidious tactic which tobacco manufacturers and their supporters have employed. While the logic of such arguments is shallow, the stirring of racial overtones may quell antismoking sentiments. For instance, antismoking ordinances have been opposed by claims that a "paternalistic" majority of white health professionals are attempting to prevent minority populations from pursuing their rights of brand preference and health life-style choice (Williams 1986). Similar sentiments came to the surface recently in New York City in response to a smoking ordinance prohibiting workers from smoking in open work areas, yet permitting those in separately enclosed offices to smoke. Since white male executives occupy most of the enclosed offices, this was interpreted as discriminatory. Members of the National Association for the Advancement of Colored People and the National Black Police Association rallied behind this issue (Milligan 1987). However, since the successful 1990 protest in Philadelphia's African American community and by the Department of Health and Human Service Secretary Dr. Louis Sullivan led R. J. Reynolds to cancel its plans to market Uptown cigarettes explicitly to black smokers, tobacco company tactics may shift—and become more subtle. The Uptown Coalition, for instance, pointed out that it was the *tobacco companies* who were being "paternalistic" by forcing two to three times as many tobacco billboards into black and Hispanic urban neighborhoods as into non-minority communities, leaving residents no choice but to be subjected to these messages.

Reducing the barriers to quitting smoking and preventing smoking onset will require attention to these and other issues. Pro-smoking social pressure and advertising should be countered with messages sensitive to ethnic and cultural variations, and with laws and ordinances that regulate the activities of the tobacco industry.

SMOKING CONTROL INTERVENTIONS

A variety of tobacco cessation programs are available to the public, yet few are well tailored to the groups at highest risk. Impediments to successful prevention efforts include a lack of research, funding, and cultural sensitivity to the unique traditions and life-styles that characterize these minority groups. As mentioned earlier, assuming homogeneity within ethnic groups may lead to weak intervention strategies. Recognizing and appealing to distinct market segments within black communities, and paying close attention to subtle differences in language and imagery associated with the subethnic Hispanic audiences is crucial for effective communications. Captivating these audiences with appropriate communications must be one of the first goals of any smoking intervention program policy. Several ongoing research projects may provide insights, models, and materials to guide interventions for the African-American community.

Smoking Control Interventions for Blacks

Supported by funding from the National Cancer Institute, researchers in Los Angeles and Chicago are targeting about 8,000 inner-city black smokers with physician advice, quit smoking materials, clinics, and other quit smoking treatment aids. Under study is the efficacy of these techniques among low-income African-American smokers, and the community's ability to respond and support such a campaign.

Another Chicago study (Manfredi et al. 1992) is evaluating the effectiveness of locally televised quit smoking programming and similar complementary quitting support offered through public housing projects. Support group leadership is provided by nonsmoking women who reside in the same area of public housing and who receive some training beforehand. A similar program in the same city will identify 400 mothers who smoke to join American Lung Association quit smoking sessions.

A media and community intervention program has been implemented in Richmond, California. Community leadership groups guided and supported networks of volunteers, who then provided lay counseling and program promotion. Intensive ethnographic research and analysis prior to the campaign led to the development of cessation training for physicians, community "Quit Nights," culturally sensitive video and print media products (disseminated through churches and community-based organizations), and local quit smoking clinics. This initiative was sponsored by the University of California at Berkeley and the Kaiser Family Foundation Research Institute in Oakland, California.

In North Carolina, a survey administered to black policyholders of the nation's largest black-owned life insurance company (North Carolina Mutual Life Insurance Company, Durham, NC) was the basis for an agent-mediated self-quitting program (Orleans et al. 1989). Current smokers exhibited a strong desire to quit and many had made previous attempts. Field agents acted as mediators providing quit smoking material and aids to policyholders who smoked. The insurance company also offered access to trained quit smoking counselors via toll-free telephone "quit lines." A *Quit for Life Guide* was developed as a companion to the American Lung Association's new *Freedom From Smoking for You and Your Family* guide. The *Quit for Life* supplement features black models, uses clear language (sixth-grade reading level), and offers tip sheets (with magnets) to be posted as reminders at home or work. Research evaluating quit rates and quitting methods is still underway.

The American Cancer Society (ACS) recently launched a series of community demonstration projects in eight ACS units across the country disseminating a new African American-focused quit smoking guide. *Pathways to Freedom* (Robinson, Orleans, James, Sutton 1992) during the November 1992 Great American Smokeout. Almost 20,000 guides were disseminated through this inititiative, relying primarily on grassroots efforts in community-based organizations and clinics. Process evaluation results indicated very favorable reactions to a guide targeted specifically at African American smokers (Orleans et al. 1993). Six-month follow-up telephone interviews with over 300 African American smokers will provide an in-depth evaluation of the guide and document self-reported quit rates.

Another intervention entitled "Know Your Body" is aimed at black primary school children in Washington, D.C., and has been found to have positive effects on smoking knowledge and attitudes. The overall program was designed to increase awareness of cardiovascular disease and its prevention. As a 5-year project still underway, preliminary results indicate that more students recognized that smoking was a serious health risk and caused heart disease.

Special cautions must be taken, however, in evaluating program results with African American smokers when biochemical verification is used. Recent findings from a field study by Wagenknecht and associates (1990) found that black smokers had higher serum cotinine levels than white smokers, suggesting racial differences in the metabolism of nicotine or the excretion of cotinine. Likewise, Henningfield (1990) summarizes findings of higher expired air carbon monoxide levels in lactose-intolerant smokers, and notes that lactose intolerance is more common in persons of African heritage.

Smoking Control Interventions for Hispanics

A few projects have been conducted with preliminary evaluations completed, to develop and test prevention and treatment programs for Hispanics. A key concept in each program has been to test the responsiveness of the community and the effectiveness of community efforts to quit smoking programming.

The "Healthy Mothers, Healthy Babies" campaign was primarily aimed at Hispanic mothers to assess health-seeking habits related to maternal and prenatal care. The results of focus groups indicated that both ethnic groups rated physicians as the most influential sources of health information, with family and friends next. The research also revealed that many women thought that smoking during pregnancy had no effect on the child (Wittenberg 1983).

"Programa A Su Salud" targeted low-income Hispanic households in a campaign utilizing mass media and community participation to encourage and support the reduction of four major health risk factors—one of which was smoking. The format for all media presentations, derived from social learning theory, featured positive role models from the immediate community. Over 500 different role models appeared in television, radio, and newspaper stories. This 5-year program was bilingual and most of the campaign themes and identifying imagery were derived through focus groups comprised of community members. In Eagle Pass, Texas, which possesses one of the lowest per capita incomes of any city in the United States, over 1,000 community volunteers were recruited and involved during the 5-year project period (Ramirez and McAlister 1988). Although there are no programs or printed materials designed for distribution outside the program, sample program materials are available upon request.

The project "Smoking Cessation Intervention in Hispanics" is based in the San Francisco Bay Area, and aims to provide culturally sensitive information on smoking health harms and quitting benefits, and to motivate and assist Hispanic smokers to stop smoking. The project includes a large mass media campaign (television, radio, newspapers, billboards), community quit smoking contests, quit smoking groups, Spanish language self-help guides *(Guia Para Dejar de Fumar),* and community volunteer support networks (Perez-Stable et al. 1991).

Two other projects have looked exclusively at the problems of smoking among

Hispanic adolescents. One has sought to develop a school-based smoking prevention curriculum aimed at Hispanic sixth and seventh graders in New York public and private schools. These groups will be followed for several years with periodic "booster" sessions planned for successive grades (Botvin et al. 1989). A second program, headed by Boston researchers, has targeted Puerto Rican teenagers and their families for intervention and study. Culturally appropriate materials have been integrated into school and community activities (McGraw et al., in press).

Recommendations for Health Education and Treatment Programs

Based on this review, it is evident that more research is needed to evaluate and identify successful black and Hispanic health behavior change programs to prevent or reduce smoking behaviors.

A mass media and small media campaign coordinated with interpersonal communications should disseminate messages sensitive to variations in local culture, community mores, and social value systems. Research also should be directed toward better comprehension of barriers to health-seeking behaviors in ethnic minority groups and subgroups. Countermarketing strategies, whether based on media advocacy or grass roots activism, should be employed whenever possible. Recent efforts by African-American communities helped to prevent the sale and marketing of Uptown brand cigarettes using these strategies.

The design of smoking cessation and prevention initiatives and their driving themes should reflect the input and values of the community. Community representation should include local businesses, local and regional health officials, opinion leaders and lay persons, and should involve active participation by a spectrum of local institutions (churches, schools, civic and fraternal organizations, health care facilities, clubs, etc.). Research would greatly benefit standardized trials, data collection, and reporting methods. The difficulty in comparing the NHIS and HHANES data is but one example of this larger problem.

Tailoring Medical Interventions for African American and Hispanic Smokers

Hispanic smokers greatly value medical advice to quit smoking, especially the advice of physicians. Regrettably, limited access to health care providers is endemic for low-income Hispanics and African Americans. When contact is made, it is often in emergency room and hospital clinic settings where preventive services and continuity of care cannot be provided. Therefore, physicians and other health care personnel should develop interventions that can be used in these locations as well as in traditional primary care settings.

Chief among the messages that health care providers must transmit is that low-rate smoking patterns are unsafe and do not diminish the serious health risk of tobacco consumption. Specific mention also should be made of the particularly dangerous aspects of menthol cigarettes (Sidney et al. 1989). Self-help materials should be an integral part of any intervention effort. Care should be taken to ensure that literacy levels are appropriate for the low-literacy client (e.g., fourth to sixth grade reading levels) and that the text and imagery reflect circumstances similar to those of the intended reader and portray the models with similar traits, culture, and life-style. Benefits and incentives for following the materials must be realistic and attuned to the cultural and community norms of a client. Intervention programs with culturally sensitive materials are now being developed and evaluated, but critical trials measuring the effectiveness of those materials have not been completed. For Hispanic audiences, one good example of a publication which incorporated many of these guidelines in its development is entitled *Guia para Dejar de Fumar* (Sabogal et al. 1988). *Pathways to Freedom* is a similarly well-tailored guide designed for African American smokers (Robinson, Orleans, James, Sutton 1992). Written at the 6th-grade reading level, it incorporates quitting techniques geared to the low-rate menthol smoking patterns common among African American smokers with guidelines for community efforts to combat tobacco advertising and promotion in the black community.

An American Cancer Society study evaluating its efficacy is now underway.

Studies show that most smokers quit on their own, but that minimal counseling can reinforce repeated efforts to quit and enhance maintenance (Glynn, Boyd, Gruman 1990). For those who find self-help materials and minimal counseling insufficient to overcome nicotine dependency, more intensive treatment, such as low-cost clinics, are widely available. Health care providers should include mechanisms for offering long-term support and relapse prevention as well as initial quitting assistance. Pharmacological therapies should be considered for those who are more severely addicted. Nicotine replacement (gum and transdermal patches) can help even the highly addicted *low-rate* smoker. While cost for these pharmacologic aids ($2–$3 per day) can tax low-income family budgets, Medicaid programs in many states include coverage for nicotine replacement.

For African Americans, quitting pro grams should be geared to the predominance of high nicotine/menthol smoking patterns and high levels of nicotine addiction suggested by lower annual quit rates compared to other ethnic groups. Cessation programs might require modifications involving special relapse prevention skills (e.g., to resist social pressures to smoke). For Hispanics, greater sensitivity to intraethnic differences requires scrutiny during all facets of media development and community organizations. More research is needed on acculturation and its effects, if any, across Hispanic subnationalities and geographic locales (Escobedo and Remington 1989; Haynes et al. 1990).

REFERENCES

American Lung Association. *Minority Outreach Institute Research Report.* Philadelphia and Montgomery County: American Lung Association, February 1990.

Andersen, R. M., Giachello, A. L., Aday, L. A. Access of Hispanics to health care and cuts in services: A state of the art overview. *Public Health Rep* 101(3):238–252, 1986.

Blendon, R. J., Aiken, L. H., Freeman, H. E., Corey, C. R. Access to medical care for Black and White Americans: A matter of continuing concern. *JAMA* 261(2):253–257, 1989.

Blum, A. Targeting minority groups by the tobacco industry. In Jones, L. A., ed. *Minorities and Cancer.* New York: Springer-Verlag, 1989, 153–162.

Botvin, G., Batson, H. W., Witts-Vitale, S., Baker, E., Dusenbery, A. A psychosocial approach to smoking prevention for urban youth. *Public Health Rep* 104(6):573–582, 198.

Castro, F. G., Newcomb, M. D., McCreary, C., Baezconde-Garbanati, L. Cigarette smokers do more than just smoke cigarettes. *Health Psychol* 8(1):107–129, 1989.

CDC (Centers for Disease Control). Cigarette smoking among adults—United States, 1991. *Morbidity and Mortality Weekly Report* 42:1–5, 1993.

———. Selected tobacco use behaviors and dietary patterns among high school students—United States, 1991. *Morbidity and Mortality Weekly Report* 41:417–421, 1992.

Coalition for Scenic Beauty. *Fact Sheet: Alcohol and Tobacco Advertising on Billboards.* 218 D Street, S.E., Washington, D.C. 20003. 1988.

Cooper, R., and Simmons, B. Cigarette smoking and ill health among Black Americans. *NY State J Med* 85:344–349, 1985.

Cummings, K. M., Giovino, G., Mendicino, A. J. Cigarette advertising and Black–White differences in brand preference. *Public Health Rep* 102(6):698–701, 1987.

Davis, R. M. Current trends in cigarette advertising and marketing. *N Engl J Med* 316:725–732, 1987.

Dusenbury, L., Kerner, J. F., Baker, E., Botvin, G., James-Ortiz, S., Zauber, A. Predictors of smoking prevalence among New York Latino youth. *Am J Public Health* 82:55–58, 1992.

Engardio, P. Fast times on Avenida Madison. *Business Week* 6 June 1988.

Escobedo, L., and Remington, P. Birth cohort analysis of prevalence of cigarette smoking among Hispanics in the United States. *JAMA* 261(1):66–69, 1989.

Feigelman, W., and Gorman, B. Toward explaining the higher incidence of cigarette smoking among Black Americans. *J Psychoactive Drugs* 21(3):299–305, 1989.

Giovino, G. 1991 NHIS Data by sex and race. Atlanta, GA: U.S. Office on Smoking and Health, 1993.

Gloede, W. F. New menthol cigarette brands battle in Pennsylvania. *Advertising Age* 36:20 January 1986.

Glynn, T. J., Boyd, G. M., Gruman, J. C. Essential elements of self-help/minimal intervention strategies for smoking cessation. *Health Educ Q* 17(3):329–345, 1990.

Haynes, S. G., Harvey, C., Montes, H., Nickens, H., Cohen, B. H. Patterns of cigarette smoking among Hispanics in the United States: Results from HHANES 1982–84. *Am J Public Health* 80:47–53, 1990.

Henningfield, J. Can genetic constitution affect the 'objective' diagnosis of nicotine dependence? *Am J Public Health* 80(9):1040–1041, 1990.

Hoffman, A., Cooper, R., Lacey, L., Mullner, R. Cigarette smoking and attitudes toward quitting among Black patients. *J Natl Med Assoc* 81(4):415–420, 1989.

McAlister, A., Ramirez, A., Galavotti, C., Gallion, K. Anti-smoking campaigns. In Rice, R. E., and Atkins, C., eds. *Public Communication Campaigns.* Newbury Park, CA: Sage, 1989, 291–307.

McGraw, S., Smith, K., Schensul, J., Carrillo, E. 1990 Aspects of socio-cultural environment of Puerto Rican adolescents in Boston associated with smoking behavior. Watertown, MA: New England Research Institute, in press.

McMahon, E. Killer billboards: The visual blight teaches kids to smoke. *Washington Post* 21 February 1988.

Manfredi, C., Lacey, L., Warnecke, R., Buis, M. Smoking-related behavior, beliefs and social environment of young black women in subsidized public housing in Chicago. *Am J Public Health* 82:267–272, 1992.

Marcus, A. C., and Crane, L. A. Current estimates of adult cigarette smoking by race/ethnicity. *National Advisory Committee Proceedings.* U.S. Department of Health and Human Services, Public Health Service, Interagency Committee on Smoking and Health, Office of Smoking and Health. DHHS Publication No. (CDC) 87-8403, Rockville, MD, 31 March 1987.

Markides, K. S., Levin, J. S., Ray, L. A. Determinants of physician utilization among Mexican-Americans: A three generation study. *Med Care* 23(3):236–246, 1985.

Markides, K. S., Krause, N., Mendes De Leon, C. Acculturation and alcohol consumption among Mexican-Americans: A three generation study. *Am J Public Health* 78(9):1178–1181, 1988.

Milligan, S. Eyes on the lies: How Black leaders and cigarette companies have turned indoor smoking into a civil rights issue. *Washington Monthly* 39, 1987.

Morbidity and Mortality Weekly Report (MMWR). Cigarette smoking among Blacks and other minority populations. *MMWR* 36(25):405–407, 1987.

National Center for Health Statistics (NCHS). *Health United States 1987 and Prevention Profile.* Washington, D.C.: U.S. Government Printing Office, 1987.

Novotny, T., Warner, K. E., Kendrick, J. E., Remington, P. L. Socioeconomic factors and racial smoking differences in the United States. *Am J Public Health* 78(9):1187–1189, 1988.

Orleans, C. T., Schoenbach, V. J., Salmon, M. A., Strecher, V. J., Kalsbeek, W., Numan, K. B., Konrad, T. R., Thompson, B. Black Americans' smoking and quitting patterns: Clinical and public health implications. Paper presented at the annual meeting of the Society of Behavior Medicine, March 1987.

Orleans, C. T., Schoenbach, V. J., Salmon, M. A., Strecher, V. J., Kalsbeek, W., Quade, D., Brooks, E. F., Konrad, T. R., Blackmon, C., Watts, C.D.A survey of smoking and quitting patterns among Black Americans. *Am J Public Health* 79(2):176–181, 1989.

Orleans, C. T., Sutton, C., James, D. Preliminary process evaluation report. American Cancer Society Pathways to Freedom Community Demonstration Project. Unpublished report. Fox Chase Cancer Center, Philadelphia, March 1993.

Pathak, D. R., Samet, J. M., Humble, C. G., Skipper, B. J. Determinates of lung cancer risk in cigarette smokers in New Mexico. *J Natl Cancer Inst* 76(4):597–604, 1986.

Perez-Stable, E. J., Marin, B., Marin, G., Brody, D. J., Benowitz, N. W. Apparent underreporting of cigarette consumption among Mexican-American smokers. *Am J Public Health* 80:1057–1061, 1990.

Perez-Stable, E. J., Sabogal, F., Marin, G., Marin, B., Otero-Sabojal, R. Evaluation of "Guia para Dejar de Fumar," a self-help guide in Spanish to quit smoking. *Public Health Rep* 106:564–570, 1991.

Pierce, J. P., Goodman, J., Gilpin, E. A., Berry, C. Technical Report on Analytic Methods and Approaches Used in the Tobacco Use in California, 1990–91 Report. Sacramento: California Department of Health Services, 1992.

Phildelphia Daily News. No Uptown in our town or any town, 16 January 1990.

Ramirez, A. G., and Fletcher, K. A. Hispanic treatment and intervention programs for smoking prevention and cessation. *The Health Consequences of Smoking: Nicotine*

Addiction. A Report of the Surgeon General. U.S. Department of Health and Human Services, Office of Smoking and Health, Rockville, MD 512–513, 1988.

Ramirez, A. G., and McAlister, A. Mass media campaign: A Su Salud. *Prev Med* 5:608–621, 1988.

Robinson, R., Barry, M., Bloch, M., et al. Report of the Tobacco Policy Research Group on Marketing and Promotions Targeted at African Americans, Latinos, and Women. *Tobacco Control* (Suppl.) 1:524–530, 1992.

Robinson, R., Orleans, C. T., James, D., Sutton, C. *Pathways to Freedom: Winning the Fight Against Tobacco.* Philadelphia, PA: Fox Chase Cancer Center, 1992.

Royce, J. M., Hymowitz, N., Corbet, K., Hartwell, T., Orlandi, M. Smoking cessation factors among African Americans and whites. *Amer J Pub Health* 83:220–226, 1993.

Sabogal, F., Marin, B., Marin, G., Otero-Sabogal, R., Perez-Stable, E. *Guia para Dejar de Fumar.* Washington, DC: National Cancer Institute. NIH Publication No. 88-3001, June 1988.

Scribner, R., and Dwyer, J. M. Acculturation and low birthweight among Latinos in the Hispanic HHANES. *Am J Public Health* 79(9):1263–1267, 1989.

Sidney, S., Tekawa, I, Friedman, G. Mentholated cigarette use among multi-phasic examines, 1979–86. *Am J Public Health Promo* 79(10):1415–1416, 1989.

Sorlie, M. P., Garcia-Palmieri, M., Costas, R., Cruz-Vidal, M., Havlik, R. Cigarette smoking and coronary heart disease in Puerto Rico. *Prev Med* 11:304–316, 1982.

Sussman, S. Two social influence perspectives of tobacco use development and prevention. *Health Educ Res* 4(2):213–223, 1989.

Tobacco Use in America Conference (TUAC). Final Report and Recommendations from the Health Community to the 101st Congress and the Bush Administration. Paper presented at the Tobacco Use in American Conference, American Medical Association, Public Affairs Group at The University of Texas M.D. Anderson Cancer Center, Houston, 27–28 January 1989.

Tuckson, R. Race, sex, economics and tobacco advertising. *J Natl Med Assoc* 81(11):1119–1124, 1989.

U.S. Department of Defense (USDOD). *Department of Defense Report on Smoking and Health in the Military.* Office of the Assistant Secretary of Defense (Health Affairs) and Office of the Assistant Secretary of Defense, Washington, DC., 1986.

U.S. Department of Health and Human Services (USDHHS). *The Health Consequences of Smoking. Cancer and Chronic Lung Disease in the Workplace. A Report of the Surgeon General.* U.S. Department of Health and Human Services, Public Health Service, Office on Smoking and Health. DHHS Publication No. (PHS) 85-50207, 1985a.

———. *Report of the Secretary's Task Force on Black and Minority Health.* U.S. Department of Health and Human Services, Office of Minority Health, Washington, D.C., 1:108, 1985b.

———. *Cancer Among Blacks and Other Minorities: Statistical Profiles.* U.S. Department of Health and Human Services, Public Health Service, National Institutes of Health, National Cancer Institute. NIH Publication No. 86-2785, March 1986.

———. Lung cancer takes high toll on Black men: Smoking major risk factor. *Closing the Gap: Minorities and Cancer.* U.S. Department of Health and Human Services, Office of Minority Health Research Center, Public Health Service, Washington, D.C., 1989.

U.S. Department of Commerce, Bureau of Census. *We, the Black Americans.* Washington, D.C.: U.S. Government Printing Office, February, 1993.

———. The Hispanic population in the United States: March 1988 (Advance Report). *Current Population Reports.* Washington, D.C.: U.S. Government Printing Office, ser. P-20, no. 431, 1988.

———. Projections of the Hispanic population: 1983–2080. *Current Population Reports.* Washington, D.C.: U.S. Government Printing Office, ser. P-25, no. 995,

Wagenknecht, L., Cutter, G., Haley, N., Sidney, S., Manolio, T., Hughes, G., Jacobs, D. Racial differences in serum cotinine levels among smokers in the coronary artery risk development in (young) adults study. *Am J Public Health* 80(9):1053–1056, 1990.

Waldron, I., and Lye, D. Employment, unemployment, occupation and smoking. *Am J Prev Med* 5(3):142–149, 1989a.

———. Family roles and smoking. *Am J Prev Med* 5(3):136–141, 1989b.

Warner, K. E. Selling smoke: Cigarette advertising and public health. Paper presented at the meeting of the American Public Health Association, Washington, D.C., 1986.

Wells, K. G., Goilding, J. M., Hough, R. L., Burnam, M. A., Karno, M. Acculturation and the probability of use of health services by Mexican-Americans. *Health Serv Res* 24(2):237–257, 1989.

Williams, L. Tobacco companies target Blacks with ads, donations and festivals. *Wall Street Journal,* 6 October 1986.

Wittenberg, C. K. Summary of market research: Healthy mothers, healthy babies campaign. *Public Health Rep* 98(4):356–359, 1983.

19

Youth Tobacco Use: Risks, Patterns, and Control

BRIAN R. FLAY

PREVALENCE AND DEMOGRAPHICS OF TOBACCO USE AMONG YOUTH

Smoking

The most reliable data on youth tobacco use come from the Monitoring the Future annual survey of high school youth conducted by the University of Michigan's Institute for Social Research (ISR) (Johnston, O'Malley, Bachman 1989; in press).[1] These data indicate that 19% of 1992 high school seniors in the United States smoked daily (more than half of them smoking 10 or more cigarettes/day) and that almost 28% smoked at least monthly. The 30-day rate of smoking among 12th graders has fallen by only 1.6 percentage points since 1981. Data from the most recent 1991 Youth Risk Behavior Survey (YRBS), another national survey of 9th–12th graders, showed a similar 17% rate of frequent cigarette use (cigarette smoking on 20 or more of the 30 days preceding the survey) for 12th-graders (CDC, 1992). Among the entire sample of 9th–12th graders, the frequent smoking rate increased from 8.4% in Grade 9 to 17% in grade 12. While smoking prevalence and rates have become increasingly similar for males and females, males tend to be heavier smokers and are far more likely than girls to use smokeless tobacco (CDC, 1992).[2]

By age 12 years, approximately 10% of U.S. youth already smoke "usually once a week." By age 15 years, this has increased to around 30%, and by age 18 years, it has reached 40%. The age of smoking initiation has declined over time. Approximately one-quarter of high school senior smokers reported starting before grade 6, and approximately one-half by grade 7 or 8. Males were somewhat more likely to try smoking before grade 7, but females caught up by grade 9, and 60–80% of youth worldwide have done so by 15 years of age (Charlton, Melia, Moyer 1990; see Table 19–1; Conrad, Flay, Hill, 1992). There are large ethnic differences in smoking initiation, with higher rates of *30-day cigarette use* among white (36%) than black (16%) or Hispanic (31%) high school students (CDC, 1991), as well as higher rates of *frequent smoking* (whites = 15.4%; blacks = 3.1%; Hispanics = 6.8%) (CDC, 1992).

The annual high school survey data are very reliable and useful for tracking national changes because of careful multistage sampling. However, they probably underestimate true rates of smoking by the nation's youth because the samples do not include the almost 30% of youth (or the much higher proportion of black youth) who do not complete high school. A number of studies demonstrate that the prevalence of smoking among school leavers is about three and a half times that for high school seniors (Flay et al. 1989; Pirie et al. 1988; Yates et al. 1988). Even among high school seniors, the prevalence of daily smoking among those without college plans is two to three times that for those with college plans (30 vs. 14% daily; 18.4 vs. 6.8% smoking 10 or more cigarettes/day). Thus, less well-educated youth

Table 19–1   Data on Smoking Prevalence (%) of 15 Year Olds, Drawn from Six Recent National Studies &
The WHO Cross National Study of Children's Health Behaviour, 1988

		Smoke Daily	Smoke Weekly	Smoke Once Per Week or More	Smoke Less than Weekly	Do Not Smoke (have tried)	Have Never Smoked	Sample No.
All	M	14.4	4.4	22.3	6.4	39.9	34.2	>5,754
countries	F	14.4	5.6	28.0	8.0	36.3	36.3	>5,934
Australia	M	—	—	25.0	—	—	—	—
	F	—	—	28.0	—	—	—	—
Austria	M	11.8	6.5	—	10.3	43.3	28.2	476
	F	13.1	7.1	—	11.8	39.1	28.9	381
Belgium	M	16.6	5.0	—	5.1	32.7	40.6	603
	F	13.5	6.2	—	5.6	29.4	45.3	502
Canada[a]	M	17.4	—	—	—	—	—	—
	F	17.8	—	—	—	—	—	—
Finland	M	29.1	6.3	—	6.3	39.9	18.4	539
	F	20.1	7.4	—	10.1	36.8	25.6	543
Hungary	M	20.4	5.9	—	8.2	39.9	25.4	562
	F	14.1	6.8	—	8.2	42.2	28.7	704
Israel	M	5.7	3.5	—	3.5	30.9	56.4	402
	F	4.1	3.4	—	6.3	21.3	64.9	559
New	M	10.0	—	—	—	—	—	—
Zealand	F	20.0	—	—	—	—	—	—
Norway	M	16.2	4.1	—	9.1	43.2	27.4	627
	F	17.6	6.3	—	14.4	35.6	26.1	568
Scotland	M	14.7	2.6	—	3.6	39.8	39.2	771
	F	15.6	4.5	—	6.7	40.0	33.3	711
Sweden	M	8.7	5.7	—	7.6	47.0	31.1	541
	F	10.9	5.6	—	7.1	37.6	38.8	521
Switzerland	M	9.5	3.6	—	10.2	35.8	40.9	279
	F	10.5	4.4	—	11.3	29.3	44.4	341
U.S.A.[b]	M	—	—	24.0	—	—	—	—
	F	—	—	29.0	—	—	—	—
Wales	M	13.1	2.4	—	4.4	41.9	38.2	954
	F	15.1	5.2	—	4.4	41.2	34.1	1104
Wales &	M	—	—	18.0	—	—	—	—
Scotland	F	—	—	27.0	—	—	—	—

[a]15–19 year olds.

[b]15 and 16 year olds.

Source: This data has been collected from a variety of studies with differing methodologies. The WHO cross-national survey statistics are courtesy of Nutbeam, N. Planning for a smoke-free generation. Smoke-free Europe. 6, see ch. 1 references. (Charlton, Melia, Moyer 1990).

are at much higher risk than better-educated youth for nicotine addiction.

Smokeless Tobacco Use

There is much more regional and individual variation in the use of smokeless tobacco than cigarettes by youth (Boyd et al. 1987; (USDHHS, 1992). Smokeless tobacco use is very much confined to males[3] (e.g., 19% vs. 1% for females in grades 9–12 (CDC, 1992), especially whites and blue-collar workers

(three times as likely as white-collar workers), and is much more prevalent in most rural than in most urban areas (e.g., 44% among high school youth in rural Southern Illinois, 20% in rural schools near Chicago in Northern Illinois, and 10% in suburban schools near Chicago) (Burton et al. 1989). Among males aged 17 to 19 years, the prevalence of snuff use increased 15 times and chewing tobacco 4 times between 1970 and 1986, while the prevalence of use among older males decreased (Novotny et al. 1989) (see Chapter 13 for more details). The 1991 Youth Risk Behavior Survey showed that white male high school students (23.6%) were significantly more likely than Hispanic (10.7%) or black (3.6%) male students to use smokeless tobacco products (CDC, 1992).

SPECIAL RISKS

Youth put themselves at special risk when they use tobacco. First, simply trying tobacco involves the risk of nicotine addiction (discussed later; see Chapter 4). Second, according to some, use of tobacco may increase the risk of subsequent addiction to other substances (Henningfield, Clayton, Pollin 1990; Kandel 1975) and other problem behaviors (Jessor and Jessor 1977).[4] Third, in the present social climate, beginning to smoke may have negative social consequences for youth. Fourth, the health effects of tobacco use are immediate and cumulative (USDHHS 1986a, 1989). Even low-level experimental smoking leads to immediate physiological changes, including changes in high density lipoprotein cholesterol levels that may be precursors to subsequent atherogenic complications (Dwyer et al. 1988), and it is well established that the earlier someone starts smoking, the greater the risk of heart disease and cancer (USDHHS 1986b).

One-quarter or more of all regular smokers eventually die of smoking-related diseases, with an average loss of 21 years of life (USDHHS 1989). If the current smoking prevalence rates were to remain the same, 20 million of the 70 million children in the United States today would become smokers.[5] At least 5 million of them would then die of smoking-related diseases.

INITIATION

Patterns of Onset

As with the adoption of most behaviors, the adoption of tobacco use by youth follows an S-shaped curve, with few starting very young, most trying it between ages 10 and 15 years, and a few not trying it until high school or later (see earlier and Table 19–1; Charlton, Melia, Moyer 1990; Flay et al.

1983). Regardless of the age of first trying tobacco, youth progress (or not) through a reasonably well-defined sequence from the first try to the acquisition of dependence or addiction (see Chapter 4; Flay et al. 1983; Leventhal and Cleary 1980). Although the process is clearly developmental, it is a stochastic one, with the probability of advancing from one stage to another always less than one.

First, the *preparatory stage* involves the formation of knowledge, beliefs, and expectations about nicotine use and the functions it can serve (definition of self as glamorous, independent, and mature; improved concentration, stress reduction, smoothing of social relations). The second stage, *initial trying,* covers the first two or three tries. These usually occur in the presence of friends, though for some they occur alone in the home. The physiological effects of and reactions to the first use (dizziness, taste, etc.) as well as the psychosocial reinforcements obtained from its use determine whether or not a person advances to the next stage (Leventhal, Fleming, Ershler 1988). The third stage, *experimentation,* involves repeated, but irregular use over an extended period, perhaps several years. It tends to be situational-specific, such as at parties, on weekends, and with special friends. The fourth stage, *regular use,* for youth means using on a regular basis, perhaps every weekend, perhaps every day on the way to or from school. Tobacco use becomes increasingly regular, over a wide variety of situations.

The fifth and final stage, *nicotine dependence or addiction* (Stepney 1984; USDHHS 1988), has occurred with the development of an internally regulated need for nicotine. Dependence is characterized by three critical factors: (1) tolerance, (2) the experience of unpleasant physiological sensations (withdrawal symptoms) upon quitting, and (3) a high probability of resuming use in the presence of challenges weeks and even months and years after quitting. About one-third of adult nicotine users were probably addicted before the end of high school (e.g., the approximately 10% of students who smoke 10 or more cigarettes/day), while two-thirds did not become addicted until after the transition to college or work.[6] The progression

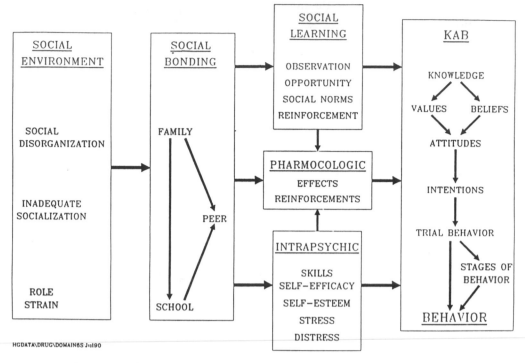

Fig. 19–1   Six domains of determinants of tobacco use. KAB = Knowledge, attitudes, and behavior. *Source:* Conrad, Flay, Hill, 1992.

from experimentation to regular use and often addiction involves multiple social, psychological, and biological factors, and different factors may play different functions at different points in the progression, and play different roles for different people (Conrad et al. 1992; Leventhal, Fleming, Ershler 1988). These factors will now be reviewed briefly.

Predictors of Initiation

Chapter 4 introduced three domains of determinants of nicotine addiction—social (social context and marketing), psychological (personal characteristics, cognition, and decision making), and biological (pharmacological processes and addiction). In this chapter, these domains are expanded upon as determinants of initiation of nicotine use (indeed any substance use and abuse (Flay and Petraitis 1991; in press) by youth (Figure 19–1). We consider the social domain in terms of social organization and disorgani-

zation, and social bonding with family, school, and peers. We consider the psychological domain in terms of social learning and intrapsychic variables, and the cognitive, attitude, and behavioral domains. The biological domain includes pharmacological processes and conditioning.

Social Organization/Disorganization

Sociologists and others (Akers 1977; Jessor and Jessor 1977) have established that social environment variables are the most distal predictors of drug use (see Figure 19–1, left side). Thus, the structure of the economic, legal, social, and educational systems of a society are determinants of behavior. In particular, role strain, or the discrepancy between aspirations and achievements, and social disorganization or breakdown may lead to disrupted socialization which, in turn, alters the social bonding and social learning variables (see Figure 19–1). These may then lead to increased substance use, for example, among the disadvantaged (c.f., Wilson 1987).[7]

Regardless of levels of socialization, the primary determinants of nicotine use by youth are probably the norms of the larger society in which they grow up and live. To the extent that youth see nicotine use as a sign of maturity, they will be motivated to use it. Tobacco advertising and promotion clearly encourages such views (Altman et al. 1987) and the tobacco industry will go to extraordinary lengths to ensure that this continues (Connolly, Orleans, Blum 1992; Warner et al.; 1992 Whelan 1984). On the other hand, the extensive antitobacco activities of the last decade have clearly discouraged such views. Overall, youth now see the consequences of substance use as more serious, and they hold less positive attitudes toward substance use than in previous years (Bachman et al. 1988). However, while this change in societal norms may have reached well-educated youth, it has not yet reached less-educated youth, or has reached them to a lesser extent. Less-educated youth are still exposed to a norm of nicotine and other substance use as an aid to coping with the hardships of life. They are still not fully informed or convinced of the seriousness of the consequences of substance use and still hold relatively positive attitudes toward use.

Social Bonding: Family, School, and Peers

Sociologists have identified social bonding (Figure 19–1) as a primary determinant of substance use and abuse and other problem behaviors, such as precocious sexuality, truancy from school or work, school dropout, and delinquency (Akers 1977; Jessor and Jessor 1977; Krohn et al. 1983). In normal social development, strong social bonds are formed between children and parents, between adolescents and schools, and between youth and other conventional social groups including conventional peers. When normal social development is disturbed, either by social disorganization (such as living in disadvantaged circumstances) or by family disruption or inadequate family support (di-

vorce, latchkey status [Richardson et al. 1989], poor family functioning) youth are more likely to form bonds with deviant peers. Such deviant bonding increases the exposure to substance use by others, disturbs patterns of social learning, and increases the probability of problem behavior.

Social Learning: Observation, Opportunity, Social Normative Beliefs, Reinforcement

Social learning variables include opportunities for observation and modeling of behavior, opportunities to use (or availability), social normative beliefs (including collective ignorance or norms), and social reinforcement (positive and negative). Bandura (1986) and Akers (1977) have developed the relations among these variables from the psychological and sociological perspectives, respectively. Any particular behavior is more likely to occur when it is differentially reinforced and is seen as desirable by important others.

As noted earlier, youth alienated from conventional culture have more opportunities than others to observe substance use and its positive functions. Substances are also more readily available, and they have more opportunities to try them. They are also more likely to overestimate the proportion of their peers who use these substances—because they are likely to be associating with groups who actually do use. For example, youth who identify themselves as belonging to groups exhibiting "problem behavior" are much more likely than others to have friends who use tobacco and to use it themselves (Mosbach and Leventhal, 1988; Sussman et al., 1990). Finally, deviant cultures reinforce these youth when they do use, for example, by acceptance into groups.

Youth alienated from conventional culture or who otherwise hang out with tobacco using peers are obviously not the only ones susceptible to social learning variables. Adolescents with strong conventional bonds may start using tobacco to imitate observed adult behaviors (Sussman 1989). Youth with tobacco using parents have many opportunities to observe nicotine use and its functions, have a ready source of tobacco, are likely to select friends from the same socioeconomic status and background, and are likely to overestimate the proportion of adults who use tobacco (Flay et al. 1983). Many studies, both cross-sectional and prospective, have found parental smoking to be the strongest predictor of smoking (often vying for first place with peer smoking, at least until youths reach puberty).

Intrapsychic: Self-esteem, Stress/Distress, Social Skills, Self-efficacy

Both sociologists and psychologists have suggested that "intrapsychic" variables might complete the link between social bonding and knowledge, attitudes, and behavior (see Figure 19–1). Sociologists and clinical psychologists suggest that poor family bonding leads to stress (inability to cope, rebelliousness, risk taking) and distress (withdrawal, self-derogation, depression). Several researchers have shown a link between stress or distress variables and substance use, including tobacco use (Covey and Tam 1990; Pierce et al. 1993; Shiffman and Wills 1985)—some as early as grade 1 (Kellam et al. 1982).

On the other hand, strong family and other conventional bonding can lead to the development of positive social skills and competencies, strong self-efficacy regarding these, and high self-esteem. Psychologists have also suggested that personality factors (e.g., locus of control) affect one's ability to cope with social situations and one's desire for, and response to, drug use (e.g., Kaplan, Martin, Robbins 1984).

Pharmacological and Conditioning Processes

Pharmacological processes may play a role at each of the stages of onset (Henningfield et al. 1990; Leventhal, Fleming, Ershler 1988). During the preparation stage, some as yet undocumented physiological changes related to subsequent attraction to substance use may be brought about by exposure to side-stream smoke (just as exposure to side-stream smoke can increase rates of childhood lung disease). Exposure to toxic sub-

stances is known to increase tolerance for them, and this may reduce the noxious deterrence of the first experience. Youth who become regular smokers less frequently report noxious effects of the first cigarette than other youth.

The first try of a cigarette seems to be dominated by negative experiences, such as coughing and burning throat. Youth experience some of these effects (tastes, burning sensations, coughing) as peripheral and some (dizziness, heart racing, headache) as systemic and central. Peripheral aversive effects serve as an initial deterrent; however, adaptation to them is often interpreted as a sign of resistance to injury, thus reinforcing the natural youthful illusions of invulnerability and encouraging further experimentation (Leventhal, Fleming, Ershler 1988; Leventhal, Glynn, Fleming 1987). Regarding the central effects, high nicotine loads appear to deter further experimentation by females but not males. Initial experiences of highs or pleasant emotions appear to encourage further experimentation and the absence of such experiences appears to discourage further experimentation. Experiences of dizziness also appear to encourage further experimentation, particularly by males who belong to groups exhibiting "problem behaviors" (Mosbach and Leventhal 1988).[8]

The situational specificity of occasional tobacco use suggests that the urge to use is a conditioned response elicited in specific contexts, consistent with a learning model (Baker, Morse, Sherman 1986; Leventhal, Fleming, Ershler 1988). Thus, youth may use tobacco in specific situations because of social cues, need for stress reduction, or something else about the situation. However, if tobacco use becomes more frequent, the addiction process can take over. For some, this will occur during high school, as a result of frequent tobacco use during breaks and before and after school. This is more likely for "problem behavior" youth who identify with "deviant" groups, such as "druggies," "dirts," or "toughs" (Mosbach and Leventhal 1988; Sussman et al., 1990); experience a chronic threat to their self-image; are often truant and away from adult surveillance (Richardson et al. 1989); and experience low levels of reinforcement from their parents, teachers, and most peers. These are the same students who are likely to have started using tobacco early, in elementary or early middle school, so they have had longer to develop a tolerance for nicotine. Early starters are less likely to try to quit during high school, but they are more likely to succeed if they do try (Ershler et al. 1989). Youth who smoke more cigarettes per day or week and who smoke more regularly, perhaps indicating greater nicotine addiction, are more likely than others to fail if they do attempt to quit (Ershler et al. 1989; Hansen et al. 1985). Others will not become addicted until they leave school and go to work or college where the social restraints against tobacco use are less rigid, though the social and policy restraints are increasing, with positive effects.

It is important to note that adolescents do not fully understand the nature of addiction (Leventhal, Fleming, Ershler 1988). When it comes to themselves, they hold illogical and contradictory beliefs about addiction. For example, they sometimes do and sometimes do not believe that they can become addicted. They sometimes do and sometimes do not believe that they would be able to tell if they were becoming addicted. They believe they will be able to stop if they do become addicted. At the same time, they believe that addiction means being unable to quit. Youth clearly underestimate the power of addiction for themselves. Ironically, youth whose parents attempted to quit and failed believe that it is easy to quit smoking, while youths whose parents quit successfully believe that it is difficult (Leventhal, Glynn, Fleming 1987).

Knowledge, Attitudes, and Behavior

The most proximal determinants to actual tobacco use are knowledge, attitudes, and behavior regarding tobacco and other substances and their use (see Figure 19–1, right side). These are, of course, precisely the variables considered in the first stage of onset, the preparation or anticipation stage.[9] They include knowledge of the physiological and social consequences of use, personal beliefs (expectancies, perceived risk, susceptibility)

regarding consequences, general values (e.g., toward health, independence), specific evaluations of the consequences, attitudes toward tobacco use and related issues, behavioral intentions, and related behaviors (e.g., alcohol use/abuse). Theories of how these variables relate to each other abound, and we have attempted to integrate them elsewhere (Flay et al. 1983, Flay and Petraitis in press). Basically, however, they all play a role in determining behavior. Since no one of them is sufficient to determine behavior on its own, they all must be considered in prevention and treatment programs.

Implications

It is clear that successful prevention of nicotine addiction and early nicotine addiction treatment programs need to consider all of the determinants discussed earlier and their interactions as we understand them. Any program that emphasizes only one or a few of the determinants or stages of onset is doomed to mediocrity at best, and probable failure. Current knowledge about prevention and early cessation will now be reviewed, and future needs discussed.

PREVENTION

The complexity of the process of acquiring nicotine addiction and the seriousness of addiction suggest that primary prevention should be chosen over the alternative of treating people once they are addicted. Researchers, health educators, and other health personnel have tried many different approaches to prevention. Though progress is being made, to date no one approach has proven totally effective. Before addressing existing approaches to prevention, the benefits of and barriers to prevention will be discussed.

Benefits of and Barriers to Prevention

The benefits of preventing youth from becoming nicotine users are clear. Unlike with alcohol, for the majority of people use is also abuse. That is, most people who use nicotine become addicted, and this leads to multiple negative consequences for society, themselves, and others in their immediate environment (see Chapters 5, 8, and 9, respectively). This is not true for alcohol, which the majority of adults (though not necessarily youth) can use without abusing. Thus, preventing addiction to nicotine has large benefits for society, the individuals concerned, and others in their environment.

The barriers to effective prevention are multiple. First, as noted earlier, is the complexity of the acquisition process. Without a full understanding of this process, plus an equally full understanding of behavior change processes in general, it is impossible to design very effective prevention programs. Second, despite the massive changes in societal norms of the last 30 years, youth still perceive many pressures to use tobacco. As noted earlier, some of these are restricted to families with adult tobacco users and to relatively alienated youth. However, the tobacco industry has ensured that some pressures to use tobacco are omnipresent. While tobacco advertising via television and radio has been banned since 1971, tobacco advertising in print media and promotion through other avenues continues at ever-increasing rates (Connolly et al. 1992; Fischer et al. 1991; Warner et al. 1992). In addition, tobacco promotion currently targets those groups least likely to resist it because of their social circumstances or aspirations (Robinson, Barry, Bloch et al. 1992). Along with other industries, until recently, the tobacco industry paid to have their products, or advertisements for their products, shown in movies. Even more insidiously, the tobacco industry imposes a form of censorship of information about the effects of nicotine, by influencing coverage of such information by magazines that are dependent on tobacco advertising revenue (Warner 1985; Warner et al. 1992); Whelan 1984).

Against this background, prevention efforts fight an uphill battle. The tobacco industry will do everything it can to prevent the development, dissemination, and implementation of effective prevention programs. As a rule, if the tobacco industry objects to an approach to prevention, it is likely that it would be an effective approach; and the less strenuous their objections, the less effective the approach. For example, the tobacco in-

dustry knew that counteradvertising was affecting sales shortly after its initiation as a result of the Fairness Doctrine in 1967; so it actually proposed the removal of all tobacco advertising from radio and television (January 1971) as long as antismoking advertising would come off as well (Senate Hearings, Commerce Committee 1969). The tobacco industry knows that increased taxes on cigarette sales reduces tobacco sales, so it strenuously objects to any attempt to apply such taxes (e.g., Proposition 99 in California and Question 1 in Massachusetts) (Slade 1992). In California, the tobacco industry believed that a multimillion dollar antismoking media campaign might be effective, so, according to press reports, it supported attempts by the California Medical Association (CMA) to have public education funds from Proposition 99 (20% of all tobacco taxes) subverted to provide funding for medical care (in addition to 45% of Proposition 99 funds already slated for this purpose) (Marr 1990; Slade 1992).[10]

Historical Approaches to Prevention

Tobacco education traditionally has consisted of information about the negative health consequences of tobacco use. While such an approach is effective in altering knowledge it typically has not effectively prevented onset. This is true both for programs imparted to school children in classrooms (Goodstadt 1978; Thompson 1978; Tobler 1986) and for broader campaigns directed to the general public through mass media (Flay 1987). Information is rarely, if ever, sufficient to alter behavior (Flay et al. 1983), regardless of how it is delivered. Thus, altering the teaching person or style (lectures, discussion, peer leaders, use of media, etc.) does not help much, if at all. In addition, information about long-term health consequences is just not salient to youth, who are focused very much on the present. Information about immediate physiological effects might be more useful, in combination with other activities (discussed later), because adolescents have limited future orientations.

As educators and researchers realized that information alone was insufficient to alter behavior, they also recognized that youth who became tobacco users often had weak self-esteem, were poor achievers, and had trouble making healthy decisions. This led to the development of "affective" approaches to smoking and drug abuse prevention. Affective programs sought to enhance self-esteem, to clarify values, and teach decision making; they often did not include information specifically about tobacco or drug use per se (Durell and Bukoski 1984; Goodstadt 1978). Programs based only on these approaches have little or no beneficial effects on tobacco use (Hansen et al. 1988; Tobler 1986).

Current Emphases in Prevention

The failure of information-based and affective approaches to prevention is probably due to not considering the broad set of social, psychological, and pharmacological determinants of tobacco use onset reviewed earlier. Consideration of the broad sets of social influences led to the development of psychosocial approaches to classroom-based smoking prevention curricula (Best et al. 1988; Evans 1986; Flay 1985; Flay et al. 1983). These fall into "social influences" programs that are specific to nicotine (and possibly other substance) use and broader "life/social competence" programs in which substance use in general, or tobacco use in particular, are not so specifically targeted (Botvin and Wills 1985). Social influence curricula typically include: (1) information on the consequences of tobacco use, with special emphasis on the short-term health and social consequences; (2) information on and the correction of estimates of the prevalence of tobacco use by peers and adults; (3) discussion of social influences from peers, family, and the media on tobacco use, and ways of dealing with them; (4) modeling to show these influences, situations, and coping behaviors on video/film or by same/age peers; (5) role-playing and explicit learning and practice of behavioral skills; and (6) the making of a public commitment regarding tobacco use intentions. The life/social skills curricula include most of these elements, together with more general self-esteem enhancement and social skills development,

though not so highly focused on the circumstances of tobacco use (Botvin and Wills 1985). Most of both types of curricula also emphasize implementation strategies, such as the use of dialectic or socratic methods (rather than didactic methods or just lecturing), active role play, and practice of skills by the students. Some include assignments with parents, or the development of activism or advocacy behavior in the community. Some emphasize the role of media and others the use of peers.

Over 50 studies of these psychosocial approaches suggest that they are somewhat effective at delaying the onset of tobacco use (Flay 1985). When implemented optimally, these programs appear to reduce the proportion of students starting to smoke by 30–50%.[11] However, it is unclear what components of the content or strategies of the programs are responsible for these positive effects. Little is known about the processes by which effective programs have their effects (see, e.g., MacKinnon et al. 1991). In addition, they have questionable long-term effects on ultimate smoking acquisition (Flay et al. 1989; Murray et al. 1989), although too few studies have included long-term follow-up to be confident about this yet.

A National Cancer Institute Advisory Panel (Glynn 1989) advised a minimum of three components for effective school-based smoking prevention: information about the short-term physiological effects and social consequences of tobacco use; information about social influences on tobacco use, especially peer, parent, and media influences; and training of resistance skills, including modeling and practice of resistance skills. The panel also recommended quality delivery by: (1) providing special training to motivated educators; and (2) emphasizing that existing curricula be implemented completely as designed rather than being adapted (except for special groups such as certain minorities).[12] Although the research evidence remains unclear (Johnson 1982), the panel recommended the use of peer assistants to trained teachers, with responsibility for carrying out specified program components such as leading discussion groups or modeling peer pressures and resistance skills. Recent data (Young et al. 1990) support the use of college-age facilitators. Parental involvement was also recommended, and research evidence supports this (Worden et al. 1987).

Emerging Approaches and Needs in Prevention

Implementation and Diffusion of Effective Approaches

The effectiveness of the recommended programs when implemented on a broad scale by regular classroom teachers rather than research staff is unclear (Best et al. 1988; Flay 1985). Because they are so different from most school-based curricula, teachers require special training to implement them correctly. In addition, effective programs need better dissemination (Best et al. 1988). It is unfortunate that at present those programs most widely disseminated are the least well evaluated, while the best evaluated are not widely available. The lack of effective dissemination strategies and policies is currently a barrier to effective prevention (Basch, Eveland, Portnoy 1986). Dissemination and diffusion policies must consider teacher training, demands on teachers' time, costs of materials, and competing educational and health priorities.

Community Interventions

School-based programs should perform better if the society at large clearly supports not using tobacco. This consideration suggests that school-based programs may be more effective when there is extensive countermarketing of tobacco use, as is already practiced in many countries.

The review of these determinants also suggests that social skills approaches to prevention might be more effective when combined with other levels of community intervention. Project STAR is a social skills program delivered by specially trained teachers to sixth and seventh grade students in Kansas City middle schools. Parents were also encouraged to participate in the program with their children, and trained to influence policy at their school. In addition, media coverage and other community involvements

support the program and reinforce its messages. Effects 2 and 3 years after initiation are impressive (Pentz et al. 1989a; Pentz et al. 1989b), and longer-term effects look promising (Pentz et al., in preparation).[13]

Pharmacological Processes

The review of determinants also suggests that prevention programs should consider the role of pharmacological processes in prevention (Henningfield et al. 1990; Leventhal et al. 1988). However, it would be a gross oversimplification to use noxious first experiences as a deterrent to further tobacco use. The symptoms must be interpreted as signs of genuine danger, and many youth do not interpret them as such. Thus, prevention programs should include efforts to influence how youth interpret the first effects of nicotine so as to strengthen their deterrent effects. Hirschman and associates (1984; Hirschman and Leventhal 1989), for example, taught students to reinterpret adaptation to noxious symptoms as the smoke killing the body's warning system, making one unaware of danger. This program reduced movement from first to later tries. Physicians and other health professionals would be credible sources for this type of information. Such an approach combined with the social influences approach should be more effective than either alone.

Developmental Sensitivity

The stage model also suggests that tobacco use prevention programs need to start in elementary school or before, and follow a developmentally sensitive path through high school and beyond. The National Cancer Institute (NCI) Advisory Panel (Glynn 1989) concluded that tobacco use prevention education conducted within a broader health focus appeared as effective as programs with an exclusive focus on tobacco use as long as the tobacco component received a minimum level of attention. They advised a minimum of five classroom sessions in each of at least 2 years. One-shot programs, whether of more than 20 sessions or only 1 to 10, are doomed to mediocre short-term success because the students are still exposed to the many influences in their environments. Those influences most salient to them, and the role they play, keep changing as children develop, enter puberty, and become young adults (Flay et al. 1983). Effective tobacco use prevention needs to do the same.[14]

Social Policy

Social policy also should play an important role in prevention. By 1992, 48 states and the District of Columbia had some restrictions or prohibitions on the sale of cigarettes to minors. But, many studies have found that "vendor compliance with the minimum-age-of-purchase laws is the exception rather than the rule" (USDHHS 1989, p. 13). We need strengthened policies regarding youth access to tobacco products at stores and vending machines and through the distribution of free samples (Altman et al. 1989; 1991; Barovich et al., 1991; Choi, Novotny, Thimis 1992; Feighery et al. 1991; Forster, Hourigan, Kelder 1992; Forster, Klapp, Jeffery 1989).

School policy clearly influences smoking onset rates (Pentz, Brannon, Charlin et al. 1989) and parents can influence school policy (e.g., Project STAR). Recent legislation against smoking in public places and worksites also help reduce smoking, and probably prevent some youth from becoming addicted smokers when they join the work force. We still need more focus on making smoke-free, or tobacco-free, other environments frequented by children and youth such as day-care settings, YMCAs, youth clubs, and discos (Pierce et al. 1993).

The efficacy of tobacco taxation, as a means of reducing tobacco consumption and discouraging use by children, has been well established (Sweanor et al. 1992). Substanial tobacco excise tax hikes are likely to figure prominently in future state and federal initiatives to curb tobacco use by children and adolescents. Following the examples of California's Proposition 99, and Massachusetts' Question 1, some portion of tobacco tax revenues can be earmarked for statewide school-based prevention programs and for mass media counter-advertising campaigns targeted especially at youth. Early results of California's Proposition 99

Tobacco Tax Initiative suggest that a modest tax increase (25-cent) is unlikely to have dramatic effects on adolescent smoking in the absence of concomitant counter-advertising, school-based programs and smoke-free school environments (Pierce, Farkas, Evans et al. 1993). The higher federal cigarette tax hikes ($1.00–$2.00 per pack) under consideration to help finance national health care reform may have more dramatic effects on tobacco consumption by children and teens (Sweanor et al. 1992).

The Role of the Medical and Public Health Sectors

No data are available regarding the effectiveness of the medical and public health sectors in tobacco use prevention. From a public health perspective, however, they should play a decisive and visible role. Pediatricians and family physicians should monitor family and child tobacco and other substance use and their precursors, with special attention to children and adolescents in high-risk groups. They should work with entire families to remove the child's exposure to tobacco use—by having parents quit, and by providing families with age-appropriate prevention materials. Parents should be encouraged to quit, not only for their own health, but for the health of their children (Cummings et al. 1989).[15] Information on the consequences of their tobacco use on their child's health can motivate parents. New portable nicotine dosimeters that assess and provide feedback of levels of household environmental tobacco smoke can be built into innovative pediatric interventions (Hammond and Leaderer 1987). Providing information to children on how they can help their parents quit, by providing social support, might also be useful.

Providing information to young children, 3–11 years of age, about the bad health effects of tobacco use can motivate them to not wish to use tobacco. Physicians could provide demonstrations to children to make the future harms of nicotine more immediate.

By puberty, information about consequences is no longer sufficient to maintain abstention, though medical advice about the effects of nicotine on athletic performance will motivate some adolescents. In addition, however, adolescents should be made aware of social influences and be provided with social skills training. Pediatricians can provide some of this directly to patients or they can work with school systems to provide it. Everybody should be aware, however, that making students aware of social pressures without successfully providing them with skills to resist such pressures may actually make the situation worse.

Physicians, nurses, physician assistants, and allied health care providers can help deliver effective prevention programs to students in schools and youth in other settings. However, they should be trained to deliver programs of proven effectiveness or programs derived from strong theory to be even more effective than existing programs, rather than focusing on only one determinant such as advertising (as the Doctors Ought to Care [DOC] program appears to do).[16] The review of determinants provided earlier in this chapter makes it clear that any approach focused on only one determinant, regardless of its assumed importance, is doomed to only partial success at best, or even failure.

Medical and public health groups can also help tobacco use prevention by actively campaigning against unfair practices by the tobacco industry and by not entering into any supportive relationships with them. The American Medical Association's support of the movement against tobacco advertising is a positive example (Fischer et al. 1991). A negative example, cited earlier, is the support obtained from the tobacco industry by the California Medical Association, in their bid to transfer public education funds derived from Proposition 99 taxation into medical care. Such a move would benefit physicians, not to mention the tobacco industry, at the expense of the long-term health of the population of California. Another potentially positive role would be to provide active support for the development and enforcement of legislation to reduce the illegal sales and free sampling of tobacco to minors (Altman et al. 1989; 1991; Jason et al. 1990) and to raise state and federal tobacco excise taxes (Sweanor et al. 1992).

EARLY CESSATION

Benefits of, Needs for, and Barriers to Early Cessation

Failure to prevent youth from starting to use tobacco gives rise to the need for effective approaches to early cessation and early nicotine addiction treatment. Unfortunately, cessation for youth is no easier than it is for adults. Indeed it may be more difficult, in that youth are less motivated by the possible consequences to their long-term health.

Youth make frequent and unsuccessful attempts to quit smoking. Over half of U.S. smoking youth attempt to quit each year. Less than one-fifth of those youth smoking 10 or more cigarettes per day are successful for even 1 month (Johnston, O'Malley, Bachman 1989). Only 5% of smoking youth believe that they will still be smoking 5 years later: in actual fact, 75% of them are still smoking 8 years later (Charlton, Melia, Moyer 1990)! This pattern is probably the same for smokeless tobacco use.

Youth report many of the same reasons for difficulty in quitting as adults—social pressure, urges, withdrawal symptoms (Leventhal, Flemming, Ershler 1988; USDHHS 1989). Data also suggest that the factors that motivate youth to attempt quitting are different from those that predict success at quitting. The reports of withdrawal symptoms and the high relapse rates, together with the fact that more than half of high school weekly smokers smoke 10 or more cigarettes per day, attest to the strength of nicotine dependence and addiction, even among youth (USDHHS 1988, 1989).

The benefits of early cessation are obvious. Many of them are the same as those discussed earlier for prevention. In addition, early cessation, for example, in high school, should help prevent addiction for many individuals when they leave the constraints of the school setting. Also, the earlier cessation the greater the long-term health benefits.

The need for early cessation opportunities are great. Youth who desire to quit have great difficulty finding a program tailored for them. Unfortunately, researchers have been slow to meet this need. Effective cessation programs for youth will need to educate them about the importance and power of addiction, and teach them how to handle social and stressful situations, as well as address all those issues of importance to adults.

The barriers to early cessation are just as great as, and similar to, those for prevention. Early cessation programs must be offered to individuals, whereas prevention programs can be offered to whole schools or classrooms of students. Schools would be an ideal location in which to offer early cessation programs. Unfortunately, the educational system usually does not support therapeutic programs during school hours, and it is difficult to motivate young tobacco users to attend a cessation program outside of school hours because of numerous competing activites with more immediate reinforcement for youth (Graham et al. 1989). However, new legislation across the country banning any smoking in schools by faculty, staff, students, or visitors may fuel increasing support for this kind of programming (Pierce et al. 1993).

Medical practices would be another ideal location in which to offer youth cessation advice, brief counseling, self-help materials, and referral to outside clinics (see Chapter 10). Unfortunately, the medical system does not reimburse such treatment, at least not at an adequate level. Of course, youth would still need to be motivated to attend such clinics if they were available. Self-help programs are only of benefit to those individuals highly motivated to quit, and most youth are not so motivated.

Existing Approaches

Many existing approaches to youth cessation are based on adult models. Adult programs are based in large part on the addiction model (see Chapters 10–16). Some research projects are investigating different combinations of traditional adult approaches and approaches derived from the newer psychosocial approaches to prevention (Burton et al. 1989). As noted earlier, some young tobacco users exhibit a wide variability in their use patterns, while others are already clearly addicted (Hahn et al. 1989). We cannot yet suggest the optimal balance of "prevention" and traditional ces-

sation approaches for youth because of the limited research in this area (USDHHS 1989, pp. 390–391).[17] Even less is known about cessation of young peoples' use of smokeless tobacco (Glover 1986; Severson et al. 1987). Much more research and program development is needed regarding cessation of both cigarette smoking and smokeless tobacco use and the proper role, if any, of nicotine replacement therapy in treating addicted youth. This is especially so for young females, who seem to find it much more difficult to quit smoking than males (Bennett, Austin, Janizewski 1986; Weissman et al. 1987).

Developing and Future Needs

Prevention programs at the high school level or later should also include a component on quitting (Leventhal, Fleming, Ershler 1988). Youth programs also need to consider pharmacological and social processes in more detail than in many adult programs. Adolescents apparently do not identify desires for tobacco as a sign of dependence or addiction and, as noted earlier, they believe that they will be aware of becoming addicted in time to avoid it.

Youth programs also need to include a *motivational* component to attract the early starters (Burton et al. 1989). Those youth who started smoking in elementary school are least motivated to want to quit, but may be more successful at doing so if they try (Ershler et al. 1989). However, in general, just as with adults, those youth who smoke more frequently and more heavily have the greatest difficulty in quitting (Ershler et al. 1989; Hansen et al. 1985).

Clearly, intensive research efforts are needed to develop educational efforts to convince youth of the importance of avoiding addiction, and to provide ways for them to do so. However, in the mean time, physicians and other health personnel can play an important role in early cessation in several ways. First, they can identify social environments that put youth at risk for early tobacco use and intervene in public and private health care settings, schools, and communities to prevent such behavior. Second, they can check the tobacco use status of adolescent patients regularly, and attempt to deter regular use of tobacco and motivate users to quit sooner rather than later. Unfortunately, exactly how best to achieve this is not yet known, so physicians and dentists also need to support and cooperate with research efforts (e.g., by participating in clinical trials) to find out. Third, physicians and other health care providers can provide young tobacco users with the skills and supports to quit, making use of existing self-help materials and adjuncts as part of a comprehensive stepped-care approach (see Chapter 10). A range of new self-help smokeless cessation materials has been developed to appeal especially to young users (USDHHS, 1992). Self-help programs are of greatest benefit to those individuals highly motivated to quit, and many youth are not so motivated, so self-help adjuncts (i.e., brief face-to-face counseling, telephone hot lines, peer counseling) should be considered along with self-help materials. Fourth, physicians can refer motivated youth to existing adult-oriented cessation programs and materials (see Chapters 10 and 11). Referral to more intensive programs is likely to be most successful when groups contain or consist exclusively of peers and are run by peers who have successfully quit. Fifth, medical personnel should do all they can to (1) support the development, dissemination, and delivery of effective tobacco cessation and nicotine treatment programs for youth; (2) oppose tobacco advertising aimed at youth and support legislation and community action to restrict access to tobacco; and (3) encourage interested youth to participate in antitobacco activities.[18]

CONCLUSIONS

Overall initiation of tobacco use among youth seems to be declining, but only marginally so among those with low educational aspirations. We have identified the stages of onset of tobacco use by youth, and several domains of variables important in the onset process—social organization, social bonding, social learning (observation, availability, social norms, reinforcement), pharmacological, intrapsychic (including social skills), and cognitive. These may have differ-

ent effects at different stages of onset, and they may also interact in complex ways. However, it is clear that successful prevention and early cessation requires consideration of all of the determinants and their interactions.

Barriers to prevention are multiple, including the complexity of the acquisition process, pressure on youth to use, and tobacco industry advertising and other promotion. Information-based approaches to prevention have failed, probably due to their lack of consideration of the psychosocial and pharmacological determinants of tobacco use. Programs based on psychosocial approaches have had some success in delaying the onset of smoking; however, these programs might be more effective when combined with community interventions, and prevention programs need to start in elementary school or before and follow a "developmentally sensitive" path through high school and beyond. Policy-based initiatives like increased excise taxes, also are unlikely to achieve maximum impact without concomitant counter-advertising and school-based prevention strategies (Pierce et al. 1993). Pharmacological processes also must be considered, and social and school policies should be addressed.

Cessation of smoking by youth is not easier than it is for adults and may even be more difficult since youth are less motivated to quit by the possible long-term consequences to their health. Youth do, however, make frequent and unsuccessful attempts to quit, and they report many of the same reasons for difficulty in quitting as adults. Youth who desire to quit have great difficulty finding programs tailored for them. Effective programs will need to educate youth about the importance and power of addiction, and teach them how to handle social and stressful situations, as well as address all those issues of importance to adults.

Physicians, other health care workers, and public health workers can and should play a more positive and visible role in prevention and cessation. Physicians, dentists and allied health care providers should monitor family tobacco and other substance use and their precursors. They should work with families to remove the child's exposure to tobacco use by having parents quit and by providing patients with age-appropriate prevention materials. Finally, physicians and other health care workers should work within their communities to alter the availability of tobacco products and the social norms surrounding their use.

EARLY NOTES

1. Data from other sources, though usually based on less representative samples, tend to be fairly consistent with those from ISR with the one exception of school dropouts (see later).
2. The 1991 Youth Risk Behavior Survey showed 19.2% of 9th–12th grade boys, versus 1.3% of girls, using smokeless tobacco at any time in the past month (CDC, 1992).
3. One exception to this is among American Indians (Hall and Dexter 1988; Schinke et al. 1987).
4. This is known as the *gateway* or *stepping stone hypothesis*. However, recent analyses question whether use of one substance actually *causes* subsequent use of other substances (Miller and Flay, under review). Rather, the mechanisms that explain the observed correlations may simply concern (1) the availability or population prevalence of use (the more available and accepted a substance is in society, the more likely it is to be tried) and (2) a learned or personality-based addiction-proneness (addiction-prone people are more likely to want to try other addictive substances and more likely to become addicted to them once they have tried or become addicted to one addictive substance).
5. About 3,000 children currently start smoking every day in the United States. During their lifetime, it is expected that of these 3,000 children, approximately 22 will be murdered (mostly while young with 1,100 life-years lost), 30 will die in traffic accidents (also mostly when young, with 1,500 life-years lost), and nearly 750 will die from smoking-related causes (with an average 21 years of life lost—15,750 life-years lost). That is, 15 times as many of these people will die because of smoking than from accidents and murders combined, with the loss of 5–6 as many life-years.
6. Even a few adults continue to smoke regularly without becoming addicted. Note that the process of addiction to nicotine is no different from the process of addiction to any other substance. However, there are differ-

ences concerning the probability of addiction (very high for nicotine and cocaine, lower for marijuana, even lower for alcohol), the speed of the addiction process (slower for nicotine, faster for cocaine), and the seriousness of the consequences of addiction (more serious in the short term for many illicit drugs and heavy use of alcohol, more serious in the long term for nicotine).

7. The extent to which this class of variables is predictive of cigarette smoking, as opposed to illicit drug use, is unclear given the lower rates of smoking among blacks compared to whites. However, the relationship of smoking to educational status in the U.S. population as a whole supports it.
8. Brandon and Baker (1986) found that adult quitters who experience dizziness upon retrial were more likely than others to relapse and returned more quickly to prequitting levels of smoking.
9. Thus, they are often considered as dependent variables rather than predictors.
10. The CMA also supported a new initiative for the 1992 ballot to enlarge the insurance net for indigent Californians. The plan was to take all but a fraction of the Proposition 99 funds raised from tobacco taxes, thereby subverting the public education fund.
11. It is not possible to determine whether one approach is better than another, e.g., life-social skills vs. social influence, because of many differences between studies in sampling, measures, and analytical strategies.
12. Dr. Thomas J. Glynn provides brief descriptions of some of these programs in *School Programs to Prevent Smoking: The National Cancer Institute Guide to Strategies that Succeed*. NIH Publication No. 90-500, January 1990. He also provides contact addresses for each program he describes.
13. The Project STAR curriculum/program is a version of Project SMART, available from the University of Southern California (see footnote 12).
14. The issue of developmental sensitivity is very important in a broader sense. Developing youth are unprepared to handle changing feelings and urges. Parents and teachers rarely discuss urges and feelings with youth. The result is that the socializaton of feelings is often left to peers. We should not neglect such basic needs in substance abuse prevention (as well as sex education and AIDS prevention).
15. Researchers at the Fox Chase Cancer Center in Philadelphia have developed materials for delivery to mothers of preschool children by

physicians and other health workers (Keintz et al. 1988; Fleisher et al. 1990). Materials may be obtained from Ms. Martha Keintz, MPH, Fox Chase Cancer Center, 7701 Burholme Ave, Philadelphia, PA 19011. (Keintz, M. K., Rimer, B, Fleisher, L., Fox, L., Engstrom, P. F. Use of multiple data sources in planning a smoking cessation program for a defined population. In Engstron, P. F., Anderson, P. N., Mortenson, L. E., eds. *Advances in Cancer Control: Cancer Control Research and the Emergence of the Oncology Product Line.* New York: Alan R. Liss, Inc., 1988.; Fleisher, L., Keintz, M. K., Rimer, B., Utt, M., Workman, S., Engstrom, P. F. Process evaluation of a minimal-contact smoking cessation program in an urban nutritional assistance [WIC] program. Fox Chase Cancer Center, Philadelphia, 1990.)

16. This is not to deny the potential benefit of DOC activities. They have clearly focused some attention on the advertising of a lethal product by an irresponsible industry. This would not have occurred nearly so soon without DOC's "guerrilla warfare" approach. However, DOC should not claim that their approach to classroom prevention is effective without proper evaluation—rather, they should work with other program developers to incorporate some of their approach into effective programs. It was good that DOC did what they could when opportunities arose, without waiting for research support, as long as they do not lose sight of the eventual need for a comprehensive approach built upon a strong research base.

17. Researchers and voluntary health organizations have developed several clinic-based and self-help cessation programs especially for youth (ACS, 1980, 1986; Bennett, Austin, Janizewski 1986; Eakin, Severson, Glasgow 1989; Glover 1986; Hulbert 1978; Severson et al. 1987; St. Pierre, Shute, Jaycox 1983; Weissman et al. 1987). However, without further research, none of them can yet be recommended confidently. However, when incorporated into a comprehensive intervention including medical advice to quit, setting a quit date, the offer of self-help materials, brief counseling and/or clinic referrals and regular follow-up, results should be better than doing nothing. (American Cancer Society, ACS. *Facilitator's Guide: Youth Smoking Cessation Clinic.* New York: American Cancer Society, 1980; ACS. *Breaking Free: Discussion Guide.* New York: American Cancer Society, 1986; Fleisher, L., Keintz, M., Rimer, B., Utt, M., Workman, S., Engs-

trom, P. F. Process evaluation of a minimal-contact smoking cessation program in an urban nutritional assistance [WIC] program. Fox Chase Cancer Center, Philadelphia, 1990; St. Pierre, R. W., Shute, R. E., Jaycox, S. Youth helping youth: A behavioral approach to the self-control of smoking. *Health Educ* 14(1):28–31, 1983.)

18. Physicians might find the publication, *Tobacco Youth Reporter* a useful resource for this purpose. It can be obtained by contacting Stop Teenage Addiction to Tobacco (STAT), PO Box 60658, Longmeadow, MA 01106-9979.

ACKNOWLEDGMENTS

Writing of this chapter was supported by research grants from the National Cancer Institute (CA44907 and CA42760), the National Heart, Lung and Blood Institute (HL42485) and the National Institute on Drug Abuse (DA03468 and DA03976). Portions of this material also appear in the report of the NHLBI Task Force on Research and Education of the Prevention and Control of Respiratory Disease, 1990. I thank Allan Best, John Elder, Tom Glynn, Ed Lichtenstein, Guy Parcel, Steve Sussman, and Nan Tobler for helpful comments.

REFERENCES

Akers, R. L. *Deviant Behavior: A Social Learning Perspective.* Belmont, CA: Wadsworth, 1977.

Altman, D. G., Slater, M. D., Albright, C. L., Maccoby, N. How an unhealthy product is sold: Cigarette advertising in magazines (1960–1985) *J Communication* 37:95–106, 1987.

Altman, D. G., Foster, V., Rasinick-Douss, L., Tye, J. C. Reducing the illegal sale of cigarettes to minors. *JAMA* 261(1):80–83, 1989.

Altman, D. G., Raesnick-Douss, L., Foster, V., Tye, J. B. Sustained effect of an educational program to reduce sales of cigarettes to minors. *Am J Pub Health* 81:891–893, 1991.

Bachman, J. G., Johnston, L. D., O'Malley, P. M., Humphrey, R. H. Explaining the recent decline in marijuana use: Differentiating the effects of perceived risks, disapproval, and general lifestyle factors. *J Health Soc Behav* 29:92–112, 1988.

Baker, T. B., Morse, E., Sherman, J. E. The motivation to use drugs: A psychobiological analysis of urges. In *Nebraska Symposium on*

Motivation. Lincoln, NE: University of Nebraska Press, 1986, 257–323.

Bandura, A. *Social Foundations of Thought and Action: A Social Cognitive Theory.* Englewood Cliffs, NJ: Prentice-Hall, 1986.

Barovich, M., Sussman, S., Dent, C. W., Stacy, A. W., Burton, D., Flay, B. R. Availability of tobacco products at stores located near public schools. *Inter J Addict,* 26(8):843–856, 1991.

Basch, C. E., Eveland, J. D., Portnoy, B. Diffusion systems for education and learning about health. *Fam Community Health* 9(2):1 26, 1986.

Bennett, G., Austin, D., Janizewski, R. Save a sweetheart: A smoking intervention in senior high school. Paper presented at 114th annual meeting of American Public Health Association, Las Vegas, 29 September 1986.

Best, J. A., Thomson, S. J., Santi, S. M., Smith, E. A., Brown, K. S. Preventing cigarette smoking among school children. *Am Rev Public Health* 9:161–201, 1988.

Botvin, G. J., and Wills, T. A. Personal and social skills training: Cognitive–behavioral approaches to substance abuse prevention. In Bell, C. S., and Battjes, R., eds. *Prevention Research: Deterring Drug Abuse Among Children and Adolescents.* NIDA Research Monograph 63. U.S. Department of Health and Human Services, Public Health Service, Alcohol, Drug Abuse, and Mental Health Administration, National Institute on Drug Abuse. DHHS Publication No. (ADM)85-1334, 1985, 8–49.

Boyd, G., et al. Use of smokeless tobacco among children and adolescents in the United States. *Prev Med* 16(3):402–421, 1987.

Brandon, T. H., and Baker, T. B. The process of relapse. Paper presented at the 20th annual convention of the Association for the Advancement of Behavior Therapy, Chicago, November 1986.

Burton, D., Graham, M., Flay, B. R., Hahn, G., Craig, S., Sussman, S., Dent, C., Stacy, A. Motivating tobacco cessation among high school students. Paper presented at the annual meeting of the Society of Public Health Educators, Chicago, October 1989.

CDC (Centers for Disease Control). Selected tobacco-use behaviors and dietary patterns among high school students. *Morbidity and Mortality Weekly Report.* 41:417–421, 1992.

———. Tobacco use among high school students. *Morbidity and Mortality Weekly Report.* 40:617–619, 1991.

Charlton, A., Melia, P., Moyer, C. *A Manual on Tobacco and Young People for the Industrialized World.* Geneva, Switzerland: International Union Against Cancer (UICC), 1990.

Choi, W. S., Novotny, T. E., Thimis, A. T. Restricting minors' access to tobacco: A review of state legislation, 1991. *Am J Prev Med* 8:19–22, 1992.

Connolly, G., Orleans, C. T., Blum, A. Snuffing tobacco out of sport. *Am J Pub Health* 82:351–353, 1992.

Conrad, K., Flay, B. R., Hill, D. Why children start smoking cigarettes: Predictors of onset. *Brit J of Addiction* 87:1711–1724, 1992.

Covey, L. S. and Tam, D. Depressive mood, the single-parent home and adolescent cigarette smoking. *Am J Pub Health* 80:1330–1333, 1990.

Cummings, K. M., Sciandra, R., Davis, S., Rimer, B Response to anti-smoking campaign aimed at mothers with young children. *Health Educ Res* 4(4):429–437, 1989.

Durell, J., and Bukoski, W. Preventing substance abuse: The state of the art. *Public Health Rep* 99(1):23–31, 1984.

Dwyer, J. H., Rieger-Ndakorerwa, G. E., Semmer, N. K., Fuchs, R., Lippert, P. Low-level cigarette smoking and longitudinal change in serum cholesterol among adolescents. *JAMA* 259(19):2857–2862, 1988.

Eakin, E., Severson, H., Glasgow, R. E. Development and evaluation of a smokeless tobacco cessation program: A pilot study. *Natl Cancer Inst Monogr* 8:95–100, 1989.

Ershler, J., Leventhal, H., Fleming, R., Glynn, K. The quitting experience for smokers in sixth through twelfth grades. *Addict Behav* 14:365–378, 1989.

Evans, R. I. Smoking in children: Developing a social psychological strategy of deterrence. *Prev Med* 5:122–127, 1976.

Feighery, E., Altman, D. G., Shaffer, G. The effects of combining education and enforcement to reduce tobacco sales to minors. *JAMA* 266:3168–3171, 1991.

Fischer, P. M., Schwartz, M. P., Richards, J. W., Goldstein, A. O., Rojas, T. Brand logo recognition by children aged 3 to 6 years: Mickey Mouse and Old Joe the Camel. *JAMA,* 266:3145–3148, 1991.

Flay, B. R. Psychosocial approaches to smoking prevention: A review of findings. *Health Psychol* 4(5):449–488, 1985.

———. *Selling the Smokeless Society: 56 Evaluated Programs and Campaigns Worldwide.* Washington, D.C.: American Public Health Association, 1987.

Flay, B. R., d'Avernas, J. R., Best, J. A., Kersell, M. W., Ryan, K. B. Cigarette smoking: Why young people do it and ways of preventing it.

In McGrath, P. J., and Firestone, P., eds. *Pediatric and Adolescent Behavioral Medicine.* New York: Springer Verlag, 1983.

Flay, B. R., Keopke, D., Thomson, S. J., Santi, S., Best, J. A., Brown, K. S. Long-term follow-up of the first Waterloo smoking prevention trial. *Am J Public Health* 79(10):1371–1376, 1989.

Flay, B. R., and Petraitis, J. M. Methodological issues in drug abuse prevention research: Theoretical foundations. In Leukefeld, C. G., and Bukoski, W. J. (eds.) *Drug abuse prevention intervention research: Methodological issues.* Washington DC: NIDA Research Monograph 107:81–109, 1991.

Flay, B. R., and Petraitis, J. The theory of triadic influence: A new theory of health behavior with implications for preventive interventions. In Albrecht, G. S. (ed.) *Advances in Medical Sociology, Vol IV: A Reconsideration of models of health behavior change.* Greenwich, CN: JAI Press, 1993 (in press).

Forster, J. L., Hourigan, M. E., Kelder, S. Locking devices on cigarette vending machines: Evaluation of a city ordinance. *Am J Pub Health* 82:1217–1219, 1992.

Forster, J. L., Hourigan, M. E., McGovern, P. Availability of cigarettes to underage youth in three communities. *Prev Med* 21:320–328, 1992.

Forster, J. L., Klepp, K. I., Jeffrey, R. W. Sources of cigarettes for tenth graders in two Minnesota cities. *Health Educ Res* 4:45–50, 1989.

Glover, E. D. Conducting smokeless tobacco cessation clinics. *Am J Public Health* 76(2):207, 1986.

Glynn, T. J. Essential elements of school-based smoking prevention programs: Research results. *J Sch Health* 59:181–188, 1989.

Goodstadt, M. S. Alcohol and drug education: Models and outcomes. *Health Educ Monogr* 6(3):263–279, 1978.

Graham, M., Burton, D., Flay, B. R., Hahn, G., Sussman, S., Craig, S., Dent, C., Stacy, A. Focus groups, high school students and tobacco cessation. Paper presented at the annual meeting of the Society of Public Health Educators, Chicago, October 1989.

Hahn, G., Sussman, S., Dent, C., Burton, D., Stacy, A., Flay, B. R. Adolescents anticipated effects of quitting the use of cigarettes and smokeless tobacco. Paper presented at the annual meeting of the Society of Public Health Educators, Chicago, October 1989.

Hall, R. L., and Dexter, D. Smokeless tobacco use and attitudes toward smokeless tobacco among Native Americans and other adolescents in the Northwest. *Am J Public Health* 78(12):1586–1588, 1988.

Hammond, S. K. and Leaderer, B. P. A diffusion monitor to measure exposure to passive smoking. *Environ Sci Technol* 21:494–497, 1987.

Hansen, W. B., Collins, L. M., Johnson, C., Graham, J. W. Self-initiated smoking cessation among high school students. *Addict Behav* 10:265–271, 1985.

Hansen, W. B., Johnson, C. A., Flay, B. R., Graham, J. W., Sobel, S. Affective and social influences approaches to the prevention of multiple substance abuse among seventh grade students: Results from Project SMART. *Prev Med* 17:135–154, 1988.

Henningfield, J. E., Clayton, R., Pollin, W. The involvement of tobacco in alcoholism and illicit drug use. *Br J Addict* 85:279–292, 1990.

Hirschman, R. S., Leventhal, H., Glynn, K. The development of smoking behavior: Conceptualization and supportive cross-sectional survey data. *J Appl Soc Psychol* 14:184–206, 1984.

Hirschman, R. S., and Leventhal, H. Preventing smoking behavior in school children: An initial test of a cognitive–developmental program. *J Appl Soc Psychol* 19:559–583, 1989.

Jason, L., Ji, P., Birkhead, S., Xaverious, P. Preventing cigarette sales to minors. Manuscript in preparation, DePaul University, Chicago, 1990.

Jessor, R., and Jessor, S. L. *Problem Behavior.* New York: Academic Press, 1977.

Johnson, C. A. Untested and erroneous assumptions underlying anti-smoking programs. In Coates, T. J., Peterson, A. C., Perry, C., eds. *Promoting Adolescent Health.* New York: Academic Press, 1982.

Johnston, L. D., O'Malley, P. M., Bachman, J. G. *Drug Use Drinking and Smoking: National Survey Results from High School, College, and Young Adult Populations. 1975–1988.* Washington, D.C.: National Institute on Drug Abuse, 1989.

Johnston, L. D., O'Malley, P. M., Bachman, O. G. *National Survey Results on Drug Use from the Monitoring to Future Study, 1975–1992. (Volume I: Secondary School Students).* Rockville, MD: National Institute on Drug Abuse, in press.

Kandel, D. B. Stages in adolescent involvement in drug use. *Science* 190:912–914, 1975.

Kaplan, H. B., Martin, S. S., Robbins, C. Pathways to adolescent drug use: Self-derogation, peer influence, weakening of social controls, and early substance use. *J Health Soc Behav* 25:270–289, 1984.

Kellam, S. G., Brown, C. H., Fleming, J. P. The prevention of teenage substance use: Longitudinal research and strategy. In Coates, T. J., Peterson, A. C., Perry, C., eds. *Promoting Adolescent Health.* New York: Academic Press, 1982.

Krohn, M. D., Massey, J. L., Skinner, W. F., Lauer, R. M. Social bonding theory and adolescent cigarette smoking: A longitudinal analysis. *J Health Soc Behav* 24:337–249, 1983.

Laugesen, M. *Health or Tobacco: An End to Tobacco Advertising and Promotion.* Wellington, New Zealand: Toxic Substances Board, P.O. Box 5013. 1989.

Leventhal, H., and Cleary, P. D. The smoking problem: A review of research and theory in behavioral risk modification. *Psychol Bull* 88:370–405, 1980.

Leventhal, H., Fleming, R., Ershler, J. Nicotine dependence and prevention. Unpublished manuscript, 1988, University of Wisconsin.

Leventhal, H., Glynn, K., Fleming, R. Is the smoking decision an "informed choice"?: Effect of smoking risk factors on smoking. *JAMA* 257:3373–3376, 1987.

MacKinnon, D. P., Johnson, C. A., Pentz, M.A.P., Dwyer, J. H., Hansen, W. B., Flay, B. R., Wang, E. Mediating mechanisms in a school-based prevention program: First year effects of the Midwestern Prevention Project. *Health Psychol* 10(3):164–172, 1991.

Marcus, A. C., Crane, L. A., Shopland, D. R., Lynn, W. R. Use of smokeless tobacco in the United States: Recent estimates from the current population survey. *Natl Cancer Inst Monogr* 8:17–24, 1989.

Marr, M. Proposition 99: The California tobacco tax initiative. Report for the Western Consortium for Public Health, Berkeley, CA, 1990.

Miller, T. Q., and Flay, B. R. Patterns of drug use. Under review. University of Illinois at Chicago.

Mosbach, P., and Leventhal, H. Peer group identification and smoking: Implications for intervention. *J Abnorm Psychol* 97(2):238–245, 1988.

Murray, D. M., Pirie, P., Luepker, R. V., Pallonen, U. Five and six-year followup results from four seventh-grade smoking prevention strategies. *J Behav Med* 12:207–218, 1989.

Novotny, T. E., Pierce, J. P., Fiore, M. C., Hatziandreu, E., Davis, R. M. Smokeless tobacco use in the United States: The Adults Use of Tobacco Surveys. *Natl Cancer Inst Monogr* 8:25–28, 1989.

Pentz, M. A., Dwyer, J. II., MacKinnon, D. P.,

Flay, B. R., Hansen, W. B., Wang, E.Y.I., Johnson, C. A. A multi-community trial for primary prevention of adolescent drug abuse: Effects on drug use prevalence. *JAMA* 261(22):3259–3266, 1989.

Pentz, M. A., MacKinnon, D. M., Dwyer J. H., Wang, E.Y.I., Hansen, W. B., Flay, B. R., Johnson, C. A. Longitudinal effects of the Midwestern Prevention Project (MPP) on regular and experimental smoking in adolescents. *Prev Med* 18:304–321, 1989.

Pentz, M. A., Brannon, B. R., Charlin, V. L., Barrett, E. J., MacKinnon, D. P., Flay, B. R. The power of policy: Relationship of smoking policy to adolescent smoking. *Am J Public Health,* in press.

Pierce, J. P., Farkas, A., Evans, N., et al. *Tobacco Use in California: A Focus on Preventing Uptake in Adolescents.* Sacramento, California: California Department of Health Services, March, 1993.

Pirie, P. L., Murray, D. M., Luepker, R. V. Smoking prevalence in a cohort of adolescents, including absentees, dropouts, and transfers. *Am J Public Health* 78(2):176–178, 1988.

Richardson, J., Dwyer, K., McGuigan, K., Hansen, W. B., Dent, C., Johnson, C. A., Sussman, S. Y., Brannon, B., Flay, B. R. Substance use among eighth grade students who take care of themselves after school. *Pediatrics* 84(3):556–566, 1989.

Robinson, R. G., Barry, M., Bloch, M., et al. Report of the Tobacco Policy Research Group on Marketing and Promotions Targeted at African Americans, Latinos and Women. *Tobacco Control* (Suppl.) *1*:S24-S30, 1992.

Schinke, S. P., Schilling, R. F., Gilchrist, L. D., Ashby, M. R., Kitajima, E. Pacific Northwest Native American youth and smokeless tobacco use. *Inter J Addict* 22(9):881–884, 1987.

Severson, H., James, L. E., Lachance, P.-A, Eakin, E. *Up to Snuff: A Handbook on Smokeless Tobacco.* Eugene, OR: Independent Video Services, 1987.

Slade, J. A retreat in the tobacco war. *JAMA* 268:524–525, 1992.

Shiffman, S., and Wills, T. A. *Coping and Substance Use.* Orlando, FL: Academic Press, 1985.

Stepney, R. Human smoking behavior and the development of dependence on tobacco smoking. In Bowman, W. C., ed. *Nicotine and the Tobacco Smoking Habit.* Oxford: Pergamon Press, 1984, 153–176.

Sussman, S. Two social influence perspectives of tobacco use development and prevention. *Health Educ Res* 4:213–223, 1989.

Sussman, S., Dent, C. W., Stacy, A., Raynor, A., Burciaga, C., Turner, G., Charlin, V., Craig, S., Hansen, W. B., Burton, D., Flay, B. R. Peer group association and adolescent tobacco use. *J Abnorm Psychol,* 99(4):349–352, 1990.

Sweanor, D., Ballin, S., Corcoran, R. D., et al. Report of the Tobacco Policy Research Study Group on Tobacco Pricing and Taxation in the United States. *Tobacco Control* (Suppl.) *1*:S31-S36, 1992.

Thompson, E. L. Smoking education programs, 1960–1976. *Am J Public Health* 68:250–257, 1978.

Tobler, N. S. Meta-analysis of 143 adolescent drug prevention programs: Quantitative outcome results of program participants compared to a control or comparison group. *J Drug Issues* 17:537–567, 1986.

U.S. Department of Health and Human Services (USDHHS). *The Health Consequences of Using Smokeless Tobacco: A Report of the Advisory Committee to the Surgeon General.* U.S. Department of Health and Human Services, Public Health Service, Centers for Disease Control, Center for Health Promotion and Education, Office on Smoking and Health. NIH Publication No. 86-2874, 1986a.

———. *Smoking and Health: A National Status Report. A Report of the Surgeon General.* U.S. Department of Health and Human Services, Public Health Service, Centers for Disease Control, Center for Health Promotion and Education, Office on Smoking and Health. DHHS Publication No. (CDC)87-8398, 1986b.

———. *Spit Tobacco and Youth* U. S. Department of Health and Human Services, Office of Inspector General, DHHS Publication No. (OE1)06-92-00500, 1992.

———. *The Health Consequences of Smoking: Nicotine Addiction. A Report of the Surgeon General.* U.S. Department of Health and Human Services, Public Health Service, Centers for Disease Control, Center for

Health Promotion and Education, Office on Smoking and Health. DHHS Publication No. (CDC)88-8406, 1988.

———. *The Health Consequences of Smoking: 25 Years of Progress. A Report of the Surgeon General.* U.S. Department of Health and Human Services, Public Health Service, Centers for Disease Control, Center for Health Promotion and Education, Office on Smoking and Health. DHHS Publication No. (CDC)89-8411, 1989.

Warner, K. E. Cigarette advertising and media coverage of smoking and health. *N Engl J Med* 312:304–388, 1985.

Warner, K. E., Goldenhar, L. M., McLaughlin, C. G. Cigarette advertising and magazine coverage of the hazards of smoking. *N Eng J Med* 326:305–309, 1992.

Weissman, W., Glasgow, R., Biglan. A., Lichtenstein, E. Development and preliminary evaluation of a cessation program for adolescent smokers. *Psychol Addict Behav* 1(2):84–91, 1987.

Whalen, E. M. *A Smoking Gun: How the Tobacco Industry Gets Away with Murder.* Philadelphia: George F. Stickley Co., 1984.

Wilson, W. J. *The Truly Disadvantaged: The Inner City, the Underclass, and Public Policy.* Chicago: The University of Chicago Press, 1987.

Worden, J. K., Flynn, B. S., Brisson, S. F., Secker-Walker, R. H., McAuliffe, T. L., Jones, R. P. An adult communication skills program to prevent adolescent smoking. *J Drug Educ* 17(1):1–9, 1987.

Yates, G. L., MacKenzie, R., Pennbridge, J., Kohen, E. A risk profile comparison of runaway and non-runaway youth. *Am J Public Health* 78(37):820–821, 1988.

Young, R. L., De Moor, C., Wildey, M. B., Gully, S., Hovell, M. F., Elder, J. P. Correlates of health facilitator performance in a tobacco-use prevention program: Implications for recruitment. *J Sch Health,* 60(9):463–467, 1990.

20

Older Smokers

BARBARA K. RIMER and C. TRACY ORLEANS

The older population is growing steadily, and by the year 2010 will represent 20% of the total U.S. population. Only recently has special attention been paid to the needs of older smokers. Older smokers experience many significant health consequences from continued smoking and derive a number of important health benefits when they stop smoking. However, they also may face special barriers when they attempt to quit after a lifetime of smoking. This chapter reviews smoking prevalence rates for older smokers, examines the health effects associated with continued smoking, the health benefits of quitting, and suggests programmatic strategies for intervention. The role of physicians is pivotal and will be discussed.

SMOKING AND HEALTH CHARACTERISTICS OF OLDER SMOKERS

Prevalence

The data summarized here derive from three sources: the National Health Interview Survey (NHIS), a national household probability survey of the U.S. adult population; the Adult Use of Tobacco Survey (AUTS), a national telephone survey of U.S. adults; and a recent American Association of Retired Persons (AARP) mail survey of AARP members throughout the United States (Rimer et al. 1990; Orleans et al. 1991).

As Table 20–1 shows, smoking rates decrease as age increases. However, there are more than 13 million American smokers aged 50 years or older; one out of five smokers is aged 50 years and older. About 28% of men and women over 50 years of age smoke, similar to the entire U.S. adult population. It

is not until after age 65 years that smoking rates show a substantial decline. Smoking rates are higher among those with less than a high school education and are especially high among minority men: 40% of Hispanic men aged 55–74 years smoke; 46% of African-American men aged 50–59 years and 31% aged 60–69 years smoke (see Chapter 6 for further discussion of smoking prevalence). As today's older minority smokers age, health care practitioners will be presented with new challenges in helping them to stop smoking.

Older smokers smoke an average of 22 cigarettes per day, and are more likely than younger smokers to smoke heavily and to have smoked for a long time. This may make quitting smoking especially difficult. In the AARP, AUTS, and NHIS surveys, about 43% of older respondents reported that they smoked 11–20 cigarettes per day. Yet, nearly half of the respondents were not concerned about the harmful effects of smoking. This may mean, in part, that older smokers are less knowledgeable about the health hazards of continued smoking. Among the AARP current smokers, 23% said they had never tried to quit, while 37% of AUTS smokers said they had never tried. Thus, there are substantial numbers of older smokers who could be motivated to attempt to quit, and who should be educated about the risks of smoking and the benefits of quitting.

Health Consequences of Continued Smoking for Older Adults

Smoking is a major risk factor in 7 of the top 14 causes of death for people aged 65 years

385

Table 20–1 Proportion of Current Smokers by Age and Sex in Three Surveys

Age (yr)	%/No. Responding	Females			Males		
		AARP	NHIS	AUTS	AARP	NHIS	AUTS
50–54	%	12.2	34.1	37.4	22.9	32.6	36.0
	n	41	882	444	48	1,058	456
55–59	%	13.6	34.7	36.9	20.3	32.2	30.9
	n	184	897	439	128	1,165	440
60–64	%	11.4	30.5	26.5	16.4	26.1	34.3
	n	352	917	449	225	1,231	463
65–69	%	9.2	24.6	22.3	12.9	20.6	26.8
	n	456	740	363	326	1,260	426
70–74	%	6.7	21.8	18.5	13.7	17.2	24.5
	n	356	610	303	256	1,113	314
75–79	%	5.7	16.1	18.1	8.7	10.4	17.4
	n	194	417	171	183	890	196
80+	%	4.2	12.0	14.1	4.8	4.6	9.5
	n	143	375	78	188	856	116
All ages	%	8.9	27.3	27.9	13.0	21.4	28.8
	n	1,726	4,838	2,247	1,354	7,573	2,411

Source: Prepared by Martha Kasper Keintz, Sc.M., Fox Chase Cancer Center.

AARP = American Association of Retired Persons Mailed Survey 1988; NHIS = National Health Interview Household Survey 1985; AUTS = Adult Use of Tobacco Telephone Survey 1986.

and older (Special Committee on Aging, U.S. Senate 1986). Smoking exerts a significant impact on morbidity from cardiovascular, cerebrovascular, and respiratory diseases (USDHHS 1984b, 1989; Howard, Toole, Frye-Pierson 1987; Salive et al. 1992). Prevalence rates for cough, phlegm, and chronic bronchitis among smokers increase with advancing age (USDHHS 1984a; Burr, Phillips, Hurst 1985). More than half of the respiratory system disease deaths among men aged 65 years and older, and more than a third of those among women of the same age, are attributable to smoking. Deaths from chronic obstructive lung disease rise to about 425 per 100,000 adults among smokers 75–84 years old compared to about 50 per 100,000 for nonsmokers (USDHHS 1984a). Men aged 65 years and older who smoke are nearly twice as likely to die from stroke, and women smokers are about 1.5 times as likely to die from stroke as nonsmokers (USDHHS 1984a).

In addition, smoking complicates illnesses and conditions that are more prevalent in older people. Conditions that may be worsened by smoking include heart disease, high blood pressure, circulatory and vascular conditions, duodenal ulcers, reductions in smell and taste, and diabetes (Achkar

1985; Moore 1986; Somerville, Faulkner, Langman 1986). Persons with diabetes who smoke are more likely to suffer serious or fatal complications, such as heart disease, blindness, and stroke (Schumacher and Smith 1988).

Current smokers in the AARP survey reported significantly more trouble breathing, frequent coughing, and tiring very easily compared to former smokers and never-smokers. Also, fewer smokers reported themselves to be "more active" than other persons their age and twice as many current as never-smokers described their health status as poor (Rimer et al. 1990). Disabilities caused by smoking-related diseases not only cause morbidity and mortality, but also compromise precious independence. In addition, smokers in both the AARP and NHIS surveys were less likely to have had blood pressure checks and pap smears compared to the overall surveyed group (see Table 20–2), and smokers in the AARP survey were less likely to have obtained a regular physical checkup, electrocardiogram (EKG), stool blood test, or mammogram than former smokers or never-smokers. Thus, smoking also appears to serve as a deterrent to preventive health care and to screening (Orleans, Rimer, Salmon 1990)—

Table 20-2 Health Care Utilization within Past Year by Smoking Status (Respondents aged 50 yrs and over)

	AARP (n = 3,147) % Responding		NHIS (n = 12,680) % Responding	
	Nonsmokers	Smokers[a]	Nonsmokers	Smokers[b]
No health care visits	14	24	21	27
No blood pressure check	13	21	20	26
No Pap smear (females only)	60	64	70	72

[a]n = 339.
[b]n = 2,943.

for the very illnesses for which their smoking places them at higher risk and for other diseases that are curable when found early although not related to smoking. Smokers in the AARP clearly were experiencing the negative consequences of their smoking. Yet, they may harbor deep-seated concerns about smoking-related health problems which could lead them to avoid regular health checkups.

Smoking can also affect drug action and metabolism for medications (Lipman 1985), such as Inderal (propanolol) (Hicks et al. 1981), and interferes with a range of other drug therapies, including antidepressants, lidocaine, pentazocine HCI, phenothiazines, and phenylbutazone. Cigarette smoking dramatically decreases serum levels of theophylline, aminophylline, and oxtriphylline (Talseth et al. 1981). Heavy smokers may need about one-half more insulin than nonsmokers (Todd 1987). The result is that drug dosages for the average older smoker may be subtherapeutic or ineffective (Greenblatt et al. 1980). Since older adults are heavier users of prescription drugs than any other age group, and many of these drugs are used to treat smoking-related illnesses, the consequences of smoking and prescription drug use interactions may be quite substantial.

Benefits of Cessation for Older Adults

Accumulating epidemiological and medical evidence reviewed in the 1990 Surgeon General's Report led to its conclusion that "it's never too late to stop smoking" (USDHHS 1990a). Older adults can achieve substantial medical and psychological benefits from quitting smoking. Stopping smoking can prevent the occurrence of some diseases, such as lung cancer and coronary heart disease (USDHHS 1989), and it also can stabilize existing conditions, such as chronic obstructive pulmonary disease (COPD), resulting in less disability and more independent functioning. This is true even for moderately ill patients who show improved survival when they stop smoking (Hermanson et al. 1988). Abramson (1985) concluded, on the basis of a review of large, prospective trials, that longevity probably can be increased by giving up smoking in the 60s and, especially for heavy smokers, even in the early 70s.

Quitting smoking exerts a protective action that increases with the number of years since stopping (Pathak et al. 1986). The benefits of quitting on coronary heart disease are almost immediate, while the benefits on respiratory function occur over a longer period of time (Gordon, Kannel, McGee 1974). Jajich, Ostfeld, and Freeman (1984) showed that while older smokers had a 52% higher risk for coronary heart disease compared to nonsmokers, quitting smoking in later life was associated with a rapid and sustained reduction in mortality from coronary heart disease. The Coronary Artery Surgery Study data showed that the benefits of quitting for participants aged 55 years and older almost immediately begin to reduce the risk of a heart attack. Smokers had a 70% higher risk of death compared to nonsmokers. The difference in survival benefits was most pronounced among the moderately ill patients (Hermanson et al. 1988).

Data from the Framingham study indicate that the risk of stroke diminishes rapidly among middle-aged and older adults who stop smoking. This is true even for those who were long-term cigarette smokers (Rowe 1985). Significant improvements in circulation and pulmonary perfusion occur rapidly when older people stop smoking, with most of the improvement occurring in the first year (Rogers et al. 1985). The cessation of cigarette smoking has a substantial salutary impact on the incidence and progression of COPD. Cigarette smokers who quit prior to developing abnormal lung function are unlikely to develop ventilatory limitations (USDHHS 1984b).

Overall, older adults who stop smoking can significantly improve the quantity and quality of their lives. The risk of coronary heart disease death among smokers who stay off cigarettes for 1–5 years is no higher than for never-smokers. Cessation leads to other benefits, including improved circulatory and respiratory function and reduced risk of COPD. However, Fries, Green, and Levine (1989) argue that the most important result of health life-style changes like stopping smoking may not be a *longer* life span, but a longer *active* life span, resulting from the prevention or compression of chronic illness in later years. In addition, although less well documented, it is expected that older quitters would achieve the same kinds of psychological benefit as documented by former smokers in the younger population (Orleans, Rimer, Salmon 1990). These would include increased self-esteem and improved sense of well-being. Smokers who adopt more adaptive coping behaviors, such as exercise, may reap other medical and psychological benefits as well. Finally, quitters will be more likely to remain independent, a freedom highly prized by older adults (Haug and Ory 1987).

Older Smokers Beliefs About Smoking

Recent analyses of the 1986 AUTS (USDHHS 1990b) data comparing smokers aged 21–49 years with smokers aged 50–74 years indicate a pervasive skepticism about smoking health harms and quitting benefits among American's older smokers (Orleans et al. 1990). Older smokers were significantly *less* likely than younger smokers to endorse or accept the link between smoking and ill-

ness (e.g., heart disease, lung cancer, emphysema, bronchitis) or to express concern about the personal health effects of smoking. Older smokers were *more* likely to view smoking as an effective coping strategy and weight control technique, with 47% of AUTS older smokers agreeing that smoking was less harmful than being 20 pounds overweight. AUTS data also showed a strong positive relationship between beliefs in smoking health harms and physician advice to quit. Smokers who had been advised to quit by a doctor were more likely than those who had not to state that smokers generally were more at risk for smoking-related diseases and conditions, to believe that smokers got more illnesses, to believe in the connection between smoking and illness, and to express concern about their personal health risks. A strong positive relationship was also found between quitting intention and past medical advice to quit. These findings underscore the need for physician advice to quit, and for health education campaigns and messages that emphasize both the harms of continued smoking and the benefits of quitting—even after 30, 40, or 50 years of smoking.

TAILORING INTERVENTIONS TO OLDER SMOKERS

Rationale

Today's older smokers matured before the release of the 1964 Surgeon General's Report which declared, for the first time in an official federal pronouncement, the health hazards of smoking. American soldiers were given cigarettes along with their C rations in World War II, and advertisements of the 1930s and 1940s proclaimed the benefits of smoking. Smoking was portrayed as not only pleasurable and sociable, but also as health-promoting. Advertisements even portrayed physicians as endorsing cigarettes during this time. It is no wonder that many older adults continue to smoke, and that 20–40% never have tried to quit (Orleans et al. 1990).

Yet, a large population of older smokers want to quit. Over 60% of AUTS smokers aged 50–74 years said they had tried to quit at least once, and 60% of those who had *not* tried to quit said they would quit if it were easy (Orleans et al. 1990). In the AARP survey noted earlier, 65% of all smokers aged 50–74 years said they were thinking about quitting in the next year—defining themselves as "contemplators" in the Prochaska and DiClemente (1983) staged model of change. However, these current smokers indicated a number of barriers to quitting: missing or craving cigarettes, losing a pleasure, being irritable, being nervous or tense, gaining weight, and boredom. Perceived barriers were greatest among the heaviest smokers, not those who had smoked the longest. Moreover, smokers' concerns about these barriers were strongly related to their quitting self-efficacy: smokers expecting more quitting difficulties reported less confidence in their ability to quit (Orleans et al. 1991). Thus, older smokers appear to be in a situation of great ambivalence—wanting to quit, but concerned about the problems associated with quitting. Moreover, their appraisal of these barriers increased with the severity of their addiction and the number of years they had smoked. In this section, some of the ways in which interventions should be tailored to the needs of older smokers will be reviewed.

Minimal-Contact Interventions for Older Smokers

The majority of smokers, both older and younger, prefer self-help methods for quitting (Fiore et al. 1990; Orleans et al. 1991). A major evaluation of eight self-help trials with adult smokers sponsored by the National Cancer Institute (NCI) showed adult quit rates ranging from 8–22% with an average quit rate of 14% 6 months after entry into the program (Cohen et al. 1989).

While there are many self-help programs, until recently, there were no self-help programs directed specifically at older adults (Bosse and Rose 1984). To overcome this deficiency, Orleans et al. (1989) developed *Clear Horizons,* a self-help smoking cessation guide designed especially for older adults. It addresses the unique quitting benefits and barriers and offers quitting strategies appropriate for older smokers. For example, the guide reviews the ways that tobacco interferes with a range of common medications, elaborates the benefits of quitting, and the risks of continued smoking even after 40–50 years of smoking, and addresses quitting motives and barriers especially important among older smokers. Four sections of the guide present information and self-change strategies appropriate for each of the five major stages of quitting: precontemplation, contemplation, action, and maintenance and relapse. *Clear Horizons* also provides tailored exercise guidelines for older adults and suggests age-appropriate substitutes for cigarettes. A clinical trial is being conducted to evaluate the impact of the targeted *Clear Horizons* guide used alone or with telephone counseling and/or with physician advice. Participants include 1,867 older smokers recruited through community and mass media sources and an additional 659 older smokers recruited through physicians' offices. Three-month follow-up guide ratings and 12-month quit rates were significantly more favorable for *Clear Horizons* than for the control NCI guide, *Clearing the Air*—a guide for smokers of all ages (Rimer et al. in press). Of course, many other self-help materials, while not specifically tailored to older smokers, could be used effectively, especially with appropriate mediation by a health professional or other trained person. These include those developed by the American Lung Association, such as *Freedom From Smoking for You and Your Family* (see Chapter 10).

The selection of self-help (or other) educational materials should be based on the learning needs of older adults. Older adults may experience age-related deficits in hearing and vision, so materials must be accessible visually and pretested for clarity of message (Rowe 1985). Although most older adults do not experience substantial cognitive deficits, some may require more time for processing and decision making. Communication can be enhanced by several techniques such as, use of large type in printed materials; repetition; use of categories to structure information; use of common, concrete words; and presenting most important information first or last (Rimer et al. 1983; Keintz et al. 1988). Any materials displayed in the office should contain pictures of older and younger people if intended for appeal to older smokers. Office posters and self-help guides should meet these criteria of accessibility to older smokers. Because older smokers are a heterogeneous population, print and other health education materials must be selected accordingly.

For many older smokers, self-help materials may not be enough. The survey of AARP members discussed earlier showed that older smokers often socialize in networks dominated by smokers (Rimer et al. 1990). They may need extra help to overcome barriers, such as, fear of failure, concern about gaining weight, losing a pleasure, or being bored. As a supplement to self-help and an alternative to clinic treatments, brief counseling by physicians, nurses, or other health professionals, lay leaders, or community counselors could address these barriers and identify methods of coping with withdrawal. Older adults will be disconcerted by abrupt, purely technical providers and will be more influenced by caring, empathic providers (Haug and Ory 1987).

Telephone counselors also may be important sources of support and planned follow-up. In September 1990, the Office on Smoking and Health launched a new campaign in conjunction with the Surgeon General's report on *The Health Benefits of Smoking Cessation* (USDHHS 1990a) and directed at older Americans. The program, "It's Never Too Late to Quit," consists of a television public station announcement and poster campaign which is cosponsored by the AARP, Administration on Aging, NCI, National Heart, Lung and Blood Institute, and the Department of Veteran's Affairs. Both programs refer older smokers who want to quit to call the NCI hot line (1-800-4-CANCER) to receive counseling and free self-quitting materials, including quitting "fact sheets" oriented especially to the older smoker. Three-month follow-up quit rates in a controlled study of the *Clear Horizons* guide for older smokers showed significantly higher quit rates for older smokers receiving the guide plus two follow-up counseling calls than for older smokers using the guide alone (12.5% *vs.* 8.8%) (Rimer et al. 1992).

Exercise may be a particularly useful strategy for helping older smokers to cope with some of the effects of withdrawal and the need to find permanent substitutes for tobacco. Even many older smokers with mobility problems can participate in low-impact aerobic exercises, such as swimming and walking. A study in California of older adults (McPhillips et al. 1989), found exercise to be positively associated with physical and emotional functioning and self-rated health.

Reaching Older Smokers Through Public Health and Mass Media Approaches

Findings from the AARP survey that almost one-third of older smokers are employed, that most belong to at least one community organization, and that most made at least one health care visit in the preceding year suggest a variety of channels for health education and quit smoking treatments aimed at older smokers, including worksites, community organizations, and medical settings. A variety of mass media channels also can be used to reach older smokers. Older adults are heavy users of the print and broadcast media, including both radio and television. Increasingly, age-tailored magazines, such as *Modern Maturity,* the magazine of the AARP, and *New Choices,* present excellent avenues for reaching targeted groups of older adults. In response to a brief announcement in *Modern Maturity* (December 1989–January 1990), we received more than 10,000 requests from older smokers for smoking cessation materials. The mass media can be used to enhance individual change by creating environments supportive of chance and by providing people with access to information (Farquahr et al. 1990).

Of course, like any other group of older adults, older smokers are heterogeneous, and no monolithic approach will be appropriate. All communications, however, should stress the benefits of quitting and harms of continued smoking since even symptomatic older smokers may deny smoking's health harms—or perhaps assume that symptoms caused by *smoking* (e.g., tiring easily, shortness of breath) are instead due to *aging.* Information that continued smoking is harmful, and quitting is beneficial, even after 50 years or more of smoking, may have a crucial impact in moving resigned or immotive smokers from pre-contemplation to contemplation and action stages. Such messages appear particularly important for smokers 65 years and older, who are most skeptical about quitting benefits. In addition, since older smokers are more likely to view smoking as an effective coping strategy and weight control technique, messages for older smokers should emphasize the long-term emotional benefits of quitting and present new findings confirming an average weight gain of only 4–6 pounds among ex-smokers (USDHHS 1990a). Messages aimed at older smokers can be communicated through print and broadcast media, as well as through peer leaders or others in the community.

An important contribution of public health smoking cessation interventions has been the refinement of mass media *in combination with* community interventions to enhance individual behavior change. For example, interpersonal networking to back-up a media campaign can provide critical support for individual behavior change (Green and McAlister 1984). In the "A Su Salud" program, simple forms of verbal cuing and reinforcement were communicated widely through brief, direct contacts of community members by volunteers (Amezcua et al. 1989). Similarly, the AARP, working in conjunction with the Fox Chase Cancer Center, has developed an educational slide tape for use by volunteer peer leaders (AARP health advocates) to inform AARP members in community settings about the benefits of quitting and to introduce effective quitting strategies (Rubenstein 1991). This community outreach will reinforce the mass media "It's never too late to quit" campaign.

Social context variables indicate specialized needs for outreach and social support among smokers aged 50 to 74 years. A high concordance in smoking status among married couples 50 years and over (Venters et al. 1984) and the substantial (19%) prevalence of network smoking (smokers reporting that "most" or "all" of their friends/family smoke) documented in the AARP survey suggest that older smokers may be insulated from mainstream nonsmoking norms/influ-

ences. Therefore, quit smoking treatments for older smokers should emphasize skills both to garner social support for quitting (even from family/friends who smoke) and to resist pressures to smoke. Using peer quitting models to communicate quitting benefits and methods could help correct for the absence of peer influences among smokers whose social networks consist predominantly of other smokers—and take advantage of the fact that the quit ratio (proportion of ever smokers who have quit) is larger in the over 55 years age group than in any other age group. Because older women smokers are more likely to live alone, and less likely to be employed for salary or wages or to belong to community organizations, special outreach may be needed to motivate and assist them.

Physician Interventions Especially for Older Smokers

In view of the fact that older adults make an average of 6.3 physician visits per year, there are a staggering 1,499,400 physician encounters annually just with older smokers who have *never* tried to quit (Rimer and Orleans 1990). In any year, if only 10% of older smokers were influenced to quit by their family physicians, this would mean 1,000,000 new ex-smokers, just among adults age 55 years and over. Medical and potential medical problems are the most critical motivating factors for stopping smoking. Thus, the role of the physician is especially important.

The significant proportion of older smokers who want to quit may be especially responsive to advice to quit from their physicians. Yet, many, by their self-report, have not been advised to do so. Physicians should assess all older patients for smoking status, advise smokers to quit, assist them in doing so, and arrange follow-up (see Chapter 10). The annual checkup, as well as acute and chronic illness visits, are all good opportunities to reinforce the importance of stopping smoking. Every failure to intervene represents a lost clinical opportunity.

In addition to following general smoke-free office environments and providing clear quitting advice and brief cessation interventions as described in Chapters 8–11, physicians should recognize some of the age-related needs of older smokers. Many symptoms, such as cough and fatigue, should be related explicitly to smoking. Unfortunately, older adults and their physicians often inappropriately disregard such symptoms as caused by aging. Symptoms are important motivational cues (Salive et al. 1992), and older patients will be more likely to stop smoking if they perceive themselves as still susceptible to the harmful effects of tobacco and able to benefit from quitting. Discussions about how the older patient's smoking interacts with prescription medications also may help motivate smokers to quit. Older adults should be cautioned especially against using other forms of tobacco, such as pipes or cigars, as a substitute for cigarettes.

For those older smokers who require more quitting assistance than can be provided by a minimal-contact medical intervention, referral to more intensive interventions, as discussed in Chapter 10, is appropriate. Older smokers who live alone or are relatively isolated from family or friends may benefit particularly from the social support formal treatments offer, as may older smokers who already have tried to quit many times on their own or with minimal-contact treatments. Recommendations made in the previous section about communicating with older adults apply as well to formal treatments as to less intensive minimal-contact treatments.

Physicians can play an equally important role with older smokers who may not yet be ready to quit. Beginning with asking about smoking, physicians and other health professionals can help to motivate precontemplators to reevaluate their smoking habit and to take actions toward quitting. Those older smokers in the AARP survey who said they were seriously thinking about quitting smoking in the next 6 months (i.e., contemplators), reported stronger beliefs in smoking health harms and quitting benefits and were more likely to have received physician advice to quit in the past year than did the precontemplators in this sample (Orleans et al. 1991). As noted earlier, physician advice to quit was strongly related to perceived

smoking health harms and intention to quit among AUTS smokers aged 50–74 years (Orleans et al. 1990). No discussion is complete without emphasizing that the patient is never too old to quit smoking and reinforcing the smoker's confidence to surmount the difficulties associated with withdrawal and ultimately benefit from quitting smoking. Since we know that smokers may avoid preventive health care (perhaps as a defensive reaction to their smoking) (Orleans, Rimer, Salmon 1990), preventive checkups always should be encouraged and reinforced. These visits, like visits for smoking-related illness, provide important opportunities for discussing the patient's personal health benefits of quitting and harms of continuing to smoke.

"Contemplators" in the AARP survey of older smokers (Orleans et al. 1991) rated fear of failure and withdrawal symptoms as *more* serious quitting barriers than did "precontemplators," reflecting perhaps a more realistic appraisal of the difficulties of stopping smoking. Consistent with this view, Prochaska and DiClemente and their colleagues (1987) have noted that precontemplators and chronic contemplators (who fail to progress into quitting stages) often exhibit unrealistic expectations of the quitting process, telling themselves that quitting is an easy task and that they can quit "any time." The challenge with such precontemplators may be to undermine their misconceptions about the ease of quitting, while at the same time bolstering their self-efficacy to overcome likely quitting difficulties.

Pharmacologic Adjuncts for Older Smokers

Nicotine replacement is especially appropriate for older smokers due to their high level of addiction. But, the older smoker is also especially likely to suffer from illnesses and conditions that contraindicate or complicate its use (e.g., recent myocardial infarction, arrhythmias, diabetes, circulatory disorders, dentures). According to Schneider (1987), many older smokers can use nicotine gum, even with dentures and extensive bridgework. As for other patients, careful instruction in proper gum use is essential. The transdermal nicotine patch (Fiore et al.

1992), however, is likely to be more appropriate for, and acceptable to, older smokers (see also Chapters 10 and 12).

Depression is the most common psychiatric diagnosis among older Americans (Carstensen 1988). A short, carefully monitored course of antidepressants may prove helpful for older smokers with a history of major depressive illness, or who report marked dysphoria following past quit attempts (Glassman et al. 1990). Regular physician follow-up is especially important when any pharmacologic adjunct is employed with older smokers.

CONCLUSION

Older smokers remain a challenge to health professionals. Medical intervention, however, should provide the backbone of efforts to motivate and assist older smokers to quit. More than 70%, or 2,310,000, Americans 55 years and over visit their physicians each year (Rimer and Orleans 1990). But, the 1986 AUTS indicated that only 55% of smokers aged 50–74 years had ever been advised to quit by a physician (Orleans et al. 1990). Following the four-step strategy outlined in the NCI's manual for physicians *How to Help Your Patients Stop Smoking* (Glynn and Manley, 1989) (Ask about smoking, Advise to quit, Assist to quit, and Arrange follow-up), provider intervention should go beyond simple advice to quit. It is critical that physicians clearly spell out the links between smoking and smoking-related symptoms and diagnoses for their older patients who smoke, taking care also to explain that improvements in these symptoms and diseases will occur with cessation. Spirometry, alveolar carbon monoxide feedback, and even feedback of elevated cotinine levels may help to increase older smokers' acceptance or awareness of their personal health risks. Discussions about how the older patient's smoking interacts with prescription medications and how quitting will pave the way to long-term improvements in well-being and health may provide new and salient information. Other health professionals caring for older Americans also should be involved—nurses, physician assistants, pharmacists, respiratory therapists, and dentists. Available evidence suggests that diligant intervention will result in significant quitting among older smokers.

ACKNOWLEDGMENTS

Writing of this chapter was supported by National Cancer Institute grant CA34856 to the Fox Chase Cancer Center. The authors are grateful to Joan Magee for clerical support.

REFERENCES

Abramson, J. H. Prevention of cardiovascular disease in the elderly. *Public Health Rev* 13(3–4):165–233, 1985.
Achkar, E. Peptic ulcer disease: current management in the elderly. *Geriatrics* 40:77–79, 82–83, 1985.
Amezcua, C., McAlister, A., Ramirez, A., Espinoza, R. Health promotion in a Mexican-American border community: Programa A Su Salud in Eagle Pass, Texas. In Bracht, N., ed. *Organizing for Community Health Promotion: A Handbook.* NY: Sage, 1989.
Bosse, R., and Rose, C. L., eds. *Smoking and Aging.* Lexington, MA: DC Health and Company, 1984.
Burr, M. L., Phillips, K. M., Hurst, D. N. Lung function in the elderly. *Thorax* 40:54–59, 1985.
Carstensen, L. L. The emerging field of behavioral gerontology. *Behav Ther* 19:159–181, 1988.
Cohen, S., Lichtenstein, E., Prochaska, J. O., et al. Debunking myths about self-quitting: Evidence from ten prospective studies of persons quitting smoking by themselves. *Am Psychol* 44:1355–1365, 1989.
Farquhar, J., Fortmann, S. P., Flora, J. A., et al. Effects of community-wide education on cardiovascular disease risk factors. *JAMA* 264(3):359–365, 1990.
Fiore, M. C., Novotny, T. E., Pierce, J. P., et al. Methods used to quit smoking in the United Sates: Do cessation programs help? *JAMA* 263(20):2760–2765, 1990.
Fiore, M. C., Jorneby, D. E., Baker, T. B., Kenford, S. L. Tobacco dependence and the nicotine patch: Clinical guidelines for effective use. *JAMA* 268:2687–2694, 1992.
Fries, J. F., Green, L. W., Levine, S. Health promotion and the compression of morbidity. *Lancet*, March 4, 481–483, 1989.
Glassman, A. H., Helzer, J. E., Covey, L. S., Cottler, L. B., Stetner, F., Tipp, J. E., Johnson, J. Smoking, smoking cessation and major depression. *JAMA* 264:1546–1549, 1990.

Glynn, T. J. and Manley, M. *How to Help Your Patients Stop Smoking: A National Cancer Institute Manual for Physicians.* U.S. Department of Health and Human Services, Public Health Service. Washington D.C.: National Institute of Health. NIH Publication No. 92-3064, 1991.

Green, L. W., and McAlister, A. L. Macro-intervention to support health behavior: Some theoretical perspectives and practical reflections. *Health Educ Q* 11:322–339, 1984.

Greenblatt, D. J., Allen, M. D., Harmatz, J. S., Shader, R. I. Diazepam disposition determinants. *Clin Pharmacol Ther* 27(3):301–312, 1980.

Gordon, T., Kannel, W., McGee, D. Death and coronary attacks in men giving up cigarette smoking. *Lancet* 2:1345–1348, 1974.

Haug, M., and Ory, M. Issues in elderly patient–provider interactions. *Research on Aging* 9(1):3–44, 1987.

Hermanson, B., Omenn, G. S., Kronmal, R. A., Gersh, B. J., and Participants in the Coronary Artery Surgery Study. Beneficial six-year outcome of smoking cessation in older men and women with coronary artery disease. *N Engl J Med* 319(21):1365–1369, 1988.

Hicks, R., Dysken, M. W., Davis, J. M., et al. The pharmacokinetics of psychotropic medication in the elderly: A review. *J Clin Psychiatry* 42(10):374–385, 1981.

Howard, G., Toole, J. F., Frye-Pierson, J. Factors influencing the survival of 451 transient ischemic attack patients. *Stroke* 18:552–557, 1987.

Jajich, C. L., Ostfeld, A. M., Freeman, D. H. Smoking and heart disease mortality in the elderly. *JAMA* 252(20):2831–2834, 1984.

Keintz, M. K., Rimer, B., Fleisher, L., Engstrom, P. Educating older adults about their increased cancer risk. *Gerontologist* 28(4):487–490, 1988.

Lipman, A. G. How smoking interferes with drug therapy. *Mod Med* 141–142, 1985.

McPhillips, J. B., Pellettera, K. M., Barrett-Connor, E., Wingard, D. L., Criqui, M. H. Exercise patterns in a population of older adults. *Am J Prev Med* 5:65–72, 1989.

Moore, S. R. Smoking and drug effects in geriatric patients. *Pharmacy Inter* 7(1):1–3, 1986.

Orleans, C. T., Rimer, B., Fleisher, L., Keintz, M. K., Telepchak, J., et al. *Clear Horizons: A Quit Smoking Guide Especially for Those 50 and Over.* Philadelphia: Fox Chase Cancer Center, May 1989.

Orleans, C. T., Rimer, B., Cristinzio, S., Jepson, C., Quade, D., Porter, C. Q., Keintz, M. K.,

Fleisher, L., Schoenbach, V. *Smoking Patterns and Quitting Motives, Barriers and Strategies among Older Smokers Aged 50–74. A Report for the American Association of Retired Persons.* Philadelphia: Fox Chase Cancer Center, December 1990.

Orleans, C. T., Rimer, B., Salmon, M. A. Long-term psychological and behavioral consequences and correlates of smoking cessation: In *The Consequences of Smoking: A Report of the Surgeon General, 1990.* U.S. Department of Health and Human Services, Rockville, MD, 532–555; 561–578, 1990.

Orleans, C. T., Rimer, B. K., Cristinzio, S., Keintz, M. K., Fleisher, L. A national survey of older smokers: Treatment needs of a growing population. *Health Psychol* 10:343–351, 1991.

Pathak, D. R., Samet, J. M., Humble, C. G., Skipper, B. J. Determinants of lung cancer risk in cigarette smokers in New Mexico. *JNCI* 76(4):597–604, 1986.

Prochaska, J. O., and DiClemente, C. C. Stages and processes of self change of smoking: Toward an integrative model of change. *J Consult Clin Psychol* 51:390–395, 1983.

Prochaska, J. O., DiClemente, C. C. and Associates. *Understanding Yourself As A Smoker.* East Greenwich, R.I. Mancini Associates, 1987.

Rimer, B., Jones, W. L., Wilson, C., et al. Planning a cancer control program for older citizens. *Gerontologist* 23(4F):384–389, 1983.

Rimer, B. K., and Orleans, C. T. Family physicians should intervene with older smokers. *Am Fam Physician* 42(4):959–965, 1990.

Rimer, B. K., Orleans, C. T., Fleisher, L. Cristinzio, S. et al. Does tailoring matter? The impact of a tailored guide on ratings and short-term smoking-related outcomes for older smokers. *Health Educ Q,* in press.

Rimer, B. K., Orleans, C. T., Keintz, M. K., et al. The older smoker: Status, challenges and opportunities for intervention. *Chest* 97:547–553, 1990.

Rogers, R. L., Meyer, J. S., Judd, B. W., Mortel, K. F. Abstention from cigarette smoking improves cerebral perfusion among elderly chronic smokers. *JAMA* 253(20):2970–2974, 1985.

Rowe, J. W. Health care of the elderly. *N Engl J Med* 312(13):827–835, 1985.

Rubenstein, L. Targeting health advocacy efforts toward the older population. *Cancer* 68:2519–2524, 1991.

Salive, M. E., Cornani-Huntley, J., LaCroix, A.

Z., Ostfeld, A. M., et al. Predictors of smoking cessation and relapse in older adults. *Am J Public Health* 82:1268–1271, 1992.

Schneider, N. G. Nicotine gum in smoking cessation: Rationale, efficacy, and proper use. *Compr Ther* 13(3):32–37, 1987.

Schumacker, M., and Smith, K. Diabetes in Utah among adults. *Am J Public Health* 78:1195–1201, 1988.

Somerville, K., Faulkner, G., Langman, M. Nonsteroidal anti-inflammatory drugs and bleeding peptic ulcer. *Lancet* 1:462–464, 1986.

Special Committee on Aging, United States Senate. *Developments in Aging,* vol. 3. Washington, D.C. U.S. Government Printing Office, 10, 1986.

Talseth, T., Boye, N. P., Kongerud, J., Bredesen, J. E. Aging, cigarette smoking and oral theophylline requirement. *Eur J Clin Pharmacol* 21:33–37, 1981.

Todd, B. Drugs and the elderly. Cigarettes and caffeine in drug interactions. *Geriatr Nurs* 8:97–98, 1987.

U.S. Department of Health and Human Services (USDHHS). *The Health Consequences of Smoking: Cardiovascular Disease: A Report of the Surgeon General.* U.S. Department of Health and Human Services, Public Health Service, Centers for Disease Control, Office on Smoking and Health. DHHS Publication No. (PHS) 84-5024, 1984a.

———. *The Health Consequences of Smoking: Chronic Obstructive Lung Disease: A Report of the Surgeon General.* U.S. Department of Health and Human Services, Public Health Service, Centers for Disease Control, Office on Smoking and Health. DHHS Publication No. (PHS) 84-50205, 1984b.

———. *Reducing the Health Consequences of Smoking: 25 Years of Progress. A Report of the Surgeon General.* U.S. Department of Health and Human Services, Public Health Service, Centers for Disease Control, Center for Health Promotion and Education, Office on Smoking and Health. DHHS Publication No. (CDC) 89-8411, prepublication version, 1989.

———. Long-term psychological and behavioral consequences and correlates of smoking cessation. In *The Health Benefits of Smoking Cessation: A Report of the Surgeon General.* U.S. Department of Health and Human Services, Public Health Service, Centers for Disease Control, Center for Health Promotion and Education, Office on Smoking and Health. DHHS Publication No. (CDC) 90-8416, 1990a, 532–555; 561–578.

———. *Smoking and Health: A National Status Report.* U.S. Department of Health and Human Services, Public Health Service, Centers for Disease Control, Center for Health Promotion and Education. DHHS Publication No. (CDC) 87-8396, 1990b.

Venters, M. H., Jacobs, D. R., Luepker, R. V., Maiman, L. A., and Gillum, R. F. Spouse concordance of smoking patterns: The Minnesota Heart Survey. *Am J Epidemiol* 120:608–616, 1984.

21

Worksite and Community Intervention for Tobacco Control

JESSIE GRUMAN and WILLIAM LYNN

For over 25 years, cigarette smoking has been identified as a primary cause of disease and death. Traditionally, models for treatment of communicable disease have been based on ridding the host or individual of the pathogen causing the disease. While many contemporary chronic diseases are not caused by a single identifiable external pathogen, the models for their treatment have developed in parallel to those of communicable diseases. Past approaches to the understanding and treatment of cigarette smoking have been consistent with this conventional model: smoking behavior has been viewed as an individual problem requiring an individual solution. Thus, smoking behavior was seen as a disease that posed a threat to the health of the smoker. Treatment of this disease was conceived of as short-term and highly tailored to the needs of the individual. This view has long shaped the behavioral and clinical investigations of smoking: most research in the field has explored individual smoking behavior and developed and tested strategies and skills by which people who smoke can be assisted in the cessation process (i.e., cured). This model has also dominated the way in which the results of such research have been practically applied: the commonly accepted means for intervening to reduce smoking has been to make cessation services available to smokers who seek help in stopping smoking, just as patients who are ill seek medical care for relief.

Over the past decade, however, there has been a growing realization that, while this model may be appropriate for the treatment of some smokers (e.g., those who seek assistance in quitting), cigarette smoking is too widespread a phenomenon (54 million in the United States) and the health consequences are too severe (420,000 deaths caused by smoking annually in the United States) to depend solely on interventions that reach so few at such great expense (Slade 1985).

Three other observations underscore the inadequacy of this model as the basis for controlling the national "epidemic" of tobacco smoking:

1. The acceptance of involuntary smoking as a cause of lung cancer and other diseases in nonsmokers has raised the profile of smoking for the general public and has contributed to a reformulation of the smoking problem as one affecting everyone, not just smokers. The threat posed by tobacco smoke pollution has expanded the population at risk to the entire population (see Chapter 7, National Research Council 1986; USDHHS 1986).
2. The extensive research and evaluation efforts directed toward different treatment methods have yielded no data that point to the preeminence of any one of them in helping smokers stop. In fact, 90% of smokers who have stopped say they have done so without the aid of a formal intervention (Fiore et al. 1988). Of those seek-

ing help, the success rate for abstinence after 1 year remains fairly constant and fairly low (20–25%), regardless of the method of intervention used. However, repeated quit attempts over time greatly increase the probability of achieving long-term, stable abstinence. These findings suggest that there are limitations to the potential of short-term individually oriented treatment in reducing total smoking prevalence in the population at large.

3. An extensive array of environmental influences at home, at work, and in the culture at large, as well as a wide variety of activities by tobacco product manufacturers (e.g., product design, marketing, and distribution) have a major impact on people who smoke or who are at risk of smoking.

Within a more comprehensive model that incorporates a public health orientation, tobacco smoke is a proximate cause of disease within the larger system, and the goal of intervention is to eliminate this proximate cause through a systems approach that includes prevention, treatment, and reduction of exposure. In practical terms, this means undertaking a concerted effort to (1) promote nonsmoking as the social norm through widespread policy changes and media messages; (2) prevent the development of nicotine dependence; (3) make support for quitting widely available to smokers; and (4) protect nonsmokers from exposure to tobacco smoke pollution.

The public health model for comprehensive smoking control suggests modifying and supplementing the traditional role of smoking cessation and requires that a range of efforts be directed toward all smokers and the general public over time in order to increase the likelihood of quitting, to reduce risk in the population at large, and to strengthen the norms and values supporting nonsmoking. Table 21–1 contrasts the traditional model of smoking intervention with the public health approach.

This public health model is based on the assumption that many of the important conditions supporting both smoking and decisions to quit smoking and to maintain abstinence are social circumstances (Blackburn and Pechacek 1984; Farquahr et al. 1985). Interventions delivered by a variety of credible sources and through a variety of channels reach much larger proportions of the smoking population than do individually directed formal treatment programs. Another important aspect of a public health approach to smoking prevention and control is that it can produce a sustained intervention effect on a large segment of the smoking population, as opposed to sporadic, high intensity contact with small groups of smokers willing to attend group or clinic programs (Green and McAlister 1984). And finally, the model predicts that the public will become protected from tobacco smoke pollution because of reduced smoking, increased avoidance of tobacco smoke by nonsmokers, and policy changes that protect nonsmokers.

In order to make significant impact on smoking prevalence before the turn of the century, smoking must be treated as the enormous public health problem it is. By intervening at both individual and environmental levels to reduce smoking, the public can be protected from the risk posed by tobacco smoke, and smokers can be provided with the motivation and skills to change their behavior, as well as an environment that consistently supports nonsmoking.

Smoking control efforts based on the public health model are becoming more common as evidence mounts about their efficacy in reducing smoking prevalence. In the following sections, the history of the investigation of this model for workplace and community-based smoking control will be briefly reviewed and current efforts described.

WORKSITES

Worksites are an ideal place to implement comprehensive smoking intervention based on a public health model. They are also an important channel for tobacco control because they are settings in which large numbers of smokers may be reached with continuous diverse messages which encourage and support abstinence (USDHHS 1985). Worksites are also an important channel for involving nonsmokers in smoking control

Table 21–1 Conventional and Public Health Models of Smoking Control

	Traditional Approach	Public Health Approach
Goal	Prevent morbidity and mortality by reducing tobacco use	Prevent morbidity and mortality by reducing tobacco use
Specific objective	To provide services for individual smokers who want help quitting	To promote nonsmoking as a cultural norm
Time frame	Short-term, limited	Long-term, sustained
Focus	Individual smoker	Entire population
Intervention	Highly tailored to the individual	1. The presentation and inescapbable cues, messages, and services supporting the nonsmoking norm 2. Modifying the agent (e.g., availability of tobacco products)
Short-term evaluation	Successful quit rates among smokers enrolled in programs	1. Changes in population prevalence over time (survey data) 2. Reduced consumption (sales data)
Long-term evaluation	Reduced morbidity and mortality	Reduced morbidity and mortality

efforts, particularly through the promotion of nonsmoking policies (American Cancer Society 1988). Additionally, worksites provide an opportunity to reach groups of smokers who are particularly at risk. For example, in 1988, 40% of blue-collar workers smoked compared to 28% of white-collar workers (USDHHS 1989), and some of these smokers are at risk of occupational exposure to carcinogens such as asbestos which have important synergistic effects with tobacco smoke (USDHHS 1985).

Tobacco use control efforts within the worksite consist of two main components: (1) clear nonsmoking policies that are strictly enforced, and (2) a continuous high level of motivation, support, and assistance for smoking cessation attempts. Examples of these intervention categories are discussed here.

Restrictive Smoking Policies in the Worksite

Early nonsmoking policies were established primarily for purposes of protecting equipment and products from the adverse effects of tobacco smoke (Fielding 1986; Glasgow 1989; Walsh and McDougall 1988). More recent nonsmoking policies reflect concerns about the adverse health effects of cigarette smoke (Ericksen 1988) and the potential costs from smoking to the company (Gaughan 1988). Estimates of excess costs

for each smoking employee range from $200 to $500 annually (USDHHS 1985).

Stimulated by a rising awareness of the health and financial costs of smoking, an increasing number of businesses have adopted policies that restrict smoking in the worksite. The 1986 Adult Use of Tobacco Survey (AUTS) found that 45% of surveyed employed adults reported smoking restrictions in their workplaces (CDC 1988). A survey conducted by the Bureau of National Affairs found that 54% of the businesses responding had policies limiting smoking at the worksite (Epstein 1987). Eighty-five percent of the worksite policies in place in 1987 had been adopted during the previous 3 years.

While the impact of smoking policies on smoking behavior has not been extensively evaluated, initial reports (Glasgow 1987; Rigotti 1989; Tager 1989) have suggested that policies that restrict smoking have little effect on smokers' behavior outside of work. In contrast, a recent study (Stillman et al. 1990) reported that a total ban in a large urban teaching hospital resulted in a 40% reduction in tobacco consumption. Another recent study (Borland et al. 1989) found that, contrary to expectation, 40% of smoking employees of an Australian public service agency supported a total ban on smoking on the premises. Some evidence suggests that policies may be important in enhancing participation in smoking cessation programs. For example, when Pacific Northwest Bell banned smoking in all of its 800 company facilities, they simultaneously offered free smoking cessation programs during work hours. During the first 6 months of the program, 1,044 employees entered the program, compared to 331 during the previous 26 months (Martin, Fehrenbach, Rosner 1986).

Increased awareness of the health risks posed to nonsmokers by exposure to environmental tobacco smoke, the necessity of protecting nonsmokers rights, and legal precedents that establish an employer's responsibility to provide a healthy, smoke-free work environment have broadened support among employees for policies that restrict smoking in individual worksites (Eriksen 1986; USDHHS 1986). These forces have also stimulated governmental efforts to restrict smoking in public and private worksites (Pertschuk and Shopland 1989; USDHHS 1986, 1989). Currently, 14 states and more than 290 cities and counties mandate the adoption of restrictive smoking policies in worksites.

Motivating, Supporting, and Assisting Smoking Cessation in the Workplace

A number of the traditional strategies for motivating and supporting smoking cessation have been applied in worksites. While they are described here as distinct strategies, they are often delivered in combination with one another and almost always are complemented by a policy that restricts smoking.

Self-Help Instruction

Self-help materials and programs are provided by about half of the worksites that sponsor smoking-related activities (Fielding and Piserchia 1989; Smoking and the Workplace—A National Survey). The popularity of this strategy reflects smoker preferences, since many smokers prefer self-help approaches over face-to-face methods (Hallett 1986; Orleans and Shipley 1982). Most evaluated worksite programs have combined self-help methods with other approaches, such as policies, support groups, and media campaigns (Bibeau et al. 1988). In general, evaluations suggest that while dropout rates for self-help methods are relatively high and initial quit rates are modest, abstinence often is maintained (Glasgow 1987). Initial quit rates average about 30% and 6-month and 1-year rates have been estimated at between 16 to 20% (Orleans and Shipley 1982) and 26% (Glasgow 1987). These long-term quit rates are particularly important in light of the low cost of delivering this intervention and smokers' preferences for this approach.

Physician's Advice

Only 15% of the companies that offer smoking cessation activities provide physician advice to stop smoking (Fielding and Piserchia 1989). This likely reflects the fact that many companies do not have physicians on staff. Physician advice is most often offered by larger companies (Glasgow 1987). Occupational health nurses are also important agents for cessation advice and are receiving increasing recognition for the role they play in advising employees.

Reviews indicate physician advice is most effective when delivered in the context of personal health care, in face-to-face interactions, and when linked to the individual's perception of personal vulnerability to illness caused by smoking. Long-term efficacy is similar to more intensive programs (Orleans and Shipley 1982). For example, brief physician advice delivered to employees at the Varian Corporation resulted in a 15% abstinence rate after 6 months. This rate did not differ from that of employees who had received extended health counseling or behavioral treatment (Meyer and Henderson 1974). Similar results were observed when physician advice was given to employees of the Cummins Engine Company (Richmond 1977). About 19% of participating smokers quit for more than 1 year. These results are especially notable since all smokers, not just those motivated to quit, were included. Overall, high-risk smokers who recognize that they are at risk for smoking-related disease achieve between 20 and 30% 1-year quit rates following physician advice (Orleans and Shipley 1982; Lichtenstein and Danaher 1978). Among otherwise healthy smokers, long-term quit rates average about 23% (Glynn 1988; Kottke et al. 1988; Schwartz

1987; Fiore et al. 1990). Improvements in these rates among otherwise healthy smokers may be achieved through the addition of nicotine gum and self-help materials (Glasgow 1989).

Physician advice programs offer other benefits as well. Improvements have been noted in general measures of functioning. One large-scale study (Rose and Hamilton 1978) found that advised employees displayed improvements in general functioning and reduced absences from work.

Formal Treatments

Following a stepped-care treatment model similar to the one presented in Chapter 10, group and other formal treatments provide an important backup to minimal contact and self-help approaches. Of the worksites offering smoking-related health promotion activities, about one in five offer smoking cessation group classes (Fielding and Piserchia 1989). As with most worksite initiatives, empirical evidence about program efficacy is scant. In general, worksite smoking cessation groups show very high initial quit rates but more modest long-term quit rates (Glasgow 1987). For example, 83% of participants in a cessation group offered to volunteers at Bell Laboratories quit smoking by the end of the program. After 6 months, only 28% remained abstinent (Bauer 1978). Levels appear to vary somewhat across worksite programs. While similar 6-month quit rates were achieved at a program offered to Ford Motor Company employees (Danaher 1980), employees of the New York Psychiatric Institute achieved only 4% abstinence at 6 months using the SmokEnders program (Kanzler, Zeidenberg, Jaffe 1976). Nationally, SmokEnders claims 70% abstinence at the end of the program and 40% at 1 year (Orleans and Shipley 1982). Lower rates are probably more typical, however (see Chapter 11).

Promising results are being obtained when these group approaches are combined with the best of more economical approaches. For example, one study (Glasgow 1987) found significantly higher quit rates among a group of employees who received self-help materials and a supplemental

media program, and who participated in co-worker led self-help groups compared to employees who received only the self-help and media materials (41% versus 21% abstinence at the end of the program).

Incentive Programs

Incentive programs are designed to enhance smokers' motivation to quit. They require limited program time, are potentially highly cost effective, and through "buddy" involvement, have the potential to involve *all* smokers (Glasgow et al., in press). Although implementation of incentive programs represents a unique opportunity within worksites, very few businesses offer such programs. Only between 1 to 3% of employers offer incentives for smoking cessation (Orleans and Shipley 1982). Further, few programs have been objectively evaluated. Abstinence rates for one such program were provided for smoking at the worksite only. Thirty-three percent of participating smokers and 25% of all smokers were abstinent at work, with no reported increase in their smoking levels outside of work (Glasgow 1987). Another incentive program combined social and normative effects with reinforcement strategies through a combination of individual prizes for cessation and group competition. Participants were recruited in the competition condition from four banks. Participants from a Savings & Loan did not participate in the competition. Although initial cessation rates were equivalent across groups, 6-month quit rates were significantly higher in the competition condition (Klesges et al. 1988).

In a review of worksite incentive programs, Glasgow (1982) found that posttreatment cessation rates ranged from 15 to 60%, with long-term cessation rates averaging about 40%. These rates are very encouraging, particularly when social networks are activated and environments supportive of long-term success are established. Incentive programs are also considered promising because they can effectively enhance participation and are cost-effective in that rewards are given only to successful quitters. It is useful to note that the characteristics associated with *participation* in worksite-based programs (e.g., the desire to quit smoking and the number of smoking-related symptoms), differ from those associated with *cessation* (e.g., the strength of the smoking habit and confidence in ability to quit) (Cummings, Hellman, Emont 1988; Glasgow et al. 1988; Hallett and Sutton 1987; Klesges, Vasey, Glasgow 1986; Klesges et al. 1988).

COMMUNITY INTERVENTIONS

Community approaches for comprehensive smoking control have been evolving since the late 1960s. The first investigations in this area were clinical trials that established that certain behaviors, such as exercise, maintaining a low-fat diet, and cigarette smoking, could be modified and if modified, might result in reduced disease risk for the individual. Individuals in these trials were randomly assigned to either intervention or control conditions. Examples of trials were the single-factor London Civil Service smoking trial (1968–70) and the multifactorial Multiple Risk Factor Intervention Trial (MRFIT) (1974–82) (USDHHS 1983). These clinical investigations have provided an important empirical foundation for the interventions which later served as component parts of the first generation of community trials.

The community-based trials that followed differed from the clinical trials in that, for the first time, entire communities were randomized into intervention or control conditions. These trials were designed to test the hypothesis that the modification of behaviors which increase an individual's risk for disease could be accomplished on a large scale—within a community, for example—and further, that such behavior modification could reduce disease incidence, morbidity, and mortality for an entire defined population.

The community-based trials included the European Multifactorial Prevention Project (1971–77) (Menotti 1983; Kornitzer and Rose 1985), the North Karelia Project (1972–77) (McAlister et al. 1982; Puska and Koskela 1983; Puska et al. 1985), the Swiss National Research Projects (1977–80) (Gutzwiller 1985), the Stanford Three Community Project (1972–78), and three studies sponsored by the National Heart, Lung and

Blood Institute: the Minnesota Heart Health Project (1980–89) (Carlaw et al. 1984), the Pawtucket Heart Health Project (1980–86) (Elder et al. 1986), and the Stanford Five Community Project (1979–87) (Farquahr et al. 1985). Table 21–2 provides an overview of these first generation community trials in relation to the traditional model for smoking control intervention and the public health model. This table illustrates that, in general, first generation studies reflected a mix of traditional and public health model characteristics. Almost all studies established goals to decrease disease incidence, morbidity, and mortality among individuals whose behaviors placed them at increased risk for disease.

Half of the studies delivered short-term interventions, while half delivered long-term interventions. In this classification, programs that lasted 10 or more years, including planning, intervention, and evaluation components, were considered long-term. The shift to long-term interventions is particularly evident among the later trials of this generation.

One of the most striking features of the data presented in Table 21–2 is the predominance of trials in which interventions were highly tailored to individual smokers. As will be discussed in more detail later, this represents the major difference between the first and second generation community trials. Finally, it is interesting that across all these trials, evaluation, while including program quit rates, addressed both prevalence of targeted behaviors and morbidity and mortality within the target communities.

Results from these trials, when combined with trials designed to investigate specific cessation techniques, strongly suggested that the simultaneous presence of a variety of smoking cessation methods coupled with cues to stop smoking, might be the most effective means of lowering smoking prevalence within a population.

Second Generation Community Trials

The Community Intervention Trial for Smoking Cessation (COMMIT)

On 30 September 1986, the National Cancer Institute's (NCI) Division of Cancer Preven-

Table 21–2 First Generation of Community-Based Smoking Control Investigations

	Traditional Model	European Multifactorial Prevention Project (1971–77)	North Karelia (1972–77)	Stanford 3 Community Project (1972–78)	Swiss National Research Project (1977–80)	Minnesota Heart Health Project (1980–89)	Pawtucket Heart Health Project (1980–86)	Stanford 5 Community Project (1979–87)	Public Health Model
Goals									
Services for the individual	X	X							X
Promote nonsmoking cultural norm			X	X	X	X	X	X	X
Timeframe									
Short-term limited	X	X		X	X				
Long-term sustained			X			X	X	X	X
Focus									
Individual smoker	X	X	X	X	X				
All affected by smoking						X	X	X	X
Intervention									
Tailored to the individual	X	X	X	X	X	X	X	X	X
Menu of options									
Delivery									
Single channel	X	X		X	X				
Multiple channels						X	X	X	
Evaluation									
Quit rates of program participants	X								
Population prevalence		X	X	X	X	X	X	X	X

tion and Control launched the Community Intervention Trial for Smoking Cessation (COMMIT). COMMIT was to be the largest smoking intervention trial in the world, involving indirectly or directly more than 6 million people in the testing of a community-based intervention protocol between June of 1988 and December 1993. Heavy smokers (25 cigarettes/day or more) are particularly targeted due to their increased cancer risk and their difficulty in quitting. Although heavy smokers represent only one-quarter of all smokers, they account for nearly half of all the lung and smoking-related cancers among smokers (USDHHS 1982).

The trial design includes 11 pairs of matched communities in North America that were matched in size, demographics, and location. Community pairs were located in western Washington (Bellingham and Longview-Kelso), western Oregon (Medford/Ashland and Albany/Corvallis), northern California (Vallejo and Hayward), New Mexico (Santa Fe and Las Cruces), Iowa (Cedar Rapids and Davenport), North Carolina (Raleigh and Greensboro), Upstate New York (Utica and Binghamton/Johnson City), metropolitan New York (Yonkers and New Rochelle), New Jersey (Paterson and Trenton), Massachusetts (Fitchburg/Leominster and Lowell), and in western Ontario in Canada (Brantford and Peterborough). Following the baseline survey, one community in each pair was selected randomly in May 1988 as the intervention site.

The primary hypothesis was that the implementation of a defined intervention protocol, delivered through multiple community groups and organizations and using limited external resources, would result in a quit rate among heavy smokers at least 10 percentage points greater than that observed in the comparison communities. The COMMIT intervention protocol focused on four primary intervention channels. Implementation was dependent on a community-based approach to smoking cessation.

The COMMIT interventions were designed to build on, coordinate, and facilitate community smoking control activities. The overall intervention goals of the trial were to:

1. Increase the priority of smoking as a public health issue;
2. Improve the community's ability to modify smoking behavior;
3. Increase the influence of existing policy and economic factors that discourage smoking; and
4. Strengthen social norms and values that support not smoking.

Results from more than 70 NCI-sponsored trials and other smoking-related behavioral research served as the basis for the COMMIT protocol of 51 mandated intervention activities. The most promising strategies were interventions offered through physicians and dentists, mass media, worksites, community organizations, and telephone hot lines. Mandated intervention activities were organized into four areas: (1) health care providers, (2) worksites and organizations, (3) cessation resources and services, and (4) public education. Specific goals and objectives were defined for each of the areas and process objectives were set for each of the 51 mandated intervention activities.

Organizational responsibility for implementation of the COMMIT protocol at the community level was vested in a Community Board. The Community Board was the link between the NCI–Research Institution partnership and the community for implementation of COMMIT activities required by the protocol. The Community Board was served by task forces corresponding to the four intervention areas. A Health Care Provider Task Force was responsible for training health care providers to implement routines for managing nicotine dependence and for nonsmoking policies in health care settings; the Worksites and Organizations Task Force had overall responsibility for promoting nonsmoking environments and providing encouragement and cessation support; the Cessation Resources and Services Task Force was responsible for increasing knowledge, awareness, and availability of cessation resources and services; and, the Public Education Task Force was responsible for working with the media and schools to promote communitywide prevention and control activities. The Community Board, working with the task forces, research institutions, and the NCI, developed an overall smoking control plan for the community and annually, during the 4-year intervention phase, prepared annual action plans for implementing the intervention activities required by the study protocol.

Evaluation of COMMIT focuses on four components: (1) outcome (monitoring changes in community smoking patterns); (2) impact (measuring the effect of COMMIT on factors thought to be important in promoting behavior change); (3) process (monitoring the quality and timeliness of intervention delivery); and (4) economic (determining the cost effectiveness of the intervention) (Matson et al. 1990–91). Evaluation of COMMIT will be accomplished by the collection of data through centrally conducted community surveys, locally conducted surveys, and an extensive system for collecting and maintaining program records.

Prior to randomization of the communities to either intervention or comparison status in May 1988, a baseline survey to determine the prevalence of cigarette smoking and to recruit cohorts of heavy and light to moderate smokers was conducted. In addition, recent quitters (having quit within 5 years of the survey) were identified to determine baseline quit rates in each of the 22 study communities. Approximately 500 heavy and 500 light to moderate smokers were identified in each of the 22 study communities. Eighty percent of these individuals have been assigned to an Endpoint Cohort that will serve as the trial's primary end point indicator. The remaining 20% of the heavy and light to moderate smokers, along with 100 recent quitters and 100 never-smokers have been assigned to an Evaluation Cohort which serves as an indicator of community change. In each of the 22 study communities, the 400 members of the Evaluation Cohort will be surveyed to assess the population-wide impact of COMMIT on: (1) intervention program awareness, receptivity, and participation; (2) acceptance of smoking as a public health problem; and (3) decline in the social acceptability of smoking. The Endpoint Cohort is followed annually throughout the intervention to determine residency and at the end of the

intervention phase will serve as the primary outcome indicator. A final prevalence survey will be conducted in all 22 study communities at the end of the intervention phase in 1993.

The COMMIT evaluation also includes a number of other data collection activities, including surveys to determine availability of cessation resources and services, smoke-free policy changes, health professionals' office and counseling practices, and worksite and organizational activities. An economic analysis is being conducted to examine the relative costs and benefits of the intervention protocol. The major elements of the COMMIT evaluation are identified in Figure 21-1.

The intervention and evaluation efforts are to continue through 1993. COMMIT will serve as a major laboratory for the study of communitywide smoking intervention and cessation and for the evaluation of specific strategies to achieve large-scale smoking cessation. COMMIT will help to establish the standards of public health intervention for smoking prevention and control and will contribute to the knowledge base to be used in the NCI's American Stop Smoking Intervention Study for Cancer Prevention (ASSIST).

The American Stop Smoking Intervention Trial for Cancer Prevention (ASSIST)

ASSIST is a collaborative effort between the NCI and the American Cancer Society, along with state and local health departments and other voluntary organizations. The ASSIST intervention model is an attempt to apply the best available tobacco control methods within the framework of the public health model.

The primary objective of ASSIST is to accelerate the decline in smoking prevalence sufficiently in all ASSIST sites combined in order to reduce smoking prevalence to less than 15% of adults by the year 2000. The secondary objective is to reduce by 50% the rates of smoking initiation among adolescents in all award sites by the year 2000. The 17 state health departments receiving ASSIST awards are Colorado, Indiana, Maine, Massachusetts, Michigan, Minnesota, Mis-

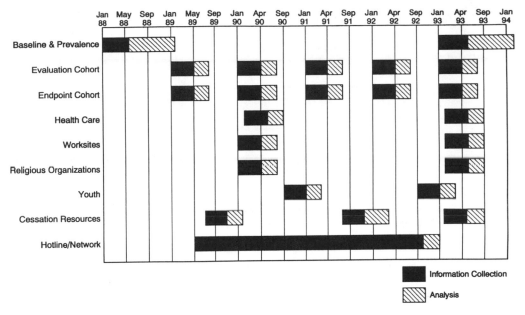

Fig. 21–1 COMMIT data collection activities and timelines, January 1988 to January 1944. *Source:* NCI COMMIT Research Group 1988.

souri, New Jersey, New Mexico, New York, North Carolina, Rhode Island, South Carolina, Virginia, Washington, Wisconsin, and West Virginia.

Through ASSIST, coalitions will be formed in award sites at the state level and in strategic metropolitan areas. ASSIST coalitions will consist of groups and agencies which will work to (1) define the smoking problem in the site, (2) develop a comprehensive smoking prevention and control plan (Phase I), and (3) implement the plan through coalition member groups. During the 5-year intervention period between 1993 and 1998, the coalitions in each of the funded sites will initiate, coordinate, and deliver a level of tobacco use prevention and control programs far in excess of current activities.

The ASSIST planning model is based on the assumptions of the public health model for tobacco control. This model provides a means for organizing and targeting the many diverse activities that make up a comprehensive initiative. A three-dimensional cube has frequently been used to illustrate interactions between person–environment disease (Heimendinger et al. 1990; Simons-

Morton et al. 1989). This planning model attempts to (1) ensure that all smokers are reached with multiple messages through multiple channels, (2) identify areas of overlap among services and channels to enhance coordination, and (3) use existing organizations and services to reach target populations.

Figure 21–2 identifies the elements critical to a tobacco control initiative, illustrates their interrelationships, and provides a structure that can be used to plan a comprehensive initiative.

Axis 1. Target Groups
The ASSIST intervention will target the following:

1. groups of smokers with relatively high smoking rates;
2. groups of smokers with secondary risk factors (e.g., occupational exposure to asbestos);
3. groups of smokers with limited access to information about smoking and cessation services;
4. groups who are at high risk for starting to smoke;

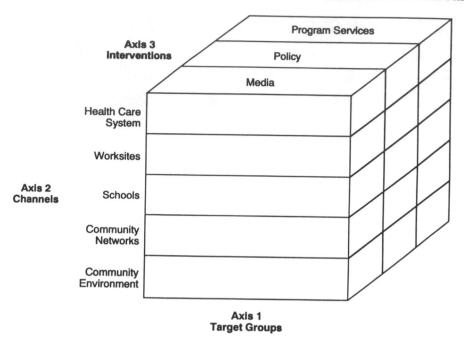

Fig. 21-2 Comprehensive smoking prevention and control. *Source:* ASSIST RFP No. NCI-CN-95165-38.

5. groups and individuals in positions to effect policy changes in relation to smoking (nonsmokers and smokers); and
6. groups and individuals able to amplify and extend effective smoking control in other ways (nonsmokers and smokers).

Because the size, identity, and location of such groups vary widely across the country, target groups must be identified for each specific site.

Axis 2. Channels for Smoking Prevention and Control.
The channels for smoking prevention and control represent the existing conduits through which most interventions will reach identified target groups. The major channels are the health care system, worksites, schools, community groups, and the community environment.

The potential for effective tobacco control intervention of the first three channels has been discussed throughout this volume. Community groups refer to groups of people who gather regularly for some mutually sanctioned purpose, such as churches, social clubs, fraternal organizations, youth groups, and so on. The community environment refers to the general physical and social milieu within an intervention site. Public policy, the mass media, and widely promoted publicly available cessation services contribute to the community norms and practices which support nonsmoking.

Axis 3. Interventions
The interventions along Axis 3 represent the three major categories of interventions in ASSIST. They are media, policy, and program services. Each category of interventions includes a variety of specific intervention strategies, some that can be delivered through all five channels (e.g., self-help materials or large community-based events such as the Great American Smokeout) and some that are most appropriately delivered within a specific channel (e.g., brief counseling by health care providers or school-based smoking prevention programs).

"Media" as used here means the collective system of communication used to disseminate information about smoking and health.

The major types of mass media are radio, television, newspapers, and magazines as well as more targeted types of media specific to individual channels, such as closed-circuit television, organizational newsletters, and neighborhood advertising papers.

The primary goals of these media interventions are to support nonsmoking behavior, increase motivation to stop smoking, inform smokers of cessation services, and enhance public support for policy changes that support smoking control.

The policy goals for ASSIST are to implement and enforce policies which:

1. ensure safe, smoke-free environments for the public and reinforce social norms and values supporting nonsmoking;
2. provide stimuli and incentives to help smokers stop and offer structural support to help them remain smoke-free; and
3. provide incentives for people to never begin smoking.

Policy-related activities including educating for changes in public legislation and regulation, and policies in private venues, as well as enforcement of existing policies.

Program Services

The mass media and policy components of a comprehensive smoking and prevention intervention raise awareness of the smoking issue and motivate people to make changes in their behavior relative to smoking. Such efforts must be accompanied by a wide range of program services that are available to guide and support individuals in making those changes. There are three main types of program services in a comprehensive smoking control effort: cessation resources, prevention resources, and smoking education. Although these program services vary widely in source, audience, intensity, structure, and purpose, all share three essential elements: (1) information about smoking, (2) compelling reasons to act, and (3) guidance about how to act effectively. The following interventions are classified as program services: (1) Cessation Resources: brief intervention by health care providers, self-help materials, dedicated stop-smoking hot lines, contests and incentives programs, group and individ-

ual smoking cessation programs; (2) Prevention Resources: school-based smoking prevention curriculums, outreach to high-risk youth through non-school channels; and (3) Smoking Education: workshops on policy development, workshops on smoking and the media, programs for the general public about the smoking issue.

The goal of program services in a smoking prevention and control effort is to ensure the high visibility and ready availability of materials and programs that support individual behavior changes consistent with the nonsmoking norms.

ASSIST will demonstrate that the implementation of a comprehensive tobacco use control intervention, when tailored to community needs, the available delivery systems, and the specific target populations, will significantly accelerate current downward trends in smoking prevalence.

California's Proposition 99: A Model State-Level Initiative

COMMIT results will be reported beginning in the fall of 1993, with full results not available or published until 1994. ASSIST results are even further off, with the intervention phase not scheduled to begin until the fall of 1993. However, evidence for the power of broad-based multi-channel public health initiatives to curb tobacco use can be found in the 1992 results of a unique experiment: California's Tobacco Tax Initiative, or Proposition 99.

In 1988, enough signatures were raised to place an initiative on the ballot in California that would raise the state's cigarette excise taxes by 25 cents per pack, with a specified portion of tax revenues earmarked for statewide programs to curb tobacco use, especially among teenagers. This tax went into effect in January 1989, with most funding for state health education programs and tobacco research programs beginning in early 1990 (Pierce et al. 1993). Although modest compared with the estimated $488 million the tobacco industry spent in California to promote cigarettes in 1989, funding for this innovative public health program has been substantial: $93 million in 1989–90, $139 million in 1990–91 for health education programs; $41 million in 1989–90, $32 million for 1990–91 for tobacco research (Slade 1992).

Three of the primary goals of Proposition 99 Tobacco Tax Initiative for the Year 1999 were to: (1) reduce cigarette smoking to a prevalence of no more than 6.5% among Californians aged 20 and over; (2) reduce the initiation of smoking by children and youth so that no more than 6.8% have become regular smokers by age 20; and (3) reduce by 75% the smoking start-up rate among teenagers. Progress towards these objectives is to be tracked by California Tobacco Surveys (funded by the initiative) (Pierce et al., 1993).

One of the highlights of California's Proposition 99 program has been a far-reaching media campaign—a counter-advertising television, radio and billboard campaign designed to deglamorize tobacco with messages targeted particularly at youth, women, and minorities. A 1991 California Department of Health study showed that "the media component of the campaign was a motivating factor for 33,000 California residents to quit smoking within the last year," and "an additional 140,000 Californians cited the campaign's advertising and marketing efforts as 'significantly related' to their decision to quit smoking." (California Department of Health Services 1991). Proposition 99-funded health education programs included multi-channel community-based cessation activities/services and prevention programs, like those of COMMIT and ASSIST.

The latest report on California's Proposition 99 entitled *Tobacco Use in California: A Focus on Preventing Uptake in Adolescents* (Pierce et al. 1993) indicated that smoking prevalence among Californians over age 18 had decreased by 24% between 1988 and 1992, a decrease substantially greater than seen in California before the Tobacco Tax Initiative and than seen elsewhere in the country during the same period—and on target with the primary program objective to reduce prevalence to 6.5% by 1999. The report concluded that: "Some of this decline was associated with the introduction of the Initiative and the tax. However, a good proportion of the decline in [smoking] prev-

alence in California may be attributed to the interventions funded by the tax initiative" (i.e., the anti-tobacco counter-advertising campaign, improved access to treatment programs/services, prevention programs) (Pierce et al. 1993, page 37).

The smoking prevalence of young adults (aged 20–24) also was on target to achieve the objective of reducing regular smoking by age 20 to no more than 6.8% by 1999. However, the impact on adolescent smoking was less clear—with substantial declines among 12- and 13-year-olds, but not among older teens. Several possible barriers to greater change in adolescent smoking rates were cited, including: the lack of smoke-free schools and the power of youth-targeted tobacco advertising, especially to convey the benefits of smoking for increased confidence in social situations and as a weight control aid. The authors of the 1993 report call for the enforcement of strict non-smoking school policies and for health education programs geared specifically towards altering the perceived benefits of smoking (Pierce et al. 1993).

The success of the California Proposition 99 initiative is likely to spawn a number of similar state-wide initiatives during the 1990s. For instance, Massachusetts voters recently voted "yes" on "Question One"— providing for a 25-cent per pack increase in Massachusetts cigarette excise taxes, with significant revenues earmarked for a state Health Protection Fund. This account will be used to fund a number of statewide initiatives complementing ongoing ASSIST activities: (1) comprehensive school health education programs, (2) workplace-based and community smoking prevention and cessation programs; (3) tobacco-related public service advertising; (4) community health centers with prenatal and maternal care programs that incorporate smoking cessation assistance; and (5) ongoing Department of Health monitoring of tobacco-related morbidity and mortality (DBIR, 1993).

CONCLUSION

The lengthy and complex group of factors that have been identified as determinants of smoking initiation, smoking, and quitting set forth a formidable challenge for those engaged in planning interventions to bring one of the twentieth century's most serious health problems under control. It is neither practical nor realistic to believe that any single approach or method will have a significant impact on population-wide smoking prevalence. The precedent for effective action has been set through numerous system-wide public health interventions in such areas as tuberculosis control, maternal and child health, HIV disease, and occupational health. It is time for tobacco use to draw upon this tradition and to be accorded top priority as a public health challenge.

REFERENCES

American Cancer Society. *Where There's No Smoke: Helping to Create a Smoke-Free Environment.* Atlanta, GA: American Cancer Society, 1988.

ASSIST RFP No. NCI-CN-95165-38.

Bauer, R. B. Bell laboratories helps employees to quit smoking. *Am Lung Assoc Bull* 64(6):11–14, July/August 1978.

Bibeau, D. L., Mullen, K. D., McLeroy, K. R., Green, L. W., Foshee, V. Evaluation of workplace smoking cessation programs: A critique. *Am J Prev Med* 4(2):87–95, 1988.

Blackburn, H., and Pechacek, T. F. Smoking cessation and the Minnesota Heart Health Program. In Forbes, W. F., Frecker, R. C., Nostbakken, D., eds. *Proceedings of the Fifth World Conference on Smoking and Health,* vol. 2. Winnipeg, Canada, July 1984, 159–164.

Borland, R., Owen, N., Hill, D., Chapman, S. Staff members' acceptance of the introduction of workplace smoking bans in the Australian public service. *Med J Aust* 151:525–528, 6 November 1989.

California Department of Health Services, *California Department of Health Services Releases New Print Advertisement for Historic Tobacco Education Campaign,* Sacramento: California Department of Health Services, July 29, 1991.

Carlaw, R. W., Mittlemark, M. B., Bracht, N., Luepker, R. Organization for a community cardiovascular health program: Experiences from the Minnesota Heart Health Program. *Health Educ Q* 11(3):243–252, Fall 1984.

Centers for Disease Control (CDC). Passive smoking: Beliefs, attitudes, and exposures—United States, 1986. *MMWR* 37(15):239–241, 22 April 1988.

Cummings, K. M., Hellmann, R., Emont, S. L. Correlates of participation in a worksite stop-smoking contest. *J Behav Med* 11(3):267–277, 1988.

Danaher, B. G. Smoking cessation programs in occupational settings. *Public Health Rep* 95(2):149–157, March–April 1980.

DBIR (Data-based Intervention Research Program), *State Cancer Legislative Database Update.* Rockville, MD: January, 1993.

Elder, J. P., McGraw, S. A., Abrams, D. B., Ferreira, A., Lasater, T. M., Longpre, H., Peterson, G. S., Schwertfeger, R., Carleton, R. A. Organizational and community approaches to community-wide prevention of heart disease: The first two years of the Pawtucket Heart Health Program. *Prev Med* 15:107–117, 1986.

Epstein, M., ed. *Where There's Smoke: Problems and Policies Concerning Smoking in the Workplace,* 2d ed. Washington, D.C.: Bureau of National Affairs, 1987.

Eriksen, M. P. Workplace smoking control: Rationale and approaches. *Adv Health Educ Promotion* 1(A):65–103, 1986.

————. Cancer prevention in workplace health promotion. *AAOHN J* 36(6):266–270, June 1988.

Farquhar, J. W., Fortmann, S. P., Maccoby, N., Haskell, W. L., Williams, P. T., Flora, J. A., Taylor, C. B., Brown, B. W., Jr., Solomon, D. S., Hulley, S. B. The Stanford five-city project: Design and methods. *Am J Epidemiol* 122(2):323–324, 1985.

Fielding, J. E. Banning worksite smoking. *Am J Public Health* 76(8):957–959, August 1986.

Fielding, J. E., and Piserchia, P. V. Frequency of worksite health promotion activities. *Am J Public Health* 79:16–20, 1989.

Fiore, M. C., Novotny, T., Lyn, W., Maklan, D., Davis, R. Smoking cessation: Data from the 1986 Adult Use of Tobacco Survey. In Aoki, M., Hisamichi, S., Tommaga, S., eds. *Smoking and Health, 1987. Proceedings of the 6th World Conference on Smoking and Health, Tokyo, November 9–12, 1987.* New York: Excerpta Medica, 1988, 189–194.

Fiore, M. C., Pierce, J. P., Remington, P. L., Fiore, B. J. Cigarette smoking: The clinician's role in cessation, prevention, and public health. *DM* 35(4):183–239, 1990.

Gaughan, S. E. Developing corporate smoking policies. *AAOHN J* 36(9):354–360, September 1988.

Glasgow, R. E. Worksite smoking cessation: Current progress and future directions. *Can J*

Public Health 78:S21–S27, November/December 1987.

————. Assessment of smoking behavior in relation to worksite smoking policies. *NY State J Med* 89(1):31–34, January 1989.

Glasgow, R. E., Hollis, J. F., Pettigrew, L., Foster, L., Givi, M. J., Morrisette, G. Implementing a year long worksite-based incentive program for smoking cessation. *Am J Health Promotion,* 5:192–199, 1991.

Glasgow, R. E., Klesges, R. C., Klesges, L. M., Somes, G. R. Variables associated with participation and outcome in a worksite smoking control program. *J Consult Clin Psychol* 56(4):617–620, 1988.

Glynn, T. J. Relative effectiveness of physician-initiated smoking cessation programs. *Cancer Bull* 40(6):359–364, 1988.

Green, L. W., and McAlister, A. L. Macro-intervention to support health behavior: Some theoretical perspectives and practical reflections. *Health Educ Q* 11(3):322–339, 1984.

Gutzwiller, F., Nater, B., Martin, J. Community-based primary prevention of cardiovascular disease in Switzerland: Methods and results of the national research program (NRP 1A). *Prev Med* 14:482–491, 1985.

Hallett, R. Smoking intervention in the workplace: Review and recommendations. *Prev Med* 15:213–231, 1986.

Hallett, R., and Sutton, S. R. Predicting participation and outcome in four workplace smoking intervention programmes. *Health Educ Res* 2(3):257–266, 1987.

Heimendinger, J., Thompson, B., Ockene, J., Sorenson, G., Abrams, D., Emmons, K., Varnes, J., Eriksen, M. P., Probart, C., Himmelstein, J. *Reducing the Risk of Cancer Through Worksite Intervention.* Philadelphia: Hanley and Belfus, 1990.

Kanzler, M., Zeidenberg, P., Jaffe, J. H. Response of medical personnel to an on-site smoking cessation program. *J Clin Psychol* 32(3):670–674, July 1976.

Klesges, R. C., Vasey, M. M., Glasgow, R. E. A worksite smoking modification competition: Potential for public health impact. *Am J Public Health* 76(2):198–200, 1986.

Klesges, R. C., Brown, K., Pascale, R. W., Murphy, M., Williams, E., Cigrang, J. A. Factors associated with participation, attrition, and outcome in a smoking cessation program at the workplace. *Health Psychol* 7(6):575–589, 1988.

Kornitzer, M., and Rose, G. WHO European collaborative trial of multifactorial prevention of coronary heart disease. *Prev Med* 14:272–278, 1985.

Kottke, T. E., Battista, R. N., DeFriese, G. H., Brekke, M. L. Attributes of successful smoking cessation interventions in medical practice. *JAMA* 259:2882–2889, 20 May 1988.

Lichtenstein, E., and Danaher, B. G. What can the physician do to assist the patient to stop smoking? In Brashear, R. E., Rhodes, M. L., eds. *Chronic Obstructive Lung Disease: Clinical Treatment and Management.* St. Louis: C. V. Mosby, 1978.

McAlister, A., Puska, P., Salonen, J. T., Tuomilehto, J., Koskela, K. Theory and action for health promotion: Illustrations from the North Karelia Project. *Am J Public Health* 72(1):43–50, January 1982.

Martin, M. J., Fehrenbach, A., Rosner, R. Ban on smoking in industry (letter). *N Engl J Med* 315(10):647–648, 4 September 1986.

Matson, M. E., Cummings, K. M., Lynn, W. R., Griffen, C., Corle, D., Pechacek, T. Evaluation plan for the Community Intervention Trial for Smoking Cessation (COMMIT). *Inter Q Clin Health Educ* 11(3):271–290, 1990–91.

Menotti, A. The European multifactorial preventive trial of coronary heart disease: Four-year experience. *Prev Med* 12:175–180, 1983.

Meyer, A. J., and Henderson, J. B. Multiple risk factor reduction in the prevention of cardiovascular disease. *Prev Med* 3:225–236, 1974.

National Cancer Institute, COMMIT Research Group (NCI). COMMIT Protocol Summary: Community Intervention Trial for Smoking Cessation. U.S. Department of Health and Human Services, National Institutes of Health, National Cancer Institute, October 1988.

National Research Council (NRC). *Environmental Tobacco Smoke: Measuring Exposures and Assessing Health Effects.* Washington, D.C.: National Academy Press, 1986.

Orleans, C. S., and Shipley, R. H. Worksite smoking cessation initiatives: Review and recommendations. *Addict Behav* 7:1–16, 1982.

Pertschuk, M., and Shopland, D. R. *Major Local Smoking Ordinances in the United States.* U.S. Department of Health and Human Services, Public Health Service, National Institutes of Health. DHHS Publication No. (NIH) 90-479, 1989.

Pierce, J., Farkas, A., Evans, N., Berry, C., Chio, W., Rosbrook, B., Johnson, M., Bal, D. G. *Tobacco Use in California: A Focus on Preventing Uptake in Adolescents.* Sacramento: California Department of Health Services, 1993.

Puska, P., and Koskela, K. Community-based strategies to fight smoking: Experiences from the North Karelia Project in Finland. *NY State J Med* 12:1335–1338, December 1983.

Puska, P., Nissinen, A., Tuomilehto, J. The community-based strategy to prevent coronary heart disease: Conclusions from the ten years of the North Karelia Project. *Ann Rev Public Health* 6:147–193, 1985.

Richmond, H. W. A fifteen-year prospective study of the incidence of coronary heart disease related to cigarette smoking habits in Cummins Engine Company management personnel with results of a vigorous anti-smoking campaign. In Steinfeld, J., Griffiths, W., Ball, K., Taylor, R. M., eds. *Smoking and Health II. Health Consequences, Education, Cessation Activities, and Governmental Action.* U.S. Department of Health, Education, and Welfare, Public Health Service, National Institutes of Health, National Cancer Institute. DHEW Publication No. (NIH) 77-1413, 1977.

Rigotti, N. A. Trends in the adoption of smoking restrictions in public places and worksites. *NY State Med* 89(1):19–26, January 1989.

Rose, G., and Hamilton, P.J.S. A randomised controlled trial of the effect on middle-aged men of advice to stop smoking. *J Epidemiol Community Health* 32(4):275–281, 1978.

Schwartz, J. L. *Review and Evaluation of Smoking Cessation Methods: The United States and Canada, 1978–1985.* U.S. Department of Health and Human Services, Public Health Service, National Institutes of Health, National Cancer Institute, Division of Cancer Prevention and Control. NIH Publication No. (NIH) 87-2940, 1987.

Simons-Morton, B. G., Brink, S. G., Simons-Morton, D. G., McIntyre, R., Chapman, M., Longoria, J., Parcel, G. S. An ecological approach to the prevention of injuries due to drinking and driving. *Health Educ Q* 16(3):397–412, Fall 1989.

Slade, J. A retreat in the tobacco war. *JAMA* 268:524–525, 1992.

Slade, J. D. A disease model of cigarette use. *NY State J Med* 85:294–298, July 1985.

Smoking and the workplace—a national survey. *J Natl Med Assoc* 72(5):527–528, 1980.

Stillman, F. A., Becker, D. M., Swank, R. T., Hantula, D., Moses, H., Glantz, S., Waranch, R. Ending smoking at the Johns Hopkins medical institutions. *JAMA* 264(12):1565–1569, 26 September 1990.

Tager, I. B. Health effects of involuntary smoking in the workplace. *NY State J Med* 89(1):27–31, January 1989.

U.S. Department of Health and Human Services (USDHHS). *The Health Consequences of Smoking: Cancer. A Report of the Surgeon General.* U.S. Department of Health and Human Services, Public Health Service, Office on Smoking and Health. DHHS Publication No. (PHS) 82-50179, 1982.

————. *The Health Consequences of Smoking: Cardiovascular Disease. A Report of the Surgeon General.* U.S. Department of Health and Human Services, Public Health Service, Office on Smoking and Health. DHHS Publication No. (PHS) 84-50204, 1983.

————. *The Health Consequences of Smoking: Cancer and Chronic Lung Disease in the Workplace. A Report of the Surgeon General.* U.S. Department of Health and Human Services, Public Health Service, Office on Smoking and Health. DHHS Publication No. (PHS) 85-50207, 1985.

————. *The Health Consequences of Involuntary Smoking: A Report of the Surgeon General.* U.S. Department of Health and Human Services, Public Health Service, Centers for Disease Control, Office on Smoking and Health. DHHS Publication No. (CDC) 87-8398, 1986.

————. *The Health Consequences of Smoking: Nicotine Addiction. A Report of the Surgeon General.* U.S. Department of Health and Human Services, Public Health Service, Centers for Disease Control, Center for Health Promotion and Education, Office on Smoking and Health. DHHS Publication No. (CDC) 88-8406, 1988.

————. *Reducing the Health Consequences of Smoking: 25 Years of Progress. A Report of the Surgeon General.* U.S. Department of Health and Human Services, Public Health Service, Centers for Disease Control, Center for Chronic Disease Prevention and Health Promotion, Office on Smoking and Health. DHHS Publication No. (CDC) 89-8411, 1989.

Walsh, D. C., and McDougall, V. Current policies regarding smoking in the workplace. *Am J Industr Med* 13:181–190, 1988.

APPENDIX A

Fagerström Test for Nicotine Dependence

ITEMS AND SCORING FOR FAGERSTRÖM TEST FOR NICOTINE DEPENDENCE

Questions	Answers	Points
1. How soon after you wake up do you smoke your first cigarette?	Within 5 minutes	3
	6–30 minutes	2
	31–60 minutes	1
	After 60 minutes	0
2. Do you find it difficult to refrain from smoking in places where it is forbidden, e.g., in church, at the library, in cinema, etc.?	Yes	1
	No	0
3. Which cigarette would you hate most to give up?	The first one in the morning	1
	All others	0
4. How many cigarettes/day do you smoke?	10 or less	0
	11–20	1
	21–30	2
	31 or more	3
5. Do you smoke more frequently during the first hours after waking than during the rest of the day?	Yes	1
	No	0
6. Do you smoke if you are so ill that you are in bed most of the day?	Yes	1
	No	0
Proposed Scoring Cut-Offs	0–2	Very Low
	3–4	Low
	5	Medium
	6–7	High (Heavy)
	8–10	Very High

Source: Adapted from Fagerström, K. O., Heatherton, T. F., Kozlowski, L. T. Nicotine addiction and its assessment. *Ear Nose Throat J* 69(11):763–767, 1992.

APPENDIX B

Mayo Foundation Nicotine Dependence Center Patient Questionnaire

MAYO NICOTINE DEPENDENCE CENTER
PATIENT QUESTIONNAIRE

Instructions

Please complete the following questionnaire by filling in the blanks and checking the appropriate boxes. The questions evaluate various aspects related to your smoking. It takes about 15 minutes and should be completed and available when the smoking cessation counselor sees you.

1. General Information

1.1 Today's date: _____ - _____ - _____
                        mo.   day   year

1.2 Your Mayo Clinic registration number: __ - __ __ __ - __ __ __

1.3 Name (please print): ☐ Mr. ☐ Mrs. ☐ Miss ☐ Ms. ☐ Other _____

_____
       First   Middle   Last

Phone: Home (__ __ __) __ __ __ - __ __ __ __

       Work (__ __ __) __ __ __ - __ __ __ __

Best time and place to contact you by phone:
                                ☐ AM   ☐ Home
Time: _____ ☐ PM at ☐ Work

1.4 Gender: ☐ Male ☐ Female

1.5 Date of birth: _____ - _____ - _____
                     mo.   day   year

1.6 Height _____ ft. _____ in. Weight _____ lbs.

1.7 Marital status:
    ☐ Single   ☐ Married   ☐ Divorced/Separated   ☐ Widowed

1.8 Race: ☐ White ☐ Black ☐ American Indian ☐ Oriental

        ☐ Other _____

1.9 Mayo Medical Center Employed: ☐ No ☐ Yes

1.10 Usual occupation/profession: _____

Present occupation/profession: □ same as above   □ retired

□ Other _____

1.11 Highest level of education _____

1.12 Reason for visit with Nicotine Dependence Consultation Service

_____

_____

1.13 Referring doctor _____

2. Smoking History   Age

2.1   How old were you when you first smoked a cigarette?   _____

2.2   How old were you when you first started regular daily cigarette smoking?   _____

                                                                         Cigarettes/day

2.3   On average, how many cigarettes are you *currently* smoking per day?   _____

2.4   *Over the past six months,* how many cigarettes did you smoke per day?   _____

2.5   On the average *of the entire time you have smoked,* how many cigarettes did you smoke per day?   _____

2.6   *When smoking the heaviest,* how many cigarettes did you smoke per day?   _____

2.7   Do you inhale cigarette smoke?
      □ Never   □ Sometimes   □ Always

2.8   List brands of cigarettes smoked:

      Starting brand _____

      Current brand _____

2.9   Please check the appropriate boxes

	Never	Past Only	Currently
Smoke a pipe?	□	□	□
Smoke cigars?	□	□	□
Chew snuff?	□	□	□
Chew tobacco?	□	□	□
Smoke other non-tobacco products?	□	□	□

2.10 When do you smoke the heaviest?—Check one answer.
      □ Mornings   □ Afternoons   □ Evenings

2.11 How soon after you wake up do you smoke your first cigarette?
      □ Immediately
      □ Within 30 minutes
      □ Between 30 minutes and 1 hour
      □ Beyond 1 hour

2.12 Which cigarette would be the most difficult to give up?
      Check one answer.
      □ First in the morning
      □ After meals

☐ During or after stressful situations
☐ During social occasions

☐ Other—specify _____

2.13 Do you find it difficult to keep from smoking in places where it is forbidden (for example in church, at the movies)?
      ☐ No   ☐ Yes

2.14 In what situations don't you smoke?—Check as many as apply.
      ☐ In public
      ☐ At work
      ☐ At home
      ☐ In presence of certain relatives (e.g., parents, grandparents, in-laws)
      ☐ In presence of my children
      ☐ At meetings
      ☐ Inside the home of non-smokers
      ☐ In my car when non-smokers are with me
      ☐ In other peoples' cars
      ☐ In restaurants
      ☐ In airplanes
      ☐ Other, specify _____

2.15 Please indicate whether or not you think you would smoke in the following situations:

Situation	Probably would not smoke	Unsure	Probably would smoke
1. When feeling anxious or under a lot of stress	☐	☐	☐
2. When wanting something in your mouth	☐	☐	☐
3. When relaxing	☐	☐	☐
4. When wanting to cheer up	☐	☐	☐
5. When wanting to keep busy	☐	☐	☐
6. When bored or trying to pass the time	☐	☐	☐
7. When around other smokers	☐	☐	☐
8. When drinking alcoholic beverages	☐	☐	☐
9. When drinking coffee or tea	☐	☐	☐
10. When talking on the telephone	☐	☐	☐
11. When in pain	☐	☐	☐
12. After meals	☐	☐	☐

2.16 Have you *in the past* had symptoms, a disease or illness you believe was caused or made worse by your smoking?

      ☐ No   ☐ Yes, please describe _____

2.17 Do you now have symptoms, a disease or illness you believe is caused by or made worse by your smoking?

      ☐ No   ☐ Yes, please describe _____

2.18 Does your desire for a cigarette ever disrupt the activities you are involved in?
      ☐ No   ☐ Yes

2.19 Do you lose time from work or other planned activities because of smoking?

      ☐ No   ☐ Yes, describe _____

2.20 Do you smoke when you are so ill that you are not able to carry on your normal activities?
☐ No   ☐ Yes

2.21 Do you use tobacco despite a serious physical disorder which you know is made worse by tobacco use?
☐ No   ☐ Yes—what is the serious physical disorder?

_____

2.22 Do you ever find yourself smoking more than you intended?

☐ No   ☐ Yes, describe _____

2.23 Has a doctor ever told you to stop smoking?

☐ No   ☐ Yes, why?_____

2.24 At this visit, has a Mayo doctor told you to stop smoking?
☐ No   ☐ Yes

3. History of Stopping Smoking

3.1   Have you tried to cut down or limit your smoking?
☐ No   ☐ Yes

3.2   _____ How many times have you *attempted* to stop smoking?

3.3   _____ How many times have you stopped smoking for at least one day?

3.4   Have you ever experienced uncomfortable symptoms when you stopped smoking?
☐ Does not apply—I have never stopped smoking.
☐ I have stopped smoking in the past but *never experienced* uncomfortable symptoms.
☐ I have stopped smoking in the past and *have experienced* uncomfortable symptoms. If yes
↓

3.5   What symptoms did you experience when you stopped smoking?—Check all that you experienced.

☐ Craving	☐ Anxiety	☐ Restlessness
☐ Decreased heart rate	☐ Increased eating	☐ Difficulty concentrating
☐ Irritability	☐ Other _____	

3.6   Since you started smoking regularly, what is the longest time you have gone without smoking anything? (Check one answer.)
☐ Never gone without smoking
☐ Less than a day
☐ At least one day but less than one week
☐ At least one week but less than one month
☐ At least one month but less than one year
☐ One year or more

3.7   Enter the number of times you have tried the following methods to stop smoking.

_____ Self-help material (for example American Lung Association material, materials from doctor, etc.)

_____ A formal cessation program (for example, with classes, group discussions, etc.)

_____ A private consultation with your doctor or mental health professional

_____ Hypnosis

_____ Nicotine medicated gum

_____ Other, please describe _____

3.8   Have you used nicotine skin patches?
      ☐ No   ☐ Yes
              ↓

> How many times? _____
>
> Any problems with the patch? _____

3.9   When was your last attempt to stop smoking?
      ☐ never attempted
      _____ hours ago   _____ days   _____ weeks   _____ months   _____ years ago

3.10 For how long did you go without smoking at that time?
      ☐ never attempted
      _____ hours   _____ days   _____ weeks   _____ months   _____ years

      How did you stop?

      Describe _____

      Why did you start again? _____

3.11 If you are still smoking, what has kept you from stopping?

      _____

      _____

4. We Would Also Like to Know How Much Support You Have for Your Efforts to Stop Smoking.

4.1   Please indicate *those relatives* who regularly smoke.—Check all that apply.
      ☐ Spouse/significant other
      ☐ Parent(s)
      ☐ Child(ren)
      ☐ Grandparent(s)
      ☐ Inlaw(s)
      ☐ None of the above

4.2   Among your close *friends,* what percentage would you say smoke?—Check one answer.
      ☐ Almost none
      ☐ About 25%
      ☐ About 50%
      ☐ About 75%
      ☐ Almost 100%

4.3 Among your *co-workers,* what percentage would you say smoke? Leave blank if not applicable, otherwise check one answer.
    ☐ Almost none
    ☐ About 25%
    ☐ About 50%
    ☐ About 75%
    ☐ Almost 100%

4.4 How much do the people closest to you want you to stop smoking?—Check one answer.
    ☐ Not at all
    ☐ Not much
    ☐ Neutral
    ☐ Somewhat
    ☐ Very much

4.5 If you were to stop smoking, how helpful would the people closest to you be?
    ☐ Not helpful
    ☐ Not much help
    ☐ Neutral
    ☐ Somewhat helpful
    ☐ Very helpful

5. Assessing Your Desire to Stop Smoking.

5.1 Are you seriously planning to stop smoking?
    ☐ Yes, have already stopped
    ☐ Yes, in the next 30 days
    ☐ Yes, in the next 6 months
    ☐ Yes, in the next year
    ☐ Undecided
    ☐ Not planning to stop

5.2 How motivated are you to stop smoking completely? (Check one answer.)
    ☐ Not at all motivated
    ☐ Not too motivated
    ☐ Neutral
    ☐ Somewhat motivated
    ☐ Very motivated

5.4 How long have you wanted to stop smoking?
    ☐ Never wanted to
    ☐ For a week or less
    ☐ A week to a year
    ☐ For over a year

5.5 If you have stopped smoking cigarettes completely, when did you stop?

    _____ - _____ - _____
     mo.   day   year

5.6 Are you ready to set a stop date?

    ☐ No ☐ Yes, Stop date _____ - _____ - _____
                               mo.   day   year

---

6. For Hospitalized Patients Only

6.1 Date of hospital admission _____ - _____ - _____
                                    mo.   day   year

6.2 Reason for hospitalization _____

_____

_____

6.3 How many days will you be in the hospital?

_____ days

6.4 Is/was surgery a part of this hospitalization?
     □ No   □ Yes

6.5 Were you aware of Mayo's Smoke-Free Policy before coming to Mayo?
     □ No   □ Yes

6.6 Did you cut back or stop smoking before/because of this hospitalization?
     □ No   □ Yes

6.7 How many hours has it been since your last cigarette?

_____ hours

6.8 How difficult do you think it will be to refrain from smoking during this hospitalization?
     □ Very easy
     □ Easy
     □ Neutral
     □ Difficult
     □ Very Difficult

---

7. For Medicare Patients Only

Medicare Patient's Acknowledgement of Noncovered Services

The coverage provided to you by Medicare is limited to medical/surgical services. Medicare **does not** cover services like the **Nicotine Dependence Consulting Service.** Should you decide to receive this service, you will personally be responsible for payment. Your signature is required below to authorize us to bill you for this service.

_____
Patient Signature

_____   _____
Patient Medicare #   Date

_____
Provider Signature

_____   _____
Billing/Pager #   Date

Any questions concerning the information in this questionnaire
should be directed to the counselor
during your appointment.

Source: Copyright 1992 Mayo Foundation, Rochester, Minnesota 55905. Reprinted with permission.

Index

Abortion, spontaneous, 282
Absorption of nicotine, 4, 25
   relationship between absorbed dosage and
      effect, 35–37
Abuse liability of nicotine, 29–31
   as a euphoriant and discriminative stimulus,
      30–31
   as a positive reinforcer, 31
   as a psychoactive drug, 30
Action (stage through which quitter may cycle),
   150
Acupuncture, 221, 233
Addiction, definitions of, 27–28
Addictive drugs. *See* Chemical dependent (CD)
   patients; Drug dependence
Additives to cigarettes, 8–9
Adrenocorticotrophic (ACTH) injections, 221,
   237
Adults. *See also* Men; Women
   expenditures for tobacco and products by
      American smokers (1988), 46
   prevalence of smoking among diabetic adults,
      80–81
   smokers (%) who have quit (1984), 59
   trends in smoking prevalence (1965–90), 91
   trends in smoking prevalence (projected to
      year 2000), 94
Adult Use of Tobacco Survey (AUTS), 385, 386,
   387, 388–89, 392
African Americans. *See* Blacks
Aids to smoking cessation, 221, 237–39
Air-cured tobacco, 5
Air pollution from tobacco smoke. *See* Indoor
   air pollution
Alaskan natives, cigarette smoking among, 92
Alcoholism. *See* Chemical dependent (CD)
   patients
Alkaloids, 24–25
Alprazolam, 255
American Association of Retired Persons
   (AARP)
   smoking and health characteristics of older
      adults, 385, 386, 387
   tailoring intervention to older smokers, 390,
      391, 392

American Cancer Society (ACS), 359
   cessation program for pregnant women, 283,
      285
   formal treatment program for smokeless
      tobacco user, 273
   FreshStart program, 233, 234
   mortality studies, 108, 121, 122
   motivational materials for cessation, 203, 271,
      272
   self-help cessation materials, 191
American Dental Association, motivational
   materials for cessation from, 203
American Heart Association, self-help cessation
   materials, 191
American Indians. *See* Native Americans
American Lung Association (ALA), 233–34
   cessation program for pregnant women 283,
      285
   self-help cessation materials, 191, 319
American Psychiatric Association's
   classification of drug addictions, 27
American Society of Addiction Medicine
   (ASAM)
   on reimbursement for treatment services,
      172
American Stop Smoking Intervention Trial for
   Cancer Prevention (ASSIST), 404–7, 408
Anger, 245
Antabuse (disulfiram), 255–56
Antidepressants, 157
   interaction between nicotine and, 332
   for older smokers, 393
Antitobacco messages. *See* Countermarketing
Anxiety, 245
Arrhythmias, 288
Arterial spasming, 288
Arterial system, delivery of inhaled nicotine to, 4
Asia
   efforts of multinational tobacco companies to
      move into, 46
   prevalence of women smoking during
      pregnancy, 283
   SLT use by Asians, 263
Asthmatics, 292
Atherosclerosis, 288